From Idea to Essay

A Rhetoric, Reader, and Handbook

THIRD EDITION

Jo Ray McCuen

Glendale College

and

Anthony C. Winkler

SCIENCE RESEARCH ASSOCIATES, INC.
Chicago, Henley-on-Thames, Sydney, Toronto

A Subsidiary of IBM

Acquisition Editor	Philip Gerould
Project Editor	Sara Boyd
Designer	Naomi Takigawa
Cover Photographer	Ernest Braun
Compositor	Interactive Composition Corporation

Library of Congress Cataloging in Publication Data

McCuen, Jo Ray, 1929–
   From idea to essay.

   Includes index.
     1. English language—Rhetoric.   2. College readers.
I. Winkler, Anthony C., joint author.   II. Title.
PE1408.M394 1982   808'.0427   82-10711
ISBN 0-574-22085-2

10 9 8 7 6 5 4

Acknowledgments

THIS IS ERIC SEVAREID ©1964 by Eric Sevareid. Reprinted by permission of the Harold Matson Company, Inc.

CRIME IN AMERICA (excerpt) Copyright © 1970 by Ramsey Clark. Reprinted by permission of Simon & Schuster, a division of Gulf and Western.

WALLACE Reprinted by permission; © 1950, 1978 The New Yorker Magazine, Inc.

THE MAN IN THE WATER Copyright 1982 Time Inc. Reprinted by permission from *Time*.

THE SHED Reprinted by permission of the author.

THE CODE Reprinted by permission; © 1957 The New Yorker Magazine, Inc.

A MISERABLE, MERRY CHRISTMAS From the *Autobiography of Lincoln Steffens*, copyright 1931 by Harcourt Brace Jovanovich, Inc.; renewed 1959 by Peter Steffens. Reprinted by permission of the publisher.

THE WILD SWANS AT COOLE From *Collected Poems* by W. B. Yeats. Copyright 1919 by Macmillan Publishing Co., Inc., renewed 1947 by Bertha Georgie Yeats. Also reprinted with the permission of M. B. Yeats, Anne Yeats, and MacMillan London Limited.

A SHACK ON THE HILLSIDE From *Phudd Hill* by Alan Devoe. Published by Julian Messner, 1937.

HANK Reprinted by permission of the author.

THE MONSTER From *Of Men and Music* by Deems Taylor. Copyright © 1937, 1965 by Deems Taylor. Reprinted by permission of Simon & Schuster, a division of Gulf & Western Corporation.

FLYING OVER AFRICA By permission of Random House, Inc., and the Rungstedlund Foundation from *Out of Africa* by Isak Dinesen, copyright by Random House, Inc., 1937, and renewed 1965 by the Rungstedlund Foundation.

THEFT Copyright 1935, 1963 by Katherine Anne Porter. Reprinted from her volume, *Flowering Judas and Other Stories,* by permission of Harcourt Brace Jovanovich, Inc.

(Continued on page 435)

Contents

Preface to the First Edition

The teaching of writing in college traditionally has swung between two polar approaches. The first approach teaches writing by fearlessly prescribing to the student the rhetorical techniques and strategies used by professional writers. Based on the belief that the interested student will automatically write better than the student whose spirit is broken by boredom, the second approach teaches writing by attempting to stimulate the student's interest. The verdict from the field is that each approach suffers from inherent limitations and deficiencies. *From Idea to Essay*—a combined rhetoric, reader, and handbook—is therefore a judicious blend of these two approaches.

From Idea to Essay is unashamedly prescriptive. The student is given thorough instruction in strategies for writing paragraphs and essays. Traditional proven labels are used. Boredom, on the other hand, is exorcised through the inclusion of stimulating stories and poems that generate a specific and different writing assignment for each unit. Before attempting the assignment, the student is treated to specific, sensible instructions on how to do it; moreover, he has the opportunity of reading two essays on the assignment—one by a professional writer, the other by a student. Each chapter closes with two additional essays and numerous alternate writing assignments. In short, the student is instructed, stimulated, and given models to follow.

From Idea to Essay is broad in the scope of its instruction and coverage. While emphasizing the essay, it also instructs the student in writing the paragraph and the research paper. Its coverage includes nine stories, nine poems, twenty-seven professional essays, nine student essays, one research paper, countless exercises, and innumerable illustrative paragraphs, making the book adaptable to a variety of quarter, semester, and trimester writing courses.

J. R. M.
A. C. W.

Preface to the Third Edition

The third edition of *From Idea to Essay* was developed in response to suggestions and criticisms from users of the second. The basic pedagogy of the book, which has proven itself so successful in teaching students how to write, remains unchanged. Each writing unit still begins with a short story chosen to trigger a writing assignment; students are still given thorough and prescriptive advice on how to do the assignments; writing models are still drawn from the work of both professional and student writers.

Nevertheless, we have made some specific changes in both structure and content. First, we have added two new units to the book. To Part I, we had added a new unit on Sentence Combining in which students are drilled in the technique of fusing kernel sentences into more complex structures. To Part II, "Writing the Essay," we have added a new unit, "Adapting the Rhetorical Modes to Essay Examinations." Our aim here is twofold: to teach students how to use the rhetorical modes in other disciplines and to show them that the rhetorical modes have a place in the real world, that they do not exist in isolation in the English classroom.

The second major change we have made is in the readings that accompany each unit. Fifteen articles, five poems, and two stories are new to this edition. As always, we have been guided in our choices by the rhetorical appropriateness of a selection, not merely by its topicality. Four of the unit writing assignments have been slightly modified; all the specific instructions for doing the writing assignments have been edited for clarity.

This revision of *From Idea to Essay* should remain appealing to those instructors who liked the second edition; those who passed up the first and second editions for whatever reason should find inducement anew for giving this edition another look.

J. R. M.
A. C. W.

Part I

Fundamentals

1

Elements of an Essay

Essay is a term not quite 400 years old. From the French *essai,* meaning "attempt," the word was used by the sixteenth-century French writer Montaigne to name the new literary form he had invented. The essay is well named, for without doubt, it is difficult to write, requiring concentration, focus, and effort.

The 500-word theme has evolved as the most common form of the essay taught in the classroom. Short enough to be written in a single class period, yet long enough to accommodate fairly complex topics, the 500-word theme forces students to pay attention to structure and to choose their words carefully. It also is about as long as the typical office memo and thus requires writing skills the student will find useful in the business world. We shall begin our discussion of the essay with a paragraph from a student's 500-word theme.

Assignment: *Write a 500-word theme about a relative.*

Student title: "My Father"

> My father is my favorite relative. I like him a lot. He grew up in Iowa and wanted to be a doctor. Instead, he became a farmer because his parents couldn't afford to send him to medical school. They couldn't afford to because they were poor and because medical school is expensive. I read someplace that the reason medical school is so expensive is because the AMA keeps the number of students low so there will be few doctors who can therefore charge high fees. Farmers, no matter what you read, don't make much money. They have to endure a lot of hardships and get little in return. Doctors, on the other hand, have an easy life. They work for themselves, make a sure income, and are looked up to by everyone in the community. Farmers, however, are just as important to any country as doctors, yet are paid less. But my father wanted to become a doctor and ended up being a farmer, just like his father. I think I want to be a farmer, too, but my Dad wants me to be a doctor. However, I don't hold this against him.

Even to the casual reader, this paragraph would appear muddled. It is glaringly disorganized, with its sentences pulling in different directions as if the writer could not decide which way to go. We may compare this paragraph to an orchestra in which each musician is playing a different tune. No matter how accurately each member of the orchestra renders the tune, the total effect will still be horribly discordant. Similarly, the individual sentences in this paragraph may be grammatical, but the paragraph as a whole is not.

There is, in fact, a grammar of the paragraph and of the essay just as there is a grammar of the sentence. *Grammar* refers to rules governing customary usage and practice in language. The "grammar" of the paragraph and the essay is a collection of commonsense guidelines and practices, generally grouped under the heading of *rhetoric,* that writers observe and English teachers struggle to impart. This unit and the next deal with some guidelines for writing the essay; Units 3 and 4 examine the guidelines for writing a paragraph and preparing an outline.

A. Purpose

Every essay must have a *purpose.* This guideline seems simple enough, but it bristles with complications. The down-to-earth student might object that the purpose of writing any essay in freshman English is to pass the course. Granting this as a sort of long-range aim, we have something quite different in mind. Purpose refers to the goal of an essay: the effect it hopes to achieve, the information or impression it intends to impart, the sentiment it wishes to arouse. With a clear purpose in mind, a writer is less likely to be seduced by irrelevant concepts and details. The student paragraph, for instance, began with the assertion "my father is my favorite relative." It then meandered to an analysis of why medical school is expensive, drifted off into a contrast between doctors and farmers, and finally petered out with an expression of the writer's ambition to become a farmer. It is difficult to discern the writer's purpose. He probably started out with no definite purpose, intending simply to pile sentence upon sentence and hope for the best. Some professional writers can and do work this way, but it is a skill acquired after reams of written work. Few beginning writers can write a good essay without having a definite purpose. Usually, such essays end up sounding as muddled as the student paragraph.

B. Strategy

Having formulated a definite purpose, writers can plan their essays before beginning to write. They can choose a *strategy* for implementing the purpose, gather relevant facts and details, and construct an outline. In effect, purpose imposes limits on the essay, while strategy enables the writer to achieve the purpose within the imposed limits.

There are nine common strategies for developing an essay, each of which is covered in a separate unit in Part II. These strategies are: narration, description, example, definition, comparison/contrast, process, classification, causal analysis, and argumentation. An essay assignment may be broadly worded to allow the student to choose a strategy for developing it—for example, "Write an essay on a favorite relative." Or it may be specifically worded to include the strategy of development that must be used—for example, "Compare and contrast your mother and father." In either case, the strategy is a means to an end—a technique for developing the essay.

Here are some possible strategies for developing a 500-word essay about a favorite relative, each based on a different purpose:

Purpose	*Strategy*
To explain why my father has become so bitter and frustrated in his middle years.	Write a *causal analysis* of why my father has become bitter.
To give the reader a vivid picture of what my father is like.	Write an essay *describing* my father—his physical looks, his personality, his habits.
To illustrate to the reader the effect of the generation gap on my relationship with my father.	Begin by *defining* the generation gap. Support this definition with specific *examples* of generation differences that have cropped up between me and my father.

In the first example, the writer has decided on the strategy of *causal analysis*. His essay will be limited to analyzing the cause of his father's bitterness. The essay in the second example will be limited to a *description;* in the third example, the essay will *define* generation gap and give *examples* of the generation gap in the writer's relationship with his father. In each case, the writer has made the assignment easier by limiting the scope of the essay.

Some students believe that what they are taught in English courses has little usefulness in the outside world. To dismiss this myth, we have selected some examples of real-world applications of the writing strategies discussed in this book. All examples were compiled from experiences either reported to the authors or lived by them.

1. You have applied for a job with a large multinational corporation and have gone successfully through a battery of screening tests. The candidates have been narrowed to a field of five. As a basis for final selection, the personnel psychologist has asked each applicant to write an essay about his or her greatest personal success. You sit down and try to think. Then you begin to write.

   Purpose: To persuade the personnel psychologist that you are the person for the job.
   Strategy: Narration.

2. You are a social worker responsible for supervising the living conditions in some state-supported nursing homes for the elderly. You find unsanitary living conditions at one nursing home and file a stop-payment order against it to cut off its state funding. Your supervisor asks you to write a description of the conditions at this nursing home in support of your action.

   Purpose: To convince the state to withdraw aid from this nursing home.
   Strategy: Description.

3. As a vocal member of your PTA group, you listen with horror as the school district officials propose curriculum changes that you are convinced will lower the standard of education. You are opposed to the changes because you have read of other districts in which such changes have not been beneficial. You meet

with other parents who share your view and a committee is formed. You are asked to find examples of other districts where similar changes have produced no advantages.

Purpose: To persuade the school district not to make the proposed changes in the curriculum.

Strategy: Example.

4. You work as a textbook salesperson for a college publisher. A sociology book published by your company is being criticized by the professors using it because it lacks a section on "deviance." You report this to your editor, who fires back a memo asking you to find out exactly what the professors mean by "deviance."

Purpose: To acquaint the editor with the professors' complaint about the text.

Strategy: Definition.

5. You are employed in the accounting division of a major department store. An employee has made a suggestion for changing the method of reporting daily income. Your boss likes the idea but is uncertain that it would be enough of an improvement over the existing method to justify the change. He asks you to write a comparison of this new method with the existing one.

Purpose: To persuade the boss to adopt the new reporting method.

Strategy: Comparison/contrast.

6. Mad about creamy chocolate pudding, you have perfected the ideal recipe. Neither riches nor fame can tempt you to share it. Love, however, does. You sit down to write out the recipe for your beloved.

Purpose: To share your recipe for perfect chocolate pudding with a friend.

Strategy: Process.

7. You work in the counseling office of a major university where entering freshmen are required to take an English test. The university is planning new English classes for its freshmen, and you are assigned to write a report dividing and classifying the incoming freshmen according to their English placement scores.

Purpose: To gather data to help with curriculum planning.

Strategy: Classification.

8. Your firm specializes in the manufacture of household brushes. Sales of one particular item—a plastic brush designed as a bathroom grout cleaner—have slumped badly. Your boss assigns you to find out why.

Purpose: To find out why sales of this brush have fallen.

Strategy: Causal analysis.

9. You and eleven other jurors have listened for two weeks to a procession of witnesses. Finally, closeted with the other jury members, you begin the painstaking evaluation of evidence. Along with four other jurors, you become convinced of the defendant's guilt, but to your amazement and dismay, the rest of the jurors have come to exactly the opposite view. Undecided himself, the foreman asks each group to prepare a written argument outlining its reasons for believing in the defendant's guilt or innocence. Your group assigns you to argue their viewpoint.

Purpose: To persuade your fellow jurors to vote in favor of a guilty verdict.

Strategy: Argument.

C. The Controlling Idea

Every essay must have a *controlling idea*. Also called a *thesis,* the controlling idea is simply a statement of what the author intends to do in the essay—what the essay will demonstrate, exemplify, prove, or implement. The controlling idea is usually placed in the first paragraph, most often as the final sentence in the first paragraph, early enough to serve both the writer and reader. The writer is served by knowing what he or she has to do, the reader by knowing what to expect. Here are three controlling ideas taken from different essays:

> The biggest piece of claptrap about the Press is that it deals almost exclusively, or even mainly, with news.
>
> T. S. Matthews, *The Power of the Press*

> While I was still a boy, I came to the conclusion that there were three grades of thinking; and since I was later to claim thinking as my hobby, I came to an even stronger conclusion—namely, that I myself could not think at all.
>
> William Golding, *Thinking as a Hobby*

> Although Boswell and Johnson belonged to the same literary club, were close friends, held the same views on the Monarchy and the English class system, there are significant differences in their literary opinions and preferences.
>
> Student essay: *A Contrast of the Literary Opinions of Boswell and Johnson*

In the first essay, we expect the author to tell us why it is claptrap to say that the Press deals with the news. We expect the second essay to catalog and explain the three grades of thinking; we expect the third to contrast the literary opinions and preferences of Boswell and Johnson.

How do you find the controlling idea? Sometimes it is implied in the way an assignment is worded. For instance, if your assignment is to write an essay comparing and contrasting the lives of two acquaintances from different social classes, the controlling idea of the assignment is clear: You must do a comparison/contrast. The broader wording of other assignments, however, may force you to find your own controlling idea and impose your own structure on the material. Suppose you are asked to write about your activities over the past year. How do you find a controlling idea?

First, begin by asking yourself some questions about the past year, "What have my activities consisted of?" "What was my state of mind most of the time?" "Did my activities repeat themselves, or did I play different roles every day?" "Have I suffered constant big upheavals, or have I led a calm existence?" "Has my family approved of me or not?" After playing with these questions and others, you hit on the following crudely worded ideas:

1. Most of the time I have been hassled with money worries.
2. Basically, it's been deadly dull of which I can't stand, making me so bored day in and day out.
3. The last year being a series of compromises.
4. Major upheavals have caused me to sink or swim as I met various Waterloos.

7

5. Why have I felt so guilty all year?

6. The first six months were misery. The second six months were ecstasy.

Each item contains a kernel idea for an essay, but each idea needs a better focus, a sharper edge, a smoother shape.

From the outset of an essay, the reader wants a clear picture of what to expect. The controlling idea obligates the writer to move in a specific direction and allows the reader to see that direction from the start. Consider the following improvements:

1. Meeting my monthly expenses on a budget of $300 has kept me anxious and depressed all year. *Divisible Terms*

   (The word *hassled* has been refined to "anxious and depressed." "Money worries" have been more specifically identified as "monthly expenses." The phrase "on a budget of $300" helps explain the writer's anxiety and worry. Develop by *examples*.)

2. Because of the deadly routine of my studies and work, the past year has been unbearably boring.

   (The main problem with the original version is incoherence. The words do not add up to a comprehensible thought. The reader gets the general meaning but has to guess where it is leading. The revision is more pointed and purposeful. Develop by *causal analysis*.)

3. The last year has been a series of compromises.

   (The original version is a sentence fragment. By replacing the participle *being* with *has been*, we turn the fragment into a complete thought. Develop by *examples*.)

4. Major upheavals required difficult decisions from me this past year.

   (The original version misuses a figure of speech. In the first place, one cannot sink or swim as one faces a Waterloo because Waterloo was a famous battlefield. Furthermore, the saying, "to meet one's Waterloo" implies one's destruction, just as the Battle of Waterloo caused Napoleon's final downfall. Figures of speech tend to blur the issue and should be avoided in the wording of a controlling idea. Develop by *examples*.)

5. Because of several serious errors in judgment, I felt guilt-ridden most of last year.

   (Our new version simply turns a question into an answer, thereby giving better direction to the content of the essay. Develop by *examples*.)

6. In contrast to my misery during the first six months of the year, I spent the second six months in a glorious, ecstatic mood.

   (The original version suggests two unrelated controlling ideas that tend to tug the reader in separate directions. The term *in contrast* links the two ideas—misery in the first six months and ecstasy in the second six months. Develop by *comparison/contrast*.)

We now can propose six guidelines on the writing of good controlling ideas. Your controlling idea must:

1. predict the content of your essay as specifically as possible without wasting words
2. be clear and coherent
3. be stated in one complete sentence
4. not be obscured by figures of speech
5. be a statement, not a question
6. move toward a single point, not diverge into two or more ideas

D. Effective Supporting Detail

A controlling idea, once expressed on paper, thereafter convinces or bores the reader according to the quality of the *supporting detail*. If the detail is vague, the controlling idea will bore; if the detail is crisp, the controlling idea will usually convince. Consider, for instance, this paragraph:

> At the turn of the century, many diseases shortened human life. People did not live very long; what life they had was miserable. If disease did not kill them, poor hygiene did. However, through improvement in medicine and public hygiene, we now live many years longer.

Convinced? Probably not, We need more detail. What diseases killed people? How was medicine improved? What improvements were made in public hygiene? How much longer do people now live? A writer doesn't need to be a genius to amass this sort of detail—all he or she needs to do is find more specific information. Consider this rewritten paragraph:

> At the turn of this century, infectious diseases were the primary health menace to this nation. Acute respiratory conditions such as pneumonia and influenza were the major killers. Tuberculosis, too, drained the nation's vitality. Gastrointestinal infections decimated the child population. A great era of environmental control helped change all this. Water and milk supplies were made safe. Engineers constructed systems to handle and treat perilous human wastes and to render them safe. Food sanitation and personal hygiene became a way of life. Continual labors of public health workers diminished death rates of mothers and their infants. Countless children were vaccinated. Tuberculosis was brought under control. True, new environmental hazards replaced the old. But people survived to suffer them. In 1900, the average person in the United States rarely eked out fifty years of life. Some twenty years have since been added to this life expectancy.
>
> Benjamin A. Kogan, *Health: Man in a Changing Environment*

By the time we read the final sentence, we are convinced simply because of the writer's generous use of detail.

Exactly what kind of supporting detail you should use will vary with your subject, but as a general rule it is always better to write in specifics rather than generalities. This means that if you are writing an essay about the ill effects of cigarette smoking, you should learn enough about your subject to be able to name not only the harmful gases given off by cigarettes but also the specific diseases they cause. Any writer who pens a sentence such as "Cigarette smoke contains a variety of dangerous gases, including carbon monoxide, formaldehyde, and hydrogen cyanide," will inevitably sound more competent than the one who merely writes, "Cigarette smoke contains many dangerous gases." And the difference between the first writer, who sounds competent, and the second, who sounds vague, is neither style, nor grammar, nor any of the other indefinables of writing that students are constantly urged to absorb. It is only that the first writer is more specific than the second. Nothing more.

E. Unity

Stick to the point of your essay. If your controlling idea is a comparison of cows and goats, write about that and nothing else. If your controlling idea is to define love, then you must define love. Good writing does not beat about the bush; it approaches the subject directly. The writer moves in the direction of his point without being distracted. This straightforward progression, called *unity*, means that every statement in the essay supports or proves the controlling idea. You introduce only material related to your controlling idea, suppressing the urge to bring up matters that are irrelevant. An essay crowded with irrelevant facts, anecdotes, or illustrations is like a quart of hearty beef soup diluted with a gallon of water.

The following excerpt is an example of writing that does not stick to the point. Notice the pieces of irrelevant information, set in italics, that are thrown in here and there, destroying the unity of the essay. Read the essay without them, and you will see how the writing is strengthened.

> The deadly routine of my studies and work turned the past year into unbearable boredom. Each day proceeded with unerring predictability, from sunrise to sunset. If I were to use a symbol to reflect my life this past year, it would be one gigantic yawn—so dull was the schedule by which I was tyrannized. *Of course, there were always a few bright accidents that invaded the boredom, but they were rare.* Every morning at 7:00 A.M. the alarm dragged me out of bed so that I could race to school in time to answer Prof. Huber's Western Civilization roll call at 8:07 A.M. For the next 50 minutes I listened to the prof drone through his battered and stained lecture notes on the meaning of *civitas,* the First Triumvirate, or the Barbarian Invasion. I took plenty of notes so that I could quote verbatim on the next test. Then I moved on to the next class, Introduction to Psychology, where the instructor always got hung up on "standard deviations," "chi square," and "correlation" because those were his graduate work specialties. Then I moved on to the next class, and the next—all equally numbing to my senses.
>
> At 1:00 P.M. it was time to report to my job as cashier of the Arco self-service gas station, located one block from where I live. *I should probably mention that I live in Bakersfield, a town whose reputation is cruelly maligned. I have found that most people think of Bakersfield as the garbage dump of creation. "How can you stand to live in that ugly place?" they often ask. "Nothing but Okies, fog, and cow dung there," they insist. But I'm defensive of my hometown, so I stick up for it.* Anyway, at the Arco station, I sat in a cage, like a monkey at the

zoo, collecting money through a barred window from citizens whose lives must have been duller than mine, judging by the way their feet dragged and their faces drooped. "That will be $8.50. Thank you, ma'am." "That will be $9.00. Thank you, sir." "No, you will have to work the pump yourself. This is self-service." I repeated myself over and over again—endlessly until I felt that my voice was floating out in the air somewhere, separate from my body. Sometimes I almost wished for a robbery to inject a moment of excitement into my life. *My friend Jimmy Davenport, who works for a posh liquor store, was held up once, and the robbers handcuffed him in the men's toilet, along with the manager of the store and two customers. He told me that he was never so scared in his life as when he looked down the barrel of that big black pistol one of the robbers stuck in his face.* But for me the most exciting event of the job was when I opened my sandwich bag to see if I was having salami or cream cheese.

F. Coherence

An essay that is clear and logical has *coherence*. Not only must its sentences be clear, logical, and grammatically correct, they must be arranged so that the reader understands the flow of thought and the relationships among sentences and words. Perhaps the best way to achieve coherence is to think of your essay as a unit rather than as individual bits and pieces. The focal point of the unit, of course, is your controlling idea. You carefully build your essay so that each sentence follows in logical sequence and so that the essay as a whole hits the reader with a clear and definite impact, as if he had been led to an address through many streets by a well-designed map.

We occasionally receive essays that sound like this:

> In the past year it's been through times of extreme highs and lows in my emotional outlook on life. The trend of any life seems to follow this general pattern. Some of the high moments were meeting new people that turned out to be much more than mere acquaintances, having the newly met person turn into a friend a person could know for the rest of their life. Also meeting and going out with a few special girls, which in our relationship between each other bloomed into a kind of affection for ourselves. Then, too, I gave top performances in the area of athletics, track and field, and also in baseball were most gratifying.
>
> The low points in my life one of them was the splitting up of my parents, watching both of them lose a little youthfulness from inside like a plant that has been cut with a sharp object, the plant will heal and continue to live but forever will be scarred. And, too, breaking up with one girl I was extremely close to. There were other low moments in my life. It occurred at times when least needed. My injuries in the sports in which I competed compounded my feelings of despair.
>
> The cycle of my life in the past year would be for me of course totally and completely unique, but in reality it probably compares to people in everyday life.

Frustrating reading, isn't it? This student's writing is *garbled*—muddled, illogical, or downright unintelligible. It reminds us of a child forcing pieces of a puzzle into the wrong spaces, creating a topsy-turvy picture. Much of this kind of writing is the result of laziness. Some students simply dash off an essay and turn it in without a second glance. They do not try out their sentences by speaking them aloud or by reading through a first draft of the essay to see how it sounds. If one of your sentences sounds choppy or senseless, strike it out and start all over again. Rewrite until the words say what you want them to say, even if it means writing in simpler sentences. As a matter of fact, if you are a chronic garbler, you should avoid embroidered, complex sentences until you have mastered simple, clear sentences.

Incoherence has numerous causes. The following rules and examples will help you to avoid the most common errors.

RULE 1:   *Avoid mixed constructions.* Here are examples of mixed constructions:

Mixed: Whereas parents insist on stifling their children's independence, they encourage rebellion.

Improved: When parents insist on stifling their children's independence, they encourage rebellion.

Mixed: With every new service on the part of government suggests that our taxes are going to be raised.

Improved: Every new service on the part of government suggests that our taxes are going to be raised.

Mixed: My mind was filled with horror at the sight of so many hungry people, which they made me feel guilty for being part of a society that neglects its poor.

Improved: My mind was filled with horror at the sight of so many hungry people. They made me feel guilty for being part of a society that neglects its poor.

Mixed constructions are confusing because they force readers into quick mental adjustments for which they aren't prepared. The writer begins with one pattern of expression but then quickly switches to another, forcing readers to correct the sentence in their minds in order to give it some coherence.

RULE 2:   *Use pronouns that refer only to identifiable antecedents.** Here is an example of incoherence resulting from poor pronoun reference:

Everybody today wants psychological advice so that *they* will tell *them* what to do. But *that's* a way of avoiding *your* problems and losing *one's* sense of responsibility, *which* is the only healthy way to survive.

A careless and inconsistent use of pronouns jumbles the ideas. The passage simply does not stick together properly. To whom do *they* and *them* refer? What does *that's* stand for? Why is there a sudden shift from *everybody* to *your* and yet another shift to *one's*? Finally, *which* seems to refer to "responsibility," creating further confusion. Now observe the revision:

Everybody today wants psychological advice from a counselor who will tell him or her what to do. But relying on counseling is a way of avoiding

---

*For an explanation of antecedent, see page 307.

problems and losing one's sense of responsibility; without responsibility a happy life is impossible.

RULE 3: *Use similar grammatical structures to achieve balance in a sentence.* This is called *parallelism.** The use of parallelism could improve the following sentence:

> Walking a beat, riding patrol cars, and the work of an undercover agent are all dangerous aspects of police work.

Walking and *riding* are similar in form, but "the work of an undercover agent" breaks the pattern. The following is an improvement:

> Walking a beat, riding patrol cars, and doing undercover work are all dangerous aspects of police work.

RULE 4: *Use transition words to help the reader move easily through your writing.* Transition words identify the logical connection between two parts of a sentence. They help the reader to move smoothly from one idea to another. For example:

Too abrupt: She searched and searched for her purse. She could not find it.

Improved: She searched and searched for her purse, *but* she could not find it.

Too abrupt: Romance may express itself in a variety of ways. A man may send a woman a dozen long-stemmed roses. A husband may plan and cook a gourmet meal.

Improved: Romance may express itself in a variety of ways. *For example*, a man may send a woman a dozen long-stemmed roses. *Or, as a romantic gesture*, a husband may plan and cook a gourmet meal.

When choosing a transition word, be certain of the type of signal you wish to send the reader—addition, contrast, specification, or conclusion (see kinds of conjunctions, p. 296).

RULE 5: *Repeat key words to attract and hold your reader's attention.* Notice the effective repetition of the word *dance* in the following excerpt from Hans Christian Andersen's *The Red Shoes:*

> The shoes would not let her do what she liked: when she wanted to go to the right, they *danced* to the left. When she wanted to *dance* up the room, the shoes *danced* down the room, and then down the stairs, through the streets and out of the town gate. Away she *danced*, and away she had to *dance*, right into the dark forest. Something shone up above the trees and she thought it was the moon, for it was a face, but it was the old soldier with the red beard. He nodded and said, "See what pretty *dancing* shoes!"
> This frightened her terribly and she wanted to throw off the red shoes, but they stuck fast. She tore off her stockings, but the shoes had grown fast to her feet. So off she *danced*, and off she had to *dance*, over fields and meadows, in rain and sunshine, by day and by night, but at night it was fearful.

The repetition of the word *dance* holds the reader's attention and reinforces the point of the fairy tale—that the red shoes were magical.

---

*For a fuller explanation of parallelism, see page 325.

2

Sentence Combining

The well-written essay has purpose, strategy, and a controlling idea behind it. It uses supporting details effectively, and consists of paragraphs that are unified and coherent. But aside from all this, a good essay—indeed, any good writing—has an even more basic component: it is composed of effective sentences. If you cannot write vigorous and expressive sentences, it is highly unlikely that you will ever write a vigorous and expressive essay. Whereas Part III of this book is devoted to grammar and designed to help you write better sentences, this chapter will drill you in sentence combining—a technique which, if practiced faithfully, has been shown to actually improve writing style and fluency.

The general theory behind sentence combining is that the human brain contains a powerful sentence-making mechanism. Everyone has a natural capacity to change sentences by adding words, deleting words, transposing words, or substituting one word for another. Practice in sentence combining is a kind of exercise for the sentence-producing mechanism of the brain; it increases the writer's fluency, promotes a more mature style, and develops a knowledge of grammar.

A. Basic Sentence Combining

In a basic sentence-combining drill, you are asked to combine two or more kernel sentences into a more complex one. A kernel sentence is the barest possible sentence, consisting only of a minimum subject and predicate. (For more on the subject and predicate of a sentence, see Unit 15, "Grammar Fundamentals.") Here, for example, are three kernel sentences:

1. The sailor ate his breakfast.
2. The breakfast consisted of eggs.
3. The sunlight streamed through the porthole.

There is nothing grammatically wrong with these three sentences. Each is plainly understandable and correct. Nevertheless, an entire essay written only in such sentences would inevitably seem childish and monotonous. One way to break the monotony and create a more mature style is to blend these simple sentences into a longer, more complex one:

While the sunlight streamed through the porthole, the sailor ate his breakfast of eggs.

Or:

As the sailor breakfasted on eggs, the sunlight streamed through the porthole.

Either of these two sentences would come as a refreshing break in any essay written mainly in kernel sentences.

The aim of sentence combining, then, is to allow you to cultivate a writing style characterized by sentence variety. And one way to achieve sentence variety is to combine kernel sentences into longer ones. Beginning with simple sentences that become progressively more complex, the exercise below asks you to combine sentence clusters into a single sentence.

Exercises

Each of the following passages is organized into clusters. Combine each cluster into a single sentence.

MODEL

Original clusters:

First Cluster:
1. A letter had landed on Jack's desk.
2. The letter was from the Security Office.
3. The letter requested a report.
4. The report was to be about the deportation of aliens.

Second Cluster:
5. The letter had an effect on Jack.
6. The effect was paralyzing.
7. The effect was paralyzing because Jack was responsible for all aliens.

Third Cluster:
8. Jack was no miracle worker.
9. Jack adopted a typical obfuscating tactic.
10. Jack made a vague reply.
11. The reply said nothing.

Possible transformation:

First Cluster Transformed: A letter from the Security Office requesting a report about the deportation of aliens landed on Jack's desk.

Second Cluster Transformed: The letter had a paralyzing effect on Jack because he was responsible for all aliens.

Third Cluster Transformed: Since Jack was no miracle worker, he simply ignored the letter and adopted the typical obfuscating tactic of sending a vague reply that said nothing.

1. a. The Dutch East India Company was chartered by the States-General of the Netherlands.
   b. It was to expand trade.
   c. It was to assure close relations between the Dutch government and its colonial enterprises in Asia.

2. a. Benjamin Franklin was an American statesman.
   b. He was a printer.
   c. He was a scientist.
   d. He was a writer.
   e. He was the son of a tallow chandler and soapmaker.

3. a. A hat provides considerable psychological security.
   b. It protects the face.
   c. It hides the face.
   d. The hiding is from curious onlookers.
   e. These onlookers threaten one's privacy.

4. a. Buddhism arose in India in the 6th century B.C.
   b. It was a protest.
   c. The protest was against the overdeveloped ritualism of the Hindus.
   d. The overdeveloped ritualism was particularly in the sacrificial cults.
   e. Sometimes these sacrificial cults even involved sacrificing human beings.

5. a. The passage of liquor laws has always been prompted by a public desire.
   b. The desire was to prevent immoderate use of intoxicants.
   c. But the passage was also prompted by the need to raise revenue.
   d. Liquor laws are legislation designed to restrict, regulate, or totally abolish the manufacture, sale, and use of alcoholic beverages.

ANSWERS   Here are some sample answers. Many other possibilities exist.

1. Chartered by the States-General of the Netherlands, the Dutch East India Company was intended to expand trade and to assure close relations between the Dutch government and its colonial enterprises in Asia.

2. Benjamin Franklin, the son of a tallow chandler and soapmaker, became an American statesman, printer, scientist, and writer.

3. A hat provides psychological security by protecting the face and hiding it from curious onlookers who threaten one's privacy.

4. Buddhism arose in India in the 6th century B.C. as a protest against the overdeveloped ritualism of the Hindus, particularly against their sacrificial cults, which often involved human sacrifices.

5. The passage of liquor laws—legislation designed to restrict, regulate, or totally abolish the manufacture, sale, and use of alcoholic beverages—has always been prompted by the public's desire to prevent immoderate use of intoxicants and by the government's need to raise revenue.

16

B. Sentence Generating

In a sentence-generating drill you are asked not merely to combine sentences, but to actually expand them using your own ideas. The aim of this drill is to teach you how to use sentence combining to produce your own varied sentences. Consider this kernel sentence:

Mr. Jones lived in a mansion.

An expanded version might read as follows (the new portions are printed in capitals):

Mr. Jones, WHO MADE MILLIONS ON THE STOCKMARKET, lived in a mansion IN A SECLUDED WOODS SURROUNDED BY VAST GREEN MEADOWS.

From expanding a single kernel sentence, you can move to expanding and combining several kernel sentences to make a paragraph. Here, for example, are four kernel sentences followed by their expansion into a paragraph:

1. The hotel kitchen upset Nick and Nora.
2. It could ruin the simplest dish.
3. Today the corned beef looked terrible.
4. They decided to cook on a hot plate in their room.

Expansion: The hotel kitchen, with its inferior service, upset Nick and Nora. It could ruin the simplest dish, even an ungarnished poached egg. Today, the corned beef looked terrible, like a lump of altogether odious black grease. They decided to cook on a hot plate in their room, thus avoiding the kitchen's inevitable bungling of meat, vegetables, and baked goods.

Sentences can be generated by the following means: coordination, subordination, relative construction, participial construction, prepositional construction, appositive, or absolute construction. An example of each follows. The generated portion appears in capital letters.

Coordination: Cassandra was a Greek prophetess, AND SHE WAS THE DAUGHTER OF PRIAM.

Subordination: ALTHOUGH IT IS STILL SOLEMN IN TONE, the Catholic requiem today reveals a more joyful attitude than it used to.

Relative Construction: The Samurai were Japanese feudal knights WHO EMERGED DURING THE 12TH-CENTURY WARS BETWEEN THE TAIRA AND MINAMOTO CLANS.

Participial Construction: Wagner's opera *Tristan and Isolde,* BASED ON GOTTFRIED VON STRASSBURG'S VERSION OF THE ARTHURIAN LEGEND, represents the fullest musical and theatrical expression of German romanticism.

Prepositional Construction: WITHOUT THE BLESSING OF LUTHER, the German peasants' cause would have ultimately met with defeat.

Appositive: It is precisely to keep infants and children from being battered—TO GIVE THEM A TEMPORARY HOME, TO FEED AND HOUSE THEM, AND TO PROVIDE SOME PSYCHOLOGICAL COUNSELING—that halfway houses have been established in many major cities.

Absolute
Construction: DINNER BEING SERVED ON A BREEZY PATIO, we all dressed warmly.

Exercises

Add at least one clause or phrase to the sentences below. Try for variety by making your clauses or phrases modify different sentence elements.

MODEL

Original
sentence: The formal gardens were turned into an enormous vegetable patch.

Transformation: The formal gardens, WHICH HAD BEEN ADMIRED FOR THEIR NEOCLASSICAL SYMMETRY, were turned into an enormous vegetable patch.

1. a. The destroyers were skulking by the eastern cove.
   b. The rear admiral had taken over only two days before.
   c. Still, his task force should have wiped out the enemy.
2. a. Members of the postwar baby boom are now young adults.
   b. They too are concerned about the effects of inflation and high interest rates.
3. a. It may seem profitless to worry about a nuclear holocaust.
   b. However, common sense dictates that we must confront the possibility honestly.
4. a. Clearly, some of the same types of people who now become smugglers or gang members probably constituted a sizable percentage of America's settlers and pioneers.
   b. This observation seems to have been true for the settlement of many countries.
   c. The fact is that privileged and exceptional individuals undoubtedly play a major role in shaping a nation, but so do the individuals at the other end of the social spectrum.
5. a. *Gone with the Wind* remains one of the world's most widely read novels.
   b. The story of Scarlett O'Hara and Rhett Butler still manages to keep readers enthralled through hundreds of pages.
   c. Today's novel readers love to escape into the idealized world of Tara and the surrounding plantations.

ANSWERS   Here are some sample answers. Many other possibilities exist.

1. TO SUPPLY THEIR STARVED, SICK GARRISON, the destroyers were skulking by the eastern cove, DROPPING MEDICAL SUPPLIES AND FOOD OVERBOARD. The rear admiral COMMANDING THE FLOTILLA had taken over only two days before, HIS FORCE

18

FORMED OF WORN-OUT UNITS WHO LONGED TO GO HOME. Still, his task force, WITH THE ADVANTAGES OF RADAR, SURPRISE, AND SUPERIOR FIREPOWER, should have wiped out the enemy.

2. Members of the postwar baby boom are now young adults WHO HOPE TO FIND GOOD JOBS AND TO BUY THEIR OWN HOMES. LIKE THEIR PARENTS' GENERATION, they too worry about the effects of inflation and high interest rates, WHICH EAT UP SAVINGS ACCOUNTS AND CAUSE BUSINESSES TO GO BANKRUPT.

3. It may seem profitless to worry about a nuclear holocaust—A THIRD WORLD WAR IN WHICH ENTIRE CONTINENTS COULD BE WIPED OUT. However, AFTER WE STUDY THE HISTORICAL TRENDS OF WORLD POWERS AND REALIZE HOW SIMPLE IT IS TO CREATE NUCLEAR POWER, common sense dictates that the possibility must be confronted honestly.

4. Clearly, some of the same types of people who now become smugglers or gang members—ADVENTURERS, MALCONTENTS, AND FUGITIVES FROM JUSTICE—probably constituted a sizable percentage of America's settlers and pioneers. This observation seems to have been true in the settlement of many areas, INCLUDING AUSTRALIA, SIBERIA, AND SOUTH AFRICA. The fact is that privileged and exceptional individuals, SUCH AS WASHINGTON AND JEFFERSON, undoubtedly play a major role in shaping a nation, but so do individuals at the other end of the social spectrum—THE POOR AND THE UNLETTERED.

5. BECAUSE OF ITS ENORMOUS ROMANTIC APPEAL, *Gone with the Wind* is still one of the world's most widely read novels. The story of Scarlett O'Hara, THE SELF-CENTERED BUT COURAGEOUS SOUTHERN BELLE, and Rhett Butler, THE DASHING, SLIGHTLY WICKED MAN OF THE WORLD, still manages to keep readers enthralled through hundreds of pages. BORED BY A DRAB INDUSTRIAL LANDSCAPE, TIRED OF STORIES ABOUT DRUGS AND DEPRESSION, AND EAGER TO EXPERIENCE A BIT OF OLD-STYLE ROMANCE, today's readers of novels love to escape into the idealized world of Tara and the surrounding plantations, WHERE KINDLY MASTERS TAKE CARE OF FAITHFUL SLAVES, WHERE MEN PLACE WOMEN ON A PEDESTAL, AND WHERE HONOR MEANS MORE THAN MONEY.

C. Judging the Sentence

Because any given passage can be written any number of different ways, all writers are faced with nearly endless possibilities of expression. Consequently, it is not enough merely to combine kernel sentences into longer ones: the combination itself must be more effective than the originals. Consider, for instance, this complex but tone-deaf sentence below. It can hardly be called an improvement over a succession of kernel sentences:

> The little red house in the ugly run-down neighborhood that had suffered through numerous attacks of violence by hideous bands of hoodlums who were poor and uneducated was finally burned down.

The point is that the ultimate aim of sentence combining is to produce more readable sentences, not merely more complex ones. To do so requires that you develop an ear for judging the best possible version of several sentences created either through sentence combining or sentence generating. In judging the various versions of sentences, you should attend to the following criteria:

1. Clarity (Which version is the clearest?)
2. Economy (Which version is the most economical?)
3. Emphasis (Which version is the most emphatic?)
4. Stylistic sophistication—wit, balance, texture, and tone (Which version sounds the best?)

Obviously, an ear for these qualities comes only with time and practice. But it is a useful exercise nevertheless to read through the following sentences and try to see why one version is preferable to the other. Even if you cannot put into words the reason for your choice, you might be able intuitively to tell which sentence is better. And when you can accurately and consistently make this kind of choice, you will be well on the way to being able to choose which of your own sentences are stronger and should be used, and which are weaker and should be edited.

Exercises

Choose from each group of two sentences below the one you find most effective, and be prepared to explain why.

MODEL

    a. Swiss watchmakers are trained by an apprentice system and they work under an accomplished master for years before they are allowed to work independently.

    b. Trained by an apprentice system, Swiss watchmakers work under an accomplished master for years before they are allowed to work independently.

Answer: The second version (b) is more emphatic, because it subordinates a participial phrase to the base sentence rather than having two base sentences joined by coordination. In this case, the information provided in the base sentence is the most important.

1. a. Groping helplessly in the dark, he was trying to turn on the light.
   b. He was, groping helplessly in the dark, trying to turn on the light.

2. a. While they were clothed in colorful uniforms, the three army captains signed the papers from headquarters.
   b. Clothed in colorful uniforms, the three army captains signed the papers from headquarters.

3. a. After a seizure, the grand mal victim will often lie stretched out, his body shivering, and his eyes are half open, and his voice is unable to utter a word.

b. After a seizure, the grand mal victim will often lie stretched out, his body shivering, his eyes half open, and his voice unable to utter a word.

4. a. *Ecumenism* is a term applied to the movement aimed at unifying rather than separating the churches of the world.
   b. *Ecumenism* is a term applied to the movement aimed at unifying rather than to separate the churches of the world.

5. a. Drinking with publishers for hours was a habit developed by the aging novelist, who was suffering from a deep depression that came from having lost popularity with his reading audience.
   b. Suffering from a deep depression caused by a loss of popularity with his reading audience, the aging novelist developed the habit of spending hours drinking with publishers.

6. a. Fire—the phenomenon of combustion as seen in light, flame, and heat—is one of the basic tools of human civilization.
   b. Fire is one of the basic tools of human civilization—as seen in light, flame, and heat.

7. a. Manufacturing gelatin, that is, removing foreign substances, boiling the material in distilled water, and purifying it of all chemicals used in freeing the gelatin from the connective tissues, is a complex process.
   b. Manufacturing gelatin is a complex process that involves removing foreign substances, boiling the material in distilled water, and purifying it of all chemicals used in freeing the gelatin from the connective tissues.

8. a. In the second version, the Madonna is holding the limp body of Jesus, a look of deep sorrow shadowing her face.
   b. In the second version, the Madonna is holding the limp body of Jesus and a look of deep sorrow is shadowing her face.

9. a. Its base corroded by water, the tower slowly leaned toward the east.
   b. Because its base had been corroded by water, the tower slowly leaned toward the east.

10. a. At several colleges in the United States, a student can get a doctoral degree without ever having to do research, taking a qualifying examination, or submitting a thesis.
    b. At several colleges in the United States, a student can get a doctoral degree without ever having to do research, take a qualifying examination, or submit a thesis.

3

The Paragraph

A. Uses of the Paragraph

Paragraph comes from the Middle Latin word *paragraphus,* meaning a sign that designated a separate part. Without question, the human brain prefers to view the whole as a collection of parts—a prejudice that has decisively affected the shape of written communication. Words are grouped into phrases, phrases into clauses, and clauses into sentences. Sentences are melded into paragraphs, paragraphs into sections, and sections into chapters. Such are the constituent parts of a book, which may or may not itself be cleaved into separate volumes.

The aim of paragraphing is to signal the introduction of a new idea, the amplification of some significant aspect of an old one, or the transition from one idea to another. In effect, the paragraph is the means by which ideas may be packaged on the page according to their importance. The reader does not have to ferret through a jumble of words for the significant points but is guided to them by the familiar paragraph indentation.

1. Paragraphs That Signal a New Idea

Consider the following two paragraphs, on the subject of how much a home town can change in thirty years:

> Sights have changed: there is a new precision about street and home, a clearing away of chicken yards, cow barns, pigeon-crested cupolas, weed lots and coulees, the dim and secret adult-free rendezvous of boys. An intricate metal "jungle gym" is a common backyard sight, the back swing uncommon. There are wide expanses of clear windows designed to let in the parlor light, fewer ornamental windows of colored glass designed to keep it out. Attic and screen porch are slowly vanishing and lovely shades of pastel are painted upon new houses, tints that once would have embarrassed farmer and merchant alike.
>
> Sounds have changed: I heard not once the clopping of a horse's hoof, nor the mourn of a coyote. I heard instead the shriek of brakes, the heavy throbbing of the once-a-day Braniff airliner into Minot, the shattering

sirens born of war, the honk of a diesel locomotive which surely cannot call to faraway places the heart of a wakeful boy like the old steam whistle in the night. You can walk down the streets of my town now and hear from open windows the intimate voices of the Washington commentators in casual converse on the great affairs of state; but you cannot hear on Sunday morning the singing in Norwegian of the Lutheran hymns; the old-country accents grow fainter in the speech of my Velva neighbors.

Eric Sevareid, This Is Eric Sevareid

The first paragraph deals with changes in sights; the second, with changes in sounds. The catalog of changes is partitioned into two paragraphs and dealt with separately. It is a little as if the writer had said to the reader, "Listen, I'm going to tell you how the sights of my home town have changed." And when he has done with that topic, he nudges the reader once again and says, "And now I'll tell you how the sounds of my home town have changed."

The division into two paragraphs here is natural and logical. A reader has the opportunity to savor the one sort of change before being treated to the other. Moreover, the writing has an intensity and concentration that would have been badly diluted had both kinds of changes been merely jumbled together in a single block of print.

2. Paragraphs That Amplify a New Aspect of an Old Idea

Writers often come to a point at which specific illustrations must be given, exceptions noted, and amplifications made. Each such turn in the writing cries out for a separate paragraph. The following is an example of such a shift:

About 900 B.C., another Asiatic people, known today as Etruscans, arrived via the sea on the western coast of central Italy in the vicinity of Rome. Etruscan origins and language, however, remain as irritatingly unknown today as do the Sumerian. But Roman legends, supported by Greek rumors, depict the Etruscans as descendants of the Hittites who had fled their disintegrating empire in the twelfth century B.C. in the aftermath of the fall of Troy.

Cruel, clever, and sexy, the Etruscans killed off the natives, invented gladiatorial games, drained the marshes, plied the seas with commerce, traversed the heartland of Europe with goods, and founded a religion built on fornication, death, and hellfire. The senior trinity of their gods consisted of a holy father, a virgin mother, and an immaculately begotten daughter. In Etruscan theology, the dead went first to purgatory for judgment, where, if found guilty, their souls were damned to various degrees of torment, the ultimate punishment being eternal hellfire. In the thirteenth century A.D., these concepts seeped into Christianity via the *Divina Commedia* of Dante, who was steeped in Etruscan mythology.

Max I. Dimont, Those Indestructible Jews

The first paragraph simply introduces the Etruscans in a general way and puzzles over their obscure origins. The second paragraph amplifies on the Etruscan char-

r. In this way the writer has separated the general from the specific, a tactic that s focus to the writing and spares the reader from having to make any dizzying p of logic.

Paragraphs That Signal a Transition

ften a writer will need to carefully bridge the gap between the ideas contained in one paragraph and those expounded in another. And where the shift in the line of thought between two paragraphs is sudden and complicated, a transition paragraph may be used to help the reader along. Here is an example:

First topic	Inside America civilized life is no finer. A President, a Senator, a man of God have been assassinated. Citizens are murdered in the streets. Riots, armed assaults, looting, burning, outbursts of hatred have increased to the point where they have become commonplace.
Transition paragraph	Life in civilized America is out of control. Nothing is out of control in the forest. Everything complies with the instinct for survival—which is the law and order of the woods.
Second topic	Although the forest looks peaceful it supports incessant warfare, most of which is hidden and silent. For thirty-five years the strong have been subduing the weak. The blueberries that once flourished on the mountain have been destroyed. All the trees are individuals, as all human beings are individuals; and every tree poses a threat to every other tree. The competition is so fierce that you can hardly penetrate some of the thickets where the lower branches of neighboring trees are interlocked in a blind competition for survival.

Brooks Atkinson, "The Warfare in the Forest
Is Not Wanton," *New York Times*,
15 March 1970

The author of these paragraphs wishes to demonstrate the difference between the respective laws of survival in the forest and in civilized society. His ultimate purpose is to conclude that the forest conducts its affairs with less rancor and malevolence than does civilized America. The first paragraph therefore describes the violence of civilized America; the third describes the violence of the forest. Squeezed in between these two is a thin transition paragraph that nudges the reader along. By such measures do writers transit their arguments from one point to another without losing the reader in the process.

B. The Shape of the Paragraph

Most paragraphs consist of three parts: a topic sentence, supporting detail, and a summary sentence. Often, but not always, a paragraph begins with its topic sentence, which states the main idea. The main idea is then developed through supporting details—examples, facts, testimonials, and other particulars. The summary sentence restates the main idea, usually by extending it slightly from its original presentation in the topic sentence. The typical paragraph that conforms to this arrangement may therefore be conceptualized as having a visual shape like the one sketched below.

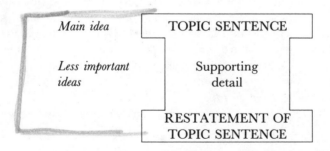

This odd-looking shape—something like an overstuffed sandwich—reminds us that paragraphs typically begin and end with generalizations, between which are crammed more specific and supportive assertions. Here is such a paragraph:

Topic sentence: *By a strange perversity in the cosmic plan, the biologically good die young.* Species are not destroyed for their shortcomings but for their achievements. The tribes that slumber in the graveyards of the past were not the most simple and undistinguished of their day, but the most complicated and con-
Supporting detail: spicuous. The magnificent sharks of the Devonian period passed with the passing of the period, but certain contemporaneous genera of primitive shellfish are still on earth. Similarly, the lizards of the Mesozoic era have long outlived the dinosaurs who were immeasurably their biologic betters.
Summary sentence: Illustrations such as these could be endlessly increased. *The price of distinction is death.*

John Hodgdon Bradley, "Is Man an Absurdity?"
Harper's Magazine, October 1936

The topic sentence of this paragraph, with which it begins, is the main idea that "the biologically good die young." Supporting details and examples are then supplied in sentences 2 through 5, while the final sentence rephrases the main idea and slightly extends it. A paragraph organized in this way is said to move from the general to the particular.

Some paragraphs are constructed in quite the opposite way, to proceed from the particular to the general, from supporting detail to the main idea. Such paragraphs may be conceptualized as having the following visual shape:

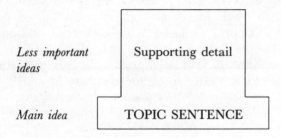

Here is a paragraph to illustrate this organization:

Supporting detail: When we watch a person walk away from us, his image shrinks in size. But since we know for a fact that he is not shrinking, we make an unconscious correcting and "see" him as retaining his full stature. Past experience tells us what his true stature is with respect to our own. Any sane and dependable expectation of the future requires that he have the same true *Topic* stature when we next encounter him. *Our perception is thus a prediction; it* *sentence:* *embraces the past and the future as well as the present.*

Warren J. Wittreich, *Visual Perception and Personality*

The paragraph opens with an example of how a person appears to shrink in size as he or she walks away from us. This fact is then explained by the topic sentence, which generalizes about perception. Paragraphs that conform to this shape are often used by writers to provide a mild change of pace. However, the other kind of paragraph, where the topic sentence precedes the supporting detail, is by far the commoner of the two.

It would be a mistake to infer from this discussion that paragraphs rigidly conform to one or the other of these two shapes. Writing is such a creative enterprise that considerable variation in paragraphs is to be expected. There is, for instance, the sort of paragraph that has the topic sentence somewhere in the midriff. Here is one such example:

As long as women were brought up and educated very differently from men and as long as their whole mode of life was different, it was safe and suitable to uphold the traditional beliefs as to certain mental sex differences. But as the differentiation in the education of the two sexes lessened so have the actual differences in their abilities and interest. *Today the survival of some of these stereotypes is a psychological strait jacket for both sexes.* Witness the fact that some 40 per cent of women undergraduates have confessed (the proportion was confirmed in two studies on widely separated college campuses) that they have occasionally "played dumb" on dates; that is, concealed some academic honor, pretended ignorance of a subject, "threw games," played down certain skills in obedience to the unwritten law that the man must be superior in those particular areas. If he *were* superior, the stratagem would not be necessary. "It embarrassed me that my 'steady' in high school," recalled a college junior in an interview, "got worse marks than I. A boy should naturally do better in school. I would never tell him my marks and would often ask him to help me with my homework." Confront the belief "a boy should naturally do better in school" with the fact that the marks of high school girls are generally somewhat superior to those of boys, probably because girls study more conscientiously. Could a surer recipe for trouble be invented?

Mirra Komarovsky, "The Bright Girl's Dilemma,"
Women in the Modern World

Such paragraphs are often found buried somewhere in the middle of an essay where the argument is the thickest. A transition sentence or two, a little preamble, and the topic sentence of the paragraph is forced to take a seat somewhere in the middle pews. What is important, however, is not where the topic sentence is actually placed, but how adequately it has been developed and proved.

Other paragraphs will routinely begin with a topic sentence, but will omit the final summary of the generalization. If the topic sentence has been adequately developed, and the point of the paragraph is quite clear, a final summarizing sentence is neither required nor desirable. The writer's aim, after all, is to make a point, not to abide by some ideal paragraph shape. Here is a paragraph that begins with a topic sentence but omits a final summarizing sentence:

Topic sentence: *It by no means follows that computers will in the immediate future exhibit human creativity, subtlety, sensitivity, or wisdom.* A classic and probably apocryphal illustration is in the field of machine translation of human languages: a language—say, English—is input and the text is output in another language—say, Chinese. After the completion of an advanced translation program, so the story goes, a delegation which included a U.S. senator was proudly taken through a demonstration of the computer system. The senator was asked to produce an English phrase for translation and promptly suggested, "Out of sight, out of mind." The machine dutifully whirred and winked and generated a piece of paper on which were printed a few Chinese characters. But the senator could not read Chinese. So, to complete the test, the program was run in reverse, the Chinese characters input and an English phrase output. The visitors crowded around the new piece of paper, which to their initial puzzlement read, "Invisible idiot."

Carl Sagan, The Dragons of Eden

In this particular paragraph, a final summarizing sentence would have all but ruined the impact of the punch line.

Finally, sometimes a topic sentence will be too complex to be developed in a single paragraph. In the following example, a single topic sentence, "There are many types of poetical obscurity," is developed in two paragraphs:

There are many types of poetical obscurity. There is the obscurity that results from the poet's being mad. This is rare. Madness in poets is as uncommon as madness in dogs. A discouraging number of reputable poets are sane beyond recall. There is also the obscurity that is the result of the poet's wishing to appear mad, even if only a little mad. This is rather common and rather dreadful. I know of nothing more distasteful than the work of a poet who has taken leave of his reason deliberately, as a commuter might of his wife.

Then there is the unintentional obscurity or muddiness that comes from the inability of some writers to express even a simple idea without stirring up the bottom. And there is the obscurity that results when a fairly large thought is crammed into a three- or four-foot line. The function of poetry is to concentrate; but sometimes over-concentration occurs, and there is no more comfort in such a poem than there is in the subway at the peak hour.

E. B. White, "Types of Poetical Obscurity"

C. The Length of the Paragraph

There are no rules governing the length of an adequately developed paragraph. The topic sentence must guide you. When you have supported and developed it to your satisfaction, you have completed your paragraph. Often, students fall into the error of writing thin, emaciated paragraphs. Look over your finished essay; if your paragraphs are all three or four lines long, something is wrong. Most likely your supportive details are inadequate, and you are probably writing empty paragraphs that sound like this:

> The defensive backfielders of football are disciplined men. They are tenacious and controlled. They must be tough and defend aggressively.

This paragraph is so empty it could float a balloon. Sentences 2 and 3 simply parrot back the content of sentence 1 without adding any detail, substantiation, examples, or proof. Here is an example of a well-developed paragraph on the same topic:

> *In the defensive backfield the aggression gets buried under more and more inhibition and discipline.* These men are like long-distance runners: They are loners, but they are nowhere near as hungry for glory as are the wide receivers. In place of the vanity and fantasies of the wide receivers, the defensive backs experience depression and rage. They have traits that can be found in offensive linemen, wide receivers, and linebackers. They are tenacious. They must learn zone and man-on-man pass-defense patterns that require incredible self-discipline in the furor of battle. They must not be led by their natural inclination, which is to follow receivers out of their zone before the quarterback releases the ball on a pass play. They must execute patterns precisely. To counter running plays, however, they must move up fast and, though lighter and weaker than the running backs they are trying to stop, hit very hard. So they need controlled and timed brutality and anger.

Arnold J. Mandell, "In Pro Football They Play
Best Who Play What They Are," *Saturday Review/World,* 5 October 1974

The topic sentence "A pig is ugly" could probably be adequately supported in 100 words; on the other hand, "Poverty is ugly" might require at least 300 words. The more restricted the topic sentence, the shorter the paragraph. Your duty is to make sure the paragraph fully supports its topic sentence.

Journalistic Paragraphs

If you have ever read a newspaper or magazine, as almost certainly you have, this discussion might strike you as odd, since popular writing often traffics in the very sort of skimpy paragraph we preach against. Indeed, as we have already said, paragraphs do come in a variety of shapes and sizes. A particularly specialized kind of paragraph has evolved from journalistic writing. Often, this sort of paragraph is no more than a sentence or two long, is entirely devoid of facts and supporting detail, and is intended to present no more than the bare bones of a case. This journalistic paragraph is designed to be gulped down at a glance from a reader crowded in a bus or squashed between commuters in a subway. Here is an example, taken from a newspaper:

> Tanzanian forces bent on driving Uganda's President Idi Amin from power launched a new attack Wednesday up a major highway leading to the capital of Kampala, diplomatic and exile sources said.
>
> The Tanzanian forces reportedly were virtually within striking distance of Entebbe Airport, Amin's main supply link with the outside world.
>
> Meanwhile, Radio Uganda claimed that Libya was sending tons of military equipment to Uganda and that Amin personally took command of his armies for a promised counterattack to begin next week.
>
> "Tanzanian Troops Drive Toward Kampala,"
> *Atlanta Constitution,* 8 March 1979

Paragraphs of this shape, skimpiness, and size, however suitable for newspaper readers, are not recommended for student essays. Newspaper writers are intent on merely supplying the bare facts to readers who are themselves too harried and rushed to want more. Student writers, on the other hand, are beset by different pressures and expectations. Teachers expect students to write fully developed paragraphs just as newspaper readers expect reporters to serve up only the bare bones of a story. If you are writing for the student newspaper, use the journalistic paragraph. But if you are writing an essay for an English class, use the more familiar, better-developed paragraph that allows you to assert a generalization and then completely support it.

D. Developmental Strategies

With considerable justification, the paragraph has frequently been called a miniature essay. Just as an essay must develop its controlling idea, so must a paragraph develop its topic sentence—in both cases, through the use of supporting detail.

Both essay and paragraph are subjected to demands of unity and coherence. Clinching the comparison, however, is the fact that both the essay and the paragraph use the same developmental strategies—narration, description, example, definition, comparison/contrast, process, classification, causal analysis, and argumentation.

Later in this book, separate units are devoted to specific instruction in the use of each strategy in writing an essay. For now, we will discuss the application of each strategy to paragraph writing.

1. Narration

To *narrate* means to tell a story. A paragraph developed by narration therefore tells a story, sometimes from the personal point of view, and sometimes from the third-person point of view. Narrative writing convinces the reader by using specific detail, by following a clear and understandable sequence, and by recounting the story in terms readers may have experienced in their own lives. Here is an example of a paragraph developed by narration:

> Every morning I lay on the floor in the front parlour watching her door. The blind was pulled down to within an inch of the sash so that I could not be seen. When she came out on the doorstep my heart leaped. I ran to the hall, seized my books and followed her. I kept her brown figure always in my eye and, when we came near the point at which our ways diverged, I quickened my pace and passed her. This happened morning after morning. I had never spoken to her, except for a few casual words, and yet her name was like a summons to all my foolish blood.
>
> James Joyce, *Araby*

The detail is specific and the sequence fast-paced and clear. Furthermore, the event recounted—of young unrequited love—is one with which most readers can identify. Unit 5 teaches how to develop an entire essay by narration.

2. Description

If narration means to tell, *description* means to show. A paragraph developed by description uses a dominant impression as a central theme to unify its descriptive detail. In the following passage, the dominant impression of Braggioni is of an expensively dressed, grossly fat man. We have italicized specific words that support this impression.

> Braggioni catches her glance solidly as if he had been waiting for it, leans forward, *balancing his paunch* between his spread knees, and sings with tremendous emphasis, weighing his words. He has, the song relates, no father and no mother, nor even a friend to console him; lonely as a wave of the sea he comes and goes, lonely as a wave. His *mouth opens round* and yearns sideways, his *balloon cheeks* grow oily with the labor of song. He *bulges* marvelously in his expensive garments. Over his lavender collar,

crushed upon a purple necktie, held by a diamond hoop: over his ammunition belt of tooled leather worked in silver, buckled cruelly around his *gasping middle:* over the tops of his glossy yellow shoes Braggioni *swells* with *ominous ripeness,* his mauve silk hose *stretched taut,* his ankles bound with the stout leather thongs of his shoes.

Katherine Anne Porter, Flowering Judas

Without a dominant impression, a passage of description runs the risk of becoming overwhelmed by irrelevant detail. Unit 6 teaches the use of a dominant impression in writing a descriptive essay.

3. Example

A paragraph developed by *example* begins with a generalization, which it then supports with specific examples. The examples must be to the point, vivid, supportive of the generalization, and clearly connected to it by an introductory phrase such as "for example," or "for instance." Here is an example:

> Temperaments are so various that there may be even more than "nine and sixty ways" of writing books. Rousseau, for example, could not compose with pen in hand: but then Chateaubriand could not compose without. Wordsworth did it while walking, riding, or in bed; but Southey, only at his desk. Shakespeare, we are told, never blotted a line; Scott could toss first drafts unread to the printer; Trollope drilled himself, watch on desk, to produce two hundred and fifty words every quarter of an hour; Hilaire Belloc, so Desmond MacCarthy once told me, claimed to have written twenty thousand of them in a day; and in ten days Balzac could turn out sixty thousand.

F. L. Lucas, Style

The generalization occurs in the first sentence, which also introduces the main idea the paragraph intends to document. Following the generalization are examples of various methods of composing used by nine different authors. The overuse of generalizations without supporting examples is a common failing of student writing. Unit 7 takes up the use of examples as a strategy in the writing of essays.

4. Definition

A *definition* says what something is and what it is not. A paragraph developed by definition therefore focuses on specifying the characteristics of the subject—first by showing the general category it belongs to, and then by distinguishing it from other items in the same category. Here is an example:

> Chemistry is that branch of science which has the task of investigating the materials out of which the universe is made. It is not concerned with the forms into which they may be fashioned. Such objects as chairs, tables, vases, bottles, or wires are of no significance in chemistry; but such sub-

stances as glass, wool, iron, sulfur, and clay, as the materials out of which they are made, are what it studies. Chemistry is concerned not only with the composition of such substances, but also with their inner structure.

John Arrend Timm, General Chemistry

The writer first places chemistry in the category of science and then differentiates it from other scientific disciplines by the nature and content of its study. This definition is short and to the point. Definitions of more abstract and complex terms such as *love* and *justice,* on the other hand, can consume several paragraphs or entire essays. Unit 8 teaches the development of an essay by definition.

5. Comparison/Contrast

Comparison/contrast paragraphs examine items for similarities and differences. The items are compared on certain specific bases, and the paragraph alternates from one to the other, indicating either similarities or differences through the use of appropriate phrases such as *on the other hand, likewise, similarly,* and *but.* In the following example, terms indicating comparison/contrast are in italics:

> The way in which culture affects language becomes clear by *comparing* how the English and Hopi languages refer to H_2O in its liquid state. English, like most other European languages, has only one word—"water"—and it pays no attention to what the substance is used for or its quantity. The Hopi of Arizona, *on the other hand,* use "pahe" to mean the large amounts of water present in natural lakes or rivers, and "keyi" for the small amounts in domestic jugs and canteens. English, *though,* makes other distinctions that Hopi does not. The speaker of English is careful to distinguish between a lake and a stream, between a waterfall and a geyser; *but* "pahe" makes no distinction among lakes, ponds, rivers, streams, waterfalls, and springs.

Peter Farb, Man at the Mercy of His Language

The basis of this comparison/contrast between English and Hopi—the way these languages refer to water—is given early in the paragraph. Having announced his intention to compare and the basis of the comparison, the writer then catalogs the similarities and differences between the English and Hopi languages on this one item.

Two common weaknesses in student essays based on comparison/contrast are: (1) failure to fairly examine both items on the same basis, thus favoring one item over another, and (2) failure to use appropriate comparison/contrast expressions, thus disguising the intent of the paragraph. Be alert to these pitfalls when writing your own comparison/contrast paragraphs. Unit 9 discusses comparison/contrast as it applies to the development of an entire essay.

6. Process

Process refers to any "how-to-do-it" writing that gives step-by-step instructions. Generally considered to be the easiest strategy for developing a paragraph or an essay, a process might give instructions on how to bake a cake, how to true a bicycle wheel, or how to play the recorder. The example we have chosen instructs the reader in how to sharpen a knife:

> The sharpening stone must be fixed in place on the table, so that it will not move around. You can do this by placing a piece of rubber inner tube or a thin piece of foam rubber under it. Or you can tack four strips of wood, if you have a rough worktable, to frame the stone and hold it in place. Put a generous puddle of oil in the stone—this will soon disappear into the surface of a new stone, and you will need to keep adding more oil. Press the knife blade flat against the stone in the puddle of oil, using your index finger. Whichever way the cutting edge of the knife faces is the side of the blade that should get a little more pressure. Move the blade around three or four times in a narrow oval about the size of your fingernail, going *counterclockwise* when the sharp edge is facing right. Now turn the blade over in the same spot on the stone, press hard, and move it around the small oval *clockwise,* with more pressure on the cutting edge that faces left. Repeat the ovals, flipping the knife blade over six or seven times, and applying lighter pressure to the blade the last two times.
>
> Florence H. Pettit, "How to Sharpen Your Knife,"
> *How to Make Whirligigs and Whimmy Diddles*

Writing about a process is usually straightforward; it is considered so easy that many teachers will not allow the student to submit a process essay for a final exam. Other than the occasional muddling of the sequence, students generally have no trouble writing process paragraphs or essays. For further instruction on this strategy, see Unit 10.

7. Classification

Classification means to divide something and group its elements into major categories and types. For a classification to be useful it must be based on a single principle and must be complete. For instance, say you had to write a paragraph classifying students according to their year in college. If your classification included only freshmen, sophomores, and seniors, it would violate the requirement of completeness by omitting all juniors. On the other hand, if your scheme included freshmen, sophomores, juniors, seniors, fraternity members, and nonfraternity members, it would no longer be based on a single principle. The first four categories refer to the student's year in college, while the fifth and sixth refer to membership or nonmembership in campus organizations.

Here is an example of a paragraph developed by classification:

> A few words about the world's reaction to the concentration camps: the terrors committed in them were experienced as uncanny by most civilized persons. It came as a shock to their pride that supposedly civilized nations could stoop to such inhuman acts. The implication that modern man has such inadequate control over his cruelty was felt as a threat. Three different psychological mechanisms were most frequently used for dealing with

the phenomenon of the concentration camp: (a) its applicability to man in general was denied by asserting (contrary to available evidence) that the acts of torture were committed by a small group of insane or perverted persons; (b) the truth of the reports were denied by ascribing them to deliberate propaganda. This method was favored by the German government which called all reports on terror in the camps horror propaganda (Greuelpropaganda); (c) the reports were believed, but the knowledge of the terror was repressed as soon as possible.

Bruno Bettelheim, The Informed Heart

The author first specifies the principle of the classifications—the psychological mechanisms used to deal with human cruelty. He then completes the classification by listing the mechanisms. Unit 11 teaches how to develop an entire essay by classification.

8. Causal Analysis

Causal analysis attempts to relate two events by asserting the occurrence of one event to be the reason for the occurrence of the other: A car engine blew up because it lacked oil. A woman slipped and fell because the pavement was slippery. A dog got rabies because it was bitten by a squirrel. Each of these statements asserts a causal relationship between two events.

Cause usually refers to an event in the past. First, the engine lacked oil, then it blew up; first, the pavement was slippery, then the woman fell; first, the dog was bitten, then it got rabies. *Effect*, on the other hand, usually refers to an event in the future. If a car engine is run without oil, it will blow up; if a well-used pavement is slippery, someone will probably fall; if a dog is bitten by a rabid squirrel, it will probably get rabies.

While cause relates two events by asserting one event as the *reason* for the other, effect relates two events by asserting one event as the *result* of another. If you write an essay giving as a reason for your father's bitterness his failure to fulfill his ambition to be a doctor, you are analyzing cause. If you write an essay analyzing what happens to a person who fails to fulfill a lifelong career ambition, you are analyzing effect. Both essays nevertheless would be considered examples of causal analysis.

Consider this paragraph, which analyzes why our age has no "great men":

Why have giants vanished from our midst? One must never neglect the role of accident in history; and accident no doubt plays a part here. But too many accidents of the same sort cease to be wholly accidental. One must inquire further. Why should our age not only be without great men but even seem actively hostile to them? Surely one reason we have so few heroes now is precisely that we had so many a generation ago. Greatness is hard for common humanity to bear. As Emerson said, "Heroism means difficulty, postponement of praise, postponement of ease, introduction of the world into the private apartment, introduction of eternity into the hours measured by the sitting-room clock." A world of heroes keeps people from living their own private lives.

Arthur M. Schlesinger, Jr., The Decline of Heroes

The following paragraph analyzes the effects of changes in the sun's nuclear balance:

> Inevitably, the solar nuclear balances will change. The hydrogen will be used up, converted into helium. The sun's core will start to burn helium in a struggle for life. The heat will increase, the sun will grow redder and swell, on the way to being a red giant star. As it expands it will bring biblical fire and brimstone to the inner planets. Mercury, Venus will melt and drop into the expanding plasma; on earth, all life will be gone long before the oceans boil and vaporize and the rocks are smelted down.

Lennard Bickel, Our Sun: The Star We Live In

Student-written causal analyses sometimes suffer from *dogmatism*—an authoritative stating of opinion as fact without sufficient evidence. Cause and effect often have a complex and frail association, which the student should assert with caution. For more on how to write a causal analysis, see Unit 12.

9. Argumentation

Argumentation, the final strategy for developing a paragraph or an essay, involves the persuasion of someone else to the writer's viewpoint. Such a paragraph will often be a combination of the strategies discussed so far, simultaneously analyzing cause, describing, comparing/contrasting, and defining. Unlike a paragraph developed by comparison/contrast, the argumentative paragraph has no definite structure but is recognizable instead by its intent. Here, for example, is a paragraph that argues that the Bible is a human document:

Description: Can any rational person believe that the Bible is anything but a human document? We now know pretty well where the various books came from, and about when they were written. We know that they were written by human beings who had no knowledge of science, little knowledge of life, and were influenced by the barbarous morality of primitive times, and were grossly ignorant of most things that men know today. *For instance,*

Example: Genesis says that God made the earth, and he made the sun to light the day and the moon to light the night, and in one clause disposes of the stars by saying that "he made the stars also." This was plainly written by someone who had no conception of the stars. Man, by the aid of his telescope, has looked out into the heavens and found stars whose diameter is as great as the distance between the earth and the sun. We know that the universe is filled with stars and suns and planets and systems. Every new telescope looking further into the heavens only discovers more and more worlds and suns and systems in the endless reaches of space. The men who wrote

Causal analysis: Genesis believed, of course, that this tiny speck of mud that we call the

35

earth was the center of the universe, the only world in space, and made for man, who was the only being worth considering. These men believed that the stars were only a little way above the earth, and were set in the firmament for man to look at, and for nothing else. Everyone today knows that this conception is not true.

Clarence Darrow, Why I Am an Agnostic

In presenting his argument, the writer resorts to a variety of strategies: he describes the men who wrote the Bible, gives an example of their misconceptions, and analyzes the probable causes of it. An argument involves the complex formulation of ideas and facts; a paragraph developed by argumentation will therefore frequently employ more than one strategy.

We do not wish to leave you with a purist's impression of paragraph development. Many paragraphs do more or less exactly conform to one strategy of development or another, but more complex paragraphs, especially those involved in the formulation of argument, will blend several strategies:

Example: We are a long, long way from understanding the complexities of individual motivation. We understand very imperfectly, *for example,* the inner pressures to excel which are present in some children and absent in
Contrast: others. We don't really know why, from earliest years, some individuals seem indomitable, while others are tossed about by events like the bird in
Causal a badminton game. Differences in energy and other physiological traits
analysis: are partially responsible. Even more important may be the role of early experiences—relations with brothers and sisters, early successes and failures. We know, *for example,* that high standards may be a means of chal-
Example: lenging and stimulating the child or, depending on the circumstances, a means of frightening and intimidating him.

John W. Gardner, Excellence

Observable in the work of many writers, the strategies of development outlined here are ideal techniques, not inviolable laws. The student writer is advised to follow them closely until he is thoroughly familiar with them. After that, he is as free to experiment, combine, blend, and modify as any other writer who has ever set words and sentences on a page.

E. Transitions Between Paragraphs

Clear transitions between paragraphs are necessary if an essay is to read smoothly. If the gap between the idea at the end of one paragraph and that at the beginning of another is too wide, the reader will lose the line of thought. Paragraphs must therefore be carefully bridged, as in the following example:

The police relationship with the community served is the most important and difficult law enforcement problem of the 1970's. Effective law enforcement depends not only on the respect and confidence of the police but on close, direct and continuous communication between the police and every segment of the population. Indeed, one is not possible without the other. Strong *community ties* provide the base for police prevention, deterrence, detection and control.

Only where *such ties* exist do police have the chance to work effectively. School authorities can then learn how to watch for, identify and report the presence of narcotics peddlers and student addicts. Students are more likely to understand the risks of LSD and refuse to joy-ride with friends in a stolen car. Slum dwellers, who know police, can complain of consumer fraud in the hope that action may result. Addicts, alcoholics and the mentally ill may find treatment through police who are in *contact* with friends, family or those in need themselves. The thief and the dangerously violent, frequently unrestrained in the ghetto, will be identified and apprehended *when the people trust the police.*

Strong police ties with residents in every block of densely populated slum areas are the only opportunity for law enforcement to measure the dimension and the nature of our vast unreported ghetto crime. Police presence can cool rather than heat angry street crowds where officers are known and respected. On campus, police can placate rather than provoke. Organized crime cannot reap the profits of gambling, narcotics traffic, loansharking and prostitution, which account for most of its income, where *police-community relations* are strong and there is law enforcement commitment to eliminate such activity. Extortion, blackmail and strong-arm tactics cannot then be safely used.

Ramsey Clark, Crime in America

The train of thought runs smoothly through these paragraphs, connected through the linking key words denoting police-community ties.

For major transitions, as from one main section of a long paper to the next, a special transitional paragraph can prepare the reader for the next section. Here is an example:

There was, however, a darker and more sinister side to the Irish character. "They are," said a land agent on the eve of the famine, "a very desperate people, with all this degree of courtesy, hospitality, and cleverness amongst them."

Transitional paragraph: To understand the Irish of the nineteenth century and their blend of courage and evasiveness, tenacity and inertia, loyalty and double-dealing, it is necessary to go back to the Penal Laws.

New topic: The Penal Laws, dating from 1695, and not repealed in their entirety until Catholic emancipation in 1829, aimed at the destruction of Catholicism in Ireland by a series of ferocious enactments. . . .

Cecil Woodham-Smith, The Great Hunger: Ireland, 1845–1849

F. Beginning and Ending Paragraphs

1. Openings That Command Attention

The opening paragraph often makes or breaks an essay. The reader who isn't grabbed by your beginning may never linger to read your brilliant middle. To get off to a good start, begin with a snappy introduction—a funny anecdote, a memorable personal experience, a provocative quotation, or a shocking statement. Avoid beginnings that start with an apology or complaint, a big, broad, abstract passage, or a trite and obvious statement. The following is an intriguing opening paragraph that arouses the reader's curiosity.

> A pickup truck drives slowly down the street. The truck stops as it comes abreast of a man sitting on a cast-iron porch and the white driver calls out, asking if the man wants a day's work. The man shakes his head and the truck moves on up the block, stopping again whenever idling men come within calling distance of the driver. At the Carry-out corner, five men debate the question briefly and shake their heads no to the truck. The truck turns the corner and repeats the same performance up the next street. In the distance, one can see one man, then another, climb into the back of the truck and sit down. It starts and stops, the truck finally disappears.
>
> Elliot Liebow, *Source*

2. Endings That Clinch

Take leave from your audience with an emphatic exit. Don't bolt or fade. Use the final paragraph to clinch the point of the essay. Here are two final paragraphs that clinch the author's case against frivolity in American education:

> If by some miracle the creative intelligence could be made as glamorous as Pat Boone, it would not be long, for example, before we ceased appointing ambassadors who know nothing of the language or the history of the country to which they are accredited. We might even go so far as to modify our idea of representative government and insist that our more important public servants be well-educated men. We might teach our children that all the material miracles that surround them are only incidentally the consequence of our extraordinary system of production and distribution, and that we wear such fine stockings only because Wallace H. Carothers, of the Du Pont Company, happened to come across Nylon while he was making a purely scientific investigation of the molecular structure of certain chemical compounds.
>
> The prestige symbols must be changed. Somehow or other the child will have to be taught the stark, chilly truth—that the intellectual is and always has been the most valuable man in the world, the one on whom we all live, the one whose ideas and discoveries and inventions afford us the opportunity for a livelihood and show us how interesting life can be. It is only when he is convinced that this is so, and that Mickey Mantle and Elvis

Presley and Rock Hudson, while doubtless estimable creatures, are mere specks of thin icing on a very large and solid cake—it is only when he deeply feels the truth of this that his natural desire to know will express itself freely, and he will learn what it is now difficult to teach him—how to read, write, calculate, speak, listen, and think.

Clifton Fadiman, Why We Must Improve Our Minds

Convince your reader that you have ended your essay not because you are tired of writing or have run out of ideas, but because nothing more needs to be said. Avoid endings that apologize for your shortcomings, insert an afterthought or trivial detail, or peter out with inconclusive or contradictory statements.

Exercises

1. Identify the topic sentence in each of the following paragraphs and state whether the material moves from the particular to the general or from the general to the particular.

    a. Everyone who makes money in the mechanical city uses the money that he makes there to escape, as far and as frequently as he can, from the inferno that is the source of his wealth. As soon as he can afford it, he moves his home out from within the city-limits into suburbia; he takes his holidays in what is still left of genuinely rural country; and, when he retires, he withdraws to die on the French Riviera or in Southern California or at Montreux or Vevey. This is not surprising, considering that the mechanized city is as repulsively ugly as the mass-produced manufactures that it pours out. It is, however, a spiritual misfortune for a worker to be alienated emotionally from the place in which he has done his work, has earned his living, and has made his mark, for good or for evil, on the history of the human race.

    Arnold Toynbee, Cities on the Move

    b. If you enjoy working out the strategy of games, tit-tat-toe or poker or chess; if you are interested in the frog who jumped up three feet and fell back two in getting out of a well, or in the fly buzzing between the noses of two approaching cyclists, or in the farmer who left land to his three sons; if you have been captivated by codes and ciphers or are interested in crossword puzzles; if you like to fool around with numbers; if music appeals to you by the sense of form which it expresses—then you will enjoy logic. You ought to be warned, perhaps. Those who take up logic get glassy-eyed and absentminded. They join a fanatical cult. But they have a good time. Theirs is one of the most durable, absorbing and inexpensive of pleasures. Logic is fun.

    Roger W. Holmes, The Rhyme of Reason

    c. Two dark spots in this otherwise bright picture must be noted.
       America's affluent society does not adequately care for its old people.

39

The elderly have a sharply declining place in the family compared with the grandparents of a simpler age. The average "home for the aged" can hardly be called an asset to the human condition.

And secondly, this affluent society is build on an exceedingly shaky foundation of natural resources. Here we connect with the liability of a degenerating environment. The United States with only some 6 percent of the world's population uses up some 40 percent of the world's annual production of raw materials. If all the world enjoyed American affluence, there would be about twelve times the current demand for raw materials—an impossible drain on the resources of this planet.

Stuart Chase, Two Cheers for Technology

d. She was a lonesome, passionate woman of dalliance, a castoff of five men and living unmarried with a sixth. But she had wit, insight and a longing for a better way. It was to her that Jesus made the first outright declaration of His universal messiahship.

She also became His first massively persuasive evangelist and the first to convey His mission beyond His Jewish homeland.

Not only did He give this extraordinary role to a woman in an age when that sex was regarded as of secondary value, but He did so to a socially tainted woman of a scorned, segregated race—a woman of Samaria.

It was a strikingly revolutionary action which shocked His disapproving male disciples and which was part of His consistent practice of defying sexist prejudices to give women equal status, a pattern that marked Him as the first and foremost champion of women's liberation.

He "vigorously promoted the dignity and equality of women in a very male-dominated society," writes theologian Leonard Swidler. "Jesus was a feminist and a very radical one."

George W. Cornell, Jesus Viewed as a Women's Liberationist

2. Identify the pattern of development used in the following paragraphs.

a. The "human condition" may be defined as a measure of the extent to which the potential for living is realized under the limitations of the inborn genes and of the environment of the Earth. Full potential means adequate food, shelter, clothing, education, and health care, plus useful and creative work and leisure for every normal baby born. The slums of Calcutta or Rio, the ghettos of the West, represent a potential close to zero.

Stuart Chase, Two Cheers for Technology

b. I have said that a scientific answer must be practical as well as sensible. This really rules out at once the panaceas which also tend to run the argument into a blind alley at this stage; the panaceas which say summarily "Get rid of them." Naturally, it does not seem to me to be sensible to get rid of scientists; but in any case, it plainly is not practical. And whatever we do with our own scientists, it very plainly is not practical to get rid of the scientists of rival nations; because if there existed the conditions for agreement among nations on this far-reaching scheme, then the conditions for war would already have disappeared. If there existed the conditions for international agreement, say to suspend all scientific research, or to abandon warlike research, or in any other way to forgo science as an instrument of nationalism—if such agreements could be reached, then they would already have disappeared. So, however we might sigh for Samuel Butler's panacea in *Erewhon*, simply to give up all machines, there is no point in talking about it. I believe it would be a disaster for mankind like the coming of the Dark Ages. But there is no point in arguing this. It just is not practical, nationally or internationally.

Jacob Bronowski, Science, the Destroyer or Creator

c. Of course, humor is often more than a laughing matter. In its more potent guises, it has a Trojan-horse nature: no one goes on guard against a gag; we let it in because it looks like a little wooden toy. Once inside, however, it can turn a city to reform, to rebellion, to resistance. Some believe, for instance, that, next to the heroic British RAF, British humor did the most to fend off German takeover in World War II. One sample will suffice: that famous story of the woman who was finally extracted from the rubble of her house during the London blitz. Asked, "Where is your husband?" she brushed brick dust off her head and arms and answered, "Fighting in Libya, the bloody coward!"

William D. Ellis, Solve That Problem—with Humor

Writing Assignments

1. Write a paragraph in which you give examples of some common superstitions in modern life.
2. Define *interview* in one paragraph.
3. Write a paragraph comparing a ten-speed bicycle with an ordinary bicycle.
4. In a paragraph, classify the general elective courses undergraduates are required to take at your school.
5. In a paragraph, state some probable reasons for the popularity of newspaper advice columns.
6. Narrate a love-at-first-sight episode in a single paragraph.
7. In one paragraph, state the effects inflation has on a working person's income.
8. Argue for or against the Equal Rights Amendment, in a paragraph.
9. In a single paragraph, outline the steps involved in any process with which you are familiar.
10. In a paragraph, describe any jogger you've ever seen.

4
Organization

A. Planning and Organization

The well-organized essay is one whose ideas lead naturally and logically from one to the other in a progression that most readers would have no difficulty following. The badly organized essay is just the opposite: its points are arranged in no logical order, and the reader can understand it only with great effort. In any kind of expository writing, organization is as at least as important as style.

The best way to organize an essay is to jot down your ideas in an outline before you actually begin writing a final draft. There are a number of advantages to organizing an essay in this way. First, it prevents a writer from getting stuck in that "I don't know what to say now" rut—a very real danger for some. Second, it allows a writer to view the essay in microcosm. Structural errors are easy to spot in an outline, but more difficult in the essay itself. Consider, for example, this plan for an essay:

> *Thesis:* A boat can sail upwind because of its keel, and because its sail acts like the wing of an airplane.
>
>   I. The keel of a sailboat acts as a counterforce against the wind.
>   A. The keel prevents the boat from capsizing.
>   B. The keel gives the boat directional stability.
>
> II. Most modern sailboats are rigged as sloops.
>   A. The sloop rigging features a mainsail and a single forward sail known as the jib.
>   B. The jib sail creates a slot that drives the wind against the outer cheek of the mainsail.
>
> III. On an upwind tack, the sail of a boat acts like the wing of an airplane.
>   A. The force of the wind creates a vacuum on the outer edge of the sails, which pulls the boat forward.
>   B. The forward motion of the boat is also accompanied by a leeward drift, which is reduced by the lateral surface of the hull and the keel.

It is immediately obvious that entry II does not belong with the other elements in the outline. This sort of irrelevancy is always less obvious during the actual writing of an essay, when one idea tends to trigger another. It is better to find and correct such structural errors in an outline, where they are easily spotted and corrected.

An outline of the essay can also tell you what supporting details you need to gather. For example, let us say that you are to write an essay on the effects of running and that one of the topics listed in your outline is "Effects on the cardio-vascular system." Right away you know that you must gather some supporting details on this topic. And once you have gathered the appropriate details, it is generally easy to incorporate them in the essay when you know what you are going to say and where you are going to say it.

B. Form and Elements of the Outline

An outline subdivides the controlling idea of the essay into a series of smaller ideas that can be developed in separate paragraphs. Numbers and letters are used to identify and order ideas according to their importance. Major ideas are slotted to the left; less important ideas are slotted to the right. Here is an example:

Controlling Idea
  I. Main Idea
     A. Sub-idea
     B. Sub-idea
        1. Subdivision of sub-idea
        2. Subdivision of sub-idea
 II. Main Idea
     A. Sub-idea
     B. Sub-idea
        1. Subdivision of a sub-idea
        2. Subdivision of a sub-idea

Every divided idea must yield at least two subcategories, since it is not possible to divide anything into fewer than two parts. Examples and details are usually not included in the outline because they are not subdivisions of ideas. Consider, for instance, the following entries:

  I. Arctic islands have become the site of rich mineral resources for Canada.
     A. The Polaris mine on Little Cornwallis contains jewel-like pockets of sparkling minerals.

The "A" entry is an example, not the subcategory of an idea.

In creating an outline, you are essentially framing out the paragraphs of the essay. The sub-ideas in the outline will eventually be incorporated into the essay as the topic sentences of its paragraphs. Sometimes a single entry will be developed into a separate paragraph; sometimes two entries will be incorporated into a single paragraph. In the outline above, the entry about the Polaris mine is simply not substantial enough to be developed into a paragraph and is therefore of little use to the writer. Such examples should be either omitted from the outline or absorbed into the idea they support. Here is an example:

I. Arctic islands, such as Little Cornwallis, have become the site of rich mineral resources for Canada.
  A. The minerals have been there for centuries, but the miners have arrived only lately.
  B. Recent advances in mining engineering have encouraged arctic developers to challenge the vast spaces and brutal temperatures.

There is an exception to this rule, however. It is this: if your essay will contain major examples that can be developed into separate paragraphs, you may include these as subcategories of your outline, as in the following example:

I. The U.S. Government has occasionally threatened communist nations with economic punishment.
  A. It has withheld grain from Russia.
  B. It has embargoed trade with Cuba.
  C. It has threatened to push Poland into default for its debt.

The rule of thumb for inclusion or omission in the outline can be stated simply: use the outline to frame out the paragraphs of the essay; include as entries those ideas that separately or in combination with another can be developed into a paragraph.

You can write either a *sentence outline* or a *topic outline*. All entries in a sentence outline are full sentences, whereas the entries in a topic outline consist of single words or phrases. The following excerpts will illustrate the difference.

TOPIC OUTLINE

Controlling idea: Two primary problems of adolescent youth

I. Extreme dependence on family
  A. Financial
  B. Emotional
II. Search for personal identity
  A. Between childhood and adulthood
  B. Difficulty of finding self in today's world
  C. Blurred social standards
  D. No official rites of passage to adulthood

SENTENCE OUTLINE

Controlling idea: Adolescent youths in our society face two primary problems.

I. Adolescents are extremely dependent on their families.
  A. Because jobs for the young don't pay well, adolescents have to depend on parents for financial support.
  B. Since parents have always provided emotional stability, adolescents feel lost without parental support.

II. Adolescents are perplexed by their search for an identity in a changing world.
   A. They are torn between acting as children and acting as adults.
   B. It is difficult for adolescents to form ideals or goals when the world is in an upheaval.
   C. Blurred social standards cause frustration and consequent insecurity in adolescents.
   D. Without official rites of passage to adulthood, adolescents in American society must establish their own rites to account for their emerging identities.

The advantage of the topic outline is that it is brief, giving an instant overview of the entire essay. A sentence outline, on the other hand, provides a complete and detailed plan of the essay. The rule of thumb is: Use topic outlines for simple subjects; use sentence outlines for complex subjects.

C. Use of the Outline

In effect, the outline is a map of what you will cover. It should tell you whether you are developing your controlling idea logically and should indicate the supporting points you need to supply. It may even suggest some details. The most important function of the outline, however, is to prevent the essay from dwelling on some topics while failing to develop others.

Consider the following student essay, which was written without an outline:

> Because of its practical uses as well as its psychological effects, my backpack is my most valuable possession. It is difficult to describe, but it resembles a chair that one places on one's hips and piles with things like sleeping bag, canteen, pots, underwear, and mosquito poison.
>
> My backpack gives me a sense of independence because it represents perseverance and self-reliance as I climb trail after trail. I know, when I set out on a trail, that for the next three or four days, my backpack and I will be challenged by the mountain, as were the old mountaineers of our country. So I fill it carefully and methodically with all the equipment I will need—from food to clothing.
>
> Campfire time is the nicest part about camping, but sitting around the campfire I sometimes wish I had a transistor radio, which is what I thought I was getting when I got my backpack.
>
> It's been a tradition in our family to go backpacking every summer, so each member of my family has his own backpack and each of us has to carry his own load up the mountain trails. As we climb, we sing, watch the beautiful scenery, and occasionally munch on some food. My favorite climb is Mt. Whitney although once I had a terrible case of altitude sickness when I reached the top. I hope that never happens again because I really suffered.

I wish I had a Kelty backpack because it is the best. Mine is just a plain orange nylon polyester backpack of some minor brand, but it will do until I can afford the Kelty. My dad surprised me with the backpack my last birthday. I had expected a transistor radio, but instead I received the backpack which pleased me enormously. I plan to use it frequently.

Here is a sketchy outline of this effort:

Controlling idea: Because of its practical uses as well as its psychological effects, my backpack is my most valuable possession.

   I. My backpack gives me a sense of independence.
     A. It represents perseverance.
     B. I feel like a mountaineer with it.
  II. Campfire time is the nicest part about camping.
     A. Sometimes I wish I had a transistor radio.
     B. I got a backpack instead.
 III. It's a tradition in our family to camp.
     A. We have a good time climbing and singing.
     B. I got sick at Mt. Whitney, my favorite climbing spot.
 IV. I wish I had a Kelty backpack.
     A. Mine is just a plain orange polyester backpack.
     B. I had expected a transistor radio.

One glance at this outline would have been enough to convince most writers that trouble loomed ahead. The student writer, however, plunged into the topic without an outline, and was thereafter blown and scattered over the page by uncontrollable gusts of inspiration.

We subdivided the controlling idea into smaller ideas, assembled them into an outline, and added a statement specifying the purpose of the essay and a suggested strategy for implementing it:

Controlling idea: Because of its practical uses as well as its psychological effects, my backpack is my most valuable possession.

   I. Description of my backpack.
     A. It is made of nylon polyester.
     B. It resembles a chair.
  II. My father gave me my backpack.
     A. It was a surprise birthday present.
     B. Backpacking is a family tradition.
 III. My backpack has practical uses.
     A. It serves as a portable restaurant.
     B. I can use it as a folding motel.
 IV. My backpack has important psychological effects.
     A. It gives me a feeling of strength and self-reliance.
     B. It gives me a feeling of independence.

Purpose: To acquaint the reader with the reasons that the backpack is your most valuable possession.

Strategy: Analysis of the reasons you value your backpack: *causal analysis.*

We gave the writer the outline and asked him to rewrite his essay. He now knew why he was writing the essay, what subtopics to cover, and which strategy to use. Limited by a definite purpose and strategy, the writer produced a revised essay improved in focus, content, and detail:

> Because of its practical uses as well as its psychological effects, my back-pack is my most valuable possession. Made of bright orange waterproof nylon polyester tied to a light aluminum frame, my backpack resembles a chair that I tie to my back and pile high with camping necessities.
>
> My dad surprised me with this pack on my eighteenth birthday. I had expected a transistor radio, but instead I received the backpack, which pleased me enormously since backpacking is a tradition in our family and everyone except me had his own personal backpack.
>
> I value my backpack for its practical uses. It is really a portable restaurant capable of carrying sixty pounds of food tucked away in its various compartments. When properly filled, my backpack will feed me for ten days in comfort and style. Whenever I get to a particularly beautiful spot, after climbing for two or three hours, I can simply set down my pack, open the food compartment, spread out a picnic of dried and canned foods and dine on a meal washed down with the tang of a mountain stream. Out in the crisp blue mountain air, the fare tastes better than that of a four-star Michelin bistro. Once the sun has disappeared and night has fallen, I can check in without a reservation, for my backpack is also a folding motel. It contains all I need: insect repellent, a propane lantern, a sleeping bag, and a portable tent. The rains can pour and the winds can howl, but I remain immune to the elements and to the mountain.
>
> I value my backpack also because of its psychological effect on me. When I am carrying it on my back, slowly inching up the mountains, one steady step at a time, I feel strong and self-reliant. In liberating me from restaurants, motels, grocery stores, my backpack helps me overcome the timidity in myself, making me feel independent and free. Sometimes I imagine myself an early American mountaineer—tough, strong, and weatherbeaten. I don't have to rely on expensive tourist traps because my backpack supplies everything I will need during the time that I will be camping out. For both its practical uses and its psychological effects, my backpack is truly my most valuable possession.

The outline for the improved essay indicates that the practical uses of the backpack and its psychological effects are roughly equal in importance, and this equality is reflected in the wording of the controlling idea: "Because of its practical uses as well as its psychological effects, my backpack is my most valuable possession." The writer has therefore attempted to give approximately equal time and space to both aspects of his subject. Having written the essay, he can then check to be sure that both ideas have been emphasized in the essay according to their importance in the outline. If he discovers that he has written five paragraphs on the practical uses of the backpack but dismissed its psychological effects in one skimpy sentence, the essay is obviously lopsided and needs to be rewritten.

Not all outlines will reflect a symmetrical and equal development of all sub-ideas. The outline on the problems of adolescent youth, for example, lists two points that need to be developed under the first sub-idea, "Adolescents are extremely dependent on their families," and four points under the second sub-idea, "Adolescents are perplexed by their search for an identity in a changing world." Common sense tells us that more space is required to develop four points under one sub-idea than two points under another. If, however, the sub-idea with the larger number of points ends up being only a skimpy paragraph, the writer has probably muddled his train of thought and produced a lopsided essay.

Exercises

1. Break down the following controlling ideas into their logical major divisions:

   a. The major strokes in tennis can be grouped into five types: the service, the topspin shot, the chop, the full volley, and the smash.
   b. Secretion of digestive juices in the stomach, constriction of the circulatory system, and an elevated heartbeat are some of the effects of smoking.
   c. *Hardhat*—used in the singular—is a term that designates a member of the working class who is usually union affiliated and politically conservative.
   d. I am an impossible spendthrift at rummage sales and estate auctions.

2. Rewrite the following outlines, correcting any defects:

   a. *Controlling idea:* A manual portable typewriter is less expensive, less distracting, and more convenient than an electric portable.

      I. The manual portable typewriter is less expensive than an electric portable.
         A. The manual typewriter has no motor or electrical wiring.
         B. The electric typewriter has an expensive motor, drive chain, and electrical grounding system.
      II. The manual portable typewriter is less distracting than an electric portable.
         A. The manual typewriter makes only the noise of its keys striking against the platen.
         B. The motor of an electric typewriter makes a constant whirring noise.
      III. The new electric portable with cartridge ribbons is troublesome to use.
         A. The cartridge ribbon feature makes a big job out of correcting a simple mistake.
         B. The cartridge ribbons are more expensive than ordinary ribbons.

IV. The manual portable is more convenient than an electric portable.
   A. The manual is lighter, smaller, and requires no electrical outlet.
   B. The electric typewriter is heavier, bulkier, and requires an electrical outlet.

b. *Controlling idea:* Buying a used car is risky because dealers sometimes falsify background information on the car; odometer readings are sometimes inaccurate; and mechanical difficulties are sometimes impossible to detect.

   I. Dealers sometimes falsify background information on the car.
      A. Background information is useful in assessing the probable conditions of a used car.
      B. Most dealers seem to sell only used cars that were owned by little old ladies.
   II. Foreign car dealers usually have good buys on domestic makes.
      A. The foreign car dealer is interested in selling one particular brand.
      B. The bluebook price on domestic cars is traditionally lower than on foreign cars.
   III. Odometer readings are sometimes inaccurate.
      A. The owner may have the odometer set back before trading in the car.
      B. An overzealous salesman may have set the odometer back.
   IV. Mechanical defects are sometimes impossible to detect.
      A. The warranty on a used car is usually limited and short.
      B. Serious mechanical problems can easily be disguised.

Part II

Writing the Essay

5

Narration

*I loved my secret place and spent many quiet,
thought-filled hours there, often making decisions that
set patterns which have followed me all my life.*

A. Reading for Ideas

The following story, "Wallace," tells of a memorable childhood friendship. As you read the story, notice the author's selection and combination of events into an uninterrupted narrative. Notice also the pace of the narrative—the glossing over of some scenes and events and the highlighting of others. Allow the story to trigger some memories of your own, and ask yourself the following questions: Have I ever met anyone like Wallace who taught me a lesson about life? What memorable experience have I had from which I have learned something?

Wallace
Richard H. Rovere

1   As a schoolboy, my relations with teachers were almost always tense and hostile. I disliked my studies and did very badly in them. There are, I have heard, inept students who bring out the best in teachers, who challenge their skill and move them to sympathy and affection. I seemed to bring out the worst in them. I think my personality had more to do with this than my poor classroom work. Anyway, something about me was deeply offensive to the pedagogic temperament.

2   Often, it took a teacher no more than a few minutes to conceive a raging dislike for me. I recall an instructor in elementary French who shied a textbook at my head the very first day I attended his class. We had never laid eyes on each other until fifteen or twenty minutes before he assaulted me. I no longer remember what, if anything, provoked him to violence. It is possible that I said something that was either insolent or intolerably stupid. I guess I often did. It is also possible that I said nothing at all. Even my silence, my humility, my acquiescence, could annoy my teachers. The very sight of me, the mere awareness of my existence on earth, could be unendurably irratating to them.

3   This was the case with my fourth-grade teacher, Miss Purdy. In order to make the acquaintance of her new students on the opening day of school, she had each one rise and give his name and address as she called the roll. Her voice was soft and gentle,

her manner sympathetic, until she came to me. Indeed, up to then I had been dreamily entertaining the hope that I was at last about to enjoy a happy association with a teacher. When Miss Purdy's eyes fell on me, however, her face suddenly twisted and darkened with revulsion. She hesitated for a few moments while she looked me up and down and thought of a suitable comment on what she saw. "Aha!" she finally said, addressing not me but my new classmates, in a voice that was now coarse and cruel. "I don't have to ask *his* name. There, boys and girls, is Mr. J. Pierpont Morgan, lounging back in his mahogany-lined office." She held each syllable of the financier's name on her lips as long as she was able to, so that my fellow-students could savor the full irony of it. I imagine my posture was a bit relaxed for the occasion, but I know well that she would not have resented anyone else's sprawl as much as she did mine. I can even hear her making some friendly, schoolmarmish quip about too much summer vacation to any other pupil. Friendly quips were never for me. In some unfortunate and mysterious fashion, my entire being rubbed Miss Purdy and all her breed the wrong way. Through-out the fourth grade, she persisted in tormenting me with her idiotic Morgan joke. "And perhaps Mr. J. P. Revere can tell us all about Vasco da Gama this morning." she would say, throwing in a little added insult by mispronouncing my surname.

4   The aversion I inspired in teachers might under certain circumstances have been turned to good account. It might have stimulated me to industry; it might have made me get high marks, just so I could prove to the world that my persecutors were motivated by prejudice and perhaps by a touch of envy; or it might have bred a monumental rebelliousness in me, a contempt for all authority, that could have become the foundation of a career as the leader of some great movement against all tyranny and oppression.

5   It did none of these things. Instead, I became, so far as my school life was concerned, a thoroughly browbeaten boy, and I accepted the hostility of my teachers as an ines-capable condition of life. In fact, I took the absolutely disastrous view that my teachers were unquestionably right in their estimate of me as a dense and altogether noxious creature who deserved, if anything, worse than he got. These teachers were, after all, men and women who had mastered the parts of speech, the multiplication tables, and a simply staggering number of imports and exports in a staggering number of countries. They could add up columns of figures the very sight of which made me dizzy and sick to the stomach. They could read "As You Like It" with pleasure—so they said, anyway, and I believed everything they said. I felt that if such knowledgeable people told me that I was stupid, they certainly must know what they were talking about. In consequence, my grades sank lower and lower, my face became more noticeably blank, my manner more mulish, and my presence in the classroom more aggravating to whoever presided over it. To be sure, I hated my teachers for their hatred of me, and I missed no chance to abuse them behind their backs, but fundamentally I shared with them the view that I was a worthless and despicable boy, as undeserving of an education as I was in-capable of absorbing one. Often, on school days, I wished that I were dead.

6   This was my attitude, at least, until my second year in preparatory school, when, at fourteen, I fell under the exhilarating, regenerative influence of my friend Wallace Duckworth. Wallace changed my whole outlook on life. It was he who freed me from my terrible awe of teachers; it was he who showed me that they could be brought to book and made fools of as easily as I could be; it was he who showed me that the gap between their knowledge and mine was not unbridgeable. Sometimes I think that I should like to become a famous man, a United States Senator or something of that sort, just to be able to repay my debt to Wallace. I should like to be so important that people would inquire into the early influences of my life and I would be able to tell them about Wallace.

54

7   I was freshly reminded of my debt to Wallace not long ago when my mother happened to come across a packet of letters I had written to her and my father during my first two years in a boarding school on Long Island. In one of these, I reported that "There's a new kid in school who's supposed to be a scientifical genius." Wallace was this genius. In a series of intelligence and aptitude tests we all took in the opening week, he achieved some incredible score, a mark that, according to the people who made up the tests, certified him as a genius and absolutely guaranteed that in later life he would join the company of Einstein, Steinmetz, and Edison. Naturally, his teachers were thrilled—but not for long.

8   Within a matter of weeks it became clear that although Wallace was unquestionably a genius, or at least an exceptionally bright boy, he was disposed to use his considerable gifts not to equip himself for a career in the service of mankind but for purely antisocial undertakings. Far from making the distinguished scholastic record everyone expected of him, he made an altogether deplorable one. He never did a lick of school work. He had picked up his scientific knowledge somewhere but evidently not from teachers. I am not sure about this, but I think Wallace's record, as long as he was in school, was even worse than mine. In my mind's eye there is a picture of the sheet of monthly averages thumbtacked to the bulletin board across the hall from the school post office; my name is one from the bottom, the bottom name being Wallace's.

9   As a matter of fact, one look at Wallace should have been enough to tell the teachers what sort of genius he was. At fourteen, he was somewhat shorter than he should have been and a good deal stouter. His face was round, owlish, and dirty. He had big, dark eyes, and his black hair, which hardly ever got cut, was arranged on his head as the four winds wanted it. He had been outfitted with attractive and fairly expensive clothes, but he changed from one suit to another only when his parents came to call on him and ordered him to get out of what he had on.

10   The two most impressive things about him were his mouth and the pockets of his jacket. By looking at his mouth, one could tell whether he was plotting evil or had recently accomplished it. If he was bent upon malevolence, his lips were all puckered up, like those of a billiard player about to make a difficult shot. After the deed was done, the pucker was replaced by a delicate, unearthly smile. How a teacher who knew anything about boys could miss the fact that both expressions were masks of Satan I'm sure I don't know. Wallace's pockets were less interesting than his mouth, perhaps, but more spectacular in a way. The side pockets of his jacket bulged out over his pudgy haunches like burro hampers. They were filled with tools—screwdrivers, pliers, files, wrenches, wire cutters, nail sets, and I don't know what else. In additon to all this, one pocket always contained a rolled-up copy of *Popular Mechanics,* while from the top of the other protruded *Scientific American* or some other such magazine. His breast pocket contained, besides a large collection of fountain pens and mechanical pencils, a picket fence of drill bits, gimlets, kitchen knives, and other pointed instruments. When he walked, he clinked and jangled and pealed.

11   Wallace lived just down the hall from me, and I got to know him one afternoon, a week or so after school started, when I was wrestling with an algebra lesson. I was really trying to get good marks at the time, for my father had threatened me with unpleasant reprisals if my grades did not show early improvement. I could make no sense of the algebra, though, and I thought that the scientific genius, who had not as yet been unmasked, might be generous enough to lend me a hand.

12   It was a study period, but I found Wallace stretched out on the floor working away at something he was learning to make from *Popular Mechanics.* He received me with courtesy, but after hearing my request he went immediately back to his tinkering. "I

could do that algebra all right," he said, "but I can't be bothered with it. Got to get this dingbat going this afternoon. Anyway, I don't care about algebra. It's too twitchy. Real engineers never do any of that stuff. It's too twitchy for them." I soon learned that "twitch" was an all-purpose word of Wallace's. It turned up in one form or another, in about every third sentence he spoke. It did duty as a noun, an adjective, a verb, and an adverb.

13   I was disappointed by his refusal of help but was fascinated by what he was doing. I stayed on and watched him as he deftly cut and spliced wires, removed and replaced screws, referring, every so often, to his magazine for further instruction. He worked silently, lips fiendishly puckered, for some time, then looked up at me and said, "Say, you know anything about that organ in the chapel?"

14   "What about it?" I asked.
"I mean do you know anything about how it works?"
"No," I said, "I don't know anything about that."

15   "Too bad," Wallace said, reaching for a pair of pliers. "I had a really twitchy idea." He worked at his wires and screws for quite a while. After perhaps ten minutes, he looked up again. "Well, anyhow," he said, "maybe you know how to get in the chapel and have a look at the organ?"

16   "Sure, that's easy," I said, "Just walk in. The chapel's always open. They keep it open so you can go in and pray if you want to, and things like that."
"Oh," was Wallace's only comment.

17   I didn't at all grasp what he had in mind until church time the following Sunday. At about six o'clock that morning, several hours before the service, he tip-toed into my room and shook me from sleep. "Hey, get dressed," he said. "Let's you and I twitch over to the chapel and have a look at the organ."

18   Game for any form of amusement, I got up and went along. In the bright, not quite frosty October morning, we scurried over the lawns to the handsome Georgian chapel. It was an hour before the rising bell.

19   Wallace had brought along a flashlight as well as his usual collection of hardware. We went to the rear of the chancel, where the organ was, and he poked the light underneath the thing and inside it for a few minutes. Then he got out his pliers and screwdrivers and performed some operations that I could neither see nor understand. We were in the chapel for only a few minutes. "There," Wallace said as he came up from under the keyboard. "I guess I got her twitched up just about right. Let's go." Back in my room, we talked softly until the rest of the school began to stir. I asked Wallace what, precisely, he had done to the organ. "You'll see," he said, with that faint, faraway smile where the pucker had been. Using my commonplace imagination, I guessed that he had fixed the organ so it would give out peculiar noises or something like that. I didn't realize that Wallace's tricks were seldom commonplace.

20   Church began as usual that Sunday morning. The headmaster delivered the invocation and then announced the number and title of the first hymn. He held up his hymnal and gave the genteel, throat-clearing cough that was his customary signal to the organist to get going. The organist came down on the keys but not a peep sounded from the pipes. He tried again. Nothing but a click.

21   When the headmaster realized that the organ wasn't working, he walked quickly to the rear and consulted in whispers with the organist. Together they made a hurried inspection of the instrument, peering inside it, snapping the electric switch back and forth, and reaching to the base plug to make certain the juice was on. Everything seemed all right, yet the organ wouldn't sound a note.

22   "Something appears to be wrong with our organ," the headmaster said when he returned to the lectern. "I regret to say that for this morning's services we shall have to—"

23   At the first word of the announcement, Wallace, who was next to me in one of the rear pews, slid out of his seat and bustled noisily down the middle aisle. It was highly unusual conduct, and every eye was on him. His gaudy magazines flapped from his pockets, his portable workshop clattered and clanked as he strode importantly to the chancel and rose on tiptoe to reach the ear of the astonished headmaster. He spoke in a stage whisper that could be heard everywhere in the chapel. "Worked around organs quite a bit, sir," he said. "Think I can get this one going in a jiffy."

24   Given the chance, the headmaster would undoubtedly have declined Wallace's kind offer. Wallace didn't give him the chance. He scooted for the organ. For perhaps a minute, he worked on it, hands flying, tools tinkling.

25   Then, stuffing the tools back into his pockets, he returned to the headmaster. "There you are, sir," he said, smiling up at him. "Think she'll go all right now." The headmaster, with great doubt in his heart, I am sure, nodded to the organist to try again. Wallace stood by, looked rather like the inventor of a new kind of airplane waiting to see his brain child take flight. He faked a look of deep anxiety, which, when a fine, clear swell came from the pipes, was replaced by a faint smile of relief, also faked. On the second or third chord, he bustled back down the aisle, looking very solemn and businesslike and ready for serious worship.

26   It was a fine performance, particularly brilliant in its timing. If Wallace had had to stay at the organ even a few seconds longer—that is if he had done a slightly more elaborate job of twitching it in the first place—he would have been ordered back to his pew before he had got done with the repairs. Moreover, someone would probably have guessed that it was he who had put it on the fritz in the first place. But no one did guess it. Not then, anyway. For weeks after that, Wallace's prestige in the school was enormous. Everyone had had from the beginning a sense of honor and pride at having a genius around, but no one up to then had realized how useful a genius could be. Wallace let on after church that Sunday that he was well up on the working not merely of organs but also of heating and plumbing systems, automobiles, radios, washing machines, and just about everything else. He said he would be pleased to help out in any emergency. Everyone thought he was wonderful.

27   "That was a real good twitch, wasn't it?" he said to me when we were by ourselves. I said that it certainly was.

28   From that time on, I was proud and happy to be Wallace's cupbearer. I find it hard now to explain exactly what his victory with the organ, and all his later victories over authority, meant to me, but I do know that they meant a very great deal. Partly, I guess, it was just the knowledge that he enjoyed my company. I was an authentic, certified dunce and he was an acknowledged genius, yet he liked being with me. Better yet was my discovery that this super-brain disliked schoolwork every bit as much as I did. He was bored silly, as I was, by "Il Penseroso" and completely unable to stir up any enthusiasm for "Silas Marner" and all the foolish goings on over Eppie. Finally, and this perhaps was what made me love him most, he had it in his power to humiliate and bring low the very people who had so often humiliated me and brought me low.

29   As I spent the long fall and winter afternoons with Wallace, being introduced by him to the early novels of H. G. Wells, which he admired extravagantly, and watching him make crystal sets, window-cleaning machines, automatic chair-rockers, and miniature steam turbines from plans in *Popular Mechanics,* I gradually absorbed bits of his liberating philosophy. "If I were you," he used to say, "I wouldn't be scared by those teachers. They don't know anything. They're twitches, those teachers, real twerpy, twitchy twitches." "Twerpy" was an adjective often used by Wallace to modify "twitch." It added several degrees of twitchiness to anything twitchy.

30   Although Wallace had refused at first to help me with my lessons, he later gave freely of his assistance. I explained to him that my father was greatly distressed about my work and that I really wanted to make him happier. Wallace was moved by this. He would read along in my Latin grammar, study out algebra problems with me, and explain things in language that seemed a lot more lucid than that of my teachers. Before long, I began to understand that half my trouble lay in my fear of my studies, my teachers, and myself. "Don't know why you get so twitched up over this stuff," Wallace would say a trifle impatiently as he helped me get the gist of a speech in "As You Like It." "There isn't anything hard about this. Fact, it's pretty good right in here. It's just those teachers who twitch it all up. I wish they'd all go soak their heads."

31   Wallace rode along for quite a while on the strength of his intelligence tests and his organ-fixing, but in time it became obvious that his disappointing classroom performance was not so much the result of failure to adjust to a new environment (as a genius, he received more tolerance in this respect than non-geniuses) as of out-and-out refusal to cooperate with the efforts being made to educate him. Even when he had learned a lesson in the course of helping me with it, he wouldn't give the teachers the satisfaction of thinking he had learned anything in their classes. Then, too, his pranks began to catch up with him. Some of them, he made no effort to conceal.

32   He was easily the greatest teacher-baiter I have ever known. His masterpiece, I think, was one he thought up for our algebra class. "Hey, you twitch," he called to me one day as I was passing his room on my way to the daily ordeal of "x"s and "y"s. "I got a good one for old twitch Potter." I went into his room, and he took down from his closet shelf a spool of shiny cooper wire. "Now, watch this," he said. He took the free end of the wire and drew it up through the left sleeve of his shirt. Then he brought it across his chest, underneath the shirt, and ran it down the right sleeve. He closed his left fist over the spool and held the free end of the wire between right thumb and forefinger. "Let's get over to that dopey class," he said, and we went.

33   When the lesson was well started, Wallace leaned back in his seat and began to play in a languorous but ostentatious manner with the wire. It glistened brightly in the strong classroom light, and it took Mr. Potter, the teacher, only a few seconds to notice that Wallace was paying no mind to the blackboard equations but was, instead, completely absorbed in the business of fingering the wire.

34   "Wallace Duckworth, what's that you're fiddling with?" Mr. Potter said.
      "Piece of wire, sir."
      "Give it to me this instant."
      "Yes, sir," Walace said, extending his hand.

35   Mr. Potter had, no doubt, bargained on getting a stray piece of wire that he could unceremoniously pitch into the wastebasket. Wallace handed him about eighteen inches of it. As Mr. Potter took it, Wallace released several inches more.
      "I want *all* that wire, Wallace," Mr. Potter said.

36   "I'm giving it to you, sir," Wallace answered, He let go of about two feet more. Mr. Potter kept pulling. His rage so far overcame his reason that he couldn't figure out what Wallace was doing. As he pulled, Wallace fed him more and more wire, and the stuff began to coil up on the floor around his feet. Guiding the wire with the fingers of his right hand, Wallace created quite a bit of tension, so that eventually Mr. Potter was pulling hand over hand, like a sailor tightening lines in a high sea. When he thought the tension was great enough, Wallace let two or three feet slip quickly through his hands, and Mr. Potter toppled to the floor, landing in a terrible tangle of wire.

37   I no longer remember all of Wallace's inventions in detail. Once, I recall, he made, in the chemistry laboratory, some kind of invisible paint—a sort of shellac, I suppose—and

covered every blackboard in the school with it. The next day, chalk skidded along the slate and left about as much impression as it would have made on a cake of ice. The dormitory he and I lived in was an old one of frame construction, and when we had fire drills, we had to climb down outside fire escapes. One night, Wallace tied a piece of flypaper securely around each rung of each ladder in the building, then rang the fire alarm. Still another time, he went back to his first love, the organ, and put several pounds of flour in the pipes, so that when the organist turned on the pumps, a cloud of flour filled the chapel. One of his favorite tricks was to take the dust jacket from a novel and wrap it around a textbook. In a Latin class, then, he would appear to be reading "Black April" when he should have been reading about the campaigns in Gaul. After several of his teachers had discovered that he had the right book in the wrong cover (he piously explained that he put the covers on to keep his books clean), he felt free to remove the textbook and really read a novel in class.

38   Wallace was expelled shortly before the Easter vacation. As the winter had drawn on, life had become duller and duller for him, and to brighten things up he had resorted to pranks of larger conception and of an increasingly anti-social character. He poured five pounds of sugar into the gasoline tank of the basketball coach's car just before the coach was to start out, with two or three of the team's best players in his car, for a game with a school about twenty-five miles away. The engine functioned adequately until the car hit an isolated spot on the highway, miles from any service place. Then it gummed up completely. The coach and the players riding with him came close to frostbite, and the game had to be called off. The adventure cost Wallace's parents a couple of hundred dollars for automobile repairs. Accused of the prank, which clearly bore his trademark, Wallace had freely admitted his guilt. It was explained to his parents that he would be given one more chance in school; another trick of any sort and he would be packed off on the first train.

39   Later, trying to justify himself to me, he said, "You don't like that coach either, do you? He's the twerpiest twitch here. All teachers are twitchy, but coaches are the worst ones of all."

40   I don't recall what I said. Wallace had not consulted me about several of his recent escapades, and although I was still loyal to him, I was beginning to have misgivings about some of them.

41   As I recall it, the affair that led directly to his expulsion was a relatively trifling one, something to do with blown fuses or short circuits. At any rate, Wallace's parents had to come and fetch him home. It was a sad occasion for me, for Wallace had built in me the foundations for a sense of security. My marks were improving, my father was happier, and I no longer cringed at the sight of a teacher. I feared, though, that without Wallace standing behind me and giving me courage, I might slip back into the old ways. I was very near to tears as I helped him pack up his turbines, his tools, and his stacks of magazines. He, however, was quite cheerful. "I suppose my Pop will put me in another one of these places, and I'll have to twitch my way out of it all over again," he said.

42   "Just remember how dumb all those teachers are," he said to me a few moments before he got into his parents' car. "They're so twitchy dumb they can't even tell if anyone else is dumb." It was rather a sweeping generalization, I later learned, but it served me well for a number of years. Whenever I was belabored by a teacher, I remembered my grimy genius friend and his reassurances. I got through school somehow or other. I still cower a bit when I find that someone I've met is a schoolteacher, but things aren't too bad and I am on reasonably civil terms with a number of teachers, and even a few professors.

4,640 words

Questions

1. What typical characteristics of youth does this story bring to light?
2. How do you explain the teachers' hostility toward the narrator?
3. How would you evaluate Wallace's influence on the narrator? Was he good or bad for him?
4. What do Wallace's tricks have in common?
5. Where in the story is there some clear indication that the narrator has matured?
6. Where in the narration, if anywhere, is there a tone of sadness?
7. What is the organization of the narration? Write an outline of it.
8. How is Wallace's use of the word *twitchy* related to the inventiveness of youth? Comment on the effectiveness of Wallace's use of this word.
9. How would you have handled Wallace if you had been his teacher?
10. What is Wallace's opinion of teachers? What generalization have you made about teachers?

La Belle Dame sans Merci
John Keats

1   O what can ail thee, Knight at arms
      Alone and palely loitering?
    The sedge has withered from the Lake,
      And no birds sing!

2   O what can ail thee, Knight at arms,
      So haggard and so woe-begone?
    The Squirrel's granary is full,
      And the harvest's done

3   I see a lily on thy brow,
      With anguish moist and fever dew;
    And on thy cheeks a fading rose
      Fast withereth too.

4   I met a Lady in the Meads,
      Full beautiful a faery's child,
    Her hair was long, her foot was light,
      And her eyes were wild.

5   I made a Garland for her head,
      And bracelets, too, and fragrant Zone;
    She look'd at me as she did love,
      And made sweet moan.

6   I set her on my pacing steed,
      And nothing else saw, all day long;
    For sidelong would she bend, and sing
      A faery's song.

7   She found me roots of relish sweet,
        And honey wild, and manna dew;
    And sure in language strange she said,
        I love thee true.

8   She took me to her elfin grot,
        And there she wept and sigh'd full sore;
    And there I shut her wild, wild eyes
        With kisses four.

9   And there she lulled me asleep,
        And there I dreamed, ah woe betide!
    The latest dream I ever dreamt,
        On the cold hill's side.

10 I saw pale Kings, and Princes too,
        Pale warriors, death pale were they all;
    They cried, La belle dame sans merci
        Thee hath in thrall!

11 I saw their starv'd lips in the gloam
        With horrid warning gaped wide—
    And I awoke, and found me here,
        On the cold hill's side.

12 And this is why I sojourn here,
        Alone and palely loitering,
    Though the sedge is withered from the Lake,
        And no birds sing.

Questions

1. The poem is a ballad and therefore tells a story. How would you summarize its plot?
2. What is the season of the year at the start of the poem? Why is this season significant?
3. How would you describe the lady that the knight is pining for? Is she real?
4. What did the knight dream? What is ironic about the revelation in the dream?
5. What did the knight awake to find? Did he dream the whole story?
6. What is the significance of the repeated line "And no birds sing"?
7. How would you describe the dominant emotion evoked by this poem?

B. How to Write a Narration

Narration tells what happened. A storyteller who begins with "Once upon a time . . ." is introducing the first step in what will probably become a bending, tortuous progression of happenings. Narration, in its widest sense, includes history, biography, personal experience, travel, and fiction—in short, any writing that recounts the events of a story in a dramatic and climactic order.

Narrate an incident or experience that taught you a lesson about life. Re-create it on paper exactly as you remember it. Keep the events in the order in which they occurred. At the end of the narrative say what the incident or experience taught you.

Specific Instructions

1. NARRATIVE WRITING MUST HAVE A CONSISTENT POINT OF VIEW.   You must decide early who you are in the story, take on the voice of your assumed character, and remain faithful to him or her for the duration of the story. For instance, if you are relating an incident from the point of view of a young boy, the language of the story should reflect his youthfulness. It would seem incongruous if, having indicated to the reader that the story is to be told from a boy's point of view, you then make him sound like an elderly college professor.

Writers resort to a variety of techniques and devices to make their prose reflect the character they have assumed as the narrator. The most common technique is playacting: the writer simply pretends to be the person who is narrating the story and tries to write the way that person would write.

This passage is taken from a story narrated from the point of view of an uneducated slave. Notice how the language is wrenched to reflect his character:

> A long time ago, in times gone by, in slavery times, there was a man named Cue. I want you to think about him. I've got a reason.
>
> He got born like the cotton in the boll or the rabbit in the pea patch. There wasn't any fine doings when he got born, but his mammy was glad to have him. Yes. He didn't get born in the Big House, or the overseer's house, or any place where the bearing was easy or the work light. No, Lord. He came out of his mammy in a field hand's cabin one sharp winter, and about the first thing he remembered was his mammy's face and the taste of a piece of bacon rind and the light and shine of the pitch-pine fire up the chimney. Well, now, he got born and there he was.
>
> Stephen Vincent Benét, Freedom's a Hard-Bought Thing

Whatever character you choose to hide behind—innocent young boy, lonely middle-aged man, or wise old woman—you must remain with him or her throughout your narrative. Don't be one character in one paragraph, only to shift suddenly to another in the next. Such an abrupt change makes the point of view choppy and inconsistent. Here is an example of the sort of shift to avoid:

> Jessica and me hated all grownups. We'd climb onto my parents' four-story apartment roof, and you can bet that we were up to no good. Gosh, sometimes we'd spit down on old lady Gunther cause she was such a grouch about us playing on her lawn. I find it rather nostalgic to reflect on those budding days of my youth, when life was free and easy and each day was the dawn of a new adventure.

Notice the sudden shift from mischievous child to reflective adult in line 4.

2. THE NARRATION MUST HAVE A THEME.   We have already pointed out that good writing must have unity—it must be centered on a controlling idea. Narration is no exception. In narrative writing, however, the controlling idea is called the "theme" and is supported by incidents rather than by "sub-ideas." For example, the theme of "Wallace"—the healthy effects of friendship on a young boy's confidence—is supported by various incidents connecting the narrator with Wallace. The incidents are united by the theme to form a complete action with a beginning, middle, and end:

Beginning: The narrator is rejected by his teachers. He meets Wallace.

Middle: The narrator admires Wallace. Wallace expresses friendship for the narrator.

End: The narrator's self-confidence rises because of the friendship to the point that he is on the verge of rejecting Wallace's disruptive tactics.

Narration establishes its theme by first raising, then resolving, conflict. The conflict gives rise to events that will determine a resolution from which the reader may infer a theme. For instance, the conflict in "Wallace" between the narrator and his teachers is raised at the very outset of the narrative. The character of Wallace is then introduced and the narrative focuses on his friendship with the narrator. Because of this friendship with the school genius, the narrator loses his fear of teachers, acquires greater self-confidence, and is on the verge of questioning his friend's pranks when Wallace is summarily expelled from school. This resolution leads us to infer the theme of the narrative—that friendship can have a healthy effect on the self-confidence of a young boy. Had the resolution of the conflict been otherwise, the reader would have inferred a different theme.

3. PACE YOUR NARRATION TO FOCUS ON IMPORTANT SCENES.   Every reader of fiction has encountered passages that read like this:

> The first time I saw her she was chasing a schnauzer in the park. Her hair was wind-blown and wild as she dodged pedestrians and bicyclists and ran screaming after the runaway schnauzer. Her calico frock billowed in furls as she tried to run in floppy leather-tonged sandals. She was as lissome and lovely as ever a woman could be. *I didn't see her for three weeks after that.* Then one Tuesday morning, as I was taking a postdigestive jog along the elm-lined footpath, I saw her again.

Three sentences are devoted to a description of the encounter between the narrator and the girl in the park; then three weeks are dismissed in a single, brief sentence. Obviously, life was not suspended during those three weeks, but because that intervening period is unimportant to the narrative, it is quickly passed over.

This is an example of *pacing,* an important and commonsense principle of narrative writing. Unimportant time, events, and scenes are dismissed as the narrative focuses on and develops in detail only what is important to its theme. A narrative about a favorite hiding place, for example, should develop the hiding place in detail, glossing over everything else as secondary or unrelated. Common sense must guide you in selecting the scenes and events to be developed, but the ultimate rule of thumb is the relevance of the material to your theme.

4. USE DETAILS TO MAKE VIVID PEOPLE AND PLACES IN YOUR NARRATIVE. People and places are the lifeblood of your narration. Make them real and imaginable through the use of detail (see Unit 6, Description). Notice how Wallace is brought to life through details:

> As a matter of fact, one look at Wallace should have been enough to tell the teachers what sort of genius he was. At fourteen, he was somewhat shorter than he should have been and a good deal stouter. His face was round, owlish and dirty. He had big, dark eyes, and his black hair, which hardly ever got cut, was arranged on his head as the four winds wanted it. He had been outfitted with attractive and fairly expensive clothes, but he changed from one suit to another only when his parents came to call on him and ordered him to get out of what he had on.

Detailed dialogue is another technique that narration uses to infuse life in a character. In "The Code" (p. 68), dialogue reveals the father as a man who will not tolerate emotional, irrational beliefs. For example, when the aunts go into hysterics over the death of the author's younger brother, calling him "a perfect baby," "a saint," "too perfect to live," the father angrily reacts:

> His face was very pale, and his eyes flashed almost feverishly. "Don't talk like that, Agnes!" he exclaimed, with a strange violence that was not anger but something much deeper. "I won't have you talking like that any more. I don't want anybody talking like that!" His whole body seemed to tremble. I have never seen him so worked up before. "Of course he was a bad boy at times!" he cried. "Every boy's bad once in a while. What do you have to change him for? Why don't you leave him as he was?"

A vivid narrative requires careful observation of people and their environment, and the inclusion of details that contribute most efficiently to a clear, vigorous, and interesting story.

On January 13, 1982, an Air Florida 737 bound from Washington, D.C., to Tampa, Florida, crashed on takeoff into the frozen Potomac, killing 78 passengers. Rescuers told afterward of the heroic behavior of an unidentified passenger who repeatedly passed to other survivors a lifeline thrown to him from a hovering helicopter. By the time all the survivors had been airlifted to safety, the man in the water had disappeared below the frozen river. The writer of this essay, which appeared in the January 25, 1982, issue of *Time* magazine, finds a lesson for all of us in this heroism.

Professional Model

The Man in the Water
Roger Rosenblatt

1   As disasters go, this one was terrible, but not unique, certainly not among the worst on the roster of U.S. air crashes. There was the unusual element of the bridge, of course, and the fact that the plane clipped it at a moment of high traffic, one routine thus intersecting another and disrupting both. Then, too, there was the location of the event. Washington, the city of form and regulations, turned chaotic, deregulated, by a blast of real winter and a single slap of metal on metal. The jets from Washington National Airport that normally swoop around the presidential monuments like famished gulls are, for the moment, emblemized by the one that fell; so there is that detail. And there was the aesthetic clash as well—blue-and-green Air Florida, the name of a flying garden, sunk down among gray chunks in a black river. All that was worth noticing, to be sure. Still, there was nothing very special in any of it, except death, which, while always special, does not necessarily bring millions to tears or to attention. Why, then, the shock here?

2   Perhaps because the nation saw in this disaster something more than a mechanical failure. Perhaps because people saw in it no failure at all, but rather something successful about their makeup. Here, after all, were two forms of nature in collision: the elements and human character. Last Wednesday, the elements, indifferent as ever, brought down Flight 90. And on that same afternoon, human nature—groping and flailing in mysteries of its own—rose to the occasion.

3   Of the four acknowledged heroes of the event, three are able to account for their behavior. Donald Usher and Eugene Windsor, a park police helicopter team, risked their lives every time they dipped the skids into the water to pick up survivors. On television, side by side in bright blue jumpsuits, they described their courage as all in the line of duty. Lenny Skutnik, a 28-year-old employee of the Congressional Budget Office, said: "It's something I never thought I would do"—referring to his jumping into the water to drag an injured woman to shore. Skutnik added that "somebody had to go in the water," delivering every hero's line that is no less admirable for its repetitions. In fact, nobody had to go into the water. That somebody actually did so is part of the reason this particular tragedy sticks in the mind.

4   But the person most responsible for the emotional impact of the disaster is the one known at first simply as "the man in the water." (Balding, probably in his fifties, an extravagant mustache.) He was seen clinging with five other survivors to the tail section of the airplane. This man was described by Usher and Windsor as appearing alert and in control. Every time they lowered a lifeline and flotation ring to him, he passed it on to another of the passengers. "In a mass casualty, you'll find people like him," said Windsor. "But I've never seen one with that commitment." When the helicopter came back for him, the man had gone under. His selflessness was one reason the story held national attention; his anonymity another. The fact that he went unidentified invested him with a universal character. For a while he was Everyman, and thus proof (as if one needed it) that no man is ordinary.

5   Still, he could never have imagined such a capacity in himself. Only minutes before his character was tested, he was sitting in the ordinary plane among the ordinary

passengers, dutifully listening to the stewardess telling him to fasten his seat belt and saying something about the "no smoking sign." So our man relaxed with the others, some of whom would owe their lives to him. Perhaps he started to read, or to doze, or to regret some harsh remark made in the office that morning. Then suddenly he knew that the trip would not be ordinary. Like every other person on that flight, he was desperate to live, which makes his final act so stunning.

6   For at some moment in the water he must have realized that he would not live if he continued to hand over the rope and ring to others. He *had* to know it, no matter how gradual the effect of the cold. In his judgment he had no choice. When the helicopter took off with what was to be the last survivor, he watched everything in the world move away from him, and he deliberately let it happen.

7   Yet there was something else about the man that kept our thoughts on him, and which keeps our thoughts on him still. He was *there,* in the essential, classic circumstance. Man in nature. The man in the water. For its part, nature cared nothing about the five passengers. Our man, on the other hand, cared totally. So the timeless battle commenced in the Potomac. For as long as that man could last, they went at each other, nature and man; the one making no distinctions of good and evil, acting on no principles, offering no lifelines; the other acting wholly on distinctions, principles and, one supposes, on faith.

8   Since it was he who lost the fight, we ought to come again to the conclusion that people are powerless in the world. In reality, we believe the reverse, and it takes the act of the man in the water to remind us of our true feelings in this matter. It is not to say that everyone would have acted as he did, or as Usher, Windsor and Skutnik. Yet whatever moved these men to challenge death on behalf of their fellows is not peculiar to them. Everyone feels the possibility in himself. That is the abiding wonder of the story. That is why we would not let go of it. If the man in the water gave a lifeline to the people gasping for survival, he was likewise giving a lifeline to those who observed him.

9   The odd thing is that we do not even really believe that the man in the water lost his fight. "Everything in Nature contains all the powers of Nature," said Emerson. Exactly. So the man in the water had his own natural powers. He could not make ice storms, or freeze the water until it froze the blood. But he could hand life over to a stranger, and that is a power of nature too. The man in the water pitted himself against an implacable, impersonal enemy; he fought it with charity; and he held it to a standoff. He was the best we can do.

1,028 words

Vocabulary

emblemized (1)
aesthetic (1)
implacable (9)

Questions

1. What collision of forces does the author see represented in this story?
2. How are paragraphs 1 and 2 linked together in the narration?
3. The author says that by remaining unidentified, the man in the water became Everyman. What does this mean? Who was Everyman?
4. How would you define heroic behavior?
5. What does the author see as the "abiding wonder" of this story?

6. Why, according to the author, do we not believe that the man in the water lost the fight with nature?
7. The author implies that since the man in the water is himself a part of nature, his heroic behavior refutes the notion of an uncaring nature. What are your views of this idea?
8. What does the author mean by "nature"? Do you agree with the author that nature is implacable and uncaring?
9. What lesson does the author infer from the story of the man in the water?
10. How is paragraph 7 developed?

Student Model

The Shed
Walter Benton

After my father lost the family business, it became necessary for him to move around the country quite a lot. It was decided that the family would move back to the farm to be close to our relatives.

We moved onto an eight-acre farm, where a little shed attached to the barn became my secret place.

The shed was old and worn. Its tin roof was streaked with rust, and the rough-hewn plank sidewalls were gray and etched with green wood rot. It was used to store grain and dried corn for the animals. It smelled of oats mixed with molasses.

I loved my secret place and spent many quiet, thought-filled hours there, often making decisions that set patterns which have followed me all my life.

At the time my parents' relationship was strained to the breaking point, and as my father's visits home became less frequent, the fights and yelling got worse. When they started, I would retire to my shed and ponder. I decided that if any institution could cause as much pain and hurt as marriage did, that I would never allow it to play a part in my life; thus, I have never had any inclination toward marriage. I also decided that if it were true that children were unplanned, unhappy, and unwanted, they too would play no role in my adult existence.

The shed became my time machine. I hid my trilogy of Horatio Hornblower's adventures, *Man Against the Sea,* and other of my favorite books under a stack of feed sacks; and in the late evening, after the chores were done, I would take my battered old kerosene lantern out to the shed and read these books over and over. The best reading was always done in the rain. The rain would patter on the tin roof, and the air would give off the sweet musty odor of wet hay and sandalwood. I remember all of these sounds, smells, and feelings even today when I get into a pensive mood. I can still hear the low hiss and sputter of my trusty old lantern as the animals pawed and moaned in the stalls next to my shed.

My little shed became my sanctuary from the world. When I was troubled or afraid or even happy, I shared my feelings with my shed, and it came as no surprise to me when I began to feel that the shed understood.

About five years ago, I returned to visit the old farm and to see my little shed, but as with so many things in life one believes will always be around, it had disappeared. A bright, shiny milking barn stood in its place, with cold concrete walls, shiny chrome pipes and neoprene tubes.

Well, another childhood memory is gone, but if you ever visit my home, there in a place of honor among my collection of leather-bound books and fine hand-cut crystal, you'll find that battered old kerosene lantern, proud and defiant, a cherished symbol of times past.

In "The Code," an old understanding between a young man and his father turns out to be a source of suffering for both of them.

Alternate Reading

The Code
Richard T. Gill

1   I remember, almost to the hour, when I first began to question my religion. I don't mean that my ideas changed radically just at that time. I was only twelve, and I continued to go to church faithfully and to say something that could pass for prayers each night before I went to sleep. But I never again felt quite the same. For the first time in my life, it had occurred to me that when I grew up I might actually leave the Methodist faith.

2   It all happened just a few days after my brother died. He was five years old, and his illness was so brief and his death so unexpected that my whole family was almost crazed with grief. My three aunts, each of whom lived within a few blocks of our house, and my mother were all firm believers in religion, and they turned in unison, and without reservation, to this last support. For about a week, a kind of religious frenzy seized our household. We would all sit in the living room—my mother, my aunts, my two sisters, and I, and sometimes Mr. Dodds, the Methodist minister, too—saying prayers in low voices, comforting one another, staying together for hours at a time, until someone remembered that we had not had dinner or that it was time for my sisters and me to be in bed.

3   I was quite swept up by the mood that had come over the house. When I went to bed, I would say the most elaborate, intricate prayers. In the past, when I had finished my "Now I lay me down to sleep," I would bless individually all the members of my immediate family and then my aunts, and let it go at that. Now, however, I felt that I had to bless everyone in the world whose name I could remember. I would go through all my friends at school, including the teachers, the principal, and the janitor, and then through the names of people I had heard my mother and father mention, some of whom I had never even met. I did not quite know what to do about my brother, whom I wanted to pray for more than for anyone else. I hesitated to take his name out of its regular order, for fear I would be committed to believing that he had really died. But then I *knew* that he had died, so at the end of my prayers, having just barely mentioned his name as I went along, I would start blessing him over and over again, until I finally fell asleep.

4   The only one of us who was unmoved by this religious fervor was my father. Oddly enough, considering what a close family we were and how strongly my mother and aunts felt about religion, my father had never shown the least interest in it. In fact, I do not think that he had ever gone to church. Partly for this reason, partly because he was a rather brusque, impatient man, I always felt that he was something of a stranger in our home. He spent a great deal of time with us children, but through it all he seemed curiously unapproachable. I think we all felt constrained when he played with us and relieved when, at last, we were left to ourselves.

5   At the time of my brother's death, he was more of a stranger than ever. Except for one occasion, he took no part in the almost constant gatherings of the family in the living room. He was not going to his office that week—we lived in a small town outside Boston—and he was always around the house, but no one ever seemed to know exactly where. One of my aunts—Sarah, my mother's eldest sister—felt very definitely that my father should not be left to himself, and she was continually saying to me, "Jack, go upstairs and see if you can find him and talk to him." I remember going timidly along the hallway on the second floor and peeking into the bedrooms, not knowing what I should say if I found him and half afraid that he would scold me for going around looking into other people's rooms. One afternoon, not finding him in any of the bedrooms, I went up into the attic, where we had a sort of playroom. I remember discovering him there by the window. He was sitting absolutely motionless in an old wicker chair, an empty pipe in his hands, staring out fixedly over the treetops. I stood in the doorway for several minutes before he was aware of me. He turned as if to say something, but then, looking at me or just above my head—I was not sure which—he seemed to lose himself in his thoughts. Finally, he gave me a strangely awkward salute with his right hand and turned again to the window.

6   About the only times my father was with the rest of us were when we had meals or when, in the days immediately following the funeral, we all went out to the cemetery, taking fresh flowers or wreaths. But even at the cemetery he always stood slightly apart—a tall, lonely figure. Once, when we were at the grave and I was nearest him, he reached over and squeezed me around the shoulders. It made me feel almost embarrassed as though he were breaking through some inviolable barrier between us. He must have felt as I did, because he at once removed his arm and looked away, as though he had never actually embraced me at all.

7   It was the one occasion when my father was sitting in the living room with us that started me to wondering about my religion. We had just returned from the cemetery—two carloads of us. It was three or four days after the funeral and just at the time when, the shock having worn off, we were all experiencing our first clear realization of what had happened. Even I, young as I was, sensed that there was a new air of desolation in our home.

8   For a long time, we all sat there in silence. Then my aunts, their eyes moist, began talking about my brother, and soon my mother joined in. They started off softly, telling of little things he had done in the days before his illness. Then they fell silent and dried their eyes, and then quickly remembered some other incident and began speaking again. Slowly the emotion mounted, and before long the words were flooding out. "God will take care of him!" my Aunt Sarah cried, almost ecstatically. "Oh, yes, He will! He will!" Presently, they were all talking in chorus—saying that my brother was happy at last and that they would all be with him again one day.

9   I believed what they were saying and I could barely hold back my tears. But swept up as I was, I had the feeling that they should not be talking that way while my father was there. The feeling was one that I did not understand at all at the moment. It was just that when I looked over to the corner where he was sitting and saw the deep, rigid lines of his face, saw him sitting there silently, all alone, I felt guilty. I wanted everyone to stop for a while—at least until he had gone upstairs. But there was no stopping the torrent once it had started.

10   "Oh, he was too perfect to live!" Aunt Agnes, my mother's youngest sister, cried. "He was never a bad boy. I've never seen a boy like that. I mean he was never even naughty. He was just too perfect."

"Oh, yes. Oh, yes," my mother sighed.

"It's true," Aunt Sarah said. "Even when he was a baby, he never really cried. There was never a baby like him. He was a saint."

"He *was* a saint!" Aunt Agnes cried. "That's why he was taken from us!"

"He was a perfect baby," my mother said.

"He was taken from us," Aunt Agnes went on, "because he was too perfect to live."

11 All through this conversation, my father's expression had been growing more and more tense. At last, while Aunt Agnes was speaking, he rose from his chair. His face was very pale, and his eyes flashed almost feverishly. "Don't talk like that, Agnes!" he exclaimed, with a strange violence that was not anger but something much deeper. "I won't have you talking like that any more. I don't want anybody talking like that!" His whole body seemed to tremble. I had never seen him so worked up before. "Of course he was a bad boy at times!" he cried. "Every boy's bad once in a while. What do you have to change him for? Why don't you leave him as he was?"

12 "But he was such a perfect baby," Aunt Sarah said.

"He *wasn't* perfect!" my father almost shouted, clenching his fist. "He was no more perfect than Jack here or Betty or Ellen. He was just an ordinary little boy. He wasn't perfect. And he wasn't a saint. He was just a little boy, and I won't have you making him over into something he wasn't!"

13 He looked as though he were going to go on talking like this, but just then he closed his eyes and ran his hand up over his forehead and through his hair. When he spoke again, his voice was subdued. "I just wish you wouldn't talk that way," he said. "That's all I mean." And then, after standing there silently for a minute, he left the living room and walked upstairs.

14 I sat watching the doorway through which he had gone. Suddenly, I had no feeling for what my mother and my aunts had been saying. It was all a mist, a dream. Out of the many words that had been spoken that day, it was those few sentences of my father's that explained to me how I felt about my brother. I wanted to be with my father to tell him so.

15 I went upstairs and found him once again in the playroom in the attic. As before, he was silent and staring out the window when I entered, and we sat without speaking for what seemed to me like half an hour or more. But I felt that he knew why I was there, and I was not uncomfortable with him.

16 Finally, he turned to me and shook his head. "I don't know what I can tell you, Jack," he said, raising his hands and letting them drop into his lap. "That's the worst part of it. There's just nothing I can say that will make it any better."

17 Though I only half understood him then, I see now that he was telling me of a drawback—that he had no refuge, no comfort, no support. He was telling me that you were all alone if you took the path that he had taken. Listening to him, I did not care about the drawback. I had begun to see what a noble thing it was for a man to bear the full loss of someone he had loved.

II

18 By the time I was thirteen or fourteen I was so thoroughly committed to my father's way of thinking that I considered it a great weakness in a man to believe in religion. I wanted to grow up to face life as he did—truthfully, without comfort, without support.

19 My attitude was never one of rebellion. Despite the early regimen of Sunday school and church that my mother had encouraged, she was wonderfully gentle with me, particularly when I began to express my doubts. She would come into my room each night after the light was out and ask me to say my prayers. Determined to be honest with her, I would explain that I could not say them sincerely, and therefore should not say

70

them at all. "Now, Jack," she would reply, very quietly and calmly, "you mustn't talk like that. You'll really feel much better if you say them." I could tell from the tone of her voice that she was hurt, but she never tried to force me in any way. Indeed, it might have been easier for me if she *had* tried to oppose my decision strenuously. As it was, I felt so bad at having wounded her that I was continually trying to make things up—running errands, surprising her by doing the dishes when she went out shopping—behaving, in short, in the most conscientious, considerate fashion. But all this never brought me any closer to her religion. On the contrary, it only served to free me for my decision *not* to believe. And for that decision, as I say, my father was responsible.

20 Part of his influence, I suppose, was in his physical quality. Even at that time—when he was in his late forties and in only moderately good health—he was a most impressive figure. He was tall and heavychested, with leathery, rough-cast features and with an easy, relaxed rhythm in his walk. He had been an athlete in his youth, and, needless to say, I was enormously proud of his various feats and told about them, with due exaggeration, all over our neighborhood. Still, the physical thing had relatively little to do with the matter. My father, by that time, regarded athletes and athletics with contempt. Now and again, he would take me into the back yard to fool around with boxing gloves, but when it came to something serious, such as my going out for football in high school, he invariably put his foot down. "It takes too much time," he would tell me. "You ought to be thinking of college and your studies. It's nonsense what they make of sports nowadays!" I always wanted to remind him of *his* school days, but I knew it was no use. He had often told me what an unforgivable waste of time he considered his youth to have been.

21 Thus, although the physical thing was there, it was very much in the background—little more, really, than the simple assumption that a man ought to know how to take care of himself. The real bond between us was spiritual, in the sense that courage, as opposed to strength, is spiritual. It was this intangible quality of courage that I wanted desperately to possess and that, it seemed to me, captured everything that was essential about my father.

22 We never talked of this quality directly. The nearest we came to it was on certain occasions during the early part of the Second World War, just before I went off to college. We would sit in the living room listening to a speech by Winston Churchill, and my father would suddenly clap his fist against his palm. "My God!" he would exclaim, fairly beaming with admiration. "That man's got the heart of a tiger!" And I would listen to the rest of the speech, thrilling to every word, and then, thinking of my father, really, I would say aloud that, of all men in the world, the one I would most like to be was Churchill.

23 Nor did we often talk about religion. Yet our religion—our rejection of religion—was the deepest statement of the bond between us. My father, perhaps out of deference to my mother and my sisters and aunts, always put his own case very mildly. "It's certainly a great philosophy," he would say of Christianity. "No one could question that. But for the rest . . ." Here he would throw up his hands and cock his head to one side, as if to say that he had tried, but simply could not manage the hurdle of divinity. This view, however mildly it may have been expressed, became mine with absolute clarity and certainty. I concluded that religion was a refuge, without the least foundation in fact. More than that, I positively objected to those—I should say those *men,* for to me it was a peculiarly masculine matter—who turned to religion for support. As I saw it, a man ought to face life as it really is, on his own two feet, without a crutch, as my father did. That was the heart of the matter. By the time I left home for college, I was so deeply committed to this view that I would have considered it a disloyalty to him, to myself, to the code we had lived by, to alter my position in the least.

24   I did not see much of my father during the next four years or so. I was home during the summer vacation after my freshman year, but then, in the middle of the next year, I went into the Army. I was shipped to the Far East for the tail end of the war, and was in Japan at the start of the Occupation. I saw my father only once or twice during my entire training period, and, naturally, during the time I was overseas I did not see him at all.

25   While I was away, his health failed badly. In 1940, before I went off to college, he had taken a job at a defense plant. The plant was only forty miles from our home, but he was working on the night shift, and commuting was extremely complicated and tiresome. And, of course, he was always willing to overexert himself out of a sense of pride. The result was that late in 1942 he had a heart attack. He came through it quite well, but he made no effort to cut down on his work and, as a consequence, suffered a second, and more serious, attack, two years later. From that time one, he was almost completely bedridden.

26   I was on my way overseas at the time of the second attack, and I learned of it in a letter from my mother. I think she was trying to spare me, or perhaps it was simply that I could not imagine so robust a man as my father being seriously ill. In any event, I had only the haziest notion of what his real condition was, so when, many months later, I finally did realize what had been going on, I was terribly surprised and shaken. One day, some time after my arrival at an American Army post in Japan, I was called to the orderly room and told that my father was critically ill and that I was to be sent home immediately. Within forty-eight hours, I was standing in the early-morning light outside my father's bedroom, with my mother and sisters at my side. They had told me, as gently as they could, that he was not very well, that he had had another attack. But it was impossible to shield me then. I no sooner stepped into the room and saw him than I realized that he would not live more than a day or two longer.

27   From that moment on, I did not want to leave him for a second. Even that night, during the periods when he was sleeping and I was of no help being there, I could not get myself to go out of the room for more than a few minutes. A practical nurse had come to sit up with him, but since I was at the bedside, she finally spent the night in the hallway. I was really quite tired, and late that night my mother and my aunts begged me to go to my room and rest for a while, but I barely heard them. I was sure he would wake up soon, and when he did, I wanted to be there to talk to him.

28   We did talk a great deal that first day and night. It was difficult for both of us. Every once in a while, my father would shift position in the bed, and I would catch a glimpse of his wasted body. It was a knife in my heart. Even worse were the times when he would reach out for my hand, his eyes misted, and begin to tell me how he felt about me. I tried to look at him, but in the end I always looked down. And, knowing that he was dying, and feeling desperately guilty, I would keep repeating to myself that he knew how I felt, that he would understand why I looked away.

29   There was another thing, too. While we talked that day, I had a vague feeling that my father was on the verge of making some sort of confession to me. It was, as I say, only the vaguest impression, and I thought very little about it. The next morning, however, I began to sense what was in the air. Apparently, Mr. Dodds, the minister, whom I barely knew, had been coming to the house lately to talk to my father. My father had not said anything about this, and I learned it only indirectly, from something my mother said to my eldest sister at the breakfast table. At the moment, I brushed the matter aside. I told myself it was natural that Mother would want my father to see the minister at the last. Nevertheless, the very mention of the minister's name caused something to tighten inside me.

30   Later that day, the matter was further complicated. After lunch, I finally did go to my room for a nap, and when I returned to my father's room, I found him and my mother talking about Mr. Dodds. The conversation ended almost as soon as I entered, but I was left with the distinct impression that they were expecting the minister to pay a visit that day, whether very shortly or at suppertime or later in the evening, I could not tell. I did not ask. In fact, I made a great effort not to think of the matter at all.

31   Then, early that evening, my father spoke to me. I knew before he said a word that the minister *was* coming. My mother had straightened up the bedroom, and fluffed up my father's pillows so that he was half sitting in the bed. No one had told me anything, but I was sure what the preparations meant. "I guess you probably know," my father said to me when we were alone, "we're having a visitor tonight. It's—ah—Mr. Dodds. You know, the minister from your mother's church."

32   I nodded, half shrugging, as if I saw nothing the least unusual in the news. "He's come here before once or twice," my father said. "Have I mentioned that? I can't remember if I've mentioned that."

      "Yes, I know. I think Mother said something, or perhaps you did. I don't remember."

      "I just thought I'd let you know. You see, your mother wanted me to talk to him. I—I've talked to him more for her sake than anything else."

      "Sure. I can understand that."

33   "I think it makes her feel a little better. I think—" Here he broke off, seeming dissatisfied with what he was saying. His eyes turned to the ceiling, and he shook his head slightly, as if to erase the memory of his words. He studied the ceiling for a long time before he spoke again. "I don't mean it was all your mother exactly," he said. "Well, what I mean is he's really quite an interesting man. I think you'd probably like him a good deal."

      "I know Mother has always liked him," I replied. "From what I gather most people seem to like him very much."

      "Well, he's that sort," my father went on, with quickening interest. "I mean, he isn't what you'd imagine at all. To tell the truth, I wish you'd talk to him a little. I wish you'd talk things over with him right from scratch." My father was looking directly at me now, his eyes flashing.

      "I'd be happy to talk with him sometime," I said. "As I say, everybody seems to think very well of him."

34   "Well, I wish you would. You see, when you're lying here day after day, you get to thinking about things. I mean, it's good to have someone to talk to." He paused for a moment. "Tell me," he said, "have you ever . . . have you ever wondered if there wasn't some truth in it? Have you ever thought about it that way at all?"

35   I made a faint gesture with my hand. "Of course, it's always possible to wonder," I replied. "I don't suppose you can ever be completely certain one way or the other."

      "I know, I know," he said, almost impatiently. "But have you ever felt—well, all in a sort of flash—that it *was* true? I mean, have you ever had that feeling?"

36   He was half raised up from the pillow now, his eyes staring into me with a feverish concentration. Suddenly, I could not look at him any longer. I lowered my head.

      "I don't mean permanently or anything like that," he went on. "But just for a few seconds. The feeling that you've been wrong all along. Have you had that feeling—ever?"

37   I could not look up. I could not move. I felt that every muscle in my body had suddenly frozen. Finally, after what seemed an eternity, I heard him sink back into the pillows. When I glanced up a moment later, he was lying there silent, his eyes closed, his lips parted, conveying somehow the image of the death that awaited him.

38   Presently, my mother came to the door. She called me into the hall to tell me that Mr. Dodds had arrived. I said that I thought my father had fallen asleep but that I would go back and see.

    It was strangely disheartening to me to discover that he was awake. He was sitting there, his eyes open, staring grimly into the gathering shadows of the evening.

    "Mr. Dodds is downstairs," I said matter-of-factly. "Mother wanted to know if you felt up to seeing him tonight."

39   For a moment, I thought he had not heard me; he gave no sign of recognition whatever. I went to the foot of the bed and repeated myself. He nodded, not answering the question but simply indicating that he had heard me. At length, he shook his head. "Tell your mother I'm a little tired tonight," he said. "Perhaps—well, perhaps some other time."

    "I could ask him to come back later, if you'd like."

    "No, no, don't bother. I—I could probably use the rest."

    I waited a few seconds. "Are you sure?" I asked. "I'm certain he could come back in an hour or so."

40   Then, suddenly, my father was looking at me. I shall never forget his face at that moment and the expression burning in his eyes. He was pleading with me to speak. And all I could say was that I would be happy to ask Mr. Dodds to come back later, if he wanted it that way. It was not enough. I knew, instinctively, at that moment that it was not enough. But I could not say anything more.

41   As quickly as it had come, the burning flickered and went out. He sank back into the pillows again. "No, you can tell him I won't be needing him tonight," he said, without interest. "Tell him not to bother waiting around." Then he turned on his side, away from me, and said no more.

42   So my father did not see Mr. Dodds that night. Nor did he ever see him again. Shortly after midnight, just after my mother and sisters had gone to bed, he died. I was at his side then, but I could not have said exactly when it occurred. He must have gone off in his sleep, painlessly, while I sat there awake beside him.

43   In the days that followed, our family was together almost constantly. Curiously enough, I did not think much about my father just then. For some reason, I felt the strongest sense of responsibility toward the family. I found myself making the arrangements for the funeral, protecting Mother from the stream of people who came to the house, speaking words of consolation to my sisters and even to my aunts. I was never alone except at night, when a kind of oblivion seized me almost as soon as my head touched the pillow. My sleep was dreamless, numb.

44   Then, two weeks after the funeral, I left for Fort Devens, where I was to be discharged from the Army. I had been there three days when I was told that my terminal leave would begin immediately and that I was free to return home. I had half expected that when I was at the Fort, separated from the family, something would break inside me. But still no emotion came. I thought of my father often during that time, but, search as I would, I could find no sign of feeling.

45   Then, when I had boarded the train for home, it happened. Suddenly, for no reason whatever, I was thinking of the expression on my father's face that last night in the bedroom. I saw him as he lay there pleading with me to speak. And I knew then what he had wanted me to say to him—that it was really all right with me, that it wouldn't change anything between us if he gave way. And then I was thinking of myself and what I had said and what I had *not* said. Not a word to help! Not a word!

46   I wanted to beg his forgiveness. I wanted to cry out aloud to him. But I was in a

crowded train, sitting with three elderly women just returning from a shopping tour. I turned my face to the window. There, silent, unnoticed, I thought of what I might have said.

4,960 words

Vocabulary

unison (2)	inviolable (6)
brusque (4)	intangible (21
constrained (4)	deference (23)

Questions

1. What was the author's childhood faith? How old was he when he thought he might give it up?
2. Why, after the death of his brother, did the narrator feel he had to bless everyone, even people whose names he had heard mentioned but whom he really didn't know?
3. What was the value of religion to the narrator's mother and aunts? Where is this stated?
4. What did the past athletic prowess of the father have to do with the code that developed between him and the narrator? How was the code related to "masculinity"?
5. What "intangible quality" drew the author to his father?
6. Examine paragraphs 24 and 26 and identify at least two examples of the author's use of pacing.
7. In paragraph 40, the narrator says of his father, "He was pleading with me to speak" and that he, the narrator, knew that his answer "was not enough." What did the narrator's father want him to say? Why didn't the narrator say it?
8. What does "The Code" have to say about role-playing and about rigid beliefs in "masculinity"?
9. How would you characterize the father's deathbed behavior? Was he courageous? Cowardly?
10. What is the significance of the final scene and the three elderly women in the train?

In this selection, Lincoln Steffens (1866–1936), journalist and author, relates a memorable Christmas of his childhood. The selection is taken from *The Autobiography of Lincoln Steffens.*

Professional Model

A Miserable, Merry Christmas
Lincoln Steffens

1   My father's business seems to have been one of slow but steady growth. He and his local partner, Llewelen Tozer, had no vices. They were devoted to their families and to "the store," which grew with the town, which, in turn, grew and changed with the State from a gambling, mining, and ranching community to one of farming, fruit-raising, and building. Immigration poured in, not gold-seekers now, but farmers, business men and home-builders, who settled, planted, reaped, and traded in the natural riches of the State, which prospered greatly, "making" the people who will tell you that they "made the State."

2   As the store made money and I was getting through the primary school, my father bought a lot uptown, at Sixteenth and K Streets, and built us a "big" house. It was off the line of the city's growth, but it was near a new grammar school for me and my sisters, who were coming along fast after me. This interested the family, not me. They were always talking about school; they had not had much of it themselves, and they thought they had missed something. My father used to write speeches, my mother verses, and their theory seems to have been that they had talents which a school would have brought to flower. They agreed, therefore, that their children's gifts should have all the schooling there was. My view, then, was that I had had a good deal of it already, and I was not interested at all. It interfered with my own business, with my own education.

3   And indeed I remember very little of the primary school. I learned to read, write, spell, and count, and reading was all right. I had a practical use for books, which I searched for ideas and parts to play with, characters to be, lives to live. The primary school was probably a good one, but I cannot remember learning anything except to read aloud "perfectly" from a teacher whom I adored and who was fond of me. She used to embrace me before the whole class and she favored me openly to the scandal of the other pupils, who called me "teacher's pet." Their scorn did not trouble me; I saw and I said that they envied me. I paid for her favor, however. When she married I had queer, unhappy feelings of resentment; I didn't want to meet her husband, and when I had to I wouldn't speak to him. He laughed, and she kissed me—happily for her, to me offensively. I never would see her again. Through with her, I fell in love immediately with Miss Kay, another grown young woman who wore glasses and had a fine, clear skin. I did not know her, I only saw her in the street, but once I followed her, found out where she lived, and used to pass her house, hoping to see her, and yet choking with embarrassment if I did. This fascination lasted for years; it was still a sort of super-romance to me when later I was "going with" another girl nearer my own age.

4   What interested me in our new neighborhood was not the school, nor the room I was to have in the house all to myself, but the stable which was built back of the house. My father let me direct the making of a stall, a little smaller than the other stalls, for my pony, and I prayed and hoped and my sister Lou believed that that meant that I would get the pony, perhaps for Christmas. I pointed out to her that there were three other stalls and

no horses at all. This I said in order that she should answer it. She could not. My father, sounded, said that some day we might have horses and a cow; meanwhile a stable added to the value of a house. "Some day" is a pain to a boy who lives in and knows only "now." My good little sisters, to comfort me, remarked that Christmas was coming, but Christmas was always coming and grown-ups were always talking about it, asking you what you wanted and then giving you what they wanted you to have. Though everybody knew what I wanted, I told them all again. My mother knew that I told God, too, every night. I wanted a pony, and to make sure that they understood, I declared that I wanted nothing else.

5   "Nothing but a pony?" my father asked.

6   "Nothing," I said.

7   "Not even a pair of high boots?"

8   That was hard. I did want boots, but I stuck to the pony. "No, not even boots."

9   "Nor candy? There ought to be something to fill your stocking with, and Santa Claus can't put a pony into a stocking."

10   That was true, and he couldn't lead a pony down the chimney either. But no. "All I want is a pony," I said. "If I can't have a pony, give me nothing, nothing."

11   Now I had been looking myself for the pony I wanted, going to sales stables, inquiring of horsemen, and I had seen several that would do. My father let me "try" them. I tried so many ponies that I was learning fast to sit a horse. I chose several, but my father always found some fault with them. I was in despair. When Christmas was at hand I had given up all hope of a pony, and on Christmas Eve I hung up my stocking along with my sisters', of whom, by the way, I now had three. I haven't mentioned them or their coming because, you understand, they were girls, and girls, young girls, counted for nothing in my manly life. They did not mind me either; they were so happy that Christmas Eve that I caught some of their merriment. I speculated on what I'd get: I hung up the biggest stocking I had, and we all went reluctantly to bed to wait till morning. Not to sleep; not right away. We were told that we must not only sleep promptly, we must not wake up till seven-thirty the next morning—or if we did, we must not go to the fireplace for our Christmas. Impossible.

12   We did sleep that night, but we woke up at six A.M. We lay in our beds and debated through the open doors whether to obey till, say, half-past six. Then we bolted. I don't know who started it, but there was a rush. We all disobeyed; we raced to disobey and get first to the fireplace in the front room downstairs. And there they were, the gifts, all sorts of wonderful things, mixed-up piles of presents; only, as I disentangled the mess, I saw that my stocking was empty; it hung limp; not a thing in it; and under and around it—nothing. My sisters had knelt down, each by her pile of gifts; they were squealing with delight, till they looked up and saw me standing there in my nightgown with nothing. They left their piles to come to me and look with me at my empty place. Nothing. They felt my stocking: nothing.

13   I don't remember whether I cried at that moment, but my sisters did. They ran with me back to my bed, and there we all cried till I became indignant. That helped some. I got up, dressed, and driving my sisters away, I went alone out into the yard, down to the stable, and there, all by myself, I wept. My mother came out to me by and by; she found me in my pony stall, sobbing on the floor, and she tried to comfort me. But I heard my father outside; he had come part way with her, and she was having some sort of angry quarrel with him. She tried to comfort me; besought me to come to breakfast. I could not; I wanted no comfort and no breakfast. She left me and went on into the house with sharp words for my father.

14   I don't know what kind of breakfast the family had. My sisters said it was "awful." They were ashamed to enjoy their own toys. They came to me, and I was rude. I ran away from

them. I went around to the front of the house, sat down on the steps, and the crying over, I ached. I was wronged, I was hurt—I can feel now what I felt then, and I am sure that if one could see the wounds upon our hearts, there would be found still upon mine a scar from that terrible Christmas morning. And my father, the practical joker, he must have been hurt, too, a little. I saw him looking out of the window. He was watching me or something for an hour or two, drawing back the curtain ever so little lest I catch him, but I saw his face, and I think I can see now the anxiety upon it, the worried impatience.

15   After—I don't know how long—surely an hour or two—I was brought to the climax of my agony by the sight of a man riding a pony down the street, a pony and a brand-new saddle; the most beautiful saddle I ever saw, and it was a boy's saddle; the man's feet were not in the stirrups; his legs were too long. The outfit was perfect; it was the realization of all my dreams, the answer to all my prayers. A fine new bridle, with a light curb bit. And the pony! As he drew near, I saw that the pony was really a small horse, what we called an Indian pony, a bay, with black mane and tail, and one white foot and a white star on his forehead. For such a horse as that I would have given, I could have forgiven, anything.

16   But the man, a disheveled fellow with a blackened eye and a fresh-cut face, came along, reading the numbers on the houses, and as my hopes—my impossible hopes— rose, he looked at our door and passed by, he and the pony, and the saddle and the bridle. Too much. I fell upon the steps, and having wept before, I broke now into such a flood of tears that I was a floating wreck when I heard a voice.

17   "Say, kid," it said, "do you know a boy named Lennie Steffens?"

18   I looked up. It was the man on the pony, back again, at our horse block.

19   "Yes," I spluttered through my tears. "That's me."

20   "Well," he said, "then this is your horse. I've been looking all over for you and your house. Why don't you put your number where it can be seen?"

21   "Get down," I said, running out to him.

22   He went on saying something about "ought to have got here at seven o'clock; told me to bring the nag here and tie him to your post and leave him for you. But, hell, I got into a drunk—and a fight—and a hospital, and—."

23   "Get down," I said.

24   He got down, and he boosted me up to the saddle. He offered to fit the stirrups to me, but I didn't want him to. I wanted to ride.

25   "What's the matter with you?" he said, angrily. "What you crying for? Don't you like the horse? He's a dandy, this horse. I know him of old. He's fine at cattle; he'll drive 'em alone."

26   I hardly heard, I could scarcely wait, but he persisted. He adjusted the stirrups, and then, finally, off I rode, slowly, at a walk, so happy, so thrilled, that I did not know what I was doing. I did not look back at the house or the man, I rode off up the street, taking note of everything—of the reins, of the pony's long mane, of the carved leather saddle. I had never seen anything so beautiful. And mine! I was going to ride up past Miss Kay's house. But I noticed on the horn of the saddle some stains like rain-drops, so I turned and trotted home, not to the house but to the stable. There was the family, father, mother, sisters, all working for me, all happy. They had been putting in place the tools of my new business: blankets, currycomb, brush, pitchfork—everything, and there was hay in the loft.

27   "What did you come back so soon for?" somebody asked. "Why didn't you go on riding?"

28   I pointed to the stains. "I wasn't going to get my new saddle rained on," I said. And my father laughed. "It isn't raining," he said. "Those are not rain-drops."

29   "They are tears," my mother gasped, and she gave my father a look which sent him off to the house. Worse still, my mother offered to wipe away the tears still running out of my eyes. I gave her such a look as she had given him, and she went off after my father, drying her own tears. My sisters remained and we all unsaddled the pony, put on his halter, led him to his stall, tied and fed him. It began really to rain; so all the rest of that memorable day we curried and combed that pony. The girls plaited his mane, forelock, and tail, while I pitch-forked hay to him and curried and brushed, curried and brushed. For a change we brought him out to drink; we led him up and down, blanketed like a race-horse; we took turns at that. But the best, the most inexhaustible fun, was to clean him. When we went reluctantly to our midday Christmas dinner, we all smelt of horse, and my sisters had to wash their faces and hands. I was asked to, but I wouldn't, till my mother bade me look in the mirror. Then I washed up—quick. My face was caked with the muddy lines of tears that had coursed over my cheeks to my mouth. Having washed away that shame, I ate my dinner, and as I ate I grew hungrier and hungrier. It was my first meal that day, and as I filled up on the turkey and the stuffing, the cranberries and the pies, the fruit and the nuts—as I swelled, I could laugh. My mother said I still choked and sobbed now and then, but I laughed, too; I saw and enjoyed my sisters' presents till—I had to go out and attend to my pony, who was there, really and truly there, the promise, the beginning, of a happy double life. And—I went and looked to make sure—there was the saddle, too, and the bridle.

30   But that Christmas, which my father had planned so carefully, was it the best or the worst I ever knew? He often asked me that; I never could answer as a boy. I think now that it was both. It covered the whole distance from broken-hearted misery to bursting happiness—too fast. A grown-up could hardly have stood it.

2,490 words

Questions

1. Conflict is at the heart of good narrative writing. In this selection, where is the reader first given an inkling of the conflict it will depict?
2. Paragraphs 1 and 2 include some unimportant details. What are the details and what purpose do they serve?
3. What does paragraph 3 tell us about the author's personality as a child?
4. The incident narrated takes place in the author's boyhood, when he was still in primary school. How does the author's style of writing reflect this youthfulness?
5. In paragraph 11, the author casually mentions that he had three sisters and then dismisses them. Why? What is this intended to reflect? His chauvinism?
6. Why did the author's parents instruct their children not to rise before 7:30 A.M.?
7. What explanation probably occurred to the author when he found nothing in his stocking?
8. Why didn't the father tell the boy that he had bought him a pony but that it had not yet been delivered?
9. Whose fault was it that the pony didn't arrive when it was supposed to?
10. In paragraph 29, the author describes the pony as "the promise, the beginning, of a happy double life." What does the term *double life* mean?

Additional Writing Assignments

1. Narrate any incident in your life in which you were forced by a role to suppress your true feelings.
2. Narrate the story of your most memorable Christmas.
3. Tell a story illustrating how you feel about your mother and your father.
4. Tell the story of the day when "everything went wrong."
5. Write a story titled "Trapped."
6. Write a story titled "My Jealousy."
7. Write a story that illustrates the way you feel about religion.
8. Narrate a story about an episode with an animal.
9. Narrate a story of how you repulsed an aggressive salesperson.
10. Write a story on a close call with death.

6

Description

*He is an old man now, as gnarled and twisted as a
cypress on a cliff above the sea.*

A. Reading for Ideas

"The Lament" is the story of a poor Russian cabdriver who is overwhelmed by the grief of losing his only son. Read the story for a dominant impression—a central theme that unifies the descriptive details. Observe carefully the accumulation of details and how they fit into the narrative. What does the story tell you about grief, about society, and about man's capacity for suffering? What is the conflict in the story? How is it finally resolved? What feelings does the story arouse in you?

The Lament
Anton Chekhov

1   It is twilight. A thick wet snow is twirling around the newly lighted street lamps, and lying in soft thin layers on roofs, on horses' backs, on people's shoulders and hats. The cabdriver Iona Potapov is quite white, and looks like a phantom; he is bent double as far as a human body can bend double; he is seated on his box; he never makes a move. If a whole snowdrift fell on him, it seems as if he would not find it necessary to shake it off. His little horse is also quite white, and remains motionless; its immobility, its angularity, and its straight wooden-looking legs, even close by, give it the appearance of a gingerbread horse worth a *kopek*. It is, no doubt, plunged in deep thought. If you were snatched from the plow, from your usual gray surroundings, and were thrown into this slough full of monstrous lights, unceasing noise, and hurrying people, you too would find it difficult not to think.

2   Iona and his little horse have not moved from their place for a long while. They left their yard before dinner, and up to now, not a fare. The evening mist is descending over the town, the white lights of the lamps replacing brighter rays, and the hubbub of the street getting louder. "Cabby for Viborg way!" suddenly hears Iona, "Cabby!"

3   Iona jumps, and through his snow-covered eyelashes sees an officer in a greatcoat, with his hood over his head.

    "Viborg way!" the officer repeats. "Are you asleep, eh? Viborg way!"

4   With a nod of assent Iona picks up the reins, in consequence of which layers of snow slip off the horse's back and neck. The officer seats himself in the sleigh, the cabdriver

smacks his lips to encourage his horse, stretches out his neck like a swan, sits up, and, more from habit than necessity, brandishes his whip. The little horse also stretches its neck, bends its wooden-looking legs, and makes a move undecidedly.

5   "What are you doing, werewolf!" is the exclamation Iona hears from the dark mass moving to and fro, as soon as they have started.

"Where the devil are you going? To the r-r-right!"

"You do not know how to drive. Keep to the right!" calls the officer angrily.

6   A coachman from a private carriage swears at him; a passerby, who has run across the road and rubbed his shoulder against the horse's nose, looks at him furiously as he sweeps the snow from his sleeve. Iona shifts about on his seat as if he were on needles, moves his elbows as if he were trying to keep his equilibrium, and gapes about like someone suffocating, who does not understand why and wherefore he is there.

7   "What scoundrels they all are!" jokes the officer; "one would think they had all entered into an agreement to jostle you or fall under your horse."

Iona looks round at the officer, and moves his lips. He evidently wants to say something, but the only sound that issues is a snuffle.

"What?" asks the officer.

8   Iona twists his mouth into a smile, and with an effort says hoarsely:

"My son, *barin,* died this week."

"Hm! What did he die of?"

Iona turns with his whole body toward his fare, and says:

"And who knows! They say high fever. He was three days in the hospital, and then died. . . . God's will be done."

"Turn round! The devil!" sounds from the darkness. "Have you popped off, old doggie, eh? Use your eyes!"

"Go on, go on," says the officer, "otherwise we shall not get there by tomorrow. Hurry up a bit!"

9   The cabdriver again stretches his neck, sits up, and, with a bad grace, brandishes his whip. Several times again he turns to look at his fare, but the latter has closed his eyes, and apparently is not disposed to listen. Having deposited the officer in the Viborg, he stops by the tavern, doubles himself up on his seat, and again remains motionless, while the snow once more begins to cover him and his horse. An hour, and another. . . . Then, along the footpath, with a squeak of galoshes, and quarreling, come three young men, two of them tall and lanky, the third one short and humpbacked.

"Cabby, the Police Bridge!" in a cracked voice calls the humpback. "The three of us for two *griveniks!*"

10   Iona picks up his reins, and smacks his lips. Two griveniks is not a fair price, but he does not mind whether it is a *rouble* or five *kopeks*—to him it is all the same now, so long as they are fares. The young men, jostling each other and using bad language, approach the sleigh, and all three at once try to get onto the seat; then begins a discussion as to which two shall sit and who shall be the one to stand. After wrangling, abusing each other, and much petulance, it is at last decided that the humpback shall stand, as he is the smallest.

11   "Now then, hurry up!" says the humpback in a twanging voice, as he takes his place and breathes on Iona's neck. "Old furry! Here, mate, what a cap you have! There is not a worse one to be found in all Petersburg! . . ."

"He-he!—he-he!" giggles Iona. "Such a . . . ."

"Now you, 'such a,' hurry up, are you going the whole way at this pace? Are you? . . . Do you want it in the neck?"

"My head feels like bursting," says one of the lanky ones. "Last night at the Donkmasovs, Vaska and I drank the whole of four bottles of cognac."

12   "I don't understand what you lie for," says the other lanky one angrily; "you lie like a brute."

"God strike me, it's the truth!"

"It's as much the truth as that a louse coughs!"

"He, he," grins Iona, "what gay young gentlemen!"

"Pshaw, go to the devil!" says the humpback indignantly.

"Are you going to get on or not, you old pest? Is that the way to drive? Use the whip a bit! Go on, devil, go on, give it to him well!"

13   Iona feels at his back the little man wriggling, and the tremble in his voice. He listens to the insults hurled at him, sees the people, and little by little the feeling of loneliness leaves him. The humpback goes on swearing until he gets mixed up in some elaborate six-foot oath, or chokes with coughing. The lankies begin to talk about a certain Nadejda Petrovna. Iona looks round at them several times; he waits for a temporary silence, then, turning round again, he murmurs;

"My son . . . died this week."

14   "We must all die," sighs the humpback, wiping his lips after an attack of coughing. "Now, hurry up, hurry up! Gentlemen, I really cannot go any farther like this! When will he get us there?"

"Well, just you stimulate him a little in the neck!"

"You old pest, do you hear, I'll bone your neck for you! If one treated the like of you with ceremony one would have to go on foot! Do you hear, old serpent Gorinytch! Or do you not care a spit?"

15   Iona hears rather than feels the blows they deal him.

"He, he," he laughs. "They are gay young gentlemen, God bless 'em!"

"Cabby, are you married?" asks a lanky one.

"I? He, he, gay young gentlemen? Now I have only a wife and the moist ground. . . . He, ho, ho . . . that is to say, the grave. My son has died, and I am alive. . . . A wonderful thing, death mistook the door . . . instead of coming to me, it went to my son. . . ."

16   Iona turns round to tell them how his son died, but at this moment, the humpback, giving a little sigh, announces, "Thank God, we have at least reached our destination," and Iona watches them disappear through the dark entrance. Once more he is alone, and again surrounded by silence. . . . His grief, which has abated for a short while, returns and rends his heart with greater force. With an anxious and hurried look, he searches among the crowds passing on either side of the street to find whether there may be just one person who will listen to him. But the crowds hurry by without noticing him or his trouble. Yet it is such an immense, illimitable grief. Should his heart break and the grief pour out, it would flow over the whole earth, so it seems, and yet no one sees it. It has managed to conceal itself in such an insignificant shell that no one can see it even by day and with a light.

17   Iona sees a hall porter with some sacking, and decides to talk to him.

"Friend, what sort of time is it?" he asks.

"Past nine. What are you standing here for? Move on."

18   Iona moves on a few steps, doubles himself up, and abandons himself to his grief. He sees it is useless to turn to people for help. In less than five minutes he straightens himself, holds up his head as if he felt some sharp pain, and gives a tug at the reins; he can bear it no longer. "The stables," he thinks, and the little horse, as if it understood, starts off at a trot.

19   About an hour and a half later Iona is seated by a large dirty stove. Around the stove, on the floor, on the benches, people are snoring; the air is thick and suffocatingly hot. Iona looks at the sleepers, scratches himself, and regrets having returned so early.

20   "I have not even earned my fodder," he thinks. "That's what's my trouble. A man who knows his job, who has had enough to eat, and his horse too, can always sleep peacefully."

21   A young cabdriver in one of the corners half gets up, grunts sleepily, and stretches toward a bucket of water.

"Do you want a drink?" Iona asks him.

"Don't I want a drink!"

"That's so? Your good health! But listen, mate—you know, my son is dead. . . . Did you hear? This week, in the hospital. . . . It's a long story."

22   Iona looks to see what effect his words have, but sees none—the young man has hidden his face and is fast asleep again. The old man sighs, and scratches his head. Just as much as the young one wants to drink, the old man wants to talk. It will soon be a week since his son died, and he has not been able to speak about it properly to anyone. One must tell it slowly and carefully; how his son fell ill, how he suffered, what he said before he died, how he died. One must describe every detail of the funeral, and the journey to the hospital to fetch the dead son's clothes. His daughter Anissia has remained in the village—one must talk about her too. Is it nothing he has to tell? Surely the listener would gasp and sigh, and sympathize with him? It is better, too, to talk to women; although they are stupid, two words are enough to make them sob.

23   "I'll go and look after my horse," thinks Iona, "there's always time to sleep. No fear of that!"

24   He puts on his coat, and goes to the stables to his horse; he thinks of the corn, the hay, the weather. When he is alone, he dares not think of his son; he can speak about him to anyone, but to think of him, and picture him to himself, is unbearably painful.

25   "Are you tucking in?" Iona asks his horse, looking at its bright eyes; "go on, tuck in, though we've not earned our corn, we can eat hay. Yes! I am too old to drive—my son could have, not I. He was a first-rate cabdriver. If only he had lived!"

26   Iona is silent for a moment, then continues:

"That's how it is, my old horse. There's no more Kuzina Ionitch. He has left us to live, and he went off pop. Now let's say, you had a foal, you were the foal's mother, and suddenly, let's say, that foal went and left you to live after him. It would be sad, wouldn't it?"

27   The little horse munches, listens, and breathes over its master's hand. . . . Iona's feelings are too much for him, and he tells the little horse the whole story.

2,048 words

Vocabulary

angularity (1)   brandishes (4)
slough (1)   petulance (10)

Questions

1. How does the title "The Lament" relate to the content of this story?
2. Death of a loved one is not the only loss probed in the story. What other sorrows are examined?
3. What is Iona's overwhelming desire throughout the story? Why does he have this desire?
4. What do all of Iona's passengers have in common?

5. In what paragraph does Iona think about the exact steps he should take in expressing his grief?

6. Examine paragraph 1, and point out some details suggesting that the story will involve some kind of grief, sadness, or loss.

7. What details create the dominant impression of a father grieving for his son? Point to specific paragraphs.

8. What is the conflict of the story? How is it resolved?

The Wild Swans at Coole
William Butler Yeats

1 The trees are in their autumn beauty,
The woodland paths are dry,
Under the October twilight the water
Mirrors a still sky;
Upon the brimming water among the stones
Are nine-and-fifty swans.

2 The nineteenth autumn has come upon me
Since I first made my count;
I saw, before I had well finished,
All suddenly mount
And scatter wheeling in great broken rings
Upon their clamorous wings.

3 I have looked upon those brilliant creatures,
And now my heart is sore.
All's changed since I, hearing at twilight,
The first time on this shore,
The bell-beat of their wings above my head,
Trod with a lighter tread.

4 Unwearied still, lover by lover,
They paddle in the cold
Companionable streams or climb the air;
Their hearts have not grown old;
Passion or conquest, wander where they will,
Attend upon them still.

5 But now they drift on the still water
Mysterious, beautiful;
Among what rushes will they build,
By what lake's edge or pool
Delight men's eyes when I awake some day
To find they have flown away?

Questions

1. The poem tells us that it is twilight, the season of autumn, the month of October. What significance do these times usually have in a poem?

2. The poet says that his heart is sore. Why? What explanation can you deduce from the poem to account for his mood?
3. What qualities does the poet attribute to the swans? By implication, what is he saying about himself?
4. What contrast is implied in this poem? What does this contrast have to do with the theme of the poem?
5. How would you interpret the final two lines of the poem?
6. How would you characterize the descriptive language of this poem?

B. How to Write a Description

A vivid description supports a dominant impression with specific details. The dominant impression of a description is its central and unifying theme. In *The Godfather*, for instance, Mario Puzo bases his description of Don Corleone's sons on the dominant impression of their resemblance to Cupid. This impression is introduced in the description of Sonny and applied to all the other sons of Don Corleone:

> Sonny Corleone was tall for a first generation American of Italian parentage, almost six feet, and his crop of bushy, curly hair made him look even taller. *His face was that of a gross Cupid, the features even but the bowshaped lips thickly sensual, the dimpled cleft chin in some curious way obscene.*

With slightly varying details, this dominant impression accommodates a description of the Don's second son, Frederico Corleone:

> He was short and burly, not handsome but with the same Cupid head of the family, the curly helmet of hair over the round face and the sensual bow-shaped lips. Only, in Fred, these lips were not sensual but granitelike.

A contrast to this dominant impression is provided in the description of Michael Corleone, the third son:

> Michael Corleone was the youngest son of the Don and the only child who had refused the great man's direction. He did not have the heavy, Cupid-shaped face of the other children, and his jet black hair was straight rather than curly. His skin was clear olive-brown that would have been called beautiful in a girl. He was handsome in a delicate way.

Writing Assignment

Describe as vividly as you can a person, a place, or an event. Begin by picking a subject that strikes you with force. If possible, accumulate details and impressions by observing your subject up close. Next, find the dominant impression created by the person, place, or event, and state it in one sentence. The dominant impression of a place might be "Ben's cafe is a dingy hole in the wall." Of a person, it might be "Alicia has a delicate beauty." Of an event, it might be "The wedding was nervewracking." Support your dominant impression with details, omitting anything irrelevant that might break the unity of the impression. Develop the dominant impression and selected supporting details into a well-shaped essay.

Specific Instructions

1. ESTABLISH THE DOMINANT IMPRESSION.   To begin, you should establish the dominant impression of whatever you wish to describe. If you are assigned to describe a place, visit the place and spend some time observing it. The details observed will often suggest a suitable dominant impression. Once chosen, this dominant impression in turn will influence your selection of details.

For example, suppose you are assigned to write a description of your local airport lobby. You visit the airport and observe the following details:

1. A man's hat falls off as he lurches down the hall to catch his plane.
2. A sailor passionately kissing a girl suddenly looks at his watch and abruptly heads toward the escalator.
3. A little girl shrieks as an elderly woman—probably her grandmother—jerks her out of the arms of her mother to rush along toward Gate 31.
4. A fat executive takes a last hurried drag from his cigar before huffing and puffing his way to the ticket counter.
5. People of all sizes, ages, and races scramble across the lobby, bumping into each other and then resuming their frantic journeys.
6. A well-manicured woman sits casually on a bench reading *Cosmopolitan* and looking bored.
7. Two uniformed porters belly-laugh over a joke during a lull in foot traffic.

Most of these details suggest a dominant impression of the airport as a place where people are *rushed*. You formulate the following controlling idea, which includes this dominant impression: "At certain hours the International Airport lobby is a throughfare for people who are *rushed.*"

The function of the dominant impression at this stage of the essay is to provide a standard for judging the relevance of details. Details that support the dominant impression are relevant; those that contradict it are irrelevant. Details 1 through 5, for instance, can be included because they support this dominant impression, but details 6 and 7 must be omitted because they contradict it. The dominant impression therefore acts as a pattern that unifies the description, preventing your essay from being mercilessly pulled in two or three different directions by irrelevant details.

2. FOCUS THE DOMINANT IMPRESSION.   The dominant impression in a description is the equivalent of the controlling idea in an essay. Like the controlling idea, it must have a focus. The following dominant impressions lack focus:

Unfocused: Toward evening the meadow becomes eerie in its forsaken barrenness as the magpies chatter happily.

Better: Toward evening the meadow becomes eerie in its forsaken barrenness as the wind howls and groans.

(Happily chattering magpies destroy the idea of "forsaken barrenness.")

Unfocused: A translucent fragility was the outstanding feature of this husky old lady.

Better: A translucent fragility gave beauty to the face of this aristocratic old lady.

("Husky" ruins the impression of fragility.)

3. SELECT SPECIFIC AND SENSORY DETAILS.   A good dominant impression will attract details the way a whirlpool sucks water toward its center. You must not only avoid irrelevant details that will obscure the dominant impression of your description, but also you must select details that are specific and appeal to the senses.

Lack of *specific details* is the biggest mistake in student descriptions. The overwhelming tendency is to fill the page with mushy generalizations—for example:

> One could tell at a look that Chaim Sachar was poor. He was always hungry, and as a result he would wander about with a hungry attitude. His continual poverty caused him to become stingy to the point where he would collect garbage to use as fuel for his stove, and he cooked poor meals.

The description never comes to life because the supporting evidence is so vague. Contrast the above with another account:

> Two small eyes, starved and frightened, peered from beneath his dishevelled eyebrows; the red rims about his eyes were reminiscent of the time when he would wash down a dish of fried liver and hard-boiled eggs with a pint of vodka every morning after prayer. Now, all day long, he wandered through the marketplace, inhaling butcher-shop odors and those from restaurants, sniffing like a dog, and occasionally napping on porters' carts. With the refuse he had collected in a basket, he fed his kitchen stove at night; then, rolling the sleeves over his hairy arms, he would grate turnips on a grater.
>
> Isaac Bashevis Singer, "The Old Man"

Now the portrait leaps at you, punctuated by specific details, including "dishevelled eyebrows," "red rims about his eyes," and "hairy arms." The first description seems to present a shadowy figure in a darkened room, while the second reveals that same figure after the lights have been turned on.

Remember too that you can appeal to your reader through all the *senses.* You can make a reader see, taste, smell, touch, and hear what you are describing:

> The winter was difficult. There was no coal, and since several tiles were missing from the stove, the apartment was filled with thick black smoke each time the old man made a fire. A crust of blue ice and snow covered the window panes by November, making the rooms constantly dark or dusky. Overnight, the water on his night table froze in the pot. No matter how many clothes he piled over him in bed, he never felt warm; his feet remained stiff, and as soon as he began to doze, the entire pile of clothes

would fall off, and he would have to climb out naked to make his bed once more. There was no kerosene; even matches were at a premium. Although he recited chapter upon chapter of the Psalms, he could not fall asleep. The wind, freely roaming about the rooms, banged the doors; even the mice left. When he hung up his shirt to dry, it would grow brittle and break, like glass.

Isaac Bashevis Singer, "The Old Man"

The passage uses details that appeal to the reader's senses:

Visual: "crust of *blue ice* and snow covered the window panes"

Auditory: "the wind, freely roaming about the room, *banged* the door"

Tactile: "No matter how many clothes he piled over him in bed, he never *felt warm.*"

4. USE FIGURES OF SPEECH. To add vividness to a description, a writer will often use colorful words and expressions. These expressions usually involve some kind of comparison, as when Washington Irving compares Ichabod Crane's head with its big nose to a "a weathercock perched upon his spindle neck to tell which way the wind blew." Here is an example of a passage containing figures of speech:

She was a little woman, with brown, dull hair very elaborately arranged, and she had prominent blue eyes behind invisible pince-nez. Her face was long, *like a sheep's;* but she gave no impression of foolishness, rather of extreme alertness; *she had the quick movements of a bird.* The most remarkable thing about her was her voice, high, metallic, and without inflection; it fell on the ear with a hard monotony, irritating to the nerves *like the pitiless clamour of the pneumatic drill.*

W. Somerset Maugham, "Rain"

A caution: avoid the obvious, trite figures of speech, such as "busy as a bee," "white as a sheet," "big as a bear." Worn and ineffective, such figures hit the reader in the face *like a truck,* and could possibly render him or her *dead as a doornail.* If you use figures of speech, make them *as fresh as a daisy.* Get the idea?

Naturalist and writer Alan Devoe (1909–1955) offers a vivid description of the hillside shack on Phudd Hill to which he used to retreat and write.

Professional Model

A Shack on the Hillside
Alan Devoe

1   Half way up the rounded green slope of that ancient earth-pile which rises behind my cottage and is known as Phudd Hill, there exists a small three-sided shack. It resembles

a dilapidated chicken-house, and this is not surprising, for it *was* a chicken-house until that day when, by such labors as those that attended the construction of the Pyramids, it was pushed, dragged, hauled and heaved to its present resting-place among the trees and undergrowth high on the hillside. There, almost invisible in its green retreat, it spends its days in slow decline, succumbing to the encroach of nature. Birch saplings have grown up through its floor and the pale green tentacles of countless voracious vines have made their way into its every interstice. Legions of ants gradually and invincibly reduce its props to sawdust, and the ancient roof rots slowly beneath the damp green lichen. To those sharp-eyed visitors who descry this shack high on the wooded slope of Phudd Hill, and who ask me about its origin and use, I explain that it is the place in which I do my writing.

2   This is rather less than accurate. It might be said more truly that this is the place in which I *mean* to do my writing. It is to this secluded high-perched aerie that daily in fair weather I clamber with my typewriter, forcing my way through tangles of black-berry briar, slipping on mossy stones and stumbling over ancient treeroots, always with the beckoning vision of a place which will have the utter stillness and the total lack of distraction requisite to concentrating. As yet this vision remains but a vision, and the writing which I have accomplished in my hillside shack is negligible.

3   There are no boards on the floor; the three walls are set solidly upon the venerable earth of Phudd Hill. It is a black and loamy earth, an earth from which a thousand or a million trees and plants have sucked up their lives, and into which have been absorbed the flesh and fiber of a myriad of withered leaves. Woodchucks have made their burrows in it, and field mice and mole through countless centuries. It has received the dung of foxes and the droppings of crows, and rain and sunlight have alternately fallen upon it since long before the time of the Mohawks. And consequently there come from this floor of earth "wild scents and subtle essences"—dim half-memories and intimations by which the process of tapping typewriter keys is dwarfed to utter unimportance. Here, resident in this dumb timeless earth, is the mystery of creation; here in this old decaying root, this wisp of dead grass, this oak leaf gnawed to a skeleton by the worms, are its evidence and its symbols. And so I have sat here long hours and days, breathing in the smell of the wet earth and of the rotting lichened boards, and writing not a line. It is such a paralysis as might have gripped one who, at the moment of witnessing some Biblical miracle, had been asked to stand upon his head or dance a jig or tell a funny story. It comes over me with a quick and tumultuous awareness that whether or no I complete my manuscript, whether I arrange my words artfully or bungle them, it will have no smallest effect upon the march of these cosmic processes all about me. Whether I sell my essay or whether I do not, whether I live or whether I die, the mute and mindless earth worms will still tunnel through this ancient soil, the hawks will still scream and wheel over Phudd Hill, the clouds will continue to cast shadows upon its hemlock-wooded slope.

4   There is no tragedy in this awareness, but a vast inrushing solace. It brings a realization of myself as a breathing, feeding, procreating, decaying unit of the cosmic entirety, born to cope with the elements as best I may and ultimately to die, precisely like that cawing crow overhead or like this cricket clambering up the mullein stalk at my feet or even like that spot of mildew on the old wood of my table top. An hour ago the sole preoccupation of my mind, the vital necessity of the moment, was to prepare a certain number of rows of typewritten words upon sheets of white paper. But I have been reproached in my petty purpose by this ancient earth, and mocked by the miracle of a cricket.

5   This minute domain which is encompassed by the walls of my shack is a theatre of endless earth-play in miniature, a ceaseless turmoil of aliveness. There are slugs traversing with infinite slowness the earthen floor; creepers crawl even more slowly but

even more implacably across the rotting roof, fighting a dumb and inarticulate and endless battle for their lives as they struggle to thrust their roots down through the crust of the rubble and into the sweet sustaining body of the soil. Roots twist with roots, and leaves grapple with leaves in the battle for the supremacy of a place in the sun. New life springs to being from the vestiges of decay; from the sour rot of last autumn's leaves in that corner there emerges the pallid white graveyard-flesh of a summer toadstool, and from the dank recesses of decaying boards there emerges a colony of newborn ants. Here is the grinding and turning of the millwheels of the universe, here the sign of the eternal processes by which mountains are flung up from the bottom of the sea and constellations propelled across the sky and the particles of colored dust arrayed upon the wings of butterflies.

6   The tranquillity of nature is the emptiest of myths. Each moth, each fly, each twig and stone and shimmering spider web is perpetually in movement, perpetually in metamorphosis. There is no single second of arrest, no minutest particle of time when this scene is static. That midge which has been caught by the spider will be transmuted into blood and nerve and muscle for other spiders, and these spiders will live their small day and die upon the surface of the earth and be absorbed into it and furnish blood and nerve and muscle for a toadstool or a maple tree. It is perpetual change and translation, of worms into birds, of bees into flowers, of each and all of them ultimately into eternal earth. This mammoth mound that is Phudd Hill itself has not always been here, baking its fir-green back in the sun, nor will it always remain. Its lifetime is no longer than the flickering of an eyelash in the infinite span of time. For all its colossal roundness, for all its immeasurable tons of weight and its prodigious girth, it is as fragile as a bee's wing and as evanescent as a puff of wood smoke. Even now as it stands here, supporting the weight of ten thousand hemlocks and bearing with ease the snows of winter and the onslaught of rains and lightning, a change is taking place in the depths of its interior earth—a change which may one day level it away, or plunge it to the bottom of an ocean or replace it with a populous city.

7   My hillside shack is a wonderful place to be when it is raining. As I sit facing the open side to the east, I can see across a dozen farms and far away to a low-lying ridge of wooded hills. It is a panorama of rolling pasture land, dotted with darker green patches that are orchards and checkered by the boundary lines of ancient stone walls. The sunlight lies upon it all, burnishing the shocks of new-cut rye, sweetening the heavy-hanging apples on a thousand trees, distilling the smell of dew-wet meadows. And then, as I sit watching, a shadow glides down the slope of Phudd Hill and spreads out over the pastures like a stain. Quickly it widens, darkening the orchards and making the red barns somber, and the distant hills grow dim. All the countryside is abruptly very still. During the past hour innumerable little fragments of sounds have been reaching my ears—the faint cackle of hens, the far-off lowing of cattle. Now these are still. Instead there comes a new sound—a soft inanimate sibilance that grows in quick crescendo until it is a pervasive rushing murmur. It is the rustle of the leaves. It begins in the topmost branches of the high hemlocks, and as it grows in force their branches creak and scrape together. And now it is coming in a faster rush, and the sumac bushes and birch saplings and little firs around my shack are swaying and bending and whispering, and the low branches of the pine tree are brushing the roof over my head. It is as though all animate life were for this moment suspended in pure arrest and the clock set back immeasurable aeons of time. It is once more the primordial planet upon which there is nothing that barks or sings or walks or squeaks or thinks, but only the cold elemental airs sighing over the earth-surface and whistling among the mute and motionless rocks. It is the moment of the rain.

8   A great drop slashes upon the burdock leaf beside me, trickles down its stem to the

mossy surface of the earth and is swallowed up. Another falls and another. The white trunks of the birches glisten moist, and tiny glittering drops bow down the grass blades. Great gusts of wind come down the side of Phudd Hill, soughing in the tops of the hemlocks and rattling the loose clapboards of my walls. The little firs and maples are bowing and bobbing frantically now, and looking out across the pastures I can see the wheat lying as flat before the wind as though a scythe had passed. Uproar and chaos are all about me, leaves whirled furiously skyward, our dirt lane a maelstrom of mud. The ants have fled in terror to their crevices and crannies, birds are huddled in the thickest undergrowth, and under every flat rock and fallen tree trunk the silvery woodlice and millepedes are seeking refuge.

9   Quite suddenly, it is over. Racked trees are abruptly still and straight, and the drumming on the roof has stopped. Only the drip from the corner of my roof upon the burdock leaves is token of the storm that has passed. And now from the furious assault of the rain, evoked from this wild excoriation of the earth, there is born the most stirring scent in the world. It rises up out of the ground at my feet, seeps through the chinks of these old moss-covered boards, is exhaled from the rainwet leaves of the maples and the drenched branches of the firs. It is redolent of the magic of new birth, as fresh and miraculous as a sunrise. It tells of dust washed away from leaves, of drying brooks replenished and made full, of the thirst of seeds in the hot fields quenched and satisfied. The dross and the grime are carried away, a myriad of weary creatures refreshed and cleansed. By slow degrees the animate world, held static for these few minutes, begins to regain its life and the eternal processes of existence to be resumed. A crow flies to the top branches of the hemlock near by, and voids his droppings on a lichened boulder below. Blades of grass, which have been bent in taut arcs by the weight of the rain, begin to straighten themselves in spasmodic jerks and to point once more at the sun. A wood nymph butterfly, its eye-marked wings still powdery dry, crawls from a tangle of leaves and ascends the stalk of a sassafras bush, and perches there in happy absorption of the returned sunlight. The wheels of the universe turn again, the aphis once more sucks at the life-blood of the vine and the spider in his damp corner of my shack sets about the spinning of new meshes to trap his prey.

10   There is a phoebe nesting in my shack now, and I have spent long hours watching her at her masonry. The special ingredients for which she has need are not to be found close at hand on Phudd Hill. To secure the suitable mud she must fly almost a quarter of a mile to the marshy pasture land that borders our creek. There in the black oozing earth—a spot that in springtime produces the first skunk-cabbages, and where the woodcocks love to probe with their long beaks—she procures her little lumps and pellets and brings them back to her nest-site, patting and molding them in place with tireless dexterity. So absorbed was I yesterday in watching her at this, and following the line of her flight across the meadows to the creek and back again, that I lost count of time. The twilight found me still rapt in watching.

11   The twilight comes early to this side of Phudd Hill. While the sun is still shining on the rolling pasture land and clovery meadows, and while its slanting rays still lie across the far-off hills, the shadows of the great hemlocks lengthen and merge and the light in my little shack grows dim. For all the heat of the sun which has beaten down upon it during the day, the floor of earth exudes now its immemorial planetary coldness. This is no sharp and menacing chill, but the tranquil and beneficent coolness of great cathedrals. It is an earth-emanation to take the ache from backs that have bent all day beneath a blazing sun, to ease the myriad eyes that have blinked and strained against the daylight glare. It is the first inflow of a miraculous peace, that peace which comes upon nature with the setting of each day's sun, that ancient pervasive benison of nothingness bestowed upon men and upon cattle, upon birds and butterflies and weary leaves, upon

everything that lives. The crows have stopped their cawing and in the green depths of the woods are quiet and at rest; the buzzing turmoil of the bumblebees, shouldering their way through the long meadow grass, is not heard now.

12   As I sat watching the darkness deepen on Phudd Hill, the countless tiny sounds of daytime dropped away one by one. All the clamor of striving and struggling, all the cries—happy or agonized—that are the voice of existence on this earth, were hushed. The raucous parleying of my neighbor's chickens diminished to a whispering and presently disappeared. The twittering of the birds—the robins and thrushes, the orioles and song-sparrows, that hunt their food on Phudd Hill and pour out their songs and beget their kind and die there—became stilled now with the approach of night. There was, presently, no sound but the riffling of a little breeze through the trees and the rubbing of one branch against another.

13   Out of unfathomable reservoirs the inhabitants of earth were drawing strength for the coming day. The chipmunk, secure in his chink in the old stone wall; the hawk, roosting motionless in the topmost branches of the towering pine; my farmer friends, seeking their beds. . . .

14   A shadowy presence, white and light as thistle seed, brushed my hand and fluttered away into the darkness. It was a luna moth.

2,414 words

Vocabulary

dilapidated (1)	metamorphosis (6)
succumbing (1)	transmuted (6)
encroach (1)	prodigious (6)
voracious (1)	evanescent (6)
interstice (1)	burnishing (7)
aerie (2)	sibilance (7)
negligible (2)	pervasive (7)
intimations (3)	primordial (7)
tumultuous (3)	maelstrom (8)
solace (4)	excoriation (9)
procreating (4)	redolent (9)
reproached (4)	dexterity (10)
encompassed (5)	immemorial (11)
traversing (5)	emanation (11)
implacably (5)	myriad (11)
inarticulate (5)	benison (11)
vestiges (5)	parleying (12)

Questions

1. In the first paragraph, the author writes that his hillside shack spends its days slowly "succumbing to the encroach of nature." What specific details does he use to reinforce and support this assertion?
2. Why does the author find it so difficult to write in the shack on Phudd Hill?
3. Around what dominant impression of Phudd Hill is paragraph 3 constructed? What specific details does the author use to support this impression?

4. What realization about himself does the author come to as he sits in his shack on Phudd Hill?
5. What pattern of organization is evident in this essay? How is the end of the essay related to its beginning?
6. What, according to the author, is the emptiest of all myths? What is your opinion of his view of nature?
7. The description in paragraph 7 appeals to at least two of the senses. To which senses do most of the images in that paragraph appeal? Find specific examples.
8. To which sense does the description in paragraph 9 appeal? What specific details does the author use in this description?
9. How does the author link paragraphs 10, 11, and 12 together?

Beginning with a dominant impression of Hank as an enduring and stubborn old man, this essay supports the portrait with appropriate details. Good use of detail is its primary strength. See, for instance, the inclusion of an anecdote, purportedly told by Hank, which also helps to characterize his spirit. A cryptic and abrupt ending is its weakness.

Student Model

Hank
Brian Peterman

The ocean, hard work, and time have shaped him. He is an old man now, as gnarled and twisted as a cypress on a cliff above the sea. For seventy years he has been a fisherman, as he will continue to be one until he dies. His name is Hank and he lives in the small town of Wrangell in Southeast Alaska, where thousands of islands, covered with evergreens and lavishly carpeted with mosses and ferns, create a maze of channels, straights, bays, and passages. During the summer months when salmon make their yearly appearance, Hank makes his in an old sturdy seiner, the *Tiny Boy II*. All the fishermen in the Southeast know him and those who know him well respectfully call him the "Old Man."

I first saw Hank on the city dock. He and a few of his crewmen were working on their nets, mending tears and adding a few new corks. Having heard stories about him all my life, I felt as if I were staring at a museum piece—a Winslow Homer painting of an old salt come to life.

Years of hardship and toil had carved deep furrows into his brow. The many lines on his face gave him a permanent look of sadness. Eyes, once sharp and piercing, had acquired a painful, tired expression, as if he had gazed at the sunset once too often. Yellow, rotten teeth were the result of careless diet and an ever-present cigarette. And he had a hacking cough that shook his whole body.

I watched Hank's leathery hands as he mended the net. Knotted, bony fingers did the work with ease. As he laced the large needle through the web, Hank told a story about an eagle that had been killed by a fish. The eagle had sunk its talons into a large sea bass that was much too heavy. Instead of being grasped from the sea, the fish dove down, and the eagle, unable to loosen its powerful grip, was pulled down with the fish.

In a desperate attempt to keep afloat, the eagle spread its wings on the water. But the bass went down just the same and the eagle's wings made a loud crack as they broke and disappeared. Hank swore he heard them snap from his boat a quarter mile away—with the engine on.

Everyone laughed and Hank laughed the loudest and then took to wheezing. When the coughing attack died down, he pulled out another unfiltered cigarette, lit it, and walked to the outhouse on the end of the dock. He had a small limp that made his baggy brown pants slip down so that every few steps he had to pull them up.

While he was gone I asked a crewman what kept the old man going. "Hell, I don't know," he said. "No one really does. This boat's all he lives for. Last year him an' his son was on the freeway in Seattle. They was goin' down the harbor an' were about 10 miles away when the old man starts to have a heart attack! His son tells him to pull the car over so's he can drive him to the hospital. Hank just grabs the wheel tighter and says 'Gotta get to my boat.' An' he did too."

The old man was walking back, his hard shoes thumping on the dock. I watched him return and asked myself, "What is it inside that man that makes him keep going?" I tried to be profound and come up with some kind of transcendental reason, such as "a fierce, passionate love for the sea" or some other dramatic phrase. But somehow it sounded funny.

However, Hank's grandson, a close friend of mine, came perhaps closest to some logical explanation. It so happens that Hank spends the winter months in an apartment in Seattle. Every summer Hank and another old fisherman have a contest to see who can catch the most salmon. The loser must treat the winner to a pair of season tickets to the Washington Huskies football games.

And Hank hates to lose bets.

The portrait below reveals a famous artist in a little-known perspective.

Alternate Reading

The Monster
Deems Taylor

1   He was an undersized little man, with a head too big for his body—a sickly little man. His nerves were bad. He had skin trouble. It was agony for him to wear anything next to his skin coarser than silk. And he had delusions of grandeur.

2   He was a monster of conceit. Never for one minute did he look at the world or at people, except in relation to himself. He was not only the most important person in the world, to himself; in his own eyes he was the only person who existed. He believed himself to be one of the greatest dramatists in the world, one of the greatest thinkers, and one of the greatest composers. To hear him talk, he was Shakespeare, and Beethoven, and Plato, rolled into one. And you would have had no difficulty in hearing him talk. He was one of the most exhausting conversationalists that ever lived. An evening with him was an evening spent in listening to a monologue. Sometimes he was brilliant; sometimes he was maddeningly tiresome. But whether he was being brilliant or dull, he had one sole topic of conversation: himself. What *he* thought and what *he* did.

3   He had a mania for being in the right. The slightest hint of disagreement, from anyone, on the most trivial point, was enough to set him off on a harangue that might last for

hours, in which he proved himself right in so many ways, and with such exhausting volubility, that in the end his hearer, stunned and deafened, would agree with him, for the sake of peace.

4   It never occurred to him that he and his doing were not of the most intense and fascinating interest to anyone with whom he came in contact. He had theories about almost any subject under the sun, including vegetarianism, the drama, politics, and music; and in support of these theories he wrote pamphlets, letters, books . . . thousands upon thousands of words, hundreds and hundreds of pages. He not only wrote these things, and published them—usually at somebody else's expense—but he would sit and read them aloud, for hours, to his friends and his family.

5   He wrote operas; and no sooner did he have the synopsis of a story, but he would invite—or rather summon—a crowd of his friends to his house and read it aloud to them. Not for criticism. For applause. When the complete poem was written, the friends had to come again, and hear *that* read aloud. Then he would publish the poem, sometimes years before the music that went with it was written. He played the piano like a composer, in the worst sense of what that implies, and he would sit down at the piano before parties that included some of the finest pianists of his time, and play for them, by the hour, his own music, needless to say. He had a composer's voice. And he would invite eminent vocalists to his house, and sing them his operas, taking all the parts.

He had the emotional stability of a six-year-old child. When he felt out of sorts, he would rave and stamp, or sink into suicidal gloom and talk darkly of going to the East to end his days as a Buddhist monk. Ten minutes later, when something pleased him, he would rush out of doors and run around the garden, or jump up and down on the sofa, or stand on his head. He could be grief-stricken over the death of a pet dog, and he could be callous and heartless to a degree that would have made a Roman emperor shudder.

7   He was almost innocent of any sense of responsibility. Not only did he seem incapable of supporting himself, but it never occurred to him that he was under any obligation to do so. He was convinced that the world owed him a living. In support of this belief, he borrowed money from everybody who was good for a loan—men, women, friends, or strangers. He wrote begging letters by the score, sometimes groveling without shame, at others loftily offering his intended benefactor the privilege of contributing to his support, and being mortally offended if the recipient declined the honor. I have found no record of his ever paying or repaying money to anyone who did not have a legal claim upon it.

8   What money he could lay his hands on he spent like an Indian rajah. The mere prospect of a performance of one of his operas was enough to set him to running up bills amounting to ten times the amount of his prospective royalties. On an income that would reduce a more scrupulous man to doing his own laundry, he would keep two servants. Without enough money in his pocket to pay his rent, he would have the walls and ceiling of his study lined with pink silk. No one will ever know—certainly he never knew—how much money he owed. We do know that his greatest benefactor gave him $6,000 to pay the most pressing of his debts in one city, and a year later had to give him $16,000 to enable him to live in another city without being thrown into jail for debt.

9   He was equally unscrupulous in other ways. An endless procession of women marched through his life. His first wife spent twenty years enduring and forgiving his infidelities. His second wife had been the wife of his most devoted friend and admirer, from whom he stole her. And even while he was trying to persuade her to leave her first husband he was writing to a friend to inquire whether he could suggest some wealthy woman—any wealthy woman—whom he could marry for her money.

10   He was completely selfish in his other personal relationships. His liking for his friends was measured solely by the completeness of their devotion to him, or by their usefulness to him, whether financial or artistic. The minute they failed him—even by so much as refusing a dinner invitation—or began to lessen in usefulness, he cast them off without a second thought. At the end of his life he had exactly one friend left whom he had known even in middle age.

11   He had a genius for making enemies. He would insult a man who disagreed with him about the weather. He would pull endless wires in order to meet some man who admired his work, and was able and anxious to be of use to him—and would proceed to make a mortal enemy of him with some idiotic and wholly uncalled-for exhibition of arrogance and bad manners. A character in one of his operas was a caricature of one of the most powerful music critics of his day. Not content with burlesquing him, he invited the critic to his house and read him the libretto aloud in front of his friends.

12   The name of this monster was Richard Wagner. Everything that I have said about him you can find on record—in newspapers, in police reports, in the testimony of people who knew him, in his own letters, between the lines of his autobiography. And the curious thing about this record is that it doesn't matter in the least.

13   Because this undersized, sickly, disagreeable, fascinating little man was right all the time. The joke was on us. He *was* one of the most stupendous musical geniuses that, up to now, the world has ever seen. The world did owe him a living. People couldn't know those things at the time, I suppose; and yet to us, who know his music, it does seem as though they should have known. What if he did talk about himself all the time? If he had talked about himself for twenty-four hours every day for the span of his life he would not have uttered half the number of words that other men have spoken and written about him since his death.

14   When you consider what he wrote—thirteen operas and music dramas, eleven of them still holding the stage, eight of them unquestionably worth ranking among the world's great musico-dramatic masterpieces—when you listen to what he wrote, the debts and heartaches that people had to endure from him don't seem much of a price. Eduard Hanslick, the critic whom he caricatured in *Die Meistersinger* and who hated him ever after, now lives only because he was caricatured in *Die Meistersinger*. The women whose hearts he broke are long since dead; and the man who could never love anyone but himself has made them deathless atonement, I think, with *Tristan und Isolde*. Think of the luxury with which for a time, at least, fate rewarded Napoleon, the man who ruined France and looted Europe; and then perhaps you will agree that a few thousand dollars' worth of debts were not too heavy a price to pay for the *Ring* trilogy.

15   What if he was faithless to his friends and to his wives? He had one mistress to whom he was faithful to the day of his death: Music. Not for a single moment did he ever compromise with what he believed, with what he dreamed. There is not a line of his music that could have been conceived by a little mind. Even when he is dull, or downright bad, he is dull in the grand manner. There is greatness about his worst mistakes. Listening to his music, one does not forgive him for what he may or may not have been. It is not a matter of forgiveness. It is a matter of being dumb with wonder that his poor brain and body didn't burst under the torment of the demon of creative energy that lived inside him, struggling, clawing, scratching to be released; tearing, shrieking at him to write the music that was in him. The miracle is that what he did in the little space of seventy years could have been done at all, even by a great genius. Is it any wonder that he had no time to be a man?

1,724 words

Questions

1. In one brief sentence, what is the dominant impression of Richard Wagner, as portrayed in this essay? Where is it first stated?
2. How does the author go about supporting this dominant impression? Give two or three examples from the text.
3. Do you agree with the author's view that Richard Wagner had a perfect right to be the monster he was? In other words, do geniuses have privileges that ordinary people do not have? Support your answer with reasons.
4. Of all the monstrosities committed by Wagner, which offended you most? Why?
5. What does the author mean when he says (paragraph 13), "The world did owe him a living."
6. In paragraph 7, why does the author use the word *innocent* rather than *void* or *free from?*
7. In what paragraph does the author lend credibility to the facts offered in this essay?

Between 1921 and 1931, Isak Dinesen (pseudonym of the Danish aristocrat Baroness Karen Blixen, 1885–1962) lived on and managed a coffee plantation in Kenya, Africa. There she became friends with Denys Finch-Hatton, an English big-game hunter, and often accompanied him in his light plane on sightseeing flights over the Kenya countryside. In this excerpt from her book *Out of Africa* (1937), Dinesen describes the African landscape as she saw it from the air. Denys Finch-Hatton was killed in a crash of his airplane and buried in the Ngong hills of Kenya shortly after the events described in this excerpt.

Flying Over Africa
Isak Dinesen

1   To Denys Finch-Hatton I owe what was, I think, the greatest, the most transporting pleasure of my life on the farm: I flew with him over Africa. There, where there are few or no roads and where you can land on the plains, flying becomes a thing of real and vital importance in your life; it opens up a world. Denys had brought out his Moth machine; it could land on my plain on the farm only a few minutes from the house, and we were up nearly every day.

2   You have tremendous views as you get up above the African highlands, surprising combinations and changes of light and colouring, the rainbow on the green sunlit land, the gigantic upright clouds and big wild black storms, all swing round you in a race and a dance. The lashing hard showers of rain whiten the air askance. The language is short

of words for the experiences of flying, and will have to invent new words with time. When you have flown over the Rift Valley and the volcanoes of Suswa and Longonot, you have travelled far and have been to the lands on the other side of the moon. You may at other times fly low enough to see the animals on the plains and to feel towards them as God did when he had just created them, and before he commissioned Adam to give them names.

3   But it is not the visions but the activity which makes you happy, and the joy and glory of the flyer is the flight itself. It is a sad hardship and slavery to people who live in towns, that in all their movements they know of one dimension only; they walk along the line as if they were led on a string. The transition from the line to the plane into the two dimensions, when you wander across a field or through a wood, is a spendid liberation to the slaves, like the French Revolution. But in the air you are taken into the full freedom of the three dimensions; after long ages of exile and dreams the homesick heart throws itself into the arms of space. The laws of gravitation and time,

"...in life's green grove,
Sport like tame beasts, none knew how
gentle they could be!"

4   Every time that I have gone up in an aeroplane and looking down have realised that I was free of the ground, I have had the consciousness of a great new discovery. "I see:" I have thought, "This was the idea. And now I understand everything."

5   One day Denys and I flew to Lake Natron, ninety miles South-East of the farm, and more than four thousand feet lower, two thousand feet above Sea level. Lake Natron is the place from where they take soda. The bottom of the lake and the shores are like some sort of whitish concrete, with a strong, sour and salt smell.

6   The sky was blue, but as we flew from the plains in over the stony and bare lower country, all colour seemed to be scorched out of it. The whole landscape below us looked like delicately marked tortoise-shell. Suddenly, in the midst of it was the lake. The white bottom, shining through the water, gives it, when seen from the air, a striking, an unbelievable azure-colour, so clear that for a moment you shut your eyes at it; the expanse of water lies in the bleak tawny land like a big bright aquamarine. We had been flying high, now we went down, and as we sank our own shade, dark-blue, floated under us upon the light-blue lake. Here live thousands of Flamingoes, although I do not know how they exist in the brackish water,—surely there are no fish here. At our approach they spread out in large circles and fans, like the rays of a setting sun, like an artful Chinese pattern of silk or porcelain, forming itself and changing, as we looked at it.

7   We landed on the white shore, that was white-hot as an oven, and lunched there, taking shelter against the sun under the wing of the aeroplane. If you stretched out your hand from the shade, the sun was so hot that it hurt you. Our bottles of beer when they first arrived with us, straight out of the ether, were pleasantly cold, but before we had finished them, in a quarter of an hour, they became as hot as a cup of tea.

8   While we were lunching, a party of Masai warriors appeared on the horizon, and approached quickly. They must have spied the aeroplane landing from a distance, and resolved to have a close look at it, and a walk of any length, even in a country like this, means nothing to a Masai. They came along, the one in front of the other, naked, tall and narrow, their weapons glinting; dark like peat on the yellow grey sand. At the feet of each of them lay and marched a small pool of shadow, these were, besides our own, the only shadows in the country as far as the eye reached. When they came up to us they fell in line, there were five of them. They stuck their heads together and began to talk to one another about the aeroplane and us. A generation ago they would have been fatal to us

to meet. After a time one of them advanced and spoke to us. As they could only speak Masai and we understood but little of the language, the conversation soon slackened, he stepped back to his fellows and a few minutes later they all turned their back upon us, and walked away, in single file, with the wide white burning salt-plain before them.

9   "Would you care," said Denys, "to fly to Naivasha? But the country lying between is very rough, we could not possibly land anywhere on the way. So we shall have to go up high and keep up at twelve thousand feet."

10   The flight from Lake Natron to Naivasha was *Das ding an sich.*[1] We took a bee-line, and kept at twelve thousand feet all the way, which is so high that there is nothing to look down for. At Lake Natron I had taken off my lambskin-lined cap, now up here the air squeezed my forehead, as cold as iced water; all my hair flew backwards as if my head was being pulled off. This path, in fact, was the same as was, in the opposite direction, every evening taken by the Roc, when, with an Elephant for her young in each talon, she swished from Uganda home to Arabia. Where you are sitting in front of your pilot, with nothing but space before you, you feel that he is carrying you upon the outstretched palms of his hands, as the Djinn carried Prince Ali through the air, and that the wings that bear you onward are his. We landed at the farm of our friends at Naivasha; the mad diminutive houses, and the very small trees surrounding them, all threw themselves flat upon their backs as they saw us descending.

11   When Denys and I had not time for long journeys we went out for a short flight over the Ngong Hills, generally about sunset. These hills, which are amongst the most beautiful in the world, are perhaps at their loveliest seen from the air, when the ridges, bare towards the four peaks mount, and run side by side with the aeroplane, or suddenly sink down and flatten out into a small lawn.

12   Here in the hills there were Buffaloes. I had even, in my very young days,—when I could not live till I had killed a specimen of each kind of African game,—shot a bull out here. Later on, when I was not so keen to shoot as to watch the wild animals, I had been out to see them again. I had camped in the hills by a spring half way to the top, bringing my servants, tents, and provisions with me, and Farah[2] and I had been up in the dark, ice cold mornings to creep and crawl through bush and long grass, in the hope of catching a glimpse of the herd; but twice I had had to go back without success. That the herd lived there, neighbours of mine to the West, was still a value in the life on the farm, but they were serious-minded, self-sufficient neighbours, the old nobility of the hills, now somehow reduced; they did not receive much.

13   But one afternoon as I was having tea with some friends of mine from up-country, outside the house, Denys came flying from Nairobi and went over our heads out West-wards; a little while after he turned and came back and landed on the farm. Lady Delamere and I drove down to the plain to fetch him up, but he would not get out of his aeroplane.

14   "The Buffalo are out feeding in the hills," he said, "come out and have a look at them."
"I cannot come," I said, "I have got a tea-party up at the house."
"But we will go and see them and be back in a quarter of an hour," said he.

15   This sounded to me like the propositions which people make to you in a dream. Lady Delamere would not fly, so I went up with him. We flew in the sun, but the hillside lay in a transparent brown shade, which soon we got into. It did not take us long to spy the Buffalo from the air. Upon one of the long rounded green ridges which run, like folds of a cloth gathered together at each peak, down the side of the Ngong mountain, a herd

---

[1]"The thing in itself."

[2]Dinesen's Somali servant, Farah Aden.

of twenty-seven Buffalo were grazing. First we saw them a long way below us, like mice moving gently on a floor, but we dived down, circling over and along their ridge, a hundred and fifty feet above them and well within shooting distance; we counted them as they peacefully blended and separated. There was one very old big black bull in the herd, one or two younger bulls, and a number of calves. The open stretch of sward upon which they walked was closed in by bush; had a stranger approached on the ground they would have heard or scented him at once, but they were not prepared for advance from the air. We had to keep moving above them all the time. They heard the noise of our machine and stopped grazing, but they did not seem to have it in them to look up. In the end they realized that something very strange was about; the old bull first walked out in front of the herd, raising his hundredweight horns, braving the unseen enemy, his four feet planted on the ground,—suddenly he began to trot down the ridge and after a moment he broke into a canter. The whole clan now followed him, stampeding head-long down, and as they switched and plunged into the bush, dust and loose stones rose in their wake. In the thicket they stopped and kept close together, it looked as if a small glade in the hill had been paved with dark grey stones. Here they believed themselves to be covered to the view, and so they were to anything moving along the ground, but they could not hide themselves from the eyes of the bird of the air. We flew up and away. It was like having been taken into the heart of the Ngong Hills by a secret unknown road.

16   When I came back to my tea party, the teapot on the stone table was still so hot that I burned my fingers on it. The Prophet had the same experience when he upset a jug of water, and the Archangel Gabriel took him, and flew with him through the seven heavens, and when he returned, the water had not yet run out of the jug.

17   In the Ngong Hills there also lived a pair of eagles. Denys in the afternoons used to say: "Let us go and visit the eagles." I have once seen one of them sitting on a stone near the top of the mountain, and getting up from it, but otherwise they spent their life up in the air. Many times we have chased one of these eagles, careening and throwing ourselves on to one wing and then to the other, and I believe that the sharp-sighted bird played with us. Once, when we were running side by side, Denys stopped his engine in mid air, and as he did so I heard the eagle screech.

18   The Natives liked the aeroplane, and for a time it was the fashion on the farm to portray her, so that I would find sheets of paper in the kitchen, or the kitchen wall itself, covered with drawings of her, with the letters ABAK carefully copied out. But they did not really take any interest in her or in our flying.

19   Natives dislike speed, as we dislike noise, it is to them, at the best, hard to bear. They are also on friendly terms with time, and the plan of beguiling or killing it does not come into their heads. In fact the more time you can give them, the happier they are, and if you commission a Kikuyu to hold your horse while you make a visit, you can see by his face that he hopes you will be a long, long time about it. He does not try to pass the time then, but sits down and lives.

20   Neither do the Natives have much sympathy with any kind of machinery or mechanics. A group of the young generation have been carried away by the enthusiasm of the European for the motor-car, but an old Kikuyu said to me of them that they would die young, and it is likely that he was right, for renegades come of a weak line of the nation. Amongst the inventions of civilization which the Natives admire and appreciate are matches, a bicycle and a rifle, still they will drop these the moment there is any talk of a cow.

21   Frank Greswolde-Williams, of the Kedong Valley, took a Masai with him to England as a Sice, and told me that a week after his arrival he rode his horses in Hyde Park as if he had been born in London. I asked this man when he came back to Africa what he found very good in England. He thought my question over with a grave face and after a long time courteously said that the white men had got very fine bridges.

22   I have never seen an old Native who, for things which moved by themselves without apparent interference by man or by the forces of Nature, expressed anything but distrust and a certain feeling of shame. The human mind turns away its eye from witchcraft as from something unseemly. It may be forced to take an interest in the effects of it, but it will have nothing to do with the inside working, and no one has ever tried to squeeze out of a witch the exact recipe for her brew.

23   Once, when Denys and I had been up, and were landing on the plain of the farm, a very old Kikuyu came up and talked to us:

24   "You were up very high to-day," he said, "we could not see you, only hear the aeroplane sing like a bee."

     I agreed that we had been up high.

     "Did you see God?" he asked.

     "No, Ndwetti," I said, "we did not see God."

25   "Aha, then you were not up high enough," he said, "but now tell me: do you think that you will be able to get up high enough to see him?"

     "I do not know, Ndwetti," I said.

26   "And you, Bedâr," he said, turning to Denys, "what do you think? Will you get up high enough in your aeroplane to see God?"

     "Really I do not know," said Denys.

27   "Then," said Ndwetti, "I do not know at all why you two go on flying."

2,634 words

Vocabulary

askance(2)
azure (6)
careening (17)
Sice (21)

Questions

1. Aside from the descriptive passages, what is the dominant rhetorical mode of this excerpt?
2. Although the author tells us little about herself directly, much is revealed about her in this excerpt. What can you infer about her personality from this excerpt?
3. Examine the description of flying in paragraphs 2, 3, and 4. What kind of imagery does the author use to describe the freedom of flight? What is the implication of this imagery?
4. Around what dominant impression of Lake Natron is the description in paragraph 7 focused?
5. Examine the description in paragraph 10. What is the purpose of the allusions to the Roc and to Prince Ali and the Djinn?
6. What kind of figurative language is prominently used in the description of the buffalo herd in paragraph 15?
7. What contrast does the author implicitly draw in the final paragraphs of this excerpt?

C. Additional Writing Assignments

1. Based on a dominant impression, write a description of your latest family dinner.
2. Using "dingy" as your dominant impression, write a description of an imaginary place. Support the impression with details.
3. Write an essay describing in detail the most *restful* spot you know.
4. Go to your local supermarket, notebook in hand. Observe the scene around you, and reduce it to a single dominant impression. Write the dominant impression and some details that support it. From these notes, develop a descriptive essay.
5. Describe the looks of your closest friend. Begin with a dominant impression and develop details to support it.
6. Describe your most valued possession, beginning with a dominant impression and supplying details.
7. Develop a descriptive essay comparing your lover (real or imaginary) to a flower, animal, or object.
8. Using sensory details, write a description of a garden in spring.
9. Go to a public park or some other place where you can observe an old person. Study his or her face, dress, and movements, and write a description of this person.
10. Write an essay fully describing your favorite television personality.

7

Example

Then, my childlike spectrum of emotions was suddenly expanded by certain events that took charge of my life.

A. Reading for Ideas

Read the story "Theft" to see if you can discover a pattern emerging from the narrator's encounters. Ask yourself the following questions: What do the encounters have in common? Does the narrator repeat any action or attitude? What personality trait does she display in all these encounters? You will discover that the encounters described provide examples of a pattern in her behavior, which in turn is a clue to the story's meaning. After reading the story, ask yourself what pattern has emerged from your own life during the past year. Try to state that pattern as a controlling idea for an essay.

Theft
Katherine Anne Porter

1   She had the purse in her hand when she came in. Standing in the middle of the floor, holding her bathrobe around her and trailing a damp towel in one hand, she surveyed the immediate past and remembered everything clearly. Yes, she had opened the flap and spread it out on the bench after she had dried the purse with her handkerchief.

2   She had intended to take the Elevated, and naturally she looked in her purse to make certain she had the fare, and was pleased to find forty cents in the coin envelope. She was going to pay her own fare, too, even if Camilo did have the habit of seeing her up the steps and dropping a nickel in the machine before he gave the turnstile a little push and sent her through it with a bow. Camilo by a series of compromises had managed to make effective a fairly complete set of smaller courtesies, ignoring the larger and more troublesome ones. She had walked with him to the station in a pouring rain, because she knew he was almost as poor as she was, and when he insisted on a taxi, she was firm and said, "You know it simply will not do." He was wearing a new hat of a pretty biscuit shade, for it never occurred to him to buy anything of a practical color; he had put it on for the first time and the rain was spoiling it. She kept thinking, "But this is dreadful, where will he get another?" She compared it with Eddie's hats that always seemed to be precisely seven years old and as if they had been quite purposely left out in the rain, and

104

yet they sat with a careless and incidental rightness on Eddie. But Camilo was far different; if he wore a shabby hat it would be merely shabby on him, and he would lose his spirits over it. If she had not feared Camilo would take it badly, for he insisted on the practice of his little ceremonies up to the point he had fixed for them, she would have said to him as they left Thora's house, "Do go home. I can surely reach the station by myself."

3   "It is written that we must be rained upon tonight," said Camilo, "so let it be together."

4   At the end of the platform stairway she staggered slightly—they were both nicely set up on Thora's cocktails—and said: "At least, Camilo, do me the favor not to climb these stairs in your present state, since for you it is only a matter of coming down again at once, and you'll certainly break your neck."

5   He made three quick bows, he was Spanish, and leaped off through the rainy darkness. She stood watching him, for he was a very graceful young man, thinking that tomorrow morning he would gaze soberly at his spoiled hat and soggy shoes and possibly associate her with his misery. As she watched, he stopped at the far corner and took off his hat and hid it under his overcoat. She felt she had betrayed him by seeing, because he would have been humiliated if he thought she even suspected him of trying to save his hat.

6   Roger's voice sounded over her shoulder above the clang of the rain falling on the stairway shed, wanting to know what she was doing out in the rain at this time of night, and did she take herself for a duck? His long, imperturbable face was steaming with water, and he tapped a bulging spot on the breast of his buttoned-up overcoat: "Hat," he said, "Come on, let's take a taxi."

7   She settled back against Roger's arm which he laid around her shoulders, and with the gesture they exchanged a glance full of long amiable associations, then she looked through the window at the rain changing the shapes of everything, and the colors. The taxi dodged in and out between the pillars of the Elevated, skidding slightly on every curve, and she said: "The more it skids the calmer I feel, so I really must be drunk."

8   "You must be," said Roger. "This bird is a homicidal maniac, and I could do with a cocktail myself this minute."

9   They waited on the traffic at Fortieth Street and Sixth Avenue, and three boys walked before the nose of the taxi. Under the globes of light they were cheerful scarecrows, all very thin and all wearing very seedy snappy-cut suits and gay neckties. They were not very sober either, and they stood for a moment wobbling in front of the car, and there was an argument going on among them. They leaned toward each other as if they were getting ready to sing, and the first one said: "When I get married it won't be jus' for getting married, I'm gonna marry for *love*, see?" and the second one said, "Aw, gwan and tell that stuff to *her*, why n't yuh?" and the third one gave a kind of hoot, and said, "Hell, dis guy? Wot the hell's he got?" and the first one said: "Aaah, shurrup yuh mush, I got plenty." Then they all squealed and scrambled across the street beating the first one on the back and pushing him around.

10   "Nuts," commented Roger, "pure nuts."

Two girls went skittering by in short transparent raincoats, one green, one red, their heads tucked against the drive of the rain. One of them was saying to the other, "Yes, I know all about *that*. But what about me? You're always so sorry for *him* . . ." and they ran on with their little pelican legs flashing back and forth.

11   The taxi backed up suddenly and leaped forward again, and after a while Roger said: "I had a letter from Stella today, and she'll be home on the twenty-sixth, so I suppose she's made up her mind and it's all settled."

"I had a sort of letter today too," she said, "making up my mind for me. I think it is time for you and Stella to do something definite."

12 When the taxi stopped on the corner of West Fifty-third Street, Roger said, "I've just enough if you'll add ten cents," so she opened her purse and gave him a dime, and he said, "That's beautiful, that purse."

"It's a birthday present," she told him, "and I like it. How's your show coming?"

"Oh, still hanging on, I guess. I don't go near the place. Nothing sold yet. I mean to keep right on the way I'm going and they can take it or leave it. I'm through with the argument."

"It's absolutely a matter of holding out, isn't it?"

"Holding out's the tough part."

"Good night, Roger."

"Good night, you should take aspirin and push yourself into a tub of hot water, you look as though you're catching cold."

"I will."

13 With the purse under her arm she went upstairs, and on the first landing Bill heard her step and poked his head out with his hair tumbled and his eyes red, and he said: "For Christ's sake, come in and have a drink with me. I've had some bad news."

14 "You're perfectly sopping," said Bill, looking at her drenched feet. They had two drinks, while Bill told how the director had thrown his play out after the cast had been picked over twice, and had gone through three rehearsals. "I said to him, 'I didn't say it was a masterpiece, I said it would make a good show.' And he said, 'It just doesn't play, do you see? It needs a doctor.' So I'm stuck, absolutely stuck," said Bill, on the edge of weeping again. "I've been crying," he told her, "in my cups." And he went on to ask her if she realized his wife was ruining him with her extravagance. "I send her ten dollars every week of my unhappy life, and I don't really have to. She threatens to jail me if I don't, but she can't do it. God, let her try it after the way she treated me! She's no right to alimony and she knows it. She keeps on saying she's got to have it for the baby and I keep on sending it because I can't bear to see anybody suffer. So I'm way behind on the piano and the victrola, both—"

"Well, this is a pretty rug, anyhow," she said.

15 Bill stared at it and blew his nose. "I got it at Ricci's for ninety-five dollars," he said. "Ricci told me it once belonged to Marie Dressler, and cost fifteen hundred dollars, but there's a burnt place on it, under the divan. Can you beat that?"

"No," she said. She was thinking about her empty purse and that she could not possibly expect a check for her latest review for another three days, and her arrangement with the basement restaurant could not last much longer if she did not pay something on account. "It's no time to speak of it," she said, "but I've been hoping you would have by now that fifty dollars you promised for my scene in the third act. Even if it doesn't play. You were to pay me for the work anyhow out of your advance."

16 "Weeping Jesus," said Bill, "you, too?" He gave a loud sob, or hiccough, in his moist handkerchief. "Your stuff was no better than mine, after all. Think of that."

"But you got something for it," she said. "Seven hundred dollars."

17 Bill said, "Do me a favor, will you? Have another drink and forget about it. I can't, you know I can't, I would if I could, but you know the fix I'm in."

"Let it go, then," she found herself saying almost in spite of herself. She had meant to be quite firm about it. They drank again without speaking, and she went to her apartment on the floor above.

18 There, she now remembered distinctly, she had taken the letter out of the purse before she spread the purse out to dry.

19 She had sat down and read the letter over again: but there were phrases that insisted on being read many times, they had a life of their own separate from the others, and when she tried to read past and around them, they moved with the movement of her

eyes, and she could not escape them . . . "thinking about you more than I mean to . . . yes, I even talk about you . . . why were you so anxious to destroy . . . even if I could see you now I would not . . . not worth all this abominable . . . the end . . ."

20   Carefully she tore the letter into narrow strips and touched a lighted match to them in the coal grate.

21   Early the next morning she was in the bathtub when the janitress knocked and then came in, calling out that she wished to examine the radiators before she started the furnace going for the winter. After moving about the room for a few minutes, the janitress went out, closing the door very sharply.

22   She came out of the bathroom to get a cigarette from the package in the purse. The purse was gone. She dressed and made coffee, and sat by the window while she drank it. Certainly the janitress had taken the purse, and certainly it would be impossible to get it back without a great deal of ridiculous excitement. Then let it go. With this decision of her mind, there rose coincidentally in her blood a deep almost murderous anger. She set the cup carefully in the center of the table, and walked steadily downstairs, three long flights and a short hall and a steep short flight into the basement, where the janitress, her face streaked with dust, was shaking up the furnace. "Will you please give me back my purse? There isn't any money in it. It was a present, and I don't want to lose it."

23   The janitress turned without straightening up and peered at her with hot flickering eyes, a red light from the furnace reflected in them. "What do you mean, your purse?"

"The gold cloth purse you took from the wooden bench in my room," she said. "I must have it back."

"Before God I never laid eyes on your purse, and that's the holy truth," said the janitress.

"Oh, well then, keep it," she said, but in a very bitter voice; "keep it if you want it so much." And she walked away.

24   She remembered how she had never locked a door in her life, on some principle of rejection in her that made her uncomfortable in the ownership of things, and her paradoxical boast before the warnings of her friends, that she had never lost a penny by theft; and she had been pleased with the bleak humility of this concrete example designed to illustrate and justify a certain fixed, otherwise baseless and general faith which ordered the movements of her life without regard to her will in the matter.

25   In this moment she felt that she had been robbed of an enormous number of valuable things, whether material or intangible: things lost or broken by her own fault, things she had forgotten and left in houses when she moved: books borrowed from her and not returned, journeys she had planned and had not made, words she had waited to hear spoken to her and had not heard, and the words she had meant to answer with; bitter alternatives and intolerable substitutes worse than nothing, and yet inescapable: the long patient suffering of dying friendships and the dark inexplicable death of love—all that she had had, and all that she had missed, were lost together, and were twice lost in this landslide of remembered losses.

26   The janitress was following her upstairs with the purse in her hand and the same deep red flickering in her eyes. The janitress thrust the purse towards her while they were still a half dozen steps apart, and said: "Don't never tell on me. I musta been crazy. I get crazy in the head sometimes, I swear I do. My son can tell you."

27   She took the purse after a moment, and the janitress went on: "I got a niece who is going on seventeen, and she's a nice girl and I thought I'd give it to her. She needs a pretty purse. I musta been crazy; I thought maybe you wouldn't mind, you leave things around and don't seem to notice much."

28   She said: "I missed this because it was a present to me from someone . . ."

The janitress said: "He'd get you another if you lost this one. My niece is young and needs pretty things, we oughta give the young ones a chance. She's got young men after her maybe will want to marry her. She oughta have nice things. She needs them bad right now. You're a grown woman, you've had your chance, you ought to know how it is!"

29   She held the purse to the janitress saying: "You don't know what you're talking about. Here, take it, I've changed my mind. I really don't want it."

30   The janitress looked up at her with hatred and said: "I don't want it either now. My niece is young and pretty, she don't need fixin' up to be pretty, she's young and pretty anyhow! I guess you need it worse than she does!"

"It wasn't really yours in the first place," she said, turning away. "You mustn't talk as if I had stolen it from you."

"It's not from me, it's from her you're stealing it," said the janitress, and went back downstairs.

31   She laid the purse on the table and sat down with a cup of chilled coffee, and thought: I was right not to be afraid of any thief but myself, who will end by leaving me nothing.

2,638 words

Questions

1. What is the marked pattern that emerges from the accumulation of actions and relationships in the narrator's life? State this pattern in the form of a single sentence that could serve as a controlling idea for the story. Which lines in the story best summarize this pattern?
2. What bearing does the title have on the story?
3. What is the crux of the narrator's relationship with Camilo?
4. What is the crux of the narrator's relationship with Roger?
5. What is the crux of the narrator's relationship with Bill?
6. How does the letter mentioned in paragraph 19 clarify the pattern in the narrator's life?
7. What does the incident with the janitress add to the story?
8. What is the narrator's state of mind? Is she happy? Unhappy? Indifferent? See paragraph 25.

Do Not Go Gentle into That Good Night
Dylan Thomas

1   Do not go gentle into that good night,
Old age should burn and rave at close of day;
Rage, rage against the dying of the light.

2   Though wise men at their end know dark is right,
Because their words had forked no lightning they
Do not go gentle into that good night.

3   Good men, the last wave by, crying how bright
Their frail deeds might have danced in a green bay,
Rage, rage against the dying of the light.

4   Wild men who caught and sang the sun in flight,
And learn, too late, they grieved it on its way
Do not go gentle into that good night.

5   Grave men, near death, who see with blinding sight
Blind eyes could blaze like meteors and be gay,
Rage, rage against the dying of the light.

6   And you, my father, there on the sad height,
Curse, bless, me now with your fierce tears, I pray.
Do not go gentle into that good night.
Rage, rage against the dying of the light.

Questions

1. What dominant pattern emerges from the examples the poet uses?
2. What does the use of refrain and repetition contribute to the poem?
3. What metaphor does the poet use to refer to his father's condition?
4. The poet urges his father not to go gentle into that "good night." In what sense is "good" used here?
5. How many rhymes does the poem use?
6. The poem is written in a tight, highly structured verse form. How does this form add to its content?

B. How to Write with Examples

An example is an illustration that unmistakably clarifies and enforces the point you are making. During the Middle Ages, most sermons ended with an *exemplum,* a little story that illustrated some important religious truth. Knowing that these stories would awaken dozing audiences and instill them with zeal or fear, the church priests told vivid tales about the evils of money and the dangers of disobedience. The example is still favored in prose writing as a means of proving a point or explaining an idea.

Writing Assignment

Write an essay in which you characterize a significant period of your life, developing the essay by examples. First, ask yourself what made the period significant. Was it successful? Frustrating? Exhilarating? Sad? Next, express the characterization in a single sentence that can function as the controlling idea of an essay. Here are some examples.

1. This past year has been characterized by many *successful* enterprises.
2. *Frustration* dogged every year of my adolescence.
3. Never have I spent a more *romantic* year than when I was eighteen.

4. When my parents moved to Reading, Massachusetts, I spent the most *serene* five years of my life.
5. The summer my brother was killed in Vietnam was pure *agony.*

Having formulated a controlling idea on how you spent this period of your life, you must now support it with examples:

Specific Instructions

1. USE EXAMPLES THAT ARE RELEVANT. An example has failed if it does not help your reader to see the general truth of what you are saying. The following example misses the point:

> As the Bible says, there is a right time for everything—even for being born and for dying. For example, the other day I failed my social science test. The day before had been beastly hot—90 degrees in the shade—and I just didn't feel like studying, so I stretched out on the couch, fanning myself and watching TV. I guess it was my time to die intellectually because when the exam was handed back, it was decorated with a big fat F.

The example used is too trivial to illustrate such a somber philosophic truth. The biblical reference deserves a more significant example. The following passage, on the other hand, uses an example that is exactly to the point:

> Some people will do the strangest things to gain fame. For example, there are those who go in for various kinds of marathons, dancing or kissing or blowing bubble gum for days at a time, to get their names in the paper or in a record book of some kind. Then there are people who sit on flagpoles or who perch on the ledges of skyscrapers for a week or more, apparently enjoying the attention they receive from the crowd below. There are people who hope to be remembered by someone because they ate the most cream pies or because they collected the most bottle tops. And there are even people who seek public notice by way of setting a record for the number of articles of clothing they can put on at one time or the number they can take off. Of course, there are a few mentally twisted individuals who seek fame at the expense of other people's property or even lives, but fortunately the great majority of people satisfy their urge to be remembered in ways that produce little more damage than tired lips or a bad case of indigestion.
>
> Sheila Y. Graham, *Writingcraft*

These examples do a good job of illustrating the idea that "Some people will do the strangest things to gain fame."

2. USE DETAILS TO MAKE YOUR EXAMPLE VIVID. The reader should be able to visualize the actual circumstances described in your example. Many student exam-

ples are ineffective because they are vague rather than vivid. Consider the vague and consequently boring example in this passage:

> There is no control over memory. Sometimes one remembers the most trivial details. For example, I remember trivial things about my father, about pieces of furniture in our house, and about insignificant places that I once visited. I even remember a particular shopping spree that took place a long time ago.

Now observe how the same passage comes to life through the use of detailed examples:

> There is no control over memory. Soon you find yourself being vague about an event which seemed so important at the time that you thought you'd never forget it. Or unable to recall the face of someone who you could have sworn was there forever. On the other hand, trivial and meaningless memories may stay with you for life. I can still shut my eyes and see Victoria grinding coffee on the pantry steps, the glass bookcase and the books in it, my father's pipe rack, the leaves of the sandbox tree, the wallpaper of the bedroom in some shabby hotel, the hairdresser in Antibes. It's in this way that I remember buying the pink Milanese-silk underclothes, the assistant who sold them to me, and coming into Bond Street holding the parcel.
>
> Jean Rhys, The New Yorker,
26 April 1976

Vividness is the basic difference between the first and second passages. The first passage lacks details while the second bristles with them.

3. WHEN NECESSARY, ESTABLISH A CLEAR CONNECTION BETWEEN YOUR EXAMPLE AND THE POINT YOU ARE MAKING. This device is particularly important when you begin an essay or a paragraph with an illustration. Consider the following:

> A 13-year-old girl has had one leg amputated, but three times a week she is put through the humiliation of being forced to change into gym shorts. Says the teacher, "Those are the rules and there's no reason you can't keep score while the other girls play."

> A high-school teacher accidentally bumps into the upraised hand of a girl who wants to ask a question. The teacher cries out that the girl is trying to strike her and that if it happens again she'll call the police.

> A first-grade teacher forces a boy to sit all day in a wastepaper basket as punishment for being noisy. When an assistant principal orders the boy's release after 2 1/2 hours, it is some minutes before he can stand up straight. He can barely limp to his seat.

Without a connecting comment, these examples are puzzling. The reader wonders what they are intended to illustrate. The sequel makes clear the connection between the examples and the point they illustrate:

> These are all documented cases of teacher ineptitude, insensitivity or brutishness. While the overwhelming majority of America's teachers are professionally competent and sensitive to children's needs, there are enough who are unfit to cause concern among both parents and school administrators.
>
> Bernard Bard, "Unfeeling Teachers?"
> *Ladies Home Journal,* March 1976

Connective expressions commonly used to introduce an example are: *for example, to illustrate, for instance,* and *a case in point is.* Frequently, however, a writer will omit a formal connective in introducing his examples provided the context makes clear what is being illustrated:

> People who sneer at "fancy theories" and prefer to rely on common sense and everyday experience are often in fact the victims of extremely vague and sweeping hypotheses. This morning's newspaper contains a letter from a young person in Pennsylvania who was once "one of a group of teenage pot smokers. Then a girl in the crowd got pregnant. Her baby was premature and deformed and needed two operations." The newspaper's adviser to the teenage lovelorn printed that letter approvingly, as evidence that the price of smoking marijuana is high.
>
> Paul Heyne and Thomas Johnson,
> *Toward Economic Understanding*

This passage clearly illustrates what is meant by "victims of . . . vague and sweeping hypotheses." No connective phrase is necessary; the connection is established by the context.

In this excerpt from *Down and Out in Paris and London* (1933), British writer George Orwell (1903–1950) explains what it is like to be poor by giving examples of the humiliations and sufferings he endured during his days of poverty in Paris.

Professional Model

Poverty
George Orwell

1   It is altogether curious, your first contact with poverty. You have thought so much about poverty—it is the thing you have feared all your life, the thing you knew would happen to you sooner or later; and it is all so utterly and prosaically different. You thought it would be quite simple; it is extraordinarily complicated. You thought it would be terrible; it is merely squalid and boring. It is the peculiar *lowness* of poverty that you

discover first; the shifts that it puts you to, the complicated meanness, the crustwiping.

2   You discover, for instance, the secrecy attaching to poverty. At a sudden stroke you have been reduced to an income of six francs a day. But of course you dare not admit it—you have got to pretend that you are living quite as usual. From the start it tangles you in a net of lies, and even with the lies you can hardly manage it. You stop sending clothes to the laundry, and the laundress catches you in the street and asks you why; you mumble something, and she, thinking you are sending the clothes elsewhere, is your enemy for life. The tobacconist keeps asking why you have cut down your smoking. There are letters you want to answer, and cannot, because stamps are too expensive. And then there are your meals—meals are the worst difficulty of all. Every day at meal-times you go out, ostensibly to a restaurant, and loaf an hour in the Luxembourg Gardens, watching the pigeons. Afterwards you smuggle your food home in your pockets. Your food is bread and margarine, or bread and wine, and even the nature of the food is governed by lies. You have to buy rye bread instead of household bread, because rye loaves, though dearer, are round and can be smuggled in your pockets. This wastes you a franc a day. Sometimes, to keep up appearances, you have to spend sixty centimes on a drink, and go correspondingly short of food. Your linen gets filthy, and you run out of soap and razor-blades. Your hair wants cutting, and you try to cut it yourself, with such fearful results that you have to go to the barber after all, and spend the equivalent of a day's food. All day you are telling lies, and expensive lies.

3   You discover the extreme precariousness of your six francs a day. Mean disasters happen and rob you of food. You have spent your last eighty centimes on half a litre of milk, and are boiling it over the spirit lamp. While it boils a bug runs down your forearm; you give the bug a flick with your nail, and it falls plop! straight in the milk. There is nothing for it but to throw the milk away and go foodless.

4   You go to the baker's to buy a pound of bread, and you wait while the girls cut a pound for another customer. She is clumsy, and cuts more than a pound. "*Pardon, monsieur,*" she says, "I suppose you don't mind paying two sous extra?" Bread is a franc a pound, and you have exactly a franc. When you think that you too might be asked to pay two sous extra, would have to confess that you could not, you bolt in panic. It is hours before you dare venture into a baker's shop again.

5   You go to the greengrocer's to spend a franc on a kilogram of potatoes. But one of the pieces that make up the franc is a Belgian piece, and the shopman refuses it. You slink out of the shop, and can never go there again.

6   You have strayed into a respectable quarter, and you see a prosperous friend coming. To avoid him you dodge into the nearest café. Once in the café you must buy something, so you spend your last fifty centimes on a glass of black coffee with a dead fly in it. One could multiply these disasters by the hundred. They are part of the process of being hard up.

7   You discover what it is like to be hungry. With bread and margarine in your belly, you go out and look into the shop windows. Everywhere there is food insulting you in huge, wasteful piles; whole dead pigs, baskets of hot loaves, great yellow blocks of butter, strings of sausages, mountains of potatoes, vast Gruyère cheeses like grindstones. A snivelling self-pity comes over you at the sight of so much food. You plan to grab a loaf and run, swallowing it before they catch you; and you refrain, from pure funk.

8   You discover the boredom which is inseparable from poverty; the times when you have nothing to do and, being underfed, can interest yourself in nothing. For half a day at a time you lie on your bed, feeling like the *jeune squelette** in Baudelaire's poem. Only

---

*"The young (female) skeleton." The poem referred to is No. 94 of Baudelaire's *Fleurs du mal*.

food could rouse you. You discover that a man who has gone even a week on bread and margarine is not a man any longer, only a belly with a few accessory organs.

10   This—one could describe it further, but it is all in the same style—is life on six francs a day. Thousands of people in Paris live it—struggling artists and students, prostitutes when their luck is sour, out of work people of all kinds. It is the suburbs, as it were, of poverty.

845 words

Vocabulary

prosaically (1)
squalid (1)
ostensibly (2)
precariousness (3)

Questions

1. What, according to Orwell, was so utterly different about poverty from the way he thought it would be?
2. Throughout the piece the author uses "you" rather than "I" in describing his encounter with poverty. What do you think he's trying to accomplish?
3. What four principal discoveries did Orwell make about poverty? What examples does he use to explain them?
4. At the beginning of the second paragraph, Orwell introduces his examples with "for instance." How does he introduce his later examples?
5. Orwell calls life on six francs a day "the suburbs of poverty." What does the phrase imply about the poverty he experienced and described?

Student Model

Expanding My Emotional Range
Marla Jenkins

For nineteen years I lived a mediocre life. Feelings of deep sadness and overpowering ecstasy were unknown to me. Then, my childlike spectrum of emotions was suddenly expanded by certain events that took charge of my life.

In the first place, I was overwhelmed by the intense sorrow and mental suffering caused by the loss of my son. Because I had never experienced death before, the finality and cruelty of the situation was incomprehensible to me. Even the absence of his toys and clutter would not convince me of his death, and I would look up expecting to see him pressing his nose against the window, laughing with the birds. Months after the funeral, as I stood washing dishes, I could feel little hands tugging at the hem of my pants, trying to get my attention. The silence of the house drove me crazier than his worst screaming ever did, and I had to sit for long hours trying to regain my sanity. I now know the sadness of death and have experienced the incongruity of life.

Although I still had moments of deep sorrow and depression, I was brought out of my gloom, by a second experience—falling in love, which unleashed an encompassing happiness, surpassed only by a sense of well-being and self-worth. The target of my affections was a most unexpected man, who entered my life suddenly and without warning, which added to the thrill and excitement of the relationship. I found myself thoroughly preoccupied with him, neglecting duties and obligations which in the past had been important, but now seemed insignificant. My school grades suffered, my boss kept yelling, "You'd better get your act together or you'll find yourself unemployed," and I had five unfinished paintings cluttering my studio. Still, I was happy with myself and my life. This man suddenly became the most important part of my life. I found myself calculating, in the corner margins of my anthropology notes, the seconds until I would see him next. For the first time in many years nothing seemed to bother me. I would wait for hours in the grocery store lines or on a traffic-congested freeway without a twinge of irritation. I found myself delighted by simple things such as the antics of a confused little spider, or the sight of a graceful formation of seagulls. Everything was suddenly beautiful, satisfying, and peaceful. I discovered that one person could cause encompassing joy in the life and mind of another person.

But soon another experience expanded my emotional horizon. Gradually, this man turned his back on my love and need, a rejection that left me totally void of all feeling. I didn't shed a single tear over his sudden departure from my life, nor speak a bitter word, for I was drained of all emotion. I quietly resumed my life from the point I had left off. Like a computerized robot, I programmed myself to accomplish the essentials, not knowing or caring if I bumped into a few walls, or if I stepped on someone's toes, or if I smiled instead of saying, "What a shame." Very quickly I organized my life with the efficiency of a bookkeeper. Only occasionally did I find myself sitting in front of a mirror trying to laugh or cry. The numbness and emptiness within me seemed a godsend. The sudden expansion of my immature range of emotions created feelings that were difficult to cope with, and I needed the time to build up my defenses in preparation for future emotional blows.

Although I now have more depth of character and intellect, I often look fondly back to the days when the tears from a skinned knee or the pleasure of a new party dress were the deepest feelings in my emotional repertoire.

This essay discusses various points of current debate about what constitutes "correct" English. The author jauntily challenges the experts by citing impressive literary precedents for usages that some grammarians love to hate.

Hopefully, They Will Shut Up
Jim Quinn

1   Almost everybody in America has an illiteracy they love to hate because it makes them feel superior to other Americans: "Anyone can do what they like," "between you and I," "input," "different than," "hopefully." Sometimes the list seems endless. We are in the middle of a great national crusade to protect the language from the people who speak it.

2   The crusaders certainly seem to be having fun. Though they claim to see the Death of English approaching at any moment, there's a kind of rosy romantic glow to their despair. You get a picture of this gallant little band of the last literates going down to defeat with *Warriner's Grade Four Grammar* in one hand and *Best-Loved Poems of*

College English Departments in the other. There are only two things wrong with this great conservative crusade of correctors: it is not conservative, and it is not correct. Though our popularizers of good grammar (let's call them pop grammarians for short) think they are defending standards and traditions, they keep attacking idioms that are centuries old. Here are a few examples:

3   **Anyone Can Do What They Like.**   We must never combine any*one* with *they,* says John Simon in his new book, *Paradigms Lost:* "that way madness lies." Simon seems to think this madness is brand-new, produced in part at least by feminists who want to overturn the old male grammar of "anyone can do what *he* wants" (and *she* better shut up about it). In fact, a wholesale confusion of number and case in pronouns has been a feature of standard English since Elizabethan times. This never hurt the writing of Shakespeare, Marlowe, Ben Jonson, Defoe, Swift, Jane Austen, Dickens, George Bernard Shaw and Oscar Wilde ("Experience is the name that everyone gives to their mistakes"). The use of *they* instead of *he,* in cases where both men and women are meant, is defended by such conservative, pre-liberation authorities as the *Oxford English Dictionary* (*OED*), our greatest historical dictionary, and Otto Jespersen, the distinguished scholarly grammarian of our language. If that be madness, as Simon says, it is a venerable and literary lunacy.

4   **Between You and I.**   "Horrible!" wrote poet W. H. Auden, giving his expert opinion in *The Harper Dictionary of Contemporary Usage.* "All debts are cleared between you and I," wrote poet William Shakespeare ("Merchant of Venice," Act III, Scene 2). Whom are we to trust? D. H. Lawrence points the way for us here. Never trust the artist, said Lawrence; always trust the art. A poet's idea of how language works is as likely to be correct as his idea of how a typewriter works. "You and I" in the accusative is an ancient (and indestructible) idiom. See the opening line of T. S. Eliot's "The Love Song of J. Alfred Prufrock": "Let us go then, you and I."

5   **Input.**   "Computer cant," said Theodore Bernstein in *Dos, Don'ts & Maybes of English Usage;* "laymen sometimes take it over to sound impressive." In fact, "input" has been around since the eighteenth century. Sir Walter Scott used it to mean "contribution" in "The Heart of Midlothian" (1818). The Supplement to the *OED* shows noncant uses in such fields as economics long before the first computer use (1948). Input is not a computer word—it's an old word borrowed by computer scientists. No harm in borrowing it back.

6   **Different Than.**   "*Different than* rather than *different from* is wrong," wrote Edwin Newman in *Strictly Speaking.* Short, simple, to the point and utterly without foundation. H. W. Fowler, in *Modern English Usage* (the bible of most pop grammarians), classes insistence on "different from" as a superstition. The *OED* notes that "different than" is considered by many to be incorrect, but that "different than" can be found in writers of all ages. Among them: Addison, Steele, Defoe, De Quincey, Coleridge, Carlyle and Thackeray. Use "different from" if you want—but criticize "different than" and you're messing with the big guys.

7   **Rhetoric.**   "Not so long ago," says William Safire, in *his* new book, *On Language,* "the predominant meaning of rhetoric was *the science of persuasion.*" Now we tend to use rhetoric to mean empty talk. Safire would like to rescue this good old word from our abuse and has a cure: use "bloviation," an old slang word dating back before 1851, for empty talk. The abuse of "rhetoric" dates back before 1851, too—to the sixteenth

century. Among users cited in the *OED:* Spenser, Milton, Swift and Swinburne, who warns against "the limp loquacity of long-winded rhetoric, so natural to men and soldiers in an hour of emergency." And so natural, also, to pop grammarians when they invent cures for which there is no disease.

8   **Hopefully, Better-Coordinated Programs Will Result.**   To John Simon, that use of "hopefully" is an infallible sign of illiteracy. "'Hopefully' so used is an abomination, its adherents should be lynched," says poet Phyllis McGinley. Adherents include Theodore Bernstein, William Safire and the editors of the *Concise Oxford, Random House, Merriam-Webster, Webster's New World* and *Standard College* dictionaries. Did Phyllis McGinley really want all of them lynched? The author of the sentence that begins this paragraph was Dr. Nathan Pusey, the former president of Harvard. Does John Simon really believe that Dr. Pusey cannot read or write? Of course not. Both Simon and McGinley were merely using the limp and fuzzy rhetoric of pop grammar, where "illiterate" means only "hasn't read my stylebook."

9   **A New Non-Worry: The Danger from the Right.**   Should we all worry that the pop grammarians will succeed and that someday soon we'll have to talk what they call Good English? Not at all. Wrongheaded objections to idioms are as much a part of the history of English as the idioms themselves—and probably always will be. There will always be gallant little bands to fling themselves, and their violent rhetoric, in front of some age-old word they have made a fad of trying to stop. And there will always be the rest of us to run right over them. That's why English is still alive.

1,026 words

Vocabulary

venerable (3)
loquacity (7)
adherents (8)

Questions

1. What is ironic about the title of this essay?
2. Why, according to the author, does everyone in America have an illiteracy they love to hate?
3. What two things does the author find wrong with the "conservative" crusade against English?
4. Aside from what he feels is the pop grammarians' niggling over minute matters of usage, what else does the author find objectionable in their crusade?
5. What phrase does the author use to introduce his examples?
6. In arguing against the pop grammarians' insistence on correctness, the author cites case after case of an offending usage in the works of great writers. What do you think of this strategy? Is an idiom necessarily correct just because a great writer has used it?
7. The author says that a poet's idea of how language works is likely to be as correct as his idea of how a typewriter works. What does he mean by this?

Why does he believe that a poet's idea of how language works is not to be trusted?

8. What is your opinion of the use of "he" as an indefinite pronoun referring to both sexes?

9. What meaning of "rhetoric" would William Safire like to restore? What substitute does he suggest we use for the current meaning of rhetoric?

10. Why does the author think we need not worry about the influence of pop grammarians?

The following selection was first published by *The New Yorker* in 1939. It is among many of the essays of James Thurber that appeared in the magazine while he was on its staff. The essay is typical of the ironic humor that made this writer famous and well-loved all over America.

Alternate Reading

Courtship Through the Ages
James Thurber

1   Surely nothing in the astonishing scheme of life can have nonplussed Nature so much as the fact that none of the females of any of the species she created really cared very much for the male, as such. For the past ten million years Nature has been busily inventing ways to make the male attractive to the female, but the whole business of courtship, from the marine annelids up to man, still lumbers heavily along, like a complicated musical comedy. I have been reading the sad and absorbing story in Volume 6 (Cole to Dama) of the *Encyclopaedia Britannica*. In this volume you can learn all about cricket, cotton, costume designing, crocodiles, crown jewels, and Coleridge, but none of these subjects is so interesting as the Courtship of Animals, which recounts the sorrowful lengths to which all males must go to arouse the interest of a lady.

2   We all know, I think, that Nature gave man whiskers and a mustache with the quaint idea in mind that these would prove attractive to the female. We all know that, far from attracting her, whiskers and mustaches only made her nervous and gloomy, so that man had to go in for somersaults, tilting with lances, and performing feats of parlor magic to win her attention; he also had to bring her candy, flowers, and the furs of animals. It is common knowledge that in spite of all these "love displays" the male is constantly being turned down, insulted, or thrown out of the house. It is rather comforting, then, to discover that the peacock, for all his gorgeous plumage, does not have a particularly easy time in courtship; none of the males in the world do. The first peahen, it turned out, was only faintly stirred by her suitor's beautiful train. She would often go quietly to sleep while he was whisking it around. The *Britannica* tells us that the peacock actually had to learn a certain little trick to wake her up and revive her interest: he had to learn to vibrate his quills so as to make a rustling sound. In ancient times man himself, observing the ways of the peacock, probably tried vibrating his whiskers to make a rustling sound; if so, it didn't get him anywhere. He had to go in for something else; so, among other things, he went in for gifts. It is not unlikely that he got this idea from certain flies and birds who were making no headway at all with rustling sounds.

3   One of the flies of the family Empidae, who had tried everything, finally hit on something pretty special. He contrived to make a glistening transparent balloon which was even larger than himself. Into this he would put sweetmeats and tidbits and he would carry the whole elaborate envelope through the air to the lady of his choice. This amused her for a time, but she finally got bored with it. She demanded silly little colorful presents, something that you couldn't eat but that would look nice around the house. So the male Empis had to go around gathering flower petals and pieces of bright paper to put into his balloon. On a courtship flight a male Empis cuts quite a figure now, but he can hardly be said to be happy. He never knows how soon the female will demand heavier presents, such as Roman coins and gold collar buttons. It seems probable that one day the courtship of the Empidae will fall down, as man's occasionally does, of its own weight.

4   The bowerbird is another creature that spends so much time courting the female that he never gets any work done. If all the male bowerbirds became nervous wrecks within the next ten or fifteen years, it would not surprise me. The female bowerbird insists that a playground be built for her with a specially constructed bower at the entrance. This bower is much more elaborate than an ordinary nest and is harder to build; it costs a lot more, too. The female will not come to the playground until the male has filled it up with a great many gifts: silvery leaves, red leaves, rose petals, shells, beads, berries, bones, dice, buttons, cigar bands, Christmas seals, and the Lord knows what else. When the female finally condescends to visit the playground, she is in a coy and silly mood and has to be chased in and out of the bower and up and down the playground before she will quit giggling and stand still long enough even to shake hands. The male bird is, of course, pretty well done in before the chase starts, because he has worn himself out hunting for eyeglass lenses and begonia blossoms. I imagine that many a bowerbird, after chasing a female for two or three hours, says the hell with it and goes home to bed. Next day, of course, he telephones someone else and the same trying ritual is gone through again. A male bowerbird is as exhausted as a night-club habitué before he is out of his twenties.

5   The male fiddler crab has a somewhat easier time, but it can hardly be said that he is sitting pretty. He has one enormously large and powerful claw, usually brilliantly colored, and you might suppose that all he had to do was reach out and grab some passing cutie. The very earliest fiddler crabs may have tried this, but, if so, they got slapped for their pains. A female crab will not tolerate any caveman stuff; she never has and she doesn't intend to start now. To attract a female, a fiddler crab has to stand on tiptoe and brandish his claw in the air. If any female in the neighborhood is interested—and you'd be surprised how many are not—she comes over and engages him in light badinage, for which he is not in the mood. As many as a hundred females may pass the time of day with him and go on about their business. By nightfall of an average courting day, a fiddler crab who has been standing on tiptoe for eight or ten hours waving a heavy claw in the air is in pretty sad shape. As in the case of all males of all species, however, he gets out of bed next morning, dashes some water on his face, and tries again.

6   The next time you encounter a male web-spinning spider, stop and reflect that he is too busy worrying about his love life to have any desire to bite you. Male web-spinning spiders have a tougher life than any other males in the animal kingdom. This is because the female web-spinning spiders have very poor eyesight. If a male lands on a female's web, she kills him before he has time to lay down his cane and gloves, mistaking him for a fly or a bumblebee who has tumbled into her trap. Before the species figured out what to do about this, millions of males were murdered by ladies they called on. It is the nature of spiders to perform a little dance in front of the female, but before a male spinner

could get near enough for the female to see who he was and what he was up to, she would lash out at him with a flat-iron or a pair of garden shears. One night, nobody knows when, a very bright male spinner lay awake worrying about calling on a lady who had been killing suitors right and left. It came to him that this business of dancing as a love display wasn't getting anybody anywhere except the grave. He decided to go in for web-twitching, or strand-vibrating. The next day he tried it on one of the near-sighted girls. Instead of dropping in on her suddenly, he stayed outside the web and began monkeying with one of its strands. He twitched it up and down and in and out with such a lilting rhythm that the female was charmed. The serenade worked beautifully; the female let him live. The *Britannica's* spider-watchers, however, report that this system is not always successful. Once in a while, even now, a female will fire three bullets into a suitor or run him through with a kitchen knife. She keeps threatening him from the moment he strikes the first low notes on the outside strings, but usually by the time he has got up to the high notes played around the center of the web, he is going to town and she spares his life.

7   Even the butterfly, as handsome a fellow as he is, can't always win a mate merely by fluttering around and showing off. Many butterflies have to have scent scales on their wings. Hepialus carries a powder puff in a perfumed pouch. He throws perfume at the ladies when they pass. The male tree cricket, Oecanthus, goes Hepialus one better by carrying a tiny bottle of wine with him and giving drinks to such doxies as he has designs on. One of the male snails throws darts to entertain the girls. So it goes, through the long list of animals, from the bristle worm and his rudimentary dance steps to man and his gift of diamonds and sapphires. The golden-eye drake raises a jet of water with his feet as he flies over a lake; Hepialus has his powder puff, Oecanthus his wine bottle, man his etchings. It is a bright and melancholy story, the age-old desire of the male for the female, the age-old desire of the female to be amused and entertained. Of all the creatures on earth, the only males who could be figured as putting any irony into their courtship are the grebes and certain other diving birds. Every now and then a courting grebe slips quietly down to the bottom of a lake and then, with a mighty "Whoosh!," pops out suddenly a few feet from his girl friend, splashing water all over her. She seems to be persuaded that this is a purely loving display, but I like to think that the grebe always has a faint hope of drowning her or scaring her to death.

8   I will close this investigation into the mournful burdens of the male with the *Britannica's* story about a certain Argus pheasant. It appears that the Argus displays himself in front of a female who stands perfectly still without moving a feather. . . . The male Argus the *Britannica* tells about was confined in a cage with a female of another species, a female who kept moving around, emptying ashtrays and fussing with lampshades all the time the male was showing off his talents. Finally, in disgust, he stalked away and began displaying in front of his water trough. He reminds me of a certain male (Homo sapiens) of my acquaintance who one night after dinner asked his wife to put down her detective magazine so that he could read her a poem of which he was very fond. She sat quietly enough until he was well into the middle of the thing, intoning with great ardor and intensity. Then suddenly there came a sharp, disconcerting *slap!* It turned out that all during the male's display, the female had been intent on a circling mosquito and had finally trapped it between the palms of her hands. The male in this case did not stalk away and display in front of a water trough; he went over to Tim's and had a flock of drinks and recited the poem to the fellas. I am sure they all told bitter stories of their own about how their displays had been interrupted by females. I am also sure that they all ended up singing "Honey, Honey, Bless Your Heart."

1,950 words

Vocabulary

annelids (1)   doxies (7)
habitué (4)   intoning (8)
badinage (5)

Questions

1. What is the controlling idea of the essay? Where is it stated?
2. Which of the examples cited is most closely allied to the human situation? What does the example reveal?
3. What does the courting grebe of paragraph 7 signify?
4. According to the essay, what is the only successful technique in courting the female? What is not enough?
5. What is ironic about the essay? How does Thurber achieve this irony?
6. Thurber's essay is a mixture of slang and scholarly language. What are some examples of both extremes? What is the effect of this mixture?
7. How does the title relate to the essay?
8. Can you think of instances in nature that would demonstrate a point of view opposite to that expressed by Thurber?
9. Does the *Encyclopaedia Britannica* really contain a section on the courtship of animals, or is this a fictional account?
10. What are the conventional courtesies men offer women today? How do they differ from courtesies of, say, the Renaissance?

Additional Writing Assignments

Illustrate the following assertions with appropriate *examples:*

1. The salaries of professional athletes are too high.
2. American cars are equipped with needless and expensive options.
3. Astrological forecasting is (is not) accurate.
4. Microcomputers are playing an increasingly important role in our lives.
5. Newspaper advice columns often reflect the common concerns of society.
6. Not all old people are fuddy-duddy, conservative, and timid.
7. Baseball games range from tense thrillers to slumberous bores.
8. Some television game shows are vulgar and tasteless.
9. Americans worry too much about their health.
10. On the whole, movies nowadays are too gory.

8

Definition

Prejudice is a judgment or opinion held in disregard
of facts that contradict it.

A. Reading for Ideas

"Arrangement in Black and White" is a story about prejudice. As you listen to the
main character in the story reveal her attitude toward blacks, ask yourself, "What
is prejudice? How is it acquired? How can it be stopped?" From your own experience, what are some examples of prejudice? Be prepared to give a one-sentence
definition of the word *prejudice*.

Arrangement in Black and White
Dorothy Parker

1   The woman with the pink velvet poppies twined round the assisted gold of her hair
traversed the crowded room at an interesting gait combining a skip with a sidle, and
clutched the lean arm of her host.

2   "Now I got you!" she said. "Now you can't get away!"

"Why, hello," said her host. "Well. How are you?"

"Oh, I'm finely," she said. "Just simply finely. Listen. I want you to do me the most
terrible favor. Will you? Will you please? Pretty please?"

3   "What is it?" said her host.

"Listen," she said. "I want to meet Walter Williams. Honestly, I'm just simply crazy
about that man. Oh, when he sings! When he sings those spirituals! Well, I said to
Burton, 'It's a good thing for you Walter Williams is colored,' I said, 'or you'd have lots
of reason to be jealous.' I'd really love to meet him. I'd like to tell him I've heard him sing.
Will you be an angel and introduce me to him?"

4   "Why, certainly," said her host. "I thought you'd met him. The party's for him. Where
is he, anyway?"

5   "He's over there by the bookcase," she said. "Let's wait till those people get through
talking to him. Well, I think you're simply marvelous, giving this perfectly marvelous party
for him, and having him meet all these white people, and all. Isn't he terribly grateful?"

6   "I hope not," said her host.

"I think it's really terribly nice," she said. "I do. I don't see why on earth it isn't perfectly all right to meet colored people. I haven't any feeling at all about it—not one single bit. Burton—oh, he's just the other way. Well, you know, he comes from Virginia, and you know how they are."

7   "Did he come tonight?" said her host.

"No, he couldn't," she said. "I'm a regular grass widow tonight. I told him when I left, 'There's no telling what I'll do,' I said. He was just so tired out, he couldn't move. Isn't it a shame?"

8   "Ah," said her host.

"Wait till I tell him I met Walter Williams!" she said. "He'll just about die. Oh, we have more arguments about colored people. I talk to him like I don't know what, I get so excited. 'Oh, don't be so silly,' I say. But I must say for Burton, he's heaps broader-minded than lots of these Southerners. He's really awfully fond of colored people. Well, he says himself, he wouldn't have white servants. And you know, he had this old colored nurse, this regular old nigger mammy, and he just simply loves her. Why, every time he goes home, he goes out in the kitchen to see her. He does, really, to this day. All he says is, he says he hasn't got a word to say against colored people as long as they keep their place. He's always doing things for them—giving them clothes and I don't know what all. The only thing he says, he says he wouldn't sit down at the table with one for a million dollars. 'Oh,' I say to him, 'you make me sick, talking like that.' I'm just terrible to him. Aren't I terrible?"

9   "Oh, no, no, no," said her host. "No, no."

"I am," she said. "I know I am. Poor Burton! Now, me, I don't feel that way at all. I haven't the slightest feeling about colored people. Why, I'm just crazy about some of them. They're just like children—just as easygoing, and always singing and laughing and everything. Aren't they the happiest things you ever saw in your life? Honestly, it makes me laugh just to hear them. Oh, I like them. I really do. Well, now, listen, I have this colored laundress, I've had her for years, and I'm devoted to her. She's a real character. And I want to tell you, I think of her as my friend. That's the way I think of her. As I say to Burton, 'Well, for Heaven's sakes, we're all human beings!' Aren't we?"

10   "Yes," said her host. "Yes, indeed."

"Now this Walter Williams," she said. "I think a man like that's a real artist. I do. I think he deserves an awful lot of credit. Goodness, I'm so crazy about music or anything, I don't care *what* color he is. I honestly think if a person's an artist, nobody ought to have any feeling at all about meeting them. That's absolutely what I say to Burton. Don't you think I'm right?"

11   "Yes," said her host. "Oh, yes."

"That's the way I feel," she said. "I just can't understand people being narrow-minded. Why, I absolutely think it's a privilege to meet a man like Walter Williams. Yes, I do. I haven't any feeling at all. Well, my goodness, the good Lord made him, just the same as He did any of us. Didn't He?"

12   "Surely," said her host. "Yes, indeed."

"That's what I say," she said. "Oh, I get so furious when people are narrow-minded about colored people. It's just all I can do not to say something. Of course, I do admit when you get a bad colored man, they're simply terrible. But as I say to Burton, there are some bad white people, too, in this world. Aren't there?"

13   "I guess there are," said her host.

"Why, I'd really be glad to have a man like Walter Williams come to my house and sing for us, some time!" she said. "Of course, I couldn't ask him on account of Burton, but I wouldn't have any feeling about it at all. Oh, can't he sing! Isn't it marvelous, the way they all have music in them? It just seems to be right *in* them. Come on, let's go on over and talk to him. Listen, what shall I do when I'm introduced? Ought I to shake hands? Or what?"

14   "Why, do whatever you want," said her host.

"I guess maybe I'd better," she said. "I wouldn't for the world have him think I had any feeling. I think I'd better shake hands, just the way I would with anybody else. That's just exactly what I'll do."

15   They reached the tall young Negro, standing by the bookcase. The host performed introductions; the Negro bowed.

16   "How do you do?" he said.

The woman with the pink velvet poppies extended her hand at the length of her arm and held it so for all the world to see, until the Negro took it, shook it, and gave it back to her.

17   "Oh, how do you do, Mr. Williams," she said. "Well, how do you do. I've just been saying, I've enjoyed your singing so awfully much. I've been to your concerts, and we have you on the phonograph and everything. Oh, I just enjoy it!"

18   She spoke with great distinctness, moving her lips meticulously, as if in parlance with the deaf.

19   "I'm so glad," he said.

"I'm just simply crazy about that 'Water Boy' thing you sing," she said. "Honestly, I can't get it out of my head. I have my husband nearly crazy, the way I go around humming it all the time. Oh, he looks just as black as the ace of—Well. Tell me, where on earth do you ever get all those songs of yours? How do you ever get hold of them?"

20   "Why," he said, "there are so many different—"

21   "I should think you'd love singing them," she said. "It must be more fun. All those darling old spirituals—oh, I just love them! Well, what are you doing, now? Are you still keeping up your singing? Why don't you have another concert, some time?"

22   "I'm having one the sixteenth of this month," he said.

"Well, I'll be there," she said. "I'll be there, if I possibly can. You can count on me. Goodness, here comes a whole raft of people to talk to you. You're just a regular guest of honor! Oh, who's that girl in white? I've seen her some place."

23   "That's Katherine Burke," said her host.

"Good Heavens," she said, "is that Katherine Burke? Why, she looks entirely different off the stage. I thought she was much better-looking. I had no idea she was so terribly dark. Why, she looks almost like—Oh, I think she's a wonderful actress! Don't you think she's a wonderful actress, Mr. Williams? Oh, I think she's marvelous. Don't you?"

24   "Yes, I do," he said.

"Oh, I do, too," she said. "Just wonderful. Well, goodness, we must give someone else a chance to talk to the guest of honor. Now, don't forget, Mr. Williams, I'm going to be at that concert if I possibly can. I'll be there applauding like everything. And if I can't come, I'm going to tell everybody I know to go, anyway. Don't you forget!"

25   "I won't," he said, "Thank you so much."

The host took her arm and piloted her into the next room.

"Oh, my dear," she said. "I nearly died! Honestly, I give you my word, I nearly passed away. Did you hear that terrible break I made? I was just going to say Katherine Burke looked almost like a nigger. I just caught myself in time. Oh, do you think he noticed?"

26   "I don't believe so," said her host.

"Well, thank goodness," she said, "because I wouldn't have embarrassed him for anything. Why, he's awfully nice. Just as nice as he can be. Nice manners, and every-thing. You know, so many colored people, you give them an inch, and they walk all over you. But he doesn't try any of that. Well, he's got more sense, I suppose. He's really nice. Don't you think so?"

27   "Yes," said her host.

"I liked him," she said. "I haven't any feeling at all because he's a colored man. I felt just as natural as I would with anybody. Talked to him as naturally, and everything. But honestly, I could hardly keep a straight face. I kept thinking of Burton. Oh, wait till I tell Burton I called him 'Mister'!"

1,556 words

Vocabulary

sidle (1)

Questions

1. What kind of person is the main character of this story? How would you describe her to someone who has not read the story?
2. The woman insists blatantly that she has no racial prejudice. "I haven't any feeling at all," she repeatedly says. What evidence have you that she is wrong? Refer to specific passages in the story.
3. What are examples of the way the woman stereotypes blacks?
4. What is Burton's attitude toward blacks? Does it differ from the woman's?
5. What is the attitude of the host toward the woman? What is his role in the story?

The poem that follows relates poignantly how a small incident can cast a long shadow.

Incident
Countee Cullen

1   Once riding in old Baltimore,
       Heart-filled, head-filled with glee,
    I saw a Baltimorean
       Keep looking straight at me.

2   Now I was eight and very small,
       And he was no whit bigger,
    And so I smiled, but he poked out
       His tongue and called me, "Nigger."

3   I saw the whole of Baltimore
       From May until December:
    Of all the things that happened there
       That's all that I remember.

Questions

1. What is the theme of this poem? State it in one complete sentence.

2. Why do you think the little boy from Baltimore called the speaker a "Nigger"? Comment on the social implications.
3. How does the title "Incident" stress the poem's theme?
4. In stanza 2, what contrast adds a sad irony to the poem?
5. How do we know that the speaker was not prepared to encounter prejudice?
6. What would your reaction be if you witnessed the incident described in the poem?

B. How to Write a Definition

Definition is the method of development used whenever it is necessary to clarify the meaning of any "fuzzy" or controversial term. In the course of an essay or a conversation, we often use words or expressions whose meanings are perfectly obvious to us, but less so to our readers or listeners. Sometimes the problem lies with the word we have used—it may be either abstract or otherwise unclear, perhaps having many different meanings. Such, for instance, is no doubt the case with the word *love*. No matter how dictionaries strain to give a single meaning to this word, their cause is a lost one. Men and women who have been blissfully in love will think the word means happiness second only to paradise. They will associate it with giving and caring, with warmth and reciprocal affection. But for many others—husbands who have been cuckolded, wives who have been betrayed, lovers who have been jilted—the word will always carry a bitter sting. No amount of semantic wrangling will ever get the one group to agree with the other. The meanings that many words have are similarly conditioned by our experience, making it necessary to define them in oral or written communication.

The *semantic triangle* is often used to explain why some words have murky meanings and others do not. Semanticists say that words evoke two responses from us. First, we may be clearly or dimly aware of the dictionary meaning of a word, which semanticists call its *referent*. For instance, the word *grapefruit* has as its referent the particular tangy citrus fruit that we all know by that name. Little disagreement is possible in this case. One may show a picture of a grapefruit, or even produce an example of the fruit itself to settle an argument over what the word means. Where the referent of a word is an object or a thing, like *grapefruit*, *textbook*, *pencil*, or *fountain pen*, the possibility of its meaning being misunderstood is lessened. "What do you mean by *paperclip*?" the puzzled Martian asks. You simply produce the thing and show it to the creature. Words that have visible referents are said to be *concrete;* words with nonvisible referents are said to be *abstract. Paperclip* is therefore a concrete word; *love* is an abstract word.

There is a second response that words evoke from us—known to semanticists as the *reference*—and here we are on unsteady ground. For the references of words are those feelings and emotions they arouse in us, and these are inseparable from our experiences with the words. Here we are entirely at the mercy of personal experiences. The jilted bridegroom will likely express the bitterest feelings about the word *love;* ask him what it means and he will probably rant on about "a sham, a charade, an illusion." On the other side, the contented husband of some 25 years will carry on about "sharing golden moments, reading the Sunday papers over coffee, bucking each other up in times of trouble" and that sort of thing. No matter how these two pore over a dictionary, they're hardly likely to reconcile their differing references about *love*. And since *love* is an abstract word with no visible referent, misunderstandings about its meaning are inevitable. It is precisely for such words that definitions are necessary.

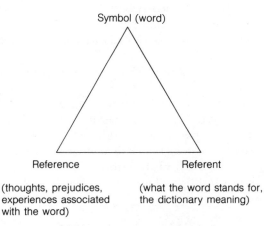

The Semantic Triangle

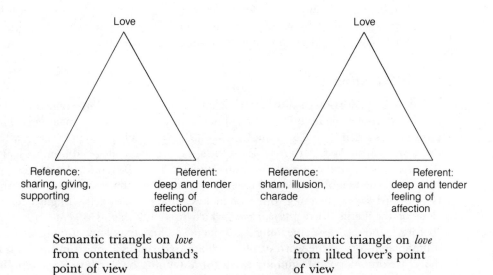

Semantic triangle on *love*
from contented husband's
point of view

Semantic triangle on *love*
from jilted lover's point
of view

The references of words are also affected by political or public experiences. During the years preceding the Second World War, for instance, Hitler repeatedly justified his designs on other countries by citing Germany's need for *Lebensraum*—

territory for political and economic expansion. Eventually, this word came to signify *German imperialism* to the allies—something entirely different from what it meant to the Germans. Similarly, in the 1960s the phrase *law and order* was widely bandied about. To some it meant repression; to others, it signified opposition to public disorder. By 1968, when candidate Richard Nixon used the phrase in his nomination acceptance speech, he was obliged to add:

> And to those why say that law and order is the code word for racism, here is a reply: Our goal is justice—justice for every American. If we are to have respect for law in America, we must have laws that deserve respect. Just as we cannot have progress without order, we cannot have order without progress.
>
> Richard Nixon, *Nomination Acceptance Speech*, 8 August 1968

This addition was necessary because the reference underlying this phrase had been so muddied that the phrase had become a polarizing catchword. Something similar seems to be happening today with the word *busing*. Used to designate the shifting of students from one school to another for the sake of racial balance, the word has provoked so many vastly differing references in the minds of those who support and those who oppose busing that it can no longer be said to have a single, clearcut meaning.

Writing Assignment

Write an essay defining the word *prejudice*. First, look up the referent of the word in a good dictionary. Choose the definition there that most closely corresponds to your own idea about the word's meaning. Then begin your essay by writing, "Prejudice is . . . ," stating and then expanding your definition.

Specific Instructions

1. USE THE ETYMOLOGY OF A WORD TO CLARIFY ITS MEANING.   The etymology of a word or phrase provides information about its origins and earliest meanings. The dictionary is a rich source of etymologies, which are usually given in brackets after the entries. From Webster's *New World Dictionary*, second college edition, we learn that the word *boycott* was derived from Captain C. C. Boycott, a land agent in Ireland whose neighbors banded together against him; that *poet* comes from the Greek word *poietes*, meaning "one who makes"; that *prejudice* is the English equivalent of the Latin word *praejudicium*, which itself is a blend of *prae*, meaning "before," and *judicium*, meaning "judgment." The etymology usually gives a thumbnail history of the word or phrase that can throw light on its meaning. It is therefore often a good beginning point for a defining essay. Here, for example, is how one writer uses etymology to help define *botulism:*

> There are life-forms which, in the course of evolution, have developed poisons designed to kill, or to prevent themselves from being eaten. Venoms are produced by a variety of animals from jellyfish to reptiles. Plants

develop a variety of poisonous substances designed to taste bad to an animal that nibbles and to kill if the animal persists.

Pride of place, however, must be taken by the product of a bacterium which is to be found everywhere and which harms no one—ordinarily. It is *Clostridium botulinum.* "Clostridium" is Latin for "little spindle," which describes its shape, and "botulinum" is from the Latin word *botulus,* which means "sausage," where it has sometimes been detected.

Isaac Asimov, "World's Most Deadly Poison . . . The Botulin Spore"
Science Digest, January 1972

This etymology tells us not only what the spore looks like, but also where it has been found.

Even if a word or term has an unknown origin, sometimes a discussion of its probable beginnings can give a useful glimpse into its background. Here, for example, a writer speculates on where the baseball term *bullpen* came from:

No one, much less the pitcher out there, knows quite why a bullpen is called as it is. One of the accepted theories is that the term is derived from the many Bull Durham tobacco signboards erected out beyond the outfield fences at the turn of the century. In 1909 the tobacco company put up 150 of these signs in baseball parks, the advertisements dominated by a large peaceful-looking domestic bull. Local merchants would pay up to $50 if a batter could hit the bull on the fly. Relief pitchers warmed up under or behind the sign, in an area many authorities believe began to be called the "bullpen."

Others suspect the word is lifted from the prison term for the detention area where defendents waited until they stood trial, an accurate enough description of the life cycle of a relief pitcher. Yet another theory suggests that the bullpen was originally the area where fans were herded behind ropes, where they had to wait until an inning was over before being seated.

George Plimpton, "The Lore of the Bullpen"

Obviously, not all words have fascinating etymologies. The recently minted, for instance, will seem as though they were spontaneously generated out of nothing as flies were once thought to be. Most such words are Americanisms. The etymologies of such words, for instance, as *hooker, blurb* (which was an arbitrary coinage), *milksop,* or *fall guy* are not especially useful. *Horse opera* seemed to have come from nowhere, and it is not especially enlightening to learn that *fiscal* comes from the Latin word *fiscus,* meaning "a basket of rushes, public chest." Yet where the etymology of a word tells something about its meaning, writers often use this information as a starting point for their definitions.

2. GIVE EXAMPLES, STATE FUNCTIONS, AND SHOW EFFECTS OF THE DEFINED TERM.   An adequate definition of a term requires more than a summary of its exact meaning. Often, it is necessary to expand on the lexical definition by giving examples, stating functions, and showing the effects of the defined term. Here, for instance, is a

rather peppy paragraph from a student essay that attempts to define love by giving an extended example of its effects:

> Love is the pitter-patter of the heart, butterflies in the tummy, the invisible symphonies that swallows dance to on silken twilit evenings; but most of all, it is a sudden, urgent lunacy. As an example, I offer the night I met Julie. I had saved for months to go to dinner at Chez François. I had the meal all planned. Appetizer: oysters sauteed in olive oil. Main course: lobster steamed in wine with herb sauce. Vegetable: eggplant stuffed with mushrooms. Wine: a white Macon, which I was just about to select when I met Julie—the cocktail waitress. I took one look in her eyes and my appetite went down the tube. I know that's slang and that I should write something more elegant, but I actually felt my appetite dropping from my belly down to my toes—as if it fell down a tube—and, with a little imagination, I thought I even saw it roll out on the carpet and scurry away like a routed mouse. The rest of the night I just kept ordering one drink after another so that Julie would come around and I could talk to her. I ate part of a lobster feeler and then abandoned the carcass to the vultures; the eggplant stayed on the plate as if some lobotomized hen had laid it there by mistake. I never touched a mushroom. All I did was drink, chat with Julie, make a desperate and inaudible moan to myself, and get roaringly drunk. $54.89 later and I ended up eating a McDonald's hamburger. That's love, brother, that's love.

A more sober example can be found in an essay by the late Scottish-born scholar Gilbert Highet, who set out to define *kitsch*. First, Mr. Highet tells us that the word *kitsch* is of Russian origin, that it "means vulgar showoff, and it is applied to anything that took a lot of trouble to make and is quite hideous." Then he proceeds to make this clearer by giving examples of kitsch:

> Of course, it is found in all the arts; think of Milan Cathedral, or the statues in Westminster Abbey, or Listz's settings of Schubert songs. There is a lot of it in the United States—for instance, the architecture of Miami, Florida, and Forest Lawn Cemetery in Los Angeles. Many of Hollywood's most ambitious historical films are superb kitsch. Most Tin Pan Alley love songs are perfect 100 per cent kitsch.
>
> Gilbert Highet, *Kitsch*

The rest of the essay simply goes on to catalog one example after another of kitsch in literature.

Another dimension may be added to a definition by an analysis of the function of a term. For example, the sewing machine may be defined as a mechanism that allows a tailor or a seamstress to stitch cloth together automatically. This definition may then be extended by stating specific functions, as follows:

> There are over 2,000 varieties of modern sewing machines designed for stitching processes in the great sewing industries making up clothing,

130

boots and shoes, corsets, hats, hosiery, etc. There are machines especially designed for sewing regular or fancy shank buttons on shoes; for sewing sweat leathers into stiff felt, soft felt or straw hats; for trimming scalloping and over-edging lace curtains; for sewing silk initials, monograms or floral designs upon material at one operation. There is a seven needle machine for making seven parallel rows of fine double chain stitching simultaneously. This machine is fitted with seven needles and seven loopers, and its capacity is 20,000 stitches per minute.

Encyclopaedia Britannica

3. CLARIFY THE DEFINITION THROUGH THE USE OF CONTRASTS.   To explain what a thing is, it is often convenient to also say what it is not. By this kind of indirection, a writer can make clear what is meant by a certain term. Here, for example, are two paragraphs taken from the essay "The Sophisticated Man" by Marya Mannes. She has already defined the sophisticated man as one who has acquired certain "perceptions, tastes, and attitudes." She then proceeds to these two paragraphs. The first sketches the sophisticated man in action; the second presents his opposite as a contrast:

Would you recognize this kind of man if you saw him across the room? I think so. He's the one with an attractive woman; conservatively dressed, but easy in his clothes. His hair is trimmed close to his head, but not too close. His hands are well-groomed, but not manicured. He does not laugh loudly or often. He is looking directly at the woman he speaks to, but he is not missing the other attractive women as they enter; a flick of the eye does it. For in all ways this man is not obvious. He would no more appear to examine a woman from the ankles up than he would move his head as he read or form the words with his lips. His senses are trained and his reflexes quick. And how did they get that way? From experience, from observation, and from deduction. He puts two and two together without adding on his fingers. He is educated in life.

Now what about that fellow over there—the one in the light-grey suit and the crew cut? He is telling a long story rather loudly to a girl who would rather not be hearing it. He is not, of course, aware of this, since he is not only a little tight but unaccustomed to watching the reactions of women. He will look down the front of her dress but not see the glaze in her eyes. He has not been educated in observation. He is, according to the dictionary, unsophisticated in that he is natural and simple and lacking in experience.

Marya Mannes, "The Sophisticated Man"

By knowing what the sophisticated man is not, we have a better idea of what he is.

4. AMPLIFY THE DEFINITION UNTIL THE MEANING IS CLEAR.   The kind of amplification that a writer should give depends, of course, on the term that is being defined. The only hard and fast rule is that one should give as much detail as is necessary to make it clear what a term or word means. Writers resort to a variety of guises

in order to accomplish this. Here, for example, a writer is defining high blood pressure. First, he says clearly what it is; then he proceeds to detail its consequences on the human body:

> High blood pressure, or hypertension, is exactly what it says, a condition in which the blood is being pumped through the vast network of arteries with unusually high force. It's difficult to say at what point the blood pressure rises from "normal" to "high," as measured by the column of mercury on the doctor's sphygmomanometer or blood pressure recorder. But generally physicians classify a person as hypertensive if his diastolic pressure—the smaller of the two-number pressure readings—is 95 millimeters of mercury or higher.
>
> Everyone experiences temporary increases in blood pressure. Emotions can push up pressure for short periods, for instance. Indeed, a patient's apprehension about a blood pressure reading can raise his pressure a bit, which is why doctors usually insist on taking three readings in a two-week period before making a firm diagnosis of hypertension.
>
> As late as the 1920's physicians didn't think high blood pressure was a threat to health. In fact, it was deemed a natural and necessary attempt by the body to keep sufficient blood flowing through arteries that were beginning to harden and narrow from age or disease.
>
> In the last few years, however, researchers have developed hard evidence that high blood pressure, if left unchecked for a few years, sharply increases the risk of a heart attack, heart failure or a stroke leading to disability and/or death. Epidemiological studies such as the Framingham study, for instance, show the rate of heart attack among men whose diastolic pressure was 105 or higher was more than twice that of men with pressures of less than 95 and three and a half times that of men with pressures of less than 85 millimeters of mercury.
>
> Jerry Bishop, *I Think I'm Having a Heart Attack*

Where necessary or appropriate, writers will often add to their definitions by elaborating in successive paragraphs on various features, functions, and characteristics of a term. The paragraphs that follow may seem to be developed according to various methods—some may seem primarily descriptive, some essentially an analysis of effect. But each is working toward the ultimate goal of the writer—to define a medieval *tournament* and explain its place in the life of a knight:

> Originating in France and referred to by others as "French combat" (*conflictus Gallicus*), tournaments started without rules or lists as an agreed-upon clash of opposing units. Though justified as training exercises, the impulse was the love of fighting. Becoming more regulated and mannered, they took two forms: jousts by individuals, and melees by groups of up to forty on a side, either *à plaisance* with blunted weapons or *à outrance* with no restraints, in which case participants might be severely wounded and not infrequently killed. Tournaments proliferated as the noble's primary occupation dwindled. Under the extended rule of mon-

archy, he had less need to protect his own fief, while a class of professional ministers was gradually taking his place around the crown. The less he had to do, the more energy he spent in tournaments artificially re-enacting his role.

A tournament might last as long as a week and on great occasions two. Opening day was spent matching and seeding the players, followed by days set apart for jousts, for melees, for a rest day before the final tourney, all interspersed with feasting and parties. These occasions were the great sporting events of the time, attracting crowds of bourgeois spectators from rich merchants to common artisans, mountebanks, food vendors, prostitutes, and pickpockets. About a hundred knights usually participated, each accompanied by two mounted squires, an armorer, and six servants in livery. The knight had of course to equip himself with painted and guilded armor and crested helmet costing from 25 to 50 livres, with a war-horse costing from 25 to 100 livres in addition to his traveling palfrey, and with banners and trappings and fine clothes. Though the expense could easily backrupt him, he might also come away richer, for the loser in combat had to pay a ransom and the winner was awarded his opponent's horse and armor, which he could sell back to him or to anyone. Gain was not recognized by chivalry, but it was present at tournaments.

Because of their extravagance, violence, and vainglory, tournaments were continually being denounced by popes and kings, from whom they drained money. In vain. When the Dominicans denounced them as a pagan circus, no one listened. When the formidable St. Bernard thundered that anyone killed in a tournament would go to Hell, he spoke for once to deaf ears. Death in a tournament was officially considered the sin of suicide by the Church, besides jeopardizing family and tenantry without cause, but even threats of excommunication had no effect. Although St. Louis condemned tournaments and Philip the Fair prohibited them during his wars, nothing could stop them permanently or dim the enthusiasm for them.

With brilliantly dressed spectators in the stands, flags and ribbons fluttering, the music of trumpets, the parade of combatants making their draped horses prance and champ on golden bridles, the glitter of harness and shields, the throwing of ladies' scarves and sleeves to their favorites, the bow of the heralds to the presiding prince who proclaimed the rules, the cry of poursuivants announcing their champions, the tournament was the peak of nobility's pride and delight in its own valor and beauty.

Barbara W. Tuchman, A Distant Mirror: The Calamitous 14th Century

It follows from all we have said in this section that the defining essay should give more than just a lexical meaning of a word, phrase, or term. Anyone can look in a dictionary and see the starkest, bare-bones summation of a referent. The essay that defines should give considerably more. It should show not only the mummified meaning of a term to be found in any dictionary, but also the living word as it exists in the mind of the individual writer.

In this essay, Gordon Allport, a well-known psychologist, gets at the root of prejudice by giving it a precise definition.

Professional Model

The Nature of Prejudice
Gordon Allport

1   Before I attempt to define prejudice, let us have in mind four instances that I think we all would agree involve prejudice.

2   The first is the case of the Cambridge University student, who said, "I despise all Americans. But," he added, a bit puzzled, "I've never met one that I didn't like."

3   The second is the case of another Englishman, who said to an American, "I think you're awfully unfair in your treatment of Negroes. How *do* Americans feel about Negroes?" The American replied, "Well, I suppose some Americans feel about Negroes just the way you feel about the Irish." The Englishman said, "Oh, come now! The Negroes are human beings!"

4   Then there's the incident that occasionally takes place in various parts of the world (in the West Indies, for example, I'm told). When an American walks down the street the natives conspicuously hold their noses till the American goes by. The case of odor is always interesting. Odor gets mixed up with prejudice because odor has great associative power. We know that some Chinese deplore the odor of Americans. Some white people think Negroes have a distinctive smell and vice versa. An intrepid psychologist recently did an experiment; it went as follows. He brought to a gymnasium an equal number of white and colored students and had them take shower baths. When they were nice and clean he had them exercise vigorously for fifteen minutes. Then he put them in different rooms, and he put a clean white sheet over each one. Then he brought his judges in, and each went to the sheeted figures and sniffed. They were to say, "white" or "black," guessing at the identity of the subject. The experiment seemed to prove that when we are sweaty we all smell bad in the same way. It's good to have experimental demonstration of the fact.

5   The fourth example I'd like to bring before you is a piece of writing that I quote. Please ask yourselves, who, in your judgment, wrote it. It's a passage about the Jews.

> The synagogue is worse than a brothel. It's a den of scoundrels. It's a criminal assembly of Jews, a place of meeting for the assassins of Christ, a den of thieves, a house of ill fame, a dwelling of iniquity. Whatever name more horrible to be found, it could never be worse than the synagogue deserves.
>
> I would say the same things about their souls. Debauchery and drunkenness have brought them to the level of lusty goat and pig. They know only one thing: to satisfy their stomachs and get drunk, kill, and beat each other up. Why should we salute them? We should have not even the slightest converse with them. They are lustful, rapacious, greedy, perfidious robbers.

6   Now who wrote that? Perhaps you say Hitler, or Goebbels, or one of our local anti-Semites? No, it was written by Saint John Chrysostom, in the fourth century A.D. Saint John Chrysostom, as you know, gave us the first liturgy in the Christian church still used in the Orthodox churches today. From it all services of the Holy Communion derive. Episcopalians will recognize him also as the author of that exalted prayer that closes the

offices of both matin and evensong in the *Book of Common Prayer*.* I include this incident to show how complex the problem is. Religious people are by no means necessarily free from prejudice. In this regard be patient even with our saints.

7   What do these four instances have in common? You notice that all of them indicate that somebody is "down" on somebody else—a feeling of rejection, or hostility. But also, in all these four instances, there is indication that the person is not "up" on his subject— not really informed about Americans, Irish, Jews, or bodily odors.

8   So I would offer, first a slang definition of prejudice: *Prejudice is being down on somebody you're not up on.* If you dislike slang, let me offer the same thought in the style of St. Thomas Aquinas. Thomists have defined prejudice as *thinking ill of others without sufficient warrant.*

9   You notice that both definitions, as well as the examples I gave, specify two ingredients of prejudice. First there is some sort of faulty generalization in thinking about a group. I'll call this the process of *categorization*. Then there is the negative, rejective, or hostile ingredient, a *feeling* tone. "Being down on something" is the hostile ingredient; "that you're not up on" is the categorization ingredient; "Thinking ill of others" is the hostile ingredient; "without sufficient warrant" is the faulty categorization.

10   Parenthetically I should say that of course there is such a thing as *positive* prejudice. We can be just as prejudiced *in favor of* as we are *against*. We can be biased in favor of our children, our neighborhood or our college. Spinoza makes the distinction neatly. He says that *love prejudice* is "thinking well of others, through love, more than is right." *Hate prejudice,* he says, is "thinking ill of others, through hate, more than is right."

840 words

Vocabulary

associative (4)	rapacious (5)	liturgy (6)
deplore (4)	perfidious (5)	matin (6)
iniquity (5)	anti-Semites (6)	

Questions

1. How does the author begin his essay? What is his purpose?
2. Why does the author think that odor often gets mixed up in prejudice?
3. The author refers to an experimental demonstration that proves that odor is not associated with race. What other firmly held beliefs have been negated by experimental demonstrations?
4. Why does the author end paragraph 6 by saying, "In this regard be patient even with our saints"?
5. What is the author's slang definition of *prejudice*? What is his more literary definition?
6. What is a present-day example of the process of categorization?
7. What is "positive prejudice"? What examples does the author supply?
8. Who is Spinoza? Look him up in your dictionary.
9. In your opinion, what are the pitfalls resulting from both negative and positive prejudice?

*The book of services and prayers used in the Church of England.

10. What is your own definition of *prejudice*? What are some of your prejudices? How do you deal with them? What prejudices in others bother you most?

Student Model

Prejudice
Michael Wilds

Prejudice is a judgment or opinion held in disregard of facts that contradict it. Any school child will tell you that prejudice is wrong. But any school child will also, with little or no prompting, tell you jokes about dumb Polacks, conniving Jews, naive prostitutes, senile teachers, or some other suitable group whom society has made the victim of one of its many biased stereotypes. Showing prejudice is a popular sport played skillfully by society since the beginning of time. It is a habit of the mind which affects all of us, invariably serving to feed our egos at the expense of someone else. In a petty way prejudice satisfies our need to feel superior without merit. After all, it is so easy to label someone "slow," "dirty," "unreliable," or "ugly," in turn causing us to seem "quick," "clean," "reliable," and "handsome" by contrast. Even a child's screaming tirade against the awful taste of spinach is usually an uninformed judgment about this much-maligned vegetable. By screaming about how "yuckie" spinach is, the child is trying to prove himself too good for such a slimy food.

Prejudice crops up in amazing places, often slipping by unrecognized. The following quotation by Charlotte Brontë serves as a case in point:

> Prejudices, it is well known, are most difficult to eradicate from the heart whose soil has never been loosened or fertilized by education; they grow there firm as weeds among the rocks.

Ironically, in this statement Miss Brontë shows her own prejudice against uneducated people and her bias in favor of the educated. The quotation is replete with implications that an educated mind is freer of prejudice than an uneducated one and that it is therefore more noble. Those of us who agree with her view can now comfortably join Miss Brontë in looking down with pity on the uneducated masses who, poor things, will always make narrow-minded, biased evaluations, so inferior to our own equitable and dispassionate ones.

It is the primary function of prejudice to demonstrate through rhetoric rather than logic the superiority of one group over another (usually, of course, one's own group). What makes Miss Brontë's quotation such a good example of a prejudicial comment is that the formula involved is standard fare. Prejudice always serves to elevate not by pointing to the achievements of its special interest, but by indicating a supposed deficiency elsewhere. As in the case of most prejudiced comments, Miss Brontë lends weight to her thesis by asserting an aggressive absolute: ". . . it is well known . . ." Other such absolutes are as follows: "Anyone will tell you . . . ," "It's an unfortunate fact that . . . ," "We all know . . . ," and so forth. Whether we are prejudiced against race, nationality, social status, food, or anything else, the elements of prejudice remain the same:

1. A desire to show superiority
2. The selection of a vulnerable target
3. The publication of a bold assertion that villifies the target but is unsupported by fact.

Prejudice will doubtless plague us always. From Moses's time to the present it has reared its ugly head in every society, coexistent with the knowledge that prejudice is wrong. If there is a way to arrest this disease, it is probably following John Locke's suggestion that "every man should let alone others' prejudices and examine his own."

One of the most emotional debates of our time concerns the issue of legalized abortion. Foes continue to lobby for a constitutional amendment against it, while supporters rally to block any attempts to repeal the Supreme Court's 1973 decision that gave women the right to decide for themselves. Crucial to the debate is the question of when life actually begins: with fertilization, as abortion foes contend, or when the fetus is capable of life outside the womb, as the Supreme Court decided in 1973. The essay that follows, which appeared in *Newsweek,* January 11, 1982, looks at the underlying definition around which much of the debate revolves: when is a human egg a human being?

Is the Human Egg a Person?
Jerry Adler and John Carey

1   A fertilized human egg is a speck of protoplasm 100 microns in diameter, roughly the diameter of a human hair and as fragile and evanescent as a spark struck from a flint. Already, nature's profligacy is working against it; between one-half and two-thirds of fertilized human eggs will fail to implant themselves in the uterus and be washed away unnoticed, a statistic that not even a constitutional amendment will alter. It is unquestionably alive, a unique entity whose destiny was forged in the ecstatic mingling of male and female gametes, within minutes of fertilization. But is it a person?

2   The question is one for philosophers, not scientists; there are no experiments in progress aimed at determining how many cells constitute a human being. But even so, scientists are being asked to take a stand on it. Later this year the Senate is expected to debate the so-called "human life" bill, sponsored by Republican Jesse Helms of North Carolina, which holds that "present-day scientific evidence indicates a significant likelihood that actual human life exists from conception." The intent of the measure is to extend constitutional protections to human embryos, thereby outlawing abortions and, in a strict interpretation, even such contraceptives as intrauterine devices, which prevent the implantation of a fertilized egg. It appears to be a partisan issue; a Senate subcommittee approved the bill on straight party lines last summer: three Republicans in favor, two Democrats opposed.

3   The bill embraces an extremely broad view of human existence, but it has at least the virtue of being unambiguous. At the other extreme is the Internal Revenue Service definition of life, which holds—for income-tax-exemption purposes—that it begins at birth. But even the straightforward language of the human-life bill has some hidden traps. Consider in vitro conception, which produced the first American-born "test-tube baby" last week: an egg is removed from an ovary, fertilized with the father's sperm and surgically implanted in the uterus. Is the newly fertilized egg, incubating in its petri dish, a person? What sort of legal obligations does that place on the technician who examines it for its suitability for implantation? Fewer than 10 percent of the implanted embryos actually develop to term. Have the rest been murdered?

4   Even some opponents of abortion have doubts about extending legal protection to

single egg cells. Normal fertilization, occurring in the Fallopian tube, cannot be detected, and the majority of fertilized eggs never take hold in the uterus. "That's a lot of little people" to contemplate losing, says Richard McCormick of the Kennedy Institute of Bioethics at Georgetown University, who favors marking human life from the time about six days after fertilization, when the embryo implants itself. At that point, even though it is a tiny hollow sphere of a few dozen cells, its effects on the mother's circulating hormones can be detected.

5   However, that definition calls attention to the inability of the fetus to live independently of the mother and to the rights of the mother over this creature so intimately a part of her. The American Medical Association, in opposing the human-life bill, said it was concerned about the legal implications for a doctor who deals with two lives in one body—and might have to jeopardize the embryo's life in treating its mother.

6   The Supreme Court attempted to address the issue in 1973, when it held that the law gives full protection to the lives of fetuses only from the time they are capable of living outside the womb, which the court fixed between 24 and 28 weeks. But viability is not absolute; it is a function of medical technology, and the implication of the Supreme Court ruling is that it is essentially the doctor who bestows life. If, as some scientists have recently predicted, embryos as young as eight weeks may someday soon be kept alive in the laboratory, will the sacred protections of the Constitution be extended accordingly? And if so, how can doctors justify aborting, say, a twelve-week fetus now?

7   Similar practical and ethical problems arise from definitions of human life that depend on one or another of the landmark events of embryonic life. One could argue that the first appearance of detectable brain waves, at about twelve weeks after conception, marks the beginning of human life—a seemingly apt choice, since a Presidential commission has recommended a definition of death that relies on the absence of brain activity. But ultrasound pictures show that the fetus is moving on its own as early as about six weeks, around the same time that it begins taking on a recognizable human form, although it is barely half an inch long. A heartbeat, which may be taken as the sine qua non of life, first begins haltingly at three to four weeks. Then again, the nervous system is not fully connected until 24 weeks. "The fetus has its thumb in its mouth at eight weeks," says obstetrician and noted abortion foe Bernard Nathanson, arguing against all such arbitrary milestones. "With better techniques, we will see a recognizable human at two weeks."

8   In the end, the Senate won't find any easy way out of the enigma by seeking answers from scientists. Even many doctors who believe that abortions are justified will concede that life begins at fertilization, and that the fetus becomes human at any point the anti-abortion groups care to specify; the problem is not determining when "actual human life" begins, but when the value of that life begins to outweigh other considerations, such as the health, or even the happiness, of the mother. And on that question, science is silent.

915 words

Vocabulary

microns (1)	ecstatic (1)	in vitro (3)	arbitrary (7)
evanescent (1)	gametes (1)	viability (6)	enigma (8)
profligacy (1)	unambiguous (3)	sine qua non (7)	

Questions

1. What will happen to between one-half and two-thirds of all fertilized human eggs?
2. The authors say that whether or not the human egg is a person is a question for philosophy, not science. Why is science unable to resolve this question?
3. What definition of life does the so-called human life bill, sponsored by Republican senator Jesse Helms, propose to use? What is your opinion of this bill?
4. Why is the presence of detectable brain waves a seemingly apt choice for determining whether the fetus is actually a human being? What objection can be raised to this criterion?
5. When does the fetus actually have a heartbeat?
6. What, according to the authors, is really the problem involved in the abortion debate?
7. What do the authors actually accomplish in their attempt at defining a person?

.

In the speech that follows, a hemophiliac provides an unforgettable definition of the dreadful disease that victimized him.

Alternate Reading

Mingled Blood
Ralph Zimmerman

1   I am a hemophiliac. To many of you, that word signifies little or nothing. A few may pause a moment and then remember that it has something to do with bleeding. Probably none of you can appreciate the gigantic impact of what those words mean to me.

2   What is this thing called hemophilia? Webster defines it as "a tendency, usually hereditary, to profuse bleeding even from slight wounds." Dr. Armand J. Quick, Professor of Biochemistry at Marquette University and recognized world authority on this topic, defines it as "a prothrombin consumption time of 8 to 13 seconds." Normal time is 15 seconds. Now do you know what hemophilia is?

3   It is by no means a 20th century phenomenon. Ancient writings reveal that Jewish rabbis upon the death of first born sons from bleeding after circumcision, allowed the parents to dispense with this ceremony for any more sons. Family laws of ancient Egypt did not permit a woman to bear any more children if the first born should die of severe bleeding from a minor wound. How odd it seems to link the pyramids of the 4th dynasty with prothrombin consumption of 1955.

4   Hemophilia has had significant influence on the pages of history. Victoria, the queen of an empire on which the sun never set, was a transmitter of this dread ailment. Through her daughter, Alice, it was passed to the Russian royal family and Czarevitch Alexis, heir apparent to the throne of Nicholas II. Alexis, the hemophilic heir apparent, was so crippled by his ailment that the Bolshevik revolters had to carry him bodily to the cellar

to execute him. And through Victoria's daughter, Beatrice, it was carried to the sons of the Spanish monarch, Alfonso XIII. While this good queen ruled her empire with an iron hand and unknowingly transmitted this mysterious affliction, my forebears, peasants of southern Germany, worked their fields, gave birth to their children, and buried their dead sons. Hemophilia shows no respect for class lines. It cares not whether your blood be red or blue.

5   For hemophilia is a hereditary disease. It afflicts only males, but paradoxically is transmitted only by females. The sons of a victim are not hemophiliacs, and do not pass it on. However, all of the daughters are transmitters. Of the transmitter daughter's children, half of the girls may be transmitters like their mother, and half of the sons may be hemophiliacs. Thus the net spreads out and on. Theoretically, it follows strict Mendelian* principles. But because it is a recessive characteristic, it may lie dormant for generation after generation. As far back as my ancestral line can be traced, there is no evidence of hemophilia until my older brother Herbert and me. The same is true of 50 per cent of America's bleeders.

6   And there are many of us. Medical authorities estimate that there are some 20,000–40,000 hemophiliacs of all types in the United States. Clinically we divide into three groups: classic hemophilia AHG, and two other less common types of hemophilia, PTC and PTA. I am a classic hemophiliac—the real McCoy.

7   What does it really mean to be a hemophiliac? The first indication comes in early childhood when a small scratch may bleed for hours. By the time the hemophiliac reaches school age, he begins to suffer from internal bleeding into muscles, joints, the stomach, the kidneys. This latter type is far more serious, for external wounds can usually be stopped in minutes with topical thromboplastin or a pressure bandage. But internal bleeding can be checked only by changes in the blood by means of transfusion or plasma injections. If internal bleeding into a muscle or joint goes unchecked repeatedly, muscle contraction and bone deformity inevitably result. My crooked left arm, the built-up heel on my right shoe, and the full length brace on my left leg offer mute but undeniable testimony to that fact. Vocal evidence you hear; weak tongue muscles are likely to produce defective L and R sounds.

8   Childhood and early adolescence are the danger periods of a hemophiliac's life. As recently as November, 1950, *The Science Digest* reported that 85 per cent of all hemophiliacs die during that period. While the figure is exaggerated, it tends to indicate this salient point: if society can keep a hemophiliac alive until after adolescence, society has saved a member. During those years, society is given a responsibility it too often refuses to accept.

9   You might ask—but what can I do? What do you expect of me? The answer lies in the title of this oration: mingled blood. For all that boy needs is blood, blood, and more blood. Blood for transfusions, blood for fresh frozen plasma, blood for serum fractions. Not Red Cross Bank Blood, for stored blood loses its clot-producing factors. But fresh blood directly from you to him in a matter of hours. Your blood, dark and thick, rich with all the complex protein fractions that make for coagulation—mingled with the thin, weak, and deficient liquid that flows in his veins. Blood directly from you to the medical researcher for transformation into fresh frozen plasma or antihemophilic globulin. During those years, his very life is flowing in your veins. No synthetic substitute has been found—only fresh blood and its derivatives.

10 Because medical science had not advanced far enough, and fresh blood not given often enough, my memories of childhood and adolescence are memories of pain and

---

*The principles of heredity as formulated by Gregor Mendel.

140

heartbreak. I remember missing school for weeks and months at a stretch—of being very proud because I attended school once for four whole weeks without missing a single day. I remember the three long years when I couldn't even walk because repeated hemorrhages had twisted my ankles and knees to pretzel-like forms. I remember being pulled to school in a wagon while other boys rode their bikes, and being pushed to my table. I remember sitting in the dark empty classroom by myself during recess while the others went out in the sun to run and play. And I remember the first terrible day at the big high school when I came on crutches and built-up shoes carrying my books in a sack around my neck.

11   But what I remember most of all is the pain. Medical authorities agree that a hemophilic joint hemorrhage is one of the most excruciating pains known to mankind. To concentrate a large amount of blood into a small compact area causes a pressure that words can never hope to describe. And how well I remember the endless pounding, squeezing pain. When you seemingly drown in your own perspiration, when your teeth ache from incessant clenching, when your tongue floats in your mouth and bombs explode back of your eyeballs; when darkness and light fuse into one hue of gray; when day becomes night and night becomes day—time stands still—and all that matters is that ugly pain. The scars of pain are not easily erased.

12   Once a hemophiliac successfully passes through the dangerous period, his need for blood steadily decreases and his health improves. The nightmare of youth is gradually hidden behind a protective curtain of objectivity that is seldom raised. In contrast to my childhood days, I can look back on more than three years of college with joy and a sense of achievement. I've had some good breaks. I've been in debate and forensics for four years and had a variety of satisfying experiences. I've been lucky in politics. My constituents, the student body at our college, elected me President of Student Government. Like so many other American youths, I've worked my way through college as a clerk in a hardware store. On warm weekends, while not a Ben Hogan at golf, I have shot an 82. And back home, a girl wears my wedding band.

13   For today, except for periodic transfusions, my life is as normal as anyone else's, and my aims and ambitions are the same as anyone else's. But now, a different type of social relationship needs to be found. Because a hemophiliac is so totally dependent on society during his early years and because his very existence is sometimes then precarious, society now tends to lag in recognizing the change. It sometimes fails to realize that this hemophiliac's life is no longer in serious question and that now his right to aspire to any new height should not be frowned on by a society still vividly remembering the past. Now, he seeks neither pity nor privilege. He wishes to be regarded not as a hemophiliac but rather a human being to be evaluated like any human being.

14   I cannot change that part of my life which is past. I cannot change my hemophilia. Therefore, I must ask you to help those hemophiliacs that need help. For I remember too well my older brother Herbert, so shattered in adolescence by hemophilia, that his tombstone reads like a blessing: "May 10, 1927–April 6, 1950, Thy Will be Done." And I ask you to help hemophiliacs because one day my grandson may need your blood. But I also must ask you to recognize a hemophiliac for what he is today; to realize that past is prologue, that weakness sometimes begets strength; that man sometimes conquers. And so I pray:

15   "God give me the courage to accept the things that I cannot change; the power to change the things which I can; and the wisdom always to know the difference between the two."

1,647 words

Vocabulary

paradoxically (5)	salient (8)	forensics (12)
dormant (5)	coagulation (9)	begets (14)
plasma (7)	synthetic (9)	

Questions

1. As noted in paragraph 9, "Mingled Blood" was originally delivered as a speech that won first prize in the men's division of the 1955 Interstate Oratorical Contest. A few months after delivering the speech, Ralph Zimmerman died, a victim of the disease he so eloquently explains. What does a knowledge of these circumstances add to your evaluation of this speech?
2. In what paragraph does the author give two definitions of hemophilia? What purpose do these definitions serve?
3. What connection between history and hemophilia does the author draw?
4. In paragraph 7, how does the author answer the question, "What does it really mean to be a hemophiliac?"
5. What is the crucial time in a hemophiliac's life?
6. How can society help save the lives of hemophiliacs?
7. What do the author's memories of childhood and adolescence consist of? Why?
8. How does the author make a hemophiliac's pain come to life in paragraph 11?
9. What request does the author make in paragraph 13?

Additional Writing Assignment

Beginning with a lexical definition and extending this definition into a full essay, define one of the following terms. Be sure that your essay answers the question, "What is it?"

1. alienation
2. truth
3. adolescence
4. fanatacism
5. marital fidelity
6. addiction
7. wit
8. autopsy
9. virtue
10. patriotism

9

Comparison / Contrast

*My two closest friends are as different as a Cape Cod
cottage and a Byzantine mosque.*

A. Reading for Ideas

In "The Use of Force" a physician called to the home of a sick child loses his temper
when she resists his attempts to treat her. As you read the story, try to compare and
contrast the personalities of the two characters involved—the physician and the
sick child. Think of specific traits each displays in the encounter. Try to understand their contrasting backgrounds, lifestyles, and personalities as revealed in
their behavior toward each other.

The Use of Force
William Carlos Williams

1   They were new patients to me, all I had was the name, Olson. Please come down as
soon as you can, my daughter is very sick.

2   When I arrived I was met by the mother, a big startled looking woman, very clean and
apologetic who merely said, Is this the doctor? and let me in. In the back, she added.
You must excuse us, doctor, we have her in the kitchen where it is warm. It is very damp
here sometimes.

3   The child was fully dressed and sitting on her father's lap near the kitchen table. He
tried to get up, but I motioned for him not to bother, took off my overcoat and started to
look things over. I could see that they were all very nervous, eyeing me up and down
distrustfully. As often, in such cases, they weren't telling me more than they had to, it was
up to me to tell them; that's why they were spending three dollars on me.

4   The child was fairly eating me up with her cold, steady eyes, and no expression to her
face whatever. She did not move and seemed, inwardly, quiet; an unusually attractive
little thing, and as strong as a heifer in appearance. But her face was flushed, she was
breathing rapidly, and I realized that she had a high fever. She had magnificent blonde
hair, in profusion. One of those picture children often reproduced in advertising leaflets
and the photogravure sections of the Sunday papers.

5   She's had a fever for three days, began the father and we don't know what it comes
from. My wife has given her things, you know, like people do, but it don't do no good.

143

And there's been a lot of sickness around. So we tho't you'd better look her over and tell us what is the matter.

6   As doctors often do I took a trial shot at it as a point of departure. Has she had a sore throat?

7   Both parents answered me together. No . . . No, she says her throat don't hurt her.

8   Does your throat hurt you? added the mother to the child. But the little girl's expression didn't change nor did she move her eyes from my face.

Have you looked?

I tried to, said the mother, but I couldn't see.

9   As it happens we had been having a number of cases of diphtheria in the school to which this child went during that month and we were all, quite apparently, thinking of that, though no one had as yet spoken of the thing.

10   Well, I said, suppose we take a look at the throat first. I smiled in my best professional manner and asking for the child's first name I said, come on, Mathilda, open your mouth and let's take a look at your throat.

11   Nothing doing.

12   Aw, come on, I coaxed, just open your mouth wide and let me take a look. Look, I said opening both hands wide. I haven't anything in my hands. Just open up and let me see.

13   Such a nice man, put in the mother. Look how kind he is to you. Come on, do what he tells you to. He won't hurt you.

14   At that I ground my teeth in disgust. If only they wouldn't use the word "hurt" I might be able to get somewhere. But I did not allow myself to be hurried or disturbed but speaking quietly and slowly I approached the child again.

15   As I moved my chair a little nearer suddenly with one cat-like movement both her hands clawed instinctively for my eyes and she almost reached them too. In fact she knocked my glasses flying and they fell, though unbroken, several feet away from me on the kitchen floor.

16   Both the mother and father almost turned themselves inside out in embarrassment and apology. You bad girl, said the mother, taking her and shaking her by one arm. Look what you've done. The nice man . . .

17   For heaven's sake, I broke in. Don't call me a nice man to her. I'm here to look at her throat on the chance that she might have diphtheria and possibly die of it. But that's nothing to her. Look here, I said to the child, we're going to look at your throat. You're old enough to understand what I'm saying. Will you open it now by yourself or shall we have to open it for you?

18   Not a move. Even her expression hadn't changed. Her breaths however were coming faster and faster. Then the battle began. I had to do it. I had to have a throat culture for her own protection. But first I told the parents that it was entirely up to them. I explained the danger but said that I would not insist on a throat examination so long as they would take the responsibility.

19   If you don't do what the doctor says you'll have to go to the hospital, the mother admonished her severely.

20   Oh yeah? I had to smile to myself. After all, I had already fallen in love with the savage brat, the parents were contemptible to me. In the ensuing struggle they grew more and more abject, crushed, exhausted while she surely rose to magnificent heights of insane fury of effort bred of her terror of me.

21   The father tried his best, and he was a big man but the fact that she was his daughter, his shame at her behavior and his dread of hurting her made him release her just at the critical moment several times when I had almost achieved success, till I wanted to kill him. But his dread also that she might have diphtheria made him tell me to go on, go

on though he himself was almost fainting, while the mother moved back and forth behind us raising and lowering her hands in an agony of apprehension.

22   Put her in front of you on your lap, I ordered, and hold both her wrists.

23   But as soon as he did the child let out a scream. Don't, you're hurting me. Let go of my hands. Let them go I tell you. Then she shrieked terrifyingly, hysterically. Stop it! Stop it! You're killing me!

24   Do you think she can stand it, doctor! said the mother.
You get out, said the husband to his wife. Do you want her to die of diphtheria? Come on now, hold her, I said.

25   Then I grasped the child's head with my left hand and tried to get the wooden tongue depressor between her teeth. She fought, with clenched teeth, desperately! But now I also had grown furious—at a child. I tried to hold myself down but I couldn't. I know how to expose a throat for inspection. And I did my best. When finally I got the wooden spatula behind the last teeth and just the point of it into the mouth cavity, she opened up for an instant but before I could see anything she came down again and gripping the wooden blade between her molars she reduced it to splinters before I could get it out again.

26   Aren't you ashamed, the mother yelled at her. Aren't you ashamed to act like that in front of the doctor?

27   Get me a smooth-handled spoon of some sort, I told the mother. We're going through with this. The child's mouth was already bleeding. Her tongue was cut and she was screaming in wild hysterical shrieks. Perhaps I should have desisted and come back in an hour or more. No doubt it would have been better. But I have seen at least two children lying dead in bed of neglect in such cases, and feeling that I must get a diagnosis now or never I went at it again. But the worst of it was that I too had got beyond reason. I could have torn the child apart in my own fury and enjoyed it. It was a pleasure to attack her. My face was burning with it.

28   The damned little brat must be protected against her own idiocy, one says to one's self at such times. Others must be protected against her. It is a social necessity. And all these things are true. But a blind fury, a feeling of adult shame, bred of a longing for muscular release are the operatives. One goes on to the end.

29   In a final unreasoning assault I overpowered the child's neck and jaws. I forced the heavy silver spoon back of her teeth and down her throat till she gagged. And there it was—both tonsils covered with membrane. She had fought valiantly to keep me from knowing her secret. She had been hiding that sore throat for three days at least and lying to her parents in order to escape just such an outcome as this.

30   Now truly she *was* furious. She had been on the defensive before, but now she attacked. Tried to get off her father's lap and fly at me while tears of defeat blinded her eyes.

1,365 words

Vocabulary

photogravure (4)
admonished (19)
abject (20)

Questions

1. What were the doctor's initial impressions of the little girl's parents?

2. From the doctor's physical description of the child and her initial responses to him, what can you infer about her and her relationship with her parents?
3. Why did the doctor feel such contempt for the child's parents?
4. How would you characterize the parents' attempts at controlling their child?
5. The narrator does not use quotation marks to indicate dialogue. What is the effect of this technique on the narrative?
6. In contrasting the child and the doctor, what class distinctions can you immediately notice between them?
7. In the end, what do the doctor and the child ironically have in common?
8. How would you characterize the tone of paragraph 20?
9. What candid admission does the narrator make about his own behavior? What does this admission tell you about him?

My Last Duchess
Robert Browning

Ferrara

1   That's my last duchess painted on the wall,
Looking as if she were alive. I call
That piece a wonder, now; Fra Pandolf's hands
Worked busily a day, and there she stands.
5   Will't please you sit and look at her? I said
"Fra Pandolf" by design, for never read
Strangers like you that pictured countenance,
The depth and passion of its earnest glance,
But to myself they turned (since none puts by
10   The curtain I have drawn for you, but I)
And seemed as they would ask me, if they durst,[1]
How such a glance came there; so, not the first
Are you to turn and ask thus. Sir, 'twas not
Her husband's presence only, called that spot
15   Of joy into the Duchess' cheek; perhaps
Fra Pandolf chanced to say, "Her mantle laps
Over my lady's wrist too much," or, "Paint
Must never hope to reproduce the faint
Half-flush that dies along her throat." Such stuff
20   Was courtesy, she thought, and cause enough
For calling up that spot of joy. She had
A heart—how shall I say?—too soon made glad,
Too easily impressed; she liked whate'er
She looked on, and her looks went everywhere.
25   Sir, 'twas all one! My favor at her breast,
The dropping of the daylight in the West,
The bough of cherries some officious fool
Broke in the orchard for her, the white mule
She rode with round the terrace—all and each

---

[1]"Dared."

146

30   Would draw from her alike the approving speech,
     Or blush, at least. She thanked men—good! but thanked
     Somehow—I know not how—as if she ranked
     My gift of a nine-hundred-years-old name
     With anybody's gift. Who'd stoop to blame
35   This sort of trifling? Even had you skill
     In speech—which I have not—to make your will
     Quite clear to such a one, and say, "Just this
     Or that in you disgusts me; here you miss,
     Or there exceed the mark"—and if she let
40   Herself be lessoned so, nor plainly set
     Her wits to yours, forsooth,[2] and made excuse—
     E'en then would be some stooping; and I choose
     Never to stoop. Oh, sir, she smiled, no doubt,
     Whene'er I passed her; but who passed without
45   Much the same smile? This grew; I gave commands;
     Then all smiles stopped together. There she stands
     As if alive. Will't please you rise? We'll meet
     The company below, then. I repeat,
     The Count your master's known munificence
50   Is ample warrant that no just pretense
     Of mine for dowry will be disallowed;
     Though his fair daughter's self, as I avowed
     At starting, is my object. Nay, we'll go
     Together down, sir. Notice Neptune, though,
55   Taming a sea-horse, thought a rarity,
     Which Claus of Innsbruck cast in bronze for me!

Vocabulary

countenance (7)	munificence (49)	disallowed (51)
mantle (16)	warrant (50)	avowed (52)
officious (27)		

Questions

1. "My Last Duchess" is a dramatic monologue; that is, a poem in which only one person speaks. Who is the speaker and what seems to be the occasion? What is the setting for the monologue?
2. While the Duke is giving the messenger a detailed description of his former wife, he inadvertently describes himself as well. A sharp contrast between wife and husband emerges. What is the contrast? Draw up two columns. In the left-hand column, list the characteristics of the Duchess; in the right-hand column, list the contrasting characteristics of the Duke.
3. What tendency of the Duchess bothered the Duke the most?
4. Why did the Duke refuse to sit down and explain to the Duchess exactly what bothered him about her so that she could then correct her behavior?
5. What specific things that make the Duchess happy are mentioned?

---

[2]"Indeed."

6. How does the Duke resolve his displeasure with the Duchess?
7. What significance, if any, do you attach to the Duke's final reference to the statue of Neptune?

B. How to Write a Comparison/Contrast

A comparison reveals the similarities and differences between two items—a contrast assumes only differences between them. Most of our private and public decisions are based on comparison and contrast: We buy a Toyota rather than a Datsun because of differences we perceive between the two. An executive hires one secretary rather than another because he perceives a difference in their skills. A student selects one history class over another because he has heard that this teacher is more interesting than that one. A person chooses one religion over another because it offers greater peace of mind. Although often carried out in a slipshod manner with little or no logic, comparison is a necessary and familiar process.

Writing Assignment

Compare and contrast two acquaintances or two people in public life who represent different social backgrounds. Base your essay on the contrast between the lifestyles they represent, taking into account such factors as attitude toward money, treatment of people, purpose in life, dependence on others, and any other important basis for comparison. Place the controlling idea at the end of the introductory paragraph, making sure that it expresses the general areas of contrast you will treat in your essay—for example, "Mark and John differ in their cultural values, their treatment of people, and their goals in life."

Specific Instructions

1. CHOOSE SUITABLE BASES FOR YOUR COMPARISON. Your assignment is to compare two people with different lifestyles. To be effective, your comparison must be systematic rather than random. The first step is therefore to establish the bases for your comparison—in this case, the three or four points on which you will examine your two choices for differences and similarities between them. For example, John, the banker's son, wears flowered shirts, gold chains, and velvet trousers, while Mark, whose father is dead, wears plain T-shirts over blue Levis. The basis of this contrast is *fashion*. You have also observed that John treats everyone with impatience, whereas Mark treats people with a polite boredom. The basis of this contrast is their *treatment of people*. John's ambition is to travel all over the world with beautiful women, while Mark's dream is to buy a horse ranch in Oregon. The basis of this contrast is their respective *goals in life*. On the other hand, John loves the music of Vivaldi and so does Mark. Both are fans of Agatha Christie and devotees of "Star Trek." Similarities therefore exist between them based on a mutual fondness for the same composer, mystery writer, and defunct television series.

2. LIMIT YOUR ESSAY TO MAJOR BASES FOR COMPARISON.   No doubt there are countless bases for comparing people—looks, talent, charm, intelligence, creativity, ability to make friends, athletic prowess, and so on. However, rambling over the infinity of differences and similarities you see between John and Mark will not necessarily give your essay structure, emphasis, or clarity. To write a structured, emphatic, and clear comparison of your two acquaintances, select the major points of difference and similarity between them and restrict your essay to a contrast based on these. Once chosen and enunciated in your controlling idea, these bases will give your essay unity and structure. You should not violate this unity and structure by slipping into areas not mentioned in the controlling idea. The following paragraph begins by announcing a comparison of two girls on the basis of looks, personality, and physical strength, and lives up to its promise:

Controlling idea: Kora and Shery, though best friends, were as different as winter and summer in their looks, personality and physical strength. Kora was tall and dark, with snappy black eyes and long silken braids that fell to her *Looks:* hips, whereas Shery looked almost frail, with soft blue eyes and a halo of golden curls framing her delicate face. Kora wasn't afraid of anyone or anything—not even Mr. Threllkeld, the burly principal. Without the slightest abashment she could confront even the town mayor and demand *Personality:* that he schedule the spring prom in the civic auditorium. Strangers didn't exist for Kora. She greeted them as she would an old acquaintance, without fear or reticence. On the other hand, Shery was painfully shy. To speak up in class was a nightmare for her, as could be seen from her high blush and whispered answers. She hated meeting new people and would always wait for Kora to take over the conversation. If someone she hardly knew attempted a conversation with her, she would begin to stammer, *Physical* look confused, and eventually excuse herself and hurriedly leave. Then, *strength:* too, Kora was physically stronger than Shery. The boys often asked her to practice basketball or baseball with them because she could hit a basket and swing a bat as well as any other tenth-grader. Unlike Kora, Shery feared any physical adventure. When Kora playfully threw her a basketball, Shery would cover her face with her hands and dodge it. When coaxed to go swimming, skating or climbing, Shery would say "I'm too chicken." Kora and Shery attracted each other as opposites, not as kindred spirits.

3. DECIDE ON THE ORGANIZATION OF YOUR COMPARISON.   Basically, there are two ways to organize a comparison assignment—vertically or horizontally. For example, you intend to compare John, who is rich, with Mark, who is poor, on the basis of their attitude toward money. Organized *vertically*, the elements of your outline would look like this:

I. John has the rich boy's contempt for money.
   a. He expects it to be there when he needs it.
   b. He never hesitates over a purchase.
   c. He buys what he wants.

II. Mark has the poor boy's reverence for money.
    a. He knows it is hard to come by.
    b. He hesitates and lingers over a purchase.
    c. He buys what he can afford.

Vertical organization requires that you first write about John on points a, b, and c, and then contrast Mark with John on these same points, as in this example:

Having always lived a life of luxury and comfort, John has a rich boy's contempt for money. He expects it to be there when he needs it; he sees it as having only a utility value, enabling him to do what he likes. He never lingers or hesitates over a purchase. For him, the object of shopping is not to agonize over the amount to be spent, but simply to find the best, most suitable, and most expeditious object that will satisfy all his wants. He has a high regard for quality, and a low regard for expense. He buys what suits him best, whether it is the most or least expensive item in the store.

Mark, on the other hand, has the poor boy's reverence and respect for money. It was not always there when he needed it; what little money he has acquired has cost him in labor, sweat, and drudgery. He spends an interminable amount of time on shopping trips, endlessly comparing prices, quality, and value and listening patiently to sales spiels and technical explanations. For him, the aim of shopping is to acquire the most for the least. He regards expense on a par with quality and usually ends up buying not his first choice nor even his second, but sometimes his third, or fourth, or even fifth, the acquisition always being dictated by his budget and seldom by quality.

Here is an outline of this same contrast organized *horizontally:*

John has contempt for money; Mark has reverence for money.

John buys without hesitation; Mark hesitates and compares prices.

John buys what he wants; Mark buys what he can afford.

Here is the horizontally organized written contrast:

Having lived a life of luxury and comfort, John has the rich boy's contempt for money. Mark, on the other hand, has the poor boy's reverence for it. John expects money to be there when he needs it and sees it as having a utility value, enabling him to do as he pleases. Mark, however, knows that money is not always there when he needs it, and that what little money he has acquired has cost him in labor, sweat, and drudgery. A pronounced difference shows up in their behavior on shopping trips. John never lingers or hesitates over a purchase; he shops for what he wants, buying always the most suitable, the most expeditious object which will satisfy all his wants. It is just the opposite with Mark. For him, shopping means acquiring the most for the least. He must choose his purchases not by quality alone, but also by expense. Frequently he ends up buying not his first choice, or even his second or third, but his fourth or fifth choice, in every case the acquisition being dictated by budget rather than by quality. John buys the best if it suits him; Mark, to the contrary, buys what he can afford.

4. USE INDICATORS TO SHOW COMPARISON/CONTRAST. A good comparison should be sprinkled with *indicators* that signal similarities and differences. For example:

Similarity	*Contrast*
likewise	but
the same as	yet
too/also	however
similarly	nevertheless
in like manner	on the contrary
	contrary to
	unlike
	the opposite of

The most common student error in comparison/contrast essays is to leave out the indicators and not complete the comparison. Consider the following:

Benjamin Franklin was a more positive American than was Jonathan Edwards. For example, he had a much more developed sense of humor, as revealed in the numerous funny anecdotes in his autobiography. He could laugh at his own mistakes and at the stupidity of the world in general. Furthermore, he was much more successful in his work, becoming famous all over the world as an inventor, writer, and statesman. Then too, Franklin was more optimistic about America. His writing reflects confidence and security in America's future; they indicate an innate pride in America's potential as well as its accomplishments.

As you can see, the above comparison is hopelessly lopsided. Claiming to draw a contrast between Benjamin Franklin and Jonathan Edwards, the writer tells us only about Franklin, leaving us to guess about Edwards. Perhaps the student simply forgot that he was comparing two figures and that he was therefore obliged to give each equal treatment. However, one way a student may forestall this sort of lapse is to mechanically and consciously sprinkle the text with indicators that force him to complete the comparison with equal treatment to all parties:

Benjamin Franklin was a more positive American than was Jonathan Edwards. First, Franklin had a developed sense of humor. He could laugh, as revealed in the numerous funny anecdotes of his autobiography. *In contrast,* the diaries of Jonathan Edwards are filled with passages in which he weeps and moans over his own sinful condition and the general wickedness of the world. Second, Benjamin Franklin was successful in everything he attempted, achieving worldwide fame as an inventor, writer, and statesman. *On the other hand,* Jonathan Edwards was doubted by most thinkers and despised by his own congregation; he ended his ministry as an outcast in the wilderness, helping the Indians. Third, Franklin was a much more optimistic man than was Jonathan Edwards. His writings show great confidence and security in America's future; they indicate an innate pride in America's potential as well as its accomplishments. *Unlike* Franklin, Edwards was burdened by a deep-seated pessimism. His sermons emphasize man's utter depravity and vileness. In his view, all men except the few elect were despicable worms and the world was damned to everlasting hell.

The second version provides a clearer contrast than the first version because the contrast indicators remind the writer to treat both sides equally.

This article by the late classicist Gilbert Highet describes a meeting between two sharply contrasting personalities of history—Alexander the Great and Diogenes. This selection originally appeared in *Horizon,* the first in a series entitled Great Confrontations.

Professional Model

Diogenes and Alexander
The Dog Has His Day
Gilbert Highet

1   Lying on the bare earth, shoeless, bearded, half-naked, he looked like a beggar or a lunatic. He was one, but not the other. He had opened his eyes with the sun at dawn, scratched, done his business like a dog at the roadside, washed at the public fountain, begged a piece of breakfast bread and a few olives, eaten them squatting on the ground, and washed them down with a few handfuls of water scooped from the spring. (Long ago he had owned a rough wooden cup, but he threw it away when he saw a boy drinking out of his hollowed hands.) Having no work to go to and no family to provide for, he was free. As the market place filled up with shoppers and merchants and gossipers and sharpers and slaves and foreigners, he had strolled through it for an hour or two. Everybody knew him, or knew of him. They would throw sharp questions at him and get sharper answers. Sometimes they threw jeers, and got jibes; sometimes bits of food, and got scant thanks; sometimes a mischievous pebble, and got a shower of stones and abuse. They were not quite sure whether he was mad or not. He knew they were mad, all mad, each in a different way; they amused him. Now he was back at his home.

2   It was not a house, not even a squatter's hut. He thought everybody lived far too elaborately, expensively, anxiously. What good is a house? No one needs privacy: natural acts are not shameful; we all do the same things, and need not hide them. No one needs beds and chairs and such furniture: the animals live healthy lives and sleep on the ground. All we require, since nature did not dress us properly, is one garment to

keep us warm, and some shelter from rain and wind. So he had one blanket—to dress him in the daytime and cover him at night—and he slept in a cask. His name was Diogenes. He was the founder of the creed called Cynicism (the word means "doggishness"); he spent much of his life in the rich, lazy, corrupt Greek city of Corinth, mocking and satirizing its people, and occasionally converting one of them.

3   His home was not a barrel made of wood: too expensive. It was a storage jar made of earthenware, something like a modern fuel tank—no doubt discarded because a break had made it useless. He was not the first to inhabit such a thing: the refugees driven into Athens by the Spartan invasion had been forced to sleep in casks. But he was the first who ever did so by choice, out of principle.

4   Diogenes was not a degenerate or a maniac. He was a philosopher who wrote plays and poems and essays expounding his doctrine; he talked to those who cared to listen; he had pupils who admired him. But he taught chiefly by example. All should live naturally, he said, for what is natural is normal and cannot possibly be evil or shameful. Live without conventions, which are artificial and false; escape complexities and superfluities and extravagances: only so can you live a free life. The rich man believes he possesses his big house with its many rooms and its elaborate furniture, his pictures and expensive clothes, his horses and his servants and his bank accounts. He does not. He depends on them, he worries about them, he spends most of his life's energy looking after them; the thought of losing them makes him sick with anxiety. They possess him. He is their slave. In order to procure a quantity of false, perishable goods he has sold the only true, lasting good, his own independence.

5   There have been many men who grew tired of human society with its complications, and went away to live simply—on a small farm, in a quiet village, in a hermit's cave, or in the darkness of anonymity. Not so Diogenes. He was not a recluse, or a stylite, or a beatnik. He was a missionary. His life's aim was clear to him: it was "to restamp the currency." (He and his father had once been convicted for counterfeiting, long before he turned to philosophy, and this phrase was Diogenes' bold, unembarrassed joke on the subject.) To restamp the currency: to take the clean metal of human life, to erase the old false conventional markings, and to imprint it with its true values.

6   The other great philosophers of the fourth century before Christ taught mainly their own private pupils. In the shady groves and cool sanctuaries of the Academy, Plato discoursed to a chosen few on the unreality of this contingent existence. Aristotle, among the books and instruments and specimens and archives and research-workers of his Lyceum, pursued investigations and gave lectures that were rightly named *esoteric,* "for those within the walls." But for Diogenes, laboratory and specimens and lecture halls and pupils were all to be found in a crowd of ordinary people. Therefore he chose to live in Athens or in the rich city of Corinth, where travelers from all over the Mediterranean world constantly came and went. And, by design, he publicly behaved in such ways as to show people what real life was. He would constantly take up their spiritual coin, ring it on a stone, and laugh at its false superscription.

7   He thought most people were only half-alive, most men only half-men. At bright noonday he walked through the market place carrying a lighted lamp and inspecting the face of everyone he met. They asked him why. Diogenes answered, "I am trying to find a *man.*"

8   To a gentleman whose servant was putting on his shoes for him, Diogenes said, "You won't be really happy until he wipes your nose for you: that will come after you lose the use of your hands."

9   Once there was a war scare so serious that it stirred even the lazy, profit-happy Corinthians. They began to drill, clean their weapons, and rebuild their neglected

fortifications. Diogenes took his old cask and began to roll it up and down, back and forward. "When you are all so busy," he said, "I felt I ought to do *something*!"

10   And so he lived—like a dog, some said, because he cared nothing for privacy and other human conventions, and because he showed his teeth and barked at those whom he disliked. Now he was lying in the sunlight, as contented as a dog on the warm ground, happier (he himself used to boast) than the Shah of Persia. Although he knew he was going to have an important visitor, he would not move.

11   The little square began to fill with people. Page boys elegantly dressed, spearmen speaking a rough foreign dialect, discreet secretaries, hard-browed officers, suave diplomats, they all gradually formed a circle centered on Diogenes. He looked them over, as a sober man looks at a crowd of tottering drunks, and shook his head. He knew who they were. They were the attendants of the conqueror of Greece, the servants of Alexander, the Macedonian king, who was visiting his newly subdued realm.

12   Only twenty, Alexander was far older and wiser than his years. Like all Macedonians he loved drinking, but he could usually handle it; and toward women he was nobly restrained and chivalrous. Like all Macedonians he loved fighting; he was a magnificent commander, but he was not merely a military automaton. He could think. At thirteen he had become a pupil of the greatest mind in Greece, Aristotle. No exact record of his schooling survives. It is clear, though, that Aristotle took the passionate, half-barbarous boy and gave him the best of Greek culture. He taught Alexander poetry; the young prince slept with the *Iliad* under his pillow and longed to emulate Achilles, who brought the mighty power of Asia to ruin. He taught him philosophy, in particular the shapes and uses of political power: a few years later Alexander was to create a supranational empire that was not merely a power system but a vehicle for the exchange of Greek and Middle Eastern cultures.

13   Aristotle taught him the principles of scientific research: during his invasion of the Persian domains Alexander took with him a large corps of scientists, and shipped hundreds of zoological specimens back to Greece for study. Indeed, it was from Aristotle that Alexander learned to seek out everything strange which might be instructive. Jugglers and stunt artists and virtuosos of the absurd he dismissed with a shrug; but on reaching India he was to spend hours discussing the problems of life and death with naked Hindu mystics, and later to see one demonstrate Yoga self-command by burning himself impassively to death.

14   Now, Alexander was in Corinth to take command of the League of Greek States which, after conquering them, his father Philip had created as a disguise for the New Macedonian Order. He was welcomed and honored and flattered. He was the man of the hour, of the century: he was unanimously appointed commander-in-chief of a new expedition against old, rich, corrupt Asia. Nearly everyone crowded to Corinth in order to congratulate him, to seek employment with him, even simply to see him: soldiers and statesmen, artists and merchants, poets and philosophers. He received their compliments graciously. Only Diogenes, although he lived in Corinth, did not visit the new monarch. With that generosity which Aristotle had taught him was a quality of the truly magnanimous man, Alexander determined to call upon Diogenes. Surely Dio-genes, the God-born, would acknowledge the conqueror's power by some gift of hoarded wisdom.

15   With his handsome face, his fiery glance, his strong supple body, his purple and gold cloak, and his air of destiny, he moved through the parting crowd, toward the Dog's kennel. When a king approaches, all rise in respect. Diogenes did not rise, he merely sat up on one elbow. When a monarch enters a precinct, all greet him with a bow or an acclamation. Diogenes said nothing.

16   There was a silence. Some years later Alexander speared his best friend to the wall,

for objecting to the exaggerated honors paid to His Majesty; but now he was still young and civil. He spoke first, with a kindly greeting. Looking at the poor broken cask, the single ragged garment, and the rough figure lying on the ground, he said, "Is there anything I can do for you, Diogenes?"

17 "Yes," said the Dog. "Stand to one side. You're blocking the sunlight."

18 There was silence, not the ominous silence preceding a burst of fury, but a hush of amazement. Slowly, Alexander turned away. A titter broke out from the elegant Greeks, who were already beginning to make jokes about the Cur that looked at the King. The Macedonian officers, after deciding that Diogenes was not worth the trouble of kicking, were starting to guffaw and nudge one another. Alexander was still silent. To those nearest him he said quietly, "If I were not Alexander, I should be Diogenes." They took it as a paradox, designed to close the awkward little scene with a polite curtain line. But Alexander meant it. He understood Cynicism as the others could not. Later he took one of Diogenes' pupils with him to India as a philosophical interpreter (it was he who spoke to the naked *saddhus*). He was what Diogenes called himself, a *cosmopolites,* "citizen of the world." Like Diogenes, he admired the heroic figure of Hercules, the mighty conqueror who labors to help mankind while all others toil and sweat only for themselves. He knew that of all men then alive in the world only Alexander the conqueror and Diogenes the beggar were truly free.

2,078 words

Vocabulary

squatter (2)	superfluities (4)	fortifications (9)
Cynicism (2)	recluse (5)	barbarous (12)
satirizing (2)	stylite (5)	supranational (12)
degenerate (4)	Lyceum (6)	mystics (13)
maniac (4)	superscription (6)	ominous (18)

Questions

1. What bases govern Highet's comparison of Diogenes and Alexander?
2. How does Highet present his comparison—vertically or horizontally?
3. In what paragraph does Highet first shift from one character to another? How is the shift accomplished?
4. What other contrast is drawn besides the contrast between Diogenes and Alexander? Point to specific passages.
5. What is the analogy used in paragraph 10?
6. What are some characteristics that Diogenes and Alexander share?
7. What are the most outstanding contrasts between the old philosopher and the young emperor?

In this essay, a student contrasts her two best friends on three points: looks, personality, and attitude toward life. The contrast is vertically organized. Its clarity is its chief strength. An occasional weakness is the writer's fondness for extravagant images and diction.

Two Friends: A Study in Contrasts
Catherine Wells

My two closest friends are as different as a Cape Cod cottage and a Byzantine mosque. Pari Ahmadi is a flamboyant dancer from Bandar, Iran, whereas Margie Warner is an unobtrusive college sophomore from Salt Lake City, Utah. The fact that both of these girls are my friends proves that my tastes are polarized. On one hand, I am drawn to the strangely exotic, but on the other hand, I need serene stability. Pari and Margie fill both of these needs. Where they differ most is in looks, personality, and attitude toward life. Let me explain.

Pari is stunning, almost embarrassingly so because everywhere we go, men turn around and give her that wow-did-you-see-that? look. Her silky black hair hangs clear down to her waist and matches her round black snappy eyes. Everything about Pari is dark and sultry. Her skin is a deep bronze with two peach spots that blend into her cheeks, giving them a look of painted velvet. Pari wears heavy makeup, but somehow on her this bit of theatricality looks right. It gives her added boldness, extra electricity. When I look at Pari's profile, I always imagine that Cleopatra looked just like her, straight-nosed and imperious. Pari wears tight-fitting dresses and pants; nothing else would look right on her voluptuous shape. She would look silly and contrived in a fluffy little flowered piqué or a sternly tailored jumpsuit. I can imagine Pari looking only one way—enticingly erotic.

Margie's looks are the exact opposite of Pari's. Whereas Pari's appearance clamors for attention, Margie's automatically fades into the background. Her looks are refined but unassuming. Nothing about her stands out. She is simply a typical medium-haired, medium-skinned, medium-sized American girl. Only her eyes hint at remarkable inner qualities. They are a deep grey and when you look into them, they seem to contain secrets worth probing. Margie has a tranquility about her that is enviable. She is not beautiful; she is not sensual; but she is serene.

If Pari and Margie differ in looks, they differ even more in personality. One might say that Pari is a stormy sky flashing with lightning whereas Margie is a soft summer breeze. Whenever I meet Pari, she takes me by storm and hurls laughter, banter, and information at me. She is violent in her tastes, either loving ecstatically or hating bitterly. For instance, in her view all classical music is a deadly bore, whereas all jazz is magically entertaining. Every acquaintance we share is either canonized or damned; there are no medians or middle levels. When we go to a movie together, it is not unusual for Pari to take turns hitting me with suspense, clinging to me in despair, or weeping audibly if the ending is sad. Her own love affairs reflect her undulant personality. Time and again I have heard her hurling angry epithets at her latest lover only to end curled up on a couch next to him, purring like a Siamese cat. Pari's personality is as exotic as her looks.

Margie is best described as quietly content. She may never soar as high with ecstasy as does Pari, but neither will she sink as low with despair. She reminds me of one of those Rembrandt portraits where the face reflects infinite harmony and balance. When I want excitement and titillation, I look for Pari, but when I want a quiet, sensible discussion, I go to Margie. Her influence on me is calming without being prissy. Her wry sense of humor, in fact, often sends me into gales of laughter because she is able to see the incongruity and hypocrisy in so much of the nonsense in our society today. "Come on, Cathy," she will gently scold when I get hostile toward my mother's nagging, "you know your mother wants only your best. Give her a break." So, she sets my life in proper perspective.

Where Pari and Margie differ most is in their philosophies of life. Pari worries me deeply because beyond her electric involvement in life is a gnawing feeling of futility. Twice already in her twenty-two years she has tried to commit suicide. These were not dramatic acts just to get attention, but acts of complete hopelessness. Despite her exotic beauty that holds many men hypnotized, Pari feels unloved, unwanted, and undesirable. When she is depressed, she hides by herself and reads Sylvia Plath or Anne Sexton. Nothing I or any of her friends say will cheer her up. The fact is that Pari has a sad, sick strain in her attitude toward life and unless she can overcome it, she will not survive to a satisfied old age. It hurts me to see Pari when she's down because her vulnerability reminds me of a magnificent bird whose wings have been clipped so that she can no longer fly or preen herself.

Margie's philosophy of life is much more stable than Pari's because it is based on a firm religious belief. Her Mormon background has led her to see life as purposeful and ultimately fulfilling when one does his duty. Margie accepts good times as well as bad times with equanimity. Often I envy her ability to face aggravations and sorrows without breaking down. Not that she is coldly stoical—no, she has plenty of emotions. But her emotions are controlled by her belief that a greater power than she is in charge of the universe. This supplies her with limitless confidence.

Pari and Margie are both my dearest friends. I love Pari because she is fascinating and alive, but I love Margie because she is strong and reliable.

In the essay below, the author describes an aquarium as a crime-ridden neighborhood where fiendish murderers lie in ambush, waiting for innocent victims.

Alternate Reading

Robbery in the Aquarium
Konrad Z. Lorenz

1   There are some terrible robbers in the pond world, and, in our aquarium, we may witness all the cruelties of an embittered struggle for existence enacted before our very eyes. If you have introduced to your aquarium a mixed catch, you will soon be able to see an example of these conflicts, for, amongst the new arrivals, there will probably be a larva of the waterbeetle Dytiscus. Considering their relative size, the voracity and cunning with which these animals destroy their prey eclipse the methods of even such notorious robbers as tigers, lions, wolves, or killer whales. These are all as lambs compared with the Dytiscus larva.

2   It is a slim, streamlined insect, rather more than two inches long. Its six legs are equipped with stout fringes of bristles which form broad oar-like blades that propel the animal with quick and sure movements through the water. The wide, flat head bears an enormous, pincer-shaped pair of jaws which are hollow and serve not only as syringes for injecting poison, but also as orifices of ingestion. The animal lies in ambush on some

157

waterplant; suddenly it shoots at lightning speed towards its prey, darts underneath it, then quickly jerks up its head and grabs the victim in its jaws. "Prey," for these creatures, is all that moves or that smells of "animal" in any way. It has often happened to me that, while standing quietly in the water of a pond, I have been "eaten" by a Dytiscus larva. Even for man, an injection of the poisonous digestive juice of this insect is extremely painful.

3   These beetle larvae are among the few animals which digest "out of doors." The glandular secretion that they inject, through their hollow forceps, into their prey, dissolves the entire inside of the latter into a liquid soup which is then sucked in through the same channel by the attacker. Even large victims, such as fat tadpoles or dragonfly larvae, which have been bitten by a Dytiscus larva, stiffen after a few defensive movements, and their inside, which, as in most water animals, is more or less transparent, becomes opaque as though fixed by formalin. The animal swells up first, then gradually shrinks to a limp bundle of skin which hangs from the deadly jaws, and is finally allowed to drop. In the confined spaces of an aquarium, a few large Dytiscus larvae will, within a few days, eat all living things over about a quarter of an inch long. What happens then? They will eat each other, if they have not already done so; this depends less on who is bigger and stronger than upon who succeeds in seizing the other first. I have often seen two nearly equal sized Dytiscus larvae each seize the other simultaneously and both die a quick death by inner dissolution. There are very few animals which, even when threatened with starvation, will attack an equal sized animal of their own species with the intention of devouring it. I only know this to be definitely true of rats and a few related rodents; that wolves do the same thing, I am much inclined to doubt, on the strength of some observations of which I shall speak later. But Dytiscus larvae devour animals of their own breed and size, even when other nourishment is at hand, and that is done, as far as I know, by no other animal.

4   A somewhat less brutal but more elegant beast of prey is the larva of the great dragonfly Aeschna. The mature insect is a true king of the air, a veritable falcon among insects, for it catches its prey when on the wing. If you shake your pond catch into a wash basin, in order to remove the worst miscreants, you will possibly find, besides Dytiscus larvae, some other streamlined insects whose remarkable method of locomotion at once attracts the attention. These slender torpedoes which are usually marked with a decorative pattern of yellow and green, shoot forward in rapid jerks, their legs pressed close to their sides. It is at first something of an enigma how they move at all. But if you observe them separately, in a shallow dish, you will see that these larvae are jet propelled. From the tip of their abdomen there squirts forth a powerful little column of water which drives the animal speedily forward. The end portion of their intestine forms a hollow bladder which is richly lined with tracheal gills and serves at the same time the purposes of respiration and of locomotion.

5   Aeschna larvae do not hunt swimming but lie in ambush: when an object of prey comes within eye range they fix it with their gaze, turn their head and body very slowly in its direction and follow all its movements attentively. This marking down of the prey can only be observed in very few other non-vertebrate animals. In contrast to the larvae of Dytiscus, those of Aeschna can see even very slow movements, such as the crawling of snails which therefore very often fall a prey to them. Slowly, very slowly, step by step, the Aeschna larva stalks its prey: it is still an inch or two away when suddenly—what was that?—the victim is struggling between the cruel jaws. Without taking a slow-motion picture of this procedure, one could only see that something tongue-like flew out from the head of the larva to its prey and drew the latter instantly within reach of the attacker's jaws. Anyone who had ever seen a chameleon eating would at once be reminded of the flicking back and forth of its sticky tongue. The "boomerang" of the Aeschna is, however,

no tongue but the metamorphosed "underlip" which consists of two movable joints with a pincer at their end.

6   The optical fixation of its prey alone makes the dragonfly larva appear strangely "intelligent" and this impression will be strengthened should some other peculiarities of its behaviour be observed. In contrast to the Dytiscus larva which will snap blindly at anything, the dragonfly larva leaves animals above a certain size severely alone, even if it has been starving for weeks. I have kept Aeschna larvae for months in a basin with fish, and have never seen them attack or damage one larger than themselves. It is a remarkable fact that the larvae will never grab at a prey which has been caught by a member of their own species and which is now moving slowly backwards and forwards between the masticating jaws; on the other hand they will at once take a piece of fresh meat moved in a like manner on the end of a glass feeding rod in front of their eyes. In my large American sun-porch aquarium I always had a few Aeschna larvae growing up: their development takes long, more than a year. Then, on a beautiful summer's day, comes the great moment; the larva climbs slowly up the stem of a plant and out of the water. There it sits for a long time and then, as in every moulting process, the outer skin on the back part of the thoracic segments bursts open and the beautiful, perfect insect unwinds itself slowly from the larval skin. After this, several hours expire before the wings have reached their full size and consistency, and this is attained by a wonderful process whereby a rapidly solidifying liquid is pumped, under high pressure, into the fine branches of the wing veins. Then you open the window wide and wish your aquarium guest good luck and *bon voyage* in its insect life.

1,430 words

Vocabulary

larva (1)	forceps (3)	tracheal (4)
voracity (1)	formalin (3)	metamorphosed (5)
pincer (2)	dissolution (3)	masticating (6)
orifices (2)	miscreants (4)	thoracic (6)
ingestion (2)		

Questions

1. The beetle larva and the dragonfly larva, both described in this essay, are alike in some ways but unlike in others. What characteristics do they share and how do they differ?
2. Throughout the essay, the beetle larva and the dragonfly larva seem more like cruel humans than beasts of prey. Why is this so?
3. The contrast is vertical, dealing first with the beetle and then with the dragonfly. Where does the contrast begin? What transitional words signal the contrast?
4. What act makes the beetle larva seem to have even less of a conscience than the dragonfly larva?
5. Which part of the description makes the dragonfly appear more attractive looking than the beetle?
6. The author states that in terms of voracity and cunning, beetle larvae and dragonfly larvae eclipse even such notorious robbers as tigers, lions, wolves, or killer whales. What is the most vicious act of biological nature you have ever witnessed? What animals were involved? Describe in detail.

In this short, amusing article, the economist John Kenneth Galbraith discovers humorous similarities between the politician and the skier.

Alternate Reading

The Politics of Skiing
John Kenneth Galbraith

1   Early this year I was writing and skiing in Switzerland. Back home, people were electioneering—New Hampshire, Florida, looking forward to Wisconsin, Nebraska. The many who were then seeking office were reaching out to persuade the few who were not.

2   My friends were calling to ask how I could bear to be absent. Senator Kennedy, Senator Tunney, Pierre Salinger stopped by for a few brief runs down the slopes or, in the case of Salinger, a quick glance in that direction. I thought them a bit reproachful. Clearly I was neglecting my civic duty. Skiing, yes, but not in an election year.

3   Eventually I yielded and came back to campaign. I slightly doubt that in an election speech I have ever persuaded anyone who wasn't previously persuaded or who wouldn't have come around anyway. People have often informed me, following one of my more impassioned efforts, and often with some vehemence, that I had confirmed them in their previous view. But I spoke and voted and even voted for myself, for I was a candidate for the Democratic delegation in Massachusetts.

4   As the year has passed and the election has approached, I've wondered about my decision. Maybe the best way to learn about politics is to go skiing. The two are alike in all particulars, but in skiing things are clearer on the whole.

5   Both politics and skiing are afflicted by professionals—the professional politician and the expert skier. The beginning of wisdom about both is to know that everything they tell you about their profession is wrong.

6   Given a choice between a smooth, straight path to his goal and a difficult and devious way of getting what he wants, the politician never hesitates. He instinctively embraces the difficult and devious.

7   In skiing, none but an idiot would choose a tortuous, steep and bumpy trail in preference to a flat slope. But the professional does and, like the politician, he thinks it is better. There is merit, he believes, in making things hard for himself.

8   In both politics and skiing, form and style count for much, performance for almost nothing. The professional politician delights in rhetoric, rejoices in the deathless phrase. What his oratory accomplishes is something else. More often than not it is ignored.

9   The professional skier tells you to keep your legs close together and lean forward and downhill. Any lunk knows that for getting safely to the bottom it's better to have your legs far apart to protect your balance. And elementary instinct tells you to keep your uphill shoulder right against the slope to protect your body from the forces of gravity. All skiing is a triumph of awkwardness over the law of gravity.

10   Both skiers and politicians attract an especially colorful train of nonfunctional hangers-on. Gstaad, where I go in the winter, rejoices each February in a brilliant—and, I believe, expanding—constellation of expensive tarts, minor and major deadbeats, major tax evaders, cosmopolitan rumpots, backgammon players, refugees from alimony, members of encounter groups, one devotee of statutory rape, one superannuated spy, and one man who is variously suspected of being an informer for the IRS and a member of the CIA.

11   None ski. Any candidate for public office, unless he is of uniquely austere demeanor and surpassing diligence, can count on attracting a similar, although possibly less interesting, range of talent.

12   Both politicians and skiers divide naturally as between liberals and conservatives. This is true for amateurs and professionals alike. The division needs no comment in the case of pols. But no less in skiing you have men (I think of myself as one) who ski circumspectly with a view to the enjoyment of the masses, who stop to assist the fallen, who fill in the cavities when they themselves take a fall as they often do, who sacrifice performance to the social conscience of the true liberal.

13   And you have men who go barreling down the mountain, scattering the population in terror before them and (one assumes) muttering phrases about the survival of the fittest and the public be damned. Since concentration is on self, the performance, though socially depraved, is technically superior. I think of my frequent skiing companion, Mr. William F. Buckley, Jr.

14   There is another resemblance between skiing and politics that has nothing to do with ideology. I mentioned at the outset that I was skiing last winter. I did so until one bright Sunday when I went out in the company of another professor of mature years. It was a day of brilliant sun; the snow was good except for occasional bare patches. Precisely when I was least expecting it—when my feeling of confidence and my sense of mastery were greatest—I fell on a rock and broke my behind. Exactly the same happens in politics. And to a lot of men in an election year.

804 words

Vocabulary

reproachful (2)   austere (11)
vehemence (3)   circumspectly (12)
tortuous (7)   depraved (13)
superannuated (10)

Questions

1. In which paragraph does the writer make it clear that he intends to compare skiing with politics? What expression of comparison does he use?
2. What basis of comparison does the author use in paragraphs 5 through 7?
3. In what aspect of form and style does the professional politician rejoice?
4. How is the comparison structured in paragraphs 8 and 9? Is it organized vertically? Horizontally?
5. Many of the paragraphs are short and crisp. What kind of paragraphs are these?
6. Who are the liberals of skiing? How does the author characterize them? According to the author, how do these skiers behave on the slopes?
7. Who are the conservatives of skiing?
8. Why is the performance of the conservative skier technically superior?
9. What final resemblance between skiers and politicians does the author propose?

C. Additional Writing Assignments

1. Compare the advantages of being old with the advantages of being young.
2. Develop an essay based on the following controlling idea: "Ignorance is different from stupidity."
3. Write an essay contrasting envy with jealousy.
4. After establishing the bases of your comparison, write an essay comparing a compact car with a large car, indicating the advantages of one over the other.
5. Compare or contrast today's society with that of your grandparents', using intimacy, individuality, and independence as your bases.
6. Write an essay comparing a teacher you find boring and one you think is interesting and stimulating.
7. From your travels in the United States and abroad, pick two cities or towns that are totally different from each another. Develop an essay describing these differences.
8. From your general knowledge of U.S. history, compare the eighteenth and twentieth centuries on three bases—for example, hygiene, education, women's rights—supplying examples that stress their differences.
9. Write an essay delineating the differences between a romantic and a realistic movie or novel. Supply examples of each.
10. What do good statesmen and good ship captains have in common? Write an essay comparing the two.

10

Process

*First of all, keep your dream journal in a notebook
small enough to carry with you all the time.*

A. Reading for Ideas

As you read through the story "How Mr. Hogan Robbed a Bank," you might
admire the meticulousness of Mr. Hogan's method even if you are repelled by his
ethics. Ask yourself whether the means ever justifies an end. In other words, if the
method is right, is the purpose also right? Also, think of some task you would like
to accomplish, and see if you can put together similar meticulous, easy-to-follow
directions for this task.

How Mr. Hogan Robbed a Bank
John Steinbeck

1   On Saturday before Labor Day, 1955, at 9:04½ A.M., Mr. Hogan robbed a bank. He
was forty-two years old, married, and the father of a boy and a girl, named John and
Joan, twelve and thirteen respectively. Mrs. Hogan's name was Joan and Mr. Hogan's
name was John, but since they called themselves Papa and Mama that left their names
free for the children, who were considered very smart for their ages, each having jumped
a grade in school. The Hogans lived at 215 East Maple Street, in a brown-shingle house
with white trim—there are two. 215 is the one across from the street light and it is the one
with the big tree in the yard, either oak or elm—the biggest tree in the whole street,
maybe in the whole town.

2   John and Joan were in bed at the time of the robbery, for it was Saturday. At 9:10 A.M.,
Mrs. Hogan was making the cup of tea she always had. Mr. Hogan went to work early.
Mrs. Hogan drank her tea slowly, scalding hot, and read her fortune in the tea leaves.
There was a cloud and a five-pointed star with two short points in the bottom of the cup,
but that was at 9:12 and the robbery was all over by then.

3   The way Mr. Hogan went about robbing the bank was very interesting. He gave it a
great deal of thought and had for a long time, but he did not discuss it with anyone. He
just read his newspaper and kept his own counsel. But he worked it out to his own
satisfaction that people went to too much trouble robbing banks and that got them in a
mess. The simpler the better, he always thought. People went in for too much hullabaloo

and hanky-panky. If you didn't do that, if you left hanky-panky out, robbing a bank would be a relatively sound venture—barring accidents, of course, of an improbable kind, but then they could happen to a man crossing the street or anything. Since Mr. Hogan's method worked fine, it proved that his thinking was sound. He often considered writing a little booklet on his technique when the how-to rage was running so high. He figured out the first sentence, which went: "To successfully rob a bank, forget all about hanky-panky."

4   Mr. Hogan was not just a clerk at Fettucci's grocery store. He was more like the manager. Mr. Hogan was in charge, even hired and fired the boy who delivered groceries after school. He even put in orders with the salesmen, sometimes when Mr. Fettucci was right in the store too, maybe talking to a customer. "You do it, John," he would say and he would nod at the customer, "John knows the ropes. Been with me—how long you been with me, John?"

5   "Sixteen years."

6   "Sixteen years. Knows the business as good as me. John, why he even banks the money."

7   And so he did. Whenever he had a moment, Mr. Hogan went into the storeroom on the alley, took off his apron, put on his necktie and coat, and went back through the store to the cash register. The checks and bills would be ready for him inside the bankbook with a rubber band around it. Then he went next door and stood at the teller's window and handed the checks and bankbook through to Mr. Cup and passed the time of day with him too. Then, when the bankbook was handed back, he checked the entry, put the rubber band around it, and walked next door to Fettucci's grocery and put the bankbook in the cash register, continued on to the storeroom, removed his coat and tie, put on his apron, and went back into the store ready for business. If there was no line at the teller's window, the whole thing didn't take more than five minutes, even passing the time of day.

8   Mr. Hogan was a man who noticed things, and when it came to robbing the bank, this trait stood him in good stead. He had noticed, for instance, where the big bills were kept right in the drawer under the counter and he had noticed also what days there were likely to be more than other days. Thursday was payday at the American Can Company's local plant, for instance, so there would be more then. Some Fridays people drew more money to tide them over the weekend. But it was even Steven, maybe not a thousand dollars difference, between Thursdays and Fridays and Saturday mornings. Saturdays were not terribly good because people didn't come to get money that early in the morning, and the bank closed at noon. But he thought it over and came to the conclusion that the Saturday before a long weekend in the summer would be the best of all. People going on trips, vacations, people with relatives visiting, and the bank closed Monday. He thought it out and looked, and sure enough the Saturday morning before Labor Day the cash drawer had twice as much money in it—he saw it when Mr. Cup pulled out the drawer.

9   Mr. Hogan thought about it during all that year, not all the time, of course, but when he had some moments. It was a busy year too. That was the year John and Joan had the mumps and Mrs. Hogan got her teeth pulled and was fitted for a denture. That was the year when Mr. Hogan was Master of the Lodge, with all the time that takes. Larry Shield died that year—he was Mrs. Hogan's brother and was buried from the Hogan house at 215 East Maple. Larry was a bachelor and had a room in the Pine Tree House and he played pool nearly every night. He worked at the Silver Diner but that closed at nine and so Larry would go to Louie's and play pool for an hour. Therefore, it was a surprise when he left enough so that after funeral expenses there were twelve hundred dollars left. And even more surprising that he left a will in Mrs. Hogan's favor, but his double-barreled twelve-gauge shotgun he left to John Hogan, Jr. Mr. Hogan was

pleased, although he never hunted. He put the shotgun away in the back of the closet in the bathroom, where he kept his things, to keep it for young John. He didn't want children handling guns and he never bought any shells. It was some of that twelve hundred that got Mrs. Hogan her dentures. Also, she bought a bicycle for John and a doll buggy and walking-talking doll for Joan—a doll with three changes of dresses and a little suitcase, complete with play make-up. Mr. Hogan thought it might spoil the children, but it didn't seem to. They made just as good marks in school and John even got a job delivering papers. It was a very busy year. Both John and Joan wanted to enter the W. R. Hearst National "I Love America" Contest and Mr. Hogan thought it was almost too much, but they promised to do the work during their summer vacation, so he finally agreed.

II

10   During that year, no one noticed any difference in Mr. Hogan. It was true, he was thinking about robbing the bank, but he only thought about it in the evening when there was neither a Lodge meeting nor a movie they wanted to go to, so it did not become an obsession and people noticed no change in him.

11   He had studied everything so carefully that the approach of Labor Day did not catch him unprepared or nervous. It was hot that summer and the hot spells were longer than usual. Saturday was the end of two weeks heat without a break and people were irritated with it and anxious to get out of town, although the country was just as hot. They didn't think of that. The children were excited because the "I Love America" Essay Contest was due to be concluded and the winners announced, and the first prize was an all-expense-paid two days trip to Washington, D.C., with every fixing—hotel room, three meals a day, and side trips in a limousine—not only for the winner, but for an accompanying chaperone; visit to the White House—shake hands with the President—everything. Mr. Hogan thought they were getting their hopes too high and he said so.

12   "You've got to be prepared to lose," he told his children. "There're probably thousands and thousands entered. You get your hopes up and it might spoil the whole autumn. Now I don't want any long faces in this house after the contest is over."

13   "I was against it from the start," he told Mrs. Hogan. That was the morning she saw the Washington Monument in her teacup, but she didn't tell anybody about that except Ruth Tyler, Bob Tyler's wife. Ruthie brought over her cards and read them in the Hogan kitchen, but she didn't find a journey. She did tell Mrs. Hogan that the cards were often wrong. The cards had said Mrs. Winkle was going on a trip to Europe and the next week Mrs. Winkle got a fishbone in her throat and choked to death. Ruthie, just thinking out loud, wondered if there was any connection between the fishbone and the ocean voyage to Europe. "You've got to interpret them right." Ruthie did say she saw money coming to the Hogans.

14   "Oh, I got that already from poor Larry," Mrs. Hogan explained.

15   "I must have got the past and future cards mixed," said Ruthie. "You've got to interpret them right."

16   Saturday dawned a blaster. The early morning weather report on the radio said "Continued hot and humid, light scattered rain Sunday night and Monday." Mrs. Hogan said, "Wouldn't you know? Labor Day." And Mr. Hogan said, "I'm sure glad we didn't plan anything." He finished his egg and mopped the plate with his toast. Mrs. Hogan said, "Did I put coffee on the list?" He took the paper from his handkerchief pocket and consulted it. "Yes, coffee, it's here."

17   "I had a crazy idea I forgot to write it down," said Mrs. Hogan. "Ruth and I are going to Altar Guild this afternoon. It's at Mrs. Alfred Drake's. You know, they just came to town. I can't wait to see their furniture."

18   "They trade with us," said Mrs. Hogan. "Opened an account last week. Are the milk bottles ready?"

19   "On the porch."

20   Mr. Hogan looked at his watch just before he picked up the bottles and it was five minutes to eight. He was about to go down the stairs, when he turned and looked back through the opened door at Mrs. Hogan. She said, "Want something, Papa?"

21   "No," he said. "No," and he walked down the steps.

22   He went down to the corner and turned right on Spooner, and Spooner runs into Main Street in two blocks, and right across from where it runs in, there is Fettucci's and the bank around the corner and the alley beside the bank. Mr. Hogan picked up a handbill in front of Fettucci's and unlocked the door. He went through to the storeroom, opened the door to the alley, and looked out. A cat tried to force its way in, but Mr. Hogan blocked it with his foot and leg and closed the door. He took off his coat and put on his long apron, tied the strings in a bowknot behind his back. Then he got the broom from behind the counter and swept out behind the counters and scooped the sweepings into a dustpan; and, going through the storeroom, he opened the door to the alley. The cat had gone away. He emptied the dustpan into the garbage can and tapped it smartly to dislodge a piece of lettuce leaf. Then he went back to the store and worked for a while on the order sheet. Mrs. Clooney came in for a half a pound of bacon. She said it was hot and Mr. Hogan agreed. "Summers are getting hotter," he said.

23   "I think so myself," said Mrs. Clooney. "How's Mrs. standing up?"

24   "Just fine," said Mr. Hogan. "She's going to Altar Guild."

25   "So am I. I just can't wait to see their furniture," said Mrs. Clooney, and she went out.

III

26   Mr. Hogan put a five-pound hunk of bacon on the slicer and stripped off the pieces and laid them on wax paper and then he put the wax paper-covered squares in the cooler cabinet. At ten minutes to nine, Mr. Hogan went to a shelf. He pushed a spaghetti box aside and took down a cereal box, which he emptied in the little closet toilet. Then, with a banana knife, he cut out the Mickey Mouse mask that was on the back. The rest of the box he took to the toilet and tore up the cardboard and flushed it down. He went into the store then and yanked a piece of string loose and tied the ends through the side holes of the mask and then he looked at his watch—a large silver Hamilton with black hands. It was two minutes to nine.

27   Perhaps the next four minutes were his only time of nervousness at all. At one minute to nine, he took the broom and went out to sweep the sidewalk and he swept it very rapidly—was sweeping it, in fact, when Mr. Warner unlocked the bank door. He said good morning to Mr. Warner and a few seconds later the bank staff of four emerged from the coffee shop. Mr. Hogan saw them across the street and he waved at them and they waved back. He finished the sidewalk and went back in the store. He laid his watch on the little step of the cash register. He sighed very deeply, more like a deep breath than a sigh. He knew that Mr. Warner would have the safe open now and he would be carrying the cash trays to the teller's window. Mr. Hogan looked at the watch on the cash register step. Mr. Kenworthy paused in the store entrance, then shook his head vaguely and walked on and Mr. Hogan let out his breath gradually. His left hand went behind his back and pulled the bowknot on his apron, and then the black hand on his watch crept up on the four-minute mark and covered it.

28   Mr. Hogan opened the charge account drawer and took out the store pistol, a silver-colored Iver Johnson .38. He moved quickly to the storeroom, slipped off his apron, put on his coat, and stuck the revolver in his side pocket. The Mickey Mouse mask he shoved up under his coat where it didn't show. He opened the alley door and looked up

166

and down and stepped quickly out, leaving the door slightly ajar. It is sixty feet to where the alley enters Main Street, and there he paused and looked up and down and then he turned his head toward the center of the street as he passed the bank window. At the bank's swinging door, he took out the mask from under his coat and put it on. Mr. Warner was just entering his office and his back was to the door. The top of Will Cup's head was visible through the teller's grill.

29   Mr. Hogan moved quickly and quietly around the end of the counter and into the teller's cage. He had the revolver in his right hand now. When Will Cup turned his head and saw the revolver, he froze. Mr. Hogan slipped his toe under the trigger of the floor alarm and motioned Will Cup to the floor with the revolver and Will went down quick. Then Mr. Hogan opened the cash drawer and with two quick movements he piled the large bills from the tray together. He made a whipping motion to Will on the floor, to indicate that he should turn over and face the wall, and Will did. Then Mr. Hogan stepped back around the counter. At the door of the bank, he took off the mask, and as he passed the window he turned his head toward the middle of the street. He moved into the alley, walked quickly to the storeroom, and entered. The cat got in. It watched him from a pile of canned goods cartons. Mr. Hogan went to the toilet closet and tore up the mask and flushed it. He took off his coat and put on his apron. He looked out into the store and then moved to the cash register. The revolver went back into the charge account drawer. He punched No Sale and, lifting the top drawer, distributed the stolen money underneath the top tray and then pulled the tray forward and closed the register, and only then did he look at his watch and it was 9:07½.

30   He was trying to get the cat out of the storeroom when the commotion boiled out of the bank. He took his broom and went out on the sidewalk. He heard all about it and offered his opinion when it was asked for. He said he didn't think the fellow could get away—where could he get to? Still, with the holiday coming up—

31   It was an exciting day. Mr. Fettucci was as proud as though it were his bank. The sirens sounded around town for hours. Hundreds of holiday travelers had to stop at the roadblocks set up all around the edge of town and several sneaky-looking men had their cars searched.

32   Mrs. Hogan heard about it over the phone and she dressed earlier than she would have ordinarily and came to the store on her way to Altar Guild. She hoped Mr. Hogan would have seen or heard something new, but he hadn't. "I don't see how the fellow can get away," he said.

33   Mrs. Hogan was so excited, she forgot her own news. She only remembered when she got to Mrs. Drake's house, but she asked permission and phoned the store the first moment she could. 'I forgot to tell you. John's won honorable mention."

34   "What?"
       "In the 'I Love America' Contest."
       "What did he win?"
       "Honorable mention."
       "Fine. Fine—Anything come with it?"

35   "Why, he'll get his picture and his name all over the country. Radio too. Maybe even television. They've already asked for a photograph of him."

36   "Fine," said Mr. Hogan. "I hope it don't spoil him." He put up the receiver and said to Mr. Fettucci, "I guess we've got a celebrity in the family."

37   Fettucci stayed open until nine on Saturdays. Mr. Hogan ate a few snacks from cold cuts, but not much, because Mrs. Hogan always kept his supper warming.

38   It was 9:05 or :06, or :07, when he got back to the brown-shingle house at 215 East Maple. He went in through the front door and out to the kitchen where the family was waiting for him.

39   "Got to wash up," he said, and went up to the bathroom. He turned the key in the bathroom door and then he flushed the toilet and turned on the water in the basin and tub while he counted the money. Eight thousand three hundred and twenty dollars. From the top shelf of the storage closet in the bathroom, he took down the big leather case that held his Knight Templar's uniform. The plumed hat lay there on its form. The white ostrich feather was a little yellow and needed changing. Mr. Hogan lifted out the hat and pried the form up from the bottom of the case. He put the money in the form and then he thought again and removed two bills and shoved them in his side pocket. Then he put the form back over the money and laid the hat on top and closed the case and shoved it back on the top shelf. Finally he washed his hands and turned off the water in the tub and the basin.

40   In the kitchen, Mrs. Hogan and the children faced him, beaming, "Guess what some young man's going on?"

41   "What?" asked Mr. Hogan.
"Radio," said John. "Monday night. Eight o'clock."
"I guess we got a celebrity in the family," said Mr. Hogan.

42   Mrs. Hogan said, "I just hope some young lady hasn't got her nose out of joint."

43   Mr. Hogan pulled up to the table and stretched his legs. "Mama, I guess I got a fine family," he said. He reached in his pocket and took out two five-dollar bills. He handed one to John. "That's for winning," he said. He poked the other bill at Joan. "And that's for being a good sport. One celebrity and one good sport. What a fine family!" He rubbed his hands together and lifted the lid of the covered dish. "Kidneys," he said. "Fine."

44   And that's how Mr. Hogan did it.

3,442 words

Questions

1. What steps are taken by Mr. Hogan to rob the bank? State them in the order in which they occur.
2. What point does this story make?
3. What are some examples of the typical middle-class life of the Hogans?
4. What detail in paragraph 9 clearly indicates Mr. Hogan's double standard?
5. What is your response to the sentence in paragraph 3, " . . . if you left hanky-panky out, robbing a bank would be a relatively sound venture . . . "?

Tract
William Carlos Williams

1   I will teach you my townspeople
how to perform a funeral—
for you have it over a troop
of artists—
unless one should scour the world—
you have the ground sense necessary.

2   See! the hearse leads.

I begin with a design for a hearse.
For Christ's sake not black—
nor white either—and not polished!
Let it be weathered—like a farm wagon—
with gilt wheels (this could be
applied fresh at small expense)
or no wheels at all:
a rough dray to drag over the ground.

3   Knock the glass out!
My God—glass, my townspeople!
For what purpose? Is it for the dead
to look out or for us to see
how well he is housed or to see
the flowers or the lack of them—
or what?
To keep the rain and snow from him?
He will have a heavier rain soon:
pebbles and dirt and what not.
Let there be no glass—
and no upholstery phew!
and no little brass rollers
and small easy wheels on the bottom—
my townspeople what are you thinking of?

4   A rough plain hearse then
with gilt wheels and no top at all.
On this the coffin lies
by its own weight.

5   No wreaths please—
especially no hot house flowers.
Some common memento is better,
something he prized and is known by:
his old clothes—a few books perhaps—
God knows what! You realize
how we are about these things
my townspeople—
something will be found—anything
even flowers if he had come to that.
So much for the hearse.

6   For heaven's sake though see to the driver!
Take off the silk hat! In fact
that's no place at all for him—
up there unceremoniously
dragging our friend out to his own dignity!
Bring him down—bring him down!
Low and inconspicuous! I'd not have him ride
on the wagon at all—damn him—
the undertaker's understrapper!
Let him hold the reins

and walk at the side
and inconspicuously too!

7   Then briefly as to yourselves:
Walk behind—as they do in France,
seventh class, or if you ride
Hell take curtains! Go with some show
of inconvenience; sit openly—
to the weather as to grief.
Or do you think you can shut grief in?
What—from us? We who have perhaps
nothing to lose? Share with us
share with us—it will be money
in your pockets.
                                    Go now
I think you are ready.

Vocabulary

dray (2)
memento (3)
unceremoniously (4)
understrapper (4)

Questions

1. In giving advice on how to perform a funeral, what major steps does the speaker advocate? List them in the order in which they are mentioned.
2. What is the poet's general purpose in advocating this kind of funeral?
3. In stanza 2, why does the speaker suggest the gilt wheels, applied fresh?
4. Why doesn't the speaker want the coffin to ride along smoothly (stanza 3)?
5. Instead of wreaths or hothouse flowers, what does the speaker suggest as a decoration for the coffin? Why?
6. What objections does the speaker have to the undertaker's driving the carriage in a silk top hat?
7. What is the most important thought contained in the final stanza?

B. How to Write a Process Paper

Describing a process, often called *process analysis,* is a common and indispensable assignment. A process paper involves step-by-step directions, such as giving someone directions to your home or writing instructions for your roommate on how to care for your plants while you're on vacation.

Writing Assignment

Choose a process with which you are thoroughly familiar and give a specific and detailed set of instructions for doing it. Here are some sample process topics: "How to detect counterfeit money," "How to train a dog in obedience," "How to make Beef Wellington," "How to write a research paper," "How a legal case reaches the Supreme Court," "How to balance a budget," "How to produce an antiflu serum."

Specific Instructions

1. BEGIN WITH A CLEAR STATEMENT OF PURPOSE. A process paper should begin by announcing the directions it intends to give: "My paper will explain the steps in assembling a dictionary." Or "The purpose of this paper is to show the easiest way to gather a good collection of rock music." Or "What follows is a summary of the basic steps involved in the scientific method of investigation." This initial announcement alerts the reader to the purpose of your process paper, giving him or her a context for the individual steps that follow.

2. ASSEMBLE ALL THE INFORMATION NECESSARY TO THE COMPLETE PROCESS. It is easier to give directions or explain the separate steps of a project when you have accurate and complete information on the process. If the process is unfamiliar and the information not at hand, you will need to do some research. Gather *all* the information you can. It is better to assemble more information than you will actually use than to overlook a detail that might have helped explain a step in the process. Collect the facts, and refer to them as you write the process.

3. DECIDE ON THE ORDER OF YOUR STEPS. Once the facts are collected, their order of presentation will usually become apparent from the process. For example, if you are analyzing the steps in planting camelias, common sense tells you that the first step is preparation of the soil. Similarly, if you are writing a paper on how an American president is elected to office, you would begin not with his inauguration, but with the election of local delegates in the primaries.

A reasonable way to begin a process paper is to outline all the steps in the order they will logically occur and to include those details necessary for a clear presentation of each step. An example of such an outline follows:

Controlling idea: My purpose is to list the basic steps in writing a book review.
  I. Read the book carefully.
      A. Look for major ideas.
      B. Mark essential pages.
  II. Think about the book.
      A. Figure out the purpose of the book.
      B. Judge the book according to how well it has fulfilled its purpose.
      C. Make mental notes of both strengths and weaknesses.
  III. Write a fair review.
      A. State the purpose of the book.
      B. Give a brief summary of the book.
      C. Explain major passages, using quotations to give a flavor of the author's style.
      D. Pass judgment on the book.

Although the sequence of a process may be extremely simple, consisting of only one or two steps, each step may be complicated by many details. For example, the process of writing good advertising copy contains two steps complicated by detail:

Controlling idea: The purpose of this paper is to show how to write good advertising copy.

I. Begin with a strong headline.
    A. Flag down all possible customers.
    B. Include key words associated with the product.
    C. Appeal to the reader's self-interest.
    D. Make the product sound new.
II. Write the body as if you were answering someone's questions.
    A. Go straight to the point.
    B. Be factual and specific.
    C. Include testimonials.
    D. Give the reader some helpful advice.
    E. Write in colloquial language.

The outline makes the process easier to write by highlighting each step along with its cluster of details. Without the aid of the outline, the writer could easily become confused.

4. EACH INDIVIDUAL STEP MUST BE CLEAR AND COMPLETE. Each step in the process must be clearly enumerated and explained; one poorly explained step can confuse an entire process. For example, suppose the third step in producing an antivenom for snake bites is to collect the serum by bleeding a horse that has been injected with the venom. A clear explanation of this step, with all the necessary details beautifully aligned, is of little use if step 1—collecting the venom by milking a snake—is never explained. A clear step-by-step presentation of material is crucial in a process paper.

A television comedian, composer, and author tells how you can appreciate man's greatest written works.

Professional Model

How to Enjoy the Classics
Steve Allen

1   Why is it? In school we learn one of the most amazing and difficult feats man has ever accomplished—*how to read*—and at the same time we learn to hate to read the things worth reading most!

2   It's happened to us all—with assignment reading! It happened to me. The teacher assigned *Moby Dick*. I didn't want to read it. So I fought it. I disliked it. I thought I won.

3   But I lost. My struggle to keep at arm's length from *Moby Dick* cost me all the good

things that can come from learning to come to terms with those special few books we call the "classics."

4   I've come back to *Moby Dick* on my own since. I *like* it. And I've discovered a new level of pleasure from it with each reading.

5   What *is* a classic? A classic is a book that gives you that exhilarating feeling, if only for a moment, that you've finally uncovered part of the meaning of life.

6   A classic is a book that's stood the test of time, a book that men and women all over the world keep reaching for throughout the ages for its special enlightenment.

7   Not many books can survive such a test. Considering all the volumes that have been produced since man first put chisel to stone, classics account for an infinitesimal share of the total—less than .001 percent. That's just a few thousand books. Of those, under 100 make up the solid core.

8   Why should you tackle the classics? Why try to enjoy them?
I suggest three good reasons:
1. Classics open up your mind.
2. Classics help you grow.
3. Classics help you understand your life, your world, yourself.

9   That last one is the big one. A classic can give you insights into yourself that you will get nowhere else. Sure, you can get pleasure out of almost any book. But a classic, once you penetrate it, lifts you up *high*! Aeschylus's *Oresteia* was written nearly 2,500 years ago—and it still knocks me out!

10   But I can hear you saying, "I've *tried* reading classics. They are hard to understand. I can't get into them."

11   Let me offer some suggestions that will help you open up this wondrous world. Pick up a classic you've always promised to try. Then take Dr. Allen's advice.

12   **Know what you're reading.**   Is it a novel, drama, biography, history? To find out, check the table of contents, read the book cover, the preface, or look up the title or author in *The Reader's Encyclopedia*.

13   **Don't read in bed.**   Classics can be tough going; I'll admit it. You need to be alert, with your senses sharp. When you read in bed you're courting sleep—and you'll blame it on the book when you start nodding off.

14   **Don't let a lot of characters throw you.**   Dostoevsky tosses fifty major characters at you in *The Brothers Karamazov*. In the very first chapter of *War and Peace*, Tolstoy bombards you with twenty-two names—long, complicated ones like Anna Pavlovna Scherer, Anatole and Prince Bolkonski. Don't scurry for cover. Stick with it. The characters will gradually sort themselves out and you'll feel as comfortable with them as you do with your own dear friends who were strangers, too, when you met them.

15   **Give the author a chance.**   Don't say "I don't get it!" too soon. Keep reading right to the end.

16   Sometimes, though, you may not be ready for the book you're trying to get into. I tackled Plato's *Republic* three times before it finally opened up to me. And man, was it worth it! So if you really can't make a go of the book in your lap, put it aside for another day, or year, and take on another one.

17   **Read in big bites.**   Don't read in short nibbles. How can you expect to get your head into anything that way? The longer you stay with it, the more you get into the rhythm and mood—and the more pleasure you get from it.

18   When you read *Zorba the Greek* try putting bouzouki music on the record player; Proust, a little Debussy; Shakespeare, Elizabethan theatre music.

19   **Read what the author read.**   To better understand where the author is coming from, as we say, read the books he once read and that impressed him. Shakespeare, for example, dipped into North's translation of Plutarch's *Lives* for the plots of *Julius Caesar, Antony and Cleopatra* and *A Midsummer Night's Dream.* It's fun to know you're reading what *he* read.

20   **Read about the author's time.**   You are the product of your time. Any author is the product of *his* time. Knowing the history of that time, the problems that he and others faced, their attitudes—will help you understand the author's point of view. *Important point:* You may not agree with the author. No problem. At least he's made you think!

21   **Read about the author's life.**   The more you know about an author's own experiences, the more you'll understand why he wrote what he wrote. You'll begin to see the auto-biographical odds and ends that are hidden in his work.

22   A writer can't help but reveal himself. Most of our surmises about Shakespeare's life come from clues found in his plays.

23   **Read the book again.**   All classics bear rereading. If after you finish the book you're intrigued but still confused, reread it then and there. It'll open up some more to you.

24   If you did read a classic a few years back and loved it, read it again. The book will have so many new things to say to you, you'll hardly believe it's the same one.

25   **A few classics to enjoy.**   You can find excellent lists of the basic classics compiled by helpful experts, like Clifton Fadiman's *Lifetime Reading Plan,* the *Harvard Classics* and Mortimer J. Adler's *Great Books.* Look into them.

26   But before you do, I'd like to suggest a few classics that can light up your life. Even though some might have been spoiled for you by the required reading stigma, try them. Try them. And *try* them.

27   1. Homer: *Iliad* and *Odyssey.* The Adam and Eve of Western literature. Read a good recent translation. My favorite is by Robert Fitzgerald.

28   2. Rabelais: *Gargantua and Pantagruel.* A Gargantuan romp. I recommend the Samuel Putnam translation.

29   3. Geoffrey Chaucer: *Canterbury Tales.* Thirty folks on a four-day pilgrimage swapping whoppers. Don't be surprised if the people you meet here are like people you know in *your* life.

30   4. Cervantes: *Don Quixote.* The first modern novel, about the lovable old Don with his "impossible dream." How could you go through life without reading it *once*?

31   5. Shakespeare: *Plays.* Shakespeare turned out 37 plays. Some are flops, some make him the greatest writer ever. All offer gold. His best: "Hamlet," "Macbeth" and "Romeo and Juliet." (See them on the stage, too.)

32   6. Charles Dickens: *Pickwick Papers.* No one can breathe life into characters the way Dickens can. Especially the inimitable Samuel Pickwick, Esq.

33   7. Mark Twain: *Huckleberry Finn.* Maybe you had to read this in school. Well, climb back on that raft with Huck and Jim. You'll find new meaning this time.

34   Of course, these few suggestions hardly scratch the surface.

35   Don't just dip your toe into the deep waters of the classics. Plunge in! Like generations of bright human beings before you, you'll find yourself invigorated to the marrow by thoughts and observations of the most gifted writers in history.

36   You still enjoy looking at classic paintings. You enjoy hearing musical classics. Good books will hold you, too.

37   Someone has said the classics are the diary of man. Open up the diary. Read about yourself—and *understand* yourself.

1,362 words

Vocabulary

infinitesimal (7)   Debussy (18)   stigma (26)
bouzouki (18)   surmises (22)   Gargantuan (28)
Proust (18)

Questions

1. How does Steve Allen define *classic*? Would his definition be suitable for a dictionary? Give reasons for your answer.
2. According to the author, classics account for only a tiny portion of the books produced so far in history. Why do you suppose so few books become classics?
3. How many specific steps does the author propose to help you enjoy the process of reading a classic? Review each step. Which step(s) do you consider the most helpful?
4. What are the titles of some bibliographies that will give you the names of the basic classics?
5. According to the author, what stigma has deterred potential readers from the classics? Explain this stigma. What experience, if any, have you had with this stigma? Offer an example.
6. In presenting his list of classics, the author admits that he has only scratched the surface. What other work(s) would you add to his list?
7. What metaphor does the author develop throughout paragraph 35? Why is it appropriate and effective?

This process essay is a step-by-step explanation of how to keep a dream journal.

Student Model

How to Keep a Dream Journal
Deborah Lott

In keeping a dream journal you not only record the mental events of sleep, but also indirectly take account of your life. Those who have kept journals for some time are amazed at how much their journals tell about past events, which at the time seemed unrelated to their dreams. Keeping a dream journal is not just an after-the-fact passive logging of dreams, but a process that will affect your dreams, and may also increase your creativity.

First of all, keep your dream journal in a notebook small enough to carry with you all the time. Thus, if you remember some aspect of a dream, you can immediately record it. At night, put the journal beside your bed along with several pens. If you awaken during the night, write down what you were dreaming, or at least the image that was in your mind when you awakened.

In the morning, wake either naturally or to music; the jolt of an alarm will blast a dream right out of memory. Allow yourself at least fifteen minutes to work on your journal before getting out of bed. If you are one of those people who "never remember dreams," set a music alarm for every two hours, beginning two hours after you go to bed. If the anxiety of this setup does not create insomnia, you should begin to remember at least fragments.

Upon awakening in the morning, don't move. Shut your eyes and attempt to recall an image. This image will trigger other images if not whole dreams. Don't try too hard—fighting too strenuously to hold on to an image may have the opposite of the desired effect and block all memory.

Write the dream on every other line of a page, recalling as much as you can as quickly as you can. Write whatever comes to mind even if there are gaps in the sequence of images, even if a scene from one dream floats into the middle of another. Indicate gaps, discrepancies, or uncertainties with a slash or question mark. If a digression occurs to you, don't deny it, asterisk the point in the narrative at which it occurs, skip two lines and write it in parentheses. The longer you keep a journal, the more spontaneously associations and digressions will occur. These may be the real meat of the journal and are not to be spurned.

Describe the dream in detail without lingering over cloudy portions. It is crucial to include as much detail as possible because no matter how vivid the dream seems at the moment, it will quickly fade. It is a common delusion to think that "shorthand" will suffice, but words laden with significance when you write them can seem absolutely flat two hours later. Recalling their importance can be as difficult as conveying the significance of an image in your own dream to someone else.

Capture the texture of the dream. What colors and shapes predominate? Are there distortions in spatial relations or in perspective? Does time pass at a normal rate or is it warped? Write descriptions as if you were delineating a foreign terrain to an alien visitor. Use drawings. Re-create the atmosphere of the dream, *what it really felt like*. As you do this, you will remember more of the dream. The process of writing the journal will be much like the process of dreaming itself— associations engender other associations; images metamorphose into other images.

Say it all. Defy the internal censors. Do not attempt to make logical stories out of your dreams or to rationalize your behavior. If something is irrational, express it that way; tax the language to express the dream. Putting a dream into words makes it seem more real; thus, you may find some resistance to expressing negative or frightening dreams. Language tends to formalize dreams, so that once written, you will always remember the dream in those words. You may wish to express some passage in two different ways when neither feels completely "right"; retain them both. Once the dream is on paper, you will be interpreting the language as much as the original experience.

Reread the narrative, filling in details, making additional notes, such as "resistance in writing this," "cloudier than the rest of the dream," "very disturbing," etc., on the blank line below.

You may then wish to engage in some tentative analysis or commentary about the dream. This process will affect your dreams. One writer was first infatuated with Freud, then Jung, and finally Reich. He reported: "When I wrote Jungian analyses, my dreams were full of huge, black oak trees, cloaked female figures, and caves. When I wrote Freudian analyses, my dreams changed until I had phalluses coming out of my ears!

With Reich I had the most visceral dreams and woke up every morning with a backache."

If you impose an analytical methodology, juxtapose the interpretation to the dream as a sort of story or myth in itself, not as a final explanation. Your journal will be more fruitful if you retain some perspective about deriving symbolic equivalences: "House equals psyche." "Big, black bear equals Daddy," etc.

The most exciting part of keeping a journal is seeing the way that dreams comment on one another, how one dream provides insight into another and into the events of your life. What once might have seemed totally unconnected dreams, if you had even remembered them, reveal fascinating connections when read together in a journal. Consider these entries:

> January 4, 1976
> Floods, everywhere in the city. Especially I remember the Tujunga area that was burned in the last forest fire. It went on for several days. Water was on the floor.

> January 12, 1976
> I had a flash of a dream in which I remembered a previous residence of Billy's and mine, the bedroom of which had many plants and an interesting architectural feature which I liked, a low box filled with soil* in which grew many plants.

> January 18, 1976
> I was in a bookstore like the Bodhi Tree. I looked at astrology books although they didn't have anything I really wanted. Then I was looking at some books on a bottom shelf near the floor. They had illustrated covers. One entitled *Jungle Doctor* showed a doctor operating on someone. I felt a sudden tugging on my heart. "I too wish to spend my life's work saving souls," I thought.

In her dreams, fire appears in association with fertility, power, and destruction. Water imagery is also prominent, being associated with fertility, and again as with fire, with destruction. Might some connection be drawn between the planter on the floor in which plants are grown in "soul" and the book about "saving souls" on the bottom shelf near the floor, in the bookstore? The jungle appears again, in proximity to fertility and to disaster:

> January 27, 1976
> I was visiting a "jungle farm." It was a residence of the strangest beasts, like Dr. Doolittle's companions. Then, the rains came—heavy, thick brown rain, turning the grounds to mud. I am reminded of the flood they had at Africa USA in '65 or '66 with the heroic tales of large beasts helping small ones to safety. Again the rains and floods!

Seen together, these dreams reveal a personal grammar of images: fire, flood, disaster, salvation—appearing in an infinite variety of representations in dream.

Once you have a body of dreams, read them all over often before going to sleep. Consider the language. What about puns? Freudian slips? Idiosyncracies of phrasing? Using a word not in your everyday vocabulary? Rewrite the endings to dreams. Rework dream plots. Program yourself to resolve a conflict left unresolved in your dreams to date. Consider the dream journal as providing a wealth of personal imagery upon which to draw for all your writing.

---

*Instead of the word *soil* she had written the word *soul*.

An experienced author reveals some effective methods a person can use to make an author's life miserable.

Alternate Reading

How to Torture an Author
Gilbert Highet

1   In more robust days than these, a hundred years ago or so, there were many heartily sadistic sports to enjoy. You could watch a bull being attacked by specially bred bulldogs whose jaws clamped fast on its nose; you could see fighting cocks trying to stab and rip each other to death; you could sit by while two men fought with bare fists for 150 rounds. That kind of thing is against the law nowadays, and the difficulty is to find a substitute for it. There is, however, one legal sport which has many variations and which produces many of the same pleasurable sensations as watching a badger fighting a pack of savage terriers. This is author-baiting.

2   The simplest way to torture an author is to get his name wrong and forget what books he has written. I once saw a woman cover John Steinbeck with flattery, and tell him that he well deserved to win the Nobel Prize for such a fine novel as *South Pacific*. A friend of mine achieved deathless fame among author-baiters when he was presented to a tall, brilliantly dressed lady of mature years who had an exotic headdress, a unique aquiline profile, long thin seaweed hands, and an air of intense though blasé distinction. 'Dame Edith,' said the introducer, 'may I present Mr. Geoffrey Winbucket?' The lady extended a fragile hand. Winbucket gazed at her with a wild surmise, and said, 'Please forgive me. I didn't catch your name. Do you write?'

3   Another vulnerable spot in writers is finance. Authors seldom make decent incomes, and they earn money very irregularly. Therefore they are more sensitive on that point than the members of any other profession, except the stage. You can make any writer yelp satisfyingly if you hit him in the pocket. There are at least four techniques for this.

4   The first is to tell him that you couldn't get hold of his new book for nearly six months after its publication, because there were so many people on the waiting list at the lending library. When he hears that you didn't think his book worth more than 15¢, and that you refused all temptations to take out your little moth-infested wallet and buy it, he will writhe.

5   The second method is to say that you bought a copy as soon as it came out, and that you have been lending it around to all your friends. 'I think twenty-five or thirty people must have read my copy of your marvelous book: it is almost coming to pieces.' It is a very strong-minded author who can think of twenty or thirty sales which you have sabotaged, deliberately sabotaged, without groaning and shaking his heavy head.

6   A third *suerte*[1] (as we *aficionados*[2] say) is to praise the author's new book highly, and then ask him to lend you a copy. 'I'm sure you must have one handy: I'll return it promptly, and keep it in a paper wrapper.' Some author-baiters even write to their victims saying that they have seen reviews of his book and would love to read it, could he send them an 'author's copy'? This implies that the author has a private store of 'author's copies,' three or four hundred extra volumes which fell out of the machine when the printer was

[1] Spanish: "trick."
[2] Spanish: "enthusiastic admirer."

not looking and are kept in a private warehouse like a wine-grower's personal stock. In fact, the author usually gets six copies free from the publisher. He keeps two for his files, and presents four to his nearest and dearest. If he gives any more copies away, he has to pay the publisher for them in his good scanty hard-earned dollars.

7   Perhaps the simplest variation of this type of torture is the fourth. If the author does know you personally and does send you a free copy of his book, don't thank him; don't write him about it; and when you do meet him next, make no reference to it whatever. Don't even mention the reviews. Contrive that he shall think it arrived, but was thrown into the garbage together with last week's newspapers.

8   By correspondence, one simple but effective method of tormenting an author is to write him a short letter saying that you know his reputation, and that you have heard he has recently published a book on a subject dear to you. Then ask, quite straight-forwardly, 'How can I get hold of your book?' The author has spent the last eight or nine months in close contact with his publisher; he may also have talked with the salesmen and met the representatives of a dozen leading booksellers. He will read this question with his stomach writhing. He will think about it all day, and wonder what to reply. The obvious answer is, 'Go to a bookstore and buy it.' But that seems too simple. The author begins to worry. He starts to think that perhaps the publisher—or someone in the publisher's office—is deliberately smothering the book, so that no copies of it have ever been sent out to the bookstores; or else that, after reaching the bookstores, they have been dissolved by cosmic rays. If you write him from, say, West Virginia, he will worry about the possibility that his books may never have penetrated to the Panhandle State, and he will start pestering his publishers to put on a special West Virginian advertising campaign, and to get copies of his book into every store in every town and at every crossroads of West Virginia. This will improve the relationship between him and the publisher, and produce a handy, cheap, self-perpetuating type of author-torture.

9   Using a different technique, you can hit an author in a tender spot by treating your own literary work as far more important than his. Remember the definition of an actor, attributed to Marlon Brando: 'An actor is a guy who, if you ain't talking about him, he ain't listening.' The same often applies to authors. Therefore when you meet one it is an excellent idea to describe your own books or the books of someone else you know. I once saw T. S. Eliot stand for a long, long time in silence, while a plump elderly lady quoted stanza after stanza of her daughter's lyrical poems to him. Mr. Eliot's face habitually expressed a deep world-weariness, illuminated by a remote and saintly good humor; but on that day, minute by minute, its lines grew deeper.

> Between the idea
> And the reality
> Falls the Shadow.[3]

10   Many, many people practice one of the most fiendish tortures which can be inflicted upon a working author. This is to send him your own unpublished work. Preferably it should be in a large heap of typescript on flimsy paper (third or fourth carbons are best), which collapses and flies out of order the moment the package is opened, so that the author must spend twenty minutes picking up the pages and getting them back into some sort of shape. There should be a covering letter, in which you write that you don't want money, but only a chance to say all that is in your heart; you *do* want detailed criticism of your writings from your victim; and you end by telling him to take steps to have your book published as soon as possible. In order to increase his agony, you should never on any account enclose a stamped addressed return envelope. He has

---

[3]Lines from T. S. Eliot's poem "The Hollow Men."

nothing else to do, between writing and publishing books, the lazy hound. Make him rummage around in his storage closet and find some brown paper and string and tie up your parcel properly for return to you: the exercise will do him good. Of course you will not have enclosed any stamps, and he has thrown out your original wrapping, so that he cannot guess how much the bundle weighs: therefore he will have to take it to the post office several miles away, and stand in line waiting to have it weighed and buy the stamps and see it dispatched, and then make his way home again. A whole morning's work will have been shot to blazes, but your author will have had some valuable exercise and a chance to develop his moral fiber.

11   To meet the author is even better. If he is meek and absent-minded, and if you catch him out of his *querencia*[4] with his self-confidence down around his ankles, then corner him. Fix him with your glittering eye. Start reading your unpublished work to him, slowly and emphatically. This will give him the same pleasure as showing him the X-ray photographs of the baby your wife is expecting in four months. James Thurber has a splendid essay on this subject in *The Middle-Aged Man on the Flying Trapeze* (Harper, 1935), called 'How to Listen to a Play.' The best way to do it, he says, is to choose a comfortable chair, get into a relaxed position, resting your head on your hand, close your eyes in rapt attention, and pass into a kind of trance. Thurber says that he can remain motionless and cataleptic for three whole acts, saying 'Fine, that's fine,' and 'Just swell,' at intervals, without taking in a single word. But the danger is that rest may pass into sleep and sleep into dream. 'For instance,' he says, 'this question occurred in the second act of a play a woman was reading to me recently: "How've you been, Jim?" "Fine!" I answered, coming out of my doze without quite knowing where I was, "How've *you* been?" That was a terrible moment for both of us.'

12   The principal form of author-baiting is called criticism. No writer really wants criticism after his book has come out. He merely wants to see it being bought steadily, so that he can relax for a few weeks before he starts thinking about the next one. He does not want to read other people's opinions of how he should have written it, or how they could have written it. Sometimes he wants to forget it altogether, because he is absorbed in planning something quite new. If a writer wants criticism after publication, he will ask for it. He never does. Therefore an effective method of tormenting him is to offer him unsolicited criticism, to thrust it on him, to send it to him in long single-spaced letters, or to back him up against a wall in the smoke and wealth and noise of a cocktail party and shout it in his ear. To stand on your two tired feet after a long day's work, breathing in the pungent and nauseating odor of other people's cigarettes, to watch a comparative stranger's mouth opening and shutting and occasionally spraying out half-chewed fragments of chopped olive and anchovy spread, and, above the concerted squawking of thirty or forty human voices, to strain in order to catch the sentences in which the stranger is vivisecting your poor quivering book—this is one of the most refined agonies which any author, however unpretentious, can be called on to endure.

13   There are several exquisite variations of this particular technique.

14   *Type 1.* Tell your author that you enjoyed his book, such as it was, but that he ought to have written a totally different work. If he has spent five years writing a biography of Boccaccio, explain to him that you were grievously disappointed because you had hoped he would give the world what he was uniquely qualified to produce, a definitive study of Savonarola.

15   *Type 2.* Express the utmost admiration for the book. Then ask him whether he really

---

[4]Spanish: "haunt" or "favorite spot."

180

wrote it. Did he have much *help* with it? How often did he (or she) consult his wife (or husband)? No doubt he must have an enormous research staff, with highly trained assistants? Make it perfectly clear that neither you nor anyone else believes the book is all his own work; and, if possible, imply that the best parts do not sound like him in the slightest degree.

16   *Type 3.* This needs a little research, but is satisfying. Praise the book highly, and go into some detail. Then ask him if he knows that the same field was covered last year rather more fully by a German writer who is expected to win the Nobel Prize.

17   *Type 4* takes a great deal of trouble, but is frequently practiced, especially in the learned professions. Read the author's book several times, with a notebook beside you. Write down every misprint, however small—even a misplaced apostrophe. Look up every citation and note every variant. Verify all the references. Collect contradictory evidence for every disputable statement. Supply extra information on every topic where your victim seems to be a little weak. Then send the whole thing to a periodical which he knows and respects, in the form of a 'review-article.' I know several men who have spent a happy and rewarding lifetime never by any means writing books themselves, but plunging poisoned daggers in the backs of colleagues who do; and after all, the Borgia[5] family lived a rich and full and rewarding life, did they not?

18   Best of all inflictions is the simplest. Show your author that the whole business of writing books is merely silly, why bother, who reads them? If you are a millionaire, or a hereditary nobleman, or a powerful official, this is your most effective form of author-baiting. The miserable Russians got a lot of it under the late Joseph Vissarionovitch Djugashvili,[6] and have had more under his successors. After the poet Ariosto presented his delightful romantic epic poem *The Madness of Roland* to his patron, the Cardinal Ippolito d'Este, the Cardinal looked through it and said, 'Where the devil did you dig up all this rubbish?' And one of the royal house of Hanover, William Henry, Duke of Gloucester (brother of George III), on hearing that the greatest living English historian had produced another volume, summed it up in an immortal piece of author-squelching: 'Another damned, thick, square book! Always scribble, scribble, scribble! Eh, Mr. Gibbon?'

2,420 words

Vocabulary

aquiline (2)	sabotaged (5)	vivisecting (12)
blasé (2)	illuminated (9)	Boccaccio (14)
surmise (2)	cataleptic (11)	Savonarola (14)

Questions

1. Within what category of literature would you place this essay? Explain your choice.
2. The author calls the sport of torturing an author "author-baiting." Where does this label come from?

---

[5]An Italian family influential in church and government from the 14th to 16th century. The family became notorious for their poison plots, incestual relationships, and other extravagant vices.
[6]Stalin.

3. Gilbert Highet offers several steps for the process of torturing an author. Some of the steps contain sub-categories. What are the main steps and what are their sub-categories? Present them in outline form.

4. In his introduction, what literary device does the author use to captivate the reader's attention? How successful is he?

5. What verbal guideposts does the author use to indicate when a new major step is to follow? Point out each guidepost.

6. What is the meaning of the reference to Joseph Vissarionovitch Djugashvili?

7. The "Mr. Gibbon" referred to in the final sentence of the essay is Edward Gibbon (1737-94). For what famous work is this venerable historian best known? If you do not already know, look up his name in an encyclopedia.

8. Which method of torturing an author do you consider the most demeaning? Why?

In this selection, Mayleas gives the prospective job-hunter a series of systematic steps to follow. The article first appeared in *Empire Magazine* and later, in condensed form, in *The Reader's Digest*.

Alternate Reading

How to Land the Job You Want
Davidyne Mayleas

1   Louis Albert, 39, lost his job as an electrical engineer when his firm made extensive cutbacks. He spent two months answering classified ads and visiting employment agencies—with zero results. Albert might still be hunting if a friend, a specialist in the employment field, had not shown him how to be his own job counselor. Albert learned how to research unlisted openings, write a forceful résumé, perform smoothly in an interview, even transform a turndown into a job.

2   Although there seemed to be a shortage of engineering jobs, Albert realized that he still persuaded potential employers to see him. This taught him something—that his naturally outgoing personality might be as great an asset as his engineering degree. When the production head of a small electronics company told him that they did not have an immediate opening, Albert told his interviewer, "You people make a fine product. I think you could use additional sales representation—someone like me who understands and talks electrical engineer's language, and who enjoys selling." The interviewer decided to send Albert to a senior vice president. Albert got a job in sales.

3   You too can be your own counselor if you put the same vigorous effort into *getting* a job as you would into *keeping* one. Follow these three basic rules, developed by placement experts:

4   1. FIND THE HIDDEN JOB MARKET.   Classified ads and agency listings reveal only a small percentage of available jobs. Some of the openings that occur through promotions, retirements, and reorganization never reach the personnel department. There are three ways to get in touch with this hidden market:

5   *Write a strong résumé with a well-directed cover letter and mail it to the appropriate department manager in the company where you'd like to work.* Don't worry whether

there's a current opening. Many managers fill vacancies by reviewing the résumés already in their files. Dennis Mollura, press-relations manager in the public-relations department of American Telephone and Telegraph, says, "In my own case, the company called me months after I sent in my résumé."

6 *Get in touch with people who work in or know the companies that interest you.* Jobs are so often filled through personal referral that Charles R. Lops, executive employment manager of the J. C. Penney Co., says, "Probably our best source for outside people comes from recommendations made by Penney associates themselves."

7 *"Drop in" on the company.* Lillian Reveille, employment manager of Equitable Life Assurance Society of the United States, reports: "A large percentage of the applicants we see are 'walk-ins'—and we do employ many of these people."

8 2. LOCATE HIDDEN OPENINGS. This step requires energy and determination to make telephone calls, see people, do research, and to keep moving despite turndowns.

9 *Contact anyone who may know of openings,* including relatives, friends, teachers, bank officers, insurance agents—anyone you know in your own or an adjacent field. When the teachers' union and employment agencies produced no teaching openings, Eric Olson, an unemployed high-school math instructor, reviewed his talent and decided that where an analytical math mind was useful, there he'd find a job. He called his insurance agent, who set up an interview with the actuarial department of one of the companies he represented. They hired Olson.

10 It's a good idea to contact not only professional or trade associations in your field, but also your local chamber of commerce and people involved in community activities. After Laura Bailey lost her job as retirement counselor in a bank's personnel department, she found a position in customer relations in another bank. Her contact: a member of the senior-citizens club that Mrs. Bailey ran on a volunteer basis.

11 *Use local or business-school libraries.* Almost every field has its own directory of companies, which provides names, addresses, products and/or services, and lists officers and other executives. Write to the company president or to the executive to whom you'd report. The vice president of personnel at Warner-Lambert Co. says, "When a résumé of someone we could use—now or in the near future—shows up 'cold' in my in-basket, that's luck for both of us."

12 *Consult telephone directories.* Sometimes the telephone company will send you free the telephone directories of various cities. Also, good-sized public libraries often have many city directories. Fred Lewis, a cabinet maker, checked the telephone directories of nine different cities where he knew furniture was manufactured. At the end of five weeks he had a sizable telephone bill, some travel expenses—and ten interviews which resulted in three job offers.

13 3. AFTER YOU FIND THE OPENING, GET THE JOB. The applicants who actually get hired are those who polish these six job-getting skills to perfection:

14 *Compose a better résumé.* A résumé is a self-advertisement, designed to get you an interview. Start by putting yourself in an employer's place. Take stock of your job history and personal achievements. Make an inventory of your skills and accomplishments that might be useful from the employer's standpoint. Choose the most important and describe them in words that stress accomplishments. Avoid such phrases as "my duties included . . . " Use action words like planned, sold, trained, managed.

15 Ask a knowledgeable business friend to review your résumé. Does it stress accomplishment rather than duties? Does it tell an employer what you can do for him? Can it be shortened? (One or two pages should suffice.) Generally, it's not wise to mention salary requirements.

16   *Write a convincing cover letter.* While the résumé may be a copy, the cover letter must be personal. Sy Mann, director of research for Aceto Chemical Co., says: "When I see a mimeographed letter that states, 'Dear Sir, I'm sincerely interested in working for your company,' I wonder, 'How many other companies got this valentine?' " Use the name and title of the person who can give you the interview, and be absolutely certain of accuracy here. Using a wrong title or misspelling a prospective employer's name may route your correspondence directly to an automatic turndown.

17   *Prepare specifically for each interview.* Research the company thoroughly; know its history and competition. Try to grasp the problems of the job you're applying for. For example, a line in an industry journal that a food company was "developing a new geriatric food" convinced one man that he should emphasize his marketing experience with vitamins rather than with frozen foods.

18   You'll increase your edge by anticipating questions the interviewer might raise. Why do you want to work with us? What can you offer us that someone else cannot? Why did you leave your last position? What are your salary requirements?

19   An employer holds an interview to get a clearer picture of your work history and accomplishments, and to look for characteristics he considers valuable. These vary with jobs. Does the position require emphasis on attention to detail or on creativity? Perseverance or aggressiveness? Prior to the interview decide what traits are most in demand. And always send a thank-you note immediately after the interview.

20   *Follow up.* They said you would hear in a week; now it's two. Call them. Don't wait and hope. Hope and act.

21   *Supply additional information.* That's the way Karen Halloway got her job as fashion director with a department store. "After my interview I sensed that the merchandise manager felt I was short on retail experience. So I wrote to him describing the 25 fashion shows I'd staged yearly for the pattern company I'd worked for."

22   *Don't take no for an answer.* Hank Newell called to find out why he had been turned down. The credit manager felt he had insufficient collection experience. Hank thanked him for his time and frankness. The next day, Hank called back saying, "My collection experience is limited, but I don't think I fully emphasized my training in credit checking." They explored this area and found Hank still not qualified. But the credit manager was so impressed with how well Hank took criticism that when Hank asked him if he could suggest other employers, he did, even going so far as to call one. Probing for leads when an interview or follow-up turns negative is a prime technique for getting personal referrals.

23   The challenge of finding a job, approached in an active, organized, realistic way, can be a valuable personal adventure. You can meet new people, develop new ideas about yourself and your career goals, and improve your skills in dealing with individuals. These in turn can contribute to your long-term job security.

1,410 words

Vocabulary

adjacent (9)
actuarial (9)

Questions

1. What is the purpose of the example given in paragraph 1?
2. What are the three basic rules of job-hunting?

3. What is the hidden job market?
4. What are the three basic ways of getting in touch with the hidden job market?
5. What three steps can you take to locate hidden openings?
6. After you find the opening, what six steps can you take to ensure that you'll get the job?
7. Whose point of view should you take in composing a résumé?
8. What sort of phrases should you avoid in writing a résumé?
9. How can you prepare specifically for each interview?
10. Examine paragraph 17. What technique does the author use there and throughout in clarifying her suggestions?

C. Additional Writing Assignments

1. If you don't already know, find out the steps involved in getting ready for a trip to Japan. Write them down as if you were explaining them to a friend.
2. You would like to have a balanced budget at the end of each month. Write a process paper on how to set up your finance sheets.
3. Write an essay explaining the several steps involved in writing a research paper. Begin with finding a subject and end with the final copy typed on white bond paper.
4. Write a 500-word essay summarizing the steps that led to the signing of either the Panama Canal Treaty or the Egypt-Israel peace agreement of 1978.
5. Delineate the major steps and details involved in writing a good contrast paper.
6. Choose your favorite hobby or sport and write a process paper on how it is best pursued.
7. Pretend that you are planning your wedding. Develop an essay in which you analyze chronologically the major events involved.
8. If you were a first-grade teacher, what events would you plan for the first day of school? Explain them in a process essay that could serve as your lesson plan.
9. Find out how to transplant a lemon tree. Write the instructions in the form of a process essay.
10. Through library research, accumulate the proper information to write an essay in which you narrate the major events that led to one of the following: the Battle of Waterloo, the bombing of Pearl Harbor, the war in Vietnam, the Revolution in Iran.

11

Classification

Therefore, if you would study the strengths,
weaknesses, and peculiar mannerisms of homo
sapiens, hie thee to your supermarket!

A. Reading for Ideas

In a story that mixes realism with symbolism and fantasy, Stanley Elkin portrays life as a neighborhood in which different types of people converge and influence each other for better or for worse.

Poetics for Bullies
Stanley Elkin

1   I'm Push the bully, and what I hate are new kids and sissies, dumb kids and smart, rich kids, poor kids, kids who wear glasses, talk funny, show off, patrol boys and wise guys and kids who pass pencils and water the plants—and cripples, *especially* cripples. I love nobody loved.

2   One time I was pushing this red-haired kid (I'm a pusher, no hitter, no belter; an aggressor of marginal violence, I hate *real* force), and his mother stuck her head out the window and shouted something I've never forgotten. "*Push,*"she yelled. "*You Push.* You pick on him because you wish you had his red hair!" It's true; I *did* wish I had his red hair. I wish I were tall, or fat, or thin. I wish I had different eyes, different hands, a mother in the supermarket. I wish I were a man, a small boy, a girl in the choir. I'm a coveter, a Boston Blackie of the heart, casing the world. Endlessly I covet and case. (Do you know what makes me cry? The Declaration of Independence. "All men are created equal." That's beautiful.)

3   If you're a bully like me, you use your head. Toughness isn't enough. You beat them up, they report you. Then where are you? I'm not even particularly strong. (I used to be strong. I used to do exercise, work out, but strength implicates you, and often isn't an advantage anyway—read the judo ads. Besides, your big bullies aren't bullies at all—they're *athletes.* With them, beating guys up is a sport.) But what I lose in size and strength I make up in courage. I'm very brave. That's a lie about bullies being cowards underneath. If you're a coward, get out of the business.

4   I'm best at torment.
     A kid has a toy bow, toy arrows. "Let Push look," I tell him.

He's suspicious, he knows me. "Go way, Push," he says, this mama-warned Push doubter.

"Come on," I say, "come on."

"No, Push. I can't. My mother said I can't."

5   I raise my arms, I spread them. I'm a bird—slow, powerful, easy, free. I move my head offering a profile like something beaked. I'm the Thunderbird. "In the school where I go I have a teacher who teaches me magic," I say. "Arnold Salamancy, give Push your arrows. Give him one, he gives back two. Push is the God of the neighborhood."

"Go way, Push," the kid says uncertain.

"Right," Push says, himself again. "Right, I'll disappear. First the fingers." My fingers ball to fists. "My forearms next." They jackknife into my upper arms. "The arms." Quick as bird-blink they snap behind my back, fit between the shoulder blades like a small knapsack. (I am double-jointed, protean.) "My head," I say.

"No, Push," the kid says, terrified. I shudder and everything comes back, falls into place from the stem of self like a shaken puppet.

"The arrow, the arrow. Two where was one." He hands me an arrow.

"*Trouble, trouble, double rubble!*" I snap it and give back the pieces.

6   Well, sure. There *is* no magic. If there were I would learn it. I would find out the words, the slow turns and strange passes, drain the bloods and get the herbs, do the fires like a vestal. I would look for the main chants. *Then* I'd change things. *Push* would!

7   But there's only casuistical trick. Sleight-of-mouth, the bully's poetics.

You know the formulas:

"Did you ever see a match burn twice?" you ask. Strike. Extinguish. Jab his flesh with the hot stub.

"Play 'Gestapo'?"

"How do you play?"

"What's your name?"

"It's Morton."

I slap him. "You're lying."

"Adam and Eve and Pinch Me Hard went down to the lake for a swim. Adam and Eve fell in. Who was left?"

"Pinch Me Hard."

I do.

Physical puns, conundrums. Push the punisher, the conundrummer!

But there has to be more than tricks in a bag of tricks.

8   I don't know what it is. Sometimes I think *I'm* the only new kid. In a room, the school, the playground, the neighborhood, I get the feeling I've just moved in, no one knows me. You know what I like? To stand in crowds. To wait with them at the airport to meet a plane. Someone asks what time it is. I'm the first to answer. Or at the ball park when the vendor comes. He passes the hot dog down the long row. I want my hands on it too. On the dollar going up, the change coming down.

9   I am ingenious, I am patient.

A kid is going downtown on the elevated train. He's got his little suit on, his shoes are shined, he wears a cap. This is a kid going to the travel bureaus, the foreign tourist offices to get brochures, maps, pictures of the mountains for a unit at his school—a kid looking for extra credit. I follow him. He comes out of the Italian Tourist Information Center. His arms are full. I move from my place at the window. I follow for two blocks and bump into him as he steps from a curb. It's a *collision*—The pamphlets fall from his arms. Pretending confusion, I walk on his paper Florence. I grind my heel in his Riviera. I climb Vesuvius and sack his Rome and dance on the Isle of Capri.

10   The Industrial Museum is a good place to find children. I cut somebody's five- or

six-year-old kid brother out of the herd of eleven- and twelve-year-olds he's come with. "*Quick,*" I say. I pull him along the corridors, up the stairs, through the halls, down to a mezzanine landing. Breathless, I pause for a minute. "I've got some gum. Do you want a stick?" He nods; I stick him. I rush him into an auditorium and abandon him. He'll be lost for hours.

11   I sidle up to a kid at the movies. "You smacked my brother," I tell him. "After the show—I'll be outside."

I break up games. I hold the ball above my head. "You want it? Take it."

I go into barber shops. There's a kid waiting. "I'm next," I tell him, "understand?"

12   One day Eugene Kraft rang my bell. Eugene is afraid of me, so he helps me. He's fifteen and there's something wrong with his saliva glands and he drools. His chin is always chapped. I tell him he has to drink a lot because he loses so much water.

"Push? Push," he says. He's wiping his chin with his tissues. "Push, there's this kid—"

"Better get a glass of water, Eugene."

"No, Push, no fooling, there's this new kid—he just moved in. You've got to see this kid."

"Eugene, get some water, please. You're drying up. I've never seen you so bad. There are deserts in you, Eugene."

"All right, Push, but then you've got to see—"

"Swallow, Eugene. You better swallow."

He gulps hard.

"Push, this is a kid and a half. Wait, you'll see."

"I'm very concerned about you, Eugene. You're dying of thirst, Eugene. Come into the kitchen with me."

13   I push him through the door. He's very excited. I've never seen him so excited. He talks at me over his shoulder, his mouth flooding, his teeth like the little stone pebbles at the bottom of a fishbowl. "He's got his sport coat, with a patch over the heart. Like a king, Push. No kidding."

"Be careful of the carpet, Eugene."

14   I turn on the taps in the sink. I mix in hot water. "Use your tissues, Eugene. Wipe your chin."

15   He wipes himself and puts the Kleenex in his pocket. All of Eugene's pockets bulge. He looks, with his bulging pockets, like a clumsy smuggler.

"Wipe, Eugene. Swallow, you're drowning."

"He's got this funny accent—you could die." Excited, he tamps at his mouth like a diner, a tubercular.

"Drink some water, Eugene."

"No, Push, I'm not thirsty—really."

"Don't be foolish, kid. That's because your mouth's so wet. Inside where it counts you're drying up. It stands to reason. Drink some water."

"He has this crazy haircut."

"*Drink,*" I command. I shake him. "*Drink!*"

"Push, I've got no glass. Give me a glass at least."

"I can't do that, Eugene. You've got a terrible disease. How could I let you use our drinking glasses? Lean under the tap and open your mouth."

16   He knows he'll have to do it, that I won't listen to him until he does. He bends into the sink.

"Push, it's *hot,*" he complains. The water splashes into his nose, it gets on his glasses and for a moment his eyes are magnified, enormous. He pulls away and scrapes his forehead on the faucet.

"Eugene, you touched it. Watch out, please. You're too close to the tap. Lean your head deeper into the sink."

"It's *hot,* Push."

"Warm water evaporates better. With your afflictions you've got to evaporate fluids before they get into your glands."

He feeds again from the tap.

"Do you think that's enough?" I ask after a while.

"I do, Push, I really do," he says. He is breathless.

"Eugene," I say seriously, "I think you'd better get yourself a canteen."

"A canteen, Push?"

"That's right. Then you'll always have water when you need it. Get one of those Boy Scout models. The two-quart kind with a canvas strap."

"But you hate the Boy Scouts, Push."

"They make very good canteens, Eugene. *And wear it!* I never want to see you without it. Buy it today."

"All right, Push."

"Promise!"

"All right, Push."

"Say it out."

He made the formal promise that I like to hear.

"Well, then," I said, "let's go see this new kid of yours."

17 He took me to the schoolyard. "Wait," he said, "you'll see." He skipped ahead.

"Eugene," I said, calling him back. "Let's understand something. No matter what this new kid is like, nothing changes as far as you and I are concerned."

"Aw, Push," he said.

"Nothing, Eugene. I mean it. You don't get out from under me."

"Sure, Push, I know that."

18 There were some kids in the far corner of the year, sitting on the ground, leaning up against the wire fence. Bats and gloves and balls lay scattered around them. (It was where they told dirty jokes. Sometimes I'd come by during the little kids' recess and tell them all about what their daddies did to their mommies.)

"There. See? Do you see him?" Eugene, despite himself, seemed hoarse.

"Be quiet," I said, checking him, freezing as a hunter might. I stared.

19 He was a *prince,* I tell you.

He was tall, tall, even sitting down. His long legs comfortable in expensive wool, the trousers of a boy who had been on ships, jets; who owned a horse, perhaps; who knew Latin—what *didn't* he know?—somebody made up, like a kid in a play with a beautiful mother and a handsome father; who took his breakfast from a sideboard, and picked, even at fourteen and fifteen and sixteen, his mail from a silver plate. He would have hobbies—stamps, stars, things lovely dead. He wore a sport coat, brown as wood, thick as heavy bark. The buttons were leather buds. His shoes seemed carved from horses' saddles, gunstocks. His clothes had once grown in nature. *What it must feel like inside those clothes,* I thought.

20 I looked at his face, his clear skin, and guessed at the bones, white as beached wood. His eyes had skies in them. His yellow hair swirled on his head like a crayoned sun.

"Look, look at him," Eugene said. "The sissy. Get him, Push."

21 He was talking to them and I moved up closer to hear his voice. It was clear, beautiful, but faintly foreign—like herb-seasoned meat.

22 When he saw me, he paused, smiling. He waved. The others didn't look at me.

"Hello there," he called. "Come over if you'd like. I've been telling the boys about tigers."

"Tigers," I said.

"Give him the 'match burn twice,' Push," Eugene whispered.

"Tigers, is it?" I said. "What do you know about tigers?" My voice was high.

"The 'match burn twice,' Push."

"Not so much as a Master *Tugjah*. I was telling the boys. In India there are men of high caste—*Tugjahs,* they're called. I was apprenticed to one once in the Southern Plains and might perhaps have earned my mastership, but the Red Chinese attacked the northern frontier and . . . well, let's just say I had to leave. At any rate, these *Tugjahs* are as intimate with the tiger as you are with dogs. I don't mean they keep them as pets. The relationship goes deeper. Your dog is a service animal, as is your elephant."

"Did you ever see a match burn twice?" I asked suddenly.

"Why, no, can you do that? Is it a special match you use?"

"No," Eugene said, "it's an ordinary match. He uses an ordinary match."

"Can you do it with one of mine, do you think?"

23   He took a matchbook from his pocket and handed it to me. The cover was exactly the material of his jacket, and in the center was a patch with a coat-of-arms identical to the one he wore over his heart.

24   I held the matchbook for a moment and then gave it back to him. "I don't feel like it," I said.

"Then some other time, perhaps," he said.

25   Eugene whispered to me. "His accent, Push, his funny *accent.*"

"Some other time, perhaps," I said. I am a good mimic. I can duplicate a particular kid's lisp, his stutter, a thickness in his throat. There were two or three here whom I had brought close to tears by holding up my mirror to their voices. I can parody their limps, their waddles, their girlish runs, their clumsy jumps. I can throw as they throw, catch as they catch. I looked around. "Some other time, perhaps," I said again. No one would look at me.

"I'm so sorry," the new one said, "we don't know each other's names. You are?"

"I'm so sorry," I said. "You are?"

26   He seemed puzzled. Then he looked sad, disappointed. No one said anything.

"It don't sound the same," Eugene whispered.

27   It was true. I sounded nothing like him. I could imitate only defects, only flaws.

28   A kid giggled.

"Shh," the prince said. He put one finger to his lips.

"Look at that," Eugene said under his breath. "He's a sissy."

He had begun to talk to them again. I squatted, a few feet away. I ran gravel through my loose fists, one bowl in an hourglass feeding another.

29   He spoke of jungles, of deserts. He told of ancient trade routes traveled by strange beasts. He described lost cities and a lake deeper than the deepest level of the sea. There was a story about a boy who had been captured by bandits. A woman in the story—it wasn't clear whether she was the boy's mother—had been tortured. His eyes clouded for a moment when he came to this part and he had to pause before continuing. Then he told how the boy escaped—it was cleverly done—and found help, mountain tribesmen riding elephants. The elephants charged the cave in which the mo—the *woman*—was still a prisoner. It might have collapsed and killed her, but one old bull rushed in and, shielding her with his body, took the weight of the crashing rocks. Your elephant is a service animal.

30   I let a piece of gravel rest on my thumb and flicked it in a high arc above his head. Some of the others who had seen me stared, but the boy kept on talking. Gradually I reduced the range, allowing the chunks of gravel to come closer to his head.

"You see?" Eugene said quietly. "He's afraid. He pretends not to notice."

31   The arcs continued to diminish. The gravel went faster, straighter. No one was listening to him now, but he kept talking.

"—of magic," he said, "what occidentals call 'a witch doctor.' There are spices that induce these effects. The *Bogdovii* was actually able to stimulate the growth of rocks with the powder. The Dutch traders were ready to go to war for the formula. Well, you can see what it could mean for the Low Countries. Without accessible quarries they've never been able to construct a permanent system of dikes. But with the *Bogdovii's* powder" —he reached out and casually caught the speeding chip as if it had been a ping-pong ball—"they could turn a grain of sand into a pebble, use the pebbles to grow stones, the stones to grow rocks. This little piece of gravel, for example, could be changed into a mountain." He dipped his thumb into his palm as I had and balanced the gravel on his nail. He flicked it; it rose from his nail like a missile and climbed an impossible arc. It disappeared. "The *Bogdovii* never revealed how it was done."

32   I stood up. Eugene tried to follow me.

"Listen," he said, "You'll get him."

"Swallow," I told him. "Swallow, you pig!"

33   I have lived my life in pursuit of the vulnerable: Push the chink seeker, wheeler dealer in the flawed cement of the personality, a collapse maker. But what isn't vulnerable, *who* isn't? There is that which is unspeakable, so I speak it, that which is unthinkable, which I think. Me and the devil, we do God's dirty work, after all.

34   I went home after I left him. I turned once at the gate, and the boys were around him still. The useless Eugene had moved closer. *He* made room for him against the fence.

35   I ran into Frank the fat boy. He made a move to cross the street, but I had seen him and he went through a clumsy retractive motion. I could tell he thought I would get him for that, but I moved by, indifferent to a grossness in which I had once delighted. As I passed he seemed puzzled, a little hurt, a little—this was astonishing—guilty. *Sure* guilty. Why *not* guilty? The forgiven tire of their exemption. Nothing could ever be forgiven, and I forgave nothing. I held them to the mark. Who else cared about the fatties, about the dummies and slobs and clowns, about the gimps and squares and oafs and fools, the kids with a mouthful of mush, all those shut-ins of the mind and heart, all those losers? Frank the fat boy knew, and passed me shyly. His wide, fat body, stiffened, forced jokishly martial when he saw me, had already become flaccid as he moved by, had already made one more forgiven surrender. Who cared?

36   The streets were full of failure. Let them. Let them be. There was a paragon, a paragon loose. What could he be doing here, why had he come, what did he want? It was impossible that this hero from India and everywhere had made his home here; that he lived as Frank the fat boy did, as Eugene did, as *I* did, in an apartment; that he shared our lives.

37   In the afternoon I looked for Eugene. He was in the park, in a tree. There was a book in his lap. He leaned against the thick trunk.

"Eugene," I called up to him.

"Push, they're closed. It's Sunday, Push. The stores are closed. I looked for the canteen. The stores are closed."

"Where is he?"

"Who, Push? What do you want, Push?"

"*Him*. Your pal. The prince. Where? Tell me, Eugene, or I'll shake you out of that tree. I'll burn you down. I swear it. Where is he?"

"No, Push. I was wrong about that guy. He's nice. He's really nice. Push, he told me about a doctor who could help me. Leave him alone, Push."

"Where, Eugene? *Where?* I count to three."

Eugene shrugged and came down the tree.

38   I found the name Eugene gave me—funny, foreign—over the bell in the outer hall. The buzzer sounded and I pushed open the door. I stood inside and looked up the carpeted

stairs, the angled bannisters.

"What is it?" She sounded old, worried.

"The new kid," I called, "the new kid."

"It's for you," I heard her say.

"Yes?" His voice, the one I couldn't mimic. I mounted the first stair. I leaned back against the wall and looked up and through the high, boxy banister poles. It was like standing inside a pipe organ.

"Yes?"

39   From where I stood at the bottom of the stairs I could see only a boot. He was wearing boots.

"Yes? What is it, please?"

"*You,*" I roared. "Glass of fashion, mold of form, it's me! It's Push the bully!"

40   I heard his soft, rapid footsteps coming down the stairs—a springy, spongy urgency. He jingled, the bastard. He had coins—I could see them: rough, golden, imperfectly round; raised, massively gowned goddesses, their heads fingered smooth, their arms gone—and keys to strange boxes, thick doors. I saw his boots. I backed away.

"I brought you down," I said.

"Be quiet, please. There's a woman who's ill. A boy who must study. There's a man with bad bones. An old man needs sleep."

"He'll get it," I said.

"We'll go outside," he said.

"No. Do you live here? What do you do? Will you be in our school? Were you telling the truth?"

"Shh. Please. You're very excited."

"Tell me your name," I said. It could be my campaign, I thought. His *name*. Scratched in new sidewalk, chalked onto walls, written on papers dropped in the street. To leave it behind like so many clues, to give him a fame, to take it away, to slash and cross out, to erase and smear—my kid's witchcraft. "Tell me your name."

"It's John," he said softly.

"What?"

"It's John."

"John what? Come on now. I'm Push the bully."

"John Williams," he said.

"John Williams? John Williams? Only that? Only John Williams?"

He smiled.

"Who's that on the bell? The name on the box?"

"She needs me," he said.

"Cut it out."

"I help her," he said.

"You stop that."

"There's a man that's in pain. A woman who's old. A husband that's worried. A wife that despairs."

"You're the bully," I said. "Your John Williams is a service animal," I yelled in the hall.

41   He turned and began to climb the stairs. His calves bloomed in their leather sheathing.

"*Lover,*" I whispered to him.

He turned to me at the landing. He shook his head sadly.

"We'll see," I said.

"We'll see what we'll see," he said.

42   That night I painted his name on the side of the gymnasium in enormous letters. In the morning it was still there, but it wasn't what I meant. There was nothing incantatory in the

huge letters, no scream, no curse. I had never traveled with a gang, there had been no togetherness in my tearing, but this thing on the wall seemed the act of vandals, the low production of ruffians. When you looked at it you were surprised they had gotten the spelling right.

43   Astonshingly, it was allowed to remain. And each day there was something more celebrational in the giant name, something of increased hospitality, lavish welcome. John Williams might have been a football hero, or someone back from the kidnappers. Finally I had to take it off myself.

44   Something had changed.

45   Eugene was not wearing his canteen. Boys didn't break off their conversations when I came up to them. One afternoon a girl winked at me. (Push has never picked on girls. *Their* submissiveness is part of their nature. They are ornamental. Don't get me wrong, please. There is a way in which they function as part of the landscape, like flowers at a funeral. They have a strange cheerfulness. They are the organizers of pep rallies and dances. They put out the Year Book. They are *born* Gray Ladies. I can't bully them.)

46   John Williams was in the school, but except for brief glimpses in the hall I never saw him. Teachers would repeat the things he had said in their other classes. They read from his papers. In the gym the coach described plays he had made, set shots he had taken. Everyone talked about him, and girls made a reference to him a sort of love signal. If it was suggested that he had smiled at one of them, the girl referred to would blush or, what was worse, look aloofly mysterious. (*Then* I could have punished her, *then* I could.) Gradually his name began to appear on all their notebooks, in the margins of their texts. (It annoyed me to remember what *I* had done on the wall.) The big canvas books, with their careful, elaborate J's and W's, took on the appearance of ancient, illuminated fables. It was the unconscious embroidery of love, hope's bright doodle. Even the administration was aware of him. In Assembly the principal announced that John Williams had broken all existing records in the school's charity drives. She had never seen good citizenship like his before, she said.

47   It's one thing to live with a bully, another to live with a hero.

48   Everyone's hatred I understood, no one's love; everyone's grievance, no one's content.

49   I saw Mimmer. Mimmer should have graduated years ago. I saw Mimmer the dummy.
"Mimmer," I said, "you're in his class."
"He's very smart."
"Yes, but is it fair? You work harder. I've seen you study. You spend hours. Nothing comes. He was born knowing. You could have used just a little of what he's got so much of. It's not fair."
"He's very clever. It's wonderful," Mimmer says.

50   Slud is crippled. He wears a shoe with a built-up heel to balance himself.
"Ah, Slud," I say, "I've seen him run."
"He has beaten the horses in the park. It's very beautiful," Slud says.
"He's handsome, isn't he, Clob?" Clob looks contagious, radioactive. He has severe acne. He is ugly *under* his acne.
"He gets the girls," Clob says.

51   He gets *everything,* I think. But I'm alone in my envy, awash in my lust. It's as if I were a prophet to the deaf. Schnooks, schnooks, I want to scream, dopes and settlers. What good does his smile do you, of what use is his good heart?

52   The other day I did something stupid. I went to the cafeteria and shoved a boy out of the way and took his place in the line. It was foolish, but their fear is almost all gone and I felt I had to show the flag. The boy only grinned and let me pass. Then someone called my name. It was *him*. I turned to face him. "Push," he said, "you forgot your silver." He

handed it to a girl in front of him and she gave it to the boy in front of her and it came to me down the long line.

53   I plot, I scheme. Snares, I think; tricks and traps. I remember the old days when there were ways to snap fingers, crush toes, ways to pull noses, twist heads and punch arms—the old-timey Flinch Law I used to impose, the gone bully magic of deceit. But nothing works against him, I think. How does he know so much? He is bully-prepared, that one, not to be trusted.

54   It is worse and worse.

55   In the cafeteria he eats with Frank. "You don't want those potatoes," he tells him. "Not the ice cream, Frank. One sandwich, remember. You lost three pounds last week." The fat boy smiles his fat love at him. John Williams puts his arm around him. He seems to squeeze him thin.

56   He's helping Mimmer to study. He goes over his lessons and teaches him tricks, short cuts. "I want you up there with me on the Honor Roll, Mimmer."

57   I see him with Slud the cripple. They go to the gym. I watch from the balcony. "Let's develop those arms, my friend." They work out with weights. Slud's muscles grow, they bloom from his bones.

58   I lean over the rail. I shout down, "He can bend iron bars. Can he peddle a bike? Can he walk on rough ground? Can he climb up a hill? Can he wait on a line? Can he dance with a girl? Can he go up a ladder or jump from a chair?"

59   Beneath me the rapt Slud sits on a bench and raises a weight. He holds it at arm's length, level with his chest. He moves it high, higher. It rises above his shoulders, his throat, his head. He bends back his neck to see what he's done. If the weight should fall now it would crush his throat. I stare down into his smile.

60   I see Eugene in the halls. I stop him. "Eugene, what's he done for you?" I ask. He smiles—he never did this—and I see his mouth's flood. "High tide," I say with satisfaction.

61   Williams has introduced Clob to a girl. They have double-dated.

62   *A week ago John Williams came to my house to see me!* I wouldn't let him in.
"Please open the door, Push. I'd like to chat with you. Will you open the door? Push? I think we ought to talk. I think I can help you to be happier."

63   I was furious. I didn't know what to say to him. "I don't want to be happier. Go way." It was what little kids used to say to me.
"*Please* let me help you."
"*Please* let me—" I began to echo. "Please let me alone."
"We ought to be friends, Push."
"No deals." I am choking, I am close to tears. What can I do? *What?* I want to kill him.

64   I double-lock the door and retreat to my room. He is still out there. I have tried to live my life so that I could keep always the lamb from my door.

65   He has gone too far this time; and I think sadly, I will have to fight him, I will have to fight him. Push pushed. I think sadly of the pain. Push pushed. I will have to fight him. Not to preserve honor but its opposite. Each time I see him I will have to fight him. And then I think—*of course!* And *I* smile. He has done *me* a favor. I know it at once. If he fights me he fails. He fails if he fights me. *Push pushed pushes!* It's physics! Natural law! I know he'll beat me, but I won't prepare, I won't train, I won't use the tricks I know. It's strength against strength, and my strength is as the strength of ten because my jaw is glass! *He doesn't know everything, not everything he doesn't.* And I think, I could go out now, he's still there, I could hit him in the hall, but I think, No, I want them to see, I want *them* to see!

66   The next day I am very excited. I look for Williams. He's not in the halls. I miss him in the cafeteria. Afterward I look for him in the schoolyard when I first saw him. (He has them organized now. He teaches them games of Tibet, games of Japan; he gets them to play lost sports of the dead.) He does not disappoint me. He is there in the yard, a circle around him, a ring of the loyal.

67   I join the ring. I shove in between two kids I have known. They try to change places; they murmur and fret.

68   Williams sees me and waves. His smile could grow flowers. "Boys," he says, "boys, make room for Push. Join hands, boys." They welcome me to the circle. One takes my hand, then another. I give to each calmly.

69   I wait. *He doesn't know everything.*

"Boys," he begins, "today we're going to learn a game that the knights of the lords and kings of old France used to play in another century. Now you may not realize it, boys, because today when we think of a knight we think, too, of his fine charger, but the fact is that a horse was a rare animal—not a domestic European animal at all, but Asian. In western Europe, for example, there was no such thing as a work horse until the eighth century. Your horse was just too expensive to be put to heavy labor in the fields. (This explains, incidentally, the prevalence of famine in western Europe, whereas famine is unrecorded in Asia until the ninth century, when Euro-Asian horse trading was at its height.) It wasn't only expensive to purchase a horse, it was expensive to keep one. A cheap fodder wasn't developed in Europe until the tenth century. Then, of course, when you consider the terrific risks that the warrior horse of a knight naturally had to run, you begin to appreciate how expensive it would have been for the lord—unless he was extremely rich—to provide all his knights with horses. He'd want to make pretty certain that the knights who got them knew how to handle a horse. (Only your knights errant—an elite, crack corps—ever had horses. We don't realize that most knights were *home* knights; *chevalier chez* they were called.)

70   "This game, then, was devised to let the lord, or king, see which of his knights had the skill and strength in his hands to control a horse. Without moving your feet, you must try to jerk the one next to you off balance. Each man has two opponents, so it's very difficult. If a man falls, or if his knee touches the ground, he's out. The circle is diminished but must close up again immediately. Now, once for practice only—"

71   "Just a minute," I interrupt.

"Yes, Push?"

I leave the circle and walk forward and hit him as hard as I can in the face.

72   He stumbles backward. The boys groan. He recovers. He rubs his jaw and smiles. I think he is going to let me hit him again. I am prepared for this. He knows what I'm up to and will use his passivity. Either way I win, but I am determined he shall hit me. I am ready to kick him, but as my foot comes up he grabs my ankle and turns it forcefully. I spin in the air. He lets go and I fall heavily on my back. I am surprised at how easy it was, but am content if they understand. I get up and am walking away, but there is an arm on my shoulder. He pulls me around roughly. He hits me.

"*Sic semper tyrannus,*"* he exults.

"Where's your other cheek?" I ask, falling backward.

"One cheek for tyrants," he shouts. He pounces on me and raises his fist and I cringe. His anger is terrific. I do not want to be hit again.

"You see? You see?" I scream at the kids, but I have lost the train of my former reasoning. I have in no way beaten him. I can't remember now what I had intended.

---

*"Thus always to tyrants."

73   He lowers his fist and gets off my chest and they cheer. "Hurrah," they yell. "Hurrah, hurrah." The word seems funny to me.

74   He offers his hand when I try to rise. It is so difficult to know what to do. Oh God, it is so difficult to know which gesture is the right one. I don't even know this. He knows everything, and I don't even know this. I am a fool on the ground, one hand behind me pushing up, the other not yet extended but itching in the palm where the need is. It is better to give than receive, surely. It is best not to need at all.

75   Appalled, guessing what I miss, I rise alone.
"Friends?" he asks. He offers to shake.
"Take it, Push." It's Eugene's voice.
"Go ahead, Push." Slud limps forward.
"Push, hatred's so ugly," Clob says, his face shining.
"You'll feel better, Push," Frank, thinner, taller, urges softly.
"Push, don't be foolish," Mimmer says.

76   I shake my head. I may be wrong. I am probably wrong. All I know at last is what feels good. "Nothing doing," I growl. "No deals." I began to talk, to spray my hatred at them. They are not an easy target even now. "Only your knights errant—your crack corps— ever have horses. Slud may dance and Clob may kiss but they'll never be good at it. *Push is no service animal.* No. *No.* Can you hear that, Williams? There isn't any magic, but your no is still stronger than your yes, and distrust is where I put my faith." I turn to the boys. "What have you settled for? Only knights errant ever have horses. *What have you settled for?* Will Mimmer do sums in his head? How do you like your lousy hunger, thin boy? Slud, you can break me but you can't catch me. And Clob will never shave without pain, and ugly, let me tell you, is *still* in the eye of the beholder!"

77   John Williams mourns for me. He grieves his gamy grief. No one has everything—not even John Williams. He doesn't have *me.* He'll never have me, I think. If my life were only to deny him that, it would almost be enough. I could do his voice now if I wanted. His corruption began when he lost me. "You," I shout, rubbing it in, "*indulger,* dispense me no dispensations. Push the bully hates your heart!"
"Shut him up, somebody," Eugene cries. His saliva spills from his mouth when he speaks.
"Swallow! *Pig, swallow!*"
He rushes toward me.

78   Suddenly I raise my arms and he stops. I feel a power in me. I am Push, Push the bully, God of the Neighborhood, its incarnation of envy and jealousy and need. I vie, strive, emulate, compete, a contender in every event there is. I didn't make myself. I probably can't save myself, but maybe that's the only need I don't have. I taste my lack and that's how I win—by having nothing to lose. It's not good enough! I want and I want and I will die wanting, but first I will have something. This time I will have something. I say it aloud. "This time, I will have something." I step toward them. The power makes me dizzy. It is enormous. They feel it. They back away. They crouch in the shadow of my outstretched wings. It isn't deceit this time but the real magic at last, the genuine thing: the cabala of my hate, of my irreconcilableness.

79   Logic is nothing. Desire is stronger.
I move toward Eugene. "*I will have something,*" I roar.
"Stand back," he shrieks, "I'll spit in your eye."
"*I will have something.* I will have terror. I will have drought. I bring the dearth. Famine's contagious. Also is thirst. Privation, privation, barrenness, void. I dry up your glands, I poison your well."

80   He is choking, gasping, chewing furiously. He opens his mouth. It is dry. His throat is parched. There is sand on his tongue.

81   They moan. They are terrified, but they move up to see. We are thrown together, Slud, Frank, Clob, Mimmer, the others, John Williams, myself. I will not be reconciled, or halve my hate. *It's* what I have, all I can keep. My bully's sour solace. It's enough, I'll make do.

82   I can't stand them near me. I move against them. I shove them away. I force them off. I press them, grasp them aside. *I push through.*

5,012 words

Vocabulary

marginal (2)	retractive (35)	celebrational (43)
protean (5)	exemption (35)	errant (69)
vestal (6)	martial (35)	gamy (77)
casuistical (7)	flaccid (35)	incarnation (78)
conundrums (7)	paragon (36)	cabala (78)
ingenious (9)	incantatory (42)	irreconcilableness (78)

Questions

1. If you were to classify the people represented in this story, how many categories would you choose, what would you label each category, and who would be in it?
2. Which aspects of Push are realistic and which are not?
3. In paragraph 78, Push gives the reader a clue to his function in the story. What is his function?
4. A careful study of John Williams reveals some Messianic overtones. In what ways is he like the Messiah?
5. Why can Push imitate only defects and flaws?
6. Why does Push refuse John Williams's friendship to the end?
7. In paragraph 72, what is the meaning of Push's question, "Where's your other cheek"?
8. What does Push mean when he tells the neighborhood boys that only knight errants ever have horses? (See paragraph 76.)

Frankie and Johnny
Anonymous

1   Frankie and Johnny were lovers, great God how they could love!
Swore to be true to each other, true as the stars up above.
He was her man, but he done her wrong.

2   Frankie she was his woman, everybody knows.
She spent her forty dollars for Johnny a suit of clothes.
He was her man, but he done her wrong.

3   Frankie and Johnny went walking, Johnny in his brand new suit.
"O good Lawd," said Frankie, "but don't my Johnny look cute?"
He was her man, but he done her wrong.

4   Frankie went down to the corner, just for a bucket of beer.
     Frankie said, "Mr. Bartender, has my loving Johnny been here?
     He is my man, he wouldn't do me wrong."

5   "I don't want to tell you no story, I don't want to tell you no lie,
     But your Johnny left here an hour ago with that lousy Nellie Blye.
     He is your man, but he's doing you wrong."

6   Frankie went back to the hotel, she didn't go there for fun,
     For under her red kimono she toted a forty-four gun.
     He was her man, but he done her wrong.

7   Frankie went down to the hotel and looked in the window so high.
     And there was her loving Johnny a-loving up Nellie Blye.
     He was her man, but he was doing her wrong.

8   Frankie threw back her kimono, took out that old forty-four.
     Root-a-toot-toot, three times she shot, right through the hardwood door.
     He was her man, but he was doing her wrong.

9   Johnny grabbed off his Stetson, crying, "O, Frankie don't shoot!"
     Frankie pulled that forty-four, went root-a-toot-toot-toot-toot.
     He was her man, but he done her wrong.

10   "Roll me over gently, roll me over slow.
     Roll me on my right side, for my left side hurts me so,
     I was her man, but I done her wrong."

11   With the first shot Johnny staggered, with the second shot he fell;
     When the last bullet got him, there was a new man's face in hell.
     He was her man, but he done her wrong.

12   "O, bring out your rubber-tired hearses, bring out your rubber-tired hacks;
     Gonna take Johnny to the graveyard and ain't gonna bring him back.
     He was my man, but he done me wrong."

14   "O, put me in that dungeon, put me in that cell,
     Put me where the northeast wind blows from the southeast corner of hell.
     I shot my man, cause he done me wrong!"

Questions

1. What kind of love is depicted in this ballad? What are its characteristics?
2. What are the main ideas of the plot in this poem?
3. On whose side of the quarrel is the narrator? How can you tell?
4. Is the narrated situation a piece of impossible fiction and romance, or could it actually happen today?

5. Assuming that you dislike crimes of passion, what alternative reaction do you suggest for a woman whose lover or husband cheats on her?
6. What other kinds of devotion besides passion have you noticed among couples?

B. How To Write a Division/Classification

Division/classification means sorting out people, objects, data, things, or ideas into various types and groups. It is a method of thinking that helps to impose order on the enormous jumble of things in the world. Biologists classify animals and plants into genera and species; the U.S. Postal Service divides the entire country into numbered regions; sociologists group people into different classes. In each case an attempt is made to impose order by division/classification—by reducing the many to the few.

As civilized humans, we are entirely addicted to thinking by division/classification. We carry classes, types, and categories on the tips of our tongues. A car is not merely a car; it is either a coupe, a sedan, or a convertible—classified by body type. Its engine is either a four, a six, or an eight—classified by number of cylinders. Its make is either domestic or foreign—classified by country of manufacture —giving rise to further subtyping as either a Ford, a Chevrolet, a Toyota, a Volkswagen, or one of the other kinds of cars. With a little reflection, almost all of us can discern similar groupings and categories lurking about the simplest object. "What kind of person is he?" we commonly ask, presuming that even people can be sorted into recognizable types.

Writing Assignment

Write an essay classifying a group, a system, an emotion, or a force into its major types. Begin with a clear statement of your classification, such as "Love can be divided into three major types: general good will, familial devotion, and romantic attraction." Then develop this controlling idea by discussing each type of love individually.

Specific Instructions

1. BASE YOUR CLASSIFICATION ON A SINGLE PRINCIPLE. In the division/classification essay, as in most nonfiction writing, clarity and intensity are children of a pure purpose. If you set out to do one thing and one thing only in an essay, you have a good chance of successfully doing it. But if you try to do two or three different things at once—unless you are a highly skilled writer—you are most likely to muddle the assignment.

To be clear and consistent, a division/classification should therefore be made according to a single principle. This simply means that once you have selected a criterion for making your division, you should concentrate exclusively on developing the categories that are thereby yielded. You should not, halfway through, switch to another principle that is likely to spawn further categories. For example, if you were writing an essay classifying cars according to their body types and suddenly switched to a classification based on number of cylinders, overlapping categories would result. Some coupes have eight cylinders; so do some sedans and some convertibles. The effect would be a tiresome double count.

The choice of a division/classification principle is sometimes dictated by the wording of an assignment, but often is left entirely to the discretion of the writer. For an essay that divides and classifies is as much a thinking as a writing assignment. Say, for example, that you are asked to write an essay dividing/classifying the people you know. Numerous criteria could be used for sorting them into categories. You could, for instance, choose degree of intimacy as your selection principle, in which case you might have an opening sentence like this:

> The people I know may be classified into mere acquaintances, casual friends, bosom buddies, and loved ones.

So far so good. If you stick to degree of intimacy as your dividing principle, you will have an essay that is at least structurally sound. But another criterion, yielding entirely different categories, could have been used. You could, for instance, have chosen to divide/classify the people you know on the basis of their politics, in which case your thesis might have read:

> The people I know fall into four different political groups: radical, liberal, conservative, and indifferent.

Or, you might have classified them on the basis of social class:

> The people in my life are classifiable into three distinct classes, each with its own peculiar way of behaving: lower class, middle class, and snooty.

Or humorously, on the basis of physique:

> My friends, relatives, and acquaintances fall neatly into three groups: the were-fats, the are-fats, and the will-be-fats.

In sum, you may make an entirely different essay out of the same assignment, depending on the principle you use to divide/classify.

But which principle should you have used? That is an unanswerable question. It depends entirely on what you can do and on what purpose you wish to achieve in your essay. If you are the solemn sort who writes stately and serious essays, you would probably do well classifying your circle of friends by their politics. If you are the jolly sort and can write in a humorous vein, you might tackle the essay that lumps your friends into fat categories. If you are the affectionate sort who values friendship, you might use degree of intimacy as your dividing principle. What matters is that, in a serious essay, you use an important principle for dividing/classifying and that you practice it consistently throughout. In other words, if you were doing a classification of books on the best-seller list, you should not base your essay on a principle as trivial as, say, whether or not the books had pictures in them. Such an essay, if meant to be serious, would be unintentionally humorous.

Finally, the use of a single principle for division/classification should be observed in the essay as a whole as well as in individual paragraphs. Here, for instance, are three paragraphs, each based upon a single principle of division:

> There are five veneral diseases, all of which can cause death. Three of these have been eliminated by modern medicine, while the other two, syphilis and gonorrhea, are on the rise once more all over the world. Both of these diseases are mainly contracted through sexual relations. These germs spread to all parts of the body and, therefore, anything the infected person uses is possibly an immediate carrier. These germs can spread to another human by an open cut if it comes in contact with the germs of an infected person.
>
> The symptoms of these diseases are usually disregarded by their victims. In infectious syphilis there are three definite stages, with a few weeks lapsing between the first two. This first stage consists of a hard chancre (SHANKer) sore in the genital area. The second stage is a rash accompanied by headaches, fever, sore throat, or loss of hair. The third stage, after a seemingly dormant period of 10 to 25 years, makes its presence known by rendering its victim blind, crippled, insane, sterile, or dead.
>
> Unlike its counterpart, gonorrhea's latent stages are more easily noticed by its victims. The first symptom is usually a burning pain during urination. The remaining factors of this disease are similar to those of syphilis, and the results are equally as devastating.
>
> Mary Kathrine Wayman, "The Unmentionable Diseases"
> *Contemporary American Speeches,* 1969

The first paragraph is a division/classification of kinds of veneral diseases; the second, of symptoms of syphilis; the third, of symptoms of gonorrhea. Because it is based upon a single principle of division/classification, each paragraph is unswervingly purposeful and clear.

2. DIVIDE THE WHOLE PIE.   Once you have been given a subject to divide/classify, be sure that you discuss the entire subject. Don't leave out a single piece. For example, if you were to classify literature into short story, drama, and poetry, a significant category would be missing: the novel. The entire subject must be included if a division/classification is to be complete.

But sometimes, especially when the division/classification is of an abstract subject whose parts are not readily apparent, it is left to the ingenuity of the writer to give an illusion of completeness. For example, consider this paragraph:

> There are three kinds of book owners. The first has all the standard sets and best-sellers—unread, untouched. (This deluded individual owns wood-pulp and ink, not books.) The second has a great many books—a few of them read through, most of them dipped into, but all of them as

clean and shiny as the day they were bought. (This person would probably like to make books his own, but is restrained by a false respect for their physical appearance.) The third has a few books or many—every one of them dog-eared and dilapidated, shaken and loosened by continual use, marked and scribbled in from front to back. (This man owns books.)

Mortimer J. Adler, "How to Mark a Book"
Saturday Review, 6 July 1940.

The division, the categories yielded, and the entire subject are obviously idiosyncratic. One cannot pounce on this piece of writing as if one knew with absolute certainty exactly what kinds of book owners there are in the world. Yet the paragraph contains recognizable types and gives the illusion of completeness. What we mean to illustrate is simply that division/classification, especially of an abstract subject, is a highly imaginative exercise. It is less a question of *being* right in such a division and more a matter of *seeming* right. The preceding paragraph contains a sensible division supported by appropriate detail and delivered in a sparklingly clear style, all of which combine to give it a sense of authenticity.

3. MAKE EACH CATEGORY IN A CLASSIFICATION SEPARATE FROM THE OTHERS.   A classification whose segments overlap acquires a fuzziness that is the mark of an inferior essay. Notice the overlapping teaching methods here:

   a. Lecture
   b. Discussion
   c. Question-answer

Question-answer and discussion overlap: there is no clear distinction between them. A discussion lesson may involve questions and answers, and a question-answer lesson may involve discussion. The classification either should be limited to lecture and discussion or it should include a third, clearly separate segment:

   a. Lecture
   b. Discussion
   c. Quizzes

4. GIVE EQUAL IMPORTANCE TO EACH SEGMENT OF THE CLASSIFICATION.   Balance plays an important role in a division essay. You must curb the tendency to pamper one segment with elaborate details while paring down another to a few barren lines. Treat each segment with equal emphasis or your essay will become obviously lopsided.

John Alan Lee, a University of Toronto sociologist, based the following article on the results of his questionnaire study on types of love. The article originally appeared in *Psychology Today,* October 1974, and was adapted by the author from his book *Colours of Love,* published in Canada by New Press.

The Styles of Loving
John Alan Lee

1   We will accept variety in almost anything, from roses and religions to politics and poetry. But when it comes to love, each of us believes we know the real thing, and we are reluctant to accept other notions. We disparage other people's experiences by calling them infatuations, mere sexual flings, unrealistic affairs.

2   For thousands of years writers and philosophers have debated the nature of love. Many recognized that there are different kinds of love, but few accepted them all as legitimate. Instead, each writer argues that his own concept of love is the best. C. S. Lewis[1] thought that true love must be unselfish and altruistic, as did sociologist Pitirim Sorokin. Stendhal,[2] by contrast, took the view that love is passionate and ecstatic. Others think that "real" love must be wedded to the Protestant ethic, forging a relationship that is mutually beneficial and productive. Definitions of love range from sexual lust to an excess of friendship.

3   The ancient Greeks and Romans were more tolerant. They had a variety of words for different and, to them, equally valid types of love. But today the concept has rigidified; most of us believe that there is only one true kind of love. We measure each relationship against this ideal in terms of degree or quantity. Does Tom love me more than Tim does? Do you love me as much as I love you? Do I love you enough? Such comparisons also assume that love comes in fixed amounts—the more I give to you, the less I have for anyone else; if you don't give me everything, you don't love me enough.

4   "There is hardly any activity, any enterprise, which is started with such tremendous hopes and expectations, and yet which fails so regularly, as love," wrote Erich Fromm. I think that part of the reason for this failure rate is that too often people are speaking different languages when they speak of love. The problem is not *how much* love they feel, but *which kind*. The way to have a mutually satisfying love affair is not to find a partner who loves "in the right amount," but one who shares the same approach to loving, the same definition of love.

5   *The Structure of Love*   My research explored the literature of love and the experiences of ordinary lovers in order to distinguish these approaches. Color served me as a useful analogy in the process. There are three primary colors—red, yellow and blue—from which all other hues are composed. And empirically I found three primary types of love, none of which could be reduced to the others, and a variety of secondary types that proved to be combinations of the basic three. In love, as in color, "primary" does not mean superior; it simply refers to basic structure. Orange is no more or less a color than red, and no less worthy. In love, as in color, one can draw as many distinctions as one wishes; I have stopped, somewhat arbitrarily, with nine types.

6   EROS   Stendhal called love a "sudden sensation of recognition and hope." He was describing the most typical symptom of eros: an immediate, powerful attraction to the physical appearance of the beloved. "The first time I saw him was several weeks before we met," a typical erotic lover said in an interview, "but I can still remember exactly the way he looked, which was just the way I dreamed my ideal lover would look." Erotic lovers typically feel a chemical or gut reaction on meeting each other; heightened

---

[1]C. S. Lewis, British novelist and critic (1898–1963).
[2]Stendhal, pen name of Marie Henri Beyle, French novelist and biographer (1783–1842).

heartbeat is not just a figment of fiction, it seems, but the erotic lover's physiological response to meeting the dream.

7   Most of my erotic respondents went to bed with their lovers soon after meeting. This was the first test of whether the affair would continue, since erotic love demands that the partner live up to the lover's concept of bodily perfection. They may try to overlook what they consider a flaw, only to find that it undermines the intensity of their attraction. There is no use trying to persuade such a lover that personal or intellectual qualities are more lasting or more important. To do so is to argue for another approach to love.

8   My erotic respondents all spoke with delight of the lover's skin, fragrance, hair, musculature, body proportions, and so on. Of course, the specific body type that each lover considered ideal varied, but all erotics had such an ideal, which they could identify easily from a series of photographs. Erotic lovers actively and imaginatively cultivate many sexual techniques to preserve delight in the partner's body. Nothing is more deadly for a serious erotic lover than to fall in love with a prudish partner.

9   Modern usage tends to define *erotic* as *sexual;* we equate erotic art with pornography. But eros is not mere sexual attraction; it is a demanding search for the lover's ideal of beauty, a concept that is as old as Pygmalion.[3] Eros involves mental as well as sexual attraction, which is faithful to the Platonic concept. Most dictionaries define Platonic love as "devoid of sensual feeling," which is certainly not what Plato had in mind. On the contrary, it was sensual feeling for the beautiful body of another person that evoked eros as the Greeks understood it.

10   *The Dream of the Ideal*   The fascination with beauty that marks eros is the basis for personal and psychological intimacy between the lovers. The erotic lover wants to know everything about the beloved, to become part of him or her. If an erotic relationship surpasses the initial hurdles of expectation and physical ideals, this desire for intimacy can sustain the relationship for years. (And this knowledge must be first-hand. The playful lover may ask a friend what so-and-so is like in bed. No erotic lover would dream of relying on such vicarious evidence.)

11   An essential component of successful erotic love is self-assurance. It takes confidence to reveal oneself intensely to another. A lover who doubts himself, who falls into self-recriminations if his love is not reciprocated, cannot sustain eros.

12   The typical erotic lovers in my sample avoided wallowing in extremes of emotion, especially the self-pity and hysteria that characterize mania. They recalled happy and secure childhoods, and reported satisfaction with work, family, and close friends. They were ready for love when it came along, but were not anxiously searching. They consider love to be important, but they do not become obsessive about it; when separated from the beloved, they do not lose their balance, become sick with desire, or turn moody. They prefer exclusive relationships but do not demand them, and they are rarely possessive or afraid of rivals. Erotic lovers seek a deep, pervasive rapport with their partners and share development and control of the relationship.

13   But because the erotic lover depends on an ideal concept of beauty, he is often disappointed. The failure of eros has littered our fiction with bitter and cynical stories of love, and caused conventional wisdom to be deeply suspicious of ideal beauty as a basis for relationships. Indeed, I found that the purer the erotic qualities of a respondent's love experience, the less his chances of a mutual, lasting relationship.

14   An erotic lover may eventually settle for less, but he or she never forgets the compromise, and rarely loses hope of realizing the dream. However, I found several cases of "love at first sight" in which initial rapture survived years of married life. The success of a few keeps the dream alive for many more.

----

[3]Pygmalion, a sculptor who made an ivory statue representing his ideal of womanhood, and then fell in love with his own creation (Greek mythology).

15   LUDUS   About the year One A.D. the Roman poet Ovid came up with the term *amor ludens,* playful love, love as a game. Ovid advised lovers to enjoy love as a pleasant pastime, but not to get too involved. The ludic lover refuses, then, to become dependent on any beloved, or to allow the partner to become overly attached to him or her, or too intimate.

16   Other types of lovers dismiss ludus as not a kind of love at all; erotic types disdain its lack of commitment, moralists condemn its promiscuity and hedonism. But to make a game of love does not diminish its value. No skilled player of bridge or tennis would excuse inept playing because "it's only a game," and ludus too has its rules, strategies, and points for skill. Ludus turns love into a series of challenges and puzzles to be solved.

17   *Ludis Strategies*   For example, ludus is most easily and most typically played with several partners at once, a guarantee against someone on either side getting too involved. "Love several persons," a 17th-century manual advises, for three lovers are safer than two, and two much safer than one. A ludic lover will often invent another lover, even a spouse, to keep the partner from becoming too attached.

18   But most of my ludic respondents had other tactics. They were careful not to date a partner too often; they never hinted at including the partner in any long-range plans; they arranged encounters in a casual, even haphazard, way: "I'll give you a call"; "See you around sometime." Such indefiniteness is designed to keep the partner from building up expectations or from becoming preoccupied with the affair.

19   Of course, as in many games, one must be on guard against cheats. Cheats in ludic love are cynical players who don't care how deeply involved the partner becomes, who may even exploit such intensity. Such players scandalize ludic lovers who believe in fair play. Insincerity and lies may be part of the game, so long as both partners understand this.

20   The ludic lover notices differences between bodies, but thinks it is stupid to specialize. As the ludic man said in *Finian's Rainbow,* when he is not near the girl he loves, he loves the girl he's near. But ludus is not simply a series of sexual encounters. A lover could get sex without the rituals of conversation, candles and wine. In ludus, the pleasure comes from playing the game, not merely winning the prize.

21   Actually, sexual gratification is only a minor part of the time and effort involved in ludic love. Of any group, ludic respondents showed the least interest in the mutual improvement of sex techniques. Their attitude was that it is easier to find a new sex partner than to work out sexual problems and explore new sexual pleasures with the current one; this view contrasts sharply with that of erotic and storgic lovers. Ludic people want sex for fun, not emotional rapport.

22   *Don Juans Aren't Always Doomed*   Ludus had enjoyed recurring popularity through history. Montesquieu[4] could write of 18th-century France: "A husband who wishes to be the only one to possess his wife would be regarded as a public killjoy." The first Don Juan emerged in Tirso de Molina's *The Trickster of Seville* in 1630, the diametric opposite of the erotic Tristan,[5] the courtly ideal. Tirso's hero conquered only four women, but a century later Mozart's Don Giovanni won a thousand and three in España alone.

23   Of course the various fates of the legendary ludic lovers reflect society's ambivalence toward them. They usually go to hell, get old and impotent, or meet their match and surrender. Rarely is ludus tolerated, much less rewarded.

24   But I was struck by the fact that most of my ludic respondents neither suffered nor regretted their ways. Like successful erotics, they play from a base of self-confidence.

---

[4]Baron de la Brède et de Montesquieu, French political philosopher, jurist, and writer (1689–1755).
[5]Tristan, a prince at King Arthur's court who fell in love with the Irish princess Iseult and died with her.

They believe in their own assets so much that they convince themselves that they do not "need" other people, like most mortals. These ludic lovers prefer to remain in perfect control of their feelings; they do not think that love is as important as work or other activities; they are thus never possessive or jealous (except as a teasing ploy in the game). They typically recall their childhoods as "average," and their current lives as "OK, but occasionally frustrating."

25   My ludic respondents seemed quite content with their detachment from intense feelings of love, but most failed the acid test of ludus: the ability to break off with a partner with whom they were through. Their intentions were ludic, but they had Victorian hangovers. They tended to prolong the relationship for the sake of the partner, until the inevitable break was painful. Ovid would not have approved. "Extinguish the fire of love gradually," he admonished, "not all at once . . . it is wicked to hate a girl you used to love."

26   The legendary ludic lovers, like Don Juan and Alfie, were generally men, and only in recent years—with the pill and penicillin—have women won entry into the game. Ludus is also frequently identified with male homosexual love; the term "gay" may have originated from the assumption that homosexuals adopt a noncommittal, playful approach to sex and love, which is not necessarily so.

27   There is a variant of this type of love that I call *manic ludus,* in which the lover alternates between a detached, devil-may-care attitude toward the partner, and a worried, lovesick desire for more attention. People in this conflicting state would like to be purely ludic, but they lack the vanity or self-sufficiency to remain aloof from intimacy. They both need and resent love, and they cannot control their emotions long enough to maintain a cool relationship.

28   STORGE (pronounced stor-gay) is, as Proudhon described it, "love without fever, tumult or folly, a peaceful and enchanting affection" such as one might have for a close sibling. It is the kind of love that sneaks up unnoticed; storgic lovers remember no special point when they fell in love. Since storgic lovers consider sex one of the most intimate forms of self-disclosure, sex occurs late in the relationship.

29   Storge is rarely the stuff of dramatic plays or romantic novels, except perhaps as a backdrop or point of comparison. In *Of Human Bondage,* the hero, Philip, follows a manic love affair with Mildred with a storgic marriage to Sally, whom he has known all along.

30   Storge superficially resembles ludus in its lack of great passion, but the origins of the two types are quite different. The ludic lover avoids intensity of feeling consciously aware of its risks. The storgic lover is unaware of intense feeling. It simply doesn't occur to him that a lover should be dewy-eyed and sentimental about a beloved. Such behavior is as out of place in storgic love as it would be for most of us in relating to a close friend. Storgic love "just comes naturally" with the passage of time and the enjoyment of shared activities. You grow accustomed to her face.

31   In most modern cities people do not live near each other long enough to develop the unself-conscious affection that is typical of storgic love. I found some such cases among people who grew up in rural areas. However, among my urban respondents, who usually had few lasting contacts with their childhood friends, there were some storgic types who based their love on friendship and companionship. This characteristic distinguishes storge from other types of love, in which the partners may not treat each other at all like friends.

32   When a storgic lover gets involved with another type of lover, serious misunderstandings are likely to occur. The goals of storge, for instance, are marriage, home and children, avoiding all the silly conflicts and entanglements of passion. But to the erotic or ludic lover, storge is a bore. Storge implies a life that is reasonable and

predictable; why make it more complicated by engaging in emotionally exhausting types of love? Erotic lovers would never understand that question.

33 *The Strengths of Storge*   Storge is a slow-burning love, rarely hectic or urgent, though of course storgic lovers may disagree and fight. But they build up a reservoir of stability that will see them through difficulties that would kill a ludic relationship and greatly strain an erotic one. The physical absence of the beloved, for instance, is much less distressing to them than to other lovers; they can survive long separations (Ulysses and Penelope are a classic example of that ability).

34   Even if a break-up occurs, storgic lovers are likely to remain good friends. A typical storgic lover would find it inconceivable that two people who had once loved each other could become enemies, simply because they had ceased to be lovers.

35   In a ludic or erotic relationship, something is happening all the time. In eros, there is always some secret to share, a misunderstanding to mend, a separation to survive with letters and poems. In ludus, inactivity quickly leads to boredom, and a search for new amusement. In storge, there are fewer campaigns to fight and fewer wounds to heal. There is a lack of ecstasy, but also a lack of despair.

36   Eros, ludus and storge are the three primary types of love, but few love affairs and few colors, are pure examples of one type. Most reds have a little yellow or blue in them, and most cases of eros have a little storge or ludus.

37   The color analogy led me to distinguish mixtures from blends (compounds). You can mix two colors and be aware of both components. But it may happen that two primary colors are so evenly blended that an entirely new color emerges, unclassifiable as a hue of either, with unique properties. This is the case with mania, a fourth color of love.

38 MANIA   The Greeks called it *theia mania,* the madness from the gods. Both Sappho and Plato, along with legions of sufferers, recorded its symptoms: agitation, sleeplessness, fever, loss of appetite, heartache. The manic lover is consumed by thoughts of the beloved. The slightest lack of enthusiasm from the partner brings anxiety and pain; each tiny sign of warmth brings instant relief, but no lasting satisfaction. The manic lover's need for attention and affection from the beloved is insatiable. Cases of mania abound in literature, for its components—furious jealousy, helpless obsession, and tragic endings—are the stuff of human conflict. Goethe made his own unhappy bout with mania the subject of his novel, *The Sorrows of Young Werther,* and Somerset Maugham did the same in *Of Human Bondage.* The manic lover alternates between peaks of ecstasy when he feels loved in return, and depths of despair when the beloved is absent. He knows his possessiveness and jealousy are self-defeating, but he can't help himself.

39 *From God's Curse to Popular Passion*   Rational lovers throughout the ages, from Lucretius[6] to Denis de Rougemont, have warned us to avoid mania like the plague. Fashions in love, of course, change. To the ancient Greeks, a person who fell head-over-heels, "madly" in love, had obviously been cursed by the gods. Many parents in the Middle Ages strongly disapproved of love matches, preferring their children to arrange "sensible marriages." But mania has gained popularity in the West since the 13th century; today many young people would consider it wrong to marry unless they loved "romantically."

40   So popular is mania in literature and love that I originally assumed it would be a primary type. But green, a color that occurs in nature more than any other, is not a primary, but a blend of yellow and blue. Similarly, the data from my interviews refused

---

[6]Titus Lucretius Carus, Roman poet and philosopher (96?–55 B.C.).

207

to reduce mania to one clear type. Instead, mania respondents derive their unique style of love from the primaries of eros and ludus.

41   These yearning, obsessed, often unhappy manic lovers are typical of frustrated eros. With eros, they share the same intensity of feeling, the same urgency to find the ideal beloved. But erotic lovers are not crushed by disappointment as manic lovers are; they keep their self-respect. Manic lovers, by contrast, are self-effacing, ambivalent, lacking in confidence. They don't have a clear idea of what they are looking for, as erotic lovers do, and they feel helpless, out of control of their emotions. "I know it was crazy, but I couldn't help myself," was a favorite explanation.

42   Oddly, manic lovers persist in falling in love with people they say they don't even like. "I hate and I love," wailed the Roman poet Catullus. "And if you ask me how, I do not know. I only feel it, and I'm torn in two." Aldous Huxley's hero in *Point Counter-Point* "wanted her against all reason, against all his ideals and principles, madly, against his wishes . . . for he didn't like Lucy, he really hated her."

43   For these reasons, some psychologists consider mania to be neurotic, unhealthy. Freud was most critical of obsessive love, and Theodor Reik, in *Of Love and Lust,* explains the obsessiveness of mania as a search for the qualities in a partner that the lover feels lacking in himself. The typical manic lover in my samples seemed to feel, as the song suggests, that he was nobody until somebody loved him.

44   Paradoxically, manic lovers also behave in ways similar to ludus. They try to hold back to manipulate the lover, to play it cool. But unlike successful ludic types, manic lovers never quite succeed at detachment. Their sense of timing is off. They try to be non-committal, only to panic and surrender in ignominious defeat.

45   *The Telephone Trauma*   Consider this typical caper. The manic realizes that he has been taking the initiative too often in calling his beloved, so he asks her to call the next time. This is a consciously ludic ploy, since no erotic or storgic lover would keep count or care. But it is part of the game in ludus to keep things in balance.

46   The hour of the expected call arrives, and the phone sits silent. The true ludic lover would not be terribly bothered; he or she would quickly make a few calls and get busy with other lovers. The manic lover falls into a frenzy of anxiety. Either he breaks down and calls the lover, or he is in such a state of emotional upset that he is incapable of ludic detachment when the lover does call: "Where were you? I was so *worried!*"

47   Manic lovers, in short, attempt to play by the rules of ludus with the passion of eros, and fail at both. They need to be loved so much that they do not let the relationship take its own course. They push things, and thereby tend to lose; mania rarely ends happily. Few lovers go to such extremes as violence or suicide, but most remain troubled by the experience for months, even years. Like malaria, it may return to seize the manic lover with bouts of nostalgia and unrest.

48   It is theoretically possible for mania to develop into lasting love, but the manic lover must find an unusual partner—who can ride out the storms of emotion, return the intensity of feeling, and ultimately convince the manic lover that he or she is lovable. A ludic partner will never tolerate the emotional extremes, and a storgic lover will be unable to reciprocate the feelings. A strong-willed erotic partner might manage it.

49   *Ludic Eros*   Mania can be reduced by resolving the underlying conditions that create and sustain the lover's lack of self-esteem and his desperate need to be in love. Then the lover may move toward a more confident eros or, perhaps, a more playful ludus. This is the part of the color chart labeled *ludic eros,* the sector between the two primaries.

50   What enables one lover to mix ludus and eros in a pleasant compromise, while another finds them compounded into mania? Having previous experience in love and

many good relationships is one factor. The manic lovers in my sample were discontented with life, but ludic-erotic lovers were basically content and knew what kind of partners they wanted. Ludic-erotic people resemble ludus in their pluralism, their desire for many relationships, but they resemble eros in their preference for clearly-defined types. They do not easily accept substitutes, as ludic types do.

51   Ludic-erotic love walks an exacting tightrope between intensity and detachment. Most people think this approach is too greedy, and therefore immoral. To the ludic-erotic lover, it is just good sense.

52   *The Art of Passionate Caution*   The tightrope isn't always easy. The lover may spend an evening in the most intense intimacy with his partner, but will always back off in a ludic direction at critical moments. Just when you, the beloved, are about to react to his passion with a murmur of confirmation, he leaps from the couch to make a cup of coffee. Or just when he is about to blurt out that he loves you; he bites his lips and says something less committal: "You really turn me on."

53   The successful combination of ludus and eros is rare, but it exists. The journals of Casanova are a classic example of the bittersweet taste of this type of love. Today many attempts at "open marriages" are in fact advocating a ludic-erotic approach to love: the spouses remain primarily involved with each other, yet may have intense involvements with others so long as these remain temporary.

54   PRAGMA is love with a shopping list, a love that seeks compatibility on practical criteria. In traditional societies, marriages were arranged on similarities of race, social class, income, and so on. In modern society the pragmatic approach to love argues that lovers should choose each other on the basis of compatible personalities, like interests and education, similar backgrounds and religious views, and the like. Computer-match services take a pragmatic view.

55   The pragmatic lover uses social activities and programs as a means to an end, and will drop them if there is no payoff in partners. By contrast, a storgic lover goes out for the activities he enjoys, and thereby meets someone who shares those interests. The storgic lover never consciously chooses a partner.

56   Pragma is not a primary type of love but a compound of storge and ludus. The pragmatic lover chooses a partner as if she had grown up with him (storge) and will use conscious manipulation to find one (ludus). Pragma is rather like manufactured storge, a faster means of achieving the time-honored version. If a relationship does not work out, the pragmatic lover will move rationally on, ludic-fashion, to search for another.

57   The pragmatic approach is not as cold as it seems. Once a sensible choice is made, more intense feelings may develop; but one must begin with a solid match that is practically based. Oriental matchmakers noted that in romantic love "the kettle is boiling when the young couple first starts out"—and cools with time, bringing disappointment. An arranged marriage, they say, is like a kettle that starts cold and slowly warms up. Pragmatic love grows over the years.

58   As pragma is the compound, so storge and ludus may combine as a mixture. The distinguishing features of a *storgic-ludic* affair are convenience and discretion. A typical example is that of a married boss and his secretary, in which the relationship is carefully managed so as to disrupt neither the boss's marriage nor the office routine. Of course, such affairs don't always stay in neat storgic-ludic boxes. In the film, *A Touch of Class*, the affair becomes too intense, threatening to interfere with the man's comfortably companionate marriage.

59   AGAPE (pronounced ah-ga-pay) is the classical Christian view of love: altruistic, univer-

salistic love that is always kind and patient, never jealous, never demanding reciprocity. When St. Paul wrote to the Corinthians that love is a duty to care about others, whether the love is deserved or not, and that love must be deeply compassionate and utterly altruistic, he used the Greek word, *agape*. But all the greater religions share this concept of love, a generous, unselfish, giving of oneself.

60   I found no saints in my sample. I have yet to interview an unqualified example of agape, although a few respondents had had brief agapic episodes in relationships that were otherwise tinged with selfishness. For instance, one of my subjects, seeing that his lover was torn between choosing him or another man, resolved to save her the pain of deciding; he bowed out gracefully. His action fell short of pure agape, however, because he continued to be interested in how well his beloved was doing, and was purely and selfishly delighted when she dropped the other man and returned to him.

61   Yet my initial sample of 112 people did contain eight case histories that came quite close to the sexual restraint, dutiful self-sacrifice, universality and altruism that characterize agape. These respondents mixed storge and eros; they had an almost religious attitude toward loving, but they fell short of the hypothetical ideal in loving the partner more than anyone else. They felt intense emotion, as erotic lovers do, along with the enduring patience and abiding affection of storge.

62   Storgic-erotic respondents felt an initial attraction to their partners, distinguishable from erotic attraction by the absence of physical symptoms of excitement. And unlike eros, these people felt little or no jealousy; they seemed to find enough pleasure in the act of loving another person so that the matter of reciprocity was almost irrelevant.

63   *Testing One's Type of Love*   Why construct a typology of love in the first place? Love is a delicate butterfly, runs a certain sentiment, that can be ruined with clumsy dissection. Who cares how many species it comes in; let it fly.

64   As far as I am concerned, any analysis that helps reduce misunderstandings is worthwhile, and there is no human endeavor more ripe for misunderstandings than love. Consider. A person who has just fallen in love is often tempted to test his sensations to prove it's "really" love. Usually such tests are based on a unidimensional concept of love, and therefore they are usually 180° wrong.

65   For example, the decision to test love by postponing sex would be disastrous for an erotic love affair, the equivalent of depriving a baby of food for a week to see if it is strong enough to live. A budding erotic love thrives on sexual intimacy. But delaying sex would be absolutely natural and right for a storgic lover, and it might be a positive incentive to a manic lover.

66   The advantage of my typology, preliminary as it is, is that it teases apart some very different definitions of love, and suggests which types of love are most compatible. Generally, the farther apart two types are on the color chart, the less likely that the lovers share a common language of love. One of my ludic respondents berated his storgic lover for trying to trap him into a commitment, while she accused him of playing games just to get her body. Different types, different languages. Eros insists on rapid intimacy, storge resents being rushed. Same feelings of "love," but opposite ways to express it.

67   Obviously, two lovers who represent unlike primaries will have trouble getting along unless they both bend toward a mixture or compromise. But it all depends on what each individual wants out of a relationship. Two storgic lovers have the best chance for a lasting relationship, and two ludic lovers have the worst chance—but they will have fun while it lasts.

68   One swallow does not a summer make, and neither does one manic binge confirm you as an obsessive lover. One playful affair in a storgic marriage does not define you

as ludus. While some people have enjoyed a variety of love experiences equally, most of us definitely prefer one type. We live with other kinds, as we live with many colors, but we still have our favorites.

5,264 words

Vocabulary

altruistic (2)	rapport (12)	insatiable (38)
ecstatic (2)	rapture (14)	self-effacing (41)
empirically (5)	disdain (16)	ignominious (44)
arbitrarily (5)	promiscuity (16)	nostalgia (47)
Platonic (9)	hedonism (16)	reciprocate (48)
devoid (9)	haphazard (18)	compatibility (54)
vicarious (10)	diametric (22)	pragmatic (54)
self-recriminations (11)	ambivalence (23)	hypothetical (61)
reciprocated (11)	impotent (23)	typology (63)
wallowing (12)	ploy (24)	unidimensional (64)
mania (12)	sibling (28)	

Questions

1. What is the basis of Lee's classification?
2. What part does the analogy to the color wheel play in this essay? How does it contribute to the classification?
3. What are the three main types of love identified in the essay?
4. Which types of love, according to the author, have the best chance for a lasting relationship? Which kind of love has the worst chance?
5. On what grounds does the author defend his study of love against the charge that love is ruined by dissection?
6. According to the author, which kind of love is at work in computer dating services?
7. Which kind of love was the author unable to find an unqualified example of? Why?

Student Model

Sociology Among the "Super Shoppers"

One of the great equalizers among civilized people is the grocery store. Housewife or harlot, wealthy or poor, each of us must occasionally lay in supplies. Through the automatic door flows a never-ending stream of human beings bent upon this common errand. Therefore, if you would study the strengths, weaknesses, and peculiar mannerisms of homo sapiens, hie thee to your supermarket!

No sooner do you park than you catch a glimpse of the "Quickie." Faster than the proverbial flying bullet he screeches through the parking lot and frantically abandons his

211

car in front of the store. Flanking it front and back are signs that say "Fire Lane—No Parking". But this is, after all, an emergency. He and his buddies have a '65 Mustang torn down in the backyard, and he is making a beer run.

Inflation brings out the "Coupon Counters." Studying the merchandise they sort and file their precious discounts—two coffees in the left hand, three cereals in the right, one for a giant Tide under the arm and, whoops—there go a dozen assorted coupons on the floor!

The "Marriage Encounter" couples are easy to spot. They gather groceries as they go through life—hand in hand. Talking over each item, seeking one another's approval, they move around the shelves. Occasionally they meet other Marriage Encounter people, and through traffic in that aisle is held up for embraces and kisses all around.

Most unattractive of the supermarket species is the "Kid Slapper." This harried housewife was forced to bring the child along, and he is not on his best behavior. "Want Cocoa Pebbles," he screams.

"No way! Shut up!" she hisses, smacking him across the cheek. Moving on, we watch the little culprit taking aim with his new cap gun. He's about to shoot her in the foot.

In almost any market you will find my favorites, the "Exotics." These customers are hard to categorize, but you know them when you spy them. California has more "Exotics" than other states, and their numbers mount in summertime. You can choose your own, but as an example I cite the six-foot-four young giant in bib overalls, tattoos, a bushy beard, and a Santa Monica tan. He wears no shoes, but in his right ear-lobe glistens a gold earring. He pushes the basket along as his "old lady," cleverly draped in an Indian madras bedspread, chooses bean sprouts and mushrooms.

Near them, in "Baked Goods" stand a group of "Peep-Show Exotics." Brief halters barely conceal burgeoning bosoms, and strategically scissored "cut-offs" top long, brown legs. Their giggles are mildly self-conscious as more sedate shoppers ogle their fleshy display. They carry off hamburger buns and cookies.

Yes, supermarkets offer more than pot-roasts and frozen vegetables. I pondered this fact only this morning as I tied my Afghan hound to the bike rack, entered the store in my magenta leotards, and presented my coupon for $2.25 off on the Napoleon Brandy. For I, too, belong to that most common of species, the genus supermarketus. Check me out.

In 1956 Dr. Martin Luther King, Jr., gained a major victory in his battle for civil rights when the Montgomery buses of Alabama began to operate on a desegregated basis. Dr. King's philosophy of nonviolent resistance, as outlined in the following selection, led to his arrest on numerous occasions and eventually to his assassination on April 4, 1968.

Alternate Reading

Three Types of Resistance to Oppression
Martin Luther King, Jr.

1   Oppressed people deal with their oppression in three characteristic ways. One way is acquiescence: the oppressed resign themselves to their doom. They tacitly adjust themselves to oppression, and thereby become conditioned to it. In every movement toward freedom some of the oppressed prefer to remain oppressed. Almost 2800 years

ago Moses set out to lead the children of Israel from the slavery of Egypt to the freedom of the promised land. He soon discovered that slaves do not always welcome their deliverers. They become accustomed to being slaves. They would rather bear those ills they have, as Shakespeare pointed out, than flee to others that they know not of. They prefer the "fleshpots of Egypt" to the ordeals of emancipation.

2   There is such a thing as the freedom of exhaustion. Some people are so worn down by the yoke of oppression that they give up. A few years ago in the slum areas of Atlanta, a Negro guitarist used to sing almost daily: "Ben down so long that down don't bother me." This is the type of negative freedom and resignation that often engulfs the life of the oppressed.

3   But this is not the way out. To accept passively an unjust system is to coöperate with that system; thereby the oppressed become as evil as the oppressor. Noncoöperation with evil is as much a moral obligation as is coöperation with good. The oppressed must never allow the conscience of the oppressor to slumber. Religion reminds every man that he is his brother's keeper. To accept injustice or segregation passively is to say to the oppressor that his actions are morally right. It is a way of allowing his conscience to fall asleep. At this moment the oppressed fails to be his brother's keeper. So acquiescence—while often the easier way—is not the moral way. It is the way of the coward. The Negro cannot win the respect of his oppressor by acquiescing; he merely increases the oppressor's arrogance and contempt. Acquiescence is interpreted as proof of the Negro's inferiority. The Negro cannot win the respect of the white people of the South or the peoples of the world if he is willing to sell the future of his children for his personal and immediate comfort and safety.

4   A second way that oppressed people sometimes deal with oppression is to resort to physical violence and corroding hatred. Violence often brings about momentary results. Nations have frequently won their independence in battle. But in spite of temporary victories, violence never brings permanent peace. It solves no social problem; it merely creates new and more complicated ones.

5   Violence as a way of achieving racial justice is both impractical and immoral. It is impractical because it is a descending spiral ending in destruction for all. The old law of an eye for an eye leaves everybody blind. It is immoral because it seeks to humiliate the opponent rather than win his understanding; it seeks to annihilate rather than to convert. Violence is immoral because it thrives on hatred rather than love. It destroys community and makes brotherhood impossible. It leaves society in monologue rather than dialogue. Violence ends by defeating itself. It creates bitterness in the survivors and brutality in the destroyers. A voice echoes through time saying to every potential Peter, "Put up your sword." History is cluttered with the wreckage of nations that failed to follow this command.

6   If the American Negro and other victims of oppression succumb to the temptation of using violence in the struggle for freedom, future generations will be the recipients of a desolate night of bitterness, and our chief legacy to them will be an endless reign of meaningless chaos. Violence is not the way.

7   The third way open to oppressed people in their quest for freedom is the way of nonviolent resistance. Like the synthesis in Hegelian philosophy, the principle of non-violent resistance seeks to reconcile the truths of two opposites—acquiescence and violence—while avoiding the extremes and immoralities of both. The nonviolent resister agrees with the person who acquiesces that one should not be physically aggressive toward his opponent; but he balances the equation by agreeing with the person of violence that evil must be resisted. He avoids the nonresistance of the former and the violent resistance of the latter. With nonviolent resistance, no individual or group need submit to any wrong, nor need anyone resort to violence in order to right a wrong.

8   It seems to me that this is the method that must guide the actions of the Negro in the present crisis in race relations. Through nonviolent resistance the Negro will be able to rise to the noble height of opposing the unjust system while loving the perpetrators of the system. The Negro must work passionately and unrelentingly for full stature as a citizen, but he must not use inferior methods to gain it. He must never come to terms with falsehood, malice, hate, or destruction.

9   Nonviolent resistance makes it possible for the Negro to remain in the South and struggle for his rights. The Negro's problem will not be solved by running away. He cannot listen to the glib suggestion of those who would urge him to migrate en masse to other sections of the country. By grasping his great opportunity in the South he can make a lasting contribution to the moral strength of the nation and set a sublime example of courage for generations yet unborn.

10   By nonviolent resistance, the Negro can also enlist all men of good will in his struggle for equality. The problem is not a purely racial one, with Negroes set against whites. In the end, it is not a struggle between people at all, but a tension between justice and injustice. Nonviolent resistance is not aimed against oppressors but against oppression. Under its banner consciences, not racial groups, are enlisted.

11   If the Negro is to achieve the goal of integration, he must organize himself into a militant and nonviolent mass movement. All three elements are indispensable. The movement for equality and justice can only be a success if it has both a mass and militant character; the barriers to be overcome require both. Nonviolence is an imperative in order to bring about ultimate community.

12   A mass movement of militant quality that is not at the same time committed to nonviolence tends to generate conflict, which in turn breeds anarchy. The support of the participants and the sympathy of the uncommitted are both inhibited by the threat that bloodshed will engulf the community. This reaction in turn encourages the opposition to threaten and resort to force. When, however, the mass movement repudiates violence while moving resolutely toward its goal, its opponents are revealed as the instigators and practioners of violence if it occurs. Then public support is magnetically attracted to the advocates of nonviolence, while those who employ violence are literally disarmed by overwhelming sentiment against their stand.

1,154 words

Vocabulary

acquiescence (1)	legacy (6)	anarchy (12)
tacitly (1)	Hegelian (7)	inhibited (12)
corroding (4)	perpetrators (8)	repudiates (12)
annihilate (5)	unrelentingly (8)	

Questions

1. What is the basis of division in this selection?
2. What are the three characteristic ways that oppressed people use to deal with their oppression?
3. What did Moses discover about the nature of slaves?
4. What is the author's criticism of acquiescence? What moral objection does he raise against it?
5. Why does the author object to violence? Why does he regard it as immoral?

6. How does nonviolent resistance reconcile the truths of two opposites? What are these opposites?
7. To what noble height does the author claim nonviolent resistance will raise the Negro?
8. What three elements are indispensable for successful nonviolent resistance?
9. According to King, what will Negroes gain by repudiating violence while resolutely moving toward their goal?

A seasoned college professor of English carefully classifies bad professors. Although Williams's judgments may seem too extravagant or far-sweeping, his basic criticisms are nevertheless legitimate—as any perceptive student will doubtless admit.

Alternate Reading

Professorial Types
George G. Williams

1   Like all other definitions, the definition of what constitutes a "good professor" must be arbitrary. My own definition would involve the following items, arranged in an ascending order of importance: (1) His students learn well what he teaches them about his subject; (2) his students learn that knowledge and the process of acquiring knowledge are an endless and irresistible source of delight; (3) his students learn to seek, in every circumstance, the best and the highest that lies *within themselves*. By these criteria, hardly one professor in several hundred would receive a grade of A-plus. Not more than one in twenty would receive an A. At least 10 per cent would receive a flat F. Not more than 10 per cent would rate a B. About 30 per cent would deserve a C, and over 40 per cent a D. These estimates are, of course, personal; there are no statistics. But they are based on nearly forty years of interested observation and experience, and they are (if anything) charitable. (I have just asked three of my nonprofessorial friends for their estimates of their former college professors. Without exception, the three rated the professors lower than I have just rated professors in general.)

2   Essentially, there is only one type of good professor. He is learned, enthusiastic about learning, original, empathic, innately suspicious of rules and regulations that endeavor to uniformize personalities, more eager to encourage students than to judge them, always conscious that appreciation is ten times more efficient as an educational device than is condemnation. This kind of professor has heartened and saved many a student who otherwise would have been lost; and though the other professors do not ordinarily respect him so much as they do their "tougher" colleagues, he is a kind of university conscience whom they cannot forget, whose existence shames them a little, and whose example influences them subtly even though they resist it. His mere presence on the campus is a continuous reminder (disturbing to the administration and to the other professors) that students are, in spite of IBM cards and efficiency-obsessed administrators, individual human beings. It is unfortunate that this professor is so rare on the campus, and a tragedy that he is becoming rarer.

3   The "bad" professors are much more various. Maybe this fact is vaguely analogous to a remark made by Dorothy Sayers many years ago, "There is only one way to make love, but there are a thousand ways to commit a murder." There is only one way to be

a good professor, but there are at least seven ways to be a bad one. Let me describe these seven types of the bad professor:

4 Worthy of first mention because he may be a very good man while being a very bad professor, is the plain stupid professor. Again, the ways to be stupid are multiple. The stupid professor may be merely ignorant—trying to teach a subject he doesn't know or understand. Or he may be too stupid to know when he is boring people, or when he is antagonizing them, or when he is amusing them at his own expense, or when he is talking over their heads, or when he is insulting their intelligence. Or he may be too stupid to adapt himself to special conditions in the classroom or about the campus, or to elicit the best from the personalities in his classes. Or his stupidity may manifest itself as an intellectual lethargy, or perhaps obduracy, as suggested in the previous section: he does not want to bother to learn anything new, or to revamp his old ideas to make them consistent with current realities. Most commonly, he is a rule-follower because rule-following simplifies life, and he needs to live a simple life.

5 The second type is the smug professor—the one with a kind of feline complacency and an imperturbable confidence that he is most clever and most knowing. He has proved to himself that he is a pretty smart fellow. For has he not received excellent grades in college, done successful graduate work, written a learned dissertation, received an accolade of various degrees, and enjoyed regular advancements in his position at the university? Has he not published articles in the learned journals? And by diligent research has he not become undisputed master of some small corner of knowledge? Why should he not consider himself rather good?

6 Besides, he is daily associated with the immature and poorly informed intellects of his students; and the contrast makes him all the more certain, consciously or subconsciously, about his own intellectual pre-eminence. His wife, in order to bolster her own confidence that she herself was pretty sharp in taking him as a husband, plays up to his concept of himself, and trains the children to do the same. I once heard a professor's small son whose mother had trained him to repeat several times daily: "Papa is a very great man." Under these conditions, how can the professor avoid becoming smug?

7 As he grows older, the smug professor becomes elegantly conventional, invariably optimistic, critical of just those things that everybody else criticizes. The apotheosis of worldliness, he associates habitually with only the right people (this equals the wealthy families in the town, and the up-and-coming professors on the campus); he participates with voluble enthusiasm in every "cultural" activity that is supported by the right people in the community; he is liberal in his religious and political views, but never so liberal as to offend the right people; he is eager to assist all students who agree with him and admire him; he disapproves of only the crassly independent mind that dares disturb his universe with a question. This type of professor is everywhere evident in every university.

8 Fortunately less common (but unfortunately still common enough) is the third type of personality produced by the intellectual obduracy characteristic of professors. This is the arrogant professor. He is never arrogant to those "from whom advancement may befall"; but he is arrogant to everybody else—to students, to graduate students, to faculty members who are his inferiors in the campus hierarchy. Most especially, if he hails from the graduate school of some famous university, he is arrogant to the yokel-like students of his new university. All the unhappiness, hostility, and scorn suffered in the graduate student's and the young instructor's soul, while he underwent the insecurities, uncertainties, deprivations, humilities, and drudgeries of his early days, finds release now that the young man has become a professor, now that the subordinate has become a master.

9 The rudeness of this professor is incredible. He has not the slightest inkling of what Emerson knew so well—that "the secret of education lies in respecting the pupil." He will

interrupt students giving oral reports in class by a continual flow of remarks: "That isn't so at all!"; "Oh, no! You've got that all wrong"; "We've had enough of that. Go sit down!" He will cut students down in class with sarcastic remarks. He will write bludgeoning comments on papers. Here are two illustrative incidents that occurred in my presence this very day:

10   I happen to pause for a moment in a colleague's office. A student comes to the door and says, "Excuse me, Dr. Blank. But did you get that paper on such-and-such a topic that I laid on your desk yesterday?"

"Oh," says Dr. Blank, "so you're the one that wrote that paper? I wondered who on earth could have written one so bad!"

11   An hour later I am walking across the campus with another colleague. A student in one of my advanced courses stops me for a moment to ask a question. My colleague, who knows the young man, says, "What! Are you taking his advanced course? I thought you were damned lucky to get through my freshman course in the same subject!"

12   Obviously, professors of this type cannot inspire a student with a desire to learn, or love of a subject, or love of a university that harbors such professors. All the student wants to do is to get out of the university, and shuffle off its unpleasant associations as quickly as possible.

13   In his extreme form this type of professor has a eunuchlike cruelty. Admittedly, the extreme form is not so frequently found; but just one in a department, or even in an entire college, is the one rotten apple that spoils the whole barrel for the student. This professor specializes in the superior stare, the supercilious tone, the calculated trick of allowing a caller to remain standing, the curt and cleverly ironical answer. He likes to make witty and cutting remarks that set everyone present roaring at the victim's expense; he writes ironical "recommendations" that ruin a young instructor's chances of employment; he asks impossible questions on oral examinations, and then acts as if the candidate were a simple idiot for not knowing the answers. All this builds up his own ego, which requires the constant and morbid sacrifice of others if it is to survive.

14   A much more common, and much less obnoxious, type is the professor who just does not care about people. He likes science or scholarship, books and libraries; he likes learning, and he may even enjoy talking about what he knows. But he has no real human warmth, friendliness, empathy, or understanding of the personalities and points of view of his students or of his colleagues.

15   I have seen him, as a mathematics professor, lecture to a class of a hundred students with a pipe in his mouth, his back to the class, and his body hiding the formulae he was writing on the board—formulae which he wrote with his right hand while his left hand followed two feet behind with the eraser. I have seen him, as an English professor, leaning on the lectern, reading lectures in a monotone from an enormous pack of little cards which he picked up one by one. I have seen him, as a biology professor, consider a laboratory exercise as an opportunity for him to do some work of his own, dump materials in the sink or on the tables, and disappear for the next four hours while the students tried to make sense out of the hastily and ambiguously written directions he had scribbled on the board at the last minute, and left with them. I have seen him, as a history professor, reading lectures from a loose-leaf notebook, the lectures consisting entirely of excerpts from the textbook which he had already assigned to the class. I have seen him, as a professor of French literature, plowing right onward in his lecture, never pausing to write name of book or author on the blackboard. I have seen him, as an engineering professor, announce to his class of 50 students at the beginning of the term that, no matter what kind of work any of them did in the course, he was going to give 5 A's, 10 B's, 20 C's, 10 D's, and 5 F's.

16   The mechanical inhumanness of such professors is quite as likely to repel the student

as the smugness and the arrogance mentioned earlier. It attracts him to the subject not at all, inspires him not at all, stimulates in him no desire for learning, or love of his university, or respect for the scholarly-scientific-intellectual ideals for which the university should stand. To be sure, this kind of professor may have something to offer a certain 10 per cent of the undergraduates, or twice that percentage of graduate students. But it is difficult to see how these percentages can be reconciled with the truism, repeated ten thousand times, from Jefferson to yesterday, that education for all the people is a necessity if democracy is to survive. A professor who can educate only one tenth, or even one fifth, of his students is hardly serving the cause of democracy—or hardly returning adequate value for all the tax money that is being spent, and the far greater amount that will be spent in the future, in an effort to educate the young people of America.

17   Just the opposite of this type of professor is the one (usually young) who tries to "pal around" with his students, be their companion and their equal. A product of early solitude and social rejection, he now overcompensates by trying to make his students like him, not respect him—make them value his friendship, not what he can teach them; make them talk about him among themselves as "a real human being," not as a person who instills in them the desire to learn; make them remember him as an agreeable personality, not as an intellectual influence; make them think of him always as a man whom they like, not as a man who taught them something. Though this professor is far from ideal, three things must be said in his favor. First, he is not a negative element in the university as is the intellectually arrogant professor; second, since young people instinctively imitate those whom they like, he may, if he is a real scholar, inadvertently influence his students to want to learn; and third, as he grows older, feels more secure in the world, does not hunger for friendship as he did in his youth, and acquires the dignity of years, he may possibly become the very highest type of teacher—one who can continually maintain an awareness within himself that he is teaching, not masses of names and faces which have little importance compared with the subject he is teaching, but individual human beings whom he is morally obligated to teach—and teach as well as he possibly can.

18   The next type of professor, though well known and powerful on the campus, is somewhat difficult to describe. Usually he has produced little in the way of published scholarship or science; he is not particularly interested in research; he is not known as a good, or even popular, teacher. But by means of certain stage properties—such as a tweed suit, a pipe, a rather deep voice, a superordinated accent, knowingness about certain backstairs matters in the history of various great professors and celebrated universities, and a peculiar manner of friendly condescension to everybody, he creates about him an atmosphere of urbanity, civilization, culture. He is just a little cynical, yet he is thoroughly optimistic when you get right down to it; he has no real ideas, yet he gives the impression that he could talk about ideas if it were not so boringly uncivilized to be serious in social intercouse; he scoffs gently at convention, yet co-operates perfectly with every convention that really matters on the campus. The trustees, the president of the university, the heads of departments, and the wealthy people of the town are invariably wild with enthusiasm about him. His complacency assures trustees, president, department heads, and citizens that all is well with the university. Any doubts they may have had are gently swept aside by the mere existence of this worldly and cultured gentleman. Disarmingly frank and humorous in criticizing matters of no consequence, he is all the more comforting when he stoutly defends the essential status quo. An excellent man for lulling and suppressing self-analysis and self-criticism.

19   The last type of professor to be mentioned here is the one who, working within the new vision of education as the output of an administrative "team," and referring to his

immediate superior as "the chief," teaches in a supremely businesslike way, with a team of assistants grading papers, a team of stenographers preparing study aids, a team of secretaries keeping records, a team of aids compiling statistics, and a continual effort by all hands to formulate new student-requirements and educational formulae, and to build up local and state-wide committees charged with this or that educational chore. To this professor-turned-executive, the students are so many items to be processed, so many completed jobs to be turned out according to schedule; education is a business, and the student is both the product and the consumer. Uniformity, efficiency, mass production, and mass consumption are the ideals. Absorbed in this dream, the professor-turned-executive loses sight of the student as a human being, a young person whose welfare is the bread of life to his parents, a separate personality whose uniqueness goes unrecognized in the pursuit of administrative efficiency and teamwork.

2,590 words

Vocabulary

arbitrary (1)	imperturbable (5)	bludgeoning (9)
empathic (2)	accolade (5)	supercilious (13)
analogous (3)	apotheosis (7)	urbanity (18)
obduracy (4)	voluble (7)	

Questions

1. According to the author, what is the most important requirement of a good professor?
2. How many categories of bad professors does the author present? Name them in the order in which they are described.
3. Why does the stupid professor like rules? What other label describes this professor?
4. Which kind of professor associates only with the wealthy families and up-and-coming professors? Why?
5. Which professor seems completely unaware of Emerson's statement that "the secret of education lies in respecting the pupil"? How does he indicate this unawareness? What is the reason for it?
6. For which kind of bad professor is there hope? Why?
7. How does the last type of professor treat education? Why is this bad?
8. What transitions does the author use for moving from one category to the next? Cite each transition.

C. Additional Writing Assignments

1. What kinds of work opportunities interest you? Write an essay classifying the categories that interest you, giving examples of each category.
2. Classify people's looks according to three or four general types, supplying vivid examples of each type.

3. Divide current television shows into three to five major types, supplying examples of each type.
4. From your experience, how many major kinds of entertainment are there? Who indulges in each? Write a classification essay answering these questions.
5. Find a basis for classifying all of the wars America has fought. Then write an essay supplying examples of each type.
6. Humans communicate with each other by various means, some including language, some not. Classify the ways humans communicate and supply examples of each way.
7. If you were to divide our society into high-brow, middle-brow, and low-brow categories, what kinds of people would you include in each? Write an essay clarifying each type.
8. All working societies pay homage to some kind of authority. Classify the major kinds of authorities and describe the characteristics of each.
9. A stereotype is a classification applied unthinkingly and without taking into account individual differences. Compose a popular stereotype of one of the following: Harvard students, car salespeople, research scientists, suburban housewives, female athletes.
10. Propose a minimum of three different bases for classifying one of the following: knowledge, humor, beauty, music, sports. Next, set up the class that each principle yields, and then develop an essay on one of the classifications.

12

Causal Analysis

The most destructive force in their love affair had been social pressure.

A. Reading for Ideas

Read "The Girls in Their Summer Dresses." See if you can describe and explain the kind of relationship that exists between Michael and Frances. Pay attention to bits of conversation and details.

The Girls in Their Summer Dresses
Irwin Shaw

1   Fifth Avenue was shining in the sun when they left the Brevoort. The sun was warm, even though it was February, and everything looked like Sunday morning—the buses and the well-dressed people walking slowly in couples and the quiet buildings with the windows closed.

2   Michael held Frances' arm tightly as they walked toward Washington Square in the sunlight. They walked lightly, almost smiling, because they had slept late and had a good breakfast and it was Sunday. Michael unbuttoned his coat and let it flap around him in the mild wind.

3   "Look out," Frances said as they crossed Eighth Street. "You'll break your neck."

4   Michael laughed and Frances laughed with him.
    "She's not so pretty," Frances said. "Anyway, not pretty enough to take a chance of breaking your neck."
    Michael laughed again. "How did you know I was looking at her?"

5   Frances cocked her head to one side and smiled at her husband under the brim of her hat. "Mike, darling," she said.
    "O.K.," he said. "Excuse me."

6   Frances patted his arm lightly and pulled him along a little faster toward Washington Square. "Let's not see anybody all day," she said. "Let's just hang around with each other. You and me. We're always up to our neck in people, drinking their Scotch or drinking our Scotch; we only see each other in bed. I want to go out with my husband all day long. I want him to talk only to me and listen only to me."

7   "What's to stop us?" Michael asked.

"The Stevensons. They want us to drop by around one o'clock and they'll drive us into the country."

"The cunning Stevensons," Mike said. "Transparent. They can whistle. They can go driving in the country by themselves."

"Is it a date?"

"It's a date."

8   Frances leaned over and kissed him on the tip of the ear.

"Darling," Michael said, "this is Fifth Avenue."

"Let me arrange a program," Frances said. "A planned Sunday in New York for a young couple with money to throw away."

"Go easy."

"First let's go to the Metropolitan Museum of Art," Frances suggested, because Michael had said during the week he wanted to go. "I haven't been there in three years and there're at least ten pictures I want to see again. Then we can take the bus down to Radio City and watch them skate. And later we'll go down to Cavanagh's and get a steak as big as a blacksmith's apron, with a bottle of wine, and after that there's a French picture at the Filmarte that everybody says—say, are you listening to me?"

9   "Sure," he said. He took his eyes off the hatless girl with the dark hair, cut dancerstyle like a helmet, who was walking past him.

10   "That's the program for the day," Frances said flatly. "Or maybe you'd just rather walk up and down Fifth Avenue."

"No," Michael said. "Not at all."

"You always look at other women," Frances said. "Everywhere. Every damned place we go."

"Now, darling," Michael said, "I look at everything. God gave me eyes and I look at women and men and subway excavations and moving pictures and the little flowers of the field. I casually inspect the universe."

"You ought to see the look in your eye," Frances said, "as you casually inspect the universe on Fifth Avenue."

"I'm a happily married man." Michael pressed her elbow tenderly. "Example for the whole twentieth century—Mr. and Mrs. Mike Loomis. Hey, let's have a drink," he said, stopping.

"We just had breakfast."

"Now listen, darling," Mike said, choosing his words with care, "it's a nice day and we both felt good and there's no reason why we have to break it up. Let's have a nice Sunday."

"All right. I don't know why I started this. Let's drop it. Let's have a good time."

11   They joined hands consciously and walked without talking among the baby carriages and the old Italian men in their Sunday clothes and the young women with Scotties in Washington Square Park.

12   "At least once a year everyone should go to the Metropolitan Museum of Art," Frances said after a while, her tone a good imitation of the tone she had used at breakfast and at the beginning of their walk. "And it's nice on Sunday. There's a lot of people looking at the pictures and you get the feeling maybe Art isn't on the decline in New York City, after all—"

13   "I want to tell you something," Michael said very seriously. "I have not touched another woman. Not once. In all the five years."

"All right," Frances said.

"You believe that, don't you?"

"All right."

14   They walked between the crowded benches, under the scrubby city-park trees.

"I try not to notice it," Frances said, "but I feel rotten inside, in my stomach, when we pass a woman and you look at her and I see that look in your eye and that's the way you looked at me the first time. In Alice Maxwell's house. Standing there in the living room, next to the radio, with a green hat on and all those people."

"I remember the hat," Michael said.

"The same look," Frances said. "And it makes me feel bad. It makes me feel terrible."

"Sh-h-h, please, darling, sh-h-h."

"I think I would like a drink now," Frances said.

15 They walked over to a bar on Eighth Street, not saying anything, Michael automatically helping her over curbstones and guiding her past automobiles. They sat near a window in the bar and the sun streamed in and there was a small, cheerful fire in the fireplace. A little Japanese waiter came over and put down some pretzels and smiled happily at them.

"What do you order after breakfast?" Michael asked.

"Brandy, I suppose," Frances said.

"Courvoisier," Michael told the waiter. "Two Courvoisiers."

16 The waiter came with the glasses and they sat drinking the brandy in the sunlight. Michael finished half his and drank a little water.

"I look at women," he said. "Correct. I don't say it's wrong or right. I look at them. If I pass them on the street and I don't look at them, I'm fooling you, I'm fooling myself."

"You look at them as though you want them," Frances said, playing with her brandy glass. "Every one of them."

"In a way," Michael said, speaking softly and not to his wife, "in a way that's true. I don't do anything about it, but it's true."

"I know it. That's why I feel bad."

"Another brandy," Michael called. "Waiter, two more brandies."

17 He sighed and closed his eyes and rubbed them gently with his fingertips. "I love the way women look. One of the things I like best about New York is the battalions of women. When I first came to New York from Ohio that was the first thing I noticed, the million wonderful women, all over the city. I walked around with my heart in my throat."

"A kid," Frances said. "That's a kid's feeling."

"Guess again," Michael said. "Guess again. I'm older now, I'm a man getting near middle age, putting on a little fat and I still love to walk along Fifth Avenue at three o'clock on the east side of the street between Fiftieth and Fifty-seventh Streets. They're all out then, shopping, in their furs and their crazy hats, everything all concentrated from all over the world into seven blocks—the best furs, the best clothes, the handsomest women, out to spend money and feeling good about it."

18 The Japanese waiter put the two drinks down, smiling with great happiness.

"Everything is all right?" he asked.

"Everything is wonderful," Michael said.

"If it's just a couple of fur coats," Frances said, "and forty-five-dollar hats—"

"It's not the fur coats. Or the hats. That's just the scenery for that particular kind of woman. Understand," he said, "you don't have to listen to this."

"I want to listen."

"I like the girls in the offices. Neat, with their eyeglasses, smart, chipper, knowing what everything is about. I like the girls on Forty-fourth Street at lunchtime, the actresses, all dressed up on nothing a week. I like the salesgirls in the stores, paying attention to you first because you're a man, leaving lady customers waiting. I got all this stuff accumulated in me because I've been thinking about it for ten years and now you've asked for it and here it is."

"Go ahead," Frances said.

"When I think of New York City, I think of all the girls on parade in the city. I don't know whether it's something special with me or whether every man in the city walks around with the same feeling inside him, but I feel as though I'm at a picnic in this city. I like to sit near the women in the theatres, the famous beauties who've taken six hours to get ready and look it. And the young girls at the football games, with the red cheeks, and when the warm weather comes, the girls in their summer dresses." He finished his drink. "That's the story."

19   Frances finished her drink and swallowed two or three times extra. "You say you love me?"

"I love you."

"I'm pretty, too," Frances said. "As pretty as any of them."

"You're beautiful," Michael said.

"I'm good for you," Frances said, pleading. "I've made a good wife, a good house-keeper, a good friend. I'd do any damn thing for you."

"I know," Michael said. He put his hand out and grasped hers.

"You'd like to be free to—" Frances said.

"Sh-h-h."

"Tell the truth." She took her hand away from under his.

Michael flicked the edge of his glass with his finger. "O.K.," he said gently. "Sometimes I feel I would like to be free."

"Well," Frances said, "any time you say."

"Don't be foolish." Michael swung his chair around to her side of the table and patted her thigh.

20   She began to cry silently into her handkerchief, bent over just enough so that nobody else in the bar would notice. "Someday," she said, crying, "you're going to make a move."

21   Michael didn't say anything. He sat watching the bartender slowly peel a lemon.

"Aren't you?" Frances asked harshly. "Come on, tell me. Talk. Aren't you?"

"Maybe," Michael said. He moved his chair back again. "How the hell do I know?"

"You know," Frances persisted. "Don't you know?"

"Yes," Michael said after a while, "I know."

22   Frances stopped crying then. Two or three snuffles into the handkerchief and she put it away and her face didn't tell anything to anybody. "At least do me one favor," she said.

"Sure."

"Stop talking about how pretty this woman is or that one. Nice eyes, nice breasts, a pretty figure, good voice." She mimicked his voice. "Keep it to yourself. I'm not interested."

23   Michael waved to the waiter. "I'll keep it to myself," he said.

Frances flicked the corners of her eyes. "Another brandy," she told the waiter.

"Two," Michael said.

"Yes, ma'am, yes, sir," said the waiter, backing away.

24   Frances regarded Michael coolly across the table. "Do you want me to call the Stevensons?" she asked. "It'll be nice in the country."

"Sure," Michael said, "Call them."

25   She got up from the table and walked across the room toward the telephone. Michael watched her walk, thinking what a pretty girl, what nice legs.

1,929 words

Questions

1. How does Frances feel about Michael? Why does she feel this way? State both

224

the *way she feels* and the *reasons* for it in a single sentence that could serve as the controlling idea for an essay about the story.

2. What role do the "girls in their summer dresses" play in the story?
3. How does Michael feel toward Frances? Support your conclusion with evidence from the story.
4. How does Michael make Frances feel when he looks at other women? Why?
5. What would your advice be to a wife whose husband looks at other women the way Michael does? Should she ignore him? Be happy that he enjoys beauty and life? Scold him? Flirt with men in order to get even? Why? Give your reasons.
6. What is your prediction about Michael and Frances' future together? Will they eventually divorce? Will the marriage survive? Why or why not?
7. Do you believe that Michael is unusual, or do his feelings toward women represent the feelings of most men?

Parents
Julius Lester

1   Linda failed to return home from a dance Friday night.
On Saturday
she admitted she had spent the night
with an Air Force lieutenant.

2   The Aults decided on a punishment
that would "wake Linda up."
They ordered her
to shoot the dog
she had owned about two years.
On Sunday,
the Aults and
Linda
took the dog into the desert
near their home.
They
had the girl
dig a shallow grave.
Then
Mrs. Ault
grasped the dog between her hands and
Mr. Ault
gave
his daughter
a .22 caliber pistol
and told her
to shoot the dog.

3   Instead,
the girl
put the pistol

to her right temple
and shot herself.

4 The police said
there were no charges
that could be filed
against the parents
except possibly

5 cruelty
to
animals.

Vocabulary

caliber (2)

Questions

1. What ostensible cause did the parents offer for ordering Linda to shoot her dog? What effect did they profess to want to achieve?
2. In your opinion, what really caused the parents to issue the horrendous order? What effect did it produce?
3. What specific act brought down on Linda the wrath of her parents?
4. Do you agree with the police that no charges could be filed against the parents, except possibly cruelty to animals?
5. What significance, if any, do you attach to the passing of time in the poem?
6. The tragic events in this poem are pared to the absolute essentials. What important details are left to the reader's imagination? What effect does such condensation have?

B. How to Write an Analysis of Cause

Causal analysis is the expression used for finding connections between events. Unconsciously, you make causal analyses every day of your life. For example, you are doing causal analysis when you try to figure out why you did poorly on an exam. You also are doing causal analysis when you decide to wear warm clothing on a mountain trip so that you won't catch a cold. In the first case, you are looking at the past to find causes; in the second case, you are looking at the future to predict results.

During your college career, you often will be required to write essays that analyze cause. Your history teacher may ask you to give the causes for the Crimean War; your health teacher may ask you to name three results of a rattlesnake bite; your aviation teacher may ask you to cite the major causes for hurricanes. Such assignments are rigorous, but you can fulfill them by drawing data and facts from textbooks or lecture notes. On occasion, you will also be asked to draw causal connections of your own and these will require particularly careful thought.

Causal analysis is tricky. Few situations can be traced directly to a single, clear cause, and for this reason even experts disagree about cause. It is commonplace to read about a murder trial in which eminent psychiatrists and psychologists disagree vehemently about a defendant's motive and state of mind. Economists argue vainly about the causes of inflation and recession; medical people constantly debate the causes of cancer. Most effects have not one but several causes, and often it is difficult, if not impossible, to determine the main cause of any event.

An effect may often be preceded by a whole chain of causes so that when you try to find the real cause, you are simply pushed further and further back from one cause to another. For instance, what is the cause of air pollution? Industrial waste. But industrial waste is caused by industry. Industry is caused by the growing needs of our exploding population. The exploding population is caused by lack of birth control, which results in part from religious beliefs. Religious beliefs come from writings in the Bible. The Bible is the word of God. Therefore, God is the cause of air pollution.

This conclusion is obviously silly. It illustrates, however, how an attempt at tracing causation can quickly lead to absurdity and serves to warn you against making haphazard, hit-or-miss, or hasty causal connections. Investigate your subject thoroughly, either from firsthand experience or by doing research. The causes for your parents' happy or miserable marriage can be identified through personal experience, but the causes of complex problems such as urban poverty or juvenile crime will require some research.

Writing Assignment

Write an essay in which you list the causes that have produced a specific situation or condition in your own life or in the life of someone you know. First, describe the situation; then probe the causes, listing them one by one. For example, you might find that two people you know treat each other with contempt, feed on each other's weaknesses, or are cruel to each other. On the other hand, you might find that the relationship is characterized by close communication and sharing, mutual respect, or a gracious attitude toward one another. Next, search for the major reasons why the relationship is the way it is. Finally, combine the description and cause into one sentence. Possible examples:

> My Aunt Marge and Uncle George live in a coldly polite atmosphere *because* my aunt has fallen in love with another man.

> Lack of money and Pete's bullheaded ways are the *reasons* my neighbors, Jan and Pete Coleman, bicker constantly.

> My grandmother and grandfather have spent fifty beautiful years together *because* they have always loved God, respected each other, and worked together toward common goals.

> Money and power have *caused* the love between Laura and Tyrone to corrode slowly.

Norman and Jennifer have had to overcome enormous hardships, but these have had *the effect* of strengthening their devotion.

Specific Instructions

1. USE THE PROPER WORD INDICATORS TO SHOW CAUSATION.

Wrong: Admissions quotas based on sex, ethnic background, or age are bad. They discriminate against the capable student.

Right: Admissions quotas based on sex, ethnic background, or age are bad *because* they discriminate against the capable student.

Whether you are listing the effects or causes of a situation, warn your reader that you intend to do a causal analysis by using such expressions as *because, therefore, since, the reason is, due to, as a result, consequently,* and *thus.* Here are some examples of causal sentences:

Chaucer is difficult to read *because* he uses antiquated English.

Because of his instability, John lost his job.

Walter is talented, practices the violin five hours a day and, *as a result,* won the Luba Lefcowitz prize for violin.

The present chaos in the world may have the following *results:* the extinction of human life, a reversion to barbarism after an atomic explosion, or the peaceful establishment of a world government.

If you are listing several causes for a certain situation, it is well to number them as in these examples:

The first cause is. . . .
The second cause is. . . .
The third cause is. . . .

As a matter of course, professional writers often use various expressions that signal what they are about to do before they do it. If they are about to define a term, they say so. If they intend to describe a vista, they tell the reader. If they are analyzing effect, they announce this in advance. It is really a commonsense strategy, and one that is highly effective. Readers are more likely to comprehend a passage whose purpose is clear to them. Here, for instance, is a paragraph that analyzes why, after the Norman Conquest, French did not replace English in England:

One might wonder why, after the Norman Conquest, French did not become the national language, replacing English entirely. The reason is that the Conquest was not a national migration, as the earlier Anglo-Saxon invasion had been. Great numbers of Normans came to England, but they came as rulers and landlords. French became the language of the court, the language of the nobility, the language of polite society, the language of literature. But it did not replace English as the language of the people. There must always have been hundreds of towns and villages in which French was never heard except when visitors of high station passed through.

Paul Roberts, Understanding English

If you are similarly analyzing the cause of a thing, or its effect, you should advise your reader that that is what you are going to do. Then you do it.

2. AMPLIFY ON THE ANALYSIS OF CAUSE. Of all assignments you will be asked to write, the analysis of cause is possibly the most mongrel. You will almost certainly—in the course of doing an essay on cause—have to write paragraphs that define, describe, and exemplify. For in any analysis of cause, it is necessary to supply background material. You may have to describe the problem, define key terms, and possibly divide and classify, even though the thrust of your essay is to explain cause or to predict effect.

It is not surprising that this is so. Essays are written with a dominant purpose or intent conceived in the mind of the writer. But a translation of this dominant intent onto the page generally requires many different kinds of paragraphs. It is a little like building a brick house. One uses not only brick, but also cement, lumber, sheetrock, tiles, and wire. Yet when the building is finished, it is indisputably a brick house, though constructed of many different kinds of material. Essays likewise have distinct and recognizable purposes. Some are intended primarily to describe; others set out to narrate; still others are written to analyze cause. Yet most are constructed of many different kinds of paragraphs.

For instance, a writer is attempting to explain why humans sleep. He is, to begin with, obliged to talk about the principal human states of mind: waking, sleeping, and dreaming. The paragraph that does this is developed by *division/classification*. But, he asks, what is sleep good for? He surveys the animal kingdom and finds that while some animals—sloths, armadillos, opossums, and bats—sleep between nineteen and twenty hours a day, there are others, such as the shrew and the porpoise, that sleep very little. He also mentions the case of humans who require only an hour or two of sleep. The paragraph that serves up all this intriguing information has been developed by *example*. He then turns his attention to the kinds of sleep—dreaming and dreamless—and discusses the results of research into each. Again, the paragraph is developed by *division/classification*. He is now ready to suggest a reason for sleep:

> Perhaps one useful hint about the original function of sleep is to be found in the fact that dolphins and whales and aquatic mammals in general seem to sleep very little. There is, by and large, no place to hide in the ocean. Could it be that, rather than increasing an animal's vulnerability, the function of sleep is to *decrease* it? Wilse Webb of the University of Florida and Ray Meddis of London University have suggested this to be the case. The sleeping style of each organism is exquisitely adapted to the ecology

229

of the animal. It is conceivable that animals who are too stupid to be quiet on their own initiative are, during periods of high risk, immobilized by the implacable arm of sleep. The point seems particularly clear for the young of predatory animals; not only are baby tigers covered with a superbly effective protective coloration, they also sleep a great deal. This is an interesting notion and probably at least partly true. It does not explain everything. Why do lions, who have few natural enemies, sleep? The question is not a very damaging objection because lions may have evolved from animals that were not the king of beasts. Likewise, adolescent gorillas, who have little to fear, nevertheless construct nests each night— perhaps because they evolved from more vulnerable predecessors. Or perhaps, once, the ancestors of lions and gorillas feared still more formidable predators.

Carl Sagan, The Dragons of Eden

The remainder of the discussion goes on to expand on this notion and to find applications of its truthfulness in the animal kingdom.

Such a paragraph mix is quite typical of an analysis of cause. The writer, however, must strive to keep on the straight-and-narrow path in pursuing the dominant purpose of the essay. It is all very well and good to sidestep to define a term or to give an example of a concept, but you must not allow these excursions to seduce you from your dominant purpose—which is to explain cause.

3. BE CAUTIOUS.   Don't be dogmatic in drawing causal connections. Since very few events are sufficient in themselves to bring about a result, it is prudent to qualify your assertions with "it appears that," "it seems to indicate," or "the evidence points to." These qualifiers show that you realize that the connection between events may be probable but not certain, thereby increasing your reliability to the reader. On the other hand, if your causal analysis is a result of personal experience, have the courage of your conviction. For example, don't say, "It appears that the cause for the many fights between my roommate and me is my roommate's sloppy housekeeping." Such a statement makes you sound wishy-washy. By all means, just say, "My roommate's sloppy housekeeping is the cause of the many fights between us."

4. FOCUS ON THE IMMEDIATE, NOT THE REMOTE CAUSE.   Causation, we pointed out earlier, has a way of multiplying back in time, with one cause leading to another and then to another, until God becomes the cause of smog. To avoid entanglement in infinity, focus on immediate rather than on remote causation. For instance, one cause of overcrowded freeways is the population explosion, but a more immediate cause is the lack of rapid transit facilities.

5. AVOID CIRCULAR REASONING ABOUT CAUSE.   The following causal statements are circular:

The freeways are overcrowded because there are too many cars.

Lung cancer is caused by the rapid and uncontrolled growth of abnormal cells in the lungs.

Beauty pageants are dehumanizing because ugly women never win them.

Each statement simply restates in the second half what is already implied in the first. Overcrowded freeways obviously have too many cars on them; lung cancer is, by definition, uncontrolled cell growth in the lungs; beauty pageants are called beauty pageants because they judge women for beauty. These revisions are better:

The freeways are overcrowded because they are inadequately engineered for need, and because rapid transit facilities are poor.

Cigarette smoking is the major cause of lung cancer.

Beauty pageants are dehumanizing because they evaluate woman as a sex object rather than as a whole, functioning person.

6. BEWARE OF IDEOLOGY IN ASSIGNING CAUSE.   Here is an example of two causal statements that are based on ideology:

The high divorce rate in Southern California is caused by the fact that the devil has chosen this section of the country for his own and has been especially busy working among couples here.

The high divorce rate in California is caused by an astrological opposition between Neptune and the Moon, and by a weak but dangerous sextile relationship between Mars and the Sun.

In a complex universe, neither statement is refutable nor demonstrable, unless one is in ideological agreement with the writer. General essays on causation, however, ought not to exert any special ideological requirement on a reader.

In this selection, Arnold Bennett (1867-1931), English novelist, presents a commonsense analysis of why some books achieve the status of a classic.

Alternate Reading

Why a Classic Is a Classic
Arnold Bennet

1   The large majority of our fellow citizens care as much about literature as they care about archaeology or the program of the Legislature. They do not ignore it; they are not quite indifferent to it. But their interest in it is faint and perfunctory; or, if their interest happens to be violent, it is spasmodic. Ask the two hundred thousand persons whose enthusiasm made the vogue of a popular novel ten years ago what they think of that novel now, and you will gather that they have utterly forgotten it, and that they would no more dream of reading it again than of reading Bishop Stubb's *Select Charters*. [1]

---

[1] A medieval history text published in 1870.

Probably if they did read it again they would not enjoy it—not because the said novel is a whit worse now than it was ten years ago; not because their taste has improved—but because they have not had sufficient practice to be able to rely on their taste as a means of permanent pleasure. They simply don't know from one day to the next what will please them.

2   In the face of this one may ask: Why does the great and universal fame of classical authors continue? The answer is that the fame of classical authors is entirely independent of the majority. Do you suppose that if the fame of Shakespeare depended on the man in the street it would survive a fortnight? The fame of classical authors is originally made, and it is maintained, by a passionate few. Even when a first-class author has enjoyed immense success during his lifetime, the majority have never appreciated him so sincerely as they have appreciated second-rate men. He has always been reinforced by the ardor of the passionate few. And in the case of an author who has emerged into glory after his death the happy sequel has been due solely to the obstinate perseverance of the few. They could not leave him alone; they would not. They kept on savoring him, and talking about him, and buying him, and they generally behaved with such eager zeal, and they were so authoritative and sure of themselves, that at last the majority grew accustomed to the sound of his name and placidly agreed to the proposition that he was a genius; the majority really did not care very much either way.

3   And it is by the passionate few that the renown of genius is kept alive from one generation to another. These few are always at work. They are always rediscovering genius. Their curiosity and enthusiasm are exhaustless, so that there is little chance of genius being ignored. And, moreover, they are always working either for or against the verdicts of the majority. The majority can make a reputation, but it is too careless to maintain it. If, by accident, the passionate few agree with the majority in a particular instance, they will frequently remind the majority that such and such a reputation has been made, and the majority will idly concur: "Ah, yes. By the way, we must not forget that such and such a reputation exists." Without that persistent memory-jogging the reputation would quickly fall into oblivion which is death. The passionate few only have their way by reason of the fact that they are genuinely interested in literature, that literature matters to them. They conquer by their obstinacy alone, by their eternal repetition of the same statements. Do you suppose they could prove to the man in the street that Shakespeare was a great artist? The said man would not even understand the terms they employed. But when he is told ten thousand times, and generation after generation, that Shakespeare was a great artist, the said man believes—not by reason, but by faith. And he too repeats that Shakespeare was a great artist, and he buys the complete works of Shakespeare and puts them on his shelves, and he goes to see the marvellous stage effects which accompany *King Lear* or *Hamlet,* and comes back religiously convinced that Shakespeare was a great artist. All because the passionate few could not keep their admiration of Shakespeare to themselves. This is not cynicism; but truth. And it is important that those who wish to form their literary taste should grasp it.

4   What causes the passionate few to make such a fuss about literature? There can be only one reply. They find a keen and lasting pleasure in literature. They enjoy literature as some men enjoy beer. The recurrence of this pleasure naturally keeps their interest in literature very much alive. They are forever making new researches, forever practising on themselves. They learn to understand themselves. They learn to know what they want. Their taste becomes surer and surer as their experience lengthens. They do not enjoy today what will seem tedious to them tomorrow. When they find a book tedious, no amount of popular clatter will persuade them that it is pleasurable; and when they find it pleasurable no chill silence of the street crowds will affect their conviction that the book

is good and permanent. They have faith in themselves. What are the qualities in a book which give keen and lasting pleasure to the passionate few? This is a question so difficult that it has never yet been completely answered. You may talk lightly about truth, insight, knowledge, wisdom, humor, and beauty, but these comfortable words do not really carry you very far, for each of them has to be defined, especially the first and last. It is all very well for Keats in his airy manner to assert that beauty is truth, truth beauty, and that that is all he knows or needs to know. I, for one, need to know a lot more. And I shall never know. Nobody, not even Hazlitt[2] nor Sainte-Beuve,[3] has ever finally explained why he thought a book beautiful. I take the first fine lines that come to hand—

> The woods of Arcady are dead,
> And over is their antique joy—

and I say that those lines are beautiful, because they give me pleasure. But why? No answer! I only know that the passionate few will, broadly, agree with me in deriving this mysterious pleasure from those lines. I am only convinced that the liveliness of our pleasure in those and many other lines by the same author will ultimately cause the majority to believe, by faith, that W. B. Yeats[4] is a genius. The one reassuring aspect of the literary affair is that the passionate few are passionate about the same things. A continuance of interest does, in actual practice, lead ultimately to the same judgments. There is only the difference in width of interest. Some of the passionate few lack catholicity, or, rather, the whole of their interest is confined to one narrow channel; they have none left over. These men help specially to vitalize the reputations of the narrower geniuses: such as Crashaw.[5] But their active predilections never contradict the general verdict of the passionate few; rather they reinforce it.

5   A classic is a work which gives pleasure to the minority which is intensely and permanently interested in literature. It lives on because the minority, eager to renew the sensation of pleasure, is eternally curious and is therefore engaged in an eternal process of rediscovery. A classic does not survive for any ethical reason. It does not survive because it conforms to certain canons, or because neglect would not kill it. It survives because it is a source of pleasure, and because the passionate few can no more neglect it than a bee can neglect a flower. The passionate few do not read "the right things" because they are right. That is to put the cart before the horse. "The right things" are the right things solely because the passionate few *like* reading them. Hence—and I now arrive at my point—the one primary essential to literary taste is a hot interest in literature. If you have that, all the rest will come. It matters nothing that at present you fail to find pleasure in certain classics. The driving impulse of your interest will force you to acquire experience, and experience will teach you the use of the means of pleasure. You do not know the secret ways of yourself: that is all. A continuance of interest must inevitably bring you to the keenest joys. But, of course, experience may be acquired judiciously or injudiciously, just as Putney may be reached via Walham Green or via Moscow.[6]

1,425 words

---

[2]William Hazlitt (1778–1830), English essayist.

[3]Charles Sainte-Beuve (1804–1869), French literary critic and writer.

[4]William Butler Yeats (1865–1939), Irish poet, playwright, and essayist.

[5]Richard Crashaw (1613?–1649), English religious poet.

[6]Putney and Walham Green are adjoining districts in London. Putney may be reached via Walham Green or via Moscow in the same way that a person in Los Angeles can fly to New York via Chicago or Buenos Aires—in other words, directly or indirectly.

Vocabulary

perfunctory (1)   catholicity (4)
spasmodic (1)   predilections (4)
concur (3)   canons (5)

Questions

1. What is the attitude of the large majority of people toward literature?
2. Why can't the large majority of people rely on their literary taste as a means of permanent pleasure?
3. What is the basis for the great fame that classical authors enjoy? Where is this stated in the essay?
4. Throughout the essay, the author frequently poses questions to himself, which he then answers. What does this self-questioning technique contribute to the essay?
5. How do the passionate few succeed in conferring fame on an author who is dead?
6. Why do the passionate few have their way in literary matters?
7. Why does the man on the street believe the proposition that Shakespeare is a great artist?
8. Why do the passionate few take such an interest in literature?
9. One man has a greater interest in literature than another. Does it follow that the literary taste of the first man is superior to that of the second? Justify your reasoning.
10. Why does a classic survive? What causes the passionate few to agree that a work is a classic?
11. What is essential to the formation of literary taste?

Student readers of this book probably will be required to do a more theoretical and abstract analysis of cause than this one. The particular assignment for which this was written allowed students to conduct an analysis of cause within a narrative.

Student Model

A Reason or Three
Donald Traylor

Don pulled the big white freightliner out of the yards, pointing it down the on-ramp and into the night. A quick check in his mirrors reflected the lights of other rigs merging from on-ramps, and he knew that most of his friends who ran this route would be forming up for a little convoy as they usually did three nights a week. He stuffed the Road Ranger transmission into thirteen and over, settled into his seat, lit a smoke, and pulled the mike to his C.B. unit from its clip.

"Break-Break. This is the White Knight, mobil truckin' north-bound on I-10 for Frisco town. How 'bout it, Cotton Mouth—you got a copy on this eighteen wheeler? We're lookin', how 'bout it?"

The C.B. cracked and suddenly the cab of the tractor was filled with the voice of his friend Cotton Mouth.

"Ten-roger-four, good buddy. You got the Cotton Mouth. Yea, you definitely got the front door, good buddy, but you better maintain that ol' double nickel for awhile. Susie homemaker up on channel twenty-one just told me that Smokey is out takin' pictures tonight from a plain brown wrapper, some place around the 76 Truck plaza. Your turn, come on."

"That's a big ten-four there, Cotton Mouth. Read you five by five and wall to wall. Guess I'll comb my hair and look real legal for the man. Your turn, go ahead."

Another quick check in the mirrors showed Don that three other trucks had joined the line and that Cotton Mouth was the last truck in the line. The C.B. hissed with greetings and truck talk.

"That's a roger on the double nickel ol' buddy. Go ahead."

"Cotton Mouth, I'm going to power down my unit for awhile. I don't have the motormouth tonight and I got some thinkin' to do. So pass the good numbers around for me. And this is the White Knight and we're gonna back on out 'a here for awhile and we're standin' by and on the side. We're gone."

Don replaced the mike in the clip, raised the squelch, lit up another smoke, and muttered to himself, "Christ, radar on the very night I want to drive my brains out." The blue green glow of the instrument panel, mixed with the gray smoke of his cigarette, matched his mood. He shifted in his seat once more and as the sixty-five-foot-long tractor trailer cut through the night with its burden of forty-two thousand pounds of steel, Don's thoughts rolled back to yesterday.

Ellen had laid the keys to his apartment on the glass-top dining room table, turned to collect a few pieces of their time together, then quietly walked out of his life.

Don grimaced as the cold icicle of pain and loss plunged into his heart. His mind slowly sorted through the memories of this love affair gone bad and he began to reflect on why they had parted.

Age had played its part. He had grown up fast and hard, his experiences far surpassing even his age. Two tours in Vietnam with a marine recon unit had put the frosting on the cake, especially the day he lay and watched his squad cut to pieces by a V.C. ambush. But when he met her, his cold, hard exterior had melted away like sugar in a rain storm. He knew he wanted this fresh, innocent girl to hold and cherish forever. But her words rang in his brain like a ricocheting bullet: "Don, I do love you, too, but don't box me in yet. Don't stunt my growth. I want to experience life as you have. I want to enjoy my youth. We have lots of time to settle down together." What she could not realize was that Don wanted to protect her from this unforgiving world and let her see only the good and not the bad. He did not want to possess her, just to love her. He knew that freedom and adventure could be horrible and ugly. Tired from the Vietnam war, he was looking for comfort and safety in a warm, stable relationship. Her needs were different. Eager for new experiences, she was looking for an open, unstructured relationship.

Religion had been another sore point between them, occasionally flaring up into angry arguments. Don was an agnostic. He had tried several formal religions but found each stultifying and hypocritical. He believed in God all right, but he was more at peace with himself when he worshiped in his own mind than when he performed church rituals. He didn't know about Heaven for sure, but he did know about Hell. He had lived in it every day of his life until he left the service. She, on the other hand, was a practicing, full-fledged Irish Roman Catholic with a head full of fine parochial school attitudes and values. He thought he had ignored most of her hints about his lack of devotion to God, in that way avoiding big destructive battles; but in the end his refusal to go to mass and his sarcasms about nuns and priests had hardened her toward him.

The most destructive force in their love affair had been social pressure. Ellen came from a proper and socially prominent family whereas Don grew up in a big family where money was always short. He blushed as he recalled one of his first meetings with her family. It was a small dinner party at her parents' Westlake home. He did not like the sympathetic glance Ellen had passed him as the afterdinner conversation turned to how nice it was that one of her old beaux had finished law school or how well her little brother was doing at Harvard Prep. Hell, man, public high school, then the service, and now night school at Riverdale City College was as well as he could do! He, too, wanted to be a lawyer, but his education would have to be assembled in segments. He had bitten his tongue a hundred times whenever her dad complained about labor ruining the country, or hippies destroying the atmosphere of their summer mansion at Lake Tahoe, or Maddy, the maid, taking advantage of them by refusing to wash down the walls. Once in a while Don couldn't help sullenly noting that Ellen's father seemed to forget that some people made a living by driving trucks during the day so that they could go to school at night. And once, when he was especially tired and grouchy, he had told her that her old man was "a fat-bellied tycoon" who lived in a fantasy world, removed from the sweat of reality. That remark had made her cry.

There it was: age, religion, and social status. Any of these problems separately and individually might have been overcome through patience and maturity. But together they combined into an overwhelming opposition. They had intruded slowly but inevitably and had gradually split Don and Ellen apart. They had blended and jelled into a sharp wedge that had lodged between them. And now he was alone without her.

Suddenly Cotton Mouth was back on the radio, just finishing a sign-off to someone. It was some time before Don realized that Cotton Mouth was trying to get his attention: "Break-break, White Knight. What happened to you, good buddy? That front door put you to sleep up there? Your turn, go ahead. Go ahead."

Don's answer was delivered in slow, measured words: "Negative, Cotton Mouth. I was just truckin'."

Himself an elderly man, the author points out the dangers of a society that worships youth while neglecting to prepare its members for old age and to seek the wisdom of its sages.

Alternate Reading

Growing Old
J. B. Priestley

1   In spite of all this "problem of the aged" stuff, all the arrangements and possible arrangements, all the national or regional councils and societies, this is a bad world, perhaps the worst there ever was, in which to reach old age.

2   To begin with, ours is a world that changes too quickly. Even I, fortunate in my work and circumstances and tougher than most old people, have now had about as much as I can take. I feel already that I am half in science fiction. The sensible world I knew how to cope with is vanishing. What a lad of twenty takes for granted, I regard with increasing horror. Those monster blocks of flats that are going up everywhere, from here to Hong

Kong! (I saw an interrelated group of them in Singapore that could house the whole population of Cambridge.) Or, where people won't live in flats, those detached or semi-detached villas that go on for ever! Or those bewildering networks of motor roads, as on Long Island or in southern California, where the cars never stop, looking at a distance like an invasion of beetles! All the more and more with less and less variety! As if sheer numbers might turn us soon into something like insects, whose lives might ultimately be controlled entirely by machines! I am willing to believe that the young see it all quite differently; I have lived too long to interpret the huge changing scene in ordinary human terms.

3   I cannot help remembering, though, that for thousands of generations not only were the old able to cope with the world but it was agreed that it was they who were better able to cope than anybody else. They were in fact respectfully consulted as experienced copers. Grandfather was not a problem but a solver of problems. And clearly there is much to be said in favour of societies that honoured old age and did not put all the emphasis on youth. All the people in those societies had something to look forward to. Everybody was moving towards the prizes and not away from them. To flatter and pamper the young for ten years is to leave them increasingly dissatisfied for the next fifty. If being young *isn't* wonderful, then why all the fuss? If it *is* wonderful, then the young creatures who enjoy it can stand being given a few orders and shouted at. Why put everybody on a conveyor belt to disenchantment and despair?

4   There would be some excuse for me if I took to drugs "for kicks" or went out at night to smash things, because after all, in what is now the fashionable view, I am old and almost done for and might as well play merry hell before I am bedridden. If I don't do these things, then it is because I have more sense and know better. But the prevailing philosophy of our society suggests I haven't more sense and don't know better, just because I am no longer young. Meanwhile, the youngsters who get up to these antics may be influenced by the idea that theirs is the only time of life worth having, that they have nothing to look forward to, so in secret despair they take something "for kicks," or satisfy their inward rage by smashing things that don't belong to them.

5   Both in life and in the arts, no doubt, it is best if there is a certain give-and-take between the generations. But if in the arts it is bad for the old to be in the saddle, it is even worse for the young to be there, galloping to nowhere. Fifty years ago, art students were taught to draw, often by severe and sarcastic professors. After that, if they had a genuinely original personal vision, they could rebel against accepted forms, each in his own way. But now we have art students who won't be taught anything, being young and therefore geniuses. This is not really a rebellion against the standards of the old but against art itself. In this growing chaos we are threatened with the disappearance of the artist himself, the man who really knows how to do something that most of us cannot do. There are signs that music, literature and the drama are going the same way.

6   When I was young we were just young, we weren't Youth. In those days, Youth hadn't arrived. Now, not only has it arrived but there seems no escaping from it. Illustrated periodicals, especially if they use colour, all appear to be passionately devoted to Youth. One of them ought to produce a special number, all deep purple and black, describing the tragedy of a thirtieth birthday. This new cult of Youth is largely an Admass device. What Admass (my term for a system, not for a number of people) wants to do—and nobody can say it isn't succeeding—is to persuade us that first and last we are con-sumers. We are here on earth to earn, spend, consume. (And this must be the lowest view humanity has ever taken of itself. The social and psychological consequences may be discovered all round us.) Youth is now the big spender. The young have more money to chuck about than anybody except the really rich. They snow pound notes on certain industries. So in those periodicals in which the advertisements and the editorial matter begin to seem all one, we have this cult of Youth. The young are switched on; the rest

of us have long been switched off; and as any sign of maturity is a disaster that must be postponed, the young will soon be younger still, schoolchildren being given more and more attention.

7   Another reason why this is a bad world to grow old in is that it is a world increasingly devoted to technology. I am no enemy of technology and gladly accept whatever benefits come my way. But its enormous importance puts the elderly into the shade. Just as we imagine that we are superior to our ancestors because we have technology and they hadn't, so our young men feel they are better than their fathers and grandfathers because they are closer to technological expertise. Yet a man may have an impressive amount of mechanical ingenuity, sufficient to put other men into space, but behave like a spoilt child or a maniac in his personal life and be hypnotised by ideas that are wildly irrational. If this is the great technological age, it is also the age of collective psychoses in which money, time and effort have been wasted on fantastic illusions. I see no signs therefore that technology, for all its benefits, makes men wiser. It is true that age is no guarantee of wisdom—and God knows it is wisdom we need—but we might agree that an increasing knowledge of electronics is not an adequate substitute.

8   There is a final reason why we who are growing old must face a sharp challenge. In the later afternoon of life, going down the other side of the hill, we look towards Death. Just as youth must prepare itself to live, we must prepare ourselves to die. This doesn't mean we must mope and sicken; on the contrary, we must live fully but in a different way, broadening our base, losing much of our egoism to religion or culture, already reaching out, we might say, to immortality. Like Cleopatra, we should have immortal longings, though our immortality should belong to the spirit of man. (As this is one of Jung's favourite themes, I refer the reader to him. Try, as a generous tasting sample, his *Psychological Reflections*, edited by Jolande Jacobi.) Now we cannot pretend we live in a society that encourages this attitude of mind. Death it tries to ignore; the very word itself is avoided. Religion and culture are both shaky. There is a pretence that we are all on the morning side of the hill, and might soon, with the help of goats' blood or sheep's glands, stay there longer and longer. But if we who are growing old are wise, we shall reject this pretence, go unprotesting down the other side of the hill:

Be absolute for death; either death or life shall thereby be the sweeter. . .

We could do with a duke or two as wise as that one.

1,378 words

Vocabulary

conveyor (3)
disenchantment (3)
ingenuity (7)

Questions

1. How many major causes does the author cite to support his contention that ours is a bad world in which to grow old? Summarize each cause.
2. What transitions does the author use to indicate that he is shifting from one cause to the next? Point out each transition.
3. According to the author, what danger lies in lavishing too much on the young? Do you agree with this view? Why or why not?

4. Why would it be more reasonable for the author to take drugs than for young people to do so?
5. In paragraph 5, what judgment on contemporary art does the author make? What will be the ultimate result?
6. What irony associated with technological advancement does the author point out in paragraph 7? What quality must accompany technological advancement if the world is to improve?
7. As we grow older and therefore closer to death, what important change should take place in our system of priorities? What is your response to this view?
8. What is the meaning of the author's reference to "goats' blood" and "sheep's glands"?

Reprinted from *The Bulletin of Atomic Scientists*, the essay that follows attempts to convince us that the danger of nuclear war is a problem of unprecedented magnitude and that the destruction resulting from such a war is unfathomable in its far-reaching implications.

Alternate Reading

The Illusion of "Survival"
H. Jack Geiger, M.D.

1   To attempt to measure and describe the consequences of a thermonuclear attack on a major American city is to confront a paradox.

2   On the one hand, the nature and magnitude of the effects of hypothetical—but eminently possible—nuclear attacks are entirely specifiable. The calculations are straightforward and only moderately complex. Indeed, over the past two decades, these consequences have been described in exquisite detail in hundreds of scientific journals, books and government publications.[1]

3   On the other hand, despite the specificity, these effects—the numbers of killed and injured, the destruction of the physical environment, the damage to the ecosphere—are unfathomable. In short, it is almost impossible fully to grasp the reality they represent, the implications they carry.

4   This is not merely because the numbers are so large as to be incomprehensible: close to 10 *million* people killed or seriously injured, for example, in consequence of a single 20-megaton explosion and the resulting firestorm on the New York metropolitan area. The difficulty occurs primarily because we are attempting to describe and understand an event that is without precedent.

---

[1] Joint Committee on Atomic Energy, U.S. Congress, *Biological and Environmental Effects of Nuclear War: Summary Analysis of Hearings, June 22–26, 1959* (Washington, D.C.: GPO, 1959); *New England Journal of Medicine* 266 (1962), pp. 1137–1144; S. Aranow, F. R. Ervin, V. W. Sidel, eds., *The Fallen Sky: Medical Consequences of Thermonuclear War* (New York: Hill and Wang, 1963); K. N. Lewis, "The Prompt and Delayed Effects of Nuclear War," *Scientific American*, 241:1 (1979), pp. 35–47; U.S. Congress, Office of Technology Assessment, *The Effects of Nuclear War*, OTA-NSO89 (Washington, D.C.: GPO, 1979).

5   Hiroshima and Nagasaki do not serve as precedents for any probable nuclear war scenario. The weapons used on those cities approximated 15 kilotons of explosive force each. At one megaton—a small weapon by contemporary standards—we are trying to imagine 70 simultaneous Hiroshima explosions. At 20 megatons we are trying to imagine 1,400 Hiroshima bombs detonated at the same moment in the same place.

6   Hiroshima and Nagasaki were single events, with effects decaying over time; today we are faced with the possibility of multiple events—a thermonuclear explosion at 10 a.m. and another at 4 p.m. At the time of Hiroshima, there was one nuclear power and the world's total arsenal comprised two or three weapons; today there are at least six nuclear powers and the total arsenal is—conservatively—in excess of 50,000 warheads.

7   But most important, Hiroshima and Nagasaki were isolated, limited disasters. They could, in time, be saved and reconstructed with help from outside. Always, we think of an "outside"; this is our intuitive model of disasters, for our historical experience is confined to single-event phenomena of limited range, duration and effect—hurricanes, earthquakes, World War II bombings, even Hiroshima and Nagasaki—in which both short-term and longer-term relief efforts could be mounted.

8   In any full-scale contemporary nuclear exchange, however, *there will be no "outside" that we can rely upon*. We cannot safely assume that there will be unaffected major areas within reach of targeted cities that will have resources that can be mobilized effectively to help the stricken targets, or that are likely to regard even making the effort as a rational enterprise. In a population-targeted attack, every major population center may be effectively destroyed.

9   In attempting to comprehend the consequences it is useful to consider the case of a single weapon and a single city. One specifies the megatonnage, the nature of the attack (air burst or ground burst, single or multiple strike), the time of year, the day of the week (workday or weekend), the time of day, the atmospheric conditions (clear or cloudy, raining or dry), and the wind patterns. The magnitudes of blast (in pounds per square inch above atmospheric pressure), heat (in calories per square centimeter) and radiation are determined at various distances from ground zero. These distances are the radii of a series of concentric circles extending outward from the point of explosion. Within each circle, given the physical forces, the nature of the buildings and terrain, and the population concentration, it is possible to calculate the numbers killed and seriously injured.

10   The U.S. Arms Control and Disarmament Agency has made such calculations for every city in the United States with a population of 25,000 or more, at weapon sizes varying from 50 kilotons to 20 megatons.[2] In San Francisco, for example, the Agency calculates that a single one-megaton air burst would kill 624,000 persons and seriously injure and incapacitate 306,000. A single 20-megaton air burst would kill 1,538,000 and seriously injure 738,000.

11   These figures are serious understatements, however. They are based on a census population distribution, that is, they make the implicit assumption that everyone is at home, when in fact a population-targeted attack is much likelier to occur on a weekday during working hours, when the population is concentrated in central-city areas closest to ground zero. And they do not allow for the probability of a firestorm or mass conflagration as the secondary consequence of a nuclear attack. A firestorm—like those at Hiroshima, and at Dresden and Hamburg after conventional bombings during World War II—may burn for days, with ambient temperatures exceeding 800° centigrade. It

---

[2]U.S. Arms Control and Disarmament Agency, "Urban Population Vulnerability in the United States" (Washington, D.C., 1979).

increases the lethal area *five-fold.*[3] It also makes all conventional sheltering attempts worse than useless. At these temperatures, and with the exhaustion of oxygen supplies and the accumulation of toxic gases, shelters become crematoria. In Dresden and Hamburg, the only survivors were those who fled their shelters.

12   A 25 percent increase in the numbers of killed and seriously injured would be a conservative adjustment for these two factors. Thus corrected, the figures for San Francisco would be that:

13   A one-megaton air burst would kill 780,000 persons (22 percent of the total Bay Area population) and seriously injure 382,000 (10.5 percent), for total casualties of 1,162,500, or 33 percent of the population.

14   A 20-megaton air burst would kill 1,923,000 persons (53 percent of all the people in the Bay Area) and seriously injure 874,000 (24 percent) for total casualties of 2,797,000, or 77.4 percent of the population.

15   The figures illustrate the lack of precedent. There is no identifiable event in human history when a million people have been killed in one place at one moment. There is no previous situation in which there were 400,000 seriously injured human beings in one place.

16   The nature of these injuries further illustrates the magnitude of the problem. Among "survivors" there will probably be tens of thousands of cases of extensive third-degree burns. And in this kind of injury, survival and recovery depend almost entirely on the availability of specialized burn-care facilities, highly and specially trained medical and allied personnel, complex laboratory equipment, almost unlimited supplies of blood and plasma, and the availability of a wide range of drugs. No such facilities would remain intact in San Francisco; the number of Bay Area burn casualties would exceed by a factor of 10 or 20 the capacity of all the burn-care centers in the United States.

17   In addition to third-degree burns, hundreds of thousands of "survivors" would suffer crushing injuries, simple and compound fractures, penetrating wounds of the skull, thorax and abdomen, and multiple lacerations with extensive hemorrhage, primarily in consequence of blast pressures and the collapse of buildings. (Many of these victims, of course, would also have serious burns.) A moderate number would have ruptured internal organs, particularly the lungs, from blast pressures. Significant numbers would be deaf in consequence of ruptured eardrums, in addition to their other injuries, and many would be blind, since—as far as 35 miles from ground zero—reflex glance at the fireball would produce serious retinal burns.

18   Superimposed on these problems would be tens of thousands of cases of acute radiation injury, superficial burns produced by beta and low-energy gamma rays, and damage due to radionucleides in specific organs. Many would die even if the most sophisticated and heroic therapy were available; others, with similar symptoms but less actual exposure, could be saved by skilled and complex treatment. In practical terms, however, there will be no way to distinguish the lethally-irradiated from the non-lethally-irradiated.

19   Finally, this burden of trauma will occur in addition to all pre-existing disease among "survivors," and this list of problems is not based on consideration of the special problems of high-risk populations—the very young and the very old, for example— which are particularly vulnerable.

20   These are the short-range problems to which a medical response must be addressed. But who will be left to respond?

---

[3]Lewis, "Prompt and Delayed Effects."

21   Physicians' offices and hospitals tend to be concentrated in central-city areas closest to ground zero. If anything, physicians will be killed and seriously injured at rates greater than those of the general population, and hospitals similarly have greater probabilities of destruction or severe damage. Of the approximately 4,000 physicians in San Francisco County, perhaps half would survive a one-megaton air burst; of the 4,647 hospital beds in the county, only a handful would remain. At 20 megatons, there would be only a few thousand physicians left in all of San Francisco, Alameda, Marin, San Mateo and Contra Costa Counties to try to care for 874,000 seriously wounded.

22   One carefully detailed study of an American city suggests that there would be 1,700 seriously injured "survivors" for every physician—and that includes physicians of all ages, types of training, states of health and location at the time of the attack.[4] If, conservatively, we estimate only 1,000 seriously wounded patients per surviving physician, if we further assume that every physician sees each patient for only 10 minutes for diagnosis and treatment, and if each such physician worked 20 hours a day, it would be eight days before all the wounded were seen once by a doctor. Most of the wounded will die without medical care of any sort. Most will die without even the simple administration of drugs for the relief of pain.

23   A closer look at these calculations reveals that they are absurd—and the absurdities have implications that extend far beyond issues of medical care.

24   Thus, the calculations assume that every surviving, uninjured physician would be willing to expose himself or herself to high levels of radiation. They assume that every physician will be able to identify the areas in which medical help is needed, get there with no expenditure of time, and find every one of the 1,000 patients. It is further assumed that physicians will spend no time on uninjured or mildly injured patients, on those with pre-existing illness requiring care, on those with acute illness unrelated to the bombing, or on those who merely believe they are injured, all of whom will demand his time and attention.

25   And all of this is happening in an area where there is no electricity, no surviving transportation system. What is left of the buildings is lying in what is left of the streets; the bridges are down, subways and tunnels are crushed; there is no effective communication system; there are no ambulances and no hospitals.

26   Finally, in each ten-minute patient visit, the "medical care" will be dispensed without x-ray, laboratory equipment, other diagnostic aids, supplies, drugs, blood, plasma, beds and the like. There will be no help from "outside." There will be no rational organization even of this primitive level of care. In short, this is not medical care at all, as we commonly understand it.

27   It is important to examine medical care scenarios not merely as an element in the essentially hopeless task of response to a nuclear attack, but as a metaphor for *all* complex human—that is to say, social—activities in the post-attack period. *What becomes clear is that all such activities require an intact social fabric*—not merely the infrastructure of electric power, transportation, communications, shelter, water or food but the social enterprises, the complex human interactions and organizations supported by that infrastructure. That social fabric is ruptured, probably irreparably, by even a single nuclear weapon. Medical care is impossible in any real sense, not only because of the damage to the physical and biological environments, but most of all because it is a complex activity that requires a high degree of social organization.

28   The same is true of most other important human activities in complex urban societies. It follows that the only true meaning of "survival" is social, not biological. Simply to tally those who are still alive, or alive and uninjured, is to make a biological body-count that

---

[4]Aranow, Ervin and Sidel, *The Fallen Sky.*

has little social meaning. The biological "survivors" in all probability have merely postponed their deaths—by days, weeks, months or at most a few years—from secondary attack-related causes. Life in the interim will bear no resemblance to life before a nuclear attack.

29   In the period from days to months after an attack, other problems of both social and medical significance will rapidly emerge. Without functioning transportation, even assuming that effective social organization continues on the "outside," no food will come into the stricken area; remaining undestroyed stocks will be depleted rapidly. Extreme water shortages will occur almost at once. The average citizen of a modern American city uses between 50 to 150 gallons of water a day; in the post-attack period, a quart a day per survivor would be generous, and there will be no easy way to assure either potability or freedom from radioactive contamination.

30   Over the first two to four weeks after the attack, thousands of short-term survivors will die of radiation sickness, particularly of infection secondary to radiation-induced lowering of resistance. The problem of mass infection is particularly ugly. Even assuming that firestorm conveniently incinerates 500,000 of the dead in a one-megaton attack, there will remain some 300,000 or more decomposing human corpses in the Bay Area. There will be no safe water supply or effective sanitation. The vectors of disease—flies, mosquitoes and other insects—will enjoy preferential survival and growth in the post-attack period because their radiation resistance is many times that of mammals. Most surviving humans will have reduced resistance to infection. It is hard to construct a scenario more likely to produce epidemic disease.

31   Finally, any *likely* population-targeted attack will assign many multi-megaton weapons to each major city, and therefore calculations based on a single one-megaton or 20-megaton strike are unrealistically conservative.

32   Other scenarios—the so-called "counterforce" exchanges aimed primarily at missile sites or various city-trading hypotheses—presumably would result in less *immediate* death and injury. But they pose medical and social problems of equal magnitude in the longer run, even if they do not almost automatically escalate into full-scale exchanges.

33   Mass evacuation of cities in a nuclear crisis, the current favorite of civil defense enthusiasts, would in itself be seen as provocative by an adversary and therefore would increase risks. According to testimony before a Senate subcommittee by representatives of the Federal Emergency Management Agency, effective evacuation would require "only eight days" from warning time to completion.

34   It is, once again, a technique aimed at short-term biological survival, not social survival: to what would the dispersed urban residents return?

35   The danger of nuclear war is a public health problem of unprecedented magnitude. It is not, however, unprecedented in *type*. There are many other medical problems to which a coherent response is not possible and for which there are no cures. One medical (and social) strategy is still available in such cases: Prevention.

2,130 words

Vocabulary

paradox (1)	kilotons (5)	retinal (17)
specifiable (2)	ambient (11)	infrastructure (27)
unfathomable (3)	crematoria (11)	vectors (30)
megaton (4)	thorax (17)	

Questions

1. How is the essay related to its title?
2. The essay is a causal analysis of effect rather than cause. What is the author's purpose in piling up so many vivid and detailed effects of a nuclear attack? In what single word is his purpose expressed?
3. What is the paradox involved in attempting to measure and describe the consequences of a thermonuclear attack on a major American city?
4. Why do Hiroshima and Nagasaki no longer serve as precedents to judge the effects of a nuclear blast?
5. What agency provides accurate calculations as to the number of killed and seriously injured in a given nuclear attack? On what American city does the author choose to focus? Why does it make a good model?
6. What two kinds of survival does the author distinguish? Describe each kind.

C. Additional Writing Assignments

1. What do you consider the major causes of juvenile crime in our country? Develop a 500-word causal analysis in which you deal with this question.
2. Think of the person in this world whom you most dislike. Describe the trait that makes you dislike him or her, and find reasons for this trait. State both the trait and the reasons for it in a controlling idea. Develop this into an essay.
3. Write an essay projecting the effects of a third world war. Begin with a controlling idea.
4. Explore the major reasons for the high dropout rate in college. Summarize these reasons in your controlling idea and develop them in an essay.
5. Think back to the last time you and your parents (or you and a friend) had a serious quarrel and write a causal analysis on the reasons for the quarrel.
6. What is your favorite city in the world? Write an essay giving detailed reasons for your choice.
7. Write a causal analysis on one of the following historical events:
   a. The Salem witch trials
   b. The Aaron Burr–Alexander Hamilton duel
   c. The 1930 depression
   d. The creation of labor unions
   Begin with a controlling idea.
8. In an essay, give your views on the high divorce rate in America. State each reason in a separate, well-developed paragraph.
9. Write a causal analysis stating three or four good effects of a college education. Supply appropriate examples for each effect.

13

Argumentation

Now I have come here today . . . to speak for life—human life and human rights.

A. Reading for Ideas

The short story "War," by Luigi Pirandello, is a subtle and moving argument against war that resurrects the universal questions men have always asked: Is war glorious? Is war worth the sacrifice of a loved one? Is there honor in dying at war? As the story progresses, you will see that it is an eloquent and persuasive argument. Use the story as a springboard to an argument of your own. Ask yourself what traditions, institutions, customs, or stereotypes bother you. Why do you dislike them? If you could do away with them, would you? Why?

War
Luigi Pirandello

1   The passengers who had left Rome by the night express had had to stop until dawn at the small station of Fabriano in order to continue their journey by the small old-fashioned local joining the main line with Sulmona.

2   At dawn, in a stuffy and smoky second-class carriage in which five people had already spent the night, a bulky woman in deep mourning was hoisted in—almost like a shapeless bundle. Behind her—puffing and moaning, followed her husband—a tiny man, thin and weakly, his face death-white, his eyes small and bright and looking shy and uneasy.

3   Having at last taken a seat he politely thanked the passengers who had helped his wife and who had made room for her; then he turned round to the woman trying to pull down the collar of her coat, and politely inquired:

4   "Are you all right, dear?"

5   The wife, instead of answering, pulled up her collar again to her eyes, so as to hide her face.

6   "Nasty world," muttered the husband with a sad smile.

7   And he felt it his duty to explain to his traveling companions that the poor woman was to be pitied for the war was taking away from her her only son, a boy of twenty to whom

245

both had devoted their entire life, even breaking up their home at Sulmona to follow him to Rome, where he had to go as a student, then allowing him to volunteer for war with an assurance, however, that at least for six months he would not be sent to the front and now, all of a sudden, receiving a wire that he was due to leave in three days' time and asking them to go and see him off.

8　　The woman under the big coat was twisting and wriggling, at times growling like a wild animal, feeling certain that all those explanations would not have aroused even a shadow of sympathy from those people who—most likely—were in the same plight as herself. One of them, who had been listening with particular attention, said:

9　　"You should thank God that your son is only leaving now for the front. Mine has been sent there the first day of the war. He has already come back twice wounded and been sent back again to the front."

10　　"What about me? I have two sons and three nephews at the front," said another passenger.

11　　"Maybe, but in our case it is our only son," ventured the husband.

12　　"What difference can it make? You may spoil your only son with excessive attentions, but you cannot love him more than you would all your other children if you had any. Paternal love is not like bread that can be broken into pieces and split amongst the children in equal shares. A father gives *all* his love to each one of his children without discrimination, whether it be one or ten, and if I am suffering now for my two sons, I am not suffering half for each of them but double . . ."

13　　"True . . . true . . . " sighed the embarrassed husband, "but suppose (of course we all hope it will never be your case) a father has two sons at the front and he loses one of them, there is still one left to console him . . . while . . ."

14　　"Yes," answered the other, getting cross, "a son left to console him but also a son left for whom he must survive, while in the case of the father of an only son if the son dies the father can die too and put an end to his distress. Which of the two positions is the worse? Don't you see how my case would be worse than yours?"

15　　"Nonsense," interrupted another traveler, a fat, red-faced man with bloodshot eyes of the palest gray.

16　　He was panting. From his bulging eyes seemed to spurt inner violence of an uncontrolled vitality which his weakened body could hardly contain.

17　　"Nonsense," he repeated, trying to cover his mouth with his hand so as to hide the two missing front teeth. "Nonsense. Do we give life to our children for our own benefit?"

18　　The other travelers stared at him in distress. The one who had had his son at the front since the first day of the war sighed: "You are right. Our children do not belong to us, they belong to the Country. . . ."

19　　"Bosh," retorted the fat traveler. "Do we think of the Country when we give life to our children? Our sons are born because . . . well, because they must be born and when they come to life they take our own life with them. This is the truth. We belong to them but they never belong to us. And when they reach twenty they are exactly what we were at their age. We too had a father and mother, but there were so many other things as well . . . girls, cigarettes, illusions, new ties . . . and the Country, of course, whose call we would have answered—when we were twenty—even if father and mother had said no. Now, at our age, the love of our Country is still great, of course, but stronger than it is the love for our children. Is there any one of us here who wouldn't gladly take his son's place at the front if he could?"

20　　There was a silence all round, everybody nodding as to approve.

21　　"Why then," continued the fat man, "shouldn't we consider the feelings of our children when they are twenty? Isn't it natural that at their age they should consider the love for their Country (I am speaking of decent boys, of course) even greater than the love for

246

us? Isn't it natural that it should be so, as after all they must look upon old boys who cannot move any more and must stay at home? If Country exists, if Country is a natural necessity, like bread, of which each of us must eat in order not to die of hunger, somebody must go to defend it. And our sons go, when they are twenty, and they don't want tears, because if they die, they die inflamed and happy (I am speaking, of course, of decent boys). Now, if one dies young and happy, without having the ugly sides of life, the boredom of it, the pettiness, the bitterness of disillusion . . . what more can we ask for him? Everyone should stop crying; everyone should laugh, as I do . . . or at least thank God—as I do—because my son, before dying, sent me a message saying that he was dying satisfied at having ended his life in the best way he could have wished. That is why, as you see, I do not even wear mourning. . . ."

22   He shook his light fawn coat as to show it; his livid lip over his missing teeth was trembling, his eyes were watery and motionless, and soon after he ended with a shrill laugh which might well have been a sob.

23   "Quite so . . . quite so . . ." agreed the others.

24   The woman who, bundled in a corner under her coat, had been sitting and listening had—for the last three months—tried to find in the words of her busband and her friends something to console her in her deep sorrow, something that might show her how a mother should resign herself to send her son not even to death but to a probable danger of life. Yet not a word had she found amongst the many which had been said . . . and her grief had been greater in seeing that nobody—as she thought—could share her feelings.

25   But now the words of the traveler amazed and almost stunned her. She suddenly realized that it wasn't the others who were wrong and could not understand her but herself who could not rise up to the same height of those fathers and mothers willing to resign themselves, without crying, not only to the departure of their sons but even to their death.

26   She lifted her head, she bent over from her corner trying to listen with great attention to the details which the fat man was giving to his companions about the way his son had fallen as a hero, for his King and his Country, happy and without regrets. It seemed to her that she had stumbled into a world she had never dreamt of, a world so far unknown to her and she was so pleased to hear everyone joining in congratulating that brave father who could so stoically speak of his child's death.

27   Then suddenly, just as if she had heard nothing of what had been said and almost as if waking up from a dream, she turned to the old man, asking him:

28   "Then . . . is your son really dead?"

29   Everybody stared at her. The old man, too, turned to look at her, fixing his great, bulging, horribly watery light gray eyes, deep in her face. For some little time he tried to answer, but words failed him. He looked and looked at her, almost as if only then—at that silly incongruous question—he had suddenly realized at last that his son was really dead—gone forever—forever. His face contracted, became horribly distorted; then he snatched in haste a handkerchief from his pocket and, to the amazement of everyone, broke into harrowing, heartrending, uncontrollable sobs.

1,576 words

Vocabulary

livid (22)	incongruous (29)
stoically (26)	harrowing (29)

1. What is the controlling idea of the story? State it in one concise sentence.
2. What is the fat man's *pretended* attitude toward the loss of a son at war? How does this contrast with his *real* attitude?
3. The story contains little action. What is the conflict of the story?
4. What exactly triggers off the sudden change in the fat man's attitude?
5. Is there any hint earlier in the story that the fat man was not as sure of his argument as he claimed to be?
6. How would you counter the fat man's argument?

Dooley Is a Traitor
James Michie

1 "So then you won't fight?"
"Yes, your Honour," I said, "that's right."
"Now is it that you simply aren't willing,
Or have you a fundamental moral objection to killing?"
Says the judge, blowing his nose
And making his words stand to attention in long rows.
I stand to attention too, but with half a grin
(In my time I've done a good many in).
"No objection at all, sir," I said.
"There's a deal of the world I'd rather see dead—
Such as Johnny Stubbs or Fred Settle or my last landlord, Mr. Syme.
Give me a gun and your blessing, your Honour, and I'll be killing
them all the time.

2 But my conscience says a clear no
To killing a crowd of gentlemen I don't know.
Why, I'd as soon think of killing a worshipful judge,
High-court, like yourself (against whom, God knows, I've got no grudge—
So far), as murder a heap of foreign folk.
If you've got no grudge, you've got no joke
To laugh at after."

3 Now the words never come flowing
Proper for me till I get the old pipe going.
And just as I was poking
Down baccy, the judge looks up sharp with "No smoking,
Mr. Dooley. We're not fighting this war for fun.
And we want a clearer reason why you refuse to carry a gun.
This war is not a personal feud, it's a fight
Against wrong ideas on behalf of the Right.
Mr. Dooley, won't you help to destroy evil ideas?"

4 "Ah, your Honour, here's
The tragedy," I said. "I'm not a man of the mind.
I couldn't find it in my heart to be unkind

To an idea. I wouldn't know one if I saw one. I haven't one of my own.
5   So I'd best be leaving other people's alone."
"Indeed," he sneers at me, "this defence is
Curious for someone with convictions in two senses.
A criminal invokes conscience to his aid
To support an individual withdrawal from a communal crusade.
Sanctioned by God, led by the Church, against a godless, churchless nation!"
6   I asked his Honour for a translation.
"You talk of conscience," he said. "What do you know of the Christian creed?"
 "Nothing, sir, except what I can read,
That's the most you can hope for from us jail-birds.
I just open the Book here and there and look at the words.
And I find when the Lord himself misliked an evil notion
He turned it into a pig and drove it squealing over a cliff into the ocean,
7   And the loony ran away
And lived to think another day.
There was a clean job done and no blood shed!
Everybody happy and forty wicked thoughts drowned dead.
A neat and Christian murder. None of your mad slaughter
Throwing away the brains with the blood and the baby with the bathwater.
8   Now I look at the war as a sportsman. It's a matter of choosing
The decentest way of losing.
Heads or tails, losers or winners,
We all lose, we're all damned sinners.
And I'd rather be with the poor cold people at the wall that's shot
Than the bloody guilty devils in the firing-line, in Hell and keeping hot."
"But what right, Dooley, what right," he cried,
"Have you to say the Lord is on your side?"
"That's a dirty crooked question," back I roared.
"I said not the Lord was on my side, but I was on the side of the Lord."
Then he was up at me and shouting.
9   But by and by he calms: "Now we're not doubting
Your sincerity, Dooley, only your arguments,
Which don't make sense."
('Hullo,' I thought, 'that's the wrong way round.
I may be skylarking a bit, but my brainpan's sound.')
Then biting his nail and sugaring his words sweet:
"Keep your head, Mr. Dooley. Religion is clearly not up your street.
But let me ask you as a plain patriotic fellow
Whether you'd stand there so smug and yellow
If the foe were attacking your own dear sister."
"I'd knock their brains out, mister,
On the floor," I said. "There," he says kindly, "I knew you were no pacifist.
10   It's your straight duty as a man to enlist.
The enemy is at the door." You could have downed
Me with a feather. "Where?" I gasp, looking round.
"Not this door," he says angered. "Don't play the clown.
But they're two thousand miles away planning to do us down.
Why, the news is full of the deeds of those murderers and rapers."
"Your Eminence," I said, "my father told me never to believe the papers
But to go by my eyes.

And at two thousand miles the poor things can't tell the truth from lies."

11   His fearful spectacles glittered like the moon: "For the last time what right
Has a man like you to refuse to fight?"
"More right," I said, "than you.
You've never murdered a man, so you don't know what it is I won't do.
I've done it in good hot blood, so haven't I the right to make bold
To declare that I shan't do it in cold?"
Then the judge rises in a great rage
And writes DOOLEY IS A TRAITOR in black upon a page
And tells me I must die.
"What, me?" says I.
"If you still won't fight."
"Well, yes, your Honour," I said, "that's right."

Questions

1. Dooley is labeled a traitor because he refuses to join the army and fight in the war. What is the controlling idea of his objection?
2. What is the judge's counterargument to Dooley's position?
3. When the judge tries to trick Dooley by bringing up the Christian creed (paragraph 6), what does Dooley answer? Why?
4. When the judge tries to trick Dooley again by asking what he would do if an enemy were suddenly to attack Dooley's sister, what is Dooley's answer?
5. How would you characterize Dooley's logic? How does his logic differ from the judge's?
6. According to Dooley, who wins in a war?
7. What supportive evidence can you present to advance either Dooley's or the judge's argument?
8. Dooley is a confessed murderer and criminal. What effect does this have on his view about war?

B. How to Write an Argument

To make an effective argument, one must reason logically, support the case by evidence, and anticipate the opposition. In a debate, one may do all these things in the give and take of arguing. But in written argument, the writer is the sole expositor of the case and must not only air his or her views, but must also raise and rebut any foreseeable counterclaims by critics.

Some arguments convince because of the merits of their argued views; others, because they are persuasively presented. Unfortunately, the merit of an argument is not necessarily related to its degree of persuasiveness. Many crooks have been very glib and convincing in advancing their fraudulent schemes and views, while many good men and women have had their ideas rejected for lack of persuasiveness. In short, to write or state a convincing argument, one needs to be more than just "right"; one needs to know how to argue persuasively.

Writing Assignment

Select a tradition, a custom, an institution, or a stereotype that you distrust or dislike and write an argument against it. Begin with a controlling idea that clearly expresses the hub of your opposition—for example, "I deplore the professionalism that infiltrates the Winter Olympic Games because it gives some countries an unfair advantage." Or, "The white wedding gown is outmoded and hypocritical." Or, "Handicapped students can usually adjust quite well to mainstream college education." Once expressed, the controlling idea should be supported by logic, evidence, and expert testimony; moreover, the argument should take into account and parry the expected replies of the opposition.

Specific Instructions

1. BASE YOUR ARGUMENT ON SOUND PREMISES.   A premise is a basic assertion that serves as the starting point of an argument. Consider, for example, the premise of a speech given by Benjamin Franklin at the Constitutional Convention held in 1787. The Convention was mulling over whether or not executive officers of the newly minted federal government should be paid for their services. Franklin made an impassioned speech against the idea of payment, beginning with the following premise:

> Sir, there are two passions which have a powerful influence in the affairs of men. These are *ambition* and *avarice:* the love of power and the love of money. Separately, each of these has great force in prompting men to action: but when united in view of the same object, they have in many minds the most violent effect.

The premise of Franklin's argument consists of his assertions about the wicked influences of ambition and avarice. He then proceeds to give examples of what he foresaw as the harmful consequences of salaried federal offices on these weaknesses in human nature. Greedy, grasping candidates would aspire to office, not for love of country, but for love of money. The best would not be called upon to serve, only the greediest. Once Franklin's premise is aired, the remainder of the argument consists mainly of demonstrating the havoc that payment to federal officers would wreak on the national character.

With some justification, the premise of an argument has often been compared to the foundation of a house. The structure of a house rests on its foundation; the integrity of an argument rests on its premise. Indeed, the premise is what the argument begins by asserting and often ends by proving. It is also the point of contention to which an opponent will most often direct a counterattack. For instance, a possible rebuttal of the Franklin argument would deny that people are as corruptible and venal as the premise implies. One might argue, instead, that good men and women are as much motivated by patriotism, morality, and/or duty as they are by avarice and ambition. And, no doubt, a strong argument could be waged on both sides, for it is the nature of premises that consist of grand assertions about human nature to be "slippery" and hard to prove or disprove.

Premises are as varied and complex as the individuals who assert them. We hold premises about the effects of the planets upon our lives, about the causes of the common cold, or about the fiery temperament of redheads. Some premises, like Franklin's, are plainly stated in the body of an argument, while others are merely implied.

Here, for example, are the theses of various arguments whose premises are implied:

Thesis: A prime reason for the increase in crime has been the reduced severity of jail sentences.

Implied premise: Severe jail sentences deter crimes.

Thesis: Abortion is a great wickedness that is in blatant opposition to the laws of God.

Implied premise: God exists, as do His laws.

Thesis: We oppose busing because we support quality education in our schools

Implied premise: Busing decreases the quality of education.

Obviously, the argument built on a shaky premise will not stand. To refute such an argument, an opponent needs merely to show that its premise is untrue or inaccurate. Few premises, however, are black-and-white, and therefore few arguments end with a clear victory on one side or the other.

a. Induction: How premises are formed A premise, we said, is a summary assertion about reality. Capital punishment deters crime, redheads are passionate people, sunspots have an effect on the world's economy—these and other generalizing statements become premises when they are used as the launching point of an argument. How do we come to believe in and to argue such generalizations?

We do so by the process of *induction*. Whenever we infer a general law or principle from a number of individual cases, we are practicing induction. It is a manner of thinking and of common-sense observation that all intelligent people use in their daily lives.

Take the case of Mr. Cochran, a gourmet cook. One day he made a mistake and stewed beef in tea, which he mistook for broth. He discovered, to his surprise, that the meat turned out especially tender. A week later, he deliberately repeated his error, with the same tender and savory result. Further trials again confirmed a conclusion that Mr. Cochran had begun to suspect: namely, that meat is tenderized when it is stewed in tea.

Though homespun and trivial, the example of Mr. Cochran is not far removed in method from the way induction is practiced by scientists. Whether conducted in the kitchen by a gourmet cook or in the laboratory by a scientist, induction involves the investigation of specific cases and the inference of general conclusions from them. Here, for instance, is a newspaper report of a medical finding that was derived from the inductive method:

Conclusion: { Thousands of children are needlessly denying themselves milk and other common foods because of allergies they don't have, a research team at the National Jewish Hospital and Research Center has concluded.

Dr. Charles D. May and Dr. S. Allan Bock, co-directors of a major clinical and research program in food allergies at the Denver hospital, said that of 71 children they have studied who were thought to have food allergies, only 25 actually had such allergies.

"That isn't to say that there aren't children who are allergic to such things as strawberries, tomatoes and chocolate," Bock said, "but it apparently is very much less common than people think."

Inductive method used to reach conclusion: { In the NJH research, which is continuing, children between the ages of 3 and 16 are "challenged" with food to which they are believed to be allergic, and their reactions are observed.

Possible bias is eliminated through the use of a double-blind technique in which neither the children nor the observers know what the patients are getting. The food is given to the patients in the form of opaque capsules. Only the person supervising the test knows what is in each capsule. It could be milk, shrimp, tomato, or one of two placebos—known whimsically as "spider teeth" and "bat wings."

The capsules are administered initially in small doses, but the dosage is increased gradually, and the patients' reactions are monitored and their reactions recorded hour by hour.

"These techniques . . . sometimes indicate that the patient can safely eat small amounts of food which, in larger quantities, might trigger reactions."

But the most significant result of the study so far is the revelation that possibly only one-third of children thought to have food allergies actually have such allergies.

Discussion of the conclusions: { This result caused May and Bock to become concerned that some people may be living with "unwarranted restrictions on optimal nutrition" because of an incorrect diagnosis of food sensitivity.

The research, if its findings are confirmed by further testing, could mean that many "allergy sufferers" can enjoy more palatable and nourishing diets.

"Doctors Find Two-Thirds of 'Allergic' Kids Aren't,"
Atlanta Constitution, 19 March 1979, p. 13A

Notice that Mr. Cochran induced his findings about the tenderizing qualities of tea after a number of experiments. Similarly, from the study of only 71 children, the doctors induced that *thousands* of children thought to have allergies do not. In both cases, random samples—of meat tenderized after stewing in tea and of children who were thought to have allergies but didn't—are taken to represent characteristics of the whole. Mr. Cochran assumes that if tea tenderizes stewed meat in fifteen trials it will do so in umpteen other instances; the doctors assume that if only 25 percent of a random sample of children thought to have allergies actually do, then this percentage should also apply to the larger population.

b. Deduction: The reasoning from premises　　Once one has discovered a general principle, it is only useful if it can be applied to different, specific cases. This is done through the method of thinking known as *deduction*. It is a kind of reasoning that uses known ideas and principles to derive information about specific, unknown cases. Consider, for instance, the possible reaction of a doctor familiar with the Denver hospital research to whom a mother has brought a child she suspects of having a food allergy. The doctor's first response is likely to be of doubt and disbelief. His thinking will doubtless run along these lines: only 25 percent of the children thought to have allergies in the Denver experiment actually did; therefore, it is unlikely that this particular child has a food allergy. Using this line of reasoning, the doctor will probably try to isolate some other cause for the mother's worry, rather than subject the child to expensive and time-consuming allergy tests.

Many scenarios may be imagined in which Mr. Cochran also makes deductions from his inductively acquired premise about the tenderizing properties of tea. There is to be a dinner party, hosted by one of Mr. Cochran's friends, to whom he had imparted his findings about the tea. Mr. Cochran arrives early only to be greeted at the door by the fretful host. The stew meat was a dreadful quality, the host tells Mr. Cochran. No doubt it will be extremely chewy and tough. The party will be ruined. Mr. Cochran asks the host whether or not he'd taken his advice and stewed the meat in tea. The host replies affirmatively, adding that the meat, however, was gristly and bad. Nevertheless, Mr. Cochran is able to reassure the host that the meat, if it had been stewed in tea, will be tender. His reasoning ran something like this: "All meat stewed in tea is tenderized; this meat was stewed in tea; therefore this meat has been tenderized."

This rather simple example demonstrates the everyday use of a *syllogism,* which is a common form of reasoning used to make deductions. Many syllogisms deduce characteristics about unknowns by classifying them in categories whose properties are known. The syllogism proposed by the Greek philosopher Socrates is a classic example:

Major premise:　　All men are mortal.

Minor premise:　　Socrates is a man.

　　Conclusion:　　Therefore Socrates is mortal.

Once identified as belonging to the category of "man," Socrates immediately assumes the known properties of that category, which include mortality.

On paper, this is a rather clear-cut example of a syllogism hardly likely to puzzle even the amateur logician. But not all deductive reasoning is as clean and simple. Here, for instance, is a pure piece of deductive reasoning that consists of a complicated series of syllogistic steps made in rapid succession:

Freud once told the story of how an East European Jew . . . observed in the train which was taking him home to his village a young man who seemed to be going there too. As the two sat alone in the compartment, the Jew, puzzled about the stranger, began to work things out: "Only peasants and Jews live there. He is not dressed like either, but still, he is reading a book, so he must be Jewish. But why to our village? Only fifty families live there, and most are poor. Oh, but wait, Mr. Shmuel, the merchant, has two daughters: one of them is married, but for the other he has been seeking a husband. Mr. Shmuel is rich, and lately has acquired airs, so he would not want anyone from the village for his daughter. He must have asked the marriage broker to find a son-in-law from the outside. But Mr. Shmuel is old and cannot travel to meet a new family, so he would probably want a son-in-law from a family he knows. This means it would have to be one that had lived in the village but moved away. Who? The Cohen family had a son. Twenty years ago they moved to Budapest. What can a Jewish boy do there? Become a doctor. Mr. Shmuel would like a doctor in the family. A doctor needs a large dowry. The boy opposite is neat, but not well dressed. Dr. Cohen. But in Budapest, Cohen wouldn't do. Probably changed his name. In Budapest? To Kovacs—a name which comes as naturally to Hungarians as Cohen to Jews."

As the train drew into the village station, the old Jew said to the young man: "Excuse me, Dr. Kovacs, if Mr. Shmuel is not waiting for you at the station, I'll take you to his home and introduce you to your betrothed." Replied the astonished young man: "How do you know who I am and where I'm going? Not a word has passed between us."

"How do I know?" said the old man with a smile. "It stands to reason."

David Abrahamsen, Nixon Versus Nixon

This is the sort of reasoning with which Sherlock Holmes made a name for himself. Using a series of premises that he had formulated from his life in the village, the old man was able to deduce the unknown from the known.

In practice, our daily processes of reasoning consist of innumerable leaps of induction and deduction. When you observe, year after year, that anyone who goes out into the rain gets wet, you are reasoning *inductively;* but when you decide to wear a raincoat to keep you from getting wet in the rain, you are reasoning *deductively.* Both forms of reasoning are essential to logical thinking. Over-reliance on deductive reasoning alone leads eventually to bigoted, stereotyped thinking, since it is only a matter of time before the premises we have accumulated in our heads become stale and inaccurate. The other side of the coin is induction practiced to an obsessive degree, in which the reasoner accepts no premises not directly yielded by his own experiments and observations. Such an insistence would create a chronic doubting Thomas, hardly able to function in a complicated world where men and women constantly presume the basic truth and accuracy of one another's reports.

c. Sound premises   A premise is sound when it accurately summarizes conditions or events that have been verified by observation and study. A sound premise is a prerequisite to a sound argument. If the premise is faulty, the argument must consequently also be faulty. Here are some examples of sound premises:

Disease is caused by germs.

Money is the basic trading medium of all industrialized countries.

Venereal disease is spread primarily by sexual contact.

Other premises lie in the borderline area of belief; that is, they are believed by some people but have not been verified by study and observation. Here are some examples of unverified premises:

A study of astrology can give us advance warning of either good or bad fortune.

Unidentified flying objects are transportation vehicles peopled with citizens from other planets.

Neither premise has been proven, and an argument based on either of them would be unsound. The following argument is faulty because its underlying premise is based on superstition:

No more than Nature desires the mating of weaker with stronger individuals, even less does she desire the blending of a higher with a lower race, since, if she did, her whole work of higher breeding, over perhaps hundreds of thousands of years, might be ruined with one blow.

Historical experience offers countless proofs of this. It shows with terrifying clarity that in every mingling of Aryan blood with that of lower peoples the result was the end of the cultured people. North America, whose population consists in by far the largest part of Germanic elements who mixed but little with the lower colored people shows a different humanity and culture from Central and South America, where the predominantly Latin immigrants often mixed with the aborigines on a large scale. By this one example, we can clearly and distinctly recognize the effect of racial mixture. The Germanic inhabitant of the American continent, who has remained racially pure and unmixed, rose to be master of the continent; he will remain the master as long as he does not fall a victim to defilement of the blood.

Adolf Hitler, *Mein Kampf*

Viewed from a modern scientific point of view, this is patent nonsense.

A wrong premise can also result from hasty generalization based on poor sampling. Notice the following argument:

In 1898, the United States declared war on Spain. In 1910, United States troops invaded Mexico. In 1917, the United States declared war on Germany. Within thirty years, the United States was involved in World War II. All these facts point to the premise my paper has set out to prove: that the United States is a warmonger.

From four instances of war during a fifty-year period it does not necessarily follow that the United States has consistently instigated war. Numerous other factors must also be considered. The conclusion and premise are improbable and shaky. Here are some other examples of hasty generalizations:

> The permissive abortion laws in America have contributed to the moral decay of our society.

> The popularization of male vasectomies as a method of birth control is a female plot to castrate the American male.

> We have nothing to fear from marijuana; it is a healthy relaxation-producing drug.

These generalizations share a lack of incontrovertible proof. They produce no evidence of careful research and sampling.

In everyday conversation we tend to ignore exceptions and play the averages, fully realizing that no one will take us literally when, for instance, we say, "Nobody makes a living in this town," or, "My company is the most radical operation this side of the Missouri." A listener accepts the fact that we are speaking in approximate terms and discounts our exaggeration. But a written argument must be more carefully constructed, and its statements painstakingly checked for accuracy.

2. AVOID COMMON FALLACIES OF THINKING.   Arguments may be corrupted in a nearly inexhaustible number of ways. But some of these ways have become well enough recognized as to be assembled into categories. The commonest fallacies are listed below under their English and Latin names.

a. Arguing in circles (*petitio principii*)   An argument is illogical if its conclusion merely repeats its major premise. Such an argument is said to "beg the question," or to be "circular." Here is an example:

> The Bible is the word of God. How do I know it is the word of God? Because in verse after verse the Old as well as the New Testament tells us that it is God speaking. When God says it's His word, that's good enough for me.

In effect, the speaker says that the Bible is the word of God because the Bible says so. A variation on this same error is shown below:

> "The citizens of New York are more sophisticated than the citizens of Los Angeles."

> "How do you know?"

> "Because New Yorkers are far less crude and boorish."

Or, in other words, New Yorkers are more sophisticated than Angelenos because New Yorkers are more sophisticated.

b. Being irrelevant (*ignoratio elenchi*)   Varieties of this error exist, many of which are to be commonly found in political speeches. The aim of the arguer who uses such tactics is to divert the reader's or listener's attention from the issue and focus it instead on unrelated matters. Different ruses may be brought to bear. The *red herring* is a favorite tactic of demagogues and unscrupulous debaters. The term comes from a practice in hunting, where the strong scent of a herring was sometimes used to distract hounds on the trail of game. Here is an example of the red-herring tactic:

> Is it lawful for the police to engage in search, seizure, and questioning of suspicious-looking people? Well, I want you to know that rape is on the increase in our country. More and more court time is spent in deciding rape cases. Soon little old ladies will not even be able to walk safely on the streets. Soon mothers will not be able to allow their daughters to even walk to the corner . . .

But the question about the legality of search and seizure is left unanswered. Instead, the whole issue is beclouded by lurid views and predictions about rape.

Another typical error of irrelevancy is the *ad hominem* argument, which attacks a person instead of an issue. Here is an example:

> Don't give Mr. Finchley a penny when he tries to collect money for a mobile unit to be used by the school to teach students fire prevention. Mr. Finchley is an avowed atheist who lives openly with a mistress.

Entirely overlooked are the pros and cons on the usefulness of the mobile unit.

The *ad populum* technique uses a similar diverting device. But here the diversion is created by an appeal to popular, though irrelevant, sentiment:

> Virgil Pettis is bound to be a wonderful president. He overcame polio when he was a teenager and he has always stuck up for the rights of little people and victims of tyranny. He is a man cut from the cloth of Lincoln and Jefferson.

This argument hopes to persuade voters to cast their lots for a candidate by dedazzling them with appeals to pity and patriotic nostalgia.

3. BE HARD-HEADED IN YOUR USE OF EVIDENCE. Nothing takes the place of facts, experience, statistics, or exhibits that supply a finite, definite, and incontestable edge to your assertions. Naturally, no one is an expert on all things, and hard evidence is often difficult to come by. However, the campus library is still a storehouse of innumerable facts, uncountable numbers, and irrefutable data. Look up the information you need. Here are some assertions of mush and assertions of granite:

Mush: Hotdogs are horrible things to eat and have been proven to be very bad for you since they are very high in fat and chemicals.

Granite: According to the U.S. Department of Agriculture, since 1937 the frankfurter has gone from 19% fat and 19.6% protein to 28% fat and only

11.7% protein. (The rest is water, salt, spices and preservatives.) This deterioration is yet another of technology's ambiguous gifts.

"The Decline and Fill of the American Hotdog," *Time*

Mush: People can reduce and lose weight. Many celebrities, including well-known actors, athletes, and politicians, have successfully lost weight. If they can, so can everyone.

Granite: People can reduce and lose weight. Alfred Hitchcock went from 365 lbs. to a weight of 200 lbs. by eating only steak and cutting down on liquor; Jackie Gleason scaled down from 280 lbs. to 221 lbs. Maria Callas likewise went from a tumorous 215 lbs. to a trim 135 lbs. Even Lyndon Johnson, when he was Vice President, lost 31 lbs. in less than 10 weeks after being elected to the post in 1961.

Jean Meyer, *Overweight: Causes, Cost, and Control*

Your evidence must be specific. All factual prose writing depends on specifics. Pack a series of pinpoint specifics in a paragraph, and it will acquire a zesty sting that will do honor to your wit and style. When the paragraph is part of an argument whose intent is to convince and persuade a reader, the specifics are even more indispensable. This applies not only to the use of facts, but to the use of general detail.

Some arguments fare badly with facts, but do better with overall detail. For instance, if you were writing an essay opposing beauty contests, facts about them would probably not dissuade your reader. Love or hate for beauty contests is not usually founded on fact alone, but on a person's underlying values. You may hate beauty contests because you think they *degrade* woman into a sex object while another person may love beauty contests because he thinks they *elevate* woman into an art object. A barrage of remorseless facts about the number of beauty contests held in America will probably not change your reader's mind about them. What you must do is draw a graphic picture showing the grotesque side of beauty contests. To do this, you desperately need specific, graphic detail. Here are two examples of arguments against beauty contests. The first is mush in its use of detail:

I am against beauty pageants because they degrade women. They show the superficial side of the contestants. They never really evaluate the inside person. The whole deal is about bosoms and legs. Then all the women watching the contestants feel inferior because they don't feel as beautiful and desirable as the girls up on the stage. To me that is degrading womanhood. When the time comes for the winner to receive the flowers and the crown, I feel depressed that our country wastes its time and money on beauty pageants.

The argument started out with a strong controlling idea but had not amounted to two sentences before we realized that the writer has little to say. His detail is weak or nonexistent. One has the urge to yell: "Prove to me that you are right! Show me!" The following has a better beginning and is sharper and more specific in the use of detail:

> I am against beauty pageants because they degrade women. By "degrade" I mean they force women to be less than what they really are. What the audience sees is a beautifully proportioned smiling mannequin, parading gracefully up and down a light-flooded ramp, to the tune of some lilting band music. Her smile is fixed, her beauty is lacquered. The master of ceremonies asks her some inane question, such as: "How does it feel to be a runner-up in the Miss Rootbeer of Indiana Contest?" The mannequin twirps a delighted giggle and spreads her lips into a wide smile that exhibits gleamingly white teeth. If the girl has an I.Q., the judges could never discern it because she is treated as if she were made of plastic, not flesh and blood. Each year, 150 such pageants are held in California alone, sponsored as advertising by big companies that sell every sort of commodity from oranges to toothpaste. And in each pageant between ten and fifty girls must go through this degrading demotion to mannequin status. The last pageant I attended was the Miss International Trade competition. And when the girls walked out on stage, I almost expected them to jump through circus hoops held by the M.C., some honey-voiced executive who stood to gain from the advertising of the pageant.

The grotesqueness of beauty contests is hammered home by effective use of detail. The author appears to have actually attended beauty pageants and to know some facts about them—the number in California each year, what questions the girls are asked, the names of certain pageants, and who profits from them. If you thought that beauty contests elevate women, here is an argument showing how they degrade. Chances are that this passage—replete with vivid details and graphic adjectives—is more likely to persuade you than the first.

Evidence is gathered through work. Checking library sources, consulting encyclopedias, and plodding through stacks of articles, books, or pamphlets is work, no question about that. But if you want to formulate a strong argument, that's what you'll have to do.

The rewards for this sort of research are numerous—some tangible, like a better grade, and some intangible, like not looking foolish. For the second reward, the best illustration we can think of comes from the current controversy about the Bermuda Triangle, an area of the Atlantic and Caribbean that is luridly billed by writers as "a graveyard of lost ships," an area where UFOs regularly capture human specimens, or giant squids burst through the surface of the sea to gobble up hapless seamen. Here is one popular version of the "disappearance" of a triangle victim, the Japanese freighter *Raifuku Maru:*

> "It's like a dagger! Come quick," the frantic voice pleaded over the wireless. "Please come, we cannot escape." Then the cries from the *Raifuku Maru* faded away into the stillness of the tranquil sea. Other ships in the Bermuda Triangle were puzzled as to why a ship would send such a

message on so calm a day. Nothing has ever been heard or seen of the freighter or its crew since that April morning in 1925.

Lawrence D. Kusche, The Bermuda Triangle Mystery Solved

The same disaster was listed in the *Dictionary of Disasters during the Age of Steam,* a work compiled from the files of Lloyd's Register of Shipping. Lloyd's is the largest and oldest maritime insurer in the world. Here is the Lloyd's account:

> The Japanese steamship *Raifuku Maru* left Boston on April 18th, 1925, for Hamburg with a cargo of wheat. Shortly after leaving port the steamship encountered very heavy weather and by the morning of the 19th was in distress. An S.O.S. call was sent out which was picked up by the White Star liner *Homeric,* 34,356 tons, Capt. Roberts, 70 miles distant. Shortly afterwards another message was received stating that all lifeboats had been smashed. A last message in broken English, "Now very danger. Come quick," came just before the Homeric sighted the derelict. The liner drove through the mountainous seas at a speed of 20 knots to the spot indicated, lat. 41 43′N., long. 61 39′W. (400 miles directly east of Boston, and 700 miles north of Bermuda), to find the *Raifuku Maru* with a list of 30 degrees and quite unmanageable. Approaching as near as she dared the liner stood by in the hope of picking up survivors, but none could survive in such a sea, and all 48 of the crew were drowned.

Assuming a love of truth, which version of the *Raifuku Maru* story would you rather have written?

4. QUOTE WITNESSES. An argument is strengthened by the support of an *authority*—a person who is generally accepted by his or her peers as an expert. Usually, he or she is an authority on a particular subject and is known to be fair and objective. For example, Jack Landau, a respected journalist known for his support of a free press, might be quoted in an argument against the gag rule that is sometimes invoked in certain trials. Or Billy Jean King might be quoted in an argument that advocates equivalent tournament purses for both male and female tennis players.

How do you find authorities and experts? By reading and by checking library sources such as the *Reader's Guide to Periodical Literature,* encyclopedias, *Who's Who,* and other reference books. Relevant personal experiences may also be used as testimonial evidence. For instance, in an argument against the legalization of marijuana, you may wish to quote a former user of the drug who has had bad experiences with it. Or, in an argument against the welfare system, you may wish to cite the case of a mother of four who has been debased and ill-treated by the system. Your own experience may also be worth quoting, providing you don't base your entire argument on it. Few arguments are flimsier than the one that waxes contentiously on the basis of a single, unrepresentative experience. Here are some examples of how testimonial evidence may be incorporated into an argument:

No witness:	Thomas Jefferson was not the moral saint students study in grade school.
With witness:	Thomas Jefferson, far from being the moral saint studied by grade school students, was a man attracted to forbidden women, as indicated by Fawn Brodie's intimate history entitled *Thomas Jefferson*.
No witness:	America is deep into the porno bit, but nobody stops the porno promoters.
With witness:	According to Morris Goldings, Boston's leading obscenity attorney, the pornography business continues to thrive because once busted, porno pushers rarely suffer conviction.
No witness:	The quality of medical care in America varies with how much you can afford to pay, and how quickly you can demonstrate your ability to pay. Accident victims are sometimes turned away by hospitals because they have no insurance or proof of financial ability to pay.
With witness:	The quality of medical care in America varies with how much you can afford to pay and how quickly you can demonstrate your ability to pay. Last summer, for instance, while climbing El Capitan in Yosemite, I fell and broke my leg. I was rescued by a group of passing hikers and driven to the nearest hospital, which refused to admit me because I had no proof of insurance. I was dressed in mountain climbing gear and sported a five-day growth of stubble on my face; my clothes had been shredded by the fall. To all appearances, I was a penniless tramp. Before the admitting nurse could dispatch me to a county hospital, one of the hikers, a well-known businessman in the area, vouched for my ability to pay. Only then was I admitted.

In sum, testimonial evidence allows you to incorporate into your argument a consensus of opinions supportive of your own views. Moreover, it permits you to add a human dimension to what might otherwise be a cut-and-dried recital of facts, figures, and statistics.

5. DON'T IGNORE THE OPPOSITION. A well-shaped argument anticipates an opponent's objection by identifying it clearly and then showing its unreasonableness. This alerts the reader to the writer's knowledge of opposing arguments. If you neglect this step in arguing, you lay yourself wide open to the accusation of ignorance. In the following argument against the wasteful extravagance of using paper grocery bags, notice how the writer anticipates two major arguments of the opposition:

Can you believe that in the most well-educated, cultured nation in the world we consume and destroy a vital part of our natural resources without a second thought? Consider the average brown paper grocery bag, which is made from the pulp of trees. One of our most vital resources is transformed into a convenience that is used no place else in the world with such careless extravagance as here in the United States. And for what? To move groceries from store to car to home—to be used briefly as a trash bag and then to be pulverized by chemical action into a city sewage plant. How foolish and spoiled we are. A billion tons of lovely trees are destroyed annually, just to satisfy our compulsive need for convenience. How shallow we are to make this tradeoff from lush green beauty to tacky brown bags. One day in the future, men will have to look at pictures to be reminded that the Ozark Mountains were breathlessly beautiful in the fall as the deep green leaves turned to shimmering gold. Personal memories they will not have.

Of course, the big industries try to make us think that high living standards are more important than beauty. For example, George I. Kneeland, Chairman of the Board and Executive Officer of the St. Regis Paper Company, insists that "providing the highest possible standard of living for America is an urgent national priority." But I ask, what kind of value system is it that places higher priority on a trivial convenience than on the survival of Mother Earth?

Another argument is that paper is biodegradable and consequently not as polluting as plastic. But plastic bags do not have to be the substitute. People all over the world adapt to grocery carts, fishnet bags, or cloth containers. We could get into the habit of doing this too and we would be stopping our insane path of ecological mass murder.

By using statistical evidence and vivid images, a famous science fiction writer demonstrates how life on our planet can become extinct if man continues to ignore the laws of ecological balance.

Professional Model

The Case Against Man
Isaac Asimov

1   The first mistake is to think of mankind as a thing in itself. It isn't. It is part of an intricate web of life. And we can't think even of life as a thing in itself. It isn't. It is part of the intricate structure of a planet bathed by energy from the Sun.

2   The Earth, in the nearly 5 billion years since it assumed approximately its present form, has undergone a vast evolution. When it first came into being, it very likely lacked what we would today call an ocean and an atmosphere. These were formed by the gradual outward movement of material as the solid interior settled together.

3   Nor were ocean, atmosphere, and solid crust independent of each other after formation. There is interaction always: evaporation, condensation, solution, weathering. Far within the solid crust there are slow, continuing changes, too, of which hot springs, volcanoes, and earthquakes are the more noticeable manifestations here on the surface.

4   Between 2 billion and 3 billion years ago, portions of the surface water, bathed by the energetic radiation from the Sun, developed complicated compounds in organization sufficiently versatile to qualify as what we call "life." Life forms have become more complex and more various ever since.

5   But the life forms are as much part of the structure of the Earth as any inanimate portion is. It is all an inseparable part of a whole. If any animal is isolated totally from other forms of life, then death by starvation will surely follow. If isolated from water, death by dehydration will follow even faster. If isolated from air, whether free or dissolved in water, death by asphyxiation will follow still faster. If isolated from the Sun, animals will survive for a time, but plants would die, and if all plants died, all animals would starve.

6   It works in reverse, too, for the inanimate portion of Earth is shaped and molded by life. The nature of the atmosphere has been changed by plant activity (which adds to the air the free oxygen it could not otherwise retain). The soil is turned by earthworms, while enormous ocean reefs are formed by coral.

7   The entire planet, plus solar energy, is one enormous intricately interrelated system. The entire planet is a life form made up of nonliving portions and a large variety of living portions (as our own body is made up of nonliving crystals in bones and nonliving water in blood, as well as of a large variety of living portions).

8   In fact, we can pursue the analogy. A man is composed of 50 trillion cells of a variety of types, all interrelated and interdependent. Loss of some of those cells, such as those making up an entire leg, will seriously handicap all the rest of the organism: serious damage to a relatively few cells in an organ, such as the heart or kidneys, may end by killing all 50 trillion.

9   In the same way, on a planetary scale, the chopping down of an entire forest may not threaten Earth's life in general, but it will produce serious changes in the life forms of the region and even in the nature of the water runoff and, therefore, in the details of geological structure. A serious decline in the bee population will affect the numbers of those plants that depend on bees for fertilization, then the numbers of those animals that depend on those particular bee-fertilized plants, and so on.

10   Or consider cell growth. Cells in those organs that suffer constant wear and tear—as in the skin or in the intestinal lining—grow and multiply all life long. Other cells, not so exposed, as in nerve and muscle, do not multiply at all in the adult, under any circumstances. Still other organs, ordinarily quiescent, as liver and bone, stand ready to grow if that is necessary to replace damage. When the proper repairs are made, growth stops.

11   In a much looser and more flexible way, the same is true of the "planet organism" (which we study in the science called ecology). If cougars grow too numerous, the deer they live on are decimated, and some of the cougars die of starvation, so that their "proper number" is restored. If too many cougars die, then the deer multiply with particular rapidity, and cougars multiply quickly in turn, till the additional predators bring down the number of deer again. Barring interference from outside, the eaters and the eaten retain their proper numbers, and both are the better for it. (If the cougars are all killed off, deer would multiply to the point where they destroy the plants they live off, and more would then die of starvation than would have died of cougars.)

12   The neat economy of growth within an organism such as a human being is sometimes—for what reason, we know not—disrupted, and a group of cells begins growing without limit. This is the dread disease of cancer, and unless that growing group of cells is somehow stopped, the wild growth will throw all the body structure out of true and end by killing the organism itself.

13   In ecology, the same would happen if, for some reason, one particular type of organism began to multiply without limit, killing its competitors and increasing its own food supply at the expense of that of others. That, too, could end in the destruction of the larger system—most or all of life and even of certain aspects of the inanimate environment.

14   And this is exactly what is happening at this moment. For thousands of years, the single species Homo sapiens, to which you and I have the dubious honor of belonging,

has been increasing in numbers. In the past couple of centuries, the rate of increase has itself increased explosively.

15   At the time of Julius Caesar, when Earth's human population is estimated to have been 150 million, that population was increasing at a rate such that it would double in 1,000 years if that rate remained steady. Today, with Earth's population estimated at about 4,000 million (26 times what it was in Caesar's time), it is increasing at a rate which, if steady, will cause it to double in 35 years.

16   The present rate of increase of Earth's swarming human population qualifies Homo sapiens as an ecological cancer, which will destroy the ecology just as surely as any ordinary cancer would destroy an organism.

17   The cure? Just what it is for any cancer. The cancerous growth must somehow be stopped.

18   Of course, it will be. If we do nothing at all, the growth will stop, as a cancerous growth in a man will stop if nothing is done. The man dies and the cancer dies with him. And, analogously, the ecology will die and man will die with it.

19   How can the human population explosion be stopped? By raising the deathrate, or by lowering the birthrate. There are no other alternatives. The deathrate will rise spontaneously and finally catastrophically, if we do nothing—and that within a few decades. To make the birthrate fall, somehow (almost *any* how, in fact), is surely preferable, and that is therefore the first order of mankind's business today.

20   Failing this, mankind would stand at the bar of abstract justice (for there may be no posterity to judge) as the mass murderer of life generally, his own included, and mass disrupter of the intricate planetary development that made life in its present glory possible in the first place.

21   Am I too pessimistic? Can we allow the present rate of population increase to continue indefinitely, or at least for a good long time? Can we count on science to develop methods for cleaning up as we pollute, for replacing wasted resources with substitutes, for finding new food, new materials, more and better life for our waxing numbers?

22   Impossible! If the numbers continue to wax at the present rate.

23   Let us begin with a few estimates (admittedly not precise, but in the rough neighborhood of the truth).

24   The total mass of living objects on Earth is perhaps 20 trillion tons. There is usually a balance between eaters and eaten that is about 1 to 10 in favor of the eaten. There would therefore be about 10 times as much plant life (the eaten) as animal life (the eaters) on Earth. There is, in other words, just a little under 2 trillion tons of animal life on Earth.

25   But this is all the animal life that can exist, given the present quantity of plant life. If more animal life is somehow produced, it will strip down the plant life, reduce the food supply, and then enough animals will starve to restore the balance. If one species of animal life increases in mass, it can only be because other species correspondingly decrease. For every additional pound of human flesh on Earth, a pound of some other form of flesh must disappear.

26   The total mass of humanity now on Earth may be estimated at about 200 million tons, or one ten-thousandth the mass of all animal life. If mankind increases in numbers ten thousandfold, then Homo sapiens will be, perforce, the *only* animal species alive on Earth. It will be a world without elephants or lions, without cats or dogs, without fish or lobsters, without worms or bugs. What's more, to support the mass of human life, all the plant world must be put to service. Only plants edible to man must remain, and only those plants most concentratedly edible and with minimum waste.

27   At the present moment, the average density of population of the Earth's land surface

is about 73 people per square mile. Increase that ten thousandfold and the average density will become 730,000 people per square mile, or more than seven times the density of the workday population of Manhattan. Even if we assume that mankind will somehow spread itself into vast cities floating on the ocean surface (or resting on the ocean floor), the average density of human life at the time when the last nonhuman animal must be killed would be 310,000 people per square mile over all the world, land and sea alike, or a little better than three times the density of modern Manhattan at noon.

28   We have the vision, then, of high-rise apartments, higher and more thickly spaced than in Manhattan at present, spreading all over the world, across all the mountains, across the Sahara Desert, across Antarctica, across all the oceans; all with their load of humanity and with no other form of animal life beside. And on the roof of all those buildings are the algae farms, with little plant cells exposed to the Sun so that they might grow rapidly and, without waste, form protein for all the mighty population of 35 trillion human beings.

29   Is that tolerable? Even if science produced all the energy and materials mankind could want, kept them all fed with algae, all educated, all amused—is the planetary high-rise tolerable?

30   And if it were, can we double the population further in 35 more years? And then double it again in another 35 years? Where will the food come from? What will persuade the algae to multiply faster than the light energy they absorb makes possible? What will speed up the Sun to add the energy to make it possible? And if vast supplies of fusion energy are added to supplement the Sun, how will we get rid of the equally vast supplies of heat that will be produced? And after the icecaps are melted and the oceans boiled into steam, what?

31   Can we bleed off the mass of humanity to other worlds? Right now, the number of human beings on Earth is increasing by 80 million per year, and each year that number goes up by 1 and a fraction percent. Can we really suppose that we can send 80 million people per year to the Moon, Mars, and elsewhere, and engineer those worlds to support those people? And even so, merely remain in the same place ourselves?

32   No! Not the most optimistic visionary in the world could honestly convince himself that space travel is the solution to our population problem, if the present rate of increase is sustained.

33   But when will this planetary high-rise culture come about? How long will it take to increase Earth's population to that impossible point at the present doubling rate of once every 35 years? If it will take 1 million years or even 100,000, then, for goodness sake, let's not worry just yet.

34   Well, we don't have that kind of time. We will reach that dead end in no more than 460 years.

35   At the rate we are going, without birth control, then even if science serves us in an absolutely ideal way, we will reach the planetary high-rise with no animals but man, with no plants but algae, with no room for even one more person, by A.D. 2430.

36   And if science serves us in less than an ideal way (as it certainly will), the end will come sooner, much sooner, and mankind will start fading long, long before he is forced to construct that building that will cover all the Earth's surface.

37   So if birth control *must* come by A.D. 2430 at the very latest, even in an ideal world of advancing science, let it come *now,* in heaven's name, while there are still oak trees in the world and daisies and tigers and butterflies, and while there is still open land and space, and before the cancer called man proves fatal to life and the planet.

2,849 words

Vocabulary

quiescent (10)   catastrophically (19)
ecology (11)   waxing (21)
decimated (11)   fusion (30)

Questions

1. What is the author's main argument? Where is it explicitly stated? What advantage does such placement have?
2. According to the author, what conditions will prevail on earth by A.D. 2430 if matters keep going the way they are?
3. How does the author use cancer as a way to clarify the problem of ecological imbalance?
4. What similarities does the author draw between the life processes of a person and those of the planet?
5. What do the statistics and mathematical calculations add to the argument?
6. According to the author, why is moving to other planets not a plausible answer?
7. Do you agree with Asimov's sense of urgency? What other world problem, if any, do you consider more important? Why?

What follows is a speech delivered in an introductory argumentation and debate class at the University of Wisconsin-Madison. Two weeks prior to the delivery of speeches, students were required to announce their propositions to class members. Lonnquist learned that his proposition was strongly opposed by all but one of the fourteen students in his class. In recognition of the audience's hostility toward his proposition, Lonnquist sought to enlist audience empathy by comparing his role to the role played by abolitionists in a time past. After reading this argument, decide whether or not his strategy was effective.

Student Model

Ghosts
Ken Lonnquist

1   There are ghosts in this room. We cannot see them, but they are here. They have come to us from a far-off place—some billowing up out of the pages of history books, others returning to us after only a short absence. Some are large; some are old; some are very young; and some are very, very small. Some are the ghosts of men and women who more than a century ago trod upon the same ground which we are treading today. Some are spirits which look to us for justice—tiny spirits that look to us for retribution for an act of wrong that was committed against them. And then there are the other ghosts—ourselves, the ghosts which we, ourselves, have become—puppets in a judgment play which is being dusted off and reenacted by history after centuries.

2   I first became aware of these ghosts when I announced to you the nature of my

discourse for today. Those who were hostile in their reaction to my subject—those who said to me, "Our minds cannot be changed," those who said in effect, "We will not listen," made me think: "What kind of a people are we? What kind of a people have we become when we will no longer listen to one another?" In that moment, I was haunted by visions of a bygone era—a time in which abolitionists were afforded much the same treatment as I had just been. For you see they, too, were involved in a titanic, moral struggle—a grave moral crisis. They were speaking out against a notion that was deeply imbedded in the minds of 19th century men and women—the notion that black men and black women were not human. They were speaking out against slavery—that wicked by-product of prejudice. At times they were ignored by indifferent masses. At times they were tarred and feathered and run out of town, and at times murdered. Never were they listened to because the men and the women of the 19th century who favored human bondage had decided that their minds could not be changed on the matter. They had decided that they would not listen.

3   Now I have come here today, as you all know, to speak for life—human life and human rights. And there is something—something about my subject, which seems strangely reminiscent—reminiscent of, and haunted by, the days, the people, and the events of the 19th century. It is more than just a parallel between the treatment that was accorded abolitionist speakers and the treatment that is accorded antiabortionist speakers today. It is deeper than that. It rests in the very heart of the issue—in the very heart of each moral struggle. You see, in the 1840s it was argued by pro slavery forces that their rights as citizens of the United States were being subverted by abolitionists who were working to eradicate slavery. "The abolitionists," they argued, "are denying us our Constitutional right to hold property." They could not see that their rights of property could not super-cede the rights of the black men and the black women to life, liberty, and the pursuit of happiness. They could not see because they did not regard black men or black women to be of human life. They were blinded by the prejudice of their age.

4   And today a similar logic has been evolved by the proponents of abortion. They argue that their rights of self-determination are being infringed upon by those who would take away the option of terminating a pregnancy. They do not recognize that they are determining the course of not one life, but two. They cannot see because they do not recognize a human life in its earliest stages to be human. Now there are many kinds of life, and what we have to ask ourselves is, "What is life? What is human life? What are the values we attach to human life? What are the rights we grant to those whom we say possess human life?" These are the questions which I believe must be asked when dealing with the matter of abortion. These are the questions over which this whole controversy rages.

5   Now the concept of life is not so difficult to understand. We look at a stone and we say, "It does not live." We look at a flower and we say, "It lives." We may crush the stone, and no change takes place. We simply have smaller stones. But if we crush the flower, it dies. A biological process has been altered, and the mysterious thing that we call life has been taken away. As I said before, there are many kinds of life. And each is distinct from all the rest. The kind of life that we possess is human life. We all recognize this to be true. But down through the course of the centuries there have been those who, for reasons of fulfilling their own ends, have attempted to qualify the definition of human life. For centuries slave holders claimed that blacks were not human. For them color was the key element in defining the humanity of an individual. Today, there are many who claim that a human being in its earliest stages is not a human being—and that the life that it possesses as a biologically functioning entity is not a human life. In their mentality, age becomes the key element in determining the humanity of an individual. Once there was a color line. Today there is an age line. But an age line definition of humanity is no more

just—is just as fallacious, and just as evil, as was the color line which existed in the past.

6   Even the textbook *The Essentials of Human Embryology* says, "The fertilized egg is the beginning of a new individual." It cannot be denied. The fertilized egg is, itself, a human being in its earliest stages. It is not a zebra—it is not a monkey—it is human. Whether or not it is a fully developed human is not the issue. The issue is humanity. And a fertilized egg is human life.

7   Look around you at the other members of this class. Just look for a moment and ask yourselves, "Was there ever a time in the existence of any of us here in which we were nonhuman?" I do not believe so.

8   Now we have laws. We do not have any laws which govern the lives of plants. We have but one law which governs the life of an animal. That animal is man. The law has been written and rewritten down through the course of the centuries—in stone, on leather, on parchment, on paper, in languages that have been lost and long forgotten. But the law has remained the same. No man, it states, may take the life of another man. Perhaps you would recognize it this way: "We hold these truths to be self-evident—that all men are created equal and are endowed by their Creator with certain unalienable rights—that among these rights are *life.*" Or this way, quite simply stated, in another book: "Thou shalt not kill." But whatever their form, the laws are there. And there were no qualifications written into these laws on the basis of race, on the basis of color, on the basis of creed, on the basis of sex—nor were there any qualifications written into these laws on the basis of age. What the whole matter boils down to is this: a human life has been determined by us, for centuries, millenia, to be sacred, and we have determined that it cannot be taken away. And a fertilized egg is human life.

9   Now for any violations of these laws to occur, especially on a grand scale as is happening today, a mentality has to have been developed through which those who are going to commit a wrong can justify their actions and can appease the guilt that they might feel—the guilt that they might feel if they had to admit that they were killing a living human entity. And this is what we have done. This is what we are doing. We have learned to call a flower a stone. Why? And how?

10   You see, we are blinded—just as Americans of another generation were blinded by prejudice—we are blinded by violence. We live in a violent society, in which the killing of a young human being means no more to us than the holding in bondage of black men and black women meant to another generation of Americans. Said E. Z. Freidenburg on this matter, "Not only do most people accept violence if it is perpetrated by legitimate authority—they also regard violence against certain kinds of people as inherently legit-imate, no matter who commits it." An abolitionist once was speaking about this condition, and he said, "You might call it a paralysis of the nerves about the heart, in a people constantly given over to selfish aims." We have become selfish. And in our selfishness, have become heartless.

11   We say that it is our right to control our bodies, and this is true. But there is a distinction that needs to be made, and that distinction is this: Preventing a pregnancy is controlling a body—controlling your body. But preventing the continuance of a human life that is not your own is murder. If you attempt to control the body of another in that fashion, you become as a slave master was—controlling the lives and the bodies of his slaves— chopping off their feet when they ran away, or murdering them if it pleased him. This was not his right; it is not our right.

12   Abortion is often argued for in terms of its beneficiality. It is better, some say, that these young human beings do not come into the world: It is better for them; it is better for the parents; it is better for society at large. And they may be right. It may be more beneficial. But what we are arguing is not beneficiality. We are not arguing pragmatism. We are not arguing convenience. We are arguing right and wrong. It was more con-

venient for slave holders to maintain a system of slavery, but it was *wrong*. A matter of principle cannot be compromised for a matter of convenience. It cannot be done.

13   Now I'd like to say something more about the whole matter. I'd like to say something particularly to the women in the room, who I think should understand more clearly what I have to say now than the men. For thousands of years women have been deprived of their rights. They have been second-class citizens, and have been, in the eyes of many, something less than human themselves. For thousands of years they have been controlled, physically and mentally, by men. They have been controlled through physical power and physical coercion, but in this age of enlightenment—in this age of feminism—it has rightly been determined that might does not make right. The fact that males might be able to physically dominate females did not make their doing so just, and it did not mean that females were not deserving of protection under the law so that they might pursue the course of their choice.

14   But today, after tens of thousands of years, the tables are turning. Today men, and *women* (who more than any man should understand the shamefulness and the unjustness and the inhumanity involved in control through physical power), have been determining not the roles that another segment of humanity will have in life, but whether or not this segment of humanity will have life at all. Under the pretext of controlling their own bodies, they are setting out on a course of controlling the bodies of others. After tens of thousands of years, they are transferring the shackles in which they themselves have languished, and against which they have struggled, onto a new segment of humanity . . . only with a difference. The shackles have been transformed into a guillotine. Why?

15   It has happened because none will do anything about it. None will stop it. We are all like ghosts in the fire. We are all involved. Although we do not hold the knife in our hand, neither do we stay the hand that does hold the knife.

16   History is repeating itself. Abraham Lincoln once said that the eyes of history were upon us, and that we would be remembered in spite of ourselves. He also said, "We are engaged in a cause, a struggle, not just for today, but for all the ensuing generations."

17   And so are we. Ghosts are crowding around us, and looking, and watching what we do. Frederick Douglas once said, in speaking of black bondage: "I hear the mournful wail of millions." Today there are the ghosts of the past—the ghosts of the present— and the ghosts of all the ensuing generations watching us, and watching the struggle that is being repeated—the struggle of human life. I, too, hear the mournful wail of millions.

With the increasing environmental awareness brought by the ecology movement and the realization that many animal species face extinction, hunting and killing seem to have fallen into public disfavor. In this selection, however, a minister undertakes the defense of the hunter and his pastime.

Alternate Reading

In Defense of Deer Hunting and Killing
Arthur C. Tennies

1   "You hunt deer?" When I nodded, my shocked colleague went on to say, "Why my whole image of you has been shattered. How can you kill such beautiful creatures?"

2   And so would many others who view the deliberate killing of deer as brutal and senseless. Such people look upon the hunter as a barbaric hangover from the distant past of the human race. To my colleague, the incongruity between the barbarism of hunting and normal civilized conduct was made more intense because I was a minister. How could I as a minister do such a thing?

3   I thought about that as I drove through the early morning darkness toward the southeastern part of Chenango County. It was a little after 5 A.M. I had gotten up at 4, something I do only in the case of an emergency or when I am going deer hunting. It was cold, the temperature in the 20s. With the ground frozen, it would be too noisy for still hunting until the sun had had a chance to thaw the frost. So it would be wait and freeze. My first thoughts about why I would hunt deer had nothing to do with the supposed barbarism of it. I thought of the foolishness of it. Wait hour after hour in the cold, feet numb, hands numb, and small chance of getting a deer.

4   I was going to hunt on Schlafer Hill on the farm of Pershing Schlafer. My choice of a place to hunt had been determined by the party permit that three of us had, which allowed us to kill one other deer of either sex besides the three bucks that we were allowed.

5   I thought about the party system in New York, the way the state controlled the size of the deer herd. The state is divided into about 40 deer-management areas. The state biologists know how many deer each area can handle, how many deer can feed on the browse available without destroying it. If there are too many deer, they will kill the plants and bushes upon which they depend. The next step is starvation for large numbers. Since the deer's natural predators were wiped out by the first settlers, the only control over their numbers now is starvation or hunting. Thus, so many deer must be killed in a deer-management area. A certain number will be killed by motor vehicles. The biologists can estimate how many will be killed on the highways and also the number of bucks that will be killed. The surplus is taken care of by issuing a set number of party permits.

6   I have often marveled at the state biologists, their skill and knowledge in managing the deer herd. As I have pondered the problems of people—poverty, starvation, injustice, and all the others—and our frantic and often futile efforts to solve these problems, I have thought, "If only we could manage the problems of people as well as we can manage a deer herd."

7   Then I realize the great difference between the two. People are not for being managed. We manage people only by robbing them of the right to choose—and the most brutal attempts to manage are ultimately frustrated by the obstinacy of human nature, its refusal to be managed. A handful of biologists may manage a deer herd and a handful of scientists may be able to put a man on the moon, but no handful of planners will ever manage the human race. And so I thought again, as the car rushed through the dark, that all of our modern management techniques would fail to come up with quick and perfect solutions to the problems of people.

8   While the darkness was still on the land, I reached the bottom of the hill. I parked the car, put on my hunting shirts, took my gun, and began the long climb up the hill. For a few minutes, I could hardly see the old road. Slowly my eyes adjusted to the dark. The trees in the woods on my right took shape and the road became clearly visible. I walked with greater confidence. As I climbed, the sun climbed toward the horizon to drive away the night. By the time I reached the top of the hill, the half-light of dawn had arrived.

9   Off to my left in the valley were lights and people, but on the hill I was alone. It had not always been that way. Once long ago the hilltop had been filled with people. Following the Revolution, white settlers came into Chenango County, and some had chosen that hilltop. I stopped and tried to picture in my mind their struggles to turn the forest into farms. I looked at the stone fence off to my right and wondered how many

days it had taken to clear the stones from the fields and pile them into a fence. The fence ran into the woods. Woods again where there had been fields or pasture.

10   I looked on down the road. I could not see the old barn down farther on the left, the only structure from the past still standing. All of the others were gone. I had seen before the crumbling stone foundations where once houses had stood. A half century or more ago, if I had stood there, I could have seen a half-dozen houses. Smoke would have been rolling out of chimneys as fires were started to chase away the cold. Men and boys would have been outside and in the barns getting the chores done. Women and girls would have been busy in the kitchen getting breakfast. The hill would have been full of people and empty of deer. Now it was empty of people and full of deer.

11   On that hill and on many others, like Bucktooth Run, is a story of the hand of a man upon the land. Before the settlers came, only a few deer lived on that hill, far fewer than there are now, because the forests provided little food for the deer. The few were soon killed off. While the disappearance of the deer was the fault of the early hunters, there was more to it than that. There was no room for deer on the hill. As my Dad, who was born on Bucktooth Run, has pointed out:

12   *These farms were worked over morning and evening by the farmers and their sons and their dogs going after the cattle. The wood lots were worked over during the winter for wood. The larger tracts of woodland were worked over by the lumbermen.*

13   *Then came World War I and the years following. Large areas of land were abandoned. Where once the woods resounded to the call of "Come, boss!" and in the winter the woods echoed the ring of the ax and whine of the saw, the sylvan stillness, for months on end, was unbroken by the human voice. Where once the deer had no place to rest from the constant activity of the busy farmer and lumberman, there was now a chance for the deer to carry on its life in solitude.*

14   *In 1900 there were no deer in much of New York. The state did some stocking shortly after that, and deer came across the border from Pennsylvania. The abandoned land provided a perfect setting for the deer and there were no natural enemies to stay their march. By the late 1930s, most of the state had a deer season.*

15   So as the farmers retreated from the hill, the deer returned. Now the hill is perfect for deer . . . some fields used by farmers, like Pershing, for pasture and hay, good feed for deer most of the year . . . brush for browse during the winter . . . woods, old and new, mixed with evergreen for cover. And most of the year, except during the hunting season, only a few people make their way to the top of the hill.

16   Let nature have her way and in another century nature's hospitality to the deer will be withdrawn as large trees again cover the hill as they did before the first white settlers came.

17   I started to walk again and felt like I had left one world, the world of technology, and entered another one, the world of nature. The rush to get things done had to give way to waiting and patience, for nature does not live at our frantic pace. The noise had to give way to quietness, for only in silence can one get close to a deer.

18   But the ground crunched beneath my feet, so I walked to a likely spot and waited. Two hours and nothing, except a few small birds. Finally the cold forced me to move. I walked and found some fresh tracks in the snow. I followed them for an hour, trying to get close enough to the deer wandering in the woods ahead of me. But I was too noisy. All I saw was the flash of brown bodies and white tails too far ahead. I waited some more. No luck. I walked to another spot where deer cross.

19   I waited another hour. It was warmer now. Finally a deer appeared, a head above a rise. It started to come nearer. Then it stopped. Something was wrong. It decided to

leave. As it turned, my gun came up and I shot. It lurched sideways, kicking and thrashing, disappearing under a pine tree. I walked to the spot. No deer. I went around the tree and there it lay. In a second it was dead.

20   I looked down at the deer, a button buck, and I thought: This is the way of nature, one creature feeding on another. Thousands of years ago our forebearers survived in just this way. They killed, gutted, butchered, and ate. Now we buy in a supermarket or order in a restaurant.

21   The first task was to gut the deer, kind of a messy process. I got my knife out, turned the deer on his back, and slit him open. I spilled the guts out on the ground. I saved the liver and heart, even though the heart had been mangled by the bullet. I cut through the diaphragm and pulled the lungs out.

22   Then I was ready to pull the deer back to the car. It was 3 p.m. when I got to the car. Time yet to hunt for a buck, so I dumped the deer into the trunk. Back up to the hill, but no luck. As night came on, I got back to the car. I tied the deer on the top of the trunk and started for home.

23   As I drove toward home, I had a sense of satisfaction. I had fitted myself to nature's way and had been successful. For a few short hours, I had marched to the beat of nature's drum, not that of our modern world. At least for me, the barrier that we had built between nature and us could still be breached.

24   Back in suburbia, I parked the car in the driveway and went into the house. Jan and the kids were eating supper.
"Any luck?" Jan asked.
"Not much."
"Did you get a deer?" one of the kids asked.
"Yup, a button buck."
Then the excited rush to see the deer, and the thrill of shared success.

25   After that there was the tedious job of butchering. I hung the deer in the garage. Then I began the task of skinning it. Once skinned, I cut the deer in half, then in quarters. Jan washed the blood and hair off of each quarter. I then cut the quarters into smaller pieces, and then Jan sliced it up into roasts, steaks, and stew meat.

26   "Can you get the brains out?" Jan wanted to know.
"I can try, but why the brains?"
"We always had brains when we butchered."
So I went to work to cut the skull open and get the brains out.
When I got back into the kitchen, Jan had a skillet on.
"Let's have some venison," she said.
"At this hour?"
"Sure."

27   So she had some brains and I had some liver. As I sat there weary, eating the liver, I thought, "This meat is on the table because I put it there." By our efforts, and ours alone, it had gone from field to table.

28   "Don't you want some brains?" Jan asked.
"No."
"But they are a delicacy."
"That may be, but I'll stick to the liver."

29   As I went to sleep that night I thought: "I suppose that no matter what I say, a lot of people will never understand why I hunt deer. Well, they don't have to, but let only vegetarians condemn me."

2,090 words

incongruity (2)
sylvan (13)

Questions

1. How, according to the author, do people regard the killing of deer? How do some people regard the hunter? Why do you think he mentions people's views of the hunter and deer killing?
2. Why do you think the author mentions that he is a minister?
3. In paragraph 3 and throughout the essay, the author emphasizes the tediousness, cold, and discomfort associated with deer hunting. Why? What purpose does this serve in his defense of deer hunting?
4. What determined the author's choice of a place to hunt?
5. What is the purpose of paragrah 5? Why does the author go into deer management in such detail?
6. Why does the author reminisce about the people who used to live on the land? What does the reminiscence have to do with his argument in favor of deer hunting?
7. Where did the deer in New York come from? How did they get there?
8. In paragraph 19, the author describes how he shot and killed a deer. What does his description contribute to his defense of deer hunting?
9. What does the author contend would happen to the deer if nature had her way?
10. The author writes: "This is the way of nature, one creature feeding on another." Do you agree with this statement? Why or why not?
11. In paragraph 20, the author compares the way our forebears survived with the way we eat today. Why? What effect does this comparison have on his defense of hunting?
12. The author makes a point of mentioning that his wife ate the brains of the deer, while he ate its liver. What is he trying to emphasize?

With gentle yet probing satire, the author encourages our health-conscious society to rejoice in its good health rather than dwell on disease.

Alternate Reading

The Health-Care System
Lewis Thomas, M.D.

1   The health-care system of this country is a staggering enterprise, in any sense of the adjective. Whatever the failures of distribution and lack of coordination, it is the gigantic scale and scope of the total collective effort that first catches the breath, and its cost. The dollar figures are almost beyond grasping. They vary from year to year, always upward, ranging from something like $10 billion in 1950 to an estimated $140 billion in

1978, with much more to come in the years just ahead, whenever a national health-insurance program is installed. The official guess is that we are now investing a round 8 percent of the GNP in Health; it could soon rise to 10 or 12 percent.

2   Those are the official numbers, and only for the dollars that flow in an authorized way—for hospital charges, physician's fees, prescribed drugs, insurance premiums, the construction of facilities, research, and the like.

3   But these dollars are only part of it. Why limit the estimates to the strictly professional costs? There is another huge marketplace, in which vast sums are exchanged for items designed for the improvement of Health.

4   The television and radio industry, no small part of the national economy, feeds on Health, or, more precisely, on disease, for a large part of its sustenance. Not just the primarily medical dramas and the illness or surgical episodes threaded through many of the nonmedical stories, in which the central human dilemma is illness: almost all the commercial announcements, in an average evening, are pitches for items to restore failed health: things for stomach gas, constipation, headaches, nervousness, sleeplessness or sleepiness, arthritis, anemia, disquiet, and the despair of malodorousness, sweat, yellowed teeth, dandruff, furuncles, piles. The food industry plays the role of surrogate physician, advertising breakfast cereals as though they were tonics, vitamins, restoratives; they are now out-hawked by the specialized Health-food industry itself, with its nonpolluted, organic, "naturally" vitalizing products. Chewing gum is sold as a tooth cleanser. Vitamins have taken the place of prayer.

5   The publishing industry, hardcover, paperbacks, magazines, and all, seems to be kept alive by Health, new techniques for achieving mental health, cures for arthritis, and diets mostly for the improvement of everything.

6   The transformation of our environment has itself become an immense industry, costing rather more than the moon, in aid of Health. Pollution is supposed to be primarily a medical problem; when the television weatherman tells whether New York's air is "acceptable" or not that day, he is talking about human lungs, he believes. Pollutants which may be impairing photosynthesis by algae in the world's oceans, or destroying all the life in topsoil, or killing all the birds are being worried about lest they cause cancer in us, for heaven's sake.

7   Tennis has become more than the national sport; it is a rigorous discipline, a form of collective physiotherapy. Jogging is done by swarms of people, out onto the streets each day in underpants, moving in a stolid sort of rapid trudge, hoping by this to stay alive. Bicycles are cures. Meditation may be good for the soul but it is even better for the blood pressure.

8   As a people, we have become obsessed with Health.

9   There is something fundamentally, radically unhealthy about all this. We do not seem to be seeking more exuberance in living as much as staving off failure, putting off dying. We have lost all confidence in the human body.

10   The new consensus is that we are badly designed, intrinsically fallible, vulnerable to a host of hostile influences inside and around us, and only precariously alive. We live in danger of falling apart at any moment, and are therefore always in need of surveillance and propping up. Without the professional attention of a health-care system, we would fall in our tracks.

11   This is a new way of looking at things, and perhaps it can only be accounted for as a manifestation of spontaneous, undirected, societal *propaganda*. We keep telling each other this sort of thing, and back it comes on television or in the weekly newsmagazines, confirming all the fears, instructing us, as in the usual final paragraph of the personal-advice columns in the daily paper, to "seek professional help." Get a checkup. Go on a diet. Meditate. Jog. Have some surgery. Take two tablets, with water. *Spring* water. If pain persists, if anomie persists, if boredom persists, see your doctor.

12   It is extraordinary that we have just now become convinced of our bad health, our constant jeopardy of disease and death, at the very time when the facts should be telling us the opposite. In a more rational world, you'd think we would be staging bicentennial ceremonies for the celebration of our general good shape. In the year 1976, out of a population of around 220 million, only 1.9 million died, or just under 1 percent, not at all a discouraging record once you accept the fact of mortality itself. The life expectancy for the whole population rose to seventy-two years, the longest stretch ever achieved in this country. Despite the persisting roster of still-unsolved major diseases—cancer, heart disease, stroke, arthritis, and the rest—most of us have a clear, unimpeded run at a longer and healthier lifetime than could have been foreseen by any earlier generation. The illnesses that plague us the most, when you count up the numbers in the U.S. Vital Statistics reports, are respiratory and gastrointestinal infections, which are, by and large, transient, reversible affairs needing not much more than Grandmother's advice for getting through safely. Thanks in great part to the improved sanitary engineering, nutrition, and housing of the past century, and in real but less part to contemporary immunization and antibiotics, we are free of the great infectious diseases, especially tuberculosis and lobar pneumonia, which used to cut us down long before our time. We are even beginning to make progress in our understanding of the mechanisms underlying the chronic illnesses still with us, and sooner or later, depending on the quality and energy of biomedical research, we will learn to cope effectively with most of these, maybe all. We will still age away and die, but the aging, and even the dying, can become a healthy process. On balance, we ought to be more pleased with ourselves than we are, and more optimistic for the future.

13   The trouble is, we are being taken in by the propaganda, and it is bad not only for the spirit of society; it will make any health-care system, no matter how large and efficient, unworkable. If people are educated to believe that they are fundamentally fragile, always on the verge of mortal disease, perpetually in need of support by health-care professionals at every side, always dependent on an imagined discipline of "preventive" medicine, there can be no limit to the numbers of doctors' offices, clinics, and hospitals required to meet the demand. In the end, we would all become doctors, spending our days screening each other for disease.

14   We are, in real life, a reasonably healthy people. Far from being ineptly put together, we are amazingly tough, durable organisms, full of health, ready for most contingencies. The new danger to our well-being, if we continue to listen to all the talk, is in becoming a nation of healthy hypochondriacs, living gingerly, worrying ourselves half to death.

15   And we do not have time for this sort of thing anymore, nor can we afford such a distraction from our other, considerably more urgent problems. Indeed, we should be worrying that our preoccupation with personal health may be a symptom of copping out, an excuse for running upstairs to recline on a couch, sniffing the air for contaminants, spraying the room with deodorants, while just outside, the whole of society is coming undone.

1,507 words

Vocabulary

collective (1)	furuncles (4)	anomie (11)
GNP (1)	surrogate (4)	lobar (12)
malodorousness (4)	photosynthesis (6)	contingencies (14)

Questions

1. What is "the health-care system" alluded to in this essay? What is the author's view of this system?
2. How do television and radio feed on health or disease for a large part of their sustenance?
3. Paragraphs 5, 6, and 7 contain considerable satire. What later statement are they meant to support? How effective are they?
4. According to the author, what attitude are we displaying by spending so much energy to make sure that we stay healthy? Why is our attitude ironic?
5. What should we be doing instead of worrying about our health?
6. If we continue as we are, what danger will we face as a nation? Why is this bad?
7. What is your response to this essay?

C. Additional Writing Assignments

1. Argue for or against recreational facilities in our nation's prisons.
2. It is often stated that newspapers give a distorted view of life because they report only the sensational. Argue for or against this proposition.
3. Should movies be subject to censorship? Rely on the rules of good argument in supporting your answer to this question.
4. Instructors of political science should never express their own political opinions in class. Argue for or against this statement.
5. Write a well-shaped argument in favor of allowing 18-year-olds to purchase liquor.
6. Write a carefully reasoned argument either for or against a nuclear freeze.
7. Write a 500-word argument supporting the statement that the American consumer is a victim of planned obsolescence.
8. Read through the editorial section in several issues of your local newspaper until you find an article containing a controlling idea with which you disagree. Counter with your own argument.
9. Write 250 words arguing that drivers should be forced by law to wear seat belts; then turn around and write 250 words arguing that drivers should *not* be forced to wear seat belts.
10. As persuasively as you can, argue in favor of a research paper requirement for freshman English.

14
Adapting the Rhetorical Modes to Essay Examinations

The rhetorical modes are ideal types. They serve the useful function of providing a writer with strategies or patterns for writing about a subject. They are not meant to bind a writer to a rigid form unalterable by imagination and insight. Rather, they are guidelines to remind us that writing is best when it is focused and organized—when it tries to do one thing at a time rather than many things.

But are these rhetorical modes applicable to writing outside the English class-room? Specifically, can they be used to develop effective essay examinations in other disciplines? Indeed so. Consider the following essay questions taken from actual examinations given at various colleges and universities throughout the country. Implicit in every one is an essay that could be organized around one or a combination of the rhetorical modes you have learned about in this book.

From philosophy: Point to a place. Can you ever point to that place again?

From physical science: Explain the implications of Heisenberg's Principle of Indeterminancy on experiments in physics.

From political science: What is MAD?

From chemistry: (1) Differentiate, first, between starch and glycogen and, second, between cellulose and starch. (2) High-compression automobile engines that operate at high temperatures are designed to oxidize hydro-carbons completely to carbon dioxide and water. In the process of attempting to completely oxidize the hydrocarbons, a non-carbon-containing pollutant is produced. What types of compounds are produced and why do high-compression engines favor the formation of these com-pounds?

From history: Explain the meaning of the Truman Doctrine.

From art history: Explain how the work of Joan Miro and Salvador Dali are both similar and different.

The first thing to notice is that essay questions in fields other than English do not usually specify the rhetorical mode you are expected to use in answering them. Often, essay questions in English classes will specifically ask you, for example, to compare and contrast two entities, or to describe a process. But few essay exams in other disciplines are so obliging. What you must do, then, is decide on the best rhetorical mode to use in organizing your answer. Usually, the wording of the question will give you a hint.

The political science question ("What is MAD?"), for instance, is obviously asking for a definition. You must say what the acronym MAD stands for, what the term means, and where it comes from. The next question, on the other hand, is asking for a comparison/contrast. You must answer by explaining how starch is different from glycogen, and cellulose from starch. Here is an excerpt from a student answer to this question:

> Both starch and glycogen are disaccharides, but starch has a d-glycosidic bond that doesn't allow a great extent of H-bonding. Therefore starch is easier to break than glycogen. Starch is found mainly in plants, whereas glycogen exists mainly in animals. Glycogen is the monomer unit of most fatty acids.

Although this is a technical answer, it is still easy to see that the student is systematically comparing and contrasting. She uses contrasting terms such as *but* and *whereas*. She says how starch and glycogen are similar and how they are different.

Sometimes, however, the rhetorical mode best suited to answer a question will not be so clearly indicated in the question's wording. You must read the question carefully and decide what it is really asking. A question that asks you to explain something may be asking for an analysis of cause, a definition, or even a comparison/contrast. For example, the physical science question ("Explain the implications of Heisenberg's Principle of Indeterminancy on experiments in physics") is really asking for an analysis of effect, though its wording does not directly say so. To answer it, you would need to discuss how physics experiments have been affected by Heisenberg's principle. On the other hand, to answer the history question, you must write an extended definition of the Truman Doctrine; and to answer the last question, whose wording also asks for an explanation, you must compare and contrast the work of Joan Miro and Salvador Dali.

Many questions may also require you to answer in an essay that blends the rhetorical modes. For example, to answer the first question ("Point to a place. Can you ever point to that same place again?"), you must first define what is philosophically meant by "a place," and then argue whether or not it is possible to point to it again. Such an essay will be developed by two primary rhetorical modes—definition and argumentation.

Consider, as another example, the second chemistry question: "High-compression automobile engines that operate at high temperatures are designed to oxidize hydrocarbons completely to carbon dioxide and water. In the process of attempting to completely oxidize the hydrocarbons, a non-carbon-containing pollutant is produced. What types of compounds are produced and why do high-compression engines favor the formation of these compounds?" Your answer should consist of paragraphs that divide and classify—specifying the types of compounds produced—as well as paragraphs that analyze cause—saying why high-compression engines produce them. Professional writers routinely produce such blend essays. The main caution for the beginner is to use sufficiently strong transitions (sentences or even entire paragraphs) to make the leap from one rhetorical mode to the other. (See the section in Unit 3 on "Transitions between Paragraphs.")

In answering any essay question, your first aim should not be to answer in a recognizable rhetorical mode but, instead, to give exactly the kind of answer that is called for. Consider, for example, this question, taken from a philosophy quiz: "In a paragraph, explain what *virtue* meant to Aristotle and give three examples of it." The question is asking you to do two things: first, to define "virtue" as Aristotle understood the term and, second, to give three examples of it. Ordinarily, you might think that one or two examples of a term are enough to define it; but in this case you are specifically asked to give three, and that is what you must do. Here is how one student answered this question:

> Aristotle defined virtue as an action lying somewhere between the twin vices of excess and deficiency. In other words, virtue is temperance or the golden mean. Let us, for example, consider wartime circumstances. The man of virtue will not cower in fear of war, but neither will he rush unthinkingly into battle. When war is inevitable, the virtuous man will bravely fight in defense of his country. Attitude toward money provides another example. The miserly hoarder of gold is no more virtuous than the wasteful spender. Virtue lies somewhere in the middle—an attitude of generosity toward need. A third example may be drawn from the way one loses or keeps one's temper. The man who throws frequent temper tantrums is not virtuous, but neither is the one who shows no anger whatsoever, even in the face of unnecessary cruelty. Virtue again lies halfway between the two extremes—in the exercise of a cool head when faced with provocation but also in the display of righteous indignation when the circumstances demand it.

The rhetorical modes, in sum, can be used to answer any kind of essay examination. You may have to combine several modes in a single essay, or you may write a single essay in a dominant mode. The point to remember is that rhetorical modes are merely patterns for organizing and expressing your thoughts. Use them, adapt them as necessary to express your ideas clearly on paper. Once you become a more experienced writer, you will probably discard the mechanical patterning behind them altogether while still heeding the principles of focus and organization that they teach.

Part III

Revising the Essay

a brief handbook

15

Grammar Fundamentals

A. The Sentence

A sentence is *a group of words that expresses a complete thought.* "Because I'm happy" and "singing in the rain" do not express complete thoughts and are therefore not sentences. The following express complete thoughts and are therefore classified as sentences:

1. Because I am happy, I like to see other people happy.
2. John is singing in the rain.

The Subject and Predicate

Every sentence is divisible into two parts—a *subject* and a *predicate.* The subject is the word or word group about which something is said; the predicate is the word or word group that asserts something about the subject:

subject	predicate
The bird	fell out of the sky.
It	angered him deeply.
All the boys	left without saying a word.

The *simple subject* of a sentence is the single word—usually a noun or pronoun—about which the sentence says something:

1. The *beggar* suddenly blinked his eyes.
2. The ugly *frog* turned into a handsome young prince.

The *simple predicate* is the verb or verb phrase that makes a statement about the subject:

1. Fred *decided* to play in the tournament.
2. Before dinner we *had welcomed* all the guests.

Complete Subjects and Predicates

The *complete subject* is the simple subject and all the words associated with it. The *complete predicate* is the simple predicate and all the words associated with it. A vertical line divides the complete subject from the complete predicate in these sentences:

1. Diseases of the mind | are often caused by the pressures of city living.
2. The regular bus driver | knows his passengers by name.

The student who is unable to distinguish between the simple subject and simple predicate, and between the complete subject and complete predicate will have trouble with the construction and punctuation of sentences.

Compound Subjects and Predicates

A compound subject is made up of two or more nouns or pronouns tied together; a compound predicate is made up of two or more verbs tied together:

1. *Terror and hate* were in their eyes.   compound subject
2. The soldier *stopped and saluted.*   compound predicate
3. *Ghosts and witches* were the main characters in the story.   compound subject
4. In the recesses of his mind, the villain *remembered and felt guilty.*   compound predicate
5. *John and Mary laughed and sang.*   compound subject/compound predicate

Exercises

Underline the simple subject once and the simple predicate twice in the following sentences. Identify the verb first. To find the subject, ask "Who or what performs the action of the verb?"

1. The teacher arrived ten minutes after the class was to begin.
2. Mary believes in the intelligence and honesty of dogs.
3. After seeing the movie twice, Alice was sure she was in love with Robert Redford.
4. At the end of the first act, the big star made his appearance.
5. People all over the world expect America to feed them.
6. Ted was elected to run as vice-president.
7. We danced in the hallway, in the cellar, and on the patio.
8. Grace, her voice controlled and her head held high, debated the issues with her rival.
9. My father, a business consultant, is going to New York on Friday.

10. At the end of the examination, Bill breathed a sigh of relief.

In the following sentences, draw a vertical line between the complete subject and the complete predicate.

1. Jane arranged her schedule to allow for study.

2. As an usher as well as a waiter, Bruce worked to save $300.

3. Alaska, with all of its natural beauty, appealed to the Smiths.

4. Playing a guitar demands skill and sensitivity.

5. Angry and tired, the dean arrived and was hit with a water balloon.

6. Separate wills are recommended for couples who have been married twice.

7. The top of Mt. Whitney offers a breathtaking view of the Sierras.

8. The undefeatable Johnson was dropped from the squad.

9. Horses, covered with flies, stood scratching their backs on the fence.

10. Honor is more important than love.

Self-Grading Exercise 1

Underline the simple subject once and the simple predicate twice in the following sentences. To find the subject, ask "Who or what performs the action of the verb?" After completing the exercise, turn to the appendix for the correct answers.

1. Libraries contain the wisdom of civilization.

2. In the district of Wymar, burglars were ransacking the stores.

3. In Hemingway's novels matadors are highly respected.

4. A clear conscience is the best sleeping pill.

5. The silver-gray vest suited his taciturn personality.

6. Most middle-class homes in the Southwest are built with air conditioning.

7. The outdoor markets in Europe attract numerous tourists.

8. Noise pollution in towns and cities blots out the sounds and silences of the outdoor world.

9. A cup of good tea or coffee must be brought me early each morning.

10. I wish to describe two kinds of tours available.

Self-Grading Exercise 2

In the following sentences, draw a vertical line between the complete subject and the complete predicate. After completing the exercise, turn to the appendix for the correct answers.

1. Television has contributed to the decline of reading skills.

2. Incensed by their rudeness, the senator left.

3. Michelangelo's work continues to attract admirers all over the world.

4. Wars go on endlessly.

5. Divorce affects children most of all.

6. Professional tennis has become big business in the United States.

7. Most people insist on paying their bills on time.

8. Within five weeks one hundred polio victims had been claimed.

9. Spain is no longer a strong world power.

10. Many areas of Saudi Arabia have experienced droughts.

B. Clauses and Phrases

The Clause

A clause is a *group of related words that forms part of a sentence.* Every clause has a subject and a predicate. There are two types of clauses: *independent* and *dependent.* An independent clause expresses a complete thought by making a complete statement, asking a question, giving a command, or making an exclamation. An independent clause, therefore, could stand alone as a complete sentence, but it is combined with other independent or dependent clauses to form a full sentence, as in the following examples:

1. John was happy at home, but he left to earn a living.

    independent clause   independent clause

2. The children played until their parents arrived.

    independent clause   dependent clause

3. Is the soldier happy because he's going home?

    independent clause   dependent clause

4. He preferred friends who were loyal.

    independent clause   dependent clause

5. The accused claimed that she was innocent.

    independent clause   dependent clause

There is a crucial difference between an independent and a dependent clause: Standing alone, an independent clause makes sense, but a dependent clause does not. A dependent clause depends for its meaning on an independent clause that either precedes or follows it. Dependent clauses are therefore said to be *subordinate* to independent clauses.

The Phrase

A phrase is a group of two or more associated words having neither subject nor predicate. A phrase does not make a complete statement, is never a clause, and is certainly not a sentence. A phrase is only part of a clause or a sentence. The following groups of words are phrases:

1. for his fiftieth birthday
2. practicing the flute
3. under the table
4. after a long time

Exercises

Label the following passages as *I* (independent clause), *D* (dependent clause), or *P* (phrase).

1. Spring has begun   _____

2. Since their parents died   _____

3. Although Sam is an atheist   _____

4. Follow the main road for a mile   _____

5. Between the two houses   _____

6. Everyone told him to stay home   _____

7. For your country   _____

8. If Mary enrolled in the class   _____

9. You may wish to return the picture today   _____

10. People who attend religious services   _____

11. Begging her to love him   _____

12. Flowers blossom   _____

13. Have you seen the five napkins   _____

14. He seldom speaks his mind   _____

15. Because she grew up in Poland   _____

Self-Grading Exercise 3

Label the following passages as *I* (independent clause), *D* (dependent clause), or *P* (phrase). After completing the exercise, turn to the appendix for the correct answers.

1. Such is my ideal _____

2. The return from the walk should coincide with the serving of tea _____

3. Not all books being suitable for mealtime reading _____

4. What one does not want is a gossipy, superficial book _____

5. Because self-concern and self-pity filled all their thoughts _____

6. The letters from his brother, now longer, arrived daily _____

7. One of the happiest men and most pleasing companions _____

8. Either condition will destroy the psyche in the end _____

9. Whenever they have set about rectifying the error _____

10. As if in all ages they had been surrounded by barbarism _____

11. He has little doubt that they should have succeeded equally well _____

12. The country was given absolute freedom _____

13. Plunged into an inferno of torturous extremes _____

14. Here their methods were the same _____

15. When I called Cleopatra a "Circe" and her love affairs "business deals" _____

16. But Homer came first _____

17. Who romanticize the worst poverty _____

18. My deep appreciation for my parents _____

19. Some discotheques don't allow clients older than twenty _____

20. With the lining of her full-length lynx coat _____

C. Sentence Types

Sentences are punctuated according to their function and their form. The examples in this section will assist you in recognizing the function a sentence serves and the forms it can take.

Classification According to Function

A *declarative sentence* states a fact or a possibility and ends with a period:

1. The pilot died in the crash. (fact)
2. The stock market may go up tomorrow. (possibility)

An *interrogative sentence* asks a question and ends with a question mark:

1. Is it true what they say about Dixie?
2. Have you decided which courses you will take?

An *imperative sentence* makes a request or gives an order:

1. Don't park your car here.
2. Turn over the cash to the cashier.

An imperative sentence ends with a period unless the command is filled with strong emotion, in which case it ends with an exclamation mark:

1. Shut your mouth, you fool!
2. It's an earthquake! Fall to the floor!

An *exclamatory sentence* expresses strong or sudden feeling and ends with an exclamation mark:

1. Oh, the pain is terrible!
2. How cruel you are!

Classification According to Form

A *simple sentence* consists of one independent clause that contains one subject and one predicate and expresses one complete thought:

1. The tree fell.
2. The heavens declare the glory of God.
3. There is no peace in being greedy.

Although a simple sentence has only one subject and one predicate, either the subject or the predicate or both may be compound. Not all simple sentences are short, for both the subject and the predicate may have many modifying words:

Staggering from his wound, inflicted during the heat of battle, and exhausted from the endless trudging through jungles, the young marine found a place near a brook shaded by trees and sat down to rest.

A *compound sentence* consists of two or more independent clauses connected by one of the following coordinating conjunctions: *and, or, nor, but, yet, for, as.* For example:

1. The flowers were blossoming, but patches of snow still covered the earth.
2. He studied hard for the examination, yet he failed.
3. Jim smiled and Fred frowned.

Occasionally, a semicolon separates the independent clauses:

He's superstitious; he never opens an umbrella inside the house.

A *complex sentence* consists of one independent clause to which one or more dependent clauses have been connected:

1. The foreman ordered the men to work because five days had elapsed.   one dependent clause
2. Since life is not perfect, we must expect to find that difficulties will confront us as we attempt to achieve our goals.   three dependent clauses

A *compound-complex sentence* consists of two or more independent clauses and at least one dependent clause.

1. The company figured the values of all the pieces of property that lay within the city limits, and the manager then wrote each property owner a letter that explained the cost of curbing.
2. The world's petroleum supply is expected to last about 30 years; while some countries are exploring alternate energy sources, others are not.

Exercises

Place the appropriate punctuation mark at the end of each of the following sentences.

1. Oh, crime and violence, how long will you continue to rob us of peace
2. This is the time for all good men to come to the aid of their country
3. Come here this minute
4. Have you, by chance, already met this gentleman
5. Help I am caught in a mousetrap
6. Go to the store and buy me a quart of milk
7. If I need you, will you be available
8. What an exciting evening
9. Should we never meet again, I wish you the best of luck
10. I asked him if he had been paid for his time

Classify each of the following sentences as (A) simple, (B) compound, (C) complex, (D) compound-complex. Justify your classification by identifying the various clauses.

1. At the end of the day, Alice made an appearance; however, she did not smile once. _____
2. Because the winter was nearly over, Maxine arranged to be home with her mother, her grandmother, and her sisters. _____
3. After he had reached the end of the road, Mr. Leffingwell began to cross the bridge. _____
4. Big Tom was dropped from the club after one month of membership; he now is trying out for the swimming team. _____
5. At the end of the race, Jane let out a yell, for she had finished in third place. _____
6. Maybelle operated an elevator for three years to save enough money to go to night school, to buy a new car, and to pay her mother's doctor bills. _____
7. In the top drawer you will find two pairs of old gloves, three torn sweaters, and a yellowed picture album. _____
8. We all believe that the U. S. Constitution must be preserved, because our liberties, which our ancestors paid for with their lives, must be nurtured with care. _____

9. After freezing all night, Nancy decided she should have worn a sweater. _____

10. When my family left for New Orleans, I thought they would return within two weeks; instead, they stayed there a full year. _____

11. My uncle, a famous poet, gave me a handwritten manuscript and asked me to take care of it for him. _____

12. Your letter was delightful; I am sure that it offended no one. _____

13. Because Tom gave the most forceful pep talk, he was asked to represent the senior class at the fine arts festival. _____

14. The mayor, his voice trembling with rage, denounced his opponent, Jack Wilson. _____

15. He flew to New York, and she drove to Chicago because she was afraid to fly with him. _____

Self-Grading Exercise 4

Place the appropriate punctuation mark at the end of each of the following sentences. After completing the exercise, turn to the appendix for the correct answers.

1. We asked him if he would be willing to do it alone

2. Are you usually alert to the problems of older people

3. Sound the alarm Then run for your life

4. I am as angry as a cornered cat

5. Do you mean to tell me that all of the money simply disappeared

6. They inquired as to whether or not we would accompany the performers

7. Heavens What a way to get attention

8. Go straight down the aisle and interrupt his conversation

9. Would you be so kind as to direct me to the British Museum

10. Whew What a terrible odor

Self-Grading Exercise 5

Classify each of the following sentences as (A) simple, (B) compound, (C) complex, (D) compound-complex. After completing the exercise, turn to the appendix for the correct answers.

1. In Paris we lived near the Louvre. _____

2. The whole school was a great temple for the worship of these mortal gods, and no boy ever went there unprepared to worship. _____

3. If you have not visited a German *Gymnasium* (high school), you may be confused about the German school system. _____

4. Their position was emphasized by special rituals; nevertheless, we refused to remain in their mansion because the atmosphere was stern and oppressive. _____

5. Strength and popularity were not enough to keep them in the club if they were not recommended by at least two members. _____

6. It is vital that they attempt a revolution when the time is ripe. _____

7. They tried to accelerate their social progress by flattering the existing leaders. _____

8. The doors opened into the study, but no one passed through them because the room was too dark to be used. _____

9. As we sat around our table, we felt the silence; however, no one ever spoke up since silence was an absolute rule. _____

10. Each study imitated the cluttered appearance of an Edwardian drawing room. _____

11. They were not like slaves, for their favors were nearly always solicited rather than compelled. _____

12. After games, gallantry was the principal topic of polite conversation. _____

13. I thought about it then, and I am still thinking about it. _____

14. He really insists that the candidate insulted him; yet, he remained seated on the podium as if he had received a compliment. _____

15. Dean Metzger has three lovely daughters, a beautiful home, and a free airline pass to travel all over the world.

16. I became a marked man, but that never stopped me from speaking my mind. _____

17. What takes so much time is waiting in line for the tickets or lining up to get in. _____

18. One must not conclude that the housekeeper's signature was forged, even though two experts testified against her. _____

19. There are two reasons for such an unusual conclusion. _____

20. The modern world is the child of doubt and inquiry, as the ancient world was the child of fear and faith. _____

D. Parts of Speech

The Verb

A verb is a word that suggests *action,* a *state of being,* or a *condition:*

1. The cat *leaped* off the roof.   action
2. The antique cup *sat* on the lace cloth.   state of being
3. Her eyes *were* big and luminous.   condition

A verb functions as the predicate or as part of the predicate in a sentence:

1. The blind man *hears.*
2. The blind man *has heard.*
3. The blind man *is* still *hearing.*

Note that verbals (participles, gerunds, or infinitives) cannot function as predicates of a sentence:

1. Participle: "*Heard* melodies are sweet . . . ." *Heard* functions as an adjective.
2. Gerund: His *hearing* is bad. *Hearing* functions as a noun.
3. Infinitive: *To hear* is important. *To hear* functions as a noun.

The Noun

Nouns are *names* of persons, animals, things, places, characteristics, or ideas. The following are nouns:

engineer	Westwood Village
dog	jealousy
box	communism

You should know the following terms that describe nouns:

1. *concrete* nouns: tangible things, such as *men, cat, towns, teachers, coat*
2. *abstract* nouns: qualities or concepts, such as *love, justice, hate, credibility, intimacy*
3. *proper* nouns: specific persons, places, things, organizations, and events, which are capitalized, such as *Mt. Everest, Mary, French, Mr. Jones, the Eiffel Tower*
4. *common* nouns: general nouns that are not capitalized, such as *chair, kite, happiness, team*
5. *collective* nouns: words that are singular, but involve a group or imply a plural meaning, such as *jury, group, family, council, committee*

Understanding these terms will help you to avoid common errors in capitalization, agreement of subject and predicate, and agreement of pronouns with their *antecedents*—the words the pronouns stand for.

The Pronoun

Pronouns are words used *in place of nouns.* For example, you may use the pronoun *she* instead of the noun *mother.* You may speak of "the *children's* toys" or "*those*" or "*theirs.*" There are nine kinds of pronouns, listed below. While it is not important that you be able to name each kind, you should be able to recognize each as a pronoun:

1. personal   *You* and *they* will help *us.*

2. interrogative   *Who* is it? *What* do you want? *Which* is best?
3. relative   The man *who* killed her is the one *that* I saw.
4. demonstrative   *This* is older than *that*.
5. indefinite   *Each* of us must accomplish *something*.
6. reciprocal   Let us help *each other* and trust *one another*.
7. reflexive   John did it *himself*. I blame *myself*.
8. intensive   *I myself* heard him. *We* need money *ourselves*.
9. possessive   Is that book *yours* or *mine*?

The Adjective

Adjectives are words that *modify* (describe or qualify) nouns and pronouns:

1. The *shiny, black* cat   The noun *cat* is modified.
2. *Morose* and *depressed,* he sat in the corner.   The pronoun *he* is modified.
3. The beggar wanted *five* nickels.   The word *nickels* is modified.

Adjectives usually precede, but sometimes follow, the nouns they modify (a *tall, handsome* man). *Appositive adjectives* immediately follow a noun and are set off by commas from the nouns they follow:

1. The attorney, *pale* with anger, jumped forward.
2. The little boy, *dusty* and *tired,* fell asleep.

Sometimes the adjective follows the predicate, in which case it is called a *predicate adjective:*

1. The sunset looks *splendid.*
2. The newlyweds seem *happy.*
3. Women are *strong.*

Occasionally, the adjective modifies the object of the sentence, in which case it is called an *objective complement:*

1. The cream sauce made her *sick.*
2. The sun turned him *crimson red.*

Possessive and demonstrative adjectives precede the nouns they point out or specify:

1. We visited *their* mansion.
2. She bought *that* coat.

The Article

The article is a kind of adjective that *limits* a noun; *the* is a definite article and *a* and *an* are indefinite articles.

1. *the* people
2. *a* balloon, *an* orange

The Adverb

Adverbs modify verbs, adjectives, and other adverbs. They are next to verbs and nouns in importance. Good writers tend to use more adverbs than adjectives. Note the use of adverbs in the following sentences:

1. Cecil will work *slowly* and *deliberately*.   adverb modifying a verb
2. My mother inherited a *surprisingly* old clock.   adverb modifying an adjective
3. She succeeded *quite* well.   adverb modifying an adverb

Most adverbs indicate time (we must leave *now*), place (they stayed *over there*), manner (she walks *awkwardly*), or degree (all the relatives were *extraordinarily* kind). Some nouns function as adverbs and are called *adverbial nouns* (he left home *Monday*).

A special group of adverbs are the *conjunctive adverbs*. The primary conjunctive adverbs are:

accordingly	indeed
also	instead
anyhow	likewise
besides	meanwhile
consequently	nevertheless
furthermore	otherwise
hence	still
henceforth	then
however	therefore
	thus

When used to connect independent clauses, the conjunctive adverb is preceded by a semicolon:

1. We doubted their word; *nevertheless,* we went along with the plan.
2. Something about the garden pleased us; *however,* we did not wish to purchase the house.
3. The manager was harsh; *moreover,* he owed us our salaries.

When a conjunctive adverb is used parenthetically, it is set off by commas:

1. You can see, *moreover,* why this is important.
2. She, *however,* denied the truth.
3. This time, *furthermore,* he was forbidden to speak.

When the adverb *there* is used to introduce a sentence, it is called an *expletive: There* is a city in Algiers where bazaars appear everywhere.

Most adverbs end in *-ly*. The few that do not are called *flat* adverbs:

1. He walked *far*.
2. He walks too *fast*.
3. They work *hard*.

The Preposition

A preposition is used to show the relationship of a noun or pronoun to some other word in the sentence. For example, in "The airplane flew *above* the clouds," the preposition *above* shows the relationship between the clouds and the airplane.

Anything else that an airplane can do in approaching clouds is likely to involve a preposition:

1. The airplane flew *into* the clouds.
2. The airplane flew *through* the clouds.
3. The airplane flew *across* the clouds.
4. The airplane flew *behind* the clouds.
5. The airplane flew *between* the clouds.
6. The airplane flew *after* the clouds.
7. The airplane flew *by* the clouds.
8. The airplane flew *over/under* the clouds.
9. The airplane flew *with* the clouds.
10. The airplane flew *out of* the clouds.
11. The airplane flew *near* the clouds.

Some prepositions, such as *for, at,* and *of,* will not work in this example.

Some words like *off, on, out, in, over,* and *up* may be used as prepositions, adverbs, or verbs:

1. He climbed *up* the ladder.   preposition
2. All of us looked *up*.   adverb
3. When I arrived in New York, I *looked* him *up*.   verb
4. He ran *out* the door.   preposition
5. Reach *out* with your hand.   adverb
6. We must *watch out* for fires.   verb

The preposition and its object form a *prepositional phrase:*

1. The dog remained *inside his kennel.*
2. Every morning he looked *underneath the table.*
3. The thief lurked *near the car.*

The Conjunction

Conjunctions are connectors and can be classified into two types: *coordinating* conjunctions and *subordinating* conjunctions. Coordinating conjunctions (*and, or, nor, but, yet, for*) are used to connect words, phrases, and clauses that are of equal importance:

1. apples *and* oranges   words
2. with them, *but* not with us   phrases
3. I love my son, *yet* he must obey me.   clauses

Subordinating conjunctions (*after, although, as, because, before, if, since, until, when, while, then*) are used to connect main clauses with subordinate clauses:

1. That man never looked us straight in the eye *when* he talked with us.
2. *If* you don't believe him, tell him so.
3. The bridge collapsed *because* it was so old.
4. She is stronger *than* any of the men are.

Relative pronouns can function as subordinators:

1. I firmly believe *that* you are wrong.

2. John returned the gift to the person *who* had given it to him.
3. He demands to know *whose* door is squeaking.

Often subordinating conjunctions consist of more than one word:

1. The sky was pitch black *even though* it was noon.
2. The doctor came *as soon as* he was called.
3. Nothing works out, *no matter how* hard I try.

A special kind of conjunction is the *correlative* conjunction, which is used in pairs:

1. They were *not only* kind *but also* generous.
2. They *neither* complained *nor* cared.

See also subordinators on pp. 347–350.

The Interjection

Interjections are words or phrases used to express strong or sudden feelings that attract attention:

1. *Hurray!* They've won.
2. *Ouch!* The horse stepped on my foot.
3. *Whew!* That's hard work.

Context and the Parts of Speech

The role of the word in a sentence always determines the part of speech it is. Context may change the role of a word:

1. He must *round* the corner at top speed.   verb
2. The audience gave the orchestra a *round* of applause.   noun
3. The baby had a perfectly *round* face.   adjective
4. Her fiance lives *round* the corner.   preposition

Exercises

Identify the part of speech of each italicized word in the following paragraphs:

I[1] went back to the *Devon School*[2] not long ago, *and*[3] *found*[4] it looking *oddly*[5] newer than *when*[6] I was a student *there*[7] fifteen years before. It seemed *more*[8] sedate *than*[9] I remembered it, more *perpendicular*[10] and straitlaced, *with*[11] *narrower*[12] windows and shinier woodwork, *as though*[13] a coat *of*[14] varnish *had been put*[15] *over*[16] everything for better preservation. *But,*[17] of course, fifteen years *before*[18] there had been a war going on. Perhaps the school wasn't as *well*[19] kept up in those days; *perhaps*[20] varnish, *along with*[21] *everything*[22] else, had gone to war.

I didn't *entirely*[23] like this glossy new *surface,*[24] *because*[25] it made the school look *like*[26] a museum, and that's exactly *what*[27] it was to me, and what I did not want it to be. In the deep, tacit way in which *feeling*[28] becomes stronger than thought, I had always *felt*[29] *that*[30] the Devon School came *into*[31] existence the *day*[32] I entered it, was vibrantly *real*[33] *while*[34] I was a student there, and then blinked out like a candle *the*[35] day I left.

John Knowles, *A Separate Peace*

1. _____

2. _____

3. _____

4. _____

5. _____

6. _____

7. _____

8. _____

9. _____

10. _____

11. _____

12. _____

13. _____

14. _____

15. _____

16. _____

17. _____

18. _____

19. _____

20. _____

21. _____

22. _____

23. _____

24. _____

25. _____

26. _____

27. _____

28. _____

29. _____

30. _____

31. _____

32. _____

33. _____

34. _____

35. _____

Self-Grading Exercise 6

Identify the part of speech of each italicized word in the following paragraphs. After completing the exercise, turn to the appendix for the correct answers.

A few years ago, an *Englishman*[1] named John David Potter *was rushed*[2] to the Newcastle General Hospital after suffering *extensive*[3] brain damage *in*[4] a brawl.

Fourteen hours *later,*[5] he stopped breathing. Ordinarily, the man *would have been declared*[6] dead, *but*[7] at that moment a kidney was needed *for*[8] transplant, and Potter was an *obvious*[9] donor.

A respirator *was applied,*[10] and *it*[11] *artificially*[12]revived Potter's *breathing.*[13] *This*[14] in turn restored his failing *heartbeat*[15] *and*[16] circulation, *thus*[17] preserving *the*[18] kidneys. These vital organs, *now*[19] strictly *dependent*[20] *upon*[21] the respirator, *were kept*[22] going 24 hours, *even though*[23] the doctors *knew*[24] *that*[25] Potter *had*[26] no chance *of*[27] *recovery.*[28] *Meanwhile,*[29] Mrs. Potter *had granted*[30] permission to remove *a*[31] kidney *for*[32] *transplant.*[33] *When*[34]*this*[35] *was done,*[36] the attending *physician*[37] ordered the respirator *turned*[38] off. For the second time, Potter *ceased*[39] breathing, and his heart stopped *forever.*[40]

Leonard A. Stevens, "When Is Death?" *Reader's Digest,* May 1969

1. _____

2. _____

3. _____

4. _____

5. _____

6. _____

7. _____

8. _____

9. _____

10. _____

11. _____

12. _____

13. _____

14. _____

15. _____

16. _____

17. _____

18. _____

19. _____

20. _____

21. _____

22. _____

23. _____

24. _____

25. _____

26. _____

27. _____

28. _____

29. _____

30. _____

31. _____

32. _____

33. _____

34. _____

35. _____

36. _____

37. _____

38. _____

39. _____

40. _____

16

Correcting
Common Errors

This unit presents the most common errors found in student essays. Most teachers use handwritten symbols to indicate student errors. For an explanation of your own errors and how to correct them, match the symbols in the margin of your paper with those provided in this unit.

frag   A sentence *fragment* results when a phrase or a dependent clause is treated as if it were a complete sentence. Correct a fragment either by attaching it to the previous sentence or by adding enough words to the fragment to make it a complete sentence:

Error: We thought about the weather. Decided to cancel the picnic.

Correction: We thought about the weather and decided to cancel the picnic.

Error: Lonely house on the block.

Correction: There was a lonely house on the block.

Error: A man doesn't call a wall warped. Unless he knows what a straight wall is.

Correction: A man doesn't call a wall warped unless he knows what a straight wall is.

Error: Birds chirping, bees buzzing, the smell of honey in the air. I knew that spring was here.

Correction: Birds were chirping, bees were buzzing, and the smell of honey hung in the air. I knew that spring was here.

CS   A *comma splice* occurs when two independent clauses are separated by a comma instead of a period or a semicolon. There are four ways of correcting a comma splice:

1. Separate the independent clauses with a period.

Error: I was deeply shaken, my favorite cousin lay ill with cancer.

Correction: I was deeply shaken. My favorite cousin lay ill with cancer.

2. Separate the independent clauses with a semicolon.

Error: The back yard was full of plums, our family ate them all.

Correction: The back yard was full of plums; our family ate them all.

3. Join the independent clauses by a comma and a coordinating conjunction.

Error: Anyone can stick flowers in a vase, few can achieve an artistic arrangement.

Correction: Anyone can stick flowers in a vase, *but* few can achieve an artistic arrangement.

4. Subordinate one independent clause to the other.

Error: You failed to come to dinner, I ate alone.

Correction: Because you failed to come to dinner, I ate alone.

Don't let a conjunctive adverb trick you into a comma splice:

Error: I hate cold weather, however, the Rocky Mountains are good for my asthma.

Correction: I hate cold weather; however, the Rocky Mountains are good for my asthma.

rt A *run-together sentence* occurs when one sentence is piled on another without any kind of punctuation, often resulting in an incoherent passage. Correct a run-together sentence by placing a period or a conjunction between the two sentences.

Error: This map also predicts California's future the San Andreas fault, which underlies Los Angeles, is heading out to sea.

Correction: This map also predicts California's future. The San Andreas fault, which underlies Los Angeles, is heading out to sea.

Error: I like her attitude she is a solid person.

Correction: I like her attitude. She is a solid person.

Error: The first year of marriage is never easy I made it harder than need be.

Correction: The first year of marriage is never easy, but I made it harder than need be.

Exercises

In the blanks at the right, enter *C* if the sentence is correct, *Frag* if it is a fragment, *CS* if it is a comma splice, or *RT* if it is a run-together sentence. Correct any sentence that is incorrect.

1. People must eat. _____

2. The countless women who need jobs. _____

3. Chicago being a city riddled with crime. _____

4. The rivers overflowed their banks the trees were swept away. _____

5. Houses were destroyed, and homes were burned. _____

6. Pet lovers in our country as well as abroad. _____

7. In particular the mayor, who had supported a transit system when he spoke to the legislature. _____

8. Irresistible also were the lovely orchards surrounding the swimming pool. _____

9. However, some crowds were vengeful. _____

10. "I cannot marry you," said the princess, "I am too ugly." _____

11. Every one of us felt the loss. _____

12. The Vietnam war was senseless it gained us nothing. _____

13. Run as fast as you can you need the practice. _____

14. Recalling his visit to Paris, my uncle smiled. _____

15. All of us visited the statue, few of us admired it. _____

16. Originally made in Taiwan but then transported to the United States. _____

17. Soon giving up trying. _____

18. She was as delicate as a butterfly. _____

19. I want to excel not only as a musician, but also as a human being. _____

20. The car weighed a ton; they could not lift it. _____

Self-Grading Exercise 7

In the blanks at the right, enter *C* if the sentence is correct, *Frag* if it is a fragment, *CS* if it is a comma splice, and *RT* if it is a run-together sentence. After completing the exercise, turn to the appendix for the correct answers.

1. Hardly as big as a powderpuff and no bigger. _____

2. Quietly this cat dozes by the fire or on her lap. _____

3. He will not sell himself for any amount of money, he will not enter into an allegiance. _____

4. Because psychologists have learned a great deal about abnormal human behavior. _____

5. There is nothing difficult here if you found this article in a children's book, you would not be surprised. _____

6. Nevertheless, the writer has prepared you for a number of questions. _____

7. Although necessity is the mother of invention. _____

8. We believe. _____

9. Once you have noted the topic sentence, the paragraph is easy to follow. _____

10. Putting your own ideas into words. _____

11. All creatures living in the wild are subject to attack by predators, their survival depends on their ability to fend off such attacks. _____

12. "I'm telling you one last time," said the policeman, "Show me your driver's license." _____

13. The battle lines are firmly drawn between the chiropractors and their foes; accordingly, the public must decide on which side to be. _____

14. Everybody knows about Chicago, the "windy city." _____

15. Consciously ignoring the poor, alienating the old, and forgetting the handicapped. _____

16. Express your thesis concisely, however, do not leave out any key words. _____

17. Of course, there is much more to reading any piece of prose, even a popular magazine article, than understanding the opening paragraph. _____

18. The manager taught them time-saving techniques and helped them improve their skills. _____

19. The winter has arrived you should get out your snow boots. _____

20. Many tourists stand admiringly in front of the *Mona Lisa,* few leave quickly. _____

agr   *An error in agreement* occurs when the subject does not agree with the verb or when a pronoun does not agree with its antecedent. Avoid errors in subject-verb agreement by learning to recognize the subject of a sentence. To avoid errors in pronoun agreement, learn which pronouns are plural and which are singular.

Errors with Verbs

Error: My family, together with numerous other families, were checked for excess baggage.

Correction: My family, together with numerous other families, was checked for excess baggage. The subject is *family.*

Error: The main issue are high taxes.

Correction: The main issue *is* high taxes. The subject is *issue.*

Error: My list of errors were so long that the teacher shook her head in despair.

Correction: My list of errors *was* so long that the teacher shook her head in despair. The subject is *list.*

Error: Either John alone or all of the boys together has to show up at the entrance.

Correction: Either John alone or all of the boys together *have* to show up at the entrance. The subject is *all.* When two subjects, one singular and one plural, are connected by *or, nor,* or *either,* the verb must agree with the nearer subject.

Error: Mary is among the girls who has collected funds to build a memorial hall.

Correction: Mary is among the girls who *have* collected funds to build a memorial hall. *Who,* subject of the dependent clause, refers to *girls,* not *Mary.*

Error: Unemployment as well as inflation affect the voters.

Correction: Unemployment as well as inflation *affects* the voters. The addition of expressions such as *together with, along with, as well as, including,* and *like* does not alter the number of the subject.

Error: A pair of scissors and some thread is standard equipment for seamstresses.

Correction: A pair of scissors and some thread *are* standard equipment for seamstresses. Subjects joined by *and* require a plural verb. Exceptions are compound subjects referring to a single person: "My lover and best friend *has* left me." *Lover* and *friend* are the same person.

Exercises

In the following sentences, change each verb that does not agree with its subject. Write the correct form in the blank, or if the sentence is correct, write *C.*

1. Neither storms nor illness delay our newspapers. _____

2. His five children and their education was his main worry. _____

3. There's much to be said for simplicity. _____

4. The importance of words are being stressed in all newspapers. _____

5. My chief concern this summer are my expenses. _____

6. Taste in books differs from student to student. _____

7. *The Three Stooges* are a wonderful movie. _____

8. Mathematics is one of my worst subjects. _____

9. Either you or I am mistaken. _____

10. My brothers as well as my sister is coming to visit me. _____

Self-Grading Exercise 8

In the following sentences, change each verb that does not agree with its subject. Write the correct form in the blank, or if the sentence is correct, write *C*. After completing the exercise, turn to the appendix for the correct answers.

1. Just one error in those endless columns of figures make the project unacceptable. _____

2. These kinds of books is pleasant to read. _____

3. Everything in this nation, world, and universe have a reason for existence. _____

4. Neither the winner nor the loser was injured. _____

5. The rate of inflation, along with the scarcity of oil, cause people to go into debt. _____

6. Not only they but also I am unhappy. _____

7. Either they or he are to drive. _____

8. There is several active ingredients in the mixture. _____

9. All three of the courses Mike is taking requires a final essay examination. _____

10. Make sure that either your sister or your brothers go. _____

11. What is her arguments supposed to prove? _____

12. The diseases we are investigating cause severe anxiety. _____

13. Does a man and a woman have to agree? _____

14. The committee has submitted a fine report. _____

15. Physics are so difficult when one uses obscure problem-solving methods. _____

16. The main problem are all of the prostitutes in town. _____

17. No matter how dreadful the weather, a cluster of onlookers watch the surfers. _____

18. The tragedy—and main argument—of the novel is that love can fail miserably. _____

19. There on the park bench sits Fritz and Jane.   _____

20. Surprisingly enough, law, not medicine or architecture, appeal to Jim.   _____

Errors with Pronouns

The following pronouns, when used as subjects, always require a singular verb: *each, either, neither, another, anyone, anybody, anything, someone, somebody, something, one, everyone, everybody, everything, nobody, nothing.*

Error: Each of the prizes were spectacular.

Correction: Each of the prizes *was* spectacular. Don't let prepositional phrases trick you into an agreement error. In the above case, *each* is the subject.

Error: Behind all the managers stand their president.

Correction: Behind all the managers *stands* their president.

Error: Everyone in that room care sincerely.

Correction: Everyone in that room *cares* sincerely.

Error: Neither of the twins plan to go to private school.

Correction: Neither of the twins *plans* to go to private school.

A pronoun must agree in number with its antecedent:

Error: Everyone who accepted the money knew that they would have to return it.

Correction: Everyone who accepted the money knew that *he* would have to return it.

Error: Anyone who visits the principal will find that they are welcome.

Correction: Anyone who visits the principal will find that *he* is welcome.

Error: Every woman who wrote demanding a ticket knew that they would get one.

Correction: Every woman who wrote demanding a ticket knew that *she* would get one.

Collective nouns are replaced by singular pronouns if they denote a single unit, but by plural pronouns if they denote a group acting separately and individually.

1. The jury rendered *its* verdict. acting as a single unit
2. The jury could not reach an agreement; *they* argued all day. acting individually
3. The whole family gave *its* view. acting as a single unit
4. The family have gone their separate ways. acting individually

case   *Case* errors most commonly occur when a student fails to distinguish between the subjective and objective cases. The subject is always a noun or pronoun that the predicate says something about. The subject answers who? or what? about the predicate. The object, on the other hand, receives the action of the verb and is not the same as the subject. Study the following diagrams:

subject   verb   object

The patient   watches   the sunset

The patient initiates the action of the verb *watched,* whereas the sunset being watched receives it. Two further examples will reinforce the difference between subject and object:

subject verb object	subject verb object
My brother hit the dog	*Americans love their country*

Problems in case arise when nouns are replaced by pronouns of the wrong case. The pronouns below are listed in the subjective case at left and in the objective case at right:

subjective	objective
I	me
you	you
he, she, it	him, her, it
we	us
they	them
who, whoever	whom, whomever

In the sentences,

1. John bit the dog.
2. The dog bit John.

a pronoun substituted for *John* must reflect in its case whether John is the subject or object of the verb *bit*—whether he initiates the action or receives it:

1. He bit the dog.
2. The dog bit him.

The subjective pronoun *he* is used in place of *John* when *John* functions in the sentence as a subject. The objective pronoun *him* is used in place of *John* when *John* functions in the sentence as an object.

Error: The coach called *he* and *I.*

Correction: The coach called *him* and *me.*   *Him* and *me* are objects because they take the action from the verb *called.*

Error: Ellen and *me* decided to wear platform heels.

Correction: *Ellen and I* decided to wear platform heels.   *Ellen and I* is a compound subject.

Prepositions always require the objective case.

Error: The teacher got a better understanding of him and *I.*

Correction: The teacher got a better understanding of him and *me.*

Error: Between you and *I,* the whole matter was a joke.

Correction: Between you and *me,* the whole matter was a joke.

Special care must be taken to use the right case with pronouns in apposition. An appositive must be in the same case as the noun or pronoun it qualifies.

Error: They told both of us—my mother and *I*—that the sale was over.

Correction: They told both of us—my mother and *me*—that the sale was over. *Me* is in the objective case since it is in apposition with *us*.

Error: Let's you and *I* make sure that the bill is paid.

Correction: Let's you and *me* make sure that the bill is paid. Let us—you and *me*. *You* and *me* must be in the objective case since they are in apposition with *us*.

The case of pronouns used in clauses must be determined by treating each clause as a separate part.

Error: I shall vote for whoever I like.

Correction: I shall vote for whomever I like. *Whomever I like* must be treated as a separate part. *Whomever* is the object of the verb *like*.

Error: Give the job to whomever is willing to work.

Correction: Give the job to whoever is willing to work. *Whoever is willing to work* must be treated as a separate part. *Whoever* is the subject of the verb *is*.

Don't allow a parenthetical expression to trick you into a wrong pronoun case.

Error: The Smiths are people whom I think will make good neighbors.

Correction: The Smiths are people *who*, I think, will make good neighbors. *Who* is the subject of *will make*.

Error: The Pennsylvania Dutch are people who, they say, we can trust.

Correction: The Pennsylvania Dutch are people whom, they say, we can trust. *Whom* is object of verb *can trust*.

A pronoun following *than* or *as* is in the subjective or the objective case depending on the implied verb:

1. He admires him more than (he admires) *her*.
2. He admires him more than *she* (admires him).
3. We are happier than *they* (are).

Use the subjective case when the pronoun follows the verb *to be:*

1. Answer the phone; it may be *she*. not *her*
2. It was *they* who rang the bell. not *them*

A possessive adjective, not an object pronoun, is used immediately in front of a gerund (noun used as a verb, such as *singing, talking, thinking*). The following are possessive adjectives:

my	our
your	their
his, her, its	whose

Error: *Him* lying is what tipped off the police.

Correction: *His* lying is what tipped off the police.

Error: *Us* checking the score helped.

Correction: *Our* checking the score helped.

Exercises

Underline the correct form of the pronoun in each of the following sentences:

1. I am more to be pitied than (he, him).

2. The saleslady (who, whom) they think stole the stockings lives next to us.

3. You must praise (whoever, whomever) does the best job.

4. During the Vietnam war some of (we, us) football players felt guilty.

5. Florence insists that I was later than (he, him).

6. Was it (she, her) who called you the other day?

7. The candidate made an excellent impression on us—my Dad and (I, me).

8. (Who, whom) do you think will set a better example?

9. We were relieved by (his, him) paying the bill.

10. Between you and (me, I), is she innocent or guilty?

11. The coach said that I swim better than (him, he).

12. (Him, his) daydreaming affected his work negatively.

13. Bud doesn't care (who, whom) he gives his cold to.

14. The pinecones were divided among the three of us—John, Bill, and (me, I).

15. (Our, us) leaving the inner city was a blessing in disguise.

16. Do you remember (me, my) telling you?

17. Can you tell me the rank of the general (who, whom), it is said, struck one of his soldiers?

18. (Whom, who) the Cubs will play next is unknown.

19. Marilyn Monroe, (who, whom) most women envied, was unhappy.

20. Give the papers to (he and I, him and me).

Self-Grading Exercise 9

Underline the correct form of the pronoun in each of the following sentences. After completing the exercise, turn to the appendix for the correct answers.

1. No one cares except (he, him).

2. I need to call (whomever, whoever) should be at the celebration.

3. His memory was so bad that he no longer knew (whom, who) she was.

4. Was it (he or she/him or her) who asked the question?

5. Between you and (I, me), the entire plan is vicious.

6. Despite the political problems in the Middle East, (him and I, he and I) traveled to Jerusalem.

7. Do you remember (my, me) getting the measles?

8. The television set was donated to the fraternity for (its, their) members.

9. (Them, Their) escaping the accident was a miracle.

10. By (who, whom) was this fabulous cake baked?

11. They may well ask (you or I, you or me) about the burglary.

12. He has no political views of his own; he will vote for (whomever, whoever) others support.

13. Robert Frost was a poet (whom, who) I admired greatly.

14. After his divorce, he consulted a psychiatrist (who, whom) he had met socially.

15. We admire you every bit as much as we do (she, her).

16. They did not wish to frighten James or (she, her).

17. (Us, We) football players require a great deal of protein.

18. It seems to me that (whomever, whoever) has the biggest car should drive.

19. Both of us—Fred and (I, me)—received an A.

20. (Who, Whom) do you trust completely?

 Errors in *point of view* occur when the writer needlessly shifts person, tense, mood, voice, discourse, or key words.

Person

Error: We have come to the place where one should either fish or cut bait.   shift from *we* to *one.*

Correction: We have come to the place where *we* should either fish or cut bait.

Error: If you turn right on LaFollet Street, one will see the sign on one's right. shift from *you* to *one.*

Correction: If you turn right on LaFollet Street, you will see the sign on your right.

Tense

Error: The weather suddenly turned windy, and clouds arise.   shift from past to present.

Correction: The weather suddenly turned windy, and clouds *arose.*

Error: William Tell takes the apple, places it on his son's head, and shot an arrow right through the middle.   shift from present to past

Correction: William Tell takes the apple, places it on his son's head, and *shoots* an arrow right through the middle.

Error: His face turned purple with rage, and he would strike his friend.   shift from past to conditional

Correction: His face turned purple with rage, and he struck his friend.

Mood

Error: People of America, why do you wait? Protect your environment and you should vote against nuclear plants.   shift from imperative to indicative

Correction: People of America, why do you wait? Protect your environment. Vote against nuclear plants.

Voice

Error: John carried Mary's pack, and her tent was also pitched by him.   shift from active to passive voice

Correction: John carried Mary's pack, and he also pitched her tent.

Discourse

Error: The minister asked Bill if he loved his fiancée and will he treat her with devotion.   shift from indirect to direct discourse

Correction: The minister asked Bill if he loved his fiancée and if he would treat her with devotion.

or

The minister asked Bill, "Do you love your fiancée and will you treat her with devotion?"

Key Words

Error: Since everyone has a primary goal in life, I too have an outstanding goal. shift from *primary* to *outstanding*

Correction: Like everyone else, I too have a primary goal in life.

Error: I want to be a perfect human being. God made me, so why not be worth-while? shift from *perfect* to *worthwhile*

Correction: I want to be a perfect human being. God made me, so why not be perfect?

Exercises

In the following sentences correct all shifts in (A) person, (B) tense, (C) mood, (D) discourse, (E) voice, or (F) key word. Identify the shift by placing the appropriate letter in the blank at the right.

1. Everyone must live according to your conscience. _____

2. She insisted loudly that "I am opposed to abortions." _____

3. A good meal is enjoyed by all of us and we like fresh air, too. _____

4. She revealed that an unknown intruder is in the room. _____

5. So far we have not mentioned poverty. So let me discuss it now. _____

6. Truth is a principle everyone should cherish because you can be a better person when we adhere to it. _____

7. Lock the door and you should turn out the lights. _____

8. The robber stole her jewelry and she was mugged by him, too. _____

9. Slowly he crept toward me and grabs for my wallet. _____

10. A straightforward question to ask the salesman is, "Why people should buy his razors?" _____

11. He helped me out by pointing out where one could find an inexpensive hotel. _____

12. The doorman opened the door; then my baggage was picked up by a porter. _____

13. In his memory he heard the melody of that old song and knew that time is passing quickly. _____

14. She was a spoiled brat, it always seems to me. _____

15. The senator's question was an intelligent one; the chairman's answer was also a wise one. _____

Self-Grading Exercise 10

In the following sentences correct all shifts in (A) person, (B) tense, (C) mood, (D) discourse, (E) voice, or (F) key word. Identify the shift by placing the appropriate letter in the blank at the right. After completing the exercise, turn to the appendix for the answers (there is more than one possible answer for each item).

1. As they listened to the music, Sir Peregrine remarked about the success of the races while his wife dreams about love. _____

2. A person must accept the fact that you can't always win. _____

3. Every secretary who worked in the office was asked to give their opinion and to say how they felt. _____

4. The airline attendants wondered why so many passengers were standing in the aisle and who gave them permission to leave their seats? _____

5. If I were wealthy and if I was living in Zaire, I'd tell Mobutu a thing or two. _____

6. He pored over all of his notes, and many library books were checked out by him. _____

7. Mrs. Olson walks into strangers' kitchens and they are told by her how to make coffee. _____

8. The professor informed us that the test would be given and asked if we are ready. _____

9. First the insane man quoted lines from Richard Lovelace; then he recites a passage from the "Song of Solomon." _____

10. "Raise the property tax—and you must impose rent control!" he yelled with fervor. _____

11. When we buy a foreign car, you have to expect poor service. _____

12. The matter suddenly came to a crisis, but just as suddenly the situation was resolved. _____

13. It is essential that he bring the document with him and that he is here by noon. _____

14. We fear the unknown whereas the known is often welcomed by us. _____

15. Our Constitution protects our right to pursue happiness; however, it does not guarantee that we shall find this satisfaction, no matter how diligently we pursue it. _____

16. The tenant claims that he paid the rent and would I convey this fact to the landlord? _____

17. The skylark gracefully lifts itself into the sky, lets out a joyful warble, and disappeared into a cloud. _____

18. The sea breeze is blowing harder and felt colder. _____

19. As you walked into the slaughterhouse, one could see hundreds of carcasses hanging on hooks. _____

20. Since most of the children loved to go swimming, the group goes to the beach. _____

ref *Reference* errors occur with the use of pronouns that do not stand for anything specific. Every pronoun must have an unmistakable *antecedent*.

Error: No one is perfect, but that doesn't mean that I shouldn't try to be *one*. The pronoun *one* has no antecedent, no specific noun for which it stands.

Correction: No one is perfect, but that doesn't mean that I shouldn't try to be.

Error: She keeps her files well organized; she gets along well with her employers; and she has ethical integrity; however, this is not enough to convince us to hire her. The antecedent of *this* is too broad; it needs to be pinpointed.

Correction: She keeps her files well organized; she gets along well with her employers; and she has ethical integrity; however, these qualities are not enough to convince us to hire her.

Error: Our neighbor, Mrs. Irwin, told my mother that *she* had not chosen the proper dress. Who had not chosen the proper dress—Mrs. Irwin or the mother? The reference is unclear.

Correction: Our neighbor, Mrs. Irwin, told my mother, "I have not chosen the proper dress." Turning the clause into direct address is the simplest way to correct this kind of reference error.

Error: His clothes were scattered all across the room which needed folding. Confusion arises because the misplaced *which* implies that the room needed folding.

Correction: His clothes, which needed folding, were scattered all across the room.

Error: In Europe they often claim that Americans eat too much ice cream. Avoid using *they* or *you* as a reference to people in general.

Correction: Europeans often claim that Americans eat too much ice cream.

Error: When the Godfather dies, it is due to a heart attack. *It* has only an implied reference.

Correction: The Godfather's death is due to a heart attack.

Error: Arthur Ashe swung his racket hard, but it went into the net. *It* stands for ball, but the word *ball* never shows up.

Correction: Arthur Ashe swung his racket hard, but the ball went into the net.

Error: When Elmer Cole's restaurant was opened, he invited all the townspeople for a free meal. A pronoun in the subjective case must not refer to an antecedent in the possessive case.

Correction: When Elmer Cole opened his restaurant, he invited all the townspeople for a free meal.

Exercises

Rewrite the following sentences to avoid confusing, implied, nonexistent, or vague pronoun references:

1. Many people are emotional but have difficulty showing them.

_____

_____

2. At the factory where I work at night, they say not to ask for salary advances.

_____

3. My dad warned my brother that he would get a promotion.

_____

_____

4. She sat by the window knitting, which was too small to let in any light.

_____

_____

5. The nuclear bomb was developed in the twentieth century; this completely changed man's approach to war.

_____

_____

6. The leading baritone didn't show up for the opening night, which caused all kinds of gossip.

_____

_____

7. In the South, you aren't understood if you have a New York accent.

_____

_____

8. Life is a cycle of happiness followed by misery, but I want to have them in equal portions.

_____

_____

9. Although it is muddy down by the river, it looks inviting.

_____

_____

10. The first chapter awakens the reader's interest in mining, which continues until the Camerons move to America.

11. The American colonists refused to pay taxes without being represented. This was the major cause of the 1776 revolution.

12. Tomorrow it may rain and damage our roof, and it should be protected.

13. The guests were perspiring and fanning themselves with the printed program; it really' bothered them.

14. The rose garden in Hoover Park is spectacular. Some of them are deep purple, almost black.

15. I went over my check stubs three times, but it never balanced properly.

Self-Grading Exercise 11

Rewrite the following sentences to avoid confusing, implied, nonexistent, or vague pronoun references. After completing the exercise, turn to the appendix for the answers (there is more than one possible answer for each item).

1. We are now expected to drive less and use public transportation; we are asked to conserve heating fuel. This is realistic.

2. They say that a tablespoon of vinegar in some sugar and oil will reduce the appetite.

_____

_____

3. In the newspaper it said that a rebirth of great art is taking place in China.

_____

_____

4. Byron carried on a lively correspondence with Shelley when he was on the Continent.

_____

_____

5. When Golda Meir died, the world was expecting it.

_____

_____

6. My brother is enormously talented, but he does not make full use of it.

_____

_____

7. During lunch John always sat alone while the other students sat together chatting away. This didn't last long, however.

_____

_____

8. In Mahatma Gandhi's room, he wanted only the sparsest of furniture.

_____

_____

9. In an interview with a group of millionaires, the master of ceremonies told the audience that they were very articulate.

_____

_____

10. Melissa invited Ruth to travel to Spain with her because she thought she was interested in Spanish history.

_____

_____

11. A psychologist has no right discussing his patients' personal problems with his friends because they could be embarrassed if their identities were discovered.

_____

_____

12. The passerby noticed a young boy dashing out of the store and running down the street, which made him wonder about it.

_____

_____

13. On our flight across the Atlantic it was beautiful.

_____

_____

14. Inside the Blue Grotto of Capri, the water was rough and dark, but it was splendid anyway.

_____

_____

15. My friend John loves to watch basketball for hours on end, but his wife doesn't approve of it.

_____

_____

dang   *Dangling modifiers* occur when words or phrases are used that have no logical relationship to any element in the sentence. These words simply "dangle" in front of the reader, causing mystification and mirth. The most frequent dangling errors are caused by (1) misused verbal phrases, and (2) misused subordinate clauses. To correct dangling elements, assign the logical subject to all verbal phrases or subordinate clauses.

Dangling: **Falling in love with Carole Lombard made me envy Clark Gable.** For this sentence to make sense, Clark Gable must be the subject of the phrase "falling in love with Carole Lombard."

Correct: I envied Clark Gable's falling in love with Carole Lombard.

Dangling: Upon reaching the age of six, my grandfather took me to school. The sentence implies that the grandfather was six years old when he took his grandchild to school.

Correct: When I reached the age of six, my grandfather took me to school.

Dangling: To understand why fat people eat, a study of self-hatred is necessary. In this sentence, *a study* becomes the subject of the infinitive *to understand,* which is obviously silly since a study can't "understand."

Correct: To understand why fat people eat, we must study self-hatred.

Dangling: Although loved by Americans, historians deny the truth of many anecdotes involving Abraham Lincoln. This sentence implies that historians are loved by Americans.

Correct: Although loved by Americans, many anecdotes involving Abraham Lincoln have been labeled as historically untrue.

misp *Misplaced modifiers* occur when modifying words, phrases, or clauses are not placed as close as possible to the words they modify. Confusing, illogical, or awkward sentences are caused by misplaced modifiers.

Confusing: We looked inside the car with our friends for the package. Were the friends inside or outside the car?

Correct: With our friends we looked inside the car for the package.

Illogical: Visitors to France can see the Eiffel Tower floating down the Seine River on a barge. In this sentence, the Eiffel Tower is floating on a barge.

Correct: Floating down the Seine River on a barge, visitors to Paris can see the Eiffel Tower.

Awkward: My husband and I expect you to instantly pay for the damage to our car. It is best never to separate *to* from its verb.

Correct: My husband and I expect you to pay for the damage to our car instantly.

Exercises

Rewrite the following sentences to eliminate the dangling or misplaced modifiers.

1. Looking down in horror the snake crawled away.

_____

_____

2. To guarantee their rights, collective bargaining was organized by the teachers.

_____

_____

320

3. She did not realize that he had had major surgery until Friday.

_____

_____

4. John had looked forward to getting married for two weeks to Mary Ellen.

_____

_____

5. Responding to consumer demands for better gasoline mileage, the Honda was promoted.

_____

_____

6. We bought ice cream cones at a small stand that cost forty cents.

_____

_____

7. She decided to immediately telephone her friend.

_____

_____

8. Arriving at the pack station, our dried food had been stolen.

_____

_____

9. I held my breath as the car slid into the curb that had raced ahead suddenly.

_____

_____

10. While dreaming about the future, lightning flashed and the rain began to pour.

_____

_____

11. My mother consented to let me use her car reluctantly.

_____

_____

12. Continue to whip the cream until tired.

_____

_____

13. To understand T. S. Eliot, the classics must be read.

_____

_____

14. Drilling my teeth, I could tell he was an excellent dentist.

_____

_____

15. He was not willing to completely give up drinking.

_____

_____

16. Looking at the mountain range from the valley, a lovely rainbow could be seen.

_____

_____

17. My uncle had warned me never to leave a gun in my car that had not been unloaded.

_____

_____

18. Now is the time to, if you want a Democrat in the White House, vote for our governor.

_____

_____

19. At the party hors d'oeuvres were served to all of the guests on silver trays.

_____

_____

Self-Grading Exercise 12

Rewrite the following sentences to eliminate the dangling or misplaced modifiers. After completing the exercise, turn to the appendix for the answers (there is more than one possible answer to each item).

1. Bowing to the audience, his violin fell to the floor.

_____

_____

2. The tiny kitten sat shivering in the corner filled with terror.

_____

_____

3. Watching from behind a bush, camera in hand, the bears seemed like harmless pets.

_____

_____

4. What the teacher needs is a list of students neatly typed.

_____

_____

5. Students will not need to pass the three conversation examinations that speak French fluently.

_____

_____

6. During World War II the Nazis only gave Jewish prisoners cabbage to eat, nothing else.

_____

_____

7. Instead of asking forgiveness, a piece of chocolate cake was her sign of repentance.

   _____

   _____

8. Even when confronted with the full truth, the facts were ignored.

   _____

   _____

9. Hearing the bell ring, the boxer's glove was flung to the ground triumphantly.

   _____

   _____

10. Out of breath, the lover ran up the stairs revealing a look of anxiety.

    _____

    _____

11. The day drew to a close with anguish, praying that God would spare the infant.

    _____

    _____

12. We not only enjoy music, but also painting and sculpture.

    _____

    _____

13. After adjourning Congress, the law was enacted immediately.

    _____

    _____

14. Scorched by the sizzling heat, jumping into the river made a great deal of sense.

    _____

    _____

15. We tried on some Givenchy pants at a Neiman-Marcus store that cost $150.

_____

_____

//   *Lack of parallelism* occurs when similar grammatical constructions are not used to express parallel ideas. The result is a disruptive break in the rhythm of writing.

Not parallel: I love swimming, hiking, and to ski.   The sentence starts with two gerunds (-ing words) but suddenly switches to an infinitive (to + a verb).

I love swimming, hiking, and skiing.

Not parallel: Community colleges are necessary because they give late bloomers a second chance; they provide free tuition for the poor; and they have always encouraged the vocational trades.   The sentence starts with two verbs in the present tense, but suddenly switches to the past tense.

Parallel: Community colleges are necessary because they give late bloomers a second chance; they provide free tuition for the poor; and they encourage the vocational trades.

Not parallel: For days the president of the club wondered whether he should pay the bills or to resign.   "He should" is followed by "to resign."

Parallel: For days the president of the club wondered whether to pay the bills or to resign.

Not parallel: Whether tired or when he is rested, he reads the paper.

Parallel: Whether tired or rested, he reads the paper.

Exercises

Rewrite the following sentences to improve parallel structure. Join participles with participles, infinitives with infinitives, noun phrases with noun phrases, and so on.

1. She was a lovely blond-haired, blue-eyed, rosy china doll.

_____

_____

2. Bright sun gleams on the water, dark shadows across the cliffs, and the delicate flowers that blossomed in the desert created a memorable picture.

_____

_____

3. I prefer to attend small dinners than going to big banquets.

_____

_____

4. What we claim to believe rarely coincides with the things we actually do.

_____

_____

5. The anthropologist traveled into heated jungles, along insect-infested rivers, and he ventured up steep mountain trails.

_____

_____

6. I tried to explain that time was short, that the firm wanted an answer, and the importance of efficiency.

_____

_____

7. Most women's fashions come from Paris, Rome, and also from New York.

_____

_____

8. As we watched through the bars of the cage we could see the monkeys eating bananas, scratching their fur, and they swung on rails.

_____

_____

9. Most teachers try not only to engage the students' attention but they also want to say something important.

_____

_____

10. Victor Hugo was a statesman and who also wrote novels, including *Les Misérables*.

_____

_____

11. Bigger social security checks would allow senior citizens to pay for decent living quarters, to get proper medical help, and they could afford sound nutrition.

_____

_____

12. Basketball, football, and the game of baseball are favorite American spectator sports.

_____

_____

13. I admire the songs of Diana Ross, formerly a member of the Supremes, but who is now on her own.

_____

_____

14. Their divorce was due to his stressful job, his hot temper, and because he disliked her friends.

_____

_____

15. You have two choices: You must take either the exam or to write a research paper.

_____

_____

Self-Grading Exercise 13

Rewrite the following sentences to improve parallel structure. Join participles with participles, infinitives with infinitives, noun phrases with noun phrases, and so on. After completing the exercise, turn to the appendix for the answers (there is more than one possible answer for each item).

1. He wanted to marry her because she was bright, pleasant, and never placed herself first.

_____

_____

2. Her boss fired her because her letters were sloppy, ungrammatical, and she didn't type well.

_____

_____

3. The handbook revealed two ways in which the unity of a paragraph could be broken: 1. one could stray away from the topic sentence, 2. excessive details obscuring the central thought.

_____

_____

4. By exercising daily, by eating proper food, and if he avoids stress, he can regain his health.

_____

_____

5. This simple man did not doubt that after death there was a paradise for good people and a hell for people who had been bad.

_____

_____

6. Most of them were either athletic or had great strength.

_____

_____

7. Handing out oil coupons seemed both intelligent and a necessity.

_____

_____

8. She insisted that he must leave and never to return.

_____

_____

9. The man is either an idealist or foolish.

_____

10. Today pocket calculators are inexpensive, durable, and it is easy to obtain them.

11. The Byronic hero was a man who felt alienated from mainstream society, who withdrew into haughty superiority, loved passionately, and felt an element of self-pity.

12. This is the case not only with policemen but also of firemen.

13. Here is what you will need to know: how to open a bank account, how to judge a contract, and selling equipment.

14. He climbed Mount Whitney not because he wanted to test his endurance but out of a sense of arrogance.

15. To err is human; forgiving is divine.

Poor diction (also called poor word usage) refers to the use of a word to mean something other than its dictionary definition or the use of a word in a way unacceptable to standards of users of *ideal English. Ideal English* can be defined as language spoken or written according to standards of educated people. It is the language of good books, magazines, and newspapers. People who follow precise standard usage rules are using ideal English, although they probably express themselves less formally in day-to-day communication—on the bus, in the laundromat, or at the supermarket.

Ideal English is the language of concentrated formality. Dun J. Li, introducing a textbook on Chinese civilization, uses *ideal English* when he states: "Of all idealogies that influenced the thinking and life of traditional China none was more important than Confucianism." On the other hand, the irate factory worker complaining about his wages uses colloquial English when he writes, "If you wasn't so darn pig-headed, you'd raise our pay." Both messages are clear, but the difference is in their levels of formality.

Use the Correct Word

Because it is highly precise, *ideal English* is generally required in student writing. Colloquial, substandard, or slang words are unacceptable in ideal English. If you are unsure about a word's meaning, we suggest that you look it up. The following glossary will help you avoid expressions that are unacceptable in ideal English.

Glossary of Word Choice

ACCEPT, EXCEPT.　To *accept* is to *receive;* to *except* is to *exclude.* (We *accepted* her into the group; we didn't let him in because C students were *excepted.*) *Except* is a preposition meaning *other than, with the exception of.* (Everyone arrived on time *except* Jim.)

ACCIDENTLY.　No such word exists. The correct word is *accidentally.*

ADVICE, ADVISE.　*Advice* is a noun; *advise* is a verb. (A person receives *advice,* but he will *advise* another.)

AFFECT, EFFECT.　*Affect* means to *influence.* (It will *affect* my health.) *Effect* is both a verb and a noun. To *effect* is to *produce, cause,* or *bring about.* (He *effected* a change.) An *effect* is a *result.* (The *effect* of the paint was ugly.)

AGGRAVATE.　*Aggravate* means *make worse.* It should not be used for *provoke* or *irritate.*

AGREE TO, AGREE WITH.　One agrees *to* a proposal but *with* a person. (I agreed *to* his plan. I agreed *with* Nancy.)

AIN'T.　Considered substandard.

ALLUSION, ILLUSION.　*Allusion* means *hint* or *indirect reference.* (The comment was an *allusion* to World War II.) *Illusion* means *false impression* or *belief.* (She is under the *illusion* that she is beautiful.)

ALL READY, ALREADY.　*All ready* means that all are ready. (The guests were *all ready.*) *Already* means *previously* or *before now.* (He had *already* moved away from town.)

ALL TOGETHER, ALTOGETHER.　*All together* means *all of a number* considered as a group. (She scolded them *all together.*) *Altogether* means *entirely, completely.* (The officer was *altogether* correct.)

AMONG, BETWEEN.　*Among* is used for more than two people or objects. (We searched *among* the many guests.) *Between* is used for two people or objects. (Divide the money *between* the two workers.)

AMOUNT, NUMBER.　*Amount* refers to uncountable things (a large *amount* of cement). *Number* refers to countable things (a large *number* of houses).

ANY PLACE, NO PLACE. Corruptions of *anywhere, nowhere.*

ANYWHERES, NOWHERES, SOMEWHERES. Corruptions of *anywhere, nowhere, somewhere.*

APPRAISE, APPRISE. *Appraise* means *estimate* (the *appraised* value of the car). *Appraise* means *inform* (*apprise* me of your decision).

APT, LIABLE, LIKELY. *Apt* means *suitable, qualified, capable* (an *apt* phrase, a man *apt* in his work). *Liable* means *susceptible, prone, responsible* (liable to be injured, *liable* for damages). *Likely* means *credible, probable, probably.* (He had a *likely* excuse. It is *likely* to rain.)

AWFUL. Colloquial when used for *disagreeable* or *very.*

BAD, BADLY. *Bad* is an adjective, *badly* an adverb. (He has a *bad* cold; he sings *badly.*)

BEING AS. Corruption of *since* or *inasmuch as.*

BESIDE, BESIDES. *Beside* is a preposition meaning *by the side of, in addition to,* or *aside from.* (He sat down *beside* her.) *Besides* is a preposition meaning *except* (He had much *besides* his good looks) and an adverb meaning *in addition, moreover.* (He received a trip and fifty dollars *besides.*)

BLAME ON. Correct idiom calls for the use of *to blame* with *for,* not *on.* (They *blamed* the driver *for* the accident, not They *blamed* the accident *on* the driver.) *Blame on* is colloquial.

BURST, BURSTED, BUST. The principal parts of the verb *burst* are *burst, burst, burst.* The use of *bursted* or *busted* for the past tense is incorrect. *Bust* is either a piece of sculpture, a part of the human body, or a slang expression for *failure.* It is sometimes incorrectly used instead of *burst* or *break.*

BUT WHAT. Use *that* instead of *but what.* (They had no doubt *that* he would win the New York primary.)

CANNOT HELP BUT. This is a mixed construction. *Cannot help* and *cannot but* are separate expressions, either of which is correct. (*He cannot but attempt it,* or *He cannot help attempting it.*) Do not write, "He *cannot help but* lose."

CAPITAL, CAPITOL. *Capital* is a city; *capitol* is a building. *Capital* is also an adjective, usually meaning *chief* or *excellent.* As a noun, *capital* means accumulated assets or wealth.

CENSOR, CENSURE. To *censor* means to *subject to censorship.* (The Vietnamese military *censored* his mail.) To *censure* means to *criticize severely.* (He was *censured* by the church.)

CHOOSE, CHOSE. *Choose* is the present tense. (Today I *choose* to stay.) *Chose* is the past tense. (Yesterday I *chose* to stay.)

CITE, SITE. To *cite* means to *quote.* (He *cited* Abraham Lincoln.) *Site* means *place* or *location.* (It was a grassy, green *site.*)

COMPLEMENT, COMPLIMENT. In its usual sense, *complement* means *something that completes.* (His suggestion was a *complement* to the general plan.) A *compliment* is an expression of courtesy or praise. (My *compliments* to the chef.)

CONSIDERABLE. The word is an adjective meaning *worthy of consideration, important.* (The idea is at least *considerable.*) When used to denote a great deal or a great many, *considerable* is colloquial or informal.

CONTINUAL, CONTINUOUS. *Continual* means *repeated often.* (The interruptions were *continual.*) *Continuous* means *going on without interruption.* (For two days the pain was *continuous.*)

CONVINCE, PERSUADE. Do not use *convince* for *persuade,* as in "I *convinced* him to do it." *Convince* means to *overcome a doubt.* (I *convinced* him of the soundness of my plan.) *Persuade* means to *induce.* (I *persuaded* him to do it.)

COUNCIL, COUNSEL. *Council* means an *assembly.* (The *council* discussed taxes.) *Counsel* means *advice.* (The teacher gave him good *counsel.*)

CREDIBLE, CREDITABLE. *Credible* means *believable.* (His evidence was not *credible.*) *Creditable* means *deserving esteem* or *admiration.* (The male lead gave a *creditable* performance.)

DIFFERENT THAN. Most authorities on usage prefer *different from* to *different than.*

DISINTERESTED. Often confused with *uninterested, disinterested* mean *unbiased, impartial.* (The judge was *disinterested.*) *Uninterested* means *bored with.* (She was *uninterested* in politics.)

DON'T. A contraction of *do not.* Do not write *he, she,* or *it don't.*

EITHER. Used only with two items, not three or more. (*Either* the teacher or the book was wrong. *Not: Either* the teacher, the book, or I was wrong.)

EMIGRANT, IMMIGRANT. A person who moves from one country to another is both an *emigrant* and an *immigrant.* He *emigrates from* one place and *immigrates to* the other.

ENTHUSED. The word is colloquial and almost always unacceptable.

EQUALLY AS. Do not use these words together; omit either *equally* or *as.* Do not write "Water is equally as necessary as air," but rather "Water is as necessary as air" or "Water and air are equally necessary."

ETC. An abbreviation of Latin *et* (and) and *cetera* (other things). It should not be preceded by *and,* nor should it be used to avoid a clear and exact ending of an idea or a sentence.

EXAM. Colloquial for examination. Compare *gym, lab, dorm, soph, prof.*

EVERYONE. This singular pronoun takes a singular verb. (Everyone *is* going.)

EXPECT. The word means *look forward to* or *foresee.* Do not use it for *suspect* or *suppose.*

FEWER, LESS. Use *fewer* to refer to items that can be numbered and *less* to refer to amount. (Where there are *fewer* machines, there is *less* noise.)

FORMALLY, FORMERLY. *Formally* means *in a formal manner.* (He was *formally* initiated last night.) *Formerly* means *at a former time.* (They *formerly* lived in Ohio.)

FUNNY. When used to mean *strange* or *queer, funny* is colloquial.

FURTHER, FARTHER. *Further* is used for ideas. (We studied the question *further.*) *Farther* is used for geographical location (*farther* down the street).

GOT. This is a correct past tense and past participle of the verb *to get.* (He *got* three traffic tickets in two days.) *Gotten* is the alternative past participle of *get.* (He had *gotten* three tickets the week before.)

GUESS. Colloquial when used for *suppose* or *believe.*

GUY. Slang when used for *boy* or *man.*

HAD OUGHT, HADN'T OUGHT. Do not use for *ought* and *ought not.*

HARDLY, SCARCELY. Do not use with a negative. "I *can't hardly* see it" borders on the illiterate. Write "I *can hardly* see it" or (if you cannot see it all all) "I *can't* see it."

HEALTHFUL, HEALTHY. Places are *healthful* (conducive to health) if persons living in them are *healthy* (having good health).

IMPLY, INFER. *Imply* means *suggest.* (His grin *implied* that he was teasing.) *Infer* means *conclude.* (I *inferred* from her look that she was teasing.)

INCIDENTLY.   There is no such word. The correct form is *incidentally,* which is derived from the adjective *incidental.*

INSIDE OF.   In expressions of time, *inside of* is colloquial for *within* (He will return *within* a week).

IRREGARDLESS.   No such word exists. Use *regardless.*

ITS, IT'S.   The form *its* is possessive. (*Its* cover is gray.) *It's* is a contraction of *it is.* (*It's* your fault.)

IT'S ME.   Formal English requires *It is I. It's me* is informal or colloquial.

KIND, SORT.   These are singular forms of nouns and should be modified accordingly (*this kind, that sort*). Do not write "*these* kind."

KIND OF, SORT OF.   Do not use these to mean *rather* as in "He was *kind of* (or *sort of*) stupid."

LAST, LATEST.   *Last* implies that there will be no more; *latest* means *most recent.* (After reading his *latest* book, I hope that it is his *last.*)

LEAVE, LET.   The use of *leave* for *let* in expressions like *leave him go* is incorrect.

LIKE, AS.   Confusion in the use of these words results from using *like* as a conjunction—"He talks *like* a gentlemen should. She spends money like she had a fortune." Use *as* or *as if* instead. (He talks *as* a gentleman should. She spends money *as if* she had a fortune.)

LOOSE, LOSE.   *Loose* means *not tight, not attached.* (The button is *loose.*) *Lose* means to *be unable to keep or find.* (Did she *lose* her diamond ring?)

LOT, LOTS.   Colloquial or informal when used to mean *many* or *much.*

MAD.   The meaning of *mad* is *insane.* Used to mean *angry,* it is informal.

MAY BE, MAYBE.   *May be* is a verb phrase. (They *may be* late.) *Maybe* used as an adverb means *perhaps.* (*Maybe* they will buy a boat.)

MEAN.   Used informally for *disagreeable.* (He has a *mean* face.) It is slang when used to mean *skillful, expert.* (He plays a *mean* tennis game.)

MEDIA.   *Media* is the plural of *medium*—a means, agency, or instrument. It is often used *incorrectly* as though it were singular, as in "The *media is* playing a big role in political races this year."

MOST.   Do not use for *almost.* "*Almost* all my friends appeared" is the correct form.

MYSELF.   Incorrect when used as a substitute for *I* or *me,* as in "He and *myself* did it" It is correctly used as an intensifier. (*I myself* shall do it) and in the reflexive. (I blame only *myself*).

NONE, NO ONE.   Singular pronouns taking irregular verb forms. (None of his reasons *is* valid. No one *is* going.

OF.   Unnecessary after such prepositions as *off, inside,* or *outside.* (He fell *off* the chair. They waited *inside* the house.)

ON ACCOUNT OF.   Do not use as a conjunction. The phrase should be followed by an object of the preposition *of* (*on account of* his illness). "He was absent *on account of* he was sick" is poor English.

ORAL, VERBAL.   *Oral* means *spoken* rather than written; *verbal* means *associated with words.* When referring to an agreement or commitment that is not in writing, *oral* should be used.

OVER WITH.   The *with* is unnecessary in such expressions as "The concert was *over with* by five o'clock."

PAST, PASSED.   *Past* is a noun, adjective, or preposition (to remember the *past;* in the *past* two weeks, one block *past* the pharmacy). *Passed* is a verb. (She *passed* by his house.)

PERSONAL, PERSONNEL.   Personal means *private*. (She expressed her *personal* view.) *Personnel* is a *body of employed people*. (The *personnel* demanded higher wages.)

PLAN ON.   Omit *on*. Standard practice calls for an infinitive or a direct object after *plan*. (They *planned to go*. They *planned a reception*.)

PRINCIPAL, PRINCIPLE.   Principal is both adjective and noun (*principal* parts, *principal* of the school, interest and *principal*). *Principle* is a noun only, meaning *code of conduct, fundamental truth or assumption* (*principles* of morality, a man of *principle*).

QUITE.   The word means *altogether, entirely*. (He was *quite* exhausted from his exertion.) It is colloquial when used for *moderately* or *very* and in expressions like *quite a few, quite a number*.

RAISE, RISE.   *Raise* requires an object. (She *raised* the cover.) *Rise* is not used with an object. (Let us *rise* and sing.)

REASON IS BECAUSE, REASON WHY.   These are not correct forms in English. Examples of correct usage are "The *reason* I stayed home is *that* I was sick," "The *reason* (not *why*) they invited us is that. . . ."

RESPECTFULLY, RESPECTIVELY.   Respectfully means *with respect*. (The young used to act *respectfully* toward their elders.) *Respectively* is used to clarify antecedents in a sentence. (The *men and women* took their seats on the right and left, respectively.)

RIGHT.   In the sense of *very* or *extremely*, *right* is colloquial. Do not write, "I'm *right* glad to know you."

SAME.   The word is an adjective, not a pronoun. Do not use it as in "We received your order and shall give *same* our immediate attention." Substitute *it* for *same*.

SET, SIT.   *Set* requires an object. (She *set* the cup on the table.) *Sit* is not used with an object. (You must *sit* in the chair.)

SHOULD OF, WOULD OF.   Do not use these forms for *should have, would have*.

SOME.   Do not use for *somewhat*, as in "She is *some* better after her illness."

STATIONARY, STATIONERY.   *Stationary* means *fixed, not moving*. *Stationery* means paper and other materials for writing letters.

STATUE, STATURE, STATUTE.   A *statue* is a piece of sculpture. *Stature* is bodily height, often used figuratively to mean *level of achievement, status,* or *importance*. A *statute* is a law or regulation.

SURE, SURELY.   *Sure* is an adjective, and *surely* is an adverb. (I am *sure* that he will arrive, but he *surely* annoys me.)

SUSPICION.   This word is a noun and should not be used for the verb *to suspect*. (His *suspicion* was right; they *suspected* the butler.)

TRY AND.   Use *try to*, not *try and*, in such expressions as "*Try to* be kind."

TYPE.   Colloquial in expressions like "this *type* book." Write "this *type of* book."

UNIQUE.   If referring to something as the *only* one of its kind, you may correctly use *unique*. (The Grand Canyon is *unique*.) The word does not mean *rare, strange,* or *remarkable*, and there are no degrees of uniqueness: Nothing can be *extremely* (almost, nearly, virtually) *unique*.

USE (USED) TO COULD.   Do not use for *once could* or *used to be able*.

VERY.   Do not use as a modifier of a past participle, as in *very burned*. English idiom calls for *badly burned* or *very badly burned*.

WAIT FOR, WAIT ON.   *To wait for* means *to look forward to, to expect*. (For days I *have waited for* you.) *To wait on* means *to serve*. (The hostess *waited on* the guests.)

WANT IN, WANT OFF, WANT OUT.   These forms are dialectal. Do not use them for *want to come in, want to get off, want to get out*.

WAY.   Colloquial when used for *away*, as in "*way* out West."

WAYS.   Colloquial when used for *way*, as in "a long *ways* to go."

WHOSE, WHO'S.   The possessive form is *whose*. (*Whose* money is this?) *Who's* is a contraction of *who is*. (*Who's* there?)

WISE.   Unacceptable when appended to a noun to convert it to an adverb as in *businesswise*.

YOUR, YOU'RE.   The possessive form is *your*. (Give me *your* address.) *You're* is a contraction of *you are*.

Exercises

Underline the correct term in each of the following sentences:

1. When they arrived at West Point, they received some practical (advise, advice) regarding the honor system.

2. During his lecture, the professor made an (allusion, illusion) to Abraham Lincoln.

3. The prime minister's illness was so (aggravated, irritated) by his drinking that he needed surgery.

4. My aunt does a (credible, creditable) job of sewing evening gowns.

5. In the past, interviewers were (disinterested, uninterested) when they interviewed candidates; now they are biased.

6. I was (enthusiastic, enthused) when they told me about the new director.

7. When we heard about the theft, we immediately (suspicioned, suspected) collusion within the company.

8. They received the news that he would return (within, inside of) a week.

9. Chris Evert's (latest, last) match gave the world of tennis something to rave about.

10. Be careful not to (loose, lose) the keys.

11. We drank the spring water (as if, like) we would never drink water again in our lives.

12. That information seriously (affects, effects) the decision.

13. The agreement was (oral, verbal), so it will not hold up in court.

14. The reason grades are necessary (is that, is because) they are a point of reference for students.

15. If I had known you were coming, I (would of, would have) baked a cake.

16. Most people improve (somewhat, some) the moment they take one spoonful of Kay's cough syrup.

17. For Christmas, I sent mother some blue (stationary, stationery) so she could write to her friends.

18. Never use a large (number, amount) of words when (less, fewer) will do.

19. We still had a long (way, ways) to trudge uphill, but none of the students complained.

20. Will the person (who's, whose) wallet this is please claim it at the front ticket booth.

21. Before the tall buildings were built, we (used to could, used to be able) to see see the ocean.

22. That scandal in her (passed, past) may keep her from getting the promotion.

23. Many Americans want to return to old-fashioned, religious (principals, principles).

24. (Regardless, irregardless) of the consequences, the ambassador stood by his post.

25. The glint in her eye (implied, inferred) more clearly than words how she really felt.

Self-Grading Exercise 14

Underline the correct term in each of the following sentences. After completing the exercise, turn to the appendix for the correct answers.

1. After noticing that the watch and the bedspread were gone, they immediately (suspicioned, suspected) his stepdaughter.

2. Dorothy insisted on keeping her (personnel, personal) opinions hidden from her students.

3. The hiring committee preferred communicating by telephone because they believed in (oral, verbal) interviews.

4. I was always told that (this type, this type of) novel was cheap and aimed at the sensation seekers.

5. (Sit, set) the flower pot in front of the brick wall, where it will look lovely.

6. The (amount, number) of registered students varies from semester to semester.

7. In the upper left-hand corner of his (stationery, stationary) one could clearly discern three modest initials.

8. Earl Warren was considered a Supreme Court justice of immense (stature, statue, statute).

9. The team that climbed Mt. Whitney included (quite a number, a rather large number) of women.

10. Twenty years and six children later, the marriage was finally (over, over with).

11. Day after day his fiancee waited (for, on) him to return from the war.

12. Thank you for the (complement, compliment)—how kind!

13. (Your, you're) either for us or against us.

14. He never returned the suitcase (like, as) he was asked to do.

15. We (can hardly, can't hardly) distinguish one twin from the other.

16. The (farther, further) he delved into St. Paul's theology, the more fascinated he became.

17. When the real estate agent had received a firm bid, he (appraised, apprised) his clients of the fact.

18. He could never be (persuaded, convinced) to travel overseas on an airplane.

19. The (site, cite) for the international hotel was near the center of town.

20. While he was in Vietnam, all of his mail was (censured, censored).

Use Concrete Words

A word is *concrete* when it refers to a *specific* object, quality, or action. "He *limped* across the road" is more concrete than "He *went* across the road." "*One hundred women* attended the dinner" is more concrete than "*Quite a few people* attended the dinner." (See also Unit 1, the section on using details.)

Vague: I like her because she is such a *nice* girl.
Concrete: I like her because she is *witty* and *vivacious*.

Vague: The lyrics of Paul Simon are *relevant*.
Concrete: The lyrics of Paul Simon *expose many fears felt by the people in our society*.

Vague: I dislike my teacher's *negative attitude* toward old people.
Concrete: I dislike my teacher's *contempt* for old people.

Exercises

Improve the following sentences by replacing the italicized vague words with more concrete words or phrases.

1. John *got* on his horse and quickly *went* away.

   _____

   _____

2. Eloise always wears such sloppy *apparel.*

   _____

   _____

3. The streets of Amsterdam are crowded with *vehicles.*

   _____

   _____

4. The lecturer was most *uninteresting.*

   _____

   _____

5. She *ate* her food *quickly.*

   _____

   _____

6. It was fascinating to watch the children *being active* on the school play-ground.

   _____

   _____

7. I was upset by this whole *business.*

   _____

   _____

8. What a *great* idea!

   _____

   _____

9. We expect to have a *wonderful* time in Palm Springs.

_____

_____

10. Eskimos are *unusual* in many *ways*.

_____

_____

11. I couldn't follow the complicated *setup* in his church.

_____

_____

12. My psychology class was one of the most *worthwhile* experiences of my college days.

_____

_____

13. Spanking is an important *element* of child rearing.

_____

_____

14. The *negative aspects* of driving huge cars outweigh the *positive aspects*.

_____

_____

15. "All the President's Men" is a *tremendous* movie.

_____

_____

16. Here are the *things* that bother me about assigning grades.

_____

_____

Self-Grading Exercise 15

Improve the following sentences by replacing the italicized vague words with more concrete words or phrases. After completing the exercise, turn to the appendix for the answers (there is more than one possible answer for each item).

1. To add to our depression, a period of *unfavorable weather* set in.

_____

_____

2. Vicky *showed great satisfaction* as she walked off the stage with her gold medal.

_____

_____

3. I liked *the advantages of living* in the city.

_____

_____

4. His extreme selfishness *had some negative consequences on his life.*

_____

_____

5. He chewed his food noisily, he talked with his mouth full, and he wiped his lips with his hand; in short, his manners were *deficient.*

_____

_____

6. For six days and nights, he *participated in a combat* with fever and death.

_____

_____

7. A delicate sea shell is a *nice thing.*

_____

_____

8. All of the fun at Joe's birthday party was ruined because the children *behaved badly.*

_____

_____

9. The Mohave Desert of California and the Sinai Desert of Palestine *have certain characteristics in common.*

_____

_____

10. Every large city *has its problems.*

_____

_____

11. She was a hopeless, desiccated old lady *going across* the street with her cane, her *entire posture* serving as a symbol of her despair.

_____

_____

12. In 1925 a terrible dust storm *went* across the Midwest, *causing considerable destruction.*

_____

_____

13. Many of the old Tin Pan Alley songs reveal poignantly *some regrettable aspects* of American life.

_____

_____

14. We tried various cleaning solutions, but the kitchen floor remained *unsightly.*

_____

_____

15. People who throw *all kinds of stuff* out of their car windows while they drive along our highways reveal a disgusting kind of vulgarity.

_____

_____

✍ **Wordiness** results when writing is overly burdened with redundant or wasted expressions. Prune your rough draft of such redundancies.

Wordy: He spent *all of his entire* life in freezing temperatures. *All* and *entire* are redundant.

Correct: He spent his entire life in freezing temperatures.

Wordy: After *the end of* the flood, Noah released the dove. *The end of* is wasted.

Correct: After the flood, Noah released the dove.

Wordy: My dress was pink and yellow *in color*. The term *in color* is wasted; pink and yellow are obviously colors.

Other redundancies of this kind are:

short *in length*	*necessary* requirements
circle *around*	*and* etc.
still persist	combined *together*
many *in number*	now *at this time*

Wordy: The Oldsmobile that was parked behind the supermarket was smeared with mud.

Correct: The Oldsmobile parked behind the supermarket was smeared with mud.

Often, relative clauses can be trimmed. Note the following:

the judge *who was* seated on the bench

the judge on the bench

the man *who was* accused

the accused man

Exercises

Revise the following sentences for economy by eliminating redundancies or wasted words.

1. The secretary who sat behind the big mahogany desk of wood seemed to be efficient.

_____

2. Most people find it difficult to express the emotion of tenderness toward other people.

3. The winner was timid and reticent about accepting the trophy.

4. Her coat, which is of the fur type, cost $2,000.

5. Worshiping ancestors is a venerable, sacred, old religious tradition among the Chinese.

6. My study of history leads me to believe that the Danes were a militant people who loved war.

7. Probably paying decent wages is usually the right thing to do in the majority of cases.

8. Workers who are employed shouldn't be allowed to collect food stamps.

9. If he wants to be President, he had better bring about new innovations in Congress.

10. Generally speaking, most of the time it is improper diet that causes gallstones.

11. All of the present clothing styles in our day and age reflect a taste for the bizarre.

12. At 10:00 P.M. at night a strange knock was heard.

13. The consensus of the majority in our class was that we should invite Dr. Boling as our keynote speaker.

14. The story dealt with a cruel murder and a tragic ending that was lamentable.

15. As a usual rule one should lock one's car while shopping.

16. There were three women who decided to volunteer for the job without being forced.

17. Neil Simon writes humorous comedies that really make you laugh.

_____

_____

18. If we don't cooperate together with the Russians, a nuclear war could annihilate the world.

_____

_____

19. Palestinians and Arabs are very different in various ways.

_____

_____

20. In this day and age it is difficult to find a musician in the entire field of music who gets at people's hearts the way Charles Witt does.

_____

_____

_____

Self-Grading Exercise 16

Revise the following sentences for economy by eliminating redundancies or wasted words. After completing the exercise, turn to the appendix for the answers (there is more than one possible answer for each item).

1. Charles Steinmetz was a man who pioneered in the field of electrical engineering.

_____

_____

2. Long-distance runners training for the Olympics run many miles a day, and they cover as many as 20 miles.

_____

_____

3. Each and every person who stood in line received a ticket.

_____

_____

4. Students today demonstrate poor writing skills for one simple reason: the reason is that they are never required to write.

_____

_____

5. My favorite poet is Emily Dickinson among all the women poets that I like best.

_____

_____

6. In the next chapter that follows we will look at and examine a theory held by Charles Darwin dealing with evolution.

_____

_____

7. In this modern world of today, it is difficult to keep up with the most recent and up-to-date advances in science.

_____

_____

8. Made of solid oak material and a rich brown in color, the table has lasted for over a hundred years of time.

_____

_____

9. One of John's most serious faults is the fact that he continously apologizes for his errors.

_____

_____

10. The method they most often used to grade objective tests was that of using a scantron machine.

_____

11. One of the most exciting events of the trip was attending a secret burial ceremony, never performed publicly.

_____

_____

12. Nevertheless, most reasonable judges are rational and do not judge defendants on the basis of feelings or emotions.

_____

_____

13. The pilot was in a terrible dilemma because a crosswind was blowing at right angles to his aircraft's line of flight.

_____

_____

14. All of the children who were observed by media reporters were tall in height.

_____

_____

15. The income from traffic fines is an important source of revenue for New York City.

_____

_____

sub The impact of an essay is lessened when its sentences are childishly short and loosely strung together. Here is an example:

> The newspaper recently contained an article. The article was about a man named Lewis Stafford. The man had passed some bogus checks. He was put in jail.

This passage would ring with more authority if its sentences were combined by subordinating the lesser ideas to the greater:

> The newspaper recently contained an article about Lewis Stafford, a man put in jail for passing bogus checks.

Subordination is the art of grammatical ranking. Faced with expressing a series of ideas in a single sentence, the writer arranges them in clauses and phrases that mirror their relative importance. In the above example, for instance, the main clause reports on the newspaper article about Lewis Stafford while the subordinate clause mentions his jailing for passing bogus checks. The writer has therefore chosen to emphasize the article in the newspaper over the jailing for bad checks. If desired, quite the reverse emphasis could have been achieved with another subordinate construction:

> Lewis Stafford was put in jail for passing bogus checks, an event recently reported in the newspaper.

The ranking of one event over another through subordination depends entirely on which event the writer deems more important and which he or she wishes to emphasize.

Subordination is achieved by combining short sentences into a single long sentence. This is done by turning main clauses into either phrases or dependent clauses:

1. Subordination by phrase. For a definition of *phrase*, see p. 287. The following are phrases:

> singing in the rain
> left alone with his friend
> with its lovely rose garden
> to lower his taxes

Note how pairs of sentences can be combined by turning one of the sentences into a phrase:

No subordination: The man left. He sang in the rain.

Subordination: The man left, singing in the rain.

No subordination: He was left alone with his friend. He confided his secret to his friend.

Subordination: Left alone with his friend, he confided his secret.

No subordination: Hoover Library stands as a monument to our city. It has a lovely rose garden.

Subordination: Hoover Library, with its lovely rose garden, stands as a monument to our city.

No subordination: He voted for Proposition 13. He did it to lower his taxes.

Subordination: To lower his taxes, he voted for Proposition 13.

2. Subordination by dependent clause. For a definition of *dependent clause,* see p. 286. The following are dependent clauses:

> although he was confronted with many alternatives
> who have lived in the Orient
> if the price of gasoline continues to rise

Notice how pairs of sentences can be combined by turning one of the sentences into a dependent clause:

No subordination: He was confronted with many alternatives. He refused to make a choice.

Subordination: Although he was confronted with many alternatives, he refused to make a choice.

No subordination: Many people have lived in the Orient. They never learned to like Oriental food.

Subordination: Many people who have lived in the Orient never learned to like Oriental food.

No subordination: The price of gasoline continues to rise. He will probably sell his car.

Subordination: If the price of gasoline continues to rise, he will probably sell his car.

Choosing the Right Subordinator

The word that introduces a dependent clause is called a *subordinator.* Your choice of subordinator will depend on the relationship you wish to establish among ideas. The following list serves to classify the various subordinators according to their logical relationship to the main clause:

Condition: If
Provided that
In case
Assuming that
Unless
Whether or not

Cause/reason: Because
Since
Considering that

Time: When
Whenever
As long as
While
Before
After
Until, till
As soon as

Extent/degree: Although
Inasmuch as
Insofar as
To the extent that

Place:	Where
	Wherever
Noun substitute:	Who
	That
	Which
	What
	Whoever
	Whom
	Whomever
	Whichever
	Whatever

See also subordinating conjunctions, p. 296.

Suppose you wish to combine the following two sentences:

> He promised to pay the rent.
> She needed the money.

Several options will be open to you, among them the following:

	because she needed the money.
	stresses cause
	as long as she needed the money.
	stresses time
	insofar as she needed the money.
He promised to pay the rent	stresses degree
	in case she needed the money.
	stresses condition
	to whoever needed the money.
	substitutes a pronoun
	for a noun

Your choice of subordinator must depend on the logic by which you wish to link the two sentences.

Exercise

Combine the sentences in each set below into a single sentence, using either dependent clauses or phrases. Try different subordinators and different combinations to see what logical effect is created.

1. a. The doctor was taking the patient's temperature.
   b. Suddenly a rock came crashing through the window.

2. a. In mid-July he was inspecting the dig.
   b. He was alerted by someone.
   c. Someone was moving along the northern edge of the plateau.

3. a. It was a bright day in May.
   b. The drums exploded.
   c. Two priests from the temple appeared.

4. a. The crowd groaned with disappointment.
   b. They had hoped to see a glamorous young girl.

5. a. Others planned the forthcoming battle.
   b. He remained alone in the shaded grove.
   c. He was meditating and praying to his god.
   d. He needed guidance from his god.

6. a. Members of the city council can ill afford to vote themselves additional fringe benefits.
   b. Their constituents mistrust them.

7. a. Alif was entirely wrong.
   b. He guessed that she was in love with Abdul.
   c. In fact, she was merely bedazzled by his brilliant lyrics.
   d. They reminded her of starry nights in Egypt.

8. a. The fraternity members all over campus carried banners.
   b. They marched back and forth tirelessly.
   c. Their signs called for an end to building nuclear reactors.

9. a. Something occurred to Madeline.
   b. Perhaps she could improve the situation.
   c. She could create an atmosphere of goodwill.

10. a. Give out these sample tubes of toothpaste.
    b. Give one to whoever asks for one.

11. a. Phil Brown regularly attends church.
    b. There he loves to hear the old hymns.
    c. He also loves to hear a rousing sermon.
    d. These make him feel purged.
    e. They give him a new lease on life.

12. a. The specific notes had faded from his memory.
    b. Yet a certain melody remained.
    c. It haunted him the rest of his life.

13. a. Such facts cannot be ignored.
    b. We want to preserve the wilderness.

14. a. Those of us who are prisoners must face the grim truth.
    b. This truth is that even our wives and lovers will leave us.
    c. We have shared the most tender and intimate moments with them.

15. a. The scientific establishment now believes that the earth was formed 10–15 billion years ago.
    b. It was formed after an explosion, or "big bang."
    c. This explosion set the universe in motion.

Combine the sentences in each set below into a single sentence, using either dependent clauses or phrases. Try different subordinators to see what logical effect is created. After completing the exercise, turn to the appendix for the answers (there is more than one possible answer for each item).

1. a. The medieval structure collapsed.
   b. Then the beginning of the modern mode of production started.

2. a. Quite a few years ago a stranger came in and bought our small valley.
   b. This was where the Sempervirens redwoods grew.
   c. At the time I was living in a little town.
   d. The little town was on the West Coast.

3. a. Writing skills can be improved.
   b. But English teachers will have to assign more writing than they now do.

4. a. We began to realize something.
   b. Resources in America are not limitless.
   c. We had thought they were.

5. a. We are an exuberant people.
   b. We are also careless and destructive.
   c. We make powerful weapons, such as the atomic bomb.
   d. We then use them to prove that they exist.

6. a. Uncountable buffalo were killed.
   b. The buffalo were stripped of their hides.
   c. They were left to rot.
   d. Thus a permanent food supply was destroyed.

7. a. He was a teacher.
   b. In that capacity he considered objections by students carefully.
   c. To him it was as if these objections had been made by colleagues.

8. a. Its roof was half torn away by wind.
   b. Its walls were blackened by fire.
   c. Its stone floors were covered with mud.
   d. This hotel looked like the ruins of a Gothic castle.

9. a. I was seventeen and extremely shy.
   b. My third-grade teacher came to visit us.

10. a. Television newscasters are victims of the rating game.
    b. They are hired and fired on the basis of how entertaining they make the news.
    c. The rating game is controlled by anti-intellectual viewers.

11. a. All four of my grandparents were unknown to one another.
    b. But they all arrived in America from the same county in Slovakia.
    c. They had experienced a severe famine.
    d. The famine was due to a potato crop failure.

12. a. Most people believed the earth was roughly 6000 years old.
    b. This idea was based on information in the Bible.
    c. It was accepted until the beginning of the nineteenth century.
    d. At that time geologists and naturalists began to suspect something.
    e. What they suspected was that the earth must have existed for a much longer period of time.

13. a. He drove along the highway like a haunted man.
    b. He was stopped by the police.

14. a. The early Incas did not have the wheel.
    b. Their architectural achievements were spectacular.

15. a. Goethe influenced Thomas Mann.
    b. We can surmise that Mann's *Dr. Faustus* is similar to Goethe's *Faust.*
    c. Both works deal with the theme of the demonic.

p *Punctuation errors* occur with the omission or misuse of one of the following marks: period (.), comma (,), semicolon (;), colon (:), dash (—), question mark (?), exclamation point (!), apostrophe ('), parentheses (()), quotation marks (". . ."), italics (underlining), and hyphen (-). The function of punctuation marks is to separate words and phrases within a sentence according to their meanings.

Frequently, meaning may be misinterpreted unless a punctuation mark is provided. Consider the following:

After we had finished the essays were read out loud.

The sentence must be reread with a pause inserted after *finished:*

After we had finished, the essays were read out loud.

The key to effective punctuation is to learn what each punctuation mark means and where it must be used.

The Period (.)

Periods are used after declarative or mildly imperative sentences, indirect questions, and abbreviations. (See also run-together sentences, p. 302.) Use ellipses—three spaced periods (. . .)—to indicate omissions from quoted material.

Declarative: We followed Mr. Smith upstairs to the conductor's room.

Imperative: Visit Old Amsterdam while you are in Holland.

Indirect question: The child asked if it was all right to pick an apple.

Abbreviation: Since we had so little money, we stayed at the Y.M.C.A.

(good men)

Ellipses: Now is the time for all . . . to come to the aid of their country.

Current usage permits the omission of the period after these and other abbreviations: TV, CIA, FBI, UN, NBC, USN. If in doubt whether to omit the period after an abbreviation, consult a dictionary.

The Comma (,)

The comma is used and misused more than any other punctuation mark. (See also comma splice, p. 301.) A writer of factual prose must learn to master the comma. While it is sometimes useful to equate commas with pauses, it is safer to follow the simple rules given below.

1. Use commas to set off phrases or clauses that interrupt the flow of a sentence or that are not essential to the meaning of a sentence. In this use, the commas sometimes function as the equivalent of parentheses.

   a. Tatyana Grosman, as her first name suggests, is Russian by birth.
   b. Mrs. Jones, while charming in every way, held doggedly to her point.
   c. My father, who is a banker, lives in New York.

2. Use a comma after a long introductory phrase or clause:

   a. Near the grove at the top of his block, someone was having a party.
   b. Since I meant my remark as a compliment, I was surprised when my boss became angry.

3. Use a comma to separate the main clause from a long clause or phrase that follows it, if the two are separated by a pause or break.

   a. Certainly no one has tried harder than Jane, although many of her ideas have proved to be disastrous when they have been put to practice.
   b. He awakened something new in me, a devotion I didn't know I was capable of.

4. Use a comma to separate long independent clauses joined by *and, but, or, for, yet, nor:*

   a. The tunnel beside the house was very dark, but after school George used it as his imaginary fortress.
   b. If he uses three or four cans of balls, then that's it, and I don't want him to come to me begging for more.

5. Use commas to separate items in a series:

   a. I felt tired, cold, and discouraged.
   b. He raised his head, closed his eyes, and let out a deep moan.

An adjective that is essential to a noun is not set off from other adjectives with a comma:

   My aunt is giving away some unusual white elephants, including a gigantic Chinese screen, several old Tiffany lamps, and a cracked ironstone platter.

6. Use a comma after words of address:

   a. Sir, that is not what I meant.
   b. Do you recall that night, Linda?

7. Use a comma to set off yes and no:

   a. Yes, the flight leaves at midnight.
   b. No, the letter has not arrived yet.

8. Use commas to set off dates and places:

   a. Miami, Florida, is humid in the summer.

   b. November 19, 1929, is my birthday.

   c. They live on 41 Parkwood Drive, Sacramento, California.

9. Use a comma to introduce quotations:

   a. Patrick Henry said, "Give me liberty or give me death!"

   b. The thief retorted, "You don't need the money."

10. Use commas to set off titles and degrees from preceding names:

   a. John Lawson, Jr., now runs the bank.

   b. Henry Knittle, M.D.

   c. Mark Hamilton, Ph.D.

The Semicolon (;)

The semicolon has three basic uses.

1. The semicolon is used to connect independent clauses so closely connected in meaning that they do not need to be separate sentences:

   a. He was a wonderful chap; we all loved him dearly.

   b. Loraine left all her money to her stepson; in this respect, she showed considerable generosity.

2. A semicolon may be used to connect independent clauses when the second clause begins with a conjunctive adverb (for a list of conjunctive adverbs, see p. 295):

   a. Joe was not a candidate; nevertheless, the gang chose him as their captain.

   b. Following her to the kitchen, I found that she had made two sandwiches; however, I was not hungry, so I did not eat.

   If the conjunctive adverb is not the first word in the second clause, the punctuation is as follows:

      The fever had subsided; my mother felt, nevertheless, that a doctor should be called.

3. The semicolon is used to separate phrases or clauses in a series when commas appear within any one of those phrases or clauses:

   a. Her estate was divided as follows: Books, diaries, and notebooks went to her agent; jewelry, furs, and clothes went to her sister; and everything else went to charity.

   b. For three days we followed a strict diet: eggs, grapefruit, and coffee on the first day; lamb chops, toast, and tomatoes on the second day; and fruit with cottage cheese on the third day.

The Colon (:)

Do not confuse the colon with the semicolon. Colons are used in the following cases:

1. Use a colon when you introduce lengthy material or lists.

   a. The following quotation from Robert Frost will support my view:
   b. Here is a list of all the camping equipment necessary to climb Mt. Wilson:
   c. Literature can be divided into four types: short story, drama, poetry, and novel.

2. Use a colon after the salutation of a formal letter, between title and subtitle of a literary work, between chapter and verse of the Bible, and between hours and minutes in time:

   a. Dear Ms. Landeen:
   b. The Ethnic Cult: New Fashion Trends
   c. I. Corinthians 3:16
   d. 10:30 A.M.

The Dash (—)

On the typewriter, the dash is made by two hyphens without spacing before, between, or after. In handwriting, the dash is an unbroken line the length of two hyphens.

1. Use the dash to indicate a sudden break in thought.

   a. The clerk's illiteracy, his lack of judgment, his poor writing skills—all added up until the company fired him.
   b. The secret of the recipe is—oh, but I promised not to tell.

2. Use dashes to set off parenthetical material that needs to be emphasized:
   a. Every house in the neighborhood—from Kenneth Road to Russel Drive—was solicited.
   b. She stood there—tall, proud, and unrelenting—daring her accusers to speak.

The Question Mark (?)

Use a question mark after a direct question. Do not use it when the question is indirect.

Direct: He asked her, "Have you had lunch?"

Indirect: He asked her if she had had lunch.

Direct: Who am I? Where am I going? Why am I here?

Do not follow a question mark with a comma or a period:

Wrong: "When will you leave?," he asked.

Correct: "When will you leave?" he asked.

The Exclamation Point (!)

Exclamation points should be used only to express surprise, disbelief, anger, or other strong emotions:

1. What an adorable baby!
2. What a rat! He couldn't have been that evil!
3. "Jinxed, by God!"

The Apostrophe (')

The apostrophe is used to show possession: "John's book" rather than "the book of John." It is also used to form contractions (can't, don't) and certain plurals.

1. Use an apostrophe to indicate possession. Note that if the plural of a noun ends with an *s* or *z* sound, only the apostrophe is added in the possessive:

   a. the attitude of the student
      the student's attitude
   b. the party of the girls
      the girls' party
   c. the home of the children
      the children's home

   Possessive pronouns do not require the apostrophe: "the book is theirs" *not* "the book is their's."

   For *inanimate* objects, *of* is preferable to the apostrophe: "The arm *of* the chair" *not* "the chair's arm."

2. Use an apostrophe to indicate an omission or abbreviation:

   a. He can't (cannot) make it.
   b. It's (it is) a perfect day.
   c. He graduated in '08.

   Caution: Place the apostrophe exactly where the omission occurs: isn't, doesn't—*not* is'nt, doe'snt.

3. Use an apostrophe to form the plural of letters, symbols, and words used as words:

   a. The English often do not pronounce their *h*'s, and they place *r*'s at the end of certain words.
   b. Instead of writing *and*'s, you can write &'s.

4. An apostrophe is *not* needed for plurals of figures:

   a. Rock groups flourished during the 1960s.
   b. The temperature was in the 90s.

Parentheses (())

Parentheses always come in pairs. Use parentheses to enclose figures, illustrations, or incidental material:

1. To make good tennis volleys, you must follow three rules: (1) Use a punching motion with your racket, (2) volley off your front leg, and (3) get your body sideways to the flight of the oncoming ball.

2. The big stars of Hollywood's glamor days **(Greta Garbo, Clark Gable, Marilyn Monroe)** exuded an aura that was bigger than life.
3. Emily Dickinson (often called "the Nun of Amherst") lived a secluded life.

Quotation Marks (" ")

Quotation marks always come in pairs, with the final set indicating the end of the quotation. The most common use of quotation marks is to indicate the exact spoken or written words of another person. There are several other uses of quotation marks as well.

1. Use quotation marks to enclose the words of someone else:
    a. Montesquieu has said: "The first motive which ought to impel us to study is the desire to augment the excellence of our nature, and to render an intelligent being yet more intelligent."
    b. With characteristic bluntness she turned to him and asked, "Are you as old as you look?"

If the passage being quoted is longer than five lines, indent it but do not use quotation marks:

The *Los Angeles Times* indicated that actress Estelle Winwood was old but still remarkably spry:

> She plays bridge for six hours a night, smokes four packs of cigarettes a day, and at 93 Estelle Winwood is the oldest active member on the rolls of the Screen Actors' Guild.
>
> Although she professes to be through with acting, her close friends don't believe her. Only recently she joined the distinguished company of Columbia Pictures' "Murder by Death," Neil Simon's spoof of mystery films. And she held her own with the likes of Alec Guinness, Peter Sellers, Maggie Smith, Peter Falk, David Niven, and Nancy Walker.

2. A quotation within a quotation is enclosed by single quotation marks:

> According to Jefferson's biographer, "The celebrated equanimity of his temper, crystallized in his pronouncement 'Peace is our passion,' extended to his private as well as his public life; his daughter Martha described how he lost his temper in her presence only two times in his life."
>
> Fawn M. Brodie, *Thomas Jefferson*

3. Use quotation marks for titles of songs, paintings, and short literary works (essays, articles, short stories, or poems):
    a. My favorite Beatles song is "Eleanor Rigby."   song
    b. "The Guest" is a story written by Camus.   short story
    c. The "Mona Lisa" by DaVinci hangs in the Louvre museum.   painting

4. Use quotation marks for words used in a special way—for instance, to show irony or to indicate that a word is slang:
    a. They killed her out of "mercy."   The author wants the reader to know that it was not genuine mercy.

b. My mother used to refer to the woman down the street as a "floozy." (slang)

When using other marks of punctuation with quoted words, follow the proper conventions.

1. Place a period or comma within quotation marks, unless material that is not quoted follows.

   a. "Very well," he said, "let's go to the bank."
   b. "The qualities that make a political leader were less obvious in Lenin than in Gladstone" (p. 451).

2. Place a colon or semicolon outside quotation marks.

   a. He reassured me, "You're a fine boy"; yet, I didn't believe him.
   b. I remember only the following words from Michael Novak's essay "White Ethnic": "Growing up in America has been an assault upon my sense of worthiness."

3. Place a question mark or exclamation point inside quotation marks when they apply to quoted matter, but outside when they do not.

   a. "Who are the eminent?" he asked bitterly.   The quoted matter is itself a question.
   b. What do you mean when you describe him as "eminent"?   The entire sentence is a question; the quoted matter is not.
   c. In the movie everyone chants, "I'm mad as hell and I won't take it anymore!"   The quoted matter is itself an exclamation.
   d. For heaven's sake, stop calling me "Big Boy"!   The entire sentence is an exclamation.

Italics (Underlining)

In longhand or typewritten material, italics are indicated by underlining; in print, italicized letters are slanted.

1. Use italics for titles of books, magazines, newspapers, movies, plays, and other long works:

   a. Most college students are required to read *Great Expectations* or *Oliver Twist.*
   b. *Harper's Bazaar* is a magazine about fashions.
   c. Although I live in California, I subscribe to the *Wall Street Journal* because it is an excellent newspaper.
   d. Mozart's *Magic Flute* is a long opera.

2. Use italics for foreign words:

   a. Everyone uses the word *détente.*
   b. I found her dress *très chic.*
   c. He gave an *apologia pro vita sua.*

3. Use italics for words, letters, and figures spoken of as such:

   a. Often the word *fortuitous* is misused.

b. In the word *knight* only *n*, *i*, and *t* are actually pronounced.

c. In the Bible, the number *7* represents perfection.

The Hyphen (-)

1. Use a hyphen for a syllable break at the end of a line:

   a. sac-ri-fi-cial
   b. nu-tri-tious
   c. lib-er-al

   If in doubt about where to break a word, check with the dictionary.

2. Use a hyphen in some compound words:

   a. brother-in-law
   b. hanky-panky
   c. self-determination
   d. vice-president
   e. two-thirds

3. Use a hyphen in compound modifiers:

   a. well-known movie
   b. blond-haired, blue-eyed baby
   c. low-grade infection

4. The hyphen is omitted when the first word of the compound modifier is an adverb ending in *ly* or an adjective ending in *ish*, or when the compound modifier follows the noun:

   a. a deceptively sweet person
   b. a plainly good meal
   c. a bluish green material
   d. is well known

Exercises

Insert commas where they are needed. If the sentence is correct, write *C* in the space provided.

1. Professor Grover as all of his students agree is one of the most exciting history teachers on campus. _____

2. Madam I beg to differ with you; that is my purse. _____

3. We were asked to check with Mr. Weaver our head custodian. _____

4. Because the water was murky cold and swift we did not go swimming. _____

5. In denouncing the hypocritical Truman encouraged honest dealings. _____

6. Let's not give up until everyone agrees with us. _____

7. Since they belong to the neighborhood they should pay for part of the damage. _____

8. Address your letter to Mrs. Margerie Freedman 320 N. Lincoln Blvd. Reading Massachusetts. _____

9. So many memories are connected with the home of my grandparents a big red brick mansion surrounded by a white picket fence. _____

10. Twice the doctor asked "Have you ever had laryngitis before?" _____

11. Relaxed and happy Jim ignored the people who were angered by his decision. _____

12. July 4 1776 is an important date for patriotic Americans. _____

13. Glistening like a diamond in the sun the lake beckoned us. _____

14. Readers of the *Times* however were not all equally impressed with the editorial on abortions. _____

15. All together some ten thousand people filled out the questionnaire. _____

16. From the mountains, from the prairies, and from numerous villages came the good news. _____

17. "My most exquisite lady" he said gallantly "you deserve the Taj Mahal." _____

18. One of her sisters lives in Paris; the other, in London. _____

19. Pat Moynihan who was once the U.S. ambassador to the United Nations is a popular lecturer. _____

20. Well Mary are you satisfied with the effect of your crass remark? _____

21. The laboratory technician has finished the gold tooth hasn't he? _____

22. Anyone who feels that this is a bad law should write to his congressman. _____

23. Outside a spectacular rainbow arched across the deep blue sky. _____

24. We walk down this street unafraid, not even thinking of danger. _____

25. Now his grandparents live in a condominium in Florida where they have no yard. _____

Punctuate the following sentences so that they read easily and clearly.

1. Shakespeare wrote many plays including the famous Hamlet

2. Listen he said if you want we can go to a movie any movie

3. The word renaissance has several pronunciations.

4. We can have the party at Johns cabin or the Fieldings apartment

5. Its overtaxed heart failing the race horse collapsed before everyones eyes.

6. The most tragic poem I can imagine is Keats Ode to Melancholy

7. Get off my lawn you swine

8. The big bands of the 40s still sell millions of records

9. Last years flowers have wilted they have withered and died

10. As far as the committee is concerned you have lost the grant nevertheless you are to take the exam one more time

11. Just as the situation appeared hopeless a surprising thing happened A number of leading American artists became interested in making lithographic prints.

12. Then in the summer of 1976 the counterrevolutionary army took over

13. Do you know the difference between the verbs compose and comprise

14. Wonderful Here comes the beer Cheers

15. He entitled his paper June Wayne Profile of a California Artist

16. He lived a stones throw from Twin Lakes

17. This is what Bertrand Russell says Science from the dawn of history and probably longer has been intimately associated with war

18. Bertrand Russell has said that Science has been intimately associated with war. (*Refer to item 17.*)

19. He received his PhD at 9 am on Sunday June 6

20. My friend asked me Did you read Bill Shirleys article Worlds First Bionic Swim Team published in the sports section of the Los Angeles Times

21. The rule is that you must sign up two days in advance. See Section 25 paragraph 2

22. Dear Sir this is in answer to your letter of May 13

23. A slight tinge of embarrassment or was it pleasure crept across his face

24. The first day we studied later in the week however we relaxed

25. The babies carriages were broken.

Insert commas where they are needed. If the sentence is correct, write *C* in the space provided. After completing the exercise, turn to the appendix for the correct answers.

1. His daughter a leader among the women had spared her father and set him afloat on the sea in a hollow chest. _____

2. As for me already old age is my companion. _____

3. He spoke slowly believing in his heart that he was telling the truth. _____

4. Great dangers lay ahead and some of the soldiers paid with their lives for drinking so heavily. _____

5. Gently he answered "I have come to my home to recover the ancient honor of my house." _____

6. These fierce women steadfastly refused to surrender to the foreign invaders. _____

7. They scorned them terrorized them and robbed them. _____

8. He insisted that he had been saved by the woman in white who had brought him to Venice an exotic city. _____

9. On November 19 1929 a star bright and luminous shot across the sky. _____

10. Let the taxpayers who reside in the county pay for a new road sign at the intersection of Broadway and Main Street. _____

11. The football players however did not care to linger in such a gloomy narrow place. _____

12. Acheron the river of woe pours into Cocytus the river of lamentation. _____

13. Sir please accept my sincere apologies for the inconvenience this has caused you. _____

14. Since hell is merely an invention of guilty minds why believe in it? _____

15. David Cotton Jr. is doing some important research in the field of high-risk pregnancies. _____

16. On his way to ask his adviser a question about a calculus course Robert arrived at an automatic gate where he blew out a tire causing his Fiat to skid into another car. _____

17. He felt himself degraded by this servile attitude and vowed revenge. _____

18. They told him "God's daylight is sweet to the old." _____

19. Yes Chicago Illinois can be windy and freezing cold in the winter. _____

20. Above some perfume bottles filled with exotic bath oils decorated
    the wall shelves. _____

Self-Grading Exercise 19

In the sentences below insert all needed marks of punctuation, including italics.
Be careful to place quotation marks in proper relation to other marks of punctuation. After completing the exercise, turn to the appendix for the correct answers.

1. According to Mythology a book by Edith Hamilton the Greeks unlike the
   Egyptians made their gods in their own image

2. Is this an exaggerated view It hardly seems so nevertheless many opponents
   of the measure dismiss it as unmenschlich

3. The search for a way to stop this vicious cycle has taxed the best minds among
   the following groups city councilmen educators and urban planners

4. Let me pose this question Could you love passionately if you knew you would
   never die

5. Who interrupted me by saying Thats enough for today

6. Dear Mr. Forsythe This is in reply to your request of May 16 1979

7. From now on please cross your t s and dot your i s

8. This is how we propose to assign the various duties The men will scrub the
   floors ceilings and walls the women will cook mend and garden the children
   will run errands clean up the yard and pick vegetables

9. But what happens when the national organizations themselves the schools the
   unions the federal government become victims of a technological culture

10. With his fifth grade education he wrote a marvelous poem entitled Languid
    Tears

11. The New Yorker is read mostly by people with keen literary interests

12. Students often find it difficult to distinguish between the words imply and infer
    in fact most people confuse their meanings

13. We currently reside at 451 Bellefontaine Drive Pasadena California

14. One of the delegates was a vegetarian the other was restricted to kosher foods

15. He yelled angrily Get out of my yard

16. Vans boats and campers are not allowed see Regulation #13

17. Have you heard the question asked What can the police department do against
    the pitiless onslaught of criminal violence

18. This my friends is how I think we can help the world in a time of tyranny by fighting for freedom

19. The age was an age of éclaircissement and self determination

20. You have arrived at your resting place she murmured softly seek no further

21. Inside the antique armoire dominated the room

22. Picture if you please an open space where twenty acrobats stand each locking hands with two different partners then imagine ten acrobats standing on the shoulders of these twenty

Cap   *Capitalization errors* result when accepted conventions of capitalizing are not followed. Commonly capitalized are words at the beginning of a sentence and the pronoun *I*. Students tend to ignore rules of capitalization. The most important rules are given here.

1. Capitalize all proper names. The following belong to the group of proper names:
   a. specific persons, places, and things but not their general classes (Jefferson, Grand Junction, Eiffel Tower, Harvard University, and Hyde Park are capitalized, but people, cities, towers, universities, and parks are not)
   b. organizations and institutions (Rotary Club, Pentagon)
   c. historical periods and events (Middle Ages, World War II)
   d. members of national, political, racial, and religious groups (Mason, Republican, Negro, Methodist)
   e. special dates on the calendar (Veterans Day), days (Wednesday), months (July).
   f. Religions (Islam, Christianity, Judaism, Methodism) but *not* ideologies (communism, socialism, atheism).

   Freshman, sophomore, junior, and *senior* are not capitalized unless associated with a specific event: "The Junior Prom will take place next Saturday."

2. In titles of literary works, capitalize all words except articles, conjunctions, and prepositions: *All the King's Men,* "The Case Against Welfare in Louisville," "The Man Without a Country." Conjunctions and prepositions of five letters or more are capitalized.

3. Capitalize titles associated with proper names: Mrs. Johnson, Ms. Mary Hanley, Judge Garcia, James R. Griedley, M.D., Henry Hadley, Jr.

4. Titles of relatives are capitalized only when they are not preceded by an article, when they are followed by a name, or in direct address:
   a. I gave the keys to Grandmother.
   b. My Grandmother Sitwell
   c. Could you help me, Grandmother?
   d. I was deeply influenced by my grandmother.

5. Unless a title is official, it is not capitalized:
   a. Peter Ferraro, President of the Valley National Bank

b. Peter Ferraro is president of a bank.

c. We shall appeal to the President (the top executive of a nation).

6. Capitalize specific courses offered in school, but not general subjects unless they contain a proper name:

a. I enrolled in Biology 120.

b. I am taking biology.

c. I failed Intermediate French.

Avoid needless capitals. For instance, the seasons (spring, summer, autumn, winter) are not capitalized unless they are personified, as in poetry ("Where are the songs of Spring?"). *North, south, east,* and *west* are not capitalized unless they refer to special regions ("He is the fastest gun in the West").

Note that abbreviations are capitalized or not capitalized according to the unabbreviated version: m.p.h. (miles per hour), M.P. (Member of Parliament), GPO (Government Printing Office), Cong. (Congress), pseud. (pseudonym).

Exercises

In the following sentences, underline the letters that should be capitalized or made lower case. If the sentence is correct, write *C* in the space at the right.

1. Our memorial day picnic was cancelled due to rain. _____

2. The headline read: "U.S. agent Fired in Investigation of Missing Ammunition." _____

3. Any mayor of a city as large as Chicago should be on good terms with the President of the United States. _____

4. The democrats will doubtless hold their convention at the cow palace in san francisco. _____

5. The tennis courts at Nibley park are always busy. _____

6. If you have to take a psychology course, take psychology 101 from Dr. Pearson, a graduate of harvard. _____

7. There is something elegant about the name "Tyrone Kelly, III, esq." _____

8. Until easter of 1949, they lived in a big white georgian home. _____

9. During the second world war, switzerland remained neutral. _____

10. I intend to exchange my capri for a toyota. _____

11. Socrates, the famous Greek philosopher, used Dialogue as a teaching method. _____

12. Some Socialists have joined the Republican Party. _____

13. She said, "the ticket entitles you to spend a night at the Holiday inn in Las Vegas." _____

14. The bible was not fully canonized until the council of Trent. _____

Write a brief sentence in which you use correctly each of the following words:

1. street _____

2. Street _____

3. Democratic _____

4. democratic _____

5. academy _____

6. Academy _____

7. biology _____

8. Biology _____

9. memorial _____

10. Memorial _____

11. father _____

12. Father _____

13. senior _____

14. Senior _____

15. against _____

16. Against _____

17. company _____

18. Company _____

Self-Grading Exercise 20

In the following sentences underline the letters that should be capitalized or made lower case. If the sentence is correct, write *C* in the space at the right. After completing the exercise, turn to the appendix for the correct answers.

1. Balloting at both the democratic and republican conventions is
   by states.   _____

2. He had taken many history courses, but none fascinated him more than introduction to western civilization. _____

3. Delta Delta Delta, the most active sorority, invited speakers from such organizations as daughters of the American revolution, national organization of Women, and the Sierra club. _____

4. The subject of the lecture was "The Treasures Of The Nile." _____

5. John Stuart Mill understood Calculus and could read greek when he was a child. _____

6. Exodus is the second book of the pentateuch. _____

7. One of his dreams was to see the Taj Mahal. _____

8. The war of the Triple Alliance was fought between Paraguay on one side and an Alliance of Argentina, brazil, and Uruguay on the other. _____

9. That is the best photograph ever taken of uncle Charlie. _____

10. As a capable and tough City attorney, he took action against one of Hollywood's swingers clubs, a place called Socrates' retreat. _____

11. John toyed with two ideas: joining the peace corps or working without pay for Cesar Chávez' United farm workers of America. _____

12. Ex-Assemblyman Waldie never ran for Office after the Summer of 1974. _____

13. Today he is Chairman of the Federal Mine Safety and Health Review Commission. _____

14. The residents of Mammoth Lakes, a mountain resort, are proud of the view of the minarets, a ragged mountain range, seen from highway 395 as one approaches the resort. _____

15. One of my favorite books is a novel entitled *in the heart of a fool.* _____

16. Some women have romantic ideas about returning to feudalism, with knights in shining armor and ladies adhering to the manners of the Middle Ages. _____

17. One of the highest mountain systems in the world is Hindu Kush, extending 500 miles from north Pakistan into northeast Afghanistan. _____

18. William S. Levey, S. J., is the vice-president of an important men's club. _____

19. I failed Organic Chemistry 101, but I passed french. _____

20. A traditional American holiday is Thanksgiving day. _____

Misspelling occurs when a word is written differently from the way it is listed in the dictionary (*recieve* instead of *receive*) or when the wrong word is used (*loose* instead of *lose*). The following list* of most commonly misspelled words will help the weak speller. Letters in italics are those that cause the most difficulty. For help in selecting the correct word, refer to the Glossary of Word Choice (p. 330).

Commonly Misspelled Words

1. acco*mm*odate	35. inter*e*st	68. pro*f*ession
2. achie*v*ement	36. *its* (*it's*)	69. promin*e*nt
3. a*c*quire	37. *led*	70. p*u*rsue
4. al*l* right	38. lo*s*e	71. qui*e*t
5. am*o*ng	39. lo*s*ing	72. rec*ei*ve
6. ap*p*ar*e*nt	40. mar*riage*	73. rec*ei*ving
7. arg*u*ment	41. me*re*	74. reco*mm*end
8. arg*ui*ng	42. ne*ce*ssary	75. refer*ring*
9. bel*ief*	43. o*cca*sion	76. rep*e*tition
10. bel*ie*ve	44. occur*red*	77. r*h*ythm
11. ben*e*ficial	45. occur*ring*	78. sen*s*e
12. ben*e*fited	46. occur*rence*	79. sep*a*rate
13. cat*e*gory	47. o*p*inion	80. sep*a*ration
14. co*m*ing	48. o*pp*or*tun*ity	81. shin*i*ng
15. compar*a*tive	49. pa*i*d	82. simil*a*r
16. con*sc*ious	50. *particular*	83. stud*y*ing
17. contr*o*versy	51. *performance*	84. su*cc*eed
18. con*trov*ersi*al*	52. person*al*	85. su*cc*ession
19. de*fi*nit*ely*	53. person*nel*	86. s*u*rprise
20. de*fi*nit*ion*	54. po*ss*e*ss*ion	87. techniqu*e*
21. de*fi*ne	55. po*ss*ible	88. tha*n*
22. de*s*cribe	56. practic*al*	89. the*n*
23. de*s*cription	57. pre*ce*de	90. th*eir*
24. disa*str*ous	58. prej*u*dice	91. ther*e*
25. *e*ffect	59. prepar*e*	92. the*y're*
26. embar*rass*	60. preval*e*nt	93. tho*rough*
27. environ*ment*	61. princip*al*	94. *to* (*too*, *two*)
28. exa*gg*erate	62. princip*le*	95. transfer*red*
29. exist*e*nce	63. privi*l*ege	96. un*ne*cessary
30. exist*e*nt	64. prob*ab*ly	97. vill*ai*n
31. experi*e*nce	65. proc*ee*d	98. wom*a*n
32. expl*a*nation	66. proc*e*dure	99. *write*
33. fa*sc*inate	67. pro*f*essor	100. wri*t*ing
34. h*ei*ght		

---

*From Thomas Clark Pollock, "Spelling Report," *College English,* XVI (November, 1954), 102–09.

Exercises

1. Some of the commonly misspelled words may not appear on either list supplied in this handbook section. If not, compile your own list of troublesome words. First, write the word correctly. Then, note the particular difficulty with it:

   bridle   I   always spell it bri*dal,* as if it came from *bride.*
   perspiration   I must be sure to pronounce it *per,* not *pre.*

2. Using the dictionary as a guide, study the list of 100 words until you know (1) what each word means, (2) how it is pronounced, and (3) how it is spelled. Study the words in groups of 20.

3. From each group of three, choose the misspelled word and write it correctly in the space provided. Check answers in the dictionary.

   a. existance, describe, personal   _____

   b. paid, particular, oportunity   _____

   c. benificial, apparent, experience   _____

   d. controversy, concious, occurred   _____

   e. preformance, similar, succeed   _____

   f. probably, marriage, predjudice   _____

   g. profession, persue, separate   _____

   h. catagory, paid, disastrous   _____

   i. effect, disasterous, mere   _____

   j. preceed, proceed, procedure   _____

   k. embarrass, exaggerate, envirement   _____

   l. prevailent, probably, existent   _____

   m. coming, heighth, professor   _____

   n. define, fascinate, posession   _____

   o. repetition, quiet, recieve   _____

Self-Grading Exercise 21

Identify the misspelled word of each sentence and spell it correctly in the space provided. After completing the exercise, turn to the appendix for the correct answers.

1. After making an appointment with the manager of the firm, he demanded to see his personal file.   _____

2. When lovers are seperated for long periods of time, their ardor cools.   _____

3. While under water, he was conscience of the fact that life is fleeting and evanescent. _____

4. Without exageration, he sounded like a genius. _____

5. To him she was a shinning star, a brilliant meteor from heaven. _____

6. Every man on board admitted that it was a most unusual occurrance. _____

7. Sons often feel pressured to enter the same proffession pursued by their fathers. _____

8. They accused him of being predjudice and reactionary. _____

9. One of the serious concerns of the younger generation is a clean enviroment. _____

10. The mystery novel ends without a clear explenation of how the murder took place. _____

11. The heighth of the building was out of proportion to its width. _____

12. The room was to small for two people. _____

13. The hero was wearing light apparel whereas the villian was wearing black. _____

14. One man or women with good typing skills could get that manuscript finished in no time. _____

15. They wore similiar clothes, but their facial characteristics were very different. _____

16. According to the committee, it was quite alright for the men to smoke. _____

17. They were lead to believe that he was a victim of his own enthusiasm. _____

18. I did not care whether or not I received the money back; it was simply a matter of principal. _____

19. Because of blustering winds she kept loosing her hat. _____

20. Just sit quietly and listen to the rythm of your heartbeats. _____

Part IV

The Research Paper

17
The Research Paper

Students often anticipate the research paper with terror and dread, but for no good reason. From the French verb *rechercher,* meaning "to seek," research requires a student to comb the library in an exhilarating and suspenseful search for information. The end product of this search is the research paper. Side benefits to the student include a mastery of the discipline involved in research and a familiarization with the library. Writing a research paper is very much a learning experience.

This chapter covers the principles of assembling library information into a research paper. The same principles, however, apply to other kinds of academic research. To begin with, we suggest the following steps in writing the research paper:

1. Choose the topic.
2. Get acquainted with the library.
3. Collect pertinent information.
4. Formulate a controlling idea and outline the paper.
5. Write the paper using proper documentation.

A. Choose the Topic

You may be assigned a specific research topic, such as a comparison of the social problems in *Oliver Twist* and *Great Expectations,* two novels by Charles Dickens. More often, however, the freshman term paper leaves the task of finding a workable topic to the student. Let us assume that your teacher has given a typical assignment—to write a ten-page research paper on a topic of your choice within the humanities or general sciences. The first problem is to find a specific topic that is challenging enough to support a ten-page research paper. Here are some topics to avoid:

1. TOPICS THAT ARE OVERLY BROAD.   A ten-page term paper, about the length of a short magazine article, cannot accommodate such massive topics as "The History of Painting," "Novels during the Victorian Age," or "The Life of Jesus Christ." To be properly covered, such topics would require an entire book.

2. TOPICS BASED ON PERSONAL OPINIONS.   Personal opinions are frequently not supportable by fact and are therefore seldom appropriate research paper topics. "Streaking Is Fun" or "Why the Counselors at Swanee College Are Stodgy Dressers" are not documentable enough to be usable topics.

3. TOPICS THAT ARE TOO CONTROVERSIAL.   A raging controversy is seldom a good topic for a term paper, because the writer frequently has a bias and is incapable of being objective. Moreover, it is easy for a writer to get bogged down in charges and countercharges and never come to a resolution. Topics such as "What Nixon Did Right in the Watergate Scandals" or "Marijuana Is No Worse than Booze" are best avoided.

4. TOPICS THAT ARE TRITE.   A trite topic will bore the reader to death and may also kill the writer's chances for a good grade. Avoid such topics as "The Advantages of a Supermarket over a Small Local Grocery" or "The Value of Motherhood to America." To spare yourself boredom, you also should avoid any topic on which you have already written another paper.

5. TOPICS THAT ARE TOO TECHNICAL.   Avoid topics involving technical terms and data that neither you nor your reader will completely understand. Papers on topics such as "Laser Geodynamic Satellites and Their Functions" or "Seismological Computations of Dilatancy in the Palmdale Bulge" generally end up as garbled horrors.

6. TOPICS THAT CAN BE DEVELOPED FROM A SINGLE SOURCE.   "How to Make Macramé Hangings" or "How to Use a Kiln" are examples of overly narrow topics that could be documented from a single accurate source. Such topics do not require enough research; moreover, they stultify a reader.

Choose a topic that generates wide-ranging research and requires documentation from several sources. Begin with some exploratory browsing through the library. Mammoth and unsuitable topics such as "Famine in Asia," "Prisons of the World," "Human Resources," or "Peoples of Africa" might occur to you at first, but eventually an offhanded remark in an article or book will trigger a question in your mind. Properly worded as a controlling idea, the answer to that question, supported by researched information and data, will be the topic of your paper.

Let us, for instance, assume that your interest in the battered child leads you to ask, "When did violence against children begin and what can be done about it?" To answer that question, you begin to search through magazine articles and books.

B. Get Acquainted with the Library

Nothing teaches efficient use of the library better than the practical experience of actual research. The following is a review of the basic research tools available in the library.

1. THE CARD CATALOG. The card catalog is an alphabetical index of all books in the library, the starting point for any research. Ask a librarian to point out the location of the card catalog, which lists all library books on three separate cards, by author, title, and subject. The cards usually are stored in small, labeled drawers.

Following are three sample cards. Technical information, useful only to the librarian, is listed on the bottom half of the card. The top half of the card contains the book title, author's name, publication data, and the call number, which indicates the location of the book in the library.

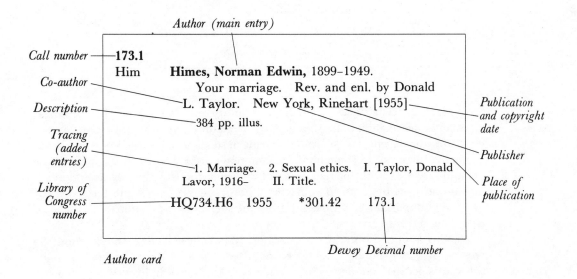

Author (main entry)

Call number — **173.1**
Him

Co-author

Description

Tracing (added entries)

Library of Congress number

Himes, Norman Edwin, 1899–1949.
Your marriage. Rev. and enl. by Donald
L. Taylor. New York, Rinehart [1955]
384 pp. illus.

1. Marriage. 2. Sexual ethics. I. Taylor, Donald
Lavor, 1916– II. Title.
HQ734.H6 1955 *301.42 173.1

Publication and copyright date

Publisher

Place of publication

Dewey Decimal number

Author card

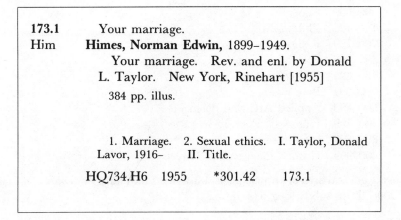

173.1 Your marriage.
Him **Himes, Norman Edwin,** 1899–1949.
Your marriage. Rev. and enl. by Donald
L. Taylor. New York, Rinehart [1955]
384 pp. illus.

1. Marriage. 2. Sexual ethics. I. Taylor, Donald
Lavor, 1916– II. Title.
HQ734.H6 1955 *301.42 173.1

Title card

```
┌──────────────────────────────────────────────────────┐
│ 173.1      MARRIAGE                                   │
│ Him      Himes, Norman Edwin, 1899–1949.             │
│             Your marriage.   Rev. and enl. by Donald │
│          L. Taylor.   New York, Rinehart [1955]      │
│             384 pp. illus.                            │
│                                                       │
│                                                       │
│             1. Marriage.   2. Sexual ethics.   I. Taylor, Donald │
│          Lavor, 1916–    II. Title.                  │
│                                                       │
│          HQ734.H6   1955      *301.42      173.1     │
│                                                       │
└──────────────────────────────────────────────────────┘
```

Subject card

2. THE STACKS.   The stacks are the actual library shelves on which books, magazines, and other materials are stored. Some large universities do not permit undergraduate readers into the stacks, preferring instead to dispense requested books through a librarian. In some libraries, commonly used works are available in the main library area, with the remainder of the collection stored in stacks and available through the librarian. If your school library allows access into the stacks, be aware that important books missing from the shelves may be on loan, in a special collection, or on reserve.

Whether admitted into the stacks or not, every college student should know the systems by which library books are organized. Through these systems, a single title can be located among vast numbers of books. American libraries use two systems for organizing books: (a) the Dewey Decimal System, and (b) the Library of Congress System. Both systems assign each book a specific "call number," marked on its spine and listed on all catalog cards for that book.

Under the Dewey Decimal System, all knowledge is divided into ten general categories and indicated by decimal notation:

000–099   General works
100–199   Philosophy
200–299   Religion
300–399   Social Sciences
400–499   Philology
500–599   Pure Science
600–699   Applied Arts and Sciences
700–799   Fine Arts, Recreation
800–899   Literature
900–999   History, Geography, Travel

Every general area of knowledge is subdivided into tens. For example, Pure Science (500–599) is subdivided as follows:

510–519   Mathematics
520–529   Astronomy

530–539 Physics
540–549 Chemistry
550–559 Geology
560–569 Paleontology
570–579 Biology
580–589 Botany
590–599 Zoology

Additional subcategories are designated as in this example:

511   Arithmetic
511.1 Systems

Invented in the 1870s, the Dewey Decimal System does not contain enough categories to adequately classify the knowledge that has accumulated since that time, especially in the sciences. Consequently, classifications are often long and awkward. Most large libraries therefore use the Library of Congress System, which contains twenty-one major categories, broken down as follows:

A. General works, Polygraphy
B. Philosophy, Religion
C. History, Auxiliary sciences
D. History, Topography (except America)
E. America (general), United States (general)
F. United States (local), America (except the United States)
G. Geography, Anthropology
H. Social Sciences (general), Statistics, Economics, Sociology
J. Political Science
K. Law
L. Education
M. Music
N. Fine Arts
P. Language and Literature
Q. Science
R. Medicine
S. Agriculture
T. Technology
U. Military Science
V. Naval Science
Z. Bibliography, Library Science

Further subdivisions are created by the addition of a letter. For example, Agriculture (S) is subdivided as follows:

SB General plant culture, soils, fertilizers, implements
SD Forestry
SF Animal culture, veterinary medicine
SH Fish culture, fisheries
SK Hunting, game protection

3. THE REFERENCE ROOM.   Reference material consists of a variety of books and indexes that synopsize and classify information and its location. Usually stored on open shelves, reference material cannot be checked out and taken home.

Indexes: The *Reader's Guide to Periodical Literature,* issued monthly, is the most important and useful index in the reference room. It lists magazine and journal articles in specific subject areas according to author, title, and subject. The monthly indexes are bound into a hardcover volume at the end of each year and stored alongside other volumes, which go back to the nineteenth century. The facsimile of a page from *Reader's Guide* (opposite) will help you interpret its listings.

Following is a list of other useful indexes:

Applied Science and Technology Index
Art Index
Bibliographic Index
Biography Index
Book Review Digest
Dramatic Index
Education Index
Index to the London Times
Monthly Catalog of United States Government Publications
Music Index
New York Times Index
Social Sciences and Humanities Index

Bookseller's lists: Consult the following works for information about books currently in print:

Books in Print (separate volumes for listings by author and by title)
Cumulative Book Index
Paperbound Books in Print
Subject Guide to Books in Print

General encyclopedias: Encyclopedias can give a general overview of a subject. The best known encyclopedias are:

Chambers's Encyclopedia, 15 vols.
Collier's Encyclopedia, 24 vols.
Columbia Encyclopedia, 1 vol.
Encyclopaedia Britannica, 24 vols.
Encyclopedia Americana, 30 vols.

Atlases and gazetteers: Atlases and gazetteers give information about places. An atlas is a collection of maps; a gazetteer is a dictionary of places. Be sure the atlas or gazetteer you use is up to date.

Columbia-Lippincott Gazetteer of the World. 2d ed. New York: Columbia University Press, 1962.
Hammond Medallion World Atlas. Maplewood, N.J.: C. S. Hammond, 1971.

CHILDREN, Adoption of. See Adoption
CHILDREN, Exceptional
    See also
  Children, Handicapped
CHILDREN, Gifted

         Education
  Gifted programs for the culturally different. E. M. Bernal, Jr. Educ
    Digest 41:28–31 My '76
CHILDREN, Handicapped
  Thelma Boston. miracle worker. M. G. Crawford. il pors Good H
    182:40+ Je '76
    See also
  Cerebral palsied children
         Education
  Education for all handicapped children. H. A. Williams, Jr. por
    Parents Mag 51:20 Je '76
  Education of the handicapped today. il Am Educ 12:6–8 Je '76
CHILDREN, Psychotic. See Mentally ill children
CHILDREN and alcohol. See Alcohol and youth
CHILDREN and television. See Television and children
CHILDREN as stockholders
  Teaching children about stocks. C. Kirk. Parents Mag 51:14 Je '76
CHILDRENS art
  Student art. See issues of School arts
    See also
  Paperwork
         Exhibitions
  Art gallery in the lobby. K. Thompson. il Sch Arts 75:35 Je '76
CHILDRENS exhibitions
    See also
  Childrens art—Exhibitions
CHILDRENS homes. See Homes, Institutional
CHILDRENS librarians
  Old strengths and new weaknesses. E. L. Heins. Horn Bk 52:250–1
    Je '76
  Skimming of memory; ed by M. Hodges. F. C. Sayers. il Horn Bk
    52:270–5 Je '76
CHILDRENS literature
    See also
  Fairy tales
         Authorship
  Books that say yes. M. L'Engle. Writer 89:9–12 Je '76
  Sprezzatura: a kind of excellence; excerpts from address. April 12,
    1975. E. L. Konigsburg. Horn Bk 52:253–61 Je '76
         Awards, prizes, etc.
  Memories of childhood; awarded to J. Reiss. A. Wolff. Sat R 3:8
    Je 12 '76
         Bibliography
  Books for the reluctant reader. A. R. Zinck and K. J. Hawkins. il
    Wilson Lib Bull 50:722–4 My '76
  Children's books: the best of the season. W. Cole. il Sat R 3:36–9
    My 15 '76
CHILDRENS sayings. See Children—Sayings
CHILDRENS stories
    See name of author for full entry
  Peachy pig. J. O'Reilly
CHILE
         Commerce
  Ray of hope from an export pickup. Bus W p48–9 My 24 '76
         Economic conditions
  Ray of hope from an export pickup. Bus W p48–9 My 24 '76
      Politics and government
  Protest in Chile. A. Bono. Commonweal 103:390–1 Je 18 '76
CHILEANS in the United States
    See also
  California—Foreign population
CHIMERAS (biology) See Mosaics (biology)
CHIMES, Electric
  Door chime. W. D. Leckey. il Pop Mech 145:107 My '76
CHINA (People's Republic)
    See also
  Agriculture—China (People's Republic)
  Education—China (People's Republic)

Subject

Title of article

Volume, pages, issue

Magazine

Cross-references

Cross-references subdividing a topic

National Atlas of the United States. Washington, D.C.: Government Printing Office, 1970.

Rand McNally Commercial Atlas and Marketing Guide. 1968–. (Annually.)

Shepherd, William R. *Historical Atlas.* 9th ed. New York: Barnes and Noble, 1964.

The Times Atlas of the World. 2d rev. ed. Boston: Houghton Mifflin, 1971.

Webster's New Geographical Dictionary. Rev. ed. Springfield, Mass.: G. & C. Merriam, 1972.

Biography: General information about well-known persons is listed in the following sources:

Biography Index. 1947–. Quarterly. Cumulated annually and every three years. An index to books and magazines.

Current Biography. 1940–. Monthly except August. Cumulated annually. Articles about living persons. Especially useful for current celebrities. See the index in each volume, which covers preceding years.

Dictionary of American Biography. 20 vols. New York: Scribner's, 1928–73. Index. Supplements. Authoritative articles on Americans no longer living who have made significant contributions to American life.

Dictionary of National Biography. 63 vols. London: Smith, Elder, 1885–1950. Supplements. The basic source of biographical information about Englishmen no longer living.

Webster's Biographical Dictionary. 2d ed. Springfield, Mass.: G. & C. Merriam, 1969.

Who's Who. London: Black, 1849–. Annually. *Who Was Who* reprints discontinued entries.

Who's Who in America. Chicago: Marquis Who's Who, Inc., 1899–. Biennially. *Who Was Who in America* reprints discontinued entries.

Dictionaries: Information about words, their meanings, and their histories is found in one or more of the following dictionaries:

A Dictionary of American English on Historical Principles. 4 vols. Chicago: University of Chicago Press, 1936–44. A historical dictionary of American words and meanings, modeled after the NED.

Funk & Wagnalls New Practical Standard Dictionary of the English Language. New York: Funk & Wagnalls, 1964.

A New English Dictionary on Historical Principles. 10 vols. Oxford: Clarendon Press, 1884–1933. Reissued in 1933 as *The Oxford English Dictionary.* 13 vols. Dated illustrative quotations portray the history of a word's meaning. Three-volume supplement in progress.

Random House Dictionary of the English Language. New York: Random House, 1966.

Webster's New Dictionary of Synonyms. Springfield, Mass.: G. & C. Merriam, 1968.

Webster's Third New International Dictionary of the English Language. Springfield, Mass.: G. & C. Merriam, 1961. (Often referred to as W III.)

Quotations: To verify the source of a quotation, check one of the following dictionaries of quotations:

Bartlett, John. *Familiar Quotations.* 14th ed. Boston: Little, Brown, 1968. Arranged chronologically by author. Index.

Evans, Bergen. *Dictionary of Quotations.* New York: Delacorte, 1968. Arranged alphabetically by subject.

Hoyt, Jehiel K. *New Cyclopedia of Practical Quotations.* New York: Funk and Wagnalls, 1940. Arranged by subject. Index.

Mencken, Henry L. *A New Dictionary of Quotations.* New York: Knopf, 1942. Arranged by subject. No index.

Oxford Dictionary of Quotations. 2d ed. New York: Oxford University Press, 1953. Arranged alphabetically by author.

Stevenson, Burton E. *The Home Book of Quotations, Classical and Modern.* 10th ed. New York: Dodd, Mead, 1967. Arranged by subject. Key-word index.

Reference works for special fields: A list of all the works that survey special fields would consume an entire volume. The following is a list, by subject area, of frequently used reference works:

Art

Art Index. 1929–. Quarterly. Cumulated annually and biennially. An author-subject index to periodicals.

Chamberlin, Mary W. *Guide to Art Reference Books.* Chicago: American Library Association, 1959.

Cummings, Paul. *A Dictionary of Contemporary American Artists.* 2d ed. New York: St. Martin's Press, 1971.

Gardner, Helen. *Art Through the Ages.* 5th ed. New York: Harcourt, Brace and World, 1970.

Groce, George C., and David H. Wallace. *The New York Historical Society's Dictionary of Artists in America,* 1564–1860. New Haven, Conn.: Yale University Press, 1957.

Lucas, E. Louise. *Art Books.* Greenwich, Conn.: New York Graphic Society, 1968.

McGraw-Hill Encyclopedia of World Art. 15 vols. New York: McGraw-Hill, 1967.

Mayer, Ralph. *A Dictionary of Art Terms and Techniques.* New York: Crowell, 1969.

Robb, David M., and Jessie J. Garrison. *Art in the Western World.* 4th ed. New York: Harper, 1963.

Sturgis, Russell. *Dictionary of Architecture and Building.* 3 vols. New York: Macmillan, 1901.

Biology

Biological Abstracts. 1926–. Semimonthly. Annual cumulations.

Biological and Agricultural Index. 1964–. Monthly except August. Annual cumulations.

Bottle, R. T. and H. V. Wyatt. *The Use of Biological Literature.* 2d ed. Hamden, Conn.: Archon, 1971.

Gray, Asa. *Gray's Manual of Botany.* New York: American Book Co., 1950.

Gray, Peter. *The Encyclopedia of the Biological Sciences.* 2d ed. New York: Van Nostrand Reinhold, 1970.

Henderson, Isabelle F. and William D. Henderson. *A Dictionary of Biological Terms.* 8th ed. Princeton, N.J.: Van Nostrand Reinhold, 1963.

Jaeger, Edmund C. *A Source-book of Biological Names and Terms.* 3d ed. Springfield, Ill.: Thomas, 1955.

Leftwich, A. W. *A Dictionary of Zoology.* 2d ed. New York: Van Nostrand Reinhold, 1967.

Walker, Ernest P. *Mammals of the World.* 3 vols. Baltimore: Johns Hopkins Press, 1964.

Willis, J. C. *A Dictionary of the Flowering Plants and Ferns.* 8th ed. New York: Cambridge University Press, 1973.

Business

Accountants' Index. 1921–. Biennially.

Bogen, Jules I. *Financial Handbook.* 4th ed. New York: Ronald, 1964.

Business Periodicals Index. 1958–. Formerly *Industrial Arts Index,* 1913–57. Subject index. Monthly except August. Annual cumulations.

Commodity Year Book. 1939–. Annual volumes except for 1943–47.

Johnson, H. Webster. *How to Use the Business Library.* 4th ed. Cincinnati: South-Western, 1972.

Munn, Glenn G. *Encyclopedia of Banking and Finance.* 6th ed. Boston: Bankers Publishing, 1962.

Poor's Register of Corporations, Directors and Executives. 1928–. Annually.

Chemistry

Chemical Abstracts. 1907–. Semimonthly. Indexed annually and every ten years.

Condensed Chemical Dictionary. 8th ed. New York: Van Nostrand Reinhold, 1971.

Crane, Evan Jay and others. *A Guide to the Literature of Chemistry.* 2d ed. New York: Wiley, 1957

Encyclopedia of Chemistry. 2d ed. New York: Reinhold, 1960.

Handbook of Chemistry and Physics. 1913–. Annual revisions.

Mellon, Melvin G. *Chemical Publications: Their Nature and Use.* 4th ed. New York: McGraw-Hill, 1965.

Thorpe, Jocelyn F., and M. A. Whiteley. *Thorpe's Dictionary of Applied Chemistry.* 12 vols. New York: Longman's, 1937–56.

Economics

Coman, Edwin T., Jr., *Sources of Business Information.* Rev. ed. Berkeley: University of California Press, 1964.

Economic Almanac. 1940–. Annually.

Economics Library Selections. 1954–. Quarterly.

Hanson, John L. *A Dictionary of Economics and Commerce.* 3d ed. London: MacDonald & Evans, 1969.

Journal of Economic Abstracts. 1963–. Quarterly.

McGraw-Hill Dictionary of Modern Economics. New York: McGraw-Hill, 1965.

Sloan, Harold S. and Arnold J. Zurcher. *Dictionary of Economics.* 5th ed. New York: Barnes and Noble, 1970.

Survey of Current Business. 1921–. Monthly.

Wall Street Journal. Five days a week.

Education

Burke, Arvid J., and Mary A. Burke. *Documentation in Education.* 5th ed. New York: Teachers College Press, 1967.

Current Index to Journals in Education. 1969–. Monthly. Semiannual and annual indexes.

Education Index. 1929–. Author-subject index. Monthly except July and August. Annual cumulations.

Encyclopedia of Education. 10 vols. New York: Macmillan, 1971.

Encyclopedia of Educational Research. 4th ed. New York: Macmillan, 1969.

Encyclopedia of Modern Education. New York: Philosophical Library, 1948.

Foskett, D. J. *How to Find Out: Educational Research.* Oxford, N.Y.: Pergamon, 1965.

Leaders in Education. 4th ed. New York: R. R. Bowker and Jacques Cattell Press, 1971.

NEA Journal. 1913–. Nine issues a year.

Research in Education. 1966–. Monthly. Abstracts prepared by Educational Research Information Center.

School and Society. 1915–. Weekly.

School Life. 1918–. Nine issues a year.

Engineering

Dalton, Blanche H. *Sources of Engineering Information.* Berkeley, Calif.: University of California Press, 1948.

Engineering Index Monthly, 1962–. Annual cumulations. Index to periodicals. Abstracts.

Jones, Franklin D., and Paul B. Schubert. *Engineering Encyclopedia.* 3d ed. 2 vols. New York: Industrial Press, 1963.

Perry, Robert H. *Engineering Manual.* 2d ed. New York: McGraw-Hill, 1967.

Souders, Mott. *The Engineer's Companion.* New York: Wiley, 1966.

Geology

Bibliography and Index of Geology. 1933–. Monthly. Annual indexes.

Dana, James D., and Edward S. Dana. *The System of Mineralogy.* 7th ed. 3 vols. New York: Wiley, 1944–62.

Geo-Science Abstracts. 1959–. Monthly. Annual index.

Loomis, Frederic B. *Field Book of Common Rocks and Minerals.* Rev. ed. New York: Putnam, 1948.

Minerals Year Book. 1933–. Annually.

Pough, Frederick H. *A Field Guide to Rocks and Minerals.* 3d ed. Boston: Houghton Mifflin, 1960.

History

Adams, James Truslow, ed. *Dictionary of American History.* 2d ed. 6 vols. New York: Scribner's, 1940–61.

America: History and Life. 1964–. Abstracts. Three issues a year.

American Historical Review. 1895–. Quarterly.

Barzun, Jacques and Henry F. Graf. *The Modern Researcher.* Rev. ed. New York: Harcourt Brace Jovanovich, 1970.

Beers, Henry P. *Bibliographies in American History.* New York: H. W. Wilson, 1942.

Cambridge Ancient History. 12 vols. New York: Cambridge University Press, 1923–29. Revision in progress.

Cambridge Medieval History. 8 vols. New York: Cambridge University Press, 1911–36. Revision in progress.

Cambridge Modern History. 13 vols. New York: Cambridge University Press, 1902–26. Revision in progress.

Commager, Henry S. *Documents of American History.* 2 vols. 7th ed. New York: Appleton-Century-Crofts, 1968.

Guide to Historical Literature. New York: Macmillan, 1961.

Historical Abstracts, 1775–1945. 1955–. Quarterly. Cumulative index every five years.

Journal of American History. 1914–. Quarterly. Formerly *Mississippi Valley Historical Review.*

Keller, Helen R. *Dictionary of Dates.* 2 vols. New York: Macmillan, 1934.

Morris, Richard B. *Encyclopedia of American History.* 4th ed. New York: Harper and Row, 1970.

Literature

Abstracts of English Studies. 1958–. Ten issues a year.

American Literature. 1929–. Quarterly. Bibliography in each number.

Benet, William R. *The Reader's Encyclopedia.* 2d ed. New York: Crowell, 1965.

Cambridge Bibliography of English Literature. 5 vols. New York: Cambridge University Press, 1940–57.

Cambridge History of American Literature. 4 vols. New York: Putnam, 1917–21. Bibliography in each volume.

Cambridge History of English Literature. 15 vols. New York: Putnam, 1907–33. Bibliography in each volume.

Columbia Dictionary of Modern European Literature. New York: Columbia University Press, 1947.

Gohdes, Clarence. *Bibliographical Guides to the Study of Literature of the U.S.A.* 3d ed. Durham, N.C.: Duke University Press, 1970.

Hart, James D. *The Oxford Companion to American Literature.* 4th ed. New York: Oxford University Press, 1965.

Harvey, Sir Paul. *The Oxford Companion to Classical Literature.* New York: Oxford University Press, 1937.

———. *The Oxford Companion to English Literature.* 4th ed. New York: Oxford University Press, 1967.

386

Holman, C. Hugh. *A Handbook to Literature.* 3d ed. Indianapolis: Odyssey Press, 1972. Thorough revision of a standard reference work with the same title by Thrall and Hibbard.

Leary, Lewis G. *Articles on American Literature, 1900–1950.* Durham, N. C.: Duke University Press, 1954. A second volume published in 1970 with the same editor, title, and publisher covers 1950–67.

New Century Classical Handbook. New York: Appleton-Century-Crofts, 1962.

PMLA. 1884–. Quarterly. Annual Bibliographies since 1921. International coverage since 1956. Bibliography issue now entitled *MLA International Bibliography.*

Spiller, Robert E. and others. *Literary History of the United States.* 3d ed. 2 vols. New York: Macmillan, 1963. Bibliography in second volume.

Year's Work in English Studies. 1921–. Annual critical surveys.

Music

Apel, Willi. *Harvard Dictionary of Music.* 2d ed. Cambridge, Mass.: Harvard University Press, 1970.

Baker, Theodore. *Biographical Dictionary of Musicians.* 5th ed. New York: Schirmer, 1965.

Barlow, Harold and Sam Morganstern. *A Dictionary of Musical Themes.* New York: Crown. 1948.

Duckles, Vincent H. *Music Reference and Research Materials.* 2d ed. New York: Free Press, 1967.

Ewen, David. *The New Encyclopedia of the Opera.* Rev. ed. New York: Hill and Wang, 1971.

Grove, Sir George. *Dictionary of Music and Musicians.* 5th ed. 10 vols. New York: St. Martin's Press, 1970. The standard encyclopedia of music, first published in 1879.

Music Educator's Journal. 1914–. Bimonthly.

Music Index. 1949–. Monthly. Annual cumulations.

The Music Quarterly. 1915–. Quarterly.

Scholes, Percy A. *The Oxford Companion to Music.* 10th ed. New York: Oxford University Press, 1970.

World of Music. 4 vols. New York: Abradale Press, 1963.

Mythology and Folklore

Bulfinch's Mythology. New York: T. Y. Crowell, 1970. New issue of a standard work.

Diehl, Katherine S. *Religions, Mythologies, Folklores: An Annotated Bibliography.* 2d ed. Metuchen, N.J.: Scarecrow Press, 1962.

Frazer, Sir James. *The Golden Bough.* 3d ed. 12 vols. New York: St. Martin's Press, 1955. A one-volume abridgment, *The New Golden Bough,* was published in 1959.

Funk & Wagnalls Standard Dictionary of Folklore, Mythology, and Legend. New York: Funk & Wagnalls, 1972. Reissue of two-volume work published in 1949–50.

Hamilton, Edith. *Mythology.* Boston: Little, Brown, 1942. Published as a paperbound Mentor Book, 1953.

Mythology of All Races. 13 vols. Boston: Archaeological Institute, 1916–32.

Radford, Edwin and Mona Radford. *Encyclopedia of Superstitions.* Rev. ed. Chester Springs, Pa.: Dufour Editions, 1969.

Thompson, Stith. *Motif-Index of Folk-Literature.* 6 vols. Bloomington, Ind.: Indiana University Press, 1955–58.

Philosophy

The Encyclopedia of Philosophy. 8 vols. New York: Macmillan, 1967.

Journal of Philosophy. 1904–. Fortnightly.

Philosopher's Index. 1967–. Quarterly. Author-subject index to periodicals.

Philosophic Abstracts. 1939–54. No longer published.

Philosophical Review. 1892–. Quarterly.

Urmson, James O., ed. *The Concise Encyclopedia of Western Philosophy and Philosophers.* New York: Hawthorn Books, 1960.

Varet, Gilbert and Paul Kurtz. *International Directory of Philosophy and Philosophers.* New York: Humanities Press, 1966.

Wiener, Philip, ed. *Dictionary of the History of Ideas.* 4 vols. New York: Scribner's, 1973.

Physics

Besancon, Robert M. *The Encyclopedia of Physics.* New York: Van Nostrand Reinhold, 1966.

Encyclopaedic Dictionary of Physics. 9 vols. London: Pergamon, 1961–64. Supplements.

Handbook of Chemistry and Physics. 1913–. Annual revisions.

Parke, Nathan G. *Guide to the Literature of Mathematics and Physics.* 2d ed. New York: Dover, 1958.

Science Abstracts. 1898–. Monthly.

Whitford, R. H. *Physics Literature: A Reference Manual.* 2d ed. Metuchen, N. J.: Scarecrow Press, 1968.

Political Science

American Political Science Review. 1906–. Quarterly.

The Book of the States. Lexington, Ky.: Council of State Governments, 1935–. Biennially.

Congressional Record. 1873–. Daily. Cumulated for each session. Annual index.

Dictionary of American Politics. 2d ed. New York: Barnes and Noble, 1968.

Dunner, Joseph. *Dictionary of Political Science.* Totowa, N. J.: Littlefield, Adams, 1970.

Harmon, R. B. *Political Science: A Bibliographical Guide.* Metuchen, N. J.: Scarecrow Press, 1965. Supplements.

Holler, Frederick L. *The Information Sources of Political Science.* Santa Barbara, Calif.: ABC-Clio, 1971.

Plano, Jack C., and Milton Greenberg. *The American Political Dictionary.* Rev. ed. New York: Holt, Rinehart & Winston, 1967.

Political Handbook and Atlas of the World. New York: Simon and Schuster, 1927–. Annual revisions.

Public Affairs Information Service. 1915–. Weekly. Cumulated five times a year and annually.

Psychology

American Journal of Psychology. 1887–. Quarterly.

Drever, James. *A Dictionary of Psychology.* Rev. ed. Baltimore: Penguin Books, 1971.

Encyclopedia of Mental Health. 6 vols. New York: Franklin Watts, 1963.

Encyclopedia of Psychology. 3 vols. New York: McGraw-Hill, 1972.

Harvard List of Books in Psychology. 4th ed. Cambridge, Mass.: Harvard University Press, 1971.

Psychology Abstracts. 1927–. Monthly.

Psychological Bulletin. 1904–. Bimonthly.

Religion

Adams, Charles J. *A Reader's Guide to the Great Religions.* New York: Free Press, 1965.

Encyclopaedia Judaica. 16 vols. New York: Macmillan, 1972.

Hastings, James. *Encyclopaedia of Religion and Ethics.* 2d. ed. 12 vols. New York: Scribner's, 1907–27.

Index to Religious Periodical Literature. 1949–. Annually. Triennial cumulations.

Interpreter's Dictionary of the Bible. 4 vols. Nashville, Tenn.: Abingdon Press, 1962.

Mead, Frank S. *Handbook of Denominations in the United States.* 5th ed. Nashville, Tenn.: Abingdon Press, 1970.

Nelson's Complete Concordance. New York: Nelson, 1957.

New Catholic Encyclopedia. 15 vols. New York: McGraw-Hill, 1967.

New Schaff-Herzog Encyclopedia of Religious Knowledge. 13 vols. Grand Rapids, Mich.: Baker Book House, 1951–58.

Oxford Dictionary of the Christian Church. New York: Oxford University Press, 1960.

Religious and Theological Abstracts. 1958–. Quarterly.

Sociology

Abstracts for Social Workers. 1965–. Quarterly.

American Journal of Sociology. 1895–. Bimonthly.

American Sociological Review, 1936–. Bimonthly.

Encyclopedia of Social Work. 1965–. Annual volumes.

Fairchild, Henry P. *Dictionary of Sociology.* Totowa, N. J.: Littlefield, Adams, 1970. Paperbound reprint of a 1944 edition.

Mitchell, G. Duncan. *A Dictionary of Sociology.* Chicago: Aldine, 1968.

Reuter, E. B. *Handbook of Sociology.* New York: Dryden Press, 1946.

Social Forces. 1922–. Quarterly.

Sociological Abstracts. 1952–. Nine issues a year.

C. Collect Pertinent Information

1. COMPILE A BIBLIOGRAPHY.   You now have a research topic, and you know how and where to collect information on it. The next step is to compile a *bibliography,* a list of useful sources of information on the topic. Purposeful reading is now one of the most important skills you can develop. You must learn to separate useless from useful information without a wasteful and slow page-by-page analysis of the source.

Skim book chapters and magazine articles to see if they contain material relevant to the topic. Read tables of contents, index pages, and subtitles of books; read the topic sentences of paragraphs. Mark pertinent passages in pencil if the source belongs to you, or if it is a library source, place a paperclip on the page. When you are reasonably sure that the source will be useful, list it on a 3 × 5 bibliography card. A typical bibliography card looks like this:

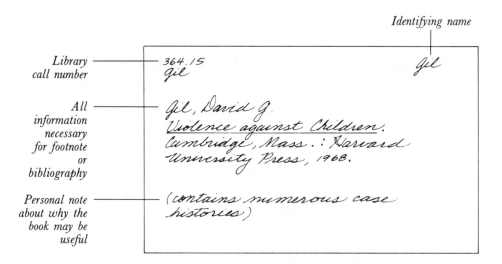

Identifying name

Library call number

All information necessary for footnote or bibliography

Personal note about why the book may be useful

> 364.15
> Gil
>
> Gil
>
> Gil, David G.
> *Violence against Children.*
> Cambridge, Mass.: Harvard
> University Press, 1968.
>
> (contains numerous case histories)

It will save you valuable time later if you note the call number of a book and the date and title of a magazine article on the bibliography card. Use a separate card for each source to simplify changes in your preliminary bibliography. To add a source, make a new card; to delete a source, remove the card on which it is entered.

2. TAKE NOTES.   By now, considerable skimming and reading should have given you an overall view of the topic. Quite likely, you have already formulated a controlling idea and are ready to begin taking notes from the sources you will use. The importance of careful note-taking cannot be overstated: accuracy and thoroughness at this stage will save literally hours of work in assembling the first draft of your paper.

Make notes on 4 x 6 cards. Any information, data, or quotation to be incorporated into the paper should be listed on the 4 x 6 note cards; call numbers and publication information on books or magazine articles should be listed on the bibliography cards. Therefore, there will be both a note card and a bibliography card for each source consulted.

The four primary forms of note-taking are: summarizing, paraphrasing, quoting, and a mixture of these.

a. *To summarize* means to condense. A condensation uses fewer words than the original. A book may be condensed into one paragraph; a paragraph may be condensed into one sentence. For example, a book citing numerous examples of child battering in the schools of Sumer, five thousand years ago, might be summarized like this on a notecard:

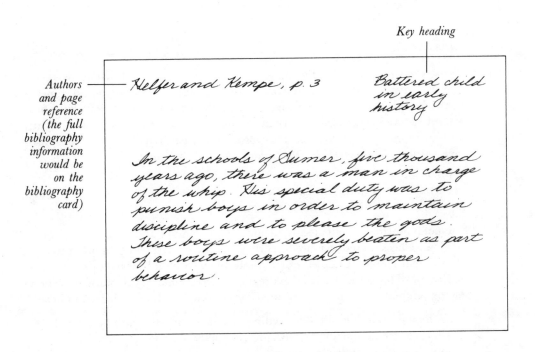

Key heading

Authors and page reference (the full bibliography information would be on the bibliography card)

Helfer and Kempe, p. 3

Battered child in early history

In the schools of Sumer, five thousand years ago, there was a man in charge of the whip. His special duty was to punish boys in order to maintain discipline and to please the gods. These boys were severely beaten as part of a routine approach to proper behavior.

b. *To paraphrase* means to restate an original source in your own words using nearly the same amount of space as the original. Here is an example of a paraphrase:

Original: The general public is not fully aware of the seriousness and prevalence of cruelty to children. The knowledge that babies suffer severe injury or death at the hands of their parents is repugnant and extremely hard to accept. Abuse of children, the greatest cause of death among children under the age of three, causes more deaths than auto accidents, leukemia, and muscular dystrophy.

c. *To quote* means to use exactly the same words as the original. Many passages may be quoted in the notes, but as few quotations as possible should appear in the actual paper. A good research paper should reveal that the writer has assimilated and established information and data in his *own* flow of thought, and therefore need not rely on the words of others. Frequent quotations also give writing a choppy effect. Use quotations only when:

(1) You want authoritative support for a statement.
(2) Something is said with exceptional literary taste.
(3) The quotation is needed for accuracy.

Quotations must meticulously include every comma and every word in the original. Check quotations for accuracy. Oddities of spelling or phrasing in the original should be copied exactly and followed by a bracketed [*sic*], which indicates, "This is the way the text reads in the original." Any omitted portion of the original quotation is indicated by ellipses (. . .) as in this example:

It is thought that because of crowding in smaller quarters and because of having larger families, "the working-class parent uses . . . punishment more than the middle-class parent."

Ellipses are not used if the quotation is integrated into a sentence and the omission is made at the beginning or end of the original. Here is an example:

Quotation to be used: Many sociologists have noted that the working-class parent uses physical punishment more than the middle-class parent.

Quotation as it appears in the paper: It is thought that because of crowding in smaller quarters and because of having larger families, "the working-class parent uses physical punishment more than the middle-class parent."

Quotations in the final paper must fit coherently into the flow of writing. Transitional sentences, based on a thorough understanding of both the quotation and its context, should be used to introduce the quotation and move the reader on to succeeding material. A well-prepared note card, with author and subject identified, will help you effectively use a quotation:

> Neill, p. 102   An authority's
>   view on
>   punishment
>
> A. S. Neill suggests that "Perhaps
> we punish because we are a Christian
> civilization. If you sin, punishment
> awaits you in the here and now,
> and Hell awaits you in the future."

Here are some additional suggestions for writing useful note cards:

a. Write in ink, not pencil, or the note cards will smudge when you shuffle them. Do not type note cards. Many libraries do not allow the use of typewriters on their premises; moreover, transcribing notes on a typewriter later wastes time and causes copying errors.

b. Use one card per idea. With one idea on each card, an outline can be created by shuffling the cards and arranging them in a logical sequence. To save money, cut your own note cards from regular paper.

c. In copying or paraphrasing material from more than one page in an original source, indicate all pages on the note card. This information is needed for footnotes or endnotes.

d. Write notes legibly or you may have to go back to an original source to decipher what you meant.

D. Formulate the Controlling Idea and Outline the Paper

1. THE CONTROLLING IDEA.   The controlling idea holds the research together and limits the paper's scope. Tinker with the wording of the controlling idea until it is abundantly clear. Acceptable controlling ideas for college papers are: (a) the *purpose* statement, and (b) the *thesis* statement.

a. The purpose statement is an initial statement of the paper's intent. It involves such phrases as "The purpose of this paper is . . . ," or "In this paper proof will be offered that . . . ," or "The intent of this paper is . . . ." Here are some sample purpose statements, taken from student papers:

   (1) The purpose of this paper is to prove that every major war in America has influenced women's fashions.
   (2) This paper will relate certain aspects of Dietrich Bonhoeffer's life to his religious views expressed in his writings.

b. The standard *thesis statement* gets directly to the controlling idea and states it:

   (1) Adolescence in American society today is characterized by the young adult's dependency on the family, his search for an identity, and the repression of his sexual drives.
   (2) The gods of the Greeks were human, with human appearances, human virtues, and human failings.
   (3) We laugh at Charlie Chaplin's movies because they reflect the bumbling creature we all fear that we might be.

2. THE OUTLINE. The next step is to outline the paper. A simple procedure for creating an outline is to assemble the note cards according to the logical sequence of their major ideas. All information relating to one major idea is placed in the same stack. For example, in the paper on child abuse, perhaps the note cards could be logically grouped into three stacks based on the following major ideas:

   I.   Violence against children by adults has been practiced throughout history.
   II. A wide variety of child-abuse cases exist today and for numerous reasons.
   III. Some effective action has been taken against child abuse, but more social cooperation and legal sanctions are needed to overcome the problem.

These three points could then be condensed into a controlling idea such as the following:

Adult violence against children, commonly practiced throughout history, occurs today for a variety of reasons in countless cases of child abuse and can be corrected only through social cooperation and legal sanctions.

A controlling idea containing three major divisions is now established. Arrange the note cards within each division into a logical sequence of information, examples, and other data. If necessary, add or delete cards. Translate the logical arrangement of the cards into an outline as in this example:

Child Abuse

Thesis: Adult violence against children, commonly practiced throughout history, occurs today for a variety of reasons in countless cases of child abuse and can be corrected only through social cooperation and legal sanctions.

I. Adult violence against children is common throughout history.

   A. The Sumerians beat children with whips to discipline them.

   B. The Romans flogged boys before the altars of Diana as a religious practice.

   C. Early Christians whipped their children on Innocents Day in memory of King Herod's massacre.

   D. During the Middle Ages, children's eyes were gouged and their bodies mutilated to make them effective beggars.

   E. The factory system allowed foremen to beat children mercilessly if they didn't work hard enough.

II. Countless cases of child abuse exist today for a variety of reasons.

   A. Numerous child-abuse cases have been recorded.

      1. On record are thousands of cases of planned falls, strangulations, and sexual assaults.

      2. Parents have assaulted children with instruments ranging from plastic bags to baseball bats.

      3. Disciplinary measures may include cigarette burns, plunges into boiling water, or starvation.

   B. Child-abuse cases exist for a variety of reasons.

      1. In a study of sixty families with beaten children, all the persecuting parents were beaten as children, indicating a revenge pattern.

      2. Some parents become abusive because they expect more love and affection from their child than the child is able to deliver.

      3. A frustrated parent will use the child's bad behavior to justify abuses.

      4. Unsatisfactory marital relationships are another frequent cause of child abuse.

III. Social cooperation and legal sanctions are needed to overcome the problem of child abuse.

   A. Although little was heard of the battered child syndrome before 1960, today all the states have adopted legislation governing reporting of battered children.

   B. But only two states, Maryland and New Jersey, have laws specifically prohibiting the use of physical force on children.

   C. Doctors and other people fear slander suits if they notify police of child abuse and an investigation does not support the charge.

   D. The other parent often protects the one inflicting the harm so that proof of battering is difficult to obtain.

   E. Society and its legal system must make further advances toward curbing child abuse.

Avoid an overly detailed outline. The rule of thumb is two pages of outline for every ten pages of writing.

E. Write and Document the Paper

With the outline completed, you are now ready to write the paper. Arrange the note cards in the sequence indicated by the outline. If properly assembled, the note cards can be expanded with transitions into a suitable first draft. Incorporate facts, opinions, data, and other information on the note cards into the first draft. Notes and bibliographic entries must be used to give credit to the authors of all material cited, quoted, or alluded to in the paper. You do not have to document your own ideas and insights, but you must acknowledge the contributions of others. This is the process of *documentation*. Summaries, paraphrases, quotations—all must be documented; otherwise your paper will be considered *plagiarized* ("stolen"), a label any self-respecting student shuns.

Documentation for research writing became standardized with publication of the Modern Language Association's *Style Sheet* in 1951 (published as the *MLA Handbook* in 1977), which makes it easier for all readers to trace the source of researched information appearing in a paper. The most common kinds of documentation are illustrated below. If you have to refer to a source for which no format is given here, either use the example most closely resembling the source, apply common sense, or check with the teacher. Bear in mind that the primary purpose of documentation is to indicate to the reader the original source of an idea.

1. Bibliography

The *bibliography* is a complete list of sources from which material or ideas were taken. The order and the punctuation of standard forms for a book and for a magazine are as follows:

Book: Author. *Title.* Volumes. Edition. Place: Publisher, Year.
Magazine: Author. "Title," *Magazine,* Volume (Issue), Pages.

STANDARD SOURCES

Book by a single author: Brodie, Fawn M. *Thomas Jefferson: An Intimate History.* New York: W. W. Norton & Company, Inc., 1974.

1. For easy alphabetizing, the author's surname comes first.
2. If the book is the work of an agency, a committee, or an organization, the name of that group replaces the name of the author.
3. If no author is given, begin the entry with the title.
4. In typing, the name of the book is underlined; in printing, it is italicized.
5. Facts of publication include: place of publication, name of publisher, and the date of publication. If more than one place is given, use only the first. Copy the publisher's name as it is listed on the title page of the book. If no date is given, use the latest copyright date or state "n.d."
6. A bibliography entry is double spaced. The second line is indented five spaces.

Book by two authors: Hallberg, Edmond C., and William G. Thomas. *When I Was Your Age.* New York: The Free Press, 1974.

The names of second (and third) authors are not inverted. Use the same order of authors' names as found on the title page of the book.

Book by several authors:	Masotti, Louis H., et al. *A Time to Burn? An Evaluation of the Present Crisis in Race Relations.* Chicago: Rand McNally, 1969.

et al. may be replaced by the English "and others" if you prefer. This form for multiple authors should be used only for books by more than three authors.

Edition of an author's work:	Plath, Aurelia S., ed. *Letters Home by Sylvia Plath.* New York: Harper and Row, 1975.

Edited work:	Arnold, Matthew. *Culture and Anarchy.* Ed. J. Dover Wilson. Cambridge: University Press, 1961.

Edited collection:	Gordon, Walter K., ed. *Literature in Critical Perspectives: An Anthology.* New York: Appleton-Century-Crofts, 1968.

Translation:	Alighieri, Dante. *The Inferno.* Trans. John Ciardi. New York: The New American Library of World Literature, 1954.

Edition other than the first:	McCrimmon, James M. *Writing with a Purpose.* 5th ed. Boston: Houghton Mifflin Company, 1974.

Other editions could be: Rev. ed. (Revised edition), 2d ed., rev. and enl. (revised and enlarged), and so on. Cite only the edition being used.

Work of more than one volume:	Harrison, G. B., et al., eds. *Major British Writers.* 2 vols. New York: Harcourt, Brace and World, 1959.

If the volumes of a multivolume work were published over a period of years, the full period is cited: 1954–1960.

Title in an edited collection:	Thoreau, Henry David. "Observation." In *The Norton Reader.* 3d ed. Ed. Arthur M. Eastman, et al. New York: W. W. Norton & Company, 1973.

1. This same form applies to short stories or poems.
2. The entry requires two titles, an author, and editor(s).
3. The title of the essay, short story, or poem is in quotation marks.
4. The title of the book is preceded by "In."

Article in a magazine:	Barthelme, Donald. "The Captured Woman." *The New Yorker,* 28 June 1976, pp. 22–25.

Berger, Brigitte. "The Coming Age of People Work." *Change,* 8 (May 1976), 24–30.

1. The first entry shows an article in a magazine published weekly.
2. The second entry shows an article in a magazine published monthly, with volume number (8) cited. If the volume number is cited, then "p." or "pp." is deleted.

Newspaper article:	Shaw, Gaylord. "Goldwater Backs Ford—His Most Difficult Decision." *Los Angeles Times,* 1 July 1976, Part I, p. 1.

1. For news stories, simply cite the headline, newspaper title, section (if each section is paged separately), column (if helpful), and page.
2. The city is underlined if it appears as part of the newspaper title on the front page.

SPECIAL SOURCES

Article from an encyclopedia:

Nicholas, Herbert George. "Churchill, Sir Winston Leonard Spencer." *Encyclopaedia Britannica* (1968), V, 747–51.

or more commonly

"Churchill, Sir Winston Leonard Spencer." *Encyclopaedia Britannica.* 1969 ed.

1. The authors of encyclopedia articles are usually listed by initials at the end of the articles; these initials are clarified in the index.
2. All facts of publication are not necessary; year and volume number suffice.
3. Watch the various spellings of *encyclopedia.*

Public document or pamphlet:

U.S. Senate *Congressional Record.* 93d Congress. 10 June 1975.

Social Security Programs in the United States. U.S. Department of Health, Education, and Welfare, March 1968.

Kruger, Jane. *Teaching as an Art.* A Conference Syllabus published by Maryland University, 1970.

1976 Foreign Currency Converter, published by Deak and Co. of Los Angeles, 1976.

Because pamphlets are distributed by a variety of organizations in a variety of nonstandard forms, the best you can do is treat them as much like books as possible, supplying place of publication, publisher, and date.

Book review:

Marcus, Greil. "Limits." Review of *Meridian* by Alice Walker. *The New Yorker,* 7 June 1976, pp. 133–36.

If the review is untitled, proceed directly with "Review of . . ."

Film:

Face to Face. Film directed by Ingmar Bergman. Starring Liv Ullmann. A Paramount Release, 1976.

1. Film titles are underlined.
2. Supply name of director, star(s), and producer.

Recording or tape:

Osborn, Alex. "Applied Imagination." Cassette, produced by Success Motivation Institute, Inc., 1972.

Roosevelt, Eleanor. "My Life with F.D.R." Cassette with regular library call number.

1. Copy all helpful information from tape or record.
2. The trend is to catalog tapes along with books.

Letter: Woolley, Morton. Personal letter. 12 Feb. 1976.

Interview: Hirshberg, Jennefer A. Personal Interview on College Grading Standards. Glendale, California, 19 Feb. 1976.

Manuscript: Zimmerman, Fred M. "Speculation: Los Angeles—1985." A working paper for the Los Angeles Goals Program. Los Angeles City Hall: Planning Department Library, 1967.

    1. No specific rules exist for the documentation of manuscripts. When you use this kind of material, stick as closely as you can to the form for books or magazines.

    2. The titles of unpublished works, no matter how long, are enclosed in quotation marks.

Radio or television program: Prokofiev, Sergei. "Romeo and Juliet" performed by the Bolshoi Ballet. Hosted by Mary Tyler Moore. CBS, 27 June 1976.

Include whatever information is needed to identify the program.

2. Endnotes or Footnotes

No firm agreement exists on whether it is better to document a research paper with footnotes or endnotes. Individual teachers usually express their preference for one form over the other. Endnotes are listed together in numerical order at the end of the paper, whereas footnotes appear at the bottom of each page where a reference is indicated in the text. Endnotes are the clear preference of the *MLA Handbook* and in time will probably replace footnotes at colleges and universities. For this reason, the sample student paper on pp. 406–416 uses endnotes. Nevertheless, many instructors prefer footnotes because they allow the reader to simply glance at the bottom of the page when checking a source. Be sure that you understand which form your instructor expects.

a. Form for Endnotes

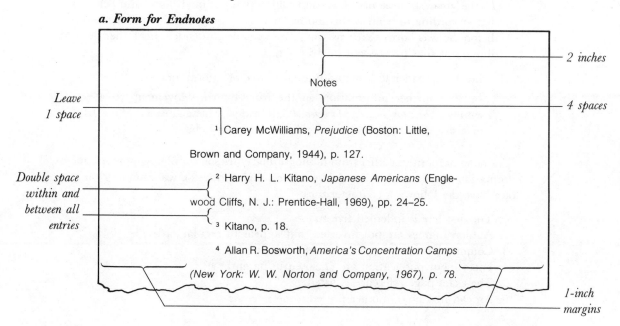

Leave 1 space

Double space within and between all entries

Notes

2 inches

4 spaces

    [1] Carey McWilliams, *Prejudice* (Boston: Little, Brown and Company, 1944), p. 127.

    [2] Harry H. L. Kitano, *Japanese Americans* (Englewood Cliffs, N. J.: Prentice-Hall, 1969), pp. 24–25.

    [3] Kitano, p. 18.

    [4] Allan R. Bosworth, *America's Concentration Camps* (New York: W. W. Norton and Company, 1967), p. 78.

1-inch margins

b. Form for Footnotes

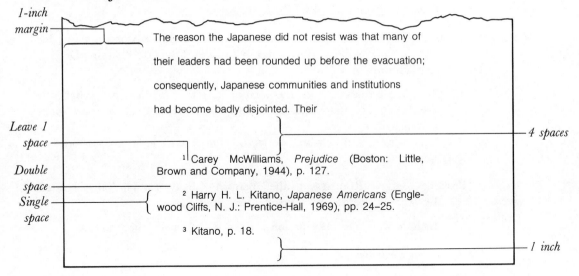

1-inch margin

The reason the Japanese did not resist was that many of

their leaders had been rounded up before the evacuation;

consequently, Japanese communities and institutions

had become badly disjointed. Their

Leave 1 space

4 spaces

[1] Carey McWilliams, *Prejudice* (Boston: Little, Brown and Company, 1944), p. 127.

Double space
Single space

[2] Harry H. L. Kitano, *Japanese Americans* (Englewood Cliffs, N. J.: Prentice-Hall, 1969), pp. 24–25.

[3] Kitano, p. 18.

1 inch

Notes have three uses:

1. To cite a specific source for borrowed material:

   [1]Jun J. Li, *The Essence of Chinese Civilization* (Princeton, New Jersey: D. Van Nostrand Company, 1967), p. 63.

2. To add an explanatory comment to the text without interrupting its main flow:

   [2]The "Cheng" referred to was known as "Ch'in Shih Huang-ti," one of the greatest emperors of ancient China, who unified the country in 221 B.C. According to hearsay, his mother had been pregnant for twelve months before he was born; that was why, some people contended, his father never found out that he was not his true son.

3. To direct the reader to some additional source of information:

   [3]For further information on the May Fourth Movement, see Chow Tse-tung, *The May Fourth Movement* (Cambridge, Massachusetts: Harvard University Press, 1960), especially the introductory chapters.

Endnotes or footnotes differ from bibliographic entries in supplying more specific information about exactly where in a work certain information was found. Primary notes have the following characteristics:

1. The first line is indented five spaces.
2. Authors' names are not inverted, but appear in regular order.
3. Commas separate the items of information.
4. Facts about publication are enclosed in parentheses.
5. The exact page reference is listed.
6. An elevated note number precedes the reference.

7. A footnote is single spaced, but separated from another footnote by a double space. An endnote is double spaced within and between each note.

STANDARD NOTES. The following notes illustrate the most common types of references that occur. Refer to the section on bibliography to adapt any reference not given here.

Book with one author: [4]Robert M. Pirsig, *Zen and the Art of Motorcycle Maintenance* (New York: William Morrow and Company, 1974), p. 29.

Subsequent reference: Pirsig, pp. 121–22.

Some teachers still insist on *ibid.,* meaning in the same place, for subsequent reference to an immediately preceding footnote, or "*Ibid.,* p. 10" if the source is the same but the page is different. However, the trend is away from Latin abbreviations.

Book with two authors: [5]William H. Masters and Virginia E. Johnson, *Human Sexual Inadequacy* (Boston: Little, Brown and Company, 1970), p. 35.

Subsequent reference: Masters and Johnson, p. 50.

Essay in an edited work: [6]Walter Lippmann, "Edison: Inventor of Invention," in *Modern Essays,* 3d ed., ed. Russell B. Nye and Arra M. Garab (Glenview, Ill.: Scott, Foresman and Company, 1963), p. 133.

Subsequent reference: Lippmann, p. 134.

Edited work: [7]William Wordsworth, *The Prelude,* ed. Ernest de Selincourt (Oxford: Clarendon Press), p. 55.

Subsequent reference: Wordsworth, p. 134.

Multivolume work: [8]Le Roy Edwin Froom, *The Prophetic Faith of Our Fathers* (Washington, D.C.: Review and Herald Publishing Association, 1954), IV, p. 382.

Subsequent reference: Froom, p. 384.

Magazine article: [9]George Leonard, "The Tattoo Taboo," *The Atlantic Monthly,* 238 (July 1976), 48.

Subsequent reference: Leonard, p. 49.

For a weekly magazine, the note would be as follows:

[10]Desmond King-Hele, "The Shape of the Earth," *Science,* 25 June 1976, p. 1293.

Subsequent reference: King-Hele, p. 1299.

Newspaper article: [11]Alpheus T. Mason, "The Right to Revolt: A Last Resort in Pursuit of Happiness," *Los Angeles Times,* 4 July 1976, Part V, p. 1.

Subsequent reference: Mason, p. 4, col. 1.

Column numbers are cited only if the page in question is cluttered with articles:

[12]"No Greater Gift, No Greater Promise," *Los Angeles Times,* 4 July 1976, Part V, p. 2.

Subsequent reference: *Los Angeles Times,* p. 2.

NOTES FOR SPECIFIC ITEMS.   As in the case of bibliography entries, a chapter such as this cannot cover all the varied possibilities involved in citing sources. We offer the most common examples. For special cases, use the form closest to your specific example, follow your common sense, or consult your instructor.

*Famous play
or poem:*
[13]William Shakespeare, *Macbeth,* III.ii.10.

The reference is to Act Three, Scene Two, Line 10.

Subsequent reference: *Macbeth,* IV.iii.20.

[14]John Milton, *Paradise Lost,* I.150.

The reference is to Book One, line 150.

Sometimes long poems also contain cantos, which are cited in small roman numerals:

[15]Edmund Spenser, *The Faerie Queene,* II.vi.26.

*Bible
passage:*
[16]John 3:16.

[17]I Kings 2:12, Revised Standard Version.

Translation is indicated only if not the King James Version.

*Public
document
or pamphlet:*
[18]U.S., *Statutes at Large 1972,* Vol. 86, 1973, Public Law 92–347.

Because public documents vary in format, you will need to improvise your own note, citing all information necessary for your reader to find the source.

[19]George S. Duggar, *The Relation of Local Government Structure to Urban Renewal.* Bureau of Public Administration, University of California at Berkeley, 1961, p. 2.

*Dissertation,
thesis, or other
manuscript material:*
[20]Joyce R. Cotton, "Evan Harrington: An Analysis of George Meredith's Revisions," Diss. University of Southern California, 1968, p. 25.

F. The Final Copy

The final copy should be clean and free of errors. Don't skimp on revising or proofreading time. If you do not type reasonably well, pay a good typist to type your paper, for the effort of a good paper is ruined by messy erasures or typographical errors.

The body of the paper should be typed on 8½″ x 11″ white bond (not erasable paper because it smudges), double spaced and properly documented, each note numbered consecutively and placed either at the bottom of the page where it occurs, or accumulated in a "Notes" section at the end of the paper if your teacher stipulates this method (see student sample paper on pages 406–416).

Quotations of five or more typewritten lines must be set off from the text by triple spacing, indented ten spaces, and double spaced. A colon ends the sentence preceding them.

> At one point in her life Sylvia Plath was deeply moved by
> a French motion picture about the temptation of Joan of
> Arc. She gives this account of her reaction:
>
> > After it was all over, I couldn't look at any-
> > one. I was crying because it was like a purge,
> > the buildup of unbelievable tension, then the
> > release, as of the soul of Joan at the stake.[6]

All of the margins of your paper should be one inch wide. For the format of title page, list of notes, and bibliography, see the sample student paper.

Following is a checklist of what your paper must include:

1. A full outline of the paper (see student sample paper)
2. A title page (see student sample paper)
3. Body of the paper
4. Footnotes or endnotes and an alphabetized bibliography
5. Note cards if your teacher requests them

Exercises

A. Unscramble the following bibliographical facts and arrange them in the proper bibliographical form.

1. A book by E. L. Doctorow, published by Random House of New York in 1975. The title of the book is *Ragtime*.
2. An article entitled "What Is the Federation Cup?" published in volume 23 of *World Tennis,* the August 1976 issue, covering pages 32–34.
3. "Good Country People," a story by Flannery O'Connor, taken from an anthology entitled *The Modern Tradition* (second edition), edited by Daniel F. Howard and published in 1972 by Little, Brown and Company of Boston.
4. Feodor Dostoevsky's famous novel *Crime and Punishment,* published by Oxford University Press, Inc. of New York (1953), in a translation by Jessie Coulson.
5. "The Dutiful Child's Promises," a selection from an anthology entitled *Readings from American Literature,* edited by Mary Edwards Calhoun and Emma Lenore MacAlarney, published by Ginn and Company of Boston, 1915.
6. A two-volume work entitled *Civilization—Past and Present,* co-authored by T. Walter Wallbank and Alastair M. Taylor, published in 1949 by Scott, Foresman and Company of Chicago.

7. An unsigned encyclopedia article under the heading "Tiryns," found in volume 22 of the 1963 edition of the *Encyclopaedia Britannica,* pp. 247–48.

8. The sixth edition of Karl C. Garrison's book entitled *Psychology of Adolescence,* published in 1965 by Prentice-Hall, of Englewood Cliffs, New Jersey.

9. An article without author from the August 9, 1976, issue of *Time.* The article appears on pages 16 and 19 and is entitled "To Plains with the Boys in the Bus."

10. A feature article by Jim Murray, entitled "The Real Olympian," which appeared in Part III of the *Los Angeles Times,* pp. 1 and 7 (Wednesday, August 4, 1976).

B. Using the biographical information provided in exercise A, convert the items below into a proper sequence of notes.

1. Page 25 of the book by Karl C. Garrison.
2. Page 50 of that same book.
3. Page 30 of volume one of the book by T. Walter Wallbank and Alastair M. Taylor.
4. Page 31 of that same book.
5. Page 90 of the book edited by Mary Edwards Calhoun and Emma Lenore MacAlarney.
6. Page 1 of the *Los Angeles Times* article.
7. Page 248 of the encyclopedia article.
8. Page 48 of Feodor Dostoevsky's novel.
9. Page 507 of Flannery O'Connor's story.
10. Page 46 of *Ragtime.*

C. From the works mentioned in this appendix, compile a list of sources that you would consult if you were to write on one of the following topics:

1. The last year of Thomas Jefferson's life
2. Research regarding the education of blind children
3. The novels of William Makepeace Thackeray
4. The myth of Europa
5. The rise of Mao Tse-tung
6. Safety in nuclear plants
7. The art of Jacques Louis David
8. Famous quotations about the value of education
9. The murder of Stanford White by Harry K. Thaw
10. The philosophy of Bertrand Russell

D. Summarize the following paragraph in one sentence:

Those who are awed by their surroundings do not think of change, no matter how miserable their condition. When our mode of life is so precarious as to make it patent that we cannot control the circumstances of our existence, we tend to stick to the proven and the familiar. We counteract a deep feeling of insecurity by making of our existence a fixed routine. We hereby acquire the illusion that we have tamed the unpredictable. Fisherfolk, nomads and farmers who have to contend with the willful elements, the creative worker who depends on inspiration, the savage awed by his surroundings—they all fear change. They face the world as they would an all-powerful jury. The abjectly poor, too, stand in awe of the world around them and are not hospitable to change. It is a dangerous life we live when hunger and cold are at our heels. There is thus a conservatism of the destitute as profound as the conservatism of the privileged, and the former is as much a factor in the perpetuation of a social order as the latter.

Eric Hoffer, The True Believer

E. Paraphrase the following paragraph so that it sounds like you.

The urge for a touch of class, for something better than others have, has put new pressure on that classic Russian institution—the queue. Customers the world-over wait in lines, but Soviet queues have a dimension all their own, like the Egyptian pyramids. They reveal a lot about the Russian predicament and the Russian psyche. And their operation is far more intricate than first meets the eye. To the passerby they look like nearly motionless files of mortals doomed to some commercial purgatory for their humble purchases. But what the outsider misses is the hidden magnetism of lines for Russians, their inner dynamics, their special etiquette.

Hedrick Smith, The Russians

G. Sample Student Paper

A student research paper is included on the following pages to give you an idea of what a good student paper looks like. It was written by a college freshman and demonstrates what any conscientious student can achieve when he or she tries. The paper follows the format set forth in the 1977 edition of the *MLA Handbook*. We have also included the sentence outline from which the paper was developed.

THE INTERNMENT OF JAPANESE AMERICANS DURING WORLD WAR II

Thesis: The internment of Japanese Americans during World War II was an
         abominable violation of American ideals.

  I. The United States government abused the rights of an entire group.
      A. Guaranteed Constitutional rights were suspended.
      B. The Japanese Americans were judged by their ancestry rather than
          by individual acts.
          1. German and Italian aliens suspected of disloyalty were treated
              more fairly than were the Japanese Americans.
          2. Efforts on the part of Japanese Americans to demonstrate loyalty
              and patriotism were futile.

 II. In a land where "all men are created equal," the underlying force behind
      the internment was extreme racial prejudice.
      A. There was a history of anti-Japanese feelings and actions in the
          United States prior to World War II.
          1. The stereotyped Japanese were viewed as a threat to Americans.
          2. Anti-Japanese legislation was already in existence.
      B. With racism to back it up, the hysteria that followed the attack on
          Pearl Harbor was aggravated by politicians, anti-Japanese groups,
          and the press.

III. The unjust suffering that Japanese Americans faced seems a paradox in a
      country where "justice for all" is proclaimed.
      A. Japanese Americans suffered severe economic losses as a result of
          the relocation.
      B. The facilities in the camps were inadequate.
      C. While Japanese Americans were living in internment camps, Japanese
          American soldiers were serving the United States in the war effort.
      D. The psychological and emotional suffering was perhaps the most tragic.

Diane L. Thomas

Professor: McCuen

English 101

May 1, 1979

The Internment of Japanese Americans during World War II

On February 19, 1942, President Franklin D. Roosevelt signed an executive order that allowed the United States government to begin the evacuation and incarceration of 110,000 Japanese Americans. The order for relocation applied to "all persons of Japanese Ancestry" and, of the total number of evacuees, 70,000 were American-born citizens. Forced to leave behind their homes, lands, and businesses, they were herded off to ten desolate camps scattered throughout the United States, surrounded by barbed-wire and under military guard, where they made their homes for nearly three years. The possibility of sabotage or espionage from among these people was the primary rationale behind this mass removal of the entire Japanese-American population in California, western Washington, Oregon, and Arizona.[1] It is difficult to imagine how this unhappy event could have happened in these United States, but it did happen. Our history books often seem to imply that we are heroes without guilt and the protectors of freedom carried on by the democratic principles for which we stand. The mass incarceration of Japanese Americans during World War II, however, is a part of our history that Americans cannot be proud of. Without a doubt, at that point in our history democracy was operating at its worst. Racial prejudice, wartime hysteria, fear, and outrage made the evacuation decision a popular one that caused us to commit what Roger Daniels called "our worst wartime mistake."[2] The internment of Japanese Americans during World War II was an abominable violation of American ideals.

By allowing the evacuation, the United States government abused the rights of an entire group. There is no question that the evacuation of men, women, and children from their homes without being charged with any crime, without trials or hearings, was a drastic invasion of the Constitutional rights of citizens.[3] Guarantees covered under the fourteenth amendment were ignored, depriving Japanese Americans of liberty and property without due process and the "equal protection of the laws" afforded other citizens.[4] All of this was done out of "military necessity" because the Japanese Americans were thought to be potentially disloyal. Even if there were saboteurs among them, such a fact does not justify suspending the rights of an entire group because of the possible guilt of a few.[5] There was not, however, one actual case of any act of sabotage or disloyalty by Japanese Americans during the entire war.

The government further abused the rights of Japanese Americans by judging them by their ancestry rather than by individual acts. Aliens and citizens alike were lumped together as a racial group whereas German and Italian aliens suspected of sabotage or espionage were handled on an individual basis. It is worth noting that, with few exceptions, the Japanese alien residents that were interned had lived in the United States from twenty to thirty years, having arrived prior to the Japanese Exclusion Act of 1924. Amazingly, the discriminating laws that were in effect made Japanese immigrants ineligible for citizenship, whereas a large percentage of German and Italian immigrants had become naturalized American citizens and, therefore, exempt from the "enemy alien" classification.[6] Army General John L. DeWitt had said, "a Jap's a Jap,"[7] and it appears that this was the policy that was followed.

Despite numerous efforts, Japanese Americans found that attempts to prove their loyalty and patriotism were futile. For example, immediately following Pearl Harbor, the Japanese American Citizens League wired President

Roosevelt pledging their cooperation: ". . . We, in our hearts are Americans

--loyal to America. We must prove that to all of you."[8] Other Japanese

Americans bought defense bonds, donated to the Red Cross, and volunteered for

civil defense and intelligence work in an effort to prove their loyalty.[9]

These patriotic actions were apparently meaningless because these same people

would soon find themselves identified as the enemy and placed in barbed-wire

enclosures.

In a land where "all men are created equal," the underlying force behind

the internment was extreme racial prejudice. Even prior to the evacuation

in 1942 the Japanese had been the victims of racism in America, particularly

on the West Coast where their population was most concentrated. When immigrants

from Japan began to arrive in the United States after 1890, they were stereo-

typed, along with other Orientals, and viewed as a threat to Americans. There

was a general feeling that the Japanese would eventually overpopulate the

country and conquer the Caucasians.[10] Economically, they were resented because

of competition in agriculture, business, and labor. The development of Japan

as a world power also contributed to this irrational fear and hatred of the

Japanese, who were described as the "yellow peril."[11]

The anti-Japanese movement in America goes back to the turn of the century

when the United States Industrial Commission made the following claim:

> The Japanese are more servile than the Chinese, but less obedient
>
> and far less desirable. They have most of the vices of the Chinese
>
> with none of the virtues. They underbid the Chinese in everything

and are as a class tricky, unreliable and dishonest.[12]

At about the same time, the slogan of politician and labor leader Dennis Kearney was "The Japs must go!" The mayor of San Francisco insisted that it was impossible for the Japanese to assimilate into our culture and that they were "not the stuff of which American citizens can be made."[13] Appropriately, the Japanese and Korean Exclusion League was formed in 1905, and a number of other anti-Japanese societies followed. There were scattered cases of individual and mob violence directed against the Japanese, the press made verbal racist attacks, and the "yellow-peril" concept continued to gain credibility.[14]

With the agitation against the Japanese came continual proposals of anti-Japanese legislation. Indeed, every session of the California legislature between 1905 and 1945 attempted to pass at least one piece of anti-Japanese legislation.[15] They were successful in 1913 when the Alien Land Law was passed, preventing Japanese from purchasing or leasing land for more than three years. In most of the western states, residence choice was restricted by covenants, intermarriage with Caucasians was forbidden, and free access to certain public places was forbidden.[16] Finally, in 1924 the agitation subsided temporarily when an exclusion act was passed specifically preventing further Japanese immigration.

With years of racism to back it up, the hysteria that persisted after Pearl Harbor was aggravated by politicians, anti-Japanese groups, and the press. Newspapers led the already frightened public to believe that Japanese saboteurs were lurking everywhere, publishing headlines like "JAP BOAT FLASHES MESSAGE ASHORE," "JAPANESE HERE SENT VITAL DATA TO TOKYO," and "JAPS PLAN COAST ATTACK

IN APRIL WARNS CHIEF OF KOREAN SPY BAND."[17] The stories, of course, were

totally unfounded. To add to the panic, former Supreme Court Justice Earl

Warren, then attorney general, testified that American-born Japanese were even

more dangerous to the security of the United States than alien Japanese.[18]

Emotional demands for action by leaders like Congressman John Rankin helped

make up the minds of the public: "I'm for catching every Japanese in America,

Alaska, and Hawaii now and putting them in concentration camps. Damn them!

Let's get rid of them now!"[19] The pressure increased, more unfounded rumors

were spread, and the fear of invasion and suspicion of sabotage eventually led

to the imprisonment of 110,000 Japanese Americans.

Considering the unjust suffering that Japanese Americans faced, it seems

a paradox that it took place in a country where there is "justice for all."

The economic losses suffered by Japanese Americans as a result of the intern-

ment has been nearly impossible to calculate. Given only a matter of days or

a few weeks between notification and evacuation, they were forced to sell their

property at prices far below its real value. Far away at relocation centers

and unable to protect their interests back home, their property that had been

stored or left to trustees was often stolen, vandalized, or sold.[20] It is

impossible to calculate the lost wages, income, and interest; but the property

losses have been estimated to be worth $400,000,000. The United States govern-

ment has repaid Japanese Americans a portion of this amount, and in 1967 the

Supreme Court ruled that an additional $10,000,000 was owed to Japanese

Americans whose dollar savings had been confiscated during the internment.[21]

To add to the miserable plight of the internees, the camps themselves

were inadequate. Small, semi-private barracks were hastily built with wood

and tar paper and often located in desolate, out-of-the-way deserts and waste-
lands. There were no cooking or plumbing facilities in the barracks, but each
block had a mess hall and a building with latrines, showers, and laundry
facilities.[22] Sanitation and protection from the elements were simply not
adequate.[23] In spite of these obstacles, cooperating communities were established in the camps and, through a lot of hard work and determination, they
led a reasonably comfortable existence.

It is ironic that while the internees were overcoming these conditions
within their barbed-wire enclosures, Japanese American soldiers were serving
the United States in the war effort. The 442nd Combat Team, an all-Japanese
volunteer unit, distinguished themselves on the battle front in Italy with
more casualties and decorations than any other unit of similar size and length
of service in the history of the army.[24] It seems incredible that while
Japanese soldiers were being injured and killed overseas, their brothers,
sisters, mothers, and fathers were back in the states imprisoned by the very
country they were fighting for. Knowing this, it must have been frustrating
for many members of the 442nd Combat Team when, at an honorary citation ceremony, President Truman said to them: "You are to be congratulated for what you
have done for this great country of ours. I think it was my predecessor who
said that Americanism is not a matter of race or creed, it is a matter of the
heart. . . ."[25]

Perhaps the most tragic of the injustices inflicted upon Japanese Americans
was the psychological and emotional suffering they experienced. The internment
was morale-killing, humiliating, and frustrating. The internees had to live
with the knowledge that they were being regarded as traitors to their country

and that they would always be judged by their ancestry rather than their actions. For those Americans, it is fair to conclude that the imprisonment represents a very bad memory that is permanently engraved in their minds.

Today the internment of 110,000 Japanese Americans in the United States is difficult to imagine, but thirty years ago it was a cold reality. Every aspect of it was diametrically opposed to the treasured ideals of America. That such a tragedy could have taken place in this country illustrates that prejudice, hate, and fear can cause us to ignore completely the rights and freedoms of which we are so proud. It should also serve as a ghastly reminder that such a tragedy should never be allowed to happen again.

Notes

[1] Dillion S. Myer, Uprooted Americans (Tucson: University of Arizona Press, 1971), p. xiii.

[2] Roger Daniels, Concentration Camps U.S.A. (New York: Holt, Rinehart and Winston, 1972), pp. xi-xii.

[3] William Petersen, "Incarceration of Japanese Americans," National Review, 8 Dec. 1972, p. 49.

[4] Janet Stevenson, "Before the Colors Fade: The Return of the Exiles," American Heritage, 20 (June 1969), 24.

[5] Carey McWilliams, Prejudice (Boston: Little, Brown and Company, 1944), pp. 109-110.

[6] Dorothy S. Thomas, The Spoilage (Los Angeles: University of California Press, 1946), p. 5.

[7] Ronald O. Haak, "Co-opting the Oppressors: The Case of the Japanese Americans," Transaction, 12 (Oct. 1970), 23.

[8] Maisie Conrat, Executive Order 9066 (Los Angeles: California Historical Society, 1972), p. 57.

[9] Audrie Girdner and Anne Loftis, The Great Betrayal (London: The Macmillan Company, 1969), p. 11.

[10] Daniels, p. 2.

[11] Myer, pp. 11-12.

[12] Conrat, p. 18.

[13] Daniels, pp. 9-10.

[14] Myer, pp. 11-14.

[15] Daniels, p. 11.

[16] Thomas, p. 2.

[17] Daniels, p. 33.

[18] Haak, p. 23.

[19] Conrat, p. 21.

[20] Conrat, p. 22.

[21] "Tule Lake Thirty Years Later," *Time*, 10 June 1974, p. 31.

[22] Myer, pp. 30-32.

[23] Conrat, p. 22.

[24] Conrat, p. 23.

[25] Myer, p. 148.

Bibliography

Conrat, Maisie. *Executive Order 9066*. Los Angeles: California Historical
Society, 1972.

Daniels, Roger. *Concentration Camps U.S.A*. New York: Holt, Rinehart and
Winston, 1972.

Girdner, Audrie, and Anne Loftis. *The Great Betrayal*. London: The
Macmillan Company, 1969.

Haak, Ronald O. "Co-opting the Oppressors: The Case of the Japanese
Americans." *Transaction*, 12 (Oct. 1970), 23-31.

McWilliams, Carey. *Prejudice*. Boston: Little, Brown and Company, 1944.

Myer, Dillion S. *Uprooted Americans*. Tucson: The University of Arizona
Press, 1971.

Petersen, William. "Incarceration of Japanese Americans." *National Review*,
9 Dec. 1972, pp. 49-50.

Stevenson, Janet. "Before the Colors Fade: The Return of the Exiles."
American Heritage, 20 (June 1969), 22-25.

Thomas, Dorothy Swaine. *The Spoilage*. Los Angeles: University of California
Press, 1946.

"Tule Lake Thirty Years Later." *Time*, 10 June 1974, p. 31.

Appendix:

answers to self-grading exercises

The answer keys that follow correspond in number to the self-grading exercises found in Part III, "Revising the Essay: A Brief Handbook."

Self-Grading Exercise 1

1. Libraries contain the wisdom of civilization.

2. In the district of Wymar, burglars were ransacking the stores.

3. In Hemingway's novels matadors are highly respected.

4. A clear conscience is the best sleeping pill.

5. The silver-gray vest suited his taciturn personality.

6. Most middle-class homes in the Southwest are built with air conditioning.

7. The outdoor markets in Europe attract numerous tourists.

8. Noise pollution in towns and cities blots out the sounds and silences of the outdoor world.

9. A cup of good tea or coffee must be brought me early each morning.

10. I wish to describe two kinds of tours available.

Self-Grading Exercise 2

1. Television | has contributed to the decline of reading skills.

2. Incensed by their rudeness, the senator | left.

3. Michelangelo's work | continues to attract admirers all over the world.

4. Wars | go on endlessly.

5. Divorce | affects children most of all.

6. Professional tennis | has become big business in the United States.

7. Most people | insist on paying their bills on time.

8. Within five weeks one hundred polio victims | had been claimed.

9. Spain | is no longer a strong world power.

10. Many areas of Saudi Arabia | have experienced droughts.

Self-Grading Exercise 3

1. I	6. I	11. I	16. I
2. I	7. P	12. I	17. D
3. P	8. I	13. P	18. P
4. I	9. D	14. I	19. I
5. D	10. D	15. D	20. P

Self-Grading Exercise 4

1. We asked him if he would be willing to do it alone.

2. Are you usually alert to the problems of older people?

3. Sound the alarm! Then run for your life!

4. I am as angry as a cornered cat.

5. Do you mean to tell me that all of the money simply disappeared?

6. They inquired as to whether or not we would accompany the performers.

7. Heavens! What a way to get attention!

8. Go straight down the aisle and interrupt his conversation.

9. Would you be so kind as to direct me to the British Museum?

10. Whew! What a terrible odor!

Self-Grading Exercise 5

1. A	6. C	11. B	16. B
2. B	7. A	12. A	17. A
3. C	8. D	13. B	18. C
4. D	9. D	14. D	19. A
5. C	10. A	15. A	20. C

1. noun
2. verb
3. adjective
4. preposition
5. adverb
6. verb
7. coordinating conjunction
8. preposition
9. adjective
10. verb
11. pronoun
12. adverb
13. noun (verbal)
14. pronoun
15. noun
16. coordinating conjunction
17. conjunctive adverb
18. article
19. adverb
20. adjective
21. preposition
22. verb
23. subordinating conjunction
24. verb
25. subordinating conjunction (relative pronoun)
26. verb
27. preposition
28. noun
29. adverb
30. verb
31. article
32. preposition
33. noun
34. adverb (subordinating conjunction)
35. pronoun
36. verb
37. noun
38. verb
39. verb
40. adverb

Self-Grading Exercise 7

1. Frag
2. C
3. CS
4. Frag
5. RT
6. C
7. Frag
8. C
9. C
10. Frag
11. CS
12. CS
13. C
14. C
15. Frag
16. CS
17. C
18. C
19. RT
20. CS

Self-Grading Exercise 8

1. makes	6. *C*	11. are	16. is
2. are	7. is	12. *C*	17. watches
3. has	8. are	13. Do	18. *C*
4. *C*	9. require	14. *C*	19. sit
5. causes	10. *C*	15. is	20. appeals

Self-Grading Exercise 9

1. him	6. he and I	11. you or me	16. her
2. whoever	7. my	12. whomever	17. We
3. who	8. its	13. whom	18. whoever
4. he or she	9. Their	14. whom	19. I
5. me	10. whom	15. her	20. Whom

Self-Grading Exercise 10

1. As they listened to the music, Sir Peregrine remarked about the success of the races while his wife dreamed about love.   B

2. A person must accept the fact that he or she can't always win.   A

3. All secretaries who worked in the office were asked to give their opinions and to say how they felt.   A

4. The airline attendants wondered why so many passengers were standing in the aisle and who had given them permission to leave their seats.   D

5. If I were wealthy and if I were living in Zaire, I'd tell Mobutu a thing or two.   C

6. He pored over all of his notes and checked out many library books.   E

7. Mrs. Olson walks into strangers' kitchens and tells them how to make coffee.   E

8. The professor informed us that the test would be given and asked if we were ready.   B

9. First the insane man quoted lines from Richard Lovelace; then he recited a passage from the "Song of Solomon."   B

10. "Raise the property tax—and impose rent control!" he yelled with fervor.   C

11. When you buy a foreign car, you have to expect poor service.   A

12. The matter suddenly came to a crisis, but just as suddenly it was resolved. _F_

13. It is essential that he bring the document with him and that he be here by noon. _C_

14. We fear the unknown whereas we often welcome the known. _E_

15. Our Constitution protects our right to pursue happiness; however, it does not guarantee that we shall find this happiness, no matter how diligently we pursue it. _F_

16. The tenant claims that he paid the rent and asked me to convey this fact to the landlord. _D_

17. The skylark gracefully lifts itself into the sky, lets out a joyful warble, and disappears into a cloud. _B_

18. The sea breeze was blowing harder and felt colder. _B_

19. As one walked into the slaughterhouse, one could see hundreds of carcasses hanging on hooks. _A_

20. Since most of the children loved to go swimming, the group went to the beach. _B_

Self-Grading Exercise 11

1. We are now expected to drive less, use public transportation, and conserve heating fuel. Saving energy is a realistic goal.

2. Some diet experts say that a tablespoon of vinegar in some sugar and oil will reduce the appetite.

3. The newspaper said that a rebirth of great art is taking place in China.

4. When Byron was on the Continent, he carried on a lively correspondence with Shelley.

5. The world was expecting Golda Meir's death.

6. My brother does not make full use of his enormous talent.

7. During lunch John always sat alone while the other students sat together chatting away. This isolation of his didn't last long, however.

8. Mahatma Gandhi wanted only the sparsest of furniture in his room.

9. In an interview with a group of millionaires, the master of ceremonies told the audience that the millionaires he interviewed were very articulate.

10. Melissa invited Ruth to travel to Spain with her because she thought Ruth was interested in Spanish history.

11. A psychologist has no right discussing his patients' personal problems with

his friends because the patients could be embarrassed if their identities were discovered.

12. The passerby wondered about the significance of the young boy's dashing out of the store and running down the street.

13. On our flight across the Atlantic the weather was beautiful.

14. Despite its dark and rough water, the Blue Grotto of Capri was a splendid sight.

15. My friend John loves to watch basketball for hours on end, but his wife doesn't approve of his doing so.

Self-Grading Exercise 12

1. As he bowed to the audience, his violin fell to the floor.

2. Filled with terror, the tiny kitten sat shivering in the corner.

3. As I watched them from behind a bush, camera in hand, the bears seemed like harmless pets.

4. What the teacher needs is a neatly typed list of students.

5. Students who speak French fluently will not need to pass the three conversation examinations.

6. During World War II the Nazis gave Jewish prisoners only cabbage to eat, nothing else.

7. Instead of asking for forgiveness, she offered a piece of chocolate cake as her sign of repentance.

8. Even when confronted with the full truth, they ignored the facts.

9. Hearing the bell ring, the boxer triumphantly flung his glove to the ground.

10. Out of breath and revealing a look of anxiety, the lover ran up the stairs.

11. The day drew to a close with anguished prayer that God would spare the infant.

12. We enjoy not only music, but also painting and sculpture.

13. The law was enacted immediately after Congress adjourned.

14. Scorched by the sizzling heat, we thought jumping into the river made a great deal of sense.

15. At a Neiman-Marcus store, we tried on some Givenchy pants that cost $150.

Self-Grading Exercise 13

1. He wanted to marry her because she was bright, pleasant, and unselfish.

2. Her boss fired her because her letters were sloppy, ungrammatical, and poorly typed.

3. The handbook revealed two ways in which the unity of a paragraph could be broken: 1. one could stray away from the topic sentence, 2. one could obscure the central thought with excessive details.

4. By exercising daily, by eating proper food, and by avoiding stress, he can regain his health.

5. This simple man did not doubt that after death there was a paradise for good people and a hell for bad people.

6. Most of them were either athletic or strong.

7. Handing out oil coupons seemed both intelligent and necessary.

8. She insisted that he must leave and never return.

9. The man is either an idealist or a fool.

10. Today pocket calculators are inexpensive, durable, and easily obtainable.

11. The Byronic hero was a man who felt alienated from mainstream society, who withdrew into haughty superiority, who loved passionately, and who felt an element of self-pity.

12. This is the case not only with policemen but also with firemen.

13. Here is what you will need to know: how to open a bank account, how to judge a contract, and how to sell equipment.

14. He climbed Mount Whitney not because he wanted to test his endurance, but because he was arrogant.

15. To err is human; to forgive is divine.

Self-Grading Exercise 14

1. After noticing that the watch and the bedspread were gone, they immediately (suspicioned, <u>suspected</u>) his stepdaughter.

2. Dorothy insisted on keeping her (personnel, <u>personal</u>) opinions hidden from her students.

3. The hiring committee preferred communicating by telephone because they believed in (<u>oral</u>, verbal) interviews.

4. I was always told that (this type, <u>this type of</u>) novel was cheap and aimed at the sensation seekers.

5. (Sit, <u>set</u>) the flower pot in front of the brick wall, where it will look lovely.

6. The (amount, <u>number</u>) of registered students varies from semester to semester.

7. In the upper left-hand corner of his (<u>stationery</u>, stationary) one could clearly discern three modest initials.

8. Earl Warren was considered a Supreme Court justice of immense (<u>stature</u>, statue, statute).

9. The team that climbed Mt. Whitney included (quite a number, <u>a rather large number</u>) of women.

10. Twenty years and six children later, the marriage was finally (<u>over</u>, over with).

11. Day after day his fiancee waited (<u>for</u>, on) him to return from the war.

12. Thank you for the (complement, <u>compliment</u>)—how kind!

13. (Your, <u>you're</u>) either for us or against us.

14. He never returned the suitcase (like, <u>as</u>) he was asked to do.

15. We (<u>can hardly</u>, can't hardly) distinguish one twin from the other.

16. The (farther, <u>further</u>) he delved into St. Paul's theology, the more fascinated he became.

17. When the real estate agent had received a firm bid, he (appraised, <u>apprised</u>) his clients of the fact.

18. He could never be (<u>persuaded</u>, convinced) to travel overseas on an airplane.

19. The (<u>site</u>, cite) for the international hotel was near the center of town.

20. While he was in Vietnam, all of his mail was (censured, <u>censored</u>).

Self-Grading Exercise 15

1. To add to our depression, a period of *driving snow* set in.

2. Vicky *beamed with pride* as she walked off the stage with her gold medal.

3. I liked *going to luxurious restaurants, visiting excellent museums, and attending the ballet* in the city.

4. His extreme selfishness *left him isolated and friendless.*

5. He chewed his food noisily, he talked with his mouth full, and he wiped his lips with his hand; in short, his manners were *disgustingly boorish.*

6. For six days and nights, he *battled* with fever and death.

7. A delicate sea shell is a *miraculous piece of sculpture.*

8. All of the fun at Joe's birthday party was ruined because the children *dropped ice cream on the carpet, left fingerprints on the windows, and broke a chair.*

9. The Mohave Desert of California and the Sinai Desert of Palestine *both experience extreme temperatures and searing winds.*

10. Every large city *suffers from overcrowded conditions, traffic congestion, and lack of green spaces.*

11. She was a hopeless, desiccated old lady *hobbling across* the street with her cane, her *stooped form* serving as a symbol of her despair.

12. In 1925 a terrible dust storm *swept* across the Midwest, *ripping chimneys off roofs, seeping through closed windows, and ruining entire vegetable crops.*

13. Many of the old Tin Pan Alley songs reveal poignantly *the poverty of the unemployed, the despair of the old, and the cold arrogance of the rich.*

14. We tried various cleaning solutions, but the kitchen floor remained *streaked with grime.*

15. People who throw *trash* out of their car windows while they drive along our highways reveal a disgusting kind of vulgarity.

Self-Grading Exercise 16

1. Charles Steinmetz was a pioneer in electrical engineering.

2. Long-distance runners training for the Olympics run as many as 20 miles a day.

3. Each person in line received a ticket.

4. Students today demonstrate poor writing skills for one simple reason: They are never required to write.

5. My favorite female poet is Emily Dickinson.

6. In the following chapter we will examine Charles Darwin's theory of evolution.

7. It is difficult to keep up with today's scientific advances.

8. Made of solid brown oak, the table has lasted for over a hundred years.

9. One of John's most serious faults is continuously apologizing for his errors.

10. Most often they graded the objective tests with a scantron machine.

11. One of the most exciting events of the trip was attending a secret burial ceremony.

12. Nevertheless, most judges are rational and do not judge defendants emotionally.

13. The pilot was in a terrible dilemma because he was flying into a crosswind.

14. All of the children observed by reporters were tall.

15. Traffic fines are an important source of revenue in New York City.

Self-Grading Exercise 17

1. When the medieval structure collapsed, the beginning of the modern mode of production started.

2. Quite a few years ago, while I was living in a little town on the West Coast, a

stranger came in and bought our valley, where the Sempervirens redwoods grew.

3. If writing skills are to be improved, English teachers will have to assign more writing than they now do.

4. We began to realize that resources in America are not limitless as we had thought.

5. While we are exuberant people, we are also destructive and careless, making powerful weapons, such as the atomic bomb, which we then use to prove that they exist.

6. Uncountable buffalo were killed, stripped of their hides, and left to rot, thus destroying a permanent food supply.

7. As a teacher he considered objections by students carefully, as if these objections had been made by colleagues.

8. Its roof half torn away by wind, its walls blackened by fire, and its stone floors covered with mud, this hotel looked like the ruins of a Gothic castle.

9. I was seventeen and extremely shy when my third-grade teacher came to visit us.

10. Hired and fired on the basis of how entertaining they make the news, television newscasters are victims of a rating game controlled by anti-intellectual viewers.

11. Although unknown to one another, all four of my grandparents arrived in America from the same county in Slovakia, where they had experienced a severe famine resulting from a potato crop failure.

12. Based on information in the Bible, most people believed the earth was roughly 6000 years old until the beginning of the nineteenth century, when geologists and naturalists began to suspect that the earth must have existed for a much longer period of time.

13. Driving along the highway like a haunted man, he was stopped by the police.

14. Considering that the early Incas did not have the wheel, their architectural accomplishments were spectacular.

15. Assuming that Goethe influenced Thomas Mann, we can surmise that Mann's *Dr. Faustus* is similar to Goethe's *Faust,* both of which deal with the theme of the demonic.

Self-Grading Exercise 18

1. His daughter, a leader among the women, had spared her father and set him afloat on the sea in a hollow chest.   _____

2. As for me, already old age is my companion.   _____

3. He spoke slowly, believing in his heart that he was telling the truth.   _____

4. Great dangers lay ahead, and some of the soldiers paid with their lives for drinking so heavily. _____

5. Gently he answered, "I have come to my home to recover the ancient honor of my house." _____

6. These fierce women steadfastly refused to surrender to the foreign invaders. _C_

7. They scorned them, terrorized them, and robbed them. _____

8. He insisted that he had been saved by the woman in white, who had brought him to Venice, an exotic city. _____

9. On November 19, 1929, a star, bright and luminous, shot across the sky. _____

10. Let the taxpayers who reside in the county pay for a new road sign at the intersection of Broadway and Main Street. _C_

11. The football players, however, did not care to linger in such a gloomy, narrow place. _____

12. Acheron, the river of woe, pours into Cocytus, the river of lamentation. _____

13. Sir, please accept my sincere apologies for the inconvenience this has caused you. _____

14. Since hell is merely an invention of guilty minds, why believe in it? _____

15. David Cotton, Jr., is doing some important research in the field of high-risk pregnancies. _____

16. On his way to ask his adviser a question about a calculus course, Robert arrived at the automatic gate, where he blew out a tire, causing his Fiat to skid into another car. _____

17. He felt himself degraded by this servile attitude and vowed revenge. _C_

18. They told him, "God's daylight is sweet to the old." _____

19. Yes, Chicago, Illinois, can be windy and freezing cold in the winter. _____

20. Above, some perfume bottles filled with exotic bath oils decorated the wall shelves. _____

Self-Grading Exercise 19

1. According to *Mythology*, a book by Edith Hamilton, the Greeks, unlike the Egyptians, made their gods in their own image.

2. Is this an exaggerated view? It hardly seems so; nevertheless, many opponents of the measure dismiss it as *unmenschlich*.

3. The search for a way to stop this vicious cycle has taxed the best minds among the following groups: city councilmen, educators, and urban planners.

4. Let me pose this question: Could you love passionately if you knew you would never die?

5. Who interrupted me by saying, "That's enough for today"?

6. Dear Mr. Forsythe: This is in reply to your request of May 16, 1979.

7. From now on, please cross your *t*'s and dot your *i*'s.

8. This is how we propose to assign the various duties: The men will scrub the floors, ceilings, and walls; the women will cook, mend, and garden; the children will run errands, clean up the yard, and pick vegetables.

9. But what happens when the national organizations themselves—the schools, the unions, the federal government—become victims of a technological culture?

10. With his fifth-grade education he wrote a marvelous poem entitled "Languid Tears."

11. *The New Yorker* is read mostly by people with keen literary interests.

12. Students often find it difficult to distinguish between the words *imply* and *infer;* in fact, most people confuse their meanings.

13. We currently reside at 451 Bellefontaine Drive, Pasadena, California.

14. One of the delegates was a vegetarian; the other was restricted to kosher foods.

15. He yelled angrily, "Get out of my yard!"

16. Vans, boats, and campers are not allowed (see Regulation #13).

17. Have you heard the question asked, "What can the police department do against the pitiless onslaught of criminal violence"?

18. This, my friends, is how I think we can help the world in a time of tyranny: by fighting for freedom.

19. The age was an age of *éclaircissement* and self-determination.

20. "You have arrived at your resting place," she murmured softly. "Seek no further."

21. Inside, the antique armoire dominated the room.

22. Picture, if you please, an open space where twenty acrobats stand, each locking hands with two different partners; then imagine ten acrobats standing on the shoulders of these twenty.

Self-Grading Exercise 20

1. Balloting at both the democratic and republican conventions is by states. _____

2. He had taken many history courses, but none fascinated him more than <u>i</u>ntroduction to <u>w</u>estern <u>c</u>ivilization. _____

3. Delta Delta Delta, the most active sorority, invited speakers from such organizations as <u>d</u>aughters of the American <u>r</u>evolution, <u>n</u>ational <u>o</u>rganization of Women, and the Sierra <u>c</u>lub. _____

4. The subject of the lecture was "The Treasures <u>O</u>f <u>T</u>he Nile." _____

5. John Stuart Mill understood <u>C</u>alculus and could read <u>g</u>reek when he was a child. _____

6. Exodus is the second book of the <u>p</u>entateuch. _____

7. One of his dreams was to see the Taj Mahal. <u>C</u>

8. The <u>w</u>ar of the Triple Alliance was fought between Paraguay on one side and an <u>A</u>lliance of Argentina, <u>b</u>razil, and Uruguay on the other. _____

9. That is the best photograph ever taken of <u>u</u>ncle Charlie. _____

10. As a capable and tough <u>C</u>ity attorney, he took action against one of Hollywood's swingers clubs, a place called Socrates' <u>r</u>etreat. _____

11. John toyed with two ideas: joining the <u>p</u>eace <u>c</u>orps or working without pay for Cesar Chávez' United <u>f</u>arm <u>w</u>orkers of America. _____

12. Ex-Assemblyman Waldie never ran for <u>O</u>ffice after the <u>S</u>ummer of 1974. _____

13. Today he is Chairman of the Federal Mine Safety and Health Review Commission. <u>C</u>

14. The residents of Mammoth Lakes, a mountain resort, are proud of the view of the <u>m</u>inarets, a ragged mountain range, seen from <u>high</u>way 395 as one approaches the resort. _____

15. One of my favorite books is a novel entitled <u>*in the heart of a fool.*</u> _____

16. Some women have romantic ideas about returning to feudalism, with knights in shining armor and ladies adhering to the manners of the Middle Ages. <u>C</u>

17. One of the highest mountain systems in the world is Hindu Kush, extending 500 miles from <u>n</u>orth Pakistan into <u>n</u>ortheast Afghanistan. _____

18. William S. Levey, S. J., is the vice-president of an important men's club. <u>C</u>

19. I failed Organic Chemistry 101, but I passed <u>f</u>rench. _____

20. A traditional American holiday is Thanksgiving <u>d</u>ay. _____

Self-Grading Exercise 21

1.	personnel	11.	height
2.	separated	12.	too
3.	conscious	13.	villain
4.	exaggeration	14.	woman
5.	shining	15.	similar
6.	occurrence	16.	all right
7.	profession	17.	led
8.	prejudiced	18.	principle
9.	environment	19.	losing
10.	explanation	20.	rhythm

Index

Acknowledgments (continued)

DO NOT GO GENTLE INTO THAT GOOD NIGHT   From the *Poems of Dylan Thomas*. Copyright 1952 by Dylan Thomas. Reprinted by permission of New Directions Publishing Corporation, J. M. Dent & Sons Ltd., and the Trustees for the Copyrights of the late Dylan Thomas.

POVERTY   From *Down and Out in Paris and London,* copyright 1933 by George Orwell; renewed 1961 by Sonia Pitt-Rivers. Reprinted by permission of Harcourt Brace Jovanovich, Inc., and the estate of the late George Orwell.

EXPANDING MY EMOTIONAL RANGE   Reprinted by permission of the author.

HOPEFULLY, THEY WILL SHUT UP   Copyright 1981, by Newsweek, Inc. All rights reserved. Reprinted by permission.

COURTSHIP THROUGH THE AGES   Copyright © 1942 James Thurber. Copyright © 1970 Helen W. Thurber and Rosemary Thurber Sauers. From *My World—and Welcome to it,* published by Harcourt Brace Jovanovich.

ARRANGEMENT IN BLACK AND WHITE   From *The Portable Dorothy Parker.* Revised and enlarged edition. Copyright 1927. Copyright © renewed 1955 by Dorothy Parker. Originally appeared in *The New Yorker.* All rights reserved. Reprinted by permission of Viking Penguin Inc.

INCIDENT   from *On These I Stand* by Countee Cullen. Copyright 1925 by Harper & Row, Publishers, Inc.; renewed 1953 by Ida M. Cullen. Reprinted by permission of the publisher.

I THINK I'M HAVING A HEART ATTACK   Reprinted by permission from Jerry Bishop's *I Think I'm Having a Heart Attack,* © Dow Jones & Company, Inc., 1974. All rights reserved.

A DISTANT MIRROR: THE CALAMITOUS 14TH CENTURY   By Barbara Tuchman, by permission of Random House, Inc., and Alfred A. Knopf.

THE NATURE OF PREJUDICE   By Gordon Allport from the 17th *Claremont Reading Conference Yearbook,* 1952. Reprinted by permission of the Claremont Reading Conference, Claremont Graduate School and the author.

PREJUDICE   Reprinted by permission of the author.

IS THE HUMAN EGG A PERSON?   Copyright 1982, by Newsweek, Inc. All rights reserved. Reprinted by permission.

MINGLED BLOOD   By Ralph Zimmerman. Published in *Winning Orations,* 1956.

THE USE OF FORCE   William Carlos Williams, *The Farmer's Daughters.* Copyright 1938 by William Carlos Williams. Reprinted by permission of New Directions Publishing Corporation.

DIOGENES AND ALEXANDER   © 1963 American Heritage Publishing Co., Inc. Reprinted by permission from *Horizon* (March 1963).

TWO FRIENDS: A STUDY IN CONTRASTS   Reprinted by permission of the author.

ROBBERY IN THE AQUARIUM   From pp. 17–21 of *King Solomon's Ring* by Konrad Z. Lorenz (Thomas Y. Crowell Company). Copyright 1952 by Harper & Row, Publishers, Inc. By permission of Harper & Row, Publishers, Inc., and Methuen & Co., Ltd.

THE POLITICS OF SKIING   By John Kenneth Galbraith. Reprinted by permission of the author. Originally printed in *Travel and Leisure,* autumn 1972.

HOW MR. HOGAN ROBBED A BANK   Copyright © 1956 by John Steinbeck. Appered originally in *The Atlantic Monthly.* Reprinted by permission of McIntosh and Otis, Inc.

TRACT   From William Carlos Williams, *Collected Earlier Poems,* Copyright 1938 by New Directions Publishing Corporation. Reprinted by permission of New Directions.

HOW TO ENJOY THE CLASSICS   By Steve Allen. Reprinted by permission from an advertisement published by International Paper Company.

HOW TO KEEP A DREAM JOURNAL   Reprinted by permission of the author.

HOW TO TORTURE AN AUTHOR   From *Explorations* by Gilbert Highet. Copyright 1971 by Gilbert Highet. Reprinted with the permission of the Oxford University Press, Inc.

HOW TO LAND THE JOB YOU WANT   Reprinted with permission from the June 1976 *Reader's Digest.* Copyright © 1976 by Reader's Digest Association, Inc.

POETICS FOR BULLIES   Copyright © 1965 by Stanley Elkin. Reprinted from *Criers and Kibitzers, Kibitzers and Criers,* by Stanley Elkin, by permission of Random House, Inc.

THE STYLES OF LOVING   By John Alan Lee. Reprinted from *Psychology Today Magazine.* Copyright © 1974 Ziff-Davis Publishing Company.

THREE TYPES OF RESISTANCE TO OPPRESSION   From pp. 211–15 in *Stride Toward Freedom* by Martin Luther King, Jr. Copyright © 1958 by Martin Luther King, Jr. Reprinted by permission of Harper & Row, Publishers, Inc.

PROFESSORIAL TYPES   From *Some of My Best Friends Are Professors* by George G. Williams. Published by Abelard Schuman Ltd., 1958.

THE GIRLS IN THEIR SUMMER DRESSES   Copyright 1939 and renewed 1967 by Irwin Shaw. Reprinted from *Selected Short Stories of Irwin Shaw,* by Irwin Shaw, by permission of the author.

PARENTS   From *Search for the New Land.* Copyright © 1969 by Julius Lester. Permission granted by The Dial Press.

WHY A CLASSIC IS A CLASSIC   By Arnold Bennett in *Literary Taste* by Arnold Bennett. Published by Doubleday & Company and A. P. Watt & Son.

A REASON OR THREE   Reprinted by permission of the author.

GROWING OLD   By J. B. Priestley. From the July 29, 1966, issue of the *New Statesman.* Reprinted by permission of the Statesman & Nation Publishing Co., Ltd.

Acknowledgments (continued)

THE ILLUSION OF SURVIVAL   Reprinted by permission of *The Bulletin of the Atomic Scientists,* a magazine of science and public affairs. Copyright © 1981 by the Educational Foundation for Nuclear Science, Chicago, Ill., 60637.

WAR   Copyright © by permission of the Pirandello Estate and Toby Cole.

DOOLEY IS A TRAITOR   Reprinted from *Possible Laughter* by James Michie. Reprinted by permission of the author.

DOCTORS FIND . . . ALLERGIC KIDS AREN'T   Reprinted by permission of the *Atlanta Constitution.*

THE CASE AGAINST MAN   Copyright © 1970 by Field Enterprises, Inc., from *Science Past–Science Future* by Isaac Asimov. Reprinted by permission.

GHOSTS   Published in the 1978 edition of *Contemporary American Speeches,* published by William C. Brown. Reprinted by permission of the author.

IN DEFENSE OF DEER HUNTING AND KILLING   Reprinted from the January 18, 1975, issue of *The National Observer.* Reprinted by permission of Dow Jones & Company, Inc.

THE HEALTH-CARE SYSTEM   From *The Medusa and the Snail: More Notes of a Biology Watcher* by Lewis Thomas. Originally published in *New England Journal of Medicine.* Reprinted by permission of Viking Penguin Inc.

COMMONLY MISSPELLED WORDS   From "Spelling Report," by Thomas Clark Pollock, from the November 1954 *College English.* Copyright 1954 by the National Council of Teachers of English. Reprinted by permission of the publisher and author.

THE INTERNMENT OF JAPANESE-AMERICANS DURING WORLD WAR II   Reprinted by permission of the author.

The Unit on Sentence Combining is adapted from "Sentence Combining," an essay Jo Ray McCuen contributed to *In the Trenches: Help for the Newly Recruited, Shellshocked, and Battle-Fatigued Teachers of Writing* (University of California, Los Angeles, 1982).